D1413290

EDUCATIONAL MEDIA AND TECHNOLOGY YEARBOOK

EDUCATIONAL MEDIA AND TECHNOLOGY YEARBOOK

Donald P. Ely, Barbara B. Minor, Editors

1995/1996 VOLUME 21

Published in Cooperation with the
ERIC® Clearinghouse on Information & Technology
and the
Association for Educational Communications
and Technology

1996

Libraries Unlimited, Inc. • Englewood, Colorado

LIBRARIES UNLIMITED, INC.
P.O. Box 6633
Englewood, CO 80155-6633
1-800-237-6124

Library of Congress Cataloging-in-Publication Data

Suggested Cataloging:

Educational media and technology yearbook,
    1996 volume 21 / Donald P. Ely and Barbara B. Minor, editors.—
Englewood, Colo.: Libraries Unlimited, 1996.
    xii, 409 p. 17x25 cm.
    Includes bibliographical references and index.
    ISBN 1-56308-359-0
    ISSN 8755-2094
    Published in cooperation with the ERIC Clearinghouse on Information
& Technology and the Association for Educational Communications and
Technology.
    1. Educational technology—yearbooks. 2. Instructional materials
centers—yearbooks. I. ERIC Clearinghouse on Information & Technology.
II. Association for Educational Communications and Technology.
III. Ely, Donald P. IV. Barbara B. Minor
LB 1028.3.E372   1996   370.778

Contents

v

Part Three
CURRENT DEVELOPMENTS

Part Four
LEADERSHIP PROFILES

Part Five
THE YEAR IN REVIEW

Part Six
ORGANIZATIONS AND ASSOCIATIONS
IN NORTH AMERICA

Part Seven
GRADUATE PROGRAMS

Part Eight
MEDIAGRAPHY
Print and Nonprint Resources

Preface

There was a time when 21 years indicated a coming of age. With this 21st volume of the *Educational Media and Technology Yearbook,* the adage no longer seems appropriate, because *EMTY* has long since become a standard reference in many libraries and professional collections.

Most standard references contain elements that readers expect to find in each new edition with up-to-date information. Volume 21 meets those expectations with the extensive listing of "Organizations and Associations in North America" and the comprehensive listing of "Graduate Programs." The "Mediagraphy" (of print and nonprint resources) was a creation of *EMTY*'s first editor, James Brown. It has continued to offer a broad overview of new materials in most media formats related to the field of media and technology. Without these important sections, the *Yearbook* would be just another collection of current articles. The coordination and preparation of these important sections are accomplished under the capable guidance of Barbara Minor.

Over the years, this publication has concentrated its efforts on North America, as there are other publications of a similar nature that focus on other parts of the world. This year, however, we have engaged several European authors who have much to say that is not culture-bound. Drs. Collis, Moonen, and Verhagen come from the University of Twente in the Netherlands. Their work is universal and they offer significant contributions to this volume. David Hawkridge, from the Open University in the United Kingdom, is another voice whose words are applicable in any culture.

The tradition of serving as a chronicle for the field of educational technology is carried out by Drs. Sullivan, Molenda, and Gustafson, and the report of the symposium on James D. Finn. This *Yearbook* is probably the only continuing publication that serves the function of reporting current trends and issues related to the profession. The tradition is carried further by publishing the biographies of leaders who have made major contributions to the field. In this issue, Robert Morgan and Paul Saettler are featured.

In addition to the changes mentioned, the 21st edition is being published in January of 1996, putting it at the beginning of the calendar year rather than at the close of the year, as was our past practice. We hope that readers will look forward each new year to a fresh edition of this work.

As the *Yearbook* enters its third decade, the current Senior Editor will retire. After more than 45 years in the field, it is time to move on to new challenges that have languished for many years. Most of them are directly related to the field, so the editor's name will still appear in the professional literature from time to time, but not as the editor of this publication. The collective efforts of the ERIC Clearinghouse on Information & Technology staff will continue to oversee the content of this book. Dr. Robert Branch will be the new Senior Editor working with Barbara Minor, who will continue as Co-Editor.

DONALD P. ELY

Contributors to the
Educational Media and Technology Yearbook 1995/1996

Don Ball
Walden University
155 Fifth Avenue South
Minneapolis, MN 55401

Robert K. Branson
College of Education
Florida State University
Tallahassee, FL 32306

Janis H. Bruwelheide
Montana State University
College of Education
213 Reid
Bozeman, MT 59717

Betty Collis
Faculty of Educational Science and
    Technology
University of Twente
Postbus 217
7500 AE Enschede
The Netherlands

Don E. Descy
Library Media Education Department
Mankato State University
P.O. Box 8400
Mankato, MN 56002-8400

Donald P. Ely, Assoc. Dir.
ERIC Clearinghouse on Information &
    Technology
4-194 Center for Science and Technology
Syracuse University
Syracuse, NY 13244-4100

Kent L. Gustafson
Department of Instructional Technology
607 Aderhold Hall
University of Georgia
Athens, GA 30602-7144

David Hawkridge
3 Leighton Road
Leighton Buzzard
Beds. L07 0AA
United Kingdom

Robert Heinich, Professor Emeritus
Indiana University
34 Middle Mountain Road
Bayfield, CO 81122

Dr. Patricia Jamison
Prince Georges County Public Schools
14201 School Lane
Upper Marlboro, MD 20772

Alan Januszewski
School of Education
204 Satterlee Hall
SUNY Potsdam
Potsdam, NY 13676

Mary Kercher
Buck Lodge Middle School
Adelphi, MD 20738

J. Randall Koetting
University of Nevada at Reno
College of Education/MS 278
9th and N. Virginia Streets
Reno, NV 89557-0029

Deborah L. Lowther
College of Education
Division of Psychology in Education
Arizona State University
Tempe, AZ 85287-0611

Larry W. Lucas, Technical Specialist
Texas Center for Educational Technology
University of North Texas
Denton, TX 76203

Charles A. MacArthur
College of Education
201 Willard Education Building
University of Delaware
Newark, DE 19716

Dr. David Malouf
8047 Glendale Road
Chevy Chase, MD 20815

Michael H. Molenda
Education 2234
Indiana University
Bloomington, IN 47405

Jef Moonen
Faculty of Educational Science and
    Technology
University of Twente
Postbus 217
7500 AE Enschede
The Netherlands

Dana Peterson
8032 Watermill Court
Baltimore, MD 21227

Virginia Pilato
12412 Silverbirch Lane
Laurel, MD 20708

Linda Roberts, Advisor for Technology
U.S. Department of Education
Office of the Deputy Secretary
400 Maryland Avenue SW
Washington, DC 20202

Dorothy G. Standish
26 Applewood Drive
Dover, DE 19901

Howard J. Sullivan
College of Education
Division of Psychology in Education
Arizona State University
Box 870611
Tempe, AZ 85287-0300

Pløn W. Verhagen
Faculty of Educational Science and
    Technology
University of Twente
Postbus 217
7500 AE Enschede
The Netherlands

Gene L. Wilkinson
Department of Instructional Technology
607 Aderhold Hall
University of Georgia
Athens, GA 30602-7144

Stanley D. Zenor, Exec. Dir.
Association for Educational Communica-
    tions and Technology
1025 Vermont Avenue, Suite 820
Washington, DC 20005

Part One
Trends and Issues

Introduction

Previous editions of *EMTY* have reported trends and issues as well as future directions. This year the focus is on the *meaning* and *perceptions* of *meaning* about the field of educational technology and how those views affect its directions. The three chapters present views of the field from inside the profession as well as from outside. The first, by David Hawkridge from the Open University in the United Kingdom, looks at social and technological factors that are facing professionals. The second, by Kent Gustafson, immediate Past President of the Association for Educational Communications and Technology (AECT), offers a direct challenge to members of AECT and to educational technologists in general. In the third, Lowther and Sullivan, from Arizona State University in the United States, explore the perceptions of educational technology by practicing professionals ("inside") and K–12 teachers ("outside"). Together these chapters represent a collective sense that the field is changing and must cope with the changes if it is to survive.

David Hawkridge asks: "How does the field transform itself from its current, time-honored position to the new era of information technology?" He reviews the contributions of scholars who have established the intellectual foundations and introduces harbingers of future directions. The challenge to the field is clear; whether or not it is confronted and acted upon is the unanswered question.

Deborah Lowther and Howard Sullivan went to the field to answer their question: "What do practicing educational technologists and K–12 teachers think about the field?" A healthy sample of the two groups responded to a survey that provided data for the researchers' analysis. Some of the findings are surprising; others are not. When this study is juxtaposed with the chapters by Hawkridge and Gustafson, it appears that educators in the United States are not as deeply concerned about changing the direction of the field as Lowther and Sullivan suggest.

All three chapters offer important signposts along the path of educational technology as a professional field.

Reforming Educational Technology*

David Hawkridge
Professor of Applied Educational Sciences
Institute of Educational Technology
The Open University, MK7 6AA, England

ABSTRACT

Educational technology today, as a field of inquiry and practice, purports to be modern, even futuristic, yet we use 1960s psychological theory as its basis. Is the quality of our performance and products as educational technologists being adversely affected by this cracked, obsolete foundation? How can educational technology be successfully reformed in the 1990s? Should we borrow from cognitive science? Why are we integrating information technology? Can we rise to the ideological challenges?

A CRACKED AND OBSOLETE FOUNDATION

The term *educational technology* came into general use in the late 1960s, after the heyday of programmed learning. Ely (1968) had two definitions: technology (hardware) use in education, and the application of behavioral science to education. If we include the period in which programmed learning was being developed, it seems as though the dominant paradigm has been the same for about 40 years. To change the language, our educational technology has a cracked and obsolete foundation.

It is time to modernize educational technology. This is not an easy task. The majority of us have clung to behavioral psychology and continue to advocate the use of familiar tools such as objectives. Many United Kingdom educational technology courses teach behavioral psychology and the systems approach. The same psychology underlies much of the thinking about performance-based models of education and the definition of competencies. Behind the jargon of our conferences on education and training are hidden assumptions about the nature of learning and what constitutes success. Behind the advice we offer as consultants there may lie a conservative worldview scarcely changed since Neil Armstrong landed on the moon.

Consider the books for 1980s courses about educational technology in British universities, polytechnics, and colleges. Romiszowski (1981) built entirely on ideas of the 1970s, derived from North American behaviorism and the systems approach. As Eraut (1989) commented, these ideas do not constitute established knowledge, though they may be useful to us, nor do they take account of constructivist views of learning. Percival and Ellington (1984) took a similar line, presenting a handbook long on techniques but short on theory.

*Developed from earlier papers published in *Educational and Training Technology International* 28(2) and *Aspects of Educational Technology XXVI: Quality in Education and Training*, edited by Malcolm Shaw and Eric Roper.

Rowntree (1974), widely used in teacher education, was anything but theoretical, perhaps because he preferred to appeal to readers' common sense rather than their knowledge of philosophy or psychology. Spencer's (1988) book on the psychological roots of educational technology depended greatly on behaviorism. He showed how Thorndike and Pavlov laid the foundations for a science of learning, but he gave Watson and Skinner, both eminent behavioral psychologists, most of the credit. He also drew particularly on Bloom, Briggs, Gagné, Keller, Mager, Popham, and Tyler, all Americans in the behaviorist mould, and he was right to do so, even if it underlined how much British educational technology had been influenced by them. Spencer did go further than this to consider briefly Piaget, Bruner, and Vygotsky, all of them interested in how children internalize what they learn as cognitive structures or models. Finally, he referred to Papert and Salomon's research, which may yet link educational technology to cognitive science.

Romiszowski (1990) summarized the position. The educational technology movement had been criticized, he said, for insisting on too-specific, product-based, uniform objectives; for placing too much emphasis on prior design and development of materials, followed by dissemination of standard messages to all learners indiscriminately; for emphasizing behaviors mastered rather than ideas processed and correction of errors rather than reflection on the implications of viewpoints; and for being shallow and superficial rather than encouraging the processing of complex, multifaceted content.

Our neglect of cognitive science may be due to its rhetorical flavor. Behaviorists stick closely to the analysis of behavior and do their best, even in the case of humans, to develop their discipline along strictly scientific, positivist lines. Cognitive scientists have much less empirical data available on which to base their theories. Like certain 19th-century psychologists, they are attempting to analyze what happens inside human beings' brains, not outside. They derive their ideas from linguistics, artificial intelligence, and psychology, but as yet cognitive scientists can tell educational technologists very little about how to guide learning according to the principles of their science. Gagné (1987) said that educational technology involves the systematic application of knowledge derived from scientific research. This is an aspiration rather than a fact. The search is still on for a science of learning, a set of normative rules that, if followed, will lead to successful teaching.

After four decades of effort by cognitive scientists, these ideas have yet to reach learners and their teachers. A large gap looms between the cognitive research laboratories and school classrooms. Artificial intelligence specialists admit that they have explored some blind alleys. Their field data are hard to interpret for practical purposes. Intelligent tutoring systems, which act like a good tutor, represent the extreme example of cognitive science applied to education. Analysis of possible errors lies at the heart of the development of intelligent tutoring systems, yet, as the behaviorists have found, human learning is extraordinarily complex, and predictions are very difficult.

Tom (1984) did suggest that even if there were no breakthroughs, cognitive scientists might have an impact on teaching by encouraging teachers to regard their pupils more as thinkers and less as behavers. At the university level, Laurillard (1993) recently launched a much more rigorous argument, and provided a framework for all teachers in higher education to apply, together with proposals for institutionalizing its use. But Briggs, Gustafson, and Tillman (1991), in revising Briggs's earlier work, remained faithful to its behaviorist origins.

INTEGRATING INFORMATION TECHNOLOGY

Educational technologists are making great use of information technology. That is not surprising. As technophiles rather than technophobes, we welcome the technology. We are continuing the line of thought we inherited from the audiovisual movement that started in the 1920s. The question is, are we exploiting information technology's special characteristics for the sake of education? We are assailed by technology-led solutions to educational problems. That is not what educational technologists stand for: We believe in student-led solutions, and technology must play an appropriate role. It is a pity that the arrival of information technology in education has let us apply the "failed" behavioral psychology all over again. Of course, many technological innovations are used at first to do faster what was done before, rather than to change the nature of what is done. For example, remember the drill-and-practice programs that flooded American schools in the late 1980s.

Challenging us are critics of information technology in education, such as Chandler (1989, 1990), who argued that computers project an ideology that conflicts with the purposes of the educators who put them into schools. The nature of information technology is certain to influence teaching and learning. For example, databases are introduced into schools to teach children how to record, sort, search for, and display data. As Chandler said, students learn "information-processing" using information technology, despite the fact that computers contain only data, not information. Data are changed into information by humans, not by computers. Computers deny the human origin of information. Humans negotiate meanings through discourse. Chandler said that this is not merely a semantic argument; the language of computers threatens to redefine the world in its own terms. He pointed out, further, that because humans give the computer power and authority, data stored elsewhere appear to lose some of their significance. Data-handling systems also distort information, diminishing the value of things they cannot record, including much everyday knowledge. Creators of databases have to be willing to tailor their intentions. Searchers have to limit the questions they ask. Chandler was worried that using computerized databases might lead students to believe that thinking is data processing. In his view, thought and memory require building and rebuilding of models of the world, not through passive data capture but through "interpretation and elaboration of information according to changing hypotheses. . . . We create ideas: computers can't." Databases disregard meaning. Computers promote the notion of their own objectivity, said Chandler. Their users often ascribe more authority to databases than to the printed word. Because databases contain standardized data, without details of sources, they seem misleadingly objective; each item carries equal weight, equal certainty. The creators' biases are invisible, the items are stripped of their origins and context. Data processing requires fragmentation of the whole, with loss of meaning, declared Chandler. It prohibits a holistic perspective.

Saettler (1990), in revising his 1968 history of our field in the United States, had nothing to say on these matters. Instead, he suggested that there was a hidden agenda in incorporating information technology into education. Improved managerial efficiency was the goal: more students taught in less time by fewer teachers using less space and at lower cost. This agenda is no longer hidden. Politicians and educators have turned to information technology as a potential means of increased efficiency, despite the fact that the evidence from cost studies is not reassuring. (The technology seems always to be an add-on cost in education.) We educational technologists must ask ourselves whether we are bringing information technology into our work in response to such an agenda. Or is it because the technology actually serves the theories we hold? Or do we believe we can exploit the technology for the benefit of learners?

IDEOLOGICAL CHALLENGES

If educational technology is to be truly modern, its practitioners must also respond to ideological challenges. Of these, the chief one comes from disciples of the Frankfurt School of critical theory, formed in 1923. Its founders, including Marcuse, studied authoritarianism. In the 1930s they began a critique of new mass media, particularly radio, and of how these were being used by the Fascists. After World War II, they mounted a critique of mass culture, which they saw as affirming the rule, or hegemony, of bourgeois values because it offered escapism and gratification, not insight. Habermas and others who came after Marcuse used critical theory to attack capitalism more directly. In particular, some critical theorists argued that capitalism was a system in which objects and the processes that produced them were valued by marketplace exchange, that is, they were turned into commodities or commodified. The commodification of the whole of society was proceeding apace, said these critics, recalling that the function of marketed objects was to profit the capitalist.

But what does critical theory have to do with educational technology? Burrell and Morgan (1979) state that proponents of critical theory "seek to reveal society for what it is, to unmask its essence and mode of operation and to lay the foundations for human emancipation through deep-seated social change" (p. 284). Translated for us, this might read "seek to reveal educational technology for what it is, to unmask its essence and mode of operation and lay the foundation for learners' emancipation through rooting it out." Harris (1987) thinks of educational technology as a species of positivism, and says that all the major authors in the field of critical theory consider positivism to be a particularly acute and modern form of domination. Bowers (1988) asserted that educational technology, far from being neutral, is a powerful force that will alienate individuals, destroy community values, and, through promoting a falsely objective view of the world, serve right-wing political and economic forces.

Critics like these find intellectual support in the work of Lyotard (1984), whose message about the "post-modern condition of knowledge" in present-day Western industrialized society is that capitalists are turning knowledge into a commodity, to be bought and sold in a marketplace which they dominate. Fox (1989), who aimed at open and distance learning, rather than directly at educational technology, saw these as a branch of the "knowledge industry." He objected that "knowledge and the opportunity to learn are benefits to be bought by private individuals rather than fundamental rights belonging to every member of a democracy" (p. 270). In the circumstances, open and distance learning could become a "dream instrument" for control of the ruled. Burt (1991) said that "educational technologists cannot escape the epistemological crisis which confronts all the other social disciplines. The new critical theory aims to address the crisis by making previously suppressed voices heard" (p. 229). Burt saw the educational and training technology literature as tending to express the ideologies of technological optimism and national economic competition, close to the dominant ideology of British and U.S. society.

This sort of criticism is hard to take for educational technologists who feel that they have frequently participated in benevolent educational reform. We are forced to admit that educational technology can be used for the wrong ends, but not that it is always used thus. It does not have a malign influence, we say. Critical theorists do not deny our good intentions; they simply say that our endeavors enhance the promotion of "falsehood and negative value."

Hlynka and Belland (1991) tried to analyze the impact of such critics on modes of inquiry in educational technology, but most of the authors in their volume of papers skirted the issues. As Webb (1991) noted, critical theory, with its emancipatory theme, is intrinsically radical. It has regenerated the Greek idea of *praxis*, roughly translated as practice subject to critical scrutiny. Bad practice will add to subjugation or oppression. Our best defense against critical theorists, if we feel we need one, is to point out that they propose substituting their own hegemony for the capitalist one, and that educational technologists desire to be slaves to neither. Critical theorists are essentially nihilistic; they offer no constructive ideas to those they accuse. Nevertheless, to be modern, we educational technologists need to develop our political consciousness and our awareness of who is suppressed, just as we should reexamine our theoretical foundations and consider why we are integrating information technology into our work.

Reforming educational technology is not a task for a day or even a year. Nor is it a task for a few reformers who want to impose their views on the rest of us. Rather, it is a process that should be continuous and pervasive, engaging all of us.

REFERENCES

Bowers, C. A. (1988). *The cultural dimensions of educational computing: Understanding the nonneutrality of technology.* New York: Teachers College Press.

Briggs, L. J., Gustafson, K. L., and Tillman, M. H. (1991). *Instructional design principles and applications.* Englewood Cliffs, NJ: Educational Technology Publications.

Burrell, G., and Morgan, G. (1979). *Sociological paradigms and organisational analysis.* London: Heinemann.

Burt, Gordon. (1991). Opinion: Culture and ideology in the training literature. *Educational and Training Technology International 28*(3), 229–37.

Chandler, D. (1989). The purpose of the computer in the classroom. In J. Beynon et al., eds. *Computers into classrooms: A critical appraisal* (Lewes, UK: Falmer Press).

Chandler, D. (1990). The educational ideology of the computer. *British Journal of Educational Technology 21*(3), 165–74.

Ely, D. P. (1968). Educational technology as instructional design. *Educational Technology 8*, 4–6 (referred to by Saettler, 1990).

Eraut, M. (1989). Conceptual frameworks and historical development. In M. Eraut, ed. *The international encyclopedia of educational technology* (Oxford: Pergamon Press).

Fox, S. (1989). The production and distribution of knowledge through open and distance learning. *Educational and Training Technology International 26*(3), 269–80.

Gagné, R., ed. (1987). *Instructional technology foundations.* Hillsdale, NJ: Lawrence Erlbaum.

Harris, D. (1987). *Openness and closure in distance education.* Lewes, UK: Falmer Press.

Hlynka, D., and Belland, J. C., eds. (1991). *Paradigms regained: The uses of illuminative, semiotic and postmodern criticism as modes of inquiry in educational technology.* Englewood Cliffs, NJ: Educational Technology Publications.

Laurillard, D. (1993). *Rethinking university teaching: A framework for the effective use of educational technology.* London: Routledge.

Lyotard, J-F. (1984). *The postmodern condition: A report on knowledge.* Minneapolis, MN: University of Minnesota Press.

Percival, F., and Ellington, H. (1984, revised 1988). *A handbook of educational technology.* London: Kogan Page.

Romiszowski, A. (1981). *Designing instructional systems.* London: Kogan Page.

Romiszowski, A. (1990). Shifting paradigms in education and training: What is the connection with telecommunications? *Educational and Training Technology International* 27(3), 233–37.

Rowntree, D. (1974, revised 1985). *Educational technology in curriculum development.* New York: Harper & Row.

Saettler, P. (1990). *The evolution of American educational technology.* Englewood, CO: Libraries Unlimited.

Spencer, K. (1988). *The psychology of educational technology and instructional media.* Beckenham, UK: Croom Helm.

Tom, Alan. (1984). *Teaching as a moral craft.* New York: Longman.

Webb, G. (1991). Epistemology, learning and educational technology. *Educational and Training Technology International* 28(2), 120–28.

Educational Media and Technology
The State of the Profession

Kent L. Gustafson
Professor, Department of Instructional Technology
The University of Georgia

The origins of this chapter are in a speech given by the author on the occasion of completing his presidency of the Association for Educational Communications and Technology (AECT). The title of the original address was "Where Are We and Where Are We Going?"

One starting point for thinking about the future of the profession is examining external forces in society that will, to a considerable degree, shape its destiny. For, in the final analysis, unless the profession both reacts and "proacts," it will limit its value to society, and this will inevitably result in diminished attention and resources for media and technology programs from the general public and key decision makers. This is a particularly important time to consider these external forces, for two reasons. First, the rate of change in society is accelerating and the number and power of these forces are expanding. Second, although there is more interest in and support for "technology" now than there has been in recent history, most of that focus is on hardware and the current obsession with what Vice-President Gore has labeled the National Information Infrastructure (NII).

Professionals with long memories will recall the halcyon days of the National Defense Education Act (NDEA), when unparalleled resources were made available by the federal government to schools for equipment with the expectation that an educational revolution would soon follow. Certainly a revolution of sorts has occurred, but it has nothing to do with the equipment that was purchased and largely gathered dust in one storage closet or another. Rather, the revolution was in the breakdown of discipline, further fragmentation of curriculum, and a general sense on the part of society and students that schools are unresponsive and bureaucratic institutions that do not serve society well. Similarly, industry has also made heavy investments in "information technology" (a fancy term for computers) while eagerly awaiting the predicted rise in worker productivity. However, most economic analyses indicate that what little productivity increase has occurred is not a result of the heavy investment in information technology.

The current hype over the NII also reminds one of the excitement generated by airborne television and other communications media that appeared to hold great promise, but in the final analysis had little impact. Although it is a little early in this chapter to ask the reader a question, here is one. "Can you provide a convincing argument for the value of expending the resources that will be required to link all first graders to the Library of Congress when we have so many other pressing needs in schools?" There are external forces that are far more pressing for the profession to deal with than providing the very limited capacity of the "on and off" ramps that are being suggested for schools. The concern here is the general lack of attention the profession is giving to the societal forces that impinge on education.

A strategic planner speaks of using a PEST analysis to identify factors likely to affect the future. By PEST he means those Political, Economic, Social, and Technological forces that strategic planners should either respond to or deliberately decide not to consider while being prepared to accept the consequences.

This list of PESTs is presented with no sense of which ones are most important to any specific individual. Therefore, they are presented in no particular order of importance and with no sense that the list is exhaustive. It is generated from the perspective of the United States, even though some of the forces are also present in other parts of the world.

- Demographic changes

- Cultural changes

- Family structure

- Children having children

- Globalization of the economy and resulting international competition

- Growing permanent economic underclass

- Globalization of communication technology

- Changing nature of the workplace and work itself

- Technology
  — Digitization
  — Communication
  — Technical convergence
  — Intelligence

- Education and training
  — Diversity
  — Accountability
  — Lifelong education and training
  — Competition from and for the private sector
  — Record amounts of hardware arriving (especially in schools)
  — Professional associations

Demographic changes are well documented in many publications, including *The Condition of Education*, an annual report compiled by the National Center for Education Statistics (1994). Among the changes are the rapidly expanding percentage of the population that is Asian, the number of practicing Muslims, and the longer life expectancies of almost all age and ethnic groups except black teenagers. Of course, some cultural changes follow demographic changes, but perhaps even more profound are the changes occurring within almost any identifiable group. To give an example, MTV is either causing or reflecting a change of culture, depending on one's point of view. The increased interest of many groups in reestablishing the roots and visibility of their cultural heritage provides additional evidence of a cultural shift away from the "melting pot" concept of American society.

Family structure is changing. The rise of the single-parent household in recent years represents a dramatic change in the meaning of *family* from the era in which many of their parents were raised. Even when two parents are present, both now work full-time outside the home, resulting in a different family than that depicted in the old TV series *Leave It to Beaver*.

Although it is possible to remain relatively value-neutral about these changes, the trend of an increasing number of children having children is especially disturbing. Among the concerns are the fact that these children will often have inadequate prenatal care and will deliver low-birth-weight babies. All the evidence indicates that many of these babies will demonstrate serious deficiencies in physical, cognitive, and social development, and will arrive in school unprepared to learn. How schools, social agencies, and society in general will deal with this growing number of children should be of profound concern to all professionals and citizens.

That economic conditions in the world are changing rapidly is certainly well known to anyone keeping up with world events. Maintaining the competitiveness of the United States in a global economy and increasingly competitive world is of concern to everyone. One particular aspect of this development deserves special attention: namely, that the last few years have seen the rise of what appears to be a growing economic underclass of individuals locked in low-paying jobs with little opportunity to improve their situation. The American dream, of economic self-sufficiency, job security, owning a home, and financial security during the golden years of retirement, is becoming a fantasy for many young adults in this country. To believe that these conditions do not represent powerful forces denies history both in the United States and around the world.

Instant global communication is another force destined to have profound impact on the profession. That one can now sit at home and communicate with others around the world via the Internet in text, sound, and visual modes is just the beginning. Voice communication is already a reality, as is two-way slow-scan video on the Internet. Interactive and on-demand video communications via satellites are already happening in the corporate world, and will become more cost-effective as the technology continues to develop. Cellular phone technology will soon be challenged by direct satellite communication, eliminating the current requirement that one be within a few miles of a cellular tower. What all this means to society and to our profession is almost the stuff of a Jules Verne novel. Someone ought to write an instructional technology "sci-fi" novel for the year 2020 to stimulate thinking about how different the world will be.

The changing nature of work and of the workplace itself is resulting in substantial restructuring of the social and economic roles of people of all ages. As new types of jobs appear, flourish, and disappear at an almost blinding rate, the impact on individuals and corporations (and hence by the profession as well) is, and will continue to be, enormous. For example, the classic notion of providing initial training to employees when starting work and then some limited update experiences as conditions change has been found to be unsatisfactory in an increasing number of work settings. Performance Support Systems (PSSs) are now being implemented in a variety of settings as an alternative to training, in an attempt to help workers be more productive and adaptable. These support systems can provide on-the-job information, guidance (perhaps via an expert system), and access to instantly updatable databases, and they hold considerable promise for selected work situations. However, discussions with professional colleagues suggest that many of them think PSSs are just another form of job aids (which admittedly some of the simpler ones are), rather than representing the emergence of a competing paradigm to conventional training. Nonetheless, many types of PSSs are really quite different from traditional training materials and their design requires something much different than the traditional instructional design process.

Four areas of technological development (digitization, communications, technical convergence, and intelligence) are reshaping the fundamental basis for the profession and will no doubt deserve greater attention in the next edition of the AECT publication (Seels and Richey, 1994) that presents the association's definition of the field.

This discussion of technological developments starts with *digitizing*, as it is the foundation for several of the other developments to be considered. It would be hard to overstate the importance of the impact of both the hardware and the software components of digitizing technology. The capacity of the hard drives on desktop machines has exploded in recent years. RAM memory is also increasing at a similar rate. But the intriguing point is not that a greater amount of what might be called traditional "number" data is being stored and manipulated. Rather, it is the fact that video and sound can be digitized, stored, retrieved, manipulated, and re-stored that makes this development so important. Similarly, it means that vast quantities of digital images, sound, and quantifiable data can be distributed over conventional phone lines, fiber optic cable, and low- and high-bandwidth broadcasting, including microwave and satellite transmission. On the software side of the digital revolution is compression technology, which vastly reduces the amount of storage or transmission capacity necessary when using digital images. As compression technology (particularly compression algorithms) continues to improve, real-time, interactive audio/video/data education and training environments will become ever more realistic and affordable.

Communication has already been alluded to, but deserves more attention. Traditionally, communication has been thought of as a one-way activity. This is the history of newspapers, radio, television, and especially classroom instruction. Currently, in the United States and other developed countries the race is on to see which service provider can establish the largest number of channels in the home or workplace. Are they wasting valuable resources? Who wants 500 channels of digital or any other kind of information on his or her workstation? Rather, users want what they want, when they want it, and they want to be able to *interact* with it. Being able to locate what is needed depends on having an efficient search engine. Being able to interact with it means that additional related information can be requested, called up for examination in different ways, and manipulated; perhaps even contact with someone who is knowledgeable about the topic can be provided. All of this interactive communication is technically possible today. All that is needed now is the infrastructure. High-level communication is already beginning to be possible with Distributed Interactive Simulation (DIS), whereby individuals around the world can simultaneously engage in a simulation, with each person's actions being immediately transmitted to all participants, who must then respond to the new conditions. Distance learning takes on an entirely different meaning in a totally interactive environment.

Convergence means that only one box is needed to handle all of a user's different data forms and communication needs, preferably via voice command. A soon-to-be-available arcade game boasts two seats for race car drivers who can compete with each other on a Le Mans-type course. (By the way, some of the most notable advances in simulation will show up first in local arcades; check with a nearby child.) The color and detail of the images is superb. What is most impressive is that, as one driver slows down, the other passes him, with the image presented being that of the approaching vehicle from the proper perspective—eventually only the tail lights are seen as it goes around the next curve. All of the images are being generated digitally rather than from existing video, and obviously in real time.

Intelligence is the fourth technological development. Fortunately, everyone's ancestors had some of this or no one would be here (and we hope it has been inherited in generous amounts). Incorporating intelligence into machines is probably the next great leap in technology. Although there is still some time before robots like the famous R2D2 from the movie *Star Wars* will be able to act in a reasonably intelligent way, intelligent "agents" that can be set to monitor external conditions or the actions of individuals in a variety of situations are now possible. Software that can be called up by the learner or practitioner to assist in decision making, demonstrate concepts or principles, interpret data, and suggest areas to explore while engaging in problem solving are all theoretically possible. Electronic Performance Support Systems (EPSS) are already being devised to assist knowledge workers in various fields. For example, in a local weather forecasting office, an "intelligent" advisor might be designed to dynamically monitor local conditions and alert the weather forecaster to conditions suggesting that a specific decision tree (e.g., does this have the potential for becoming a flash flood?) or standard operating procedure (e.g., alert other offices statewide) be examined for applicability. The question for the educational technology profession then becomes, "What amount of what type of initial training is necessary, and what type of EPSS should be designed and how will it be supported?" It seems safe to predict that, in the future, learning and performance will begin to be viewed as a continuum rather than a dichotomy.

Having described many of the external forces affecting the profession, it is now time to consider some of those that are internal. These forces are not completely independent of the external ones, as all are part of a larger interdependent and interactive system. Nonetheless, there is some value in examining them individually from an internal perspective.

Diversity in the school and in the workplace reflects the demographic and cultural changes mentioned earlier. However, the increased value society now places on diversity has added to the complexity of the issue. In the past, diversity was often dealt with by segregation. Although legal segregation disappeared many years ago, segregation by housing, economic status, ethnic background, and other factors continues today. The profession has a great stake in how issues like integration, maintaining social and cultural identity, valuing the individual, and providing meaningful educational opportunities for all evolve and play out over time.

Although the concept of accountability has been around for many years, clearly there is a growing mood in the country that schools must be more accountable for their output. Historically, accountability has been limited to proper expenditure of inputs and providing a reasonably safe educational environment. It seems that increased accountability for the quality of the "product" is being added to the school's list, as it has been for other service agencies in the community.

The demand for lifelong education and training provides both an opportunity and a challenge to the profession. Much of traditional lifelong education might be characterized as enrichment. That is, individuals for intrinsic or extrinsic reasons seek opportunities to learn and grow, but the experiences often lack intensity, structure, and rigor. That is, it is "nice to do," but not necessarily essential, and in many instances does not have major consequences for the participants. Although the demand by adults for enrichment experiences is likely to continue and even expand, a second theme of lifelong learning is emerging. This latter theme is based on the idea that access to high-quality and functionally relevant continuing education will have significant impact on one's future employment and economic well-being. How schools, colleges and universities, employers, and other education providers respond to this demand will shape their futures.

Significant competition from the private sector is a recent phenomenon that schools and colleges are only now beginning to recognize and understand. Educators in the public sector have had a virtual monopoly on providing education in the K–12 sector for many years, but the power of home schooling, after-school programs, educational materials marketed directly to parents of school-age children, and the contracts being drawn today between private industry and school boards to take over and operate public schools should not be underestimated. At the college level, the explosion of distance education degree programs is only now beginning to be heard on traditional college campuses. Whereas in the past only a few "quality" participants were in the business of offering distance education degree programs, their ranks are expanding to include many well-known names from among existing colleges and universities. One of the areas in which at-a-distance degree programs are proliferating most rapidly is the field of instructional technology.

In many schools, computer hardware is being acquired in record amounts. However, the supporting infrastructure is rarely present. Inservice training, adequate technical support, changes in class organization and scheduling, and provision of networking and connectivity to the outside world are among the most important missing ingredients. Teachers, students, administrators, and parents are ill-prepared to capitalize on any of the potential value all of this hardware might possess. A recent report about the Detroit schools provides a depressing example of the lack of impact of computer hardware. It was reported that despite Detroit's having spent more than $24 million on computers over a three-year period, extremely low test scores had not improved (*Heller Report*, 1995). There may be many such reports over the next few years as objective assessments confirm that no significant value has been added by all these expenditures. The result is likely to be public and political disillusionment with the whole concept of technology and all of the people who have been its advocates. The profession seems to have two options. One is to work very hard to educate fellow educators, the public, and the political establishment to the fact that simply throwing hardware at schools will not solve the problems, while we also offer sound advice and assistance on what really needs to be done. The second is to start building a "blame" list of teachers and administrators who just didn't work hard enough or were not "true believers" who were responsible for the failure.

The message should by now be quite clear: Infusion of equipment technology rarely has any significant impact. Those who consider themselves to be instructional designers might quickly defend the view that the profession is already aware of that fact. Nonetheless, the impact of the field has been largely limited to a small subset of industry training, while schools and most industry training go merrily about their business of not responding to either the educational technologists or the external changes affecting them.

Intellectual leadership from both universities and professional associations must create a sense of need, and then provide encouragement and support to professionals in the field. Such support and guidance are essential if the field is to make effective use of current technologies in response to the challenges faced by education in a rapidly changing social environment and workplace.

REFERENCES

The Heller Report 6 (March 1995), 3.

Seels, Barbara, and Richey, Rita C. (1994). *Instructional technology: The definition and domains of the field.* Washington, DC: Association for Educational Communications and Technology.

U.S. Department of Education. National Center for Education Statistics. (1994). *The condition of education, 1994.* (NCES 94–149). Washington, DC: Author.

Perceptions of Educational Technology
Among K–12 Teachers
and Educational Technologists*

Deborah L. Lowther
Howard J. Sullivan
Arizona State University

What do teachers think about educational technology? Much of the work in our field is conducted without a good database of teacher opinions (Aust and Padmanabhan, 1994). Yet recent research indicates that educational technologists believe our field will have increased involvement in teacher education and educational reform (Sullivan, Igoe, Klein, Jones, and Savenye, 1993).

The purpose of the present research was to study the perceptions of grade K–12 teachers and of educational technology faculty and graduate students about five topic areas related to educational technology: instructional design, cooperative learning, learner control, school reform, and computers and media. Subjects who were currently teaching at the time of the study were also asked to report the degree to which they use a key practice in each of these five topic areas in their teaching.

METHOD

The sample was drawn from nine universities that have well-known educational technology programs: Arizona State, Florida State, Georgia, University of Memphis, Minnesota, Pennsylvania State, South Alabama, Syracuse, and Utah State. The sample consisted of 477 respondents representing four groups: 41 educational technology faculty, 249 educational technology graduate students (93 doctoral students and 156 master's students), 137 grade K–8 teachers, and 50 grade 9–12 teachers. Sixty-two percent of the respondents were females and 38 percent were male.

The data were collected using the Educational Technology Survey, an instrument constructed for this study and consisting of 30 items covering the 5 topic areas listed earlier and implementation of one key practice from each area in one's teaching. Five items for each of the five topic areas and for implementation were included on the survey to constitute the total of thirty items. Each item consisted of a statement and a five-point Likert-type scale of agreement that ranges from strongly agree to strongly disagree. The Cronbach Alpha reliability coefficient across all 30 items was .84.

This article is adapted and reprinted with permission of the Association for Education Communications and Technology. The original article, titled "Teacher and Technologist Beliefs about Educational Technology," was published in *Educational Technology Research and Development 42*(4), 73–87 (1994).

One faculty member from each of the nine universities served as a contact person for his or her university. The contact person distributed and collected all surveys at the university and returned them to the researchers. All K–12 teachers in the study were from graduate education courses outside the educational technology area, and the final sample included at least one such class from each university.

Mean scores were calculated on a 1 (strongly agree) to 5 (strongly disagree) basis within each topic area for the four respondent groups: educational technology faculty, educational technology graduate students, K–8 teachers, and 9–12 teachers. Multivariate analyses of variance (MANOVAs) were used to test for significant differences between respondent groups by topic area. The MANOVAs yielded significant overall differences for each topic area, and therefore were followed by univariate analyses and Tukey HSD tests to identify significant differences between respondent groups by item.

RESULTS AND DISCUSSION

The overall mean score for the survey, as shown in Table 1, was 2.27. The mean scores by respondent group were educational technology faculty 2.32, educational technology graduate students 2.26, K–8 teachers 2.22, and 9–12 teachers 2.38.

Table 1
Mean Scores by Topic Area and Respondent Group

Topic Area N	Ed Tech Faculty [41]	Ed Tech Graduate Students [249]	K–8 Teachers [137]	9–12 Teachers [50]	Overall [477]
Instructional Design	1.82	1.77	2.04	2.07	1.88
Cooperative Learning	2.38	2.42	2.10	2.51	2.34
Learner Control	2.50	2.39	2.23	2.35	2.35
School Reform	2.64	2.40	2.33	2.39	2.40
Computers and Media	2.53	2.47	2.52	2.54	2.50
N[a]	[40]	[78]	[134]	[49]	[301]
Implementation	2.07	2.10	2.11	2.42	2.15
TOTALS	2.32	2.26	2.22	2.38	2.27

Note. Scores are based on 1 = Strongly Agree to 5 = Strongly Disagree
[a]The implementation N is reported separately from the overall N because items in the implementation area were answered only by respondents who are teachers.

The mean scores for the 5 items from the 30-item survey with the highest level of agreement and the 5 items with the lowest level of agreement are shown in Table 2. All 5 items that showed the strongest level of agreement dealt with instructional design. Respondents agreed most strongly (M = 1.50) with the statement "Teacher training programs should include at least one course in the design of effective instructional programs."

Table 2

Items with Highest and Lowest Overall Mean Scores

Rank	Question	Mean
	Highest Agreement	
1	Teacher training programs should include at least one course in the design of effective instructional programs.	1.50
2	Good instructional programs include instructional objectives, student practice, and evaluation of how well students have learned.	1.63
3	Teachers should have specific instructional objectives for their classroom instruction.	1.64
4	Teachers should study models and systems for designing effective instructional programs.	1.67
5	I use instructional objectives with students in my class(es), provide instruction and practice on the learning content for the objectives, and assess student performance on them.	1.70
	Lowest Agreement	
26	Computer-delivered instruction is capable of carrying out many of the human aspects of instruction.	2.69
27	By the year 2010, more instruction in the schools will be delivered by computers and other media than by textbooks and teachers.	2.88
28	Instructional programs developed by trained instructional designers and developers (that is, people specifically trained to design and develop instructional programs) result in greater learning than instructional programs developed by teachers.	3.00
29	Computer-delivered instruction is more effective than textbook-based instruction.	3.00
30	Most students are able to select appropriate learning objectives and learning strategies for themselves.	3.30

Three of the five lowest-rated items dealt with computer delivery of instruction. Respondents disagreed most strongly with the item "Most students are able to select their own learning objectives and learning strategies" (M = 3.30). The next two lowest-ranking items dealt with the ideas that instructional programs developed by trained instructional designers result in greater learning than instructional programs developed by teachers (M = 3.00), and that computer-delivered instruction is more effective than textbook-based instruction (M = 3.00).

Statistical analyses of the survey scores revealed that there were significant differences between respondent groups at the $p<.05$ level on 16 of the 30 survey items. In all, there were 32 significant differences on these 16 items. The most notable pattern in the data was the large number of significant differences (19 of the 32 total differences) between K–8 teachers and the two educational technology groups. This pattern, of course, reveals that there are important differences between elementary teachers and educational technologists in their perceptions of key topic areas in the educational technology field. Thirteen of these nineteen significant differences were associated with positive attitudes of the K–8 teachers toward cooperative learning, learner control, and school reform. Most such differences reflected that the K–8 teachers had greater confidence in their students' ability to work in cooperative groups and to make good learner control decisions than the educational technologists did. A few differences between K–8 teachers and educational technologists indicated greater confidence in teachers on the part of K–8 teachers and in educational technologists on the part of educational technology faculty and/or graduate students.

Respondents had high overall agreement (M = 1.88) with positive statements in the Instructional Design area. Educational technology faculty and graduate students agreed more strongly than K–8 and 9–12 teachers with statements in this topic area, but most of the difference was due to their much stronger agreement with the statement "Instructional programs developed by trained instructional designers and developers result in greater learning than instructional programs developed by teachers" (M = 2.70 for educational technology faculty and graduate students combined, and 3.45 for K–8 and 9–12 teachers combined). Educational technologists clearly believe that they can produce more effective instructional programs than teachers, probably because of their training and their use of a systematic design and development approach. Teachers, in contrast, believe that they can produce better instructional programs than instructional designers, most likely because of their greater familiarity with the students and the schools. This latter idea was captured in a comment written by one of the K–8 teachers, "Who are these people [instructional designers] who sit in their ivory palaces and have no real understanding of students?"

There was moderate agreement (M = 2.34) with positive statements in the Cooperative Learning area, and much stronger agreement by K–8 teachers than by any of the other three respondent groups. K–8 teachers agreed significantly more strongly with positive statements about cooperative learning than educational technology graduate students on all five items, and than educational technology faculty and 9–12 teachers on two of the five items each. The positive attitudes of K–8 teachers toward cooperative learning may be partly due to the fact that many of them spend the entire day in self-contained classrooms, where it may be beneficial to use a greater variety of instructional strategies. Cooperative learning can contribute to this variety because of the high levels of learner activity and social interaction associated with it.

Respondents also showed moderate agreement (M = 2.35) with statements in the Learner Control area. They generally agreed with statements that were in favor of giving students more control over their instruction. For example, they agreed that learners should be actively involved in selecting what and how they learn and (somewhat surprisingly) that it is as important to allow students to adapt instruction to their individual interests and learning styles as it is to increase learner achievement. Yet they disagreed (M = 3.30, the lowest mean among the 30 items) with the statement "Most students are able to select appropriate learning objectives and learning strategies for themselves." It seems ironic that respondents agree that learners should be involved in selecting what and how they learn, yet they disagree that students are able to do that, i.e., select appropriate objectives and learning strategies for themselves.

Also of interest in the Learner Control area is the fact that K–8 teachers agreed significantly more strongly than both educational technology faculty and graduate students with the idea that students are able to select appropriate objectives and learning strategies for themselves. Thus, teachers of younger (K–8) students indicated more confidence in their students' ability to select appropriate learning objectives and strategies for themselves than teachers of older students. K–8 teachers are generally considered to have a caring, humanistic attitude toward their students, and their greater confidence in them may partly reflect this attitude. In addition, there is research evidence (Igoe, 1989; Shen, 1994) that younger students themselves have greater self-confidence toward school and desire more challenge than older students, and the K–8 teachers' attitudes could be influenced by their students' perceptions.

Respondents showed moderate agreement (M = 2.40) with items related to School Reform as well. They agreed quite strongly that greater use of technology in the classrooms will be an important feature of school reform, but were relatively neutral (M = 2.88) on the idea that more instruction in the schools will be delivered by computers and other media than by textbooks or teachers by the year 2010. Responses by graduate students and K–8 teachers to two items in this area reflected somewhat self-oriented opinions of these two groups toward their own roles in the school reform movement. Graduate students agreed significantly more strongly than either K–8 teachers or faculty that instructional designers will influence the reform and restructuring of schools. K–8 teachers, in contrast, agreed significantly more strongly than graduate students that classroom teachers will play a major role in the reform and restructuring of schools.

The educational technology faculty overall mean (M = 2.64) in the School Reform area was well below the means (2.33 to 2.40) for the other three groups. All five of the school reform items were stated in the future tense. Faculty skepticism in this area may be at least partly a function of their greater experience with past change movements in the schools. These change movements were often associated with technological advances or a new curriculum orientation, but seldom yielded the promise originally predicted for them.

Respondents also showed moderate agreement with statements in the Computers and Media area, although this area had the lowest overall mean (M = 2.50) of the five topic areas. Both educational technology faculty and graduate students agreed significantly more strongly than the K–8 teachers with the statement "Computer-delivered instruction is capable of carrying out many of the human aspects of instruction." This difference may reflect greater knowledge about and confidence in computer technology among educational technology faculty and graduate students than among K–8 teachers. However, K–8 teachers may also show less agreement with it because they may believe more strongly that personal identification and interaction with students are the key to humanizing instruction.

Respondents had a neutral response (M = 3.00)—which tied for the second lowest agreement on the 30-item survey—to the Computers and Media statement "Computer-delivered instruction is more effective than textbook-based instruction." This result is interesting in light of the numerous articles in the educational technology literature that cite the advantages of computer-based instruction (e.g., Kinzie, Sullivan, and Berdel, 1988; Park and Gittelman, 1992; Rieber, 1992; Robyler, 1988; Tobin and Dawson, 1992). The mean scores for this item do not reflect the enthusiasm for the use of computer-based instruction often found in the professional literature in our field, although the item does not, of course, specifically address the use of computers for specialized instructional purposes.

The overall responses for the Implementation area ($\underline{M}$ = 2.15) generally indicate that the respondents use the practices covered in the survey in their classrooms, at least according to their self-reports. Respondents agreed most strongly that they use instructional design practices (objectives, instruction and practice, assessment) with their classes and least strongly that "I frequently have students in my class(es) use computers for instructional purposes." There was a wide range of mean scores (2.00 for educational technology faculty to 3.42 for 9–12 teachers) on the latter item, with faculty, graduate students, and K–8 teachers all agreeing significantly more strongly with the statement than grades 9–12 teachers. Eighty-seven percent of the K–8 teachers, but only 57 percent of the 912 teachers responded in the introduction section of the survey that computers were available for their use at school. Thus, the lower agreement by 9–12 teachers may be due in part to lack of availability of computers for general faculty and student use at the 9–12 level.

The topic area with the highest agreement, Instructional Design, and the one with the lowest agreement, Computers and Media, are the two most closely associated with educational technology. It seems likely that the high level of agreement for instructional design reflects the fact that the concepts associated with instructional design have been well established since the 1960s, and that many people consider them to be the core concepts of educational technology. Further, these concepts are general enough that they are very relevant to teachers, even though teachers may not fully understand their application to the design and development of instructional materials or programs. Computers, however, are newer in the schools than instructional design concepts, at least in terms of their general availability. Computers are still expensive, they are not yet as easy to apply to most instruction as basic instructional design concepts, and many people have concerns about their general effectiveness for instructional purposes (Weber, 1994).

The results indicate different perceptions among the four respondent groups. K–8 teachers had the strongest overall agreement with the entire survey and the highest level of agreement among the four groups on 13 of the 30 items. They differed from one or more groups on 15 of the 16 items that had significant differences, with significantly higher agreement on 11 of these items. K–8 teachers had much more positive attitudes toward cooperative learning than the other three respondent groups and somewhat more positive attitudes toward learner control and school reform. Clearly, they like cooperative learning and they show considerable confidence in their students' learner-control abilities, in spite of their students' youth. In contrast, they agree less strongly than educational technology personnel that instructional designers will influence school reform, that instructional designers develop more effective instructional programs than teachers, and that computers are capable of carrying out many human aspects of instruction.

Grade 9–12 teachers had the lowest overall level of agreement with items on the survey and the lowest agreement with 11 of the 30 survey items. They differed significantly from one or more groups on 7 of the 16 items that had significant differences, and they had the lower agreement on 6 of these 7 items. Grade 9–12 teachers are commonly considered to have more of a subject-matter orientation and less of a concern with instructional methodology than K–8 teachers. Several of the topic areas in the survey deal mainly with methodology, including instructional design, cooperative learning, and learner control. The lower level of overall agreement by 9–12 teachers may be due in part to their emphasis on subject-matter content over different instructional approaches.

The educational technology graduate students had the second highest overall agreement on the 30-item survey. Their relatively high agreement was due in part to their scores in the Instructional Design area, in which they had the strongest agreement on four of the five items. Their responses generally indicated that they felt at least as strongly as educational technology faculty about the importance and influence of both instructional design and educational technology. Their significant differences on 13 items with K–8 teachers revealed that educational technology graduate students have greater confidence in educational technology and educational technologists, whereas K–8 teachers have greater confidence in teachers and in students working under cooperative learning and learner control.

The educational technology faculty had the lowest level of agreement on 13 of the 30 survey items. Faculty had high agreement with statements in the Instructional Design area, but relatively low agreement in both School Reform and Computers and Media. Their School Reform score was the lowest mean score for any respondent group across all five topic areas. As noted earlier, the relatively low faculty agreement in this area may reflect a skepticism about major future changes that is grounded in past change movements that were weaker than projected.

CONCLUSIONS

The results suggest certain approaches that may be useful to educational technologists who design instructional programs for the schools and who teach instructional design courses. School programs are likely to have greater credibility among teachers if it is clear that one or more teachers played an important role in their development. This can be done through field testing, of course, but teacher involvement throughout the development process would also be desirable. Instructional designers can also cater to elementary teachers' preferences by incorporating many opportunities for cooperative learning and learner control into school programs. University instructors in instructional design courses could emphasize the importance of teacher involvement in the design process to students in their courses.

This study yielded information on the attitudes and beliefs of educational technologists and teachers about several important areas in educational technology. Overall, all four respondent groups revealed positive perceptions about these areas. Differences in perceptions were greatest between the educational technologists and the K–8 teachers. Awareness of teacher perceptions of educational technology and sensitivity to these perceptions in our work can help to ensure the success of our educational technology classes and the instructional programs that we develop for the schools.

REFERENCES

Aust, R., and Padmanabhan, S. (1994). Empowering teachers with technology: An agenda for research and development. In *Proceedings of the Annual Conference of the Association for Educational Communications and Technology,* ed. M. R. Simonson, N. Maushak, and K. Abu-Omar (Washington, DC: Association for Educational Communications and Technology), 15–29.

Igoe, A. R. (1989). *Patterns of learner characteristics and career preferences among male and female students.* Unpublished master's thesis, Arizona State University, Tempe, AZ.

Kinzie, M. B., Sullivan, H. J., and Berdel, R. L. (1988). Learner control and achievement in science computer-assisted instruction. *Journal of Educational Psychology 80*(3), 299–303.

Park, O., and Gittelman, S. S. (1992). Selective use of animation and feedback in computer-based instruction. *Educational Technology Research and Development 40*(4), 27–38.

Rieber, L. P. (1992). Computer-based microworlds: A bridge between constructivism and direct instruction. *Educational Technology Research and Development 40*(1), 93–106.

Robyler, M. D. (1988). Fundamental problems and principles of designing effective course-ware. In *Instructional designs for microcomputer courseware*, ed. D. Jonassen (Hillsdale, NJ: Lawrence Erlbaum), 7–33.

Shen, S. (1994). *Student attributes and occupational preferences of Chinese and American adolescents.* Unpublished doctoral dissertation, Arizona State University, Tempe, AZ.

Sullivan, H. J., Igoe, A. R., Klein, J. D., Jones, E. E., and Savenye, W. C. (1993). Perspectives on the future of educational technology. *Educational Technology Research and Development 41*(2), 97–110.

Tobin, K., and Dawson, G. (1992). Constraints to curriculum reform: Teachers and the myths of schooling. *Educational Technology Research and Development 40*(1), 81–92.

Weber, J. (1994). Learning a costly lesson on computers. *Los Angeles Times,* 14 May, 1, 20–21.

Part Two
The Profession

Introduction

Part Two extends some of the trends and issues described in Part One. The emphasis here is on the past contributions of James D. Finn, an influential figure and early leader in the field, and future needs for research on the profession.

Randy Koetting set the stage for a symposium held at the 1994 AECT convention on the occasion of the 25th anniversary of James D. Finn's death. Koetting's articulate and provocative introduction leads to individual perceptions of three authors who review Finn's contributions to the profession from their special perspectives. Robert Heinich, Professor Emeritus, Indiana University, did his doctoral work with Finn. In his section, he reviews Finn's influence on the curriculum of instructional technology from five viewpoints. Ely, who worked closely with Finn on several national projects, describes Finn's role in creating and shaping a professional association for the field. Januszewski, who never knew Finn personally but has studied his work extensively, considers Finn's contributions to the intellectual and theoretical development of instructional technology.

The chapter by Michael Molenda is the first publication of his concern about research on the profession. Molenda contends that educational technologists ought to know more about themselves as professionals—for instance, such matters as definition, types of positions, compensation, marketplace demands for personnel, professional preparation, professional organizations, and workplace matters. There is actually very little information about these topics in the current literature. Molenda outlines the areas in which further research is needed to gain a better picture of the status and direction of individuals who call themselves educational (or instructional) technologists.

The *Yearbook* is one of the few places where concerns about the profession and its population are regularly recorded. These chapters help to review one important era from the past and to chart the course ahead.

On the Importance of Historical Understanding Within Our Own Work*

J. Randall Koetting
Associate Professor, Department of Curriculum and Instruction
University of Nevada-Reno

My contribution to this section of the text is by way of an introduction. I want to speak to the critical importance of having an historical understanding or perspective as we write and study and teach. The ideas we use in our work, as well as the ways we talk about our work in educational technology, have a foundation that we must be concerned with. The ideas come from "somewhere," from the thoughts and writings of someone or group, as well as "somewhere/one" before them, and so on. That is part of studying history; that is part of understanding or studying any discipline, as well as the influences on our own thoughts within and outside that discipline.

As I reflected on what approach I would take in writing this introduction to the following essays on the work and person of James Finn, I wanted to maintain the spirit of the past several editions of the *Educational Media and Technology Yearbook* in their representation of influential thinkers through profiles or brief biographies. What these profiles and biographies represented to me was the subtlety of differential influences and experiences and how these influences and experiences affect us in our work and in our personal and professional lives.

I will not do an analysis of the three essays that follow. The authors speak for themselves. Nor will I present a biographical profile of James Finn. Rather, I write from the perspective of knowing a person and his work, and not knowing the person, but knowing the work of the person. I use an essay by Ralph Waldo Emerson (1883) entitled "Uses of Great Men" as a basis for my reflections.

I would like to start with a brief comment on reading Emerson in the 1990s. Today Emerson probably would not use the term *men*, but rather "Uses of Great 'Scholars' " or great "Thinkers," or "Uses of Great Individuals as Role Models," or some such title. Although the language of Emerson's essay may seem stilted, flowery or grandiose, as well as sexist, I think the content of what Emerson presented is very much in keeping with the spirit of the essays and brief biographies that have appeared in the *Yearbooks*, as well as the following essays on the work of James Finn. I will not alter Emerson's language of the 1880s, and yet I am quite sensitive to issues of gender it raises.

---

*This article is dedicated to Dr. Russell L. Dobson, Professor Emeritus, Oklahoma State University: Mentor, colleague, friend.

KNOWING THE PERSON AND KNOWING THE WORK

Being a true contemporary of a person (e.g., a contemporary of James Finn), knowing him personally as well as his work and struggles with the work and study, can add a dimension of mutual respect that is shown to colleagues who share the same struggles. If we are truly fortunate, "knowing" a person can go beyond the relationship of colleague or teacher to be that of a mentor. There is the privilege of knowing and talking with each other. The value of a colleague, teacher, or mentor is suggested by Emerson:

> I can say that by another which I cannot do alone. I can say to you what I cannot first say to myself. Other men are lenses through which we read our own minds (Emerson, 1883, p. 11).

Scholarship does not exist in isolation. There is a time for personal study and reflection, and a time for dialogue. It is in the dialogue and study that we challenge our thinking and push it further. Scholarship demands the company and the conversation of others. I believe we can have a sense of this when we share a specific research interest with a colleague, when we struggle through similar life or professional struggles, and so on. We know what this means to us, because we continue to come to conferences, we continue to maintain professional ties with each other, we continue to take an interest in each other's work. We continue our conversations.

Emerson reminds us that greatness, the "great person," comes from "nature," that is, he or she is part of humankind. And "great person's" greatness is unique. Yet that greatness/great person must somehow be related to us

> and our life receive from him some promise of explanation. "I cannot tell what I would know; but I have observed there are persons who, in their character and actions, answer questions which I have not skill to put" (Emerson 1883, p. 12).

Knowing the person, we begin to know the work of the person in a different, personal way. We can talk of the person himself or herself. We can interpret writings from the vantage point of personal knowledge of the person, as well as the work itself. We can agree with, as well as engage in critique of, the person and the work. We can get answers, or perhaps rather a direction or insight into questions we do not know how to ask.

KNOWING A PERSON FROM HIS OR HER WORK

> *"True genius will not impoverish, but will liberate, and add new senses."*
> (Emerson 1883, p. 23)

Knowing a person's work—a person's work in relation to his or her study (e.g., the work of James Finn)—yet not knowing the person provides a distance. This distance can promote a certain respect for the person, and allow us to listen more objectively. For a person who studies the work of an author, there is a responsibility, and sometimes a burden, to re-present the author through his or her own words, as well as through his or her own historical time frame. Hence we may develop a perspective that is critical of the work of the person, as well as identifying his or her historical significance and stature. The "true genius" that Emerson refers to will challenge us to push beyond our own knowledge boundaries. The true genius can liberate and provide new understandings. This is the emancipatory potential of education.

Not personally knowing James Finn (and many other scholars who are not our contemporaries, whom we may not know personally), we can read his (their) essays and works. Through the study of James Finn's work we can "see" the philosopher/scholar, we can see the man with a strong vision for the future of a professional association for the field of instructional technology. We can see a man rooted in his times yet looking ahead, a person who gives form and shape to a national organization. We can see how he differed with others of his time. I can view James Finn within our present context and wonder whether it is possible for one person today to provide the political and educational agenda for an organization, particularly an organization that has grown in size to the membership of the Association for Educational Communications and Technology.

As we live in academia, what can we rely on in our work? There are texts. There is the need to pay attention to the people with whom we work and interact, and whom we meet year after year at our professional conferences and other meeting arenas. There are many scholars among us who have important, thoughtful, and challenging positions—radical views, such as Finn's work must have seemed during his time. Reading the work of and interacting with people who differ with our positions or who challenge the mainstream voices of the field can challenge us to consider new possibilities. Emerson comments:

> We are equally served by receiving and by imparting [knowledge]. Men who know the same things are not long the best of company for each other. But bring to each an intelligent person of another experience, and it is as if you let off water from a lake by cutting a lower basin. It seems a mechanical advantage, and great benefit it is to each speaker, as he can now paint out his thought to himself (Emerson 1883, p. 35).

As we cannot engage James Finn in this conversation, we must work with each other to understand our intellectual history, in which James Finn was a major participant. We must bring that intellectual foundation and history to our understanding of ourselves today. We must take those ideas further, expanding explanations and understandings and creating new "knowledge." It is one way in which we can "use" the "great" men, women, and ideas of intellectual history. Emerson states that:

> Within the limits of human education and agency, we may say that great men exist that there may be greater men. The destiny of organized nature is amelioration, and who can tell its limits? It is for man to tame the chaos; on every side, whilst he lives, to scatter the seeds of science and of song, that climate, corn, animals, men, may be milder, and the germs of love and benefit may be multiplied (Emerson 1883, p. 38).

Emerson's language may not be our language, or the language we hear in relation to education today. Yet it is a language that identifies the possibilities open to us in our interactions with each other as we study, teach, and do research. We need to pay attention to each other. We are also building upon, and making history.

CONCLUDING COMMENT

Emerson starts his essay with the following thought:

> It is natural to believe in great men. . . . The world is upheld by the veracity of good men: they make the earth wholesome. They who lived with them found life glad and nutritious. Life is sweet and tolerable only in our belief in such society (Emerson 1883, p. 9).

This sense of the use of great individuals is a positive, humane commentary for our present context. Living in academia can be a liberating experience. Our studies, research, and teaching can open us to the work and lives of many people. If we are open to these diverse experiences, our lives may be peopled with great individuals. If we are fortunate, we are privileged to know and interact with them.

REFERENCE

Emerson, Ralph Waldo. (1883). Uses of great men. In *Representative men. Vol. IV, Emerson's complete works* (Cambridge: Riverside Press).

Finn and the Curriculum
of Instructional Technology

Robert Heinich
Professor Emeritus
Indiana University

The influence of James D. Finn on the curriculum of instructional technology manifested itself in five ways: (1) a broad view of the field that maintained a connection with related disciplines; (2) expansion of the literature of the field; (3) the introduction of courses based on the cutting edge of technology; (4) the unabashed acknowledgment that media and machines (generically speaking) are at the heart of the field; and (5) perhaps most important, the impact of technology on institutions.

The first course I took from Finn was at Colorado State College of Education (now the University of Northern Colorado) in 1947. The title was "Communication, Education, and Propaganda." This was my introduction to Finn's insistence that the study of general communication was an integral part of the field, a position he emphasized in his article on needed research in volume one, number one of *A-V Communication Review* (1953). When he went to the University of Southern California (USC), he introduced a course on communications. This connection was long ignored by much of the field, but recent developments in computer networks and satellite transmissions are reconnecting us with the societal implications of communications and proving the wisdom of Finn.

This spirit of inquiry extended into sociology, anthropology, and other disciplines, as a perusal of his references in articles such as *A Walk on the Altered Side* (1962) will affirm. As a result, he was recognized as someone with broad-ranging concerns and invited to participate in "think-tanks" such as Robert Hutchins's Center for the Study of Democratic Institutions in Santa Barbara.

In 1956, he and Charlie Hoban separately but collaboratively pushed the field into the concept of systems, Charlie at Okoboji and Jim in a series of journal articles. He quickly saw that the work going on in systems engineering and operations research had implications for instructional technology. In the spring of 1963, USC was the first to offer a course in designing instructional systems (taught by Len Silvern), which is now a standard part, in some form, of the curriculum of every graduate program.

When new technologies came on the horizon, Finn explored their potential through the introduction of courses. For example, USC offered the first course in multi-image productions, an outgrowth of his presentations on the Technological Development Project. He was using electronic student response systems in the 1960s. Technology to Finn was a process, a way of solving problems, but he also knew that media and machines often made the process possible—and transferable.

I mentioned the Technological Development Project, funded by the U.S. Office of Education and administered through the National Education Association (NEA). (At that time the Association for Educational Communications and Technology was the Division of

Audio-Visual Instruction (DAVI), a department of NEA.) The project explored the implications of technology in education. One of its most significant outcomes was the first codification of technology. Finn commissioned Don Ely of Syracuse University to head that part of the project. The result has had a continuing influence on the curriculum of the field and set in motion the basis for periodic review of the intellectual foundations of instructional technology.

Finn's interest in the relationship between technology and culture, as studied by sociologists, anthropologists, and historians of technology, led him to investigate the potential changes that technology could effect in education. He recognized that, while the culture at large embraced technology, the subculture of education kept technology on the periphery of its activities. (Larry Cuban's book *Teachers and Machines: The Classroom Use of Technology Since 1920* is an accurate analysis of why.) But he was convinced that eventually technology would force itself into the mainstream, and that when it did, the institution of education as we know it would not be the same. Some of his most provocative writings, such as "The Franks Had the Right Idea" (1964), were extrapolations into education of how certain technological innovations changed history. His 1960 article, "Technology and the Instructional Process," was an attempt to demonstrate how this might happen with the technology of the period, using the systems approach that he and Hoban had written about in 1956. The technology we have today is far more likely to bring about the changes he anticipated.

James D. Finn died at the peak of his intellectual powers. His legacy is still felt in the curricula of instructional technology programs. But we lost an irreplaceable giant. We can only speculate on what his ultimate contribution would have been.

REFERENCES

Cuban, L. (1986). *Teachers and machines: The classroom use of technology since 1920.* New York: Teachers College Press.

Finn, J. D. (1953). Professionalizing the audio-visual field. *Audio-Visual Communication Review 1*(1), 6–17.

Finn, J. D. (1960, Winter). Technology and the instructional process. *Audio-Visual Communication Review 8*(5), 5–26.

Finn, J. D. (1962, October). A walk on the altered side. *Phi Delta Kappan 44*(1), 29–34.

Finn, J. D. (1964, April). The Franks had the right idea. *NEA Journal 53*(4), 24–27.

James D. Finn and the Development of a Professional Association for the Field of Instructional Technology

Donald P. Ely
Professor of Education, Syracuse University

In 1957, I wrote my first fan letter. It was to Jim Finn. At that time he was editor of *Teaching Tools* magazine. I don't remember the editorial that moved me to write, but I do remember him well and the ideas he generated.

I first met Jim Finn in 1958 when I visited the University of Southern California to do some research on my dissertation. I asked him if I could attend the class he was teaching that evening, thinking that it would be focused on some aspect of instructional technology, but, to my surprise, it was a Philosophy of Education course. Jim was a person of multiple intellectual dimensions. His dean, Irving Melbo, said: "Dr. Finn was at heart a philosopher" (Lane 1974, p. 120).

After these initial encounters, I met and worked with Jim many times until his untimely death. He encouraged and supported my effort to define the field and to try to bring some order to its terminology. (He called it the "French Academy for the Preservation of the Language.") As a result of his prodding (and some money he had obtained from his U.S. Office of Education), I coordinated the publication of *The Audiovisual Process in Education: A Definition and a Glossary of Related Terms,* published in 1963. I managed the Washington office of the Technological Development Project after Lee Campion left to head the Educational Communications Program in New York state. Jim, Charlie Schuller (of Michigan State University), and I founded the consortium known first as the Special Media Institutes, which later (with Jack Edling from Teaching Research of the Oregon State System of Higher Education and various leaders from Indiana University) became the University Consortium for Instructional Development and Technology (UCIDT). Subsequently, Arizona State University, Florida State University, and the University of Georgia became active members. The major product of our early effort, first envisioned by Finn, was the Instructional Development Institute (IDI), which has had a lasting impact on our field.

My professional career has been deeply influenced by James Finn. His *vision* was contagious; his *intellect* was marked by *curiosity* and *depth of understanding*. He had that special quality of mind that took apparently isolated facts and, with his talent for creative extrapolation, made sense by identifying trends and issues facing the field. Most of his ideas were well founded in the history and philosophy of education.

FINN'S CONTRIBUTIONS TO THE DEVELOPMENT
OF A PROFESSIONAL ASSOCIATION IN
INSTRUCTIONAL TECHNOLOGY

There is no better place to start with Finn's contribution to the development of a professional association than the principles he so eloquently articulated in the first issue of *Audio-Visual Communication Review* (*AVCR*) in 1953, a journal that he helped to found. In the classic article, "Professionalizing the Audio-Visual Field," Finn spelled out the characteristics of a profession:

> A profession has, at least, these characteristics: (a) an intellectual technique, (b) an application of that technique to the practical affairs of man, (c) a period of long training necessary before entering into the profession, (d) an association of the members of the profession into a closely knit group with a high quality of communication between members, (e) a series of standards and a statement of ethics which is enforced, and (f) an organized body of intellectual theory constantly expanding by research (1953, p. 7).

In regard to the association characteristic, Finn had already targeted the Department of Audio Visual Instruction of the National Education Association as the group to lead the field into the professional spotlight. He had already begun "communication between members" by founding *Teaching Tools* magazine and, later, *AVCR*. His energy and visibility brought about his election to the presidency of DAVI. During this term of office (1961-1962), he initiated projects and programs at a furious pace while serving as chief spokesman for the field. His work did not go unrecognized.

To fulfill the challenges and requirements of the presidential office, Finn obtained a $102,000 grant from the U.S. Office of Education and called it the Technological Development Project. He set up offices in Los Angeles and Washington, DC—right in the NEA building. He recruited me to head the definition and terminology effort that produced the first published glossary in the field. He organized an invitational seminar on the Education of the AV Communication Specialist at the 1960 DAVI convention, which featured such participants as Marshall McLuhan, George Gerbner, Ole Larson, and a dozen others of similar stature. Another monograph came from that conference. Both of these efforts helped to advance the profession toward the criteria he had defined earlier.

Meanwhile, from the "bully pulpit" of his DAVI presidency, he addressed the staid members of the John Dewey Society at their annual conference. He published "A Walk on the Altered Side" in the *Phi Delta Kappan* in 1962 and was quoted (out of context, much to his chagrin) in *Time* magazine. The denouement of his presidential year was his presidential address at the 1961 DAVI convention in Miami Beach, when he enraged the humanists with his "Tradition in the Iron Mask" speech, which held that the humanists had restrained the technologists who were trying to bring about technological changes in education, just as Dumas's character had held his twin brother in bondage. He relished these opportunities to awaken traditionalists to the impending movement of instructional technology. Especially noteworthy were his challenges (in print) to A. Whitney Griswold, president of Yale, and Rudolf Flesch, author of *Why Johnny Can't Read*, and invitations to address groups of intellectuals at the Center for the Study of Democratic Institutions and Harvard University. He was in his element in the dens of intellectuals and public figures.

But these were not ego trips. They were forays into the educational holy of holies. He shared his writings and presentations with the instructional technology (IT) community. Most of us stood on the sidelines, cheering him on, as he scored points for emerging field. We were beginning to believe that there was a field of instructional technology and we saw Finn as our prophet. No one since, in my opinion, has come close to Finn in this regard. He not only emboldened those of us who were making inroads at schools, colleges, and universities across the country, but he also empowered his students at USC to pick up the torch and carry it with pride.

I don't recall how important Finn considered the name change of our professional association. He did make a case for "Instructional Technology" at the Milwaukee convention in 1965. Others supported changes that would incorporate "Learning Resources," "Educational Communications," and "Audiovisual Education." Finn's arguments could be used today:

> If, as an organization of professionals, we understand what technology is and understand that our jobs, whatever they may be—producer, designer, administrator, research worker, teacher, educator—are the management and operation of the technological function within the social institution of education at any level, we have a future. . . . Properly constructed, the concept of instructional or educational technology is totally integrative. It provides a common ground for all professionals, no matter in what aspect of the field they are working. . . . The concept is so completely viable that it will not only provide new status for our group, but will, for the first time, threaten the status of others. We can, I repeat, make no other choice but to call ourselves the Department of Instructional (or Educational) Technology (1965, p. 193).

The compromise, "Association for Educational Communications and Technology" (AECT) was reached a year later at the Atlantic City convention. He succeeded in getting "technology" into the name, but that was not a major issue on his agenda. His concern was more conceptual, and his hopes for the association were more political than show.

AECT honored Finn by publishing a volume of his writings, *Extending Education Through Technology*, edited by Ron McBeath, one of his doctoral graduates. Four of his doctoral graduates became presidents of DAVI (AECT)—Bob Gerletti, Bob Heinich, Mendel Sherman, and John Vergis. Other graduates who have contributed to the association and the field include Bob Casey, Paul Saettler, Ken Silber, Ron McBeath, and C. J. Wallington. The tradition of the Past Presidents group and an annual dinner for them at the national convention was initiated by Finn.

It is difficult to add it all up and say "The total is the sum of Finn's contributions to our professional association." The total is *more* than the sum of the parts. More, in that the vision Finn possessed has been passed on to others—colleagues and former students. His ideas have been with us at every convention; his advocacy for the profession persists; and AECT, as a professional association, has come a long way in meeting the criteria he established for us in 1953.

REFERENCES

Finn, J. D. (1953). Professionalizing the audio-visual field. *Audio-Visual Communication Review 1*(1), 6–17.

Finn, J. D. (1961). The tradition in the Iron Mask. *Audiovisual Instruction 6*(6), 238–43.

Finn, J. D. (1965). Instructional technology. *Audiovisual Instruction 10*(3), 192–94.

Lane, Mary C. (1974). *The Melbo years.* Los Angeles, CA: University of Southern California Press.

McBeath, Ron, ed. (1972). *Extending education through technology: Selected writings by James D. Finn.* Washington, DC: Association for Educational Communications and Technology.

BIBLIOGRAPHY

The history of instructional technology. (1965). 16mm film produced by Robert Wagner, The Ohio State University.

The teacher of tomorrow. (1965). 16mm film produced by Robert Wagner, The Ohio State University.

James D. Finn and the Process
of Educational Technology

Alan Januszewski
SUNY Potsdam

James D. Finn's contribution to the development of the process view of educational technology can best be analyzed in light of his desire to upgrade the status of the audiovisual education movement to a professional field of study. Finn's assessment of the need for the first definition of the field in 1963 and his effort to change the name of the field to *educational technology* in 1965 are just two examples of his contribution to the process view of educational technology.

Finn covered much ground in his writing about the concepts and techniques of the field. This included the systems concept, the importance of instructional programming, the difference between a scientific and an empirical approach to developing instruction, and the relationship between the teacher and technology. But Finn's interest in the process view of the field can be traced to his earliest writings. In 1953 he evaluated the audiovisual field as a candidate for professional status and identified six characteristics of a profession:

> (a) an intellectual technique, (b) an application of that technique to the practical affairs of man, (c) a period of long training necessary before entering into the profession, (d) an association of the members of the profession into a closely knit group with a high quality of communication between members, (e) a series of standards and a statement of ethics which is enforced, and (f) an organized body of intellectual theory constantly expanded by research (1953, p. 7).

Of these six characteristics of a profession, the two that were most important to the development of Finn's process view of educational technology were (1) an intellectual technique and (2) a body of intellectual theory expanded by research. In fact, Finn sought to have the intellectual technique of the field based on theory that was supported by research.

Finn argued that "the most fundamental and most important characteristic of a profession is that the skills involved are founded upon a body of intellectual theory and research" (1953, p. 8). Once he had established the importance of systematic theory and research for professional status, Finn further explained his position by saying that "this systematic theory is constantly being expanded by research and thinking *within* the profession" (1953, p. 8). Finn did not believe that a profession was simply knowledge from a particular academic subject put into practice. Rather, he was arguing that a profession conducts its own research and theory development to complement the research and theory that it adapts or adopts from other academic areas of study.

In 1953, Finn was generally satisfied that "the audiovisual member does possess an intellectual technique" (p. 8), but it was not clear just what that technique was. Finn described the technique as thinking "reflectively in such varied areas as the critical evaluation of materials, the visualization of abstract concepts, the improvement of instruction, and in many aspects of planning and administration" (1953, p. 8). Finn never clearly articulated what he meant by the phrase "thinking reflectively," but it does seem likely that he meant it as the application of research and theory to professional practice.

Finn believed that the audiovisual field was plagued by a "lack of theoretical direction" and attributed this to a general "lack of content" in the field. He also charged that there was an absence of "intellectual meat" in the meetings and professional journals of the field (1953, p. 14). In his argument promoting the development of a theoretical base for the audiovisual field, Finn warned that:

> Without a theory which produces hypotheses for research, there can be no expanding knowledge and technique. And without a constant attempt to assess practice so that the theoretical implications may be teased out, there can be no assurance that we will ever have a theory or that our practice will make sense (1953, p. 14).

Finn spent much of his career rectifying this deficiency in theory and research in the audiovisual field.

Agreement with Finn's criteria and reasoning about professions is not at issue here. What is important is that this argument was largely accepted by, and had a profound effect on, the leadership of the audiovisual field. It also established the direction for Finn's future scholarship.

The view that technology was primarily a process became a favorite theme for Finn. Although he was the acknowledged leader in the early movement to establish educational technology as a process (Heinich 1968; Ely 1970; AECT 1977), Finn was not always consistent with the label that he used to describe the complex processes involved in audiovisual education.

Finn's earlier writings (1955, 1957) concentrated on the concept of automation in education. As part of his analysis of the possibilities of automation for education, Finn wrote that "automation is not a manless [sic], machine-operated production. *Its primary characteristic is a process—a way of thinking involving patterns and self-regulation* [my emphasis]. It is here that the educational implications are tremendous" (1955, p. 145).

Two years later Finn produced the first in a series of three articles about the potential for automation in education for *AV Communication Review*, "Automation and Education: General Aspects" (1957). In that article Finn identified the important characteristics of automation and its associated processes as: "(a) the concept of systems; (b) the flow and control of information; (c) scientific analysis and long-range planning; (d) an increase in the need for wise decision making; and (e) a high-level technology" (pp. 115-16).

Initially, Finn considered automation to be an expansion—an outgrowth—of technology. The fifth characteristic of automation that Finn identified, that automation included "a high-level technology," showed that at this point in his thinking Finn drew a distinction between automation and technology. Soon, however, this distinction became blurred.

Finn frequently used the terms *technical* and *technology* in his early writings (1953, 1955, 1956). But it was in the early 1960s that Finn changed the label of those complex educational processes which interested him from "automation" to "technology."

Finn spent a substantial part of his professional life trying to dispel the image that technology was just machines. In 1960, Finn wrote that "technology, however, is more than an invention—more than machines. It is a process and a way of thinking" (1960b, p. 142). Finn then explained the relationship of technology to the instructional process, saying that:

[One] must remember that, in addition to machinery, technology includes processes, systems, management, and control mechanisms both human and non human, and above all, the attitude discussed by [Charles] Beard—a way of looking at problems as to their interest and difficulty (broadly conceived) of those solutions. This is the context in which the educator must study technology (p. 145).

In 1961 Finn made only minor revisions of his earlier descriptions of technology. In an article analyzing audiovisual needs for the preparation of teachers, he argued that "technology . . . is much more than machines; technology involves systems, control mechanisms, patterns of organization, and a way of approaching problems" (1961, p. 209).

In opposition to the view that technology is a device or series of devices, Finn argued that machines were "symbols . . . and must be thought of in connection with systems, organizational patterns, utilization practices, and so forth, to present a true technological picture" (1961, p. 210). Later, as part of a speech delivered to the John Dewey Society in 1962, Finn said that "technology is not, as many of the technically illiterate seem to think, a collection of gadgets, of hardware, of instrumentation. It is instead, best described as a way of thinking about certain classes of problems and their solutions" (1962, p. 70).

In 1964 he wrote that "Technology is not just hardware—or even hardware and materials. Technology is a way of organizing, a way of thinking, involving at the center, to be sure, man-machine systems, but including systems of organization, patterns of use, tests of economic feasibility" (1964, p. 295).

Finn followed that with "Instructional technology [should] be viewed as defined in this paper—a complex pattern of man-machine systems and organizations based on concepts of feasibility" (1966b, p. 247).

It is unclear whether Finn decided that technology, which in 1957 he considered a condition of automation, had to be determined and clarified as part of a desired automated state of education, or if he decided to change the label of the object that he was talking about all along, "automation," to "technology." In either case, certain specific themes continued to appear throughout his writing.

There is a great deal of similarity and consistency in the way in which Finn described automation and technology. He argued that automation was a process and a way of thinking (1955, 1957), and that technology was a process and a way of thinking (1960b, 1961). He further stated that automation included systems, controls, scientific analysis, and planning (1955, 1957), and that technology included systems, controls, and management and/or organization (1960a, 1961). Finn's discussions of the need for scientific analysis and planning in automation (1957) are very similar to the discussions of management and organization included in his conceptions of technology (1961, 1962).

Although Finn's descriptions of automation and technology remained similar over the years, one important facet did seem to shift within Finn's writing on technology: the relationship of technology to problems. In 1960, Finn viewed technology as "a way of looking at problems" (1960a). In 1961, Finn stated that technology is "a way of approaching problems." It could be argued that "looking at problems" means defining problems, and that "approaching problems" means defining problems but also includes taking some action to solve a problem. The phrases "looking at problems" and "approaching problems" both infer a way to begin to solve problems. Both phrases infer a certain "attitude" (1960a) toward professional practice. This attitude would directly affect the intellectual technique of the audiovisual profession.

In 1962 a not-so-subtle shift occurred in Finn's outlook, which carried on through his subsequent discussions of the process of technology and problem solving (1965b, 1966b). It was the view that technology is "a way of thinking about *certain classes* [my emphasis] of problems." It is clear from this statement that Finn believed that there were limitations to technology's problem-solving ability. It seems to mean that technology either cannot solve, or should not be used to solve, all problems. Considering Finn's optimistic view of technology, one could easily conclude that his position prior to 1962 was that technology was essentially the technique to be used to look at or approach all educational problems.

It is difficult to assess what prompted Finn to make this further clarification of his position. Perhaps it was the fact that this 1962 statement was part of his address to the John Dewey Society. The prospect of talking with educational philosophers may have provided Finn with reason to reflect on his ideas concerning technology as a way of thinking. What is certain is that this shift or clarification in Finn's writing on technology remained a part of his thinking for the rest of his professional life.

The implication of this shift by Finn is not recognized by those members of the field who describe educational technology as simply "a problem solving approach to education." It does not seem as though Finn intended educational technology to be viewed as an all-encompassing approach to education, as was inferred by later definitions of educational technology published in the field.

Another look at his analyses of technology reveals that even Finn, the great proponent of technology as process, conceded that machines and materials were a major part of instructional technology. This is best seen in his discussion aimed at changing the name of the professional organization and the field to instructional technology. There he stated that "machines, materials, methods of use, [and] systems are all part of the pattern of rational mechanisms operating as means to educational ends. And, as Hobban has said, machines are central to this concept even though they alone are not technology" (Finn 1965a, p. 193). This statement is consistent with his prior writings on technology (1960a, 1960b, 1961), all of which include machines as an essential component of technology. For Finn, it seemed that if there were no machines there could be no technology.

CONCLUSION

Three conclusions can be drawn from this brief exploration of Finn's writing about the process view of educational technology and the intellectual technique of our field. First, Finn was a man with a vision for his profession. But it is often the case that individuals with long-range visions focus on broad ideas and do not always develop those ideas into specific concepts. This seems to be the case with Finn, as he never provided a specific statement of his definition of *technology*. Second, Finn changed his ideas on technology over time. This is exemplified by his discussions on problems in technology and his use of the terms *automation* and *technology* to refer to the same idea. Third, Finn has been misinterpreted by others in the field, specifically in the areas of problem solving and educational technology. What is certain is that the ideas Finn articulated were changed or reoriented by the membership of the field. This is simply a playing out of the premise that ideas change over time.

No matter how one views his writing and his influence on the process of educational technology, Finn had a long-range vision that gave direction to his work. He also had the drive to gain that direction—to professionalize the audiovisual field by developing the process view of educational technology.

REFERENCES

Association for Educational Communications and Technology. (1977). *The definition of educational technology.* Washington, DC: Author.

Ely, D. P. (1970). Toward a philosophy of Instructional Technology. *The British Journal of Educational Technology 1*(2), 81–94.

Finn, J. D. (1953). Professionalizing the audio-visual field. *Audio-Visual Communication Review 1*(1), 6–17.

Finn, J. D. (1955, Fall). A look at the future of AV communication. *Audio-Visual Communication Review 3*(4), 244–56.

Finn, J. D. (1956). AV development and the concept of systems. *Teaching Tools 3*(4), 163–64.

Finn, J. D. (1957, Winter). Automation and education: General aspects. *Audio-Visual Communication Review 5*(1), 343–60.

Finn, J. D. (1960a). Automation and education: A new theory for instructional technology. *Audio-Visual Communication Review 8*(1), 5–26.

Finn, J. D. (1960b, November). Teaching machines: Auto-instructional devices for the teacher. *NEA Journal 49*(8), 41–44.

Finn, J. D. (1961). New techniques for teaching in the sixties. In *Teacher Education: Direction for the sixties* (American Association of Colleges for Teacher Education, National Education Association), 31–42.

Finn, J. D. (1962, October). A walk on the altered side. *Phi Delta Kappan 44*(1), 29–34.

Finn, J. D. (1964, April). The Franks had the right idea. *NEA Journal 53*(4), 24–27.

Finn, J. D. (1965a). Instructional technology. *Audiovisual Instruction 10*(3), 192–94.

Finn, J. D. (1965b, December). The marginal media man. Part 1: The great paradox. *Audiovisual Instruction 10*(10), 762–65.

Finn, J. D. (1966a, February). The emerging technology of education. In *Educational implications of technological change,* Appendix, Vol. 4, Technology and the American economy. Prepared for the National Commission on Technology, Automation, and Economic Progress (Washington, DC: U.S. Government Printing Office), 33–52.

Finn, J. D. (1966b). *Educational technology, innovation, and Title III.* Prepared for Projects to Advance Creativity in Education (PACE).

Heinich, R. (1968). Is there a field of educational communications and technology? *Audiovisual Instruction 18*(5), 44–46.

Note: The articles, reports, and chapters written by Finn in this reference list include the page numbers from the original sources of publication. However, many of the quotations cited in the text use the page numbers from the book *Extending Education Through Technology, Selected Writings by James D. Finn,* ed. Ron McBeath (Washington, DC: AECT, 1972). This volume is a compilation of the best of Finn's writing and has been very useful in my research. I have checked many of the papers of this volume against the original and find them to be most accurate. For practical purposes, in this study I have used McBeath's volume instead of many of the original articles.

An Agenda for Research on the Educational Media and Technology Profession

Michael H. Molenda
Associate Professor, School of Education
Indiana University

INTRODUCTION

Who are we? Where are we going? What useful purpose do we serve? Such introspective questions—although annoying to some—are necessary questions for a profession to ask of itself periodically. During the late 1980s, the Board of Directors of the Association for Educational Communications and Technology (AECT) undertook strategic planning for the future of the association. They began by looking at the members who constitute the organization and who populate the educational media and technology (em/t) profession. As they did so, they realized that there are many questions about "who we are" and "where we are going" that could not be answered with any degree of certainty. The data either did not exist or were not readily accessible.

This dearth of information about the profession was considered serious enough to set up a task force, later a committee, on "Research on the Profession." This committee, chaired first by George Grimes and later by Michael Molenda, operated from 1990 to 1994 with the charge of doing something to remedy this information gap. The group decided that a long-term solution must include the promotion of continuing research about the educational media and technology profession and the establishment of a mechanism for making this research available to those seeking information.

Fortunately, the committee discovered early that Donald P. Ely, Director of the ERIC Clearinghouse on Information and Technology, had already committed the Clearinghouse to serving the storage and dissemination functions envisioned by the committee. From that point, the committee focused on a strategy of:

- staking out the territory to be included in "research on the profession,"

- determining where the knowledge gaps are, and

- encouraging further research to fill those knowledge gaps.

This report is the first effort to stake out the territory or identify the domain of knowledge to be covered. It is the hope of the committee that this agenda will stimulate interest among researchers and apprentice researchers. It comprises a set of questions, the answers to which cast light on who we are, where we are going, and what useful purpose we serve.

A pre-publication draft of this agenda was presented at the 1995 AECT annual convention by Michael Molenda and J. Fred Olive. Reactions were given by Donald Ely, Sandy Patton, and Philip Doughty. Each made valuable substantive suggestions, which have been incorporated in this first published version.

THE AGENDA

I. Definition of the Field

A. *Boundaries:* What is the currently accepted definition of the educational media and technology (em/t) field?
- within the profession
- among outside individuals and groups

B. *Image:* How is the field perceived?
- within the profession
- among outside individuals and groups

C. *Historical Perspective:* How have perceptions changed over time?

D. *Justification for Existence:* Are em/t specialists needed? What valuable functions do they serve within the organization? Within society? What potential harm might be caused by ignorant, incompetent, or unethical practice? Are employers well informed about qualifications em/t professionals should possess?

II. Positions Held

A. *Position Titles:* What positions are currently held by em/t professionals
- in schools?
- in higher education?
- in business/industry?
- in government?
- other?

B. *Marketplace:* What sorts of positions are currently being advertised?

C. *Qualifications:* What entry qualifications are expected by employers?

D. *Marketplace Status:* Is there a balance between supply and demand of graduates?

E. *Roles:* How are the roles of em/t specialists defined?
- What different roles are defined and advocated within the field?
- What different roles are actually being played by practitioners?
- What do exemplary performers do that makes them exemplary?

F. *Career Paths:* What are typical career paths followed by em/t professionals?

G. *Position/Role Trends:* Is there a pattern of change in the types of positions available, the supply of qualified applicants, the roles played, or career paths?

III. Compensation Versus Demands

A. *Compensation Status:* What are the current salary ranges for different positions? Other compensation?

B. *Compensation Variables:* Do salaries vary by educational level? Geographical location? Workplace? Gender? Other variables?

C. *Compensation Trends:* Is there a pattern of change in salaries or other compensation?

D. *Job Demands:* What responsibilities do em/t professionals have? What special stresses are they subjected to?

E. *Job Demand Trends:* How are job demands changing? How are stresses changing?

IV. Professional Preparation and Standards

A. *Academic Study Opportunities:* Where are degrees in em/t offered?
- Master's
- Specialist/Certificate
- Doctoral

B. *Distribution of Students:* How many students graduate from each program/degree?
- Male/female
- Minorities
- International

C. *Academic Curricula:* What are the curricula offered in these programs? How do they differ?

D. *Core Curriculum:* To what extent is there agreement on a "core curriculum"?

E. *Program Quality:* Are there evaluative data about these programs (e.g., relative to relevance of curricula to career preparedness)?

F. *Preparation/Practice Match:* What sorts of training are most valuable in helping students become successful practitioners?

G. *Academic Program Trends:* Are the number or type of programs or graduates changing? Are the curricula changing? Are the programs flourishing, declining, remaining steady?

H. *Continuing Professional Development:* What sorts of continuing education are needed? Wanted?

I. *Standards:* What standards of professional competence or ethical codes are advocated? Enforced?

V. Communications

A. *Communications Among Professionals:* How do professionals communicate among themselves?
- adequacy of journals and periodicals
- accessibility of publications

B. *Information Sources:* How is needed information stored and retrieved?
- accessibility of print and electronic databases

C. *Linkages:* How do professionals, individually and in groups, connect with others?
- on a local and regional basis?
- on a national basis?
- on an international basis?

VI. Professional Organizations

A. *Membership:* Which professional organizations do em/t professionals belong to?
- national level
- regional level
- state level
- local level

B. *Membership Overlap:* To what degree is there overlap in membership among associations?

C. *Association Functions:* What sorts of services are offered or activities undertaken by these associations?

D. *Association Leadership:* Who holds leadership positions in these associations? How are positions of leadership gained? What provision is made for leadership development?

E. *Association Trends:* Any change in the pattern of association membership? How are internal and external forces affecting the growth and health of professional organizations?

VII. The Workplace

A. *Workplace Settings:* In what organizational settings do em/t professionals work (e.g., school or college media centers, local or state school agencies, university academic departments, corporations, etc.)?

B. *Workplace Satisfaction:* Do em/t professionals experience satisfaction with their workplace environment?

C. *Job Satisfaction:* Do em/t professionals experience satisfaction in their jobs?

D. *Workplace Trends:* Are these organizational settings declining or growing in number? Are they declining or growing in financial support? Are roles changing? In what ways?

VIII. External Forces

A. *Societal Forces:* What societal forces are affecting the profession? What are the forces that assist or impede the appropriate adoption of technology in education?

B. *Governance Forces:* What changes are taking place in the governance of public K–12 education? Public and private higher education? How are these governance changes affecting the em/t profession? How do these forces aid or impede the appropriate adoption of technology?

C. *Workplace Forces:* What workplace forces are affecting the profession?

D. *Technological Forces:* How are technological forces affecting the profession? How does change in technology itself affect the adoption or rejection of technology in education and training?

E. *Historical Patterns and Trends:* Historically, what has been the impact of various external forces on the size of, shape of, or directions taken by the field?

CONCLUSION

Understanding who we are, why we exist, and where we are going may seem to be esoteric concerns best left to existential philosophers. But they are of immediate practical importance as well. Every day we encounter newer, more powerful software promising to make everyone an instant expert on graphic design, presentations, multimedia production, even instructional development. This leads people to ask, "Why do we need instructional technologists any more?" Does the educational media and technology field have an answer?

Association for
Educational Communications and Technology

Stanley D. Zenor
Executive Director

The year 1994 was one of new direction, excitement, and energy for the Association for Educational Communications and Technology (AECT). Virtually every area of the association was affected by new initiatives, ventures, membership services, and activities during the year.

The 1994 national convention, February 16-20, at the Opryland Hotel in Nashville, Tennessee, marked the debut of the association's International Computing and Instructional Technology Exposition (InCITE). After three years of extensive planning and preparation, AECT once again provided its members with an exposition featuring instructional technology hardware and software, held in conjunction with its annual convention. The convention and exposition were enthusiastically received by a record number of participants. The presentation sessions were filled to capacity throughout the convention and the exhibitors experienced heavy traffic as participants sought out the newest software and hardware products.

Following the convention, an AECT gopher was established on the Internet through the University of South Dakota at Vermillion. The gopher quickly gained recognition as a resource for instructional technologists. Throughout the year, the gopher contained information about AECT and AECT publications, conventions, seminars, and conferences, division newsletters, job placement information, and other items of interest to both members and nonmembers. During this same period, the association's listserve at the University of West Virginia, AECT L, served as a focal point for individuals discussing a wide range of topics related to AECT and the profession. As a result of its experience in 1994, the association will expand its presence on the Internet in 1995.

Following many months of work, thought, debate, and revision, the AECT Board of Directors adopted the Vision 2000 Strategic Plan in the summer of 1994. The board adopted as its first priority the expansion of electronic membership services. During the fall, the association worked with a commercial vendor to establish an AECT domain on the Internet. The AECT gopher and listserv will move to the aect.org Internet domain in the spring of 1995. Plans are in place to expand the resources available through the gopher and to develop an AECT home page on the World Wide Web. The association views the aect.org domain as an important new mechanism to deliver membership services and information to AECT members and instructional technology professionals.

During 1994, the Board of Directors approved the formation of 2 new special-interest divisions, bringing the number of AECT divisions to 11. The Systemic Change in Education Division (CHANGE) focuses on promoting systemic change in schools, business, higher education and technical institutes, primarily through systems design approaches, to meet learner needs, improve the quality of education, and enable technology to reach its potential in all educational settings. The CHANGE division is growing rapidly, attracting new members to the association and capturing the interest of existing members. The second new division, the Division of Learning and Performance Environments (DLPE), is focused on human learning and performance through the use of computer-based technology; that is, the design, development, evaluation, assessment, and implementation of learning environments and performance support systems for adults. The Board of Directors' approval of both new divisions is recognition that AECT must evolve to better serve the needs and interests of its members as the field and profession evolve.

The association's publication program continued to expand in 1994. Following nearly five years of research and writing, the association published *Instructional Technology: The Definition and Domains of the Field,* by Barbara Seels and Rita Richey. This book, a landmark publication for the field, addresses new developments in the theory and practice in the field and reexamines the definition of the field outlined in *The Definition of Educational Technology,* which was published by AECT in 1977. The association also published *Distance Education: A Review of the Literature, Educational Technology: A Review of the Literature,* and *Quality Management for Educational Technology Services.* Additionally, the association continued to work with other publishers to make their books available through AECT.

As a result of actions taken by the Board of Directors, the success of the association's new InCITE Exposition, and the increased emphasis on delivering new and expanded membership services, AECT has positioned itself as the leading association for educational and instructional technologists working to promote, implement, and manage the effective application of technology in the teaching/learning process at all levels.

Part Three
Current Developments

Introduction

The theme that runs through this section is innovation. What is new? What are the cutting-edge movements within the field that help to make it grow in an ever-changing world? Several "hot topics" are included in this section. They appear to be quite separate, yet all of them are related, in some way, to educational media and technology.

The increasing importance of *information technology* is recognized in the report on "Putting the Information Infrastructure to Work," with its emphasis on education. The increasing use of computer software across country borders is presented in the chapter on "The Evolution of Educational Software Portability." Concerns about the knowledge and skills required by teachers to use information technology appropriately are discussed in the chapter on "Mentoring Model for Technology Education for Teachers" and the closely related chapter, "Ignite Technology: Making the Difference with Staff Development." And what could be more contemporary than "The Internet: Resources for Educational Technology"?

Traditional interests about media applications have not been forgotten in this edition of *EMTY*. "Visualization and Effective Instruction" is accompanied by "Functions and Design of Video Components in Multi-Media Applications," both written by Dutch authors.

As in past years, there is an article on a new academic program in educational technology. This year it is the graduate program at Walden University, which is being offered at a distance. The design indicates that the program will practice what it teaches—appropriate use of media and technology to achieve learning objectives.

Assistance for school library media specialists in designing programs to meet the needs of changing school environments is also provided in "Library Media Standards and Guidelines: A Survey of Resources for K–12 Program Planning and Evaluation." This survey of current materials available in all 50 states and the District of Columbia updates a similar survey reported in the 1983 edition of the *Yearbook*.

Current ERIC Digests from the Clearinghouse on Information & Technology focus on the topics of telephones in the classroom and copyright, both on the cutting edge of the field.

The menu is rich with current resources to keep readers up-to-date on new developments. Pick and choose the items that will satisfy your professional appetite.

New Walden University Master's Program Cultivates the Innovative Power of Teachers

Don Ball
Walden University
Minneapolis, Minnesota

WHO WILL REFORM THE PUBLIC SCHOOLS?

Pity the public school. Never in our nation's history have so many citizens demanded so much out of so few teachers, staff, and administrators. Indeed, this nation's public schools are in a tightening vise. While many districts try to accommodate the needs of a booming student population, taxpayers have begun to put the brakes on growing school budgets.

In spite of this fiscal conservatism, the push for higher-quality education has never been stronger. A vocal contingent of parents, politicians, and industrialists complain that today's students are ill-equipped to meet the challenges of the Information Age. "Clearly, there's agreement around the country that major reform efforts need to be initiated for grades K through 12," says Jeff Konzak, Vice President for Administration of Walden University, a Minneapolis-based university that offers graduate-level distance-learning programs in education, administration/management, and health and human services. "The question is not *whether* the public schools need reform, but *how*," he says.

For Walden, the *how* of educational reform is a well-traversed terrain. Only months ago, the university wrapped up two years of preparation and unveiled its first master's degree program. The subject: Educational Change and Technology Innovation.

Behind the development of this program was a distinguished advisory board and group of founding faculty, whose members were carefully chosen from select school districts and the finest graduate schools of education across the nation. Among these founders were such luminaries as Dr. Gloria Chernay, Executive Director of the Association of Teacher Educators (ATE); Dr. Rodney Earle, Associate Professor of Teacher Education at the College of Education, Brigham Young University; and Dr. William J. Stockebrand, international consultant and Superintendent of the American Schools, Monterrey, Mexico.

After countless sessions of debate, reflection, and planning, these educators developed the premise for Walden's program—the notion that one of the best ways to empower educators is through the innovative application of technology. "There have been many attempts to reform public schools since the 1980s," Konzak says. "Some efforts have focused on structure, governance, site-based management, or student-teacher ratios. Technology, however, is a particularly strong lever for change," he says.

It's not just the application of technology, cautions advisory board and faculty member George Gustafson. "It's how you apply it. While most institutions focus either on innovation, change, or technology, we decided to create a program that would put all three elements together," said Gustafson, who is also Superintendent of Schools for the Gateway Regional School District in Worthington, Massachusetts.

ANOTHER TECHNOLOGICAL REVOLUTION?

For teachers who remember the 1970s, this talk of technology may seem familiar. Back then, federal grants brought a flood of audiovisual technology into the classroom. "Those grants helped spread the use of projectors and film, but it never got around to causing any major innovations," says Andy Abbott, Walden's Executive Director of Information Technology and a veteran teacher of 22 years.

Today's technology is different, says Abbott. The personal computer—and its ability to integrate text, sound, and video images—makes possible innovations that weren't imaginable 20 years ago. "We have the ability to use technology in an individualized manner. For example, you could use a computer as a tester, scorer, and remedial teacher. That allows the teacher to focus on more productive tasks, such as being a mentor and guide," he explains.

"With computers, the whats and the whens of education can be handled by the computers. In any particular subject, a significant number of concepts or data can be stored in tape, video, or computer format and students can recall that anytime," explains Bill Grady, professor at the University of Colorado's Graduate School of Education and former president of the National Council for Accreditation of Teacher Education (NCATE). Grady served as a consultant to Walden in the development of its new master's program.

"The teacher's job will call for a more inquiring approach to learning. Assuming that the technology offers the basic learning in a subject, the teacher will then help kids assimilate disparate information," he says. Need proof? Grady points to the schools of South Korea, which have applied technology in such a manner. Last year, they produced the world's top students in math and science.

Besides its ability to revolutionize the classroom, technology may also appeal to budget-minded administrators. "The public school system is a labor-intensive enterprise. And it's not likely that the American taxpayers are going to tax themselves at an increasing rate for increased labor costs," says Grady. "The application of technology, however, will probably extend the school day. You can't double the number of hours that teachers can teach, but at little extra cost you can increase the number of hours that technology is available to students," he says.

A LESSON IN CHANGE

To be sure, technology holds great promise for education. But how does the average teacher introduce that potential into the realities of the classroom? Walden's new Master of Science program suggests a two-pronged approach which, in fact, it makes use of by focusing on both the power of technology and the dynamics of organizational change. "While there are other master's-level programs in educational technology, most of those are geared toward media and library specialists. They're not focused on empowering the nation's teachers and helping them understand how to propose and implement change," Konzak says.

Walden offers a curriculum that spans the breadth of two disciplines. Drawing on numerous courses, including "Change Theory and Human Behavior," "Economics of Education in an Environment of Change," and "Computer Technology and Multimedia in Education," students will learn not just how to revolutionize their own classrooms, but also their schools and districts. By the fall of 1995, Walden will have provided its students with access to a unique electronic database that will serve as an information clearinghouse. Among its riches, this database will contain case studies and research in progress involving the application of technology in K–12 schools.

The importance of understanding change can't be oversold, says Abbott. "Introducing innovations requires diplomacy and savvy. Change tends to be feared, so you have to know how to work with your colleagues. You don't want to anger them because you're doing wonderful things in your classroom," he says.

HANDS-ON LEARNING . . . FROM A DISTANCE

Although it may be inspiring, no amount of textbook learning will guarantee the metamorphosis of a teacher into a supercharged "change agent." Consequently, Walden's new program takes a decidedly hands-on approach. In addition to an ample load of course work in technology and change theory, students are required to make practical applications of their learnings.

"Because Walden is a distance-learning institution, the curriculum is delivered to teachers across the country using technology itself," says Konzak. Indeed, students receive some of their course materials in the form of multimedia CD-ROMs. "In addition to discussing the use of technology, teachers actively use technologies they'll need in the classroom, such as interactive multimedia, computer conferencing, and use of the Internet," he says.

At the heart of Walden's "virtual campus" is the Walden Information Network (WIN), a computer network that keeps students and faculty in touch electronically. Using WIN, students can submit assignments, confer with professors, and participate in electronic "class discussions" of course material. WIN also provides access to the vast resources of the Internet.

Graduate library resources are provided by an innovative partnership with Indiana University, Bloomington. Walden students are served by a full-time librarian and given electronic access and borrowing privileges at one of the finest graduate library systems available.

To give students a hands-on orientation, Walden provides first-year students with a five-day practicum, offered each summer. "This residency allows students to interact with each other and other star practitioners. The purpose of this very focused session is to understand specific innovations in detail and experience new applications of interactive multimedia. This prepares students for the final project, which is to propose and/or implement an innovation in their own school," says Grady.

TEACH IT AND THEY WILL COME

With the roll-out of its new M.S. degree, Walden is counting on the belief that legions of educators are hungry for change. "We think there are 3 million teachers out there who are receptive to change and in need of empowerment," Konzak says.

Bill Grady agrees. "I think it's going to attract some interesting students. They'll be excitable people, teachers who care about the students in their classes and who want to provide the best environment," he says. "By offering this program, we're saying that they can do it—they can make significant, far-reaching changes."

APPENDIX A: ABOUT WALDEN UNIVERSITY

Walden University is a private graduate university serving mostly students in pursuit of a Ph.D. The university was founded in 1970 to meet the needs of the growing number of doctoral students unable to meet the residency requirements of traditional universities. It is one of the few alternative doctoral-level institutions to be recognized by an accrediting body.

Since accreditation by the North Central Association of Colleges and Schools in 1990, Walden University has grown rapidly to a current enrollment of approximately 900 students enrolled in the areas of Administration/Management, Education, Health Services, and Human Services.

Unlike students at a traditional campus, Walden Students are typically in their 40s. Most have already obtained a master's degree and are employed full time. Walden students have, as Thoreau phrased it, "many more lives to live."

APPENDIX B:
WALDEN'S MASTER'S PROGRAM: UP CLOSE

Degree:

Master of Science, Educational Change and Technology Innovation

Who should apply:

Active, licensed teachers, K–12; administrators; district staff; media specialists; computer resource center specialists; and State Department of Education staff.

Curriculum:

The curriculum for this program requires 48 quarter credit hours of study, including:

- Nine three-credit-hour distance-learning courses
- One six-credit-hour summer-session laboratory course
- One three-credit-hour summer-session seminar
- Twelve credit hours consisting of two practicums, a final project paper, and a seminar

Courses include:

1. Learning Theories, Motivation, and Relationship to Technology
2. Family and Societal Factors in Education
3. Critical Survey of Educational Innovations Utilizing Technology
4. Education Structures and Decision Making Processes
5. Computer Technology and Multimedia in Education
6. Survey of Alternative School Reform Initiatives
7. Economics of Education in an Environment of Change
8. Change Theory and Human Behavior

9. Outcomes Based Assessment and Program Evaluation

10. Organizational Behavior and Educational Systems (Summer Session—3 credit hours)

11. Course Development and Delivery Utilizing Technology (Summer Session—6 credit hours)

Admissions criteria:

1. Bachelor's degree from an accredited institution

2. Minimum of two years of teaching experience or equivalent experience in an educational setting

3. Completed application form with transcripts of undergraduate work

4. Written goal statement (four pages) describing teaching experience, personal development goals, and interest in educational change

5. Two letters of recommendation

6. Completion of telephone interview with program faculty or program director

7. Computer literacy and access to personal computer with modem and CD-ROM drive

For more information:

Call (800) 444-6795 to speak with an admissions counselor.

A Transformation of Learning:
Use of the NII for Education and Lifelong Learning*
Putting the Information Infrastructure to Work:
A Report of the Information Infrastructure Task Force
Committee on Applications and Technology**

Linda Roberts
Chair of the Education Working Committee
U.S. Department of Education

Today, we have a dream for a different kind of superhighway that can save lives, create jobs and give every American, young and old, the chance for the best education available to anyone, anywhere.

I challenge you . . . to connect all of our classrooms, all of our libraries, and all of our hospitals and clinics by the year 2000.

Vice President Albert Gore
speaking to communications industry leaders, January 11, 1994

PART I: WHAT IS THE APPLICATION AREA?

Description of Education and Lifelong Learning

Communications technology is transforming the way we live by connecting us with information and each other. The National Information Infrastructure (NII) promises every business, government agency, hospital, home, library, and school in the nation access anywhere to voice, data, full-motion video, and multimedia applications. The impact of these capabilities on learning—for the children, for higher education students, and for lifelong learners—will be substantial.

The way Americans teach, learn, transmit, and access information remains largely unchanged from a century ago. We find the following conditions in American education and training:

- The textbook remains the basic unit of instruction. Absorption of its contents tends to be the measure of educational success.

- Teachers and instructors use "chalk and talk" to convey information. Students are often recipients of instruction rather than active participants in learning.

NIST (National Institute of Standards and Technology) Special Publication 857. The original report is available on the Internet.
**For additional information, contact Dr. Linda Roberts, Chair of the Education Working Committee. Dr. Roberts is a Special Advisor to the U.S. Department of Education on Educational Technology and coordinator of the department's educational technology activities.

- School teachers work largely in isolation from their peers. Teachers interact with their colleagues for only a few moments each day. Most other professionals collaborate, exchange information, and develop new skills on a daily basis.

- Although half of the nation's school teachers use passive video materials for instruction, only a small fraction have access to interactive video, computer networks, or even telephones in the classroom.

- Although computers are a frequent sight in America's classrooms and training sites, they are usually used simply as electronic workbooks. Interactive, high-performance uses of technology, such as networked teams collaborating to solve real-world problems, retrieving information from electronic libraries, and performing scientific experiments in simulated environments, are all too uncommon.

- "U.S. schooling is a conservative institution, which adopts new practice and technology slowly. Highly regulated and financed from a limited revenue base, schools serve many educational and social purposes, subject to local consent. The use of computer technology, with its demands on teacher professional development, physical space, time in the instructional day, and budget . . . has found a place in classroom practice and school organization slowly and tentatively" (Melmed 1993).

Events of the last two decades have proven that we can do better. We have found that most American children are capable of learning at dramatically higher levels—levels of performance we now expect only of our best students. We have learned this from research in cognitive science, from the educational achievements of other countries, and from pioneering efforts in our own schools. Moreover, after 35 years of research, we have found that technology can be the key to higher levels of achievement. (U.S. Congress, Office of Technology Assessment 1988).

Similarly, in the American workplace we have found that workers can achieve levels of productivity and quality equal to the best in the world. (U.S. Congress, Office of Technology Assessment 1990). Well-educated, well-trained, motivated workers can produce high-quality goods and services at low cost, enhance industrial productivity and competitiveness, and sustain high living standards. High-quality education and training pay off for the individual whose skills are upgraded, for the company seeking a competitive edge, and for the nation in achieving overall productivity and competitiveness.

Our major foreign competitors place much greater emphasis on developing and maintaining workforce skills than we do. Experienced production workers at Japanese auto assembly plants, for example, receive three times as much training each year as their American counterparts. Research in our country has shown that workers who receive formal job training are 30 percent more productive than those who do not. Again, we have found that technology is the key to making training accessible and affordable especially for small- to medium-sized firms with few resources of their own to devote to producing and implementing the training and lifelong learning their workers need and for workers who, on their own, are attempting to improve their skills or transfer them to new areas of endeavor.

Finally, in preparing students for the workplace, we have learned that interactive, high-performance technology can produce immersive, real-world instructional environments. These environments can smooth long-term school-to-work transitions while helping to meet the immediate objectives of both schools and workplaces. Our efforts to develop this capability have been fragmentary and short-lived at best.

A Vision for the Use of the National Information Infrastructure

The National Information Infrastructure (NII) will be the vehicle for improving education and lifelong learning throughout America in ways we now know are critically important. Our nation will become a place where students of all ages and abilities reach the highest standards of academic achievement. Teachers, engineers, business managers, and all knowledge workers will constantly be exposed to new methods, and will collaborate and share ideas with one another.

Through the NII, students of all ages will use multimedia electronic libraries and museums containing text, images, video, music, simulations, and instructional software. The NII will give teachers, students, workers, and instructors access to a great variety of instructional resources and to each other. It will give educators and managers new tools for improving the operations and productivity of their institutions.

The NII will remove school walls as barriers to learning in several ways. It will provide access to the world beyond the classroom. It will also permit both teachers and students access to the tools of learning and their peers—outside the classroom and outside the typical nine-to-three school day. It will enable family members to stay in contact with their children's schools. The NII will permit students, workers, and instructors to converse with scientists, scholars, and experts around the globe.

Workplaces will become lifelong learning environments, supporting larger numbers of high-skill, high-wage jobs. Printed books made the content of great instruction widely and inexpensively available in the 18th century. The interactive capabilities of the NII will make both the content and the interactions of great teaching universally and inexpensively available in the 21st century.

Education and Lifelong Learning Applications for the NII

The NII will provide the backbone for a lifelong learning society. Education and training communities will better accommodate an enormous diversity of learners in an equally diverse variety of settings. In addition to schools and workplaces, interconnected, high-performance applications will extend interactive learning to community centers, libraries, and homes. Education, training, and lifelong learning applications available from the NII may include:

- Multimedia interactive learning programs delivered to homes to immigrant children and their parents to collaborate on learning English as a second language.

- Troubleshooting and operating applications that access the computer-assisted-design (CAD) databases used to design workplace technology and to integrate the CAD data with instructional and job-aiding capabilities to provide just-in-time training and maintenance assistance.

- Comprehensive interconnectivity for students that allows them to receive and complete assignments, collaborate with students in distant locations on school projects, and interact with teachers and outside experts to receive help, hints, and critiques.

- Simulated learning activities such as laboratory experiments and archeological digs.

- Universal access interfaces for computers and telecommunications devices for students, worker, and others with disabilities to allow access to the NII.

- Affordable, portable personal learning assistance that taps into the NII from any location at any time and provides multimedia access to any NII information resource.

- Immersive, realistic interactive simulations that allow emergency teams made up of geographically dispersed members to practice together on infrequently used procedures that may be urgently needed to meet local exigencies.

The Educational Benefits of Technology

Evidence from research, schools, and workplaces around the country tells us that communications technologies are powerful tools in reaching the highest levels of educational performance.

- Students with disabilities, who previously had at best limited access to most educational and reference materials, will have fuller access and will have the ability to participate in the learning experience with their peers.

- A 1993 survey of studies on the effectiveness of technology in schools concluded that "courses for which computer-based networks were used increased student-student and student-teacher interaction, increased student-teacher interaction with lower-performing students, and did not decrease the traditional forms of communications used" (*Report on the effectiveness of technology* 1993).

- Research on the costs of instruction delivered via distance learning, videotape, teleconferencing, and computer software indicates that savings are often achieved with no loss of effectiveness. Distance learning vastly broadens the learning environment, often providing teaching resources simply not available heretofore. Technology-based methods have a positive impact on learner motivation and frequently save instructional time. Savings in training time produce benefits both by reducing training costs and by shortening the time required to become and remain productive in the workplace.

- A review of computer-based instruction used in military training found that students reach similar levels of achievement in 30 percent less time than they need using more standard approaches to training (Orlansky and String 1979).

- A congressionally mandated review covering 47 comparisons of multimedia instruction with more conventional approaches to instruction found time savings of 30 percent, improved achievement, cost savings of 30 to 40 percent, and a direct, positive link between amount of interactivity provided and instructional effectiveness (Fletcher 1991).

- A comparison of peer tutoring, adult tutoring, reduced class size, increased length of the school day, and computer-based instruction found computer-based instruction to be the least expensive instructional approach for raising mathematics scores by a given amount (Fletcher, Hawley, and Piele 1990).

- A landmark study of the use of technology for persons with disabilities found that "almost three-quarters of school-age children were able to remain in a classroom, and 45 percent were able to reduce school-related services" (National Council on Disability 1993).

Of course, these benefits depend upon several contextual factors, including the instructional methods used, the quality of the applications, the availability of professional development for educators, the accessibility of instructional materials, the presence of school technology support staff, and family involvement (Becker 1994). We must learn through experience how best to ensure that the benefits we intend to obtain from NII-based applications become routinely realized in practice.

Telecommunications networks provide a range of resources to students and educators that were never before available or affordable. Students and workers can now gain access to mentoring, advice, and assistance from scientists, engineers, researchers, business leaders, technicians, and local experts around the globe through the Internet, using a level of access and connectivity that was previously unimaginable. High school students in West Virginia, for example, can now study Russian via satellite and telephone with a teacher hundreds of miles away. Few West Virginia school districts could afford to offer such a course any other way. Less well understood are changes in the types of learning that occur with the use of certain technologies. Current evidence suggests that some technology applications are more effective than traditional instructional methods in building complex problem-solving capabilities for synthesizing information and in improving writing quality. The effects are achieved in part by permitting alternate methods of reaching and motivating learners.

The Clinton Administration's National Information Infrastructure initiative can trigger a transformation of education, training, and lifelong learning by making new tools available to educators, instructors, students, and workers, and can help them reach dramatically higher levels of performance and productivity. The impact of this transformation in teaching and learning is inestimable, but clearly enormous. Knowledge drives today's global marketplace. The NII will permit us to take learning beyond the limitations of traditional school buildings. It will take our educators and learners to worldwide resources. Learning will be our way of life.

PART II: WHERE ARE WE NOW?

Today, compelling teaching and learning applications are the exception, not the rule. Several federal agencies provide services that meet specific, focused needs, while hundreds of state and local networks and private service providers have begun to address the technology needs of education. Current uses, though expanding rapidly, reach only a small number of technologically literate school communities.

Current application of NII capabilities to workplace training is more extensive and technologically advanced than educational applications, yet it lags well behind what is needed and available. The story of workplace training seems to be a case of the haves receiving more and the have-nots remaining neglected. Small firms, those with 100 employees or fewer, provide about 35 percent of total U.S. employment, but they lack the expertise to provide in-house training, the resources to pay for outside training, and sufficient numbers of people who need training at any one time to justify focused training efforts. Larger firms are more likely to provide training than smaller ones, but the training they provide is mostly limited to college-educated technicians and managers. The lower the level of skills possessed, the less likely the worker is to receive training from any source. Transportable, quality-controlled training and lifelong learning could be made readily and inexpensively accessible using the NII and will have a major impact on improving worker skills and workplace productivity.

Although much remains to be done, the opportunities offered by the NII put many of the needed capabilities within reach of schools, homes, and workplaces.

Current Uses of Telecommunications for Education

The existing telecommunications infrastructure is composed of telephone, broadcast, cable, and electronic networks. It is used for education, training, and lifelong learning in five basic ways: (1) instructing with video; (2) gathering information from remote libraries and databases; (3) communicating using two-way asynchronous capabilities such as e-mail and information bulletin boards; (4) distance learning; and (5) electronic transfer of instructional software and simulations.

- **Instructional video.** Seventy-five percent of America's schools have cable television, and half of its teachers use video material in their courses (Corporation for Public Broadcasting 1991). The Stars Schools program is reaching 200,000 students in 48 states with advanced placement courses in mathematics, science, and foreign-language instruction using fiber optics, computers, and satellites (Withrow 1994). Cassette videotapes for instruction are widely used in schools and workplaces, and the development of these videotapes for both education and training has become a vigorous industry.

- **Information collection.** This activity includes location and retrieval of documents such as lesson plans and research reports, but it also includes newer data sources such as CAD databases for workplace technologies and equipment, and multimedia information retrieval from digital libraries that can be accessed by students, workers, or people in homes, libraries, and museums. More than 60,000 electronic bulletin boards are used by more than 12 million Americans every day (*Investor's Business Daily* 1994). The annual rate of gopher traffic on the Internet, which directly represents an effort to use NII facilities to gather information, is growing at an annual rate of approximately 1,000 percent (Treese 1993). The Department of Education has a gopher server that points to or contains educational research information, such as the AskERIC service and information from sources such as CNN, Academy One, and the Educational Testing Service. NASA Spacelink makes lesson plans on space flight and related science topics available on the Internet.

- **Two-way communication.** This includes communication via electronic mail and conferencing among teachers, students, workers, mentors, technicians, and subject-matter experts of every sort. Approximately one-quarter of the teachers in Texas regularly sign on to the Texas Education Network, or TENET, to share information, exchange mail, and find resources. A professor at Virginia Polytechnic Institute and State University teaches a writing course entirely online. Students swap writing projects and discuss their assignments online. In the workplace, electronic mail was used by more than 12 million workers, and by 1995 had more than 27 million worker users. Just less than one-sixth of U.S. homes now have at least one computer connected to a modem, and this percentage is growing rapidly (Melmed 1993). As of July 1993, there were four Internet hosts for every 1,000 people in the United States. There are now 60 countries on the Internet. About 137 countries can now be reached by electronic mail (Treese 1993).

- **Distance learning.** Hundreds of thousands of students in schools, community colleges, and universities now take courses via one- and two-way video and two-way audio communication. In South Carolina, high school students across the state study with a teacher of Russian based in Columbia through South Carolina Educational Television. Boise State University offers a master's degree program conducted entirely over networked computers to students all over the country. The Department of Defense is investing well over $1 billion in the development and implementation of networked distributed interactive simulation. This technology, which allows dispersed learners to engage in collaborative problem-solving activities in real time, is now ready for transfer to schools and workplaces outside of the defense sector.

- **Transfer of instructional software and simulations.** Instructional programs, simulations, materials, and databases can all be accessed over the NII and delivered to schools, homes, libraries, and workplaces wherever and whenever it is desirable to do so. Currently, there are massive exchanges of software, databases, and files using the Internet, but relatively little of this activity occurs in the service of education, training, and lifelong learning.

Nonetheless, compelling applications that will become indispensable to teachers, students, and workers are not yet available. All the capabilities of computer-based instruction and multimedia instruction can be distributed using NII facilities to schools, workplaces, homes, libraries, museums, community centers, store fronts—wherever and whenever people wish to learn. Yet the infrastructure and applications to support this level of accessibility for education, training, and lifelong learning uses have yet to be developed. Until compelling applications are available, educators will not realize the potential of the NII.

Efforts to Build the NII for Education and Lifelong Learning: Roles of the Private, Nonprofit, and Public Sectors

Successful implementation of the NII to serve the nation's education and lifelong learning needs will require significant contributions by the private sector, state and local governments, the federal government, and the nonprofit sector.

- The private sector's role in providing telecommunications services and applications for education and lifelong learning has been expanding rapidly in recent years, and should continue to do so. The private sector will build the telecommunications infrastructure and must also make 75 percent to 95 percent of the nation's investments in applications development for education and lifelong learning. The private sector also supports the bulk of job training costs. On the telecommunications side, Pacific Bell has committed to providing data links for all California schools, colleges, and universities. On the applications side, the Software Publishers Association reports that education is its fastest-growing product category, with more than 700 firms currently producing educational software.

- State and local governments provide 93 percent of the nation's investment in elementary and secondary education and provide a large percentage of the investment in higher education. Accordingly, most of the spending on hardware, software, professional development, and support services will come from state and local public funds. In addition, states are in a position to remove regulatory and tariff barriers to NII access in local communities.

- The federal government has three principal responsibilities. It facilitates private-sector investment in infrastructure and applications for education and lifelong learning by creating incentives; removing regulatory barriers; establishing standards;

supporting research, evaluation, and prototype development; developing visionary "benchmark" applications; and providing assistance to the education and training communities. It communicates a vision for the education, training, and lifelong learning uses of the NII. Most importantly, it promotes access for all learners to the resources of the NII.

- Thousands of private nonprofit organizations, ranging from large national industry associations to small, informal groups serving Internet users with specialized interests, now serve critical roles as providers of information, technical assistance, and valuable applications.

Key Federal Agencies

Although almost every federal agency supports instructional activities that involve telecommunications technology, 11 agencies actively support the development of instructional uses of the future NII.

The **Department of Agriculture** collaborates with land-grant colleges and universities to make an array of information and expertise available online and to provide distance learning opportunities to urban and rural communities.

The **Department of Commerce** provides support and direct funding for telecommunications infrastructure planning and development, and plans to support improvements in workplace training using the NII. Commerce's National Institute of Standards and Technology supports standards development.

The **Department of Defense** provides lifelong education and training to hundreds of thousands of military personnel. It supports research and development for education and training and is expected to transfer knowledge and software to schools and nondefense workplaces under its Dual-Use and Technology Reinvestment programs. The Department of Defense Dependents Schools are expected to serve as a testbed for new applications.

The **Department of Education** advocates for the needs of all learners in the development of the NII. The department is the principal source of federal support for distance learning, via the Star Schools Program. In fiscal year 1995, the department will also support applications and programming development, pilot projects, teacher networks, research, and planning grants to states and districts.

The **Department of Energy** is in the forefront in the development and use of information technologies, such as high-performance computing, high-speed networking, data storage and databases, and other information services and system integration technology. The department is developing K-12 computing and communication applications that support a new learning paradigm and take advantage of the regional presence and capabilities of the department's laboratories. Emphasis is placed on reaching a broad range of students, including women and underrepresented minorities. The department will initiate pilot projects that have scalability as an important characteristic, so that schools can bridge the period until network and system costs decline to the point that the education establishment can take over this support. Another key technology initiative is the development of digital libraries that will enable users speedy and economical access to Department of Energy information over an electronic data highway.

The **Department of Housing and Urban Development (HUD)** has undertaken an initiative to develop the capability to provide training to HUD employees and clients by linking trainers to students who may be thousands of miles apart. This distance learning network makes use of computer, interactive video, satellite, and telecommunications technologies, and will be implemented under the auspices of the recently established HUD Training Academy.

The **Department of the Interior** has several activities under way to implement the NII within the department. One of these is the National Biological Information Infrastructure, which will allow users to access, manipulate, organize, and use biological data and information from a variety of sources.

The **Department of Labor** has direct and indirect interaction with employers, workers, business and labor organizations, and other government entities, and administers most federal training programs. The department hopes to use the NII to enhance the skills, education, and training of the American workforce.

The **Federal Communications Commission** regulates interstate and foreign telecommunications by radio, television, wire, satellite, and cable. The FCC is responsible for the orderly development and operation of broadcast services and the provision of rapid, efficient, nationwide telephone and telegraph services at reasonable rates.

The **National Aeronautics and Space Administration** continues to build on its High Performance Computing and Communications (HPCC) program, its aeronautics and space science research and engineering missions, and its existing education outreach infrastructure to facilitate the general development of the NII to support mathematics, science, and engineering education in K–12 education. This program consists of pilot projects at seven NASA Centers involving many of their local schools and school districts. The goal of the K–12 effort will be to produce and distribute curriculum materials to a very broad user community over the Internet. A video is in production in cooperation with the Department of Education to provide guidance on appropriate steps for implementing Internet access and utilization in the classroom. NASA continues to operate and improve its "Spacelink" computer information system for the education community, principally teachers and students.

The **National Science Foundation** supports research on digital libraries for capturing, categorizing, and organizing data of all forms (text, images, sound, speech) in electronic form to allow utilization of networked databases distributed around the nation and the world. A networking infrastructure for education programs will establish testbeds and implement prototypes that explore the role of electronic networks in support of reformed education. The NSF will also support the development of national facilities and centers such as NSFNET, High Performance Computing and Communications Centers, and National Challenge Centers needed to support the research, education, and training activities required to broaden the impact of the NII.

In addition, the High-Performance Computing and Communications initiative, an interagency effort under the aegis of the Office of Science and Technology Policy, includes several components that directly support the development of NII uses for education, training, and lifelong learning. These include:

- The **National Research and Education Network (NREN).** The NREN will establish a very fast communications infrastructure for research and educational use. NREN efforts include increasing the availability of advanced network products and services at affordable cost to research and education communities.

- **Information Infrastructure Technology and Applications (IITA).** This component supports the development of software, interfaces, and tools necessary for educational use of the NII, including access to digital libraries.

State and Local Agencies

States and local communities have initiatives to provide Internet access and high-speed access to the NII for education and lifelong learning.

More than half the states sponsor broad educational networking. In some states, the state government has led the effort; in others, regional or local organizations have taken the initiative as illustrated in the following examples.

- The **Iowa Communications Network (ICN)** currently includes more than 2,600 miles of fiber optic cable that links together 15 regional centers, 3 regent universities, and Iowa Public Television. Current uses include 63 semester-long distance learning courses offered in the fall of 1993, workshops and seminars for educators, and town meetings. Ultimately, ICN will link up every college and high school in the state. The state has invested more than $100 million in ICN so far ("Information Infrastates" 1993, p. 19).

- In May 1993, North Carolina Governor Jim Hunt announced the North Carolina Information Highway, an effort to link educational, medical, economic development, and public safety organizations statewide. In January 1994, Governor Hunt announced the first 106 sites to be linked up to the information highway, most of which are educational institutions. The state legislature created a school technology commission to examine the technology needs of the state's schools. The legislature was scheduled to vote on a $350 million proposal to fund educational technology in late 1994.

- In Ohio, a number of local and statewide organizations are now working to increase access to networks for educational use. These include the State of Ohio Network for Integrated Communications, which provides connectivity for all state agencies; the Ohio Educational Computer Network, charged with developing K–12 educational links; Cleveland FreeNet, a regional network; and the Ohio Academic Resources Network, linking up colleges and universities. Comparatively little state money has been spent to build these networks (Information intrastates 1993, p. 19).

Use of Telecommunications Technologies in Schools

Although computers and some communications capabilities are present in American schools, high-speed communications technology is limited to very few classrooms. Substantial local infrastructure investments will be necessary to realize the promise of NII applications. The installed base of computers, modems, networks, and video technology indicates that growth has been, at best, uneven. Because education and training application development has not kept pace with other grand challenges for types of NII applications, most schools, communities, and state and local governing bodies have neither recognized nor acted on the need to build the technological capability to access the information superhighway. A key but not well-understood requirement is technical expertise to install and maintain high-speed connections to the NII. Once the high-speed communications linkages of the NII are brought to the schoolhouse door, the challenge is to build the internal high-speed linkages within the building to connect the user hardware.

The installed base of computers in American elementary and secondary schools is largely incapable of supporting multimedia graphical applications, because of obsolete or obsolescent hardware. Although 80 percent of the base consists of 55 percent Apple IIs and 24 percent IBM PCs, XTs, ATs, or similar-class machines, with limited modern graphic or multimedia capabilities; only the part of the base made of 10 percent Apple Macintoshes and 8 percent IBM compatible 386s or 486s is capable of supporting high-level applications. The number of computers in the schools, 2.5 million, is equivalent to one per classroom (Melmed 1993). In a 1993 survey of National Education Association members, only 4 percent of teachers reported having a modem in the classroom, whereas 38 percent reported having access to a modem somewhere in the school building (Princeton Survey Research Associates 1993). Another survey found that of 550 educators who are actively involved in using telecommunications, less than half have access to the Internet. They use the Internet services twice as often for professional activities as for student learning activities (Honey and Henriquez 1993).

Use of Telecommunications Technologies in the Workplace

Well-designed technology-based training can provide greater mastery of material in less time and with higher employee satisfaction than the average classroom lecture, yet classroom instruction remains the most common formal training method in the United States (U.S. Congress, Office of Technology Assessment 1990). Most corporate trainers have insufficient experience with technology to use it confidently or to design courses around it. Although 35 million adults have difficulties with common literacy tasks, no more than 15 percent of literacy providers use them regularly for instruction, and many do not use them at all (U.S. Congress, Office of Technology Assessment 1993). Despite the explosion of cable, public, and commercial television channels, only a few instructional television programs target adult literacy. This situation remains despite the privacy and accessibility that technology and the NII offer adult learners.

The issue is not limited to the literacy training adults need to obtain and keep employment. Even among those who are prepared to benefit from them, the immersing, tutorial interactions of instruction and especially instructional simulations that are now available from high-performance technology are rarely found in the workplace. Even the capabilities of just-in-time and just-enough training and job performance aiding are rarely employed to their useful limits.

Equity and Access

Computer technology is unevenly distributed in our schools today when measured by computer density (the ratio of computers to students). Schools in the top quintile have nine times as many computers as those in the bottom quintile. Computer density in the schools is not strongly correlated with socioeconomic, racial, or ethnic patterns, however. Lower-than-average computer densities are found in large schools, urban schools, both private and parochial schools, and schools with large numbers of Hispanic students. Because the installed base is 80 percent obsolete, it is not a significant indicator of utilization of modern technology.

Distribution of video technologies such as distance learning equipment, VCRs, and cable TV is more even. Schools in rural and poor areas actually have higher densities of these types of equipment. For instance, every school in West Virginia, regardless of its location, has a satellite receive-only dish providing ready access to televised courses.

Dramatic disparities appear in the area of computer networking. Instructional networks are most prevalent in the Northeast, in suburban schools, in schools where parents' education is "said to be above average," and also in elementary schools receiving Chapter 1 support, a reasonable measure of poverty.

Although most schools' use of technology is far below what they desire, because the technology is not affordable, a small number of schools have made substantial investments in technology. Such schools achieve greater "high-end" technology usage. Higher socioeconomic-level schools also are more likely to be high-end technology users.

A disparity in technology investments between small and large firms is noted. Small firms can make only limited investments in training, with or without NII support. When such investments are made, they appear to pay off. A Canadian study found that successful companies innovate and spend more on technology than those that are less successful (U.S. Congress, Office of Technology Assessment 1990). However, entry-level training to facilitate school-to-work transitions remains everyone's stepchild. Some of the entry-level training needs are being met by electronic home learning. In fact, education software sales for the first three quarters of 1993 were up 46 percent from the same period in 1992 (The Heller Report 1994). Nonetheless, the situated apprenticeship training and basic skills training that form the foundation for entry-level training that could be provided through the NII remain to be developed. Without accessibility to such workplace training technical capabilities, intractable inequities are likely to remain.

PART III: WHERE DO WE WANT TO BE?

The goal of the Clinton Administration—as stated by Vice President Al Gore—is for all citizens to use the NII from every home, library, workplace, community center, and classroom in the nation. The NII will support lifelong learning opportunities for an enormously diverse community of learners.

This goal implies nothing short of a complete transformation of American education and lifelong learning. The NII will enable education to become a lifelong enterprise for all Americans, integrating and substantially enhancing school, community, and workplace learning and providing opportunities accessible to all.

Immediate Objectives

We propose the following objectives as goals for the near term:

- Schools, libraries, workplaces, and other learning sites will have high-speed access to the NII, capable of supporting interactive, multimedia applications.

- Interactive, multimedia, high-quality educational applications for students in the basic learning areas and at different skill levels will be affordable and readily available in the marketplace.

- Schools will have internal networking capabilities and hardware capable of supporting high-quality applications.

- High-quality basic skills training that provides every motivated worker with the verbal and quantitative skills needed to learn and perform job-relevant tasks will be available in every workplace.

The following conditions should exist in support of these goals:

- Educators and the public will understand the potential of the NII to support high-performance learning environments, and they will be able to use NII resources effectively. Examples of the effective use of the NII for education, training, and lifelong learning, and evidence of concrete instructional benefits, will be widely available.

- All states, and a majority of school districts, will have comprehensive plans in place for the integration of technology into education and lifelong learning, will have linked those plans to systemic education improvement plans, and will have begun implementation of these plans. At a minimum, these plans will address the challenges of diminished budgets while meeting requirements for increased investments in technology, professional development, maintenance, and technical support; provision for access by users with disabilities; broadband access to classrooms and other learning sites; and changes in regulatory structures to facilitate infrastructure and applications investments.

- Investment by all levels of government in research, development, and evaluation, implementation, and technical support will increase dramatically. The investments will include professional development and technical assistance for teachers, school administrators, instructors, and managers in the use of information technologies. Providers of professional development and technical assistance will be encouraged to offer quality, easily accessible services in a variety of ways—including access through the NII. A majority of teachers will have access to personal telecommunications devices and networking services to support continuing professional growth and interchange of professional information.

- The demand for high-quality software packages and tools for education, training, and lifelong learning will grow rapidly and substantially such that the private sector will make massive new investments in the infrastructure and increase the quality and accessibility of software packages and tools.

- Multimedia education and training packages will become portable so that they can be delivered across the NII and used when they reach their destination regardless of the hardware platform installed there.

- Strategies and standards will be available for making at least the current-generation applications accessible to users with disabilities or who are experiencing limitations due to aging.

Long-Term Goals

To serve the needs of the educational community in the long term, an improved NII must have the following attributes:

- **Convenient and equitable access.** Connection to every American classroom, public library, and other learning location will ensure that NII applications are available to all citizens as instructional tools and not available just as special, rationed services. Affordable workplace and home access will give all learners access to NII resources whenever and wherever they are needed, will enable family members to be fully involved in the education of their children, and will allow workers to participate in a productive, lifelong-learning society.

- **High-speed transmission capability.** The NII will permit the interactive transmission of voice, video, data, multimedia applications, and other digitized information at the capacities needed to support education, training, and lifelong learning.

- **Easy use.** User interfaces will be simple and easy to use. Networks and applications will be interoperable, to permit easy access from all hardware platforms to the widest possible array of resources. The NII will have directories and other exploration tools that allow students, teachers, and workers to make their way conveniently through the massive amounts of available information. Tools to help users identify resources will be developed.

- **Technological simplification.** Telecommunications hardware and software will be simplified so that connecting a computer to the NII is no more complex than connecting a telephone.

- **Accessibility.** User interfaces and information must accommodate users with a widespread range of abilities through built-in interface options, flexibility, and compatibility with special access technologies.

- **Security.** The NII will accommodate security systems adequate to protect privacy, maintain the confidentiality of sensitive information, and safeguard intellectual property rights. The network must also accommodate varying levels of access to resources in education and training settings.

- **Content.** The NII must offer information, communication, and learning opportunities that meet high standards of quality and help America reach the National Education Goals.

- **Portability.** Interactive courseware will have the same operating interoperability—"plug and play"—now available in high-fidelity audio systems. Investments in multimedia education and training programs will be preserved through NII delivery using interoperability standards in the development of software and hardware.

- **Instructional delivery.** Instructional delivery will provide workers with a "PhD in a pocket." Instruction and job performance aids will be delivered on a device that resembles a pocket calculator. Every complex device will include sufficient embedded training and user assistance to make it easily usable.

- **Instructional intelligence.** Instructional intelligence will support integrated individualized tutoring that integrates goal setting, instruction, job performance aid, and decision aid into a single package. Natural-language interaction will be an essential feature of this capability.

- **Institutional integration.** Institutional integration will be the most difficult challenge to meet. The new instructional capabilities will first have to be integrated into the routine, daily practice of our current instructional and workplace institutions. Just-in-time and just-enough training that is universally available will not only change the ways people are treated in the workplace but also the workplace itself.

PART IV: HOW ARE WE GOING TO GET THERE?

Making the NII a reality for education will require significant capital investments by the private sector and commitments to meet continuing operating costs. Federal, state, and local governments need to create the conditions in which this investment can proceed, and will play a critical role in "jump starting" educational applications and access to the network. The following questions are intended to focus attention on the most important issues for federal policy.

Access

How can the federal government facilitate the connectivity needs of schools and other learning sites? Should schools that have traditionally been underserved be given special attention with respect to network access and access to the information resources relevant to their needs? Should schools and other learning sites be given universal service to ensure the delivery of service at the same affordable rates as most American homes?

How can the NII be made accessible in a variety of learning environments? How can the NII allow individual learners access to the resources they need when and where they want access? How can the NII provide the capability for learning on demand through education and training programs funded by the federal government?

What incentives, regulatory actions, or other activities within the private sector and state and local government are needed to encourage investments to connect educational institutions and other learning sites to the NII?

Should the Federal Communications Commission propose regulations that enhance the availability of advanced telecommunications services to all educational institutions by mechanisms such as preferential rates for telecommunications services? Are there alternative means of achieving this public requirement?

Should the federal government collect and publicly report data to monitor progress in areas such as the extent of network access in schools?

Professional Development

Teachers, administrators, instructors, and others need access to professional development opportunities on a much wider scale than is now the case. How can the federal government facilitate access to on-site and online assistance? Should professional development be expanded to include the new role of teachers and trainers as guides and mentors rather than their present role as the primary information provider in the classroom?

Development of Education and Training Applications

Should the federal government target investments for the development of high-quality applications for education, training, and lifelong learning use of the NII that meet challenging content and performance standards? What incentives and guidelines should be developed to encourage software developers and other producers of education and training materials to participate in developing new technologies and applications to address the needs of diverse and special needs populations?

Research and Development

What categories of research and development should be identified across the agencies of the federal government to ensure that technology-supported learning is pursued in conjunction with the development of the NII? Should the federal government require evaluation of all supported projects?

How can the teachers, trainers, and other educators who are actively using the NII best be supported and their work disseminated? How can the intellectual property rights of those creating applications of the NII for learning best be protected?

Planning

How can the federal government best support state and local efforts to develop and implement technology plans? Should the federal government ensure a coordinated approach among states? Within each state?

Technical Assistance

How can technical assistance best be provided by the federal government in response to a general or specific request from any segment of the learning community? Should the federal government establish specialized teams (composed of federal staff or contractors) to assist schools, districts, state agencies? Should technical assistance networks of expert staffs be available to answer questions about NII uses for education and lifelong learning? Should planning tools be developed and disseminated, such as videotapes, planning guides, directories, resource listings, and other forms of information?

Partnership

What is the role of the federal government in developing sustained public and private partnerships to support education and training uses of the NII?

How can the federal government best promote the goals of the NII and its application to education and lifelong learning with the public, with state and local governments, and with the education and training communities?

What role should the federal government play in making public and private information resources available to schools, institutions of higher education, training institutions, libraries, and other institutions of learning?

How can the federal government facilitate a public-private partnership for the development of interoperability standards, application quality standards, and effectiveness standards to facilitate the development of high-quality telecommunications and applications?

How can the federal government best ensure collaboration among its agencies to bring together technical expertise and application development to expand the use of the NII for education and training?

How can the federal government best support research and evaluation on the education and training applications of current and emerging technologies to the NII?

REFERENCES

Becker, Henry Jay. (1994). How our best computer-using teachers differ from other teachers: Implications for realizing the benefits of computers in schools. *Journal of Research on Computing in Education 26*, 291–321.

Corporation for Public Broadcasting. (1991, Spring). *Study of school uses of television and video.* Washington, DC: Author.

Fletcher, J. D. (1991). Effectiveness and cost of interactive videodisc instruction. *Machine Mediated Learning 3*, 361–85.

Fletcher, J. D., Hawley, D. E., and Piele, P. K. (1990). Costs, effects, and utility of microcomputer assisted instruction in the classroom. *American Educational Research Journal 27*, 783–806.

The Heller Report. (1994, January). *5*(3).

Honey, M., and Henriquez, A. (1993). *Telecommunications and K-12 educators: Findings from a national survey.* New York: Bank Street College of Education.

Information intrastates. (1993, October). *State Government News,* publication of the Council of State Governments.

Investor's Business Daily. (1994, February 17).

Melmed, Arthur. (1993, June). *A learning infrastructure for all Americans.* Fairfax, VA: Institute of Public Policy, George Mason University.

National Council on Disability. (1993, March 4). *Study on the financing of assistive technology devices and services for individuals with disabilities: A report to the President and the Congress of the United States.*

Orlansky, J., and String, J. (1979). *Cost-effectiveness of computer based instruction in military training.* IDA Paper P-1375. Alexandria, VA: Institute for Defense Analyses.

Princeton Survey Research Associates. (1993, Spring). *NEA communications survey.* Weighted sample of 1,206 NEA member teachers.

Report on the effectiveness of technology in schools 1990-1992. (1993). Conducted by Interactive Educational Systems Design and commissioned by the Software Publishers Association, 1993, p. 2.

Treese, Win. (1993, December). *Internet index.*

U.S. Congress, Office of Technology Assessment. (1988, September). *Power on! New tools for teaching and learning.* OTA-SET-379. Washington, DC: Government Printing Office.

U.S. Congress, Office of Technology Assessment. (1990). *Worker training: Competing in the new international economy.* OTA-ITE-457. Washington, DC: Government Printing Office.

U.S. Congress, Office of Technology Assessment. (1993). *Adult literacy and new technologies: Tools for a lifetime.* OTA-SET-550. Washington, DC: Government Printing Office.

Withrow, F. (1994, March 2). Personal communication.

The Internet
Resources for Educational Technologists

Don E. Descy
Library Media Education Department
Mankato State University

Three years ago I attended a workshop in Texas and learned about something called "The Internet." At the end of the six hours, I was absolutely overwhelmed by this new technology. Deep down inside, though, I knew I was experiencing the cutting edge. Now, three years later, I am still overwhelmed, not by the technology, but by the speed of change in the technology. I would not dream of presenting a workshop like the one I sat through. It was an outstanding presentation in its day, but now that presentation is as dated as the Model-T. Aside from the addition of the World Wide Web, the Internet itself has changed little. It is the access software technology surrounding the Internet that has changed considerably. The Internet is now (almost) user-friendly. With this in mind, let's look at a variety of ways the Internet can be utilized by a media technologist.

As you may know, the Internet is not a computer network but rather a network of computer networks. If we had to place a specific date on its beginnings, we would have to say that it began as ARPANET (Advanced Research Projects Agency Network), a U.S. Defense Department network, in 1969.

The common thread enabling all member networks to work smoothly together is that all of the networks must use the same set of rules, called *protocols*, to ensure interconnectivity. This set of rules is called Transmission Control Protocol/Internet Protocol (TCP/IP). Thanks to TCP/IP, one can use a Macintosh to go through a university VAX to get files stored on an IBM in some other part of the world. (We don't have to worry about the type of computer anyone on the "Net" is using: TCP/IP makes the connections transparent!) No one knows exactly how many networks or computers are connected to the Internet at present, because so many new people and networks are being connected every day. Currently it is estimated that the Internet interconnects more than 15,000 networks and reaches 35 million people. The Internet is not a specific "thing," governed by a specific organization, so these are only best-guess estimates.

In this chapter I review three basic Internet functions and highlight useful resources for media technologists in each. This review is followed by a brief discussion of several useful tools to aid in exploring network resources, finding e-mail addresses and file archives, and obtaining files.

INTERNET BASICS

The three basic Internet functions are communications, remote logon, and file transfer. Of these, communications is most heavily utilized. On the Internet, a colleague (or group of colleagues) is (are) only a few keystrokes away. Electronic mail (e-mail) is the most common means of communications. Much e-mail is sent from one individual to another individual.

It is also possible to join groups of colleagues with similar interests in a discussion group. Online discussion groups are called LISTSERVs. Being a member of a LISTSERV is similar to being at a constant professional conference. Letters sent to the LISTSERV computer will be distributed to all LISTSERV members. There are well over a thousand LISTSERVs for educators, with several hundred of these ideal for educational technologists. Some of the better (and more general) ones are EDTECH (listserv@msu.edu); AECT-L "Association for Educational Communications and Technology—List" (listserv@wvnvm.wvnet.edu); AERA "American Educational Research Association" (listserv@asuvm.inre.asu.edu); LM_NET "Library Media Specialist Network" (listserv@suvm.bitnet); and MAC-L "Macintosh news and information—List" (mac-l@yalevm.bitnet). The AECT Gopher (sunbird.usd.edu 72) contains a list of several hundred LISTSERVs of interest to media technologists.

A second function of the Internet is to enable users to log on to a remote computer. Remote login is referred to as "Telnet" after the Telnet protocol part of the TCP/IP protocol suite. Telnet enables a person to log on to a distant computer and, in effect, use his or her own computer as a remote terminal for the distant computer. Telnet is a real-time connection; that is, as keys are pressed on the keyboard, responses are activated on the distant computer. Using the Telnet protocol, it is possible to log on to remote libraries to access their catalogs, or to log on to remote databases to search for other information. It is possible to interact with other computers through simulations and games. Telnet also allows persons to log on to their own computers from someplace else. Telnet requires the user to enter specific computer addresses and passwords. It is fast being replaced by gophers and the World Wide Web, which do not require the user to enter either addresses or passwords.

The last general category of Internet activity is FTP or File Transfer Protocol. FTP enables the user to transfer files from one computer to another. There are tens of thousands of files residing on other computers just waiting to be downloaded. These files include freeware and shareware software applications, text files (from how-to-do something to complete textbooks), sounds, and graphics. Like Telnet, FTP requires addresses and passwords and also the knowledge of a strict set of commands to initiate responses on the host computer.

Freeware applications, such as Fetch from Dartmouth College, have made file transfer much easier by automating the command structure. Unfortunately, Fetch is only available for the Macintosh. Fetch can be FTPed from ftp.dartmouth.edu in the directory pub/mac/fetch. Once you use Fetch, you will never FTP the old way again.

The following list of files can be FTPed. These files contain some of the most common questions asked by participants in Internet classes and at workshops.

Academic Lists (713k in 12 files). This is a compilation of academic discussion groups, e-newsletters, e-journals, Usenet newsgroups, interest groups, and the like listed by discipline. First FTP the "readme" file to read the contents of the other files—some files are keyword-searchable.

   Address: ftp.ncsa.uiuc.edu
   Directory: education/education_resources/academic_lists
   File: readme

An Educator's Guide to E-Mail Lists (114k). This is a very good collection of LISTSERVs for educators. You may be surprised at what is here!

   Address: nic.umass.edu
   Directory: pub/ednet
   File: educatrs.lst

An Educator's Guide to Usenet Newsgroups (46k). Not all newsgroups are available on all computers so you may have to ask for the one that you are interested in. This list is grouped by subject area.

    Address: nic.umass.edu
    Directory: pub/ednet
    File: edusenet.gde

Answers to Commonly Asked "Primary and Secondary School Internet User" Questions (113k). This is a handy guide. Many people use this in workshops or as one of the first files for FTP practice.

    Address: nic.merit.edu
    Directory: documents/fyi
    File: fyi_22.txt

EFF'S Guide to the Internet (formerly **Big Dummy's Guide to the Internet**) (386k). A great introductory guide to the Internet. This one is very popular.

    Address: ftp.eff.org
    Directory: pub/net_info/eff_net_guide
    File: netguide.eff

Incomplete Guide to the Internet and Other Telecommunications Opportunities Especially for Teachers and Students, K-12 (1158k in 18 files). This is a how-to manual for beginner and intermediate users of the Internet, as well as a resource guide and reference manual for the more advanced user.

    Address: ftp.ncsa.uiuc.edu
    Directory: education/education_resources/incomplete_guide/
        dec_1993_edition/MS_word
        (also other formats and README files)

Merit's Network Information Center FYI Papers (1817k in 25 files). This is a collection of 25 titles covering a wide variety of information about the Internet. Site security, network infrastructure, privacy, network resources, and choosing a name for your computer are some of the topics included. I have mentioned others in this list. FTP the "index.fyi" file first.

    Address: nic.merit.edu
    Directory: documents/fyi
    File: index.fyi (5k)
        fyi_05.txt (Naming your computer: 18k)
        fyi_08.txt (Site security handbook: 249k)
        fyi_15.txt (Privacy and accuracy in databases: 9k)

Navigating the Internet: An Interactive Workshop (293k in 37 files). This is Richard J. Smith's e-mail-based introductory Internet course. The entire course covers e-mail, Telnet, FTP, Internet resources, and UNIX computing basics. This is very well written and easy to understand.

    Address: ftp.sura.net
    Directory: pub/nic/training

Net Etiquette Guide (16k). The proper way to send e-mail and communicate on the Net is covered in this manual. It contains useful information for people new to the Net—and some veterans as well.

> Address: ftp.sura.net
> Directory: pub/nic/internetliterature
> File: netiquette.txt

Search Techniques for Informational Resources (40k). This document is designed to help the new user access and utilize search tools available on the network. Also included are suggestions on where to start the search and how to ask the right questions to find the information you want.

> Address: ftp.sura.net
> Directory: pub/nic
> File search.techniques

SURAnet Guide to Selected Internet Resources (175k). This is a very complete guide to Internet resources. Introductory Internet resources, network services, directory services, network tools, informational resources, and software are just some of the topics covered. This one is updated regularly.

> Address: ftp.sura.net
> Directory: pub/nic
> File: infoguide.x-xx.txt (where x-xx is the most recent date: 10-94 as of this writing)

SURAnet How-to Guides. SURAnet has created four guides that cover basic information for Internet users. Guides on e-mail, FTP, Telnet, and using the UNIX text editor can be found here.

> Address: ftp.sura.net
> Directory: pub/nic/network.services.guides
> File: how.to.email.guide (13k)
>   how.to.ftp.guide (7k)
>   how.to.telnet.guide (3k)
>   how.to.use.vi.guide (4k)

The Guide to Network Resource Tools (244k.txt, 528k.ps). This guide covers almost anything you would like to know about the Internet. Topics include exploring the network, searching databases, finding network resources, finding people and computers, obtaining files, and networked interest groups. Guides in Cyrillic (Russian) and Kamenicky code (Czech national characters) can also be FTPed from here.

> Address: ftp.earn.net
> Directory: pub/doc
> File: resource-tools-guide.txt (text version)
> File: resource-tools-guide.ps (post script)

HELPFUL TOOLS TO EASE YOUR INTERNET TRAVELS

Many individuals and groups around the world are designing tools to improve accessibility to Internet resources. These tools help individuals locate that one username, Internet address, or file among the millions that are out there . . . and, happily, most of these tools are user-friendly.

I start with the Gopher. This text-based menuing system is probably the one tool that first opened the Internet to the masses. Next I discuss the World Wide Web (WWW). WWW is the fastest growing part of the Internet and is based on a concept called hypertext. WWW has added color graphics, movement, and sounds to the Internet. I finish by discussing a variety of other tools designed to increase user efficiency in utilizing Internet resources.

Gopher

Gopher was developed in 1991 to aid individuals at the University of Minnesota to find information they needed in various online databases around the university. This information was made available through a series of hierarchical menus, which is the basis of the Gopher system. Once an individual reaches the point in the menu with the specific information, addresses, passwords, and commands hidden behind the menu item are executed and the Gopher software searches out and retrieves the information. These addresses, passwords, and commands are not seen and need not be known by the user. Menu items have been expanded to include databases, FTP sites, archives, online library catalogs, Netfind, WAIS (Wide Area Information Server), and thousands of other gophers all around the world. This information is said to reside in "Gopherspace."

There are several ways to access a gopher. One method involves installing special software on your computer. This is called "Gopher client" software and is available via anonymous FTP from boombox.micro.umn.edu. (First look in the directory /pub/gopher and then in the directory for the type of computer that is of interest.) The second method of accessing Gopher is to establish a gopher site (hole) on your computer. It is possible to set up a gopher site on many types of computers, including desktop Mac or PC, or large VAX or UNIX, machines. The third and easiest way to access Gopher is to simply Telnet to a remote gopher.

Here are a few gophers that are of particular interest. At the machine prompt, type telnet, skip a space, and type the hostname.

Hostname	Login	Location
consultant.micro.umn.edu	gopher	University of Minnesota
gopher.msu.edu	gopher	Michigan State
gopher.ebone.net	gopher	Europe

The following are subject-specific gophers. At the machine prompt, type the hostname. No login is required.

Hostname	Location
gopher gopher.ed.gov	U.S. Department of Education Gopher
gopher ernest.ccs.carleton.ca 419	Canada's SchoolNet Gopher
gopher informns.k12.mn.us 70	K–12 Gopher in Minnesota
gopher sunbird.usd.edu 72	The AECT gopher

There is also an interesting LISTSERV devoted to the sharing of interesting gopher finds (no technical questions please!). This is the gopherjewelslist. To subscribe, e-mail to listproc@einet.net, leave the subject line blank, and send this message: *subscribe gopherjewelslist (your name).* Example: *subscribe gopherjewelslist Don E. Descy.*

The latest FAQ (fact) sheet about gophers can be obtained through any gopher or by anonymous FTP in the /pub/usenet/news.answers/gopher-faq directory at pitman-ager.mit.edu.

World Wide Web

World Wide Web (WWW or W3) is a new tool that was developed by CERN, the European Particle Physics Laboratory in Geneva, in 1991. WWW allows the user to browse information servers around the world using hypertext technology. Hypertext allows text and nontext objects to be linked during a search. WWW has been called the most advanced information system on the Internet. Universities, businesses, governments, and many elementary and secondary schools now have WWW sites of their own.

WWW, like Gopher, is an information delivery system. They differ in how they deliver the information. Gopher is a point-and-click menu-driven system (i.e., clicking on a menu item takes you to another menu, text file, etc.). WWW is not menu-driven, but rather is based on a concept called *hypertext*. With hypertext, each word or graphic can be linked to some other part of the text, another document, graphic, database, sound, video, and three-dimensional, movable objects. One of the beauties of WWW is that it is in color. As with Gopher, the user really doesn't know (or care?) where the links are obtaining their information. A short WWW session may access information from computers located all around the world.

To access World Wide Web, one needs a program called a WWW "browser" or "client" that will allow a person to connect to the remote WWW "server." This WWW browser may be on a desktop computer or at a remote mainframe computer. If a computer has Telnet capabilities, it is possible to try a remote WWW browser. Although these remote browsers give one an idea of how WWW works, they lack full functionality (color, graphics, etc.). With WWW, there really is nothing like the real thing! Here are four remote browsers to try:

Rutgers University CWIS (campus-wide information system):
Telnet info.rutgers.edu
Arrows select, <enter> links

Finnish University and Research Network (FUNET):
Telnet info.funet.fi
Login: www
Select service: www
Select interface: lynx
Terminal type: vt100
Arrows select, <enter> links

University of Kansas:
Telnet hnsource.cc.ukans.edu
Login: www (This is not on the menu but do it anyway!)
Arrows select, <enter> links

European Centre for Particle Physics (CERN), Switzerland:
Telnet info.cern.ch
Enter number to follow link

The very best way to travel around the Web is with browser software on your computer. Most of it is copyrighted but free for academic use. The five most popular browsers are Lynx, NCSA's Mosaic, Netscape, Cello, and CERN's LineMode browser. Unfortunately, if you are not directly connected to the Internet through your organization's network and have to dial in, you need to have a special dial-up connection such as PPP (Point to Point Protocol), SLIP (Serial Line Internet Protocol), or ARA (Apple Remote Access) for these browsers to function properly.

The new favorite browser is Netscape. Netscape has a wonderful graphical interface and is available in versions for MS Windows, Macintosh, and UNIX platforms. All three versions are available at ftp.mcom.com in the Netscape folder.

Another popular browser is NCSA's Mosaic. NCSA's Mosaic may be retrieved by anonymous FTP from ftp.ncsa.uiuc.edu in the directory /Mac/Mosaic (for NCSAMosaicMac) or /Mosaic/Mosaic-binaries (for other platforms).

A year ago there was very little to look at on the Web. Now there are many very interesting places to browse. Below are a few World Wide Web sites that contain information relevant to the media technologist:

A Ton of Web Sites (a master list)
    URL: http://www.mit.edu:8001/people/mkgray/comprehensive.html

Adaptive Technology Resource Center—University of Toronto
    URL: http://www.utirc.utoronto.ca/AdTech/ATRCmain.html

Cisco Education Catalog (Start here—you may never go anywhere else)
    URL: http://sunsite.unc.edu/cisco/edu-arch.html

Cool Site of the Day (Takes you to a different place every day)
    URL: http://www.infi.net/cool.html

Educational Technology Initiatives in the UK
    URL: http://www.liv.ac.uk/ctichem/etinituk.html

Educational Technology Virtual Library (large!)
    URL: http://tecfa.unige.ch/info-edu-comp.html

Hillside Elementary School (first elementary school server—check out what third- and sixth-graders can do!), Cottage Grove, MN
    URL: http://hillside.coled.umn.edu

Hotlist of K-12 Internet School Sites (schools online in the United States and abroad)
    URL: http://toons.cc.ndsu.nodak.edu/~sackmann/k12.html

Instructional Technology Connections—University of Colorado
    URL: gopher://ccnucd.denver.colorado.edu/hO/UCD/dept/edu/IT/itcon.html

Mankato State University Library Media Education WWW Server
    URL: http://lmewww.mankato.msus.edu

National Council for Educational Technology Information Service (UK)
    URL: http://ncet.csv.warwick.ac.uk/index/html

NCSA Mosaic Home Page (the Mosaic starting point)
    URL: http://www.ncsa.uiuc.edu/SDG/Software/Mosaic/NCSAMosaicHome.html

Spider's Pick of the Day (like Cool Site)
    URL: http://gagme.wwa.com/~boba/pick.html

U.S. Department of Education Technology Initiatives
    URL: http://www.ed.gov/techno.html

Vincent Voice Library at Michigan State (voice clips from all over)
    URL: http://web.msu.edu/vincent/index.html

Weather Maps/Movies (current satellite and radar weather infrared and visible images and movies)
    URL: http://rs560.cl.msu.edu/weather

WWW Sites of Interest to Education (many good places to look)
    URL: http://www.informns.k12.mn.us/hotlist.html

OTHER INTERNET TOOLS

Alex: Alex is a database that allows users to access files in FTP sites around the world. It is still in the experimental stage of development. You can FTP further information from alex.sp.cs.cmu.edu. Start with the README in the doc directory.

Archie: Archie was developed by the McGill University Computer Center (Canada) to help a user find the file he or she wants from more than 800 anonymous FTP sites (computers) containing more than one million files. When a search term is typed in, Archie searches for file names that contain the search term. Archie is updated every month. One may Telnet to many different Archie servers including: archie.mcgill.ca (Canada); archie.sura.net (MD); archie.ans.net (NY); archie.doc.ic.ac.uk (United Kingdom); archie.funet.fi (Finland/ Continental Europe); and archie.au (Australia).

HYTELNET: HYTELNET is a hypertext database of Internet sites. Peter Scott of the University of Saskatchewan is the author. It currently contains more than 1,300 libraries, Freenets, Campus-Wide Information servers, WAIS, Gopher, and WWW sites. Telnet to access.usask.ca and log in as hytelnet (all lowercase). There is also a new gopherized HYTELNET database found in l/internet/hytelnet at liberty.uc.wlu.edu 70.

Jughead: (Jonzy's Universal Gopher Hierarchy Excavation And Display) is a database of Gopher links. Word searches (it is possible to use OR, NOT, and AND connectors) will help find high-level menu items, but not individual file names at this time. To examine Jughead at Washington & Lee gopher liberty.uc.wlu.edu 70 and go to 4. Finding gopher resources.

Netfind: Netfind is designed to search computers to locate someone's e-mail address. Enter the name of the person and some location information and Netfind tries to locate the e-mail address. Telephone numbers, snail-mail (U.S. Postal Service) addresses, and work locations may also be found. Many computers (such as the one that my account is on at MSU) do not allow Netfind searches. To try Netfind, Telnet to bruno.cs.colorado.edu and log in as netfind.

Veronica: (Very Easy Rodent-Oriented Net-wide Index to Computer Archives) is an index of menus found on Gopher servers. This allows for the simultaneous search of hundreds of Gopher menus by keyword. The resulting menus can then be accessed directly by selecting from the resulting menu list. Access Veronica through one of the Gopher sites previously listed.

WAIS: WAIS (Wide Area Information Server) is similar to Archie but is capable of doing an in-depth search of close to 500 databases worldwide. WAIS searches the actual articles for the words specified. WAIS then sends a list of documents that may be helpful, and a "score" evaluating the utility of each of the listed documents. To try WAIS, Telnet to quake.think.com and log in as wais.

WHOIS: WHOIS is a directory of networks, hosts, domains, and more than 70,000 people maintained by the Defense Data Network Information Center. Most of the addresses pertain to people working on Internet research or projects. Telnet to nic.ddn.mil. No login is required.

Three years ago, very few people had heard of the Internet. At that time only a few academics used it for e-mail and some file transfer. Now, thousands of teachers and students are on board. The information available on computers and in heads around the world is endless. Climb on board and watch a whole new world open up before you. But be warned: What you learn today may be outdated tomorrow. You will need to keep in touch with the latest resources through magazines, books, and information from the Internet itself.

The Evolution of Educational
Software Portability

Betty Collis
Faculty of Educational Science and Technology
University of Twente
Enschede, The Netherlands

The portability of educational software relates to the likelihood that computer-based learning materials will be used in settings other than those in which they were originally designed and produced. Portability, and the related issue of technology transfer, have been of interest in education for many years, although recently some of the initial concerns about educational software, especially those relating to technical aspects of portability, seem to be less frequent topics of educational discussion than they were in the 1980s. However, it is likely that new interest in the portability of computer-related learning materials will emerge as a consequence of worldwide developments in computer technologies, telecommunications technologies, and human-computer interaction. In this review, the evolution of interest in issues relating to the portability of educational software is examined, a number of projects and experiences are summarized, and emerging issues are considered.

MOTIVATIONS FOR EDUCATIONAL
SOFTWARE PORTABILITY

In 1976, Alfred Bork wrote that:

> An important issue for developers of computer-based learning materials is the one of transferability to other locations beyond the campus on which the initial material was developed. Much discussion goes on about this problem, informally and in the literature, but much of this discussion appears to be based on very simplistic solutions, which do not examine the full range of problems associated with transferability (p. 1).

Before a discussion of this "full range of problems," it is useful to consider general motivations concerning educational software portability. Why is portability of interest? There are motivations relating to economics, strategic and social impulses, and motivations relating to the science and practice of educational technology (for an analysis, see Collis and De Diana 1990).

Motivations Related to Economics and Practicality

Educational software development is a labor-intensive, costly process. Because of this, there is a natural desire to reuse components of software whenever possible. For at least a decade, standard practices in software engineering, such as structured programming, modularity and abstraction, information hiding, and object-oriented development, have also been seen as important for the subset of educational software (Ratcliff 1987). Time and cost of development are central motivations, as well as better quality control. These aspects are magnified in less-developed or small countries and in increasingly complex software. It has long been noted that "small countries simply cannot fund the major cost of their own educational software development" (IFIP Working Conference 1989), and that it is not only limited financial means but also limited qualified manpower and limited access to up-to-date development tools and environments that stymie local design and production of quality educational software in many countries. (Oualid [1989], for example, discusses this problem in the context of Arabic countries.) This resource problem continues, as software becomes increasingly complex.

> The amount of effort which goes into producing high quality multimedia material is usually very large and the level of skills required very high. This is the reason why it is extremely important for the future of the field of the application of multimedia interactive technology to education to find efficient ways to share the efforts of courseware development (Olimpo, Chioccariello, Tavella, and Trentin 1992, p. 535).

Another reason for increasing the portability potential of educational software relates to strengthening the market for the product, from the perspectives of both the consumer and the producer. The educational buyer is only willing or able to pay a certain maximum amount for software products, even though the development costs of the software may be much higher. Thus, economies of scale, or continuing subsidization, must occur for educational software to be put into practice. Increasing the portability of the software is one way to increase the purchase base (Oliveira 1990).

Strategic and Social Motivations

Another set of motivations for educational software portability is driven more by social and strategic motivations than by cost and production reasons. Many who work in less-developed countries are struck by the "desperate need for instructional resources" (Ely 1989). For many countries, technology transfer is seen as "fundamental for human survival, where recurrent problems can no longer be met adequately by traditional means and practices" (Wolansky and Iyewarun 1989). Those with more abundant resources, including educational resources, have a moral obligation to see that such resources are extended to those in need.

Also, in many settings, computer-related educational resources are seen as vital ways to compensate for inadequate local educational conditions (a motivation that also stimulates distance-education delivery in many countries); in these settings, increasing the likelihood of portability of software is seen as a strategic as well as a socially responsible task. In the Province of Ontario in Canada, for example, the Ministry of Education commissioned the development of a particular software package for electronics instruction specifically so that quality electronics education could be had in remote, small schools in the geographically dispersed province, even as it was available in large urban schools (Collis, Moonen, Wetter-ling, and Oliveira 1991).

Motivations Related to the Science of Educational Technology

In addition, there is ongoing interest in the portability of educational software from a more scientific perspective. Careful analysis of different situations in which the same or an adapted set of learning materials is used can yield much insight into the interaction of context with software characteristics and the relationship of this interaction to learning. Learning more about what hinders, or stimulates, diffusion of an educational resource across different settings is fundamental to better design of the resource, as well as to better educational decision making about the resource. Also, better-designed software may also become more portable software and vice versa; thus, the study of portability is valuable not only to extend diffusion, but also to improve the design and development of computer-related educational resources in general (De Diana and Collis 1990).

Critical also is support for the decision to develop or adapt or use existing software. One focus for portability research is how better to handle the local adaptation of materials. Parallel to this is the study of how to design software that anticipates localization, "writing the software in the first place so that it is simple to customize it" (Hall, Preece, Hudson, and Jin 1993, p. 10). These are important considerations, not only for educational software, but also for educational media more generally.

Thus, motivations for improving the portability of educational software are plentiful. But many problems confront the success of portability, as Bork noted in 1976, and as is still the case in the mid-1990s. Bork called for a systematic examination of factors that limit portability; this examination has now taken place many times and in many different settings. An overview of some of the findings of these examinations follows.

ANALYSES OF FACTORS THAT INFLUENCE EDUCATIONAL SOFTWARE PORTABILITY

Factors Identified from Technology Transfer Experiences

Many analyses of factors associated with successful, and often unsuccessful, transfer of educational media from one country and culture to another have been done. All have direct relevance to the subset of educational media involving computers. One such example is Michel's analysis of the transferability of educational radio and television to less-developed countries (1987). Michel presents 15 "lessons" that illustrate key factors in the relationships among the exporting and importing countries that have influenced the application of broadcast technology. He pays particular attention to the motives, status, and levels of knowledge of those who participate in the transfer efforts; to sociopolitical conditions in the countries involved, including sensitivities related to nationalism; to the availability of personnel qualified to deal with the transfer; to economic issues; and to the expectations held by those involved about what the media can accomplish. He concludes with some strategic guidelines, including:

> Assess the short-term and long-term impact of the imported technology on the cultural, economic, and political autonomy of the country (Michel 1987, p. 142).

Technical and Pedagogical Factors

Bork, in his 1976 review, also analyzed short-term and long-term factors, but in relation to the portability of educational software. He identified two dimensions, each having both short- and long-term aspects. One dimension relates to technical aspects, the second to "innovative teaching aspects." He noted that most attention was focused on the technical aspects. He predicted, though, that technical preoccupations would gradually fade (he foresaw massive wide-area networking being a large factor in this, a prediction that is now coming true 20 years later), but that the issues involved with innovative learning would continue to stymie portability attempts. Bork's predictions and analyses, made 20 years earlier, are indeed proving to be accurate.

European Analyses

As another example directly relating to the portability of educational software, the "Summer University" sponsored in 1987 and 1988 by the Commission of the European Communities brought together educational software-development experts from throughout Europe to find common paths toward the creation of a European educational software market. The initiative involved an examination of the problems affecting the portability of educational software, and also the problems of "getting educationalists and computer scientists to work together," and had as its aim the development of a European methodology that would take into account the problems of portability. In particular, these problems were identified as:

- Problems of vocabulary
- Semantic problems
- Problems of culture and environment
- Teaching problems
- Problems related to the "ergonomic necessities of different languages"
- Technical problems related to different computer platforms
- Computer-language problems
- Problems related to lack of standard interfaces and module libraries (Ballini and Poly 1988).

The methodology developed by the group was tested on a set of educational computer packages, but it cannot be said that the two-year initiative has led to a marked improvement in the portability of educational software packages in Europe.

As an example of another European analysis of the portability of educational software, a more recent study (Fyfe and Fearn 1990) focused on commercial textbook and educational media publishers and their willingness to become involved in educational software distribution (either locally made or coming from somewhere else. In addition to technical and educational issues, particular attention was given to:

- Commercial issues, such as customs and duty regulations between countries and methods for arranging payment and currency for payment;
- Copyright and ownership issues when different countries are involved;

- Human resource issues relating to trained personnel who know both the software and the market in the countries involved; such people "do not exist, forcing companies to use local distributors who know the market but may not know the software and are less accountable to the software developers" (p. 3).

The general conclusion again was that transnational educational software portability was not likely to be seen by commercial publishers as a viable task.

Other groups of European practitioners have also examined the educational software portability problem. For example, from the human-computer interaction community, an "HCI Layer Model" was developed that identified factors related to the sensory motor level, the perceptual level, the interface organization level, the application level, and the curriculum level (DELTA OSIRIS 1989). One of the main conclusions of this multinational study was

> There is an inadequate "relationship between pedagogic demand and technology offer. . . . The problem is at the curricular/applications level and the way in which this interfaces with the broader social conditions within which such [portability] activity takes place" (p. 22).

Synthesis of Factors

On the basis of a synthesis of many such analyses, coming from different perspectives and continents, Collis and De Diana made, in 1990, the following categorization of factors influencing the portability of educational software:

1. **Technical factors**

   - mechanisms for human-computer interaction
   - program architecture
   - authoring tools and environments
   - operating-system-level factors
   - hardware characteristics
   - network and interconnectivity aspects

2. **Educational factors**

   - educational need and relevance
   - curriculum fit
   - instructional approach
   - tone and style of educational interactions
   - classroom context in which the software will be used
   - teacher-related considerations

3. **Social/cultural factors**

   - language for interaction with the software
   - tone and style of communication
   - issues related to cultural identity
   - political sensitivities
   - cultural perception of the roles of teacher and student
   - local references and assumptions

4. Organizational issues

- institutional decision-making procedures
- copyright and ownership
- cost-related issues
- marketing and distribution issues
- maintenance
- management of the design, development, and distribution processes (Collis and De Diana 1990, pp. 155-56).

It is one thing to analyze the problem—many have done this. But what is the progress with respect to educational software portability itself? To address this question, a number of major cases and projects formed to directly address the educational-software portability problem are described next. The examples are clustered relative to their predominant focus: technical issues, educational issues, or social and cultural factors. To demonstrate the evolution of issues over time, the examples span nearly a decade.

PROGRESS? SAMPLE CASES

Technical Issues Focus

Different Platforms. Many projects have focused on technical issues hampering portability. A major example was the "EASI" software portability effort in Ontario, Canada, which evolved during the period 1983 to 1990. EASI, which stood for "Educational Application Software Interface," was a major initiative through which the Ministry of Education attempted to stimulate the development of software tools so that developers would create educational software according to a set of procedures and standards defined by EASI rather than a particular operating system. The EASI software tools would thus permit the developer to produce a version of the program for each of a list of different microcomputer systems eligible for subsidized acquisition by schools, with little if any further programming (McLean 1989). The initiative was in direct response to the fact that a variety of computers were present in schools, thus splintering the market for any quality educational software development. To attack the problem, in 1983 the Ministry released a set of minimal functional requirements that a computer had to meet to qualify for a position on the supported list. Then, over the period 1983 to 1988, the EASI interface was developed, and vendors wishing support for educational software development from the Ministry were told that they had to accommodate the requirements of EASI as a common software portability environment in their source code. The components of EASI were a standard C compiler and its library, and a C-callable library of primitive routines permitting access to any of the listed platforms.

The project failed. The office responsible for it disappeared after a change of government in the early 1990s. The computers on the target list rapidly changed or became obsolete. The market for educational software was not robust enough in Ontario to motivate vendors to pursue the exercise without long-term government subsidy. The idea of a machine-independent platform continues to be of interest, but is left to be addressed by the major vendors themselves rather than educational specialists or ministries of education. A key decision in Ontario, that of officially subsidizing a wide variety of computer systems so that schools could choose the platform they wished, was politically motivated and led directly to the paralysis of what had begun in the early 1980s as a major international example of concentrated stimulation of educational software development.

Many other projects have also taken place, attempting to address educational software portability at the delivery-system level. Another large-scale example was the Department of Defense (DoD) courseware portability initiative in the United States. This initiative had as its goal the increased capacity to share interactive courseware across a wide range of Defense training settings, in order to "lower the per-unit costs of ICW, lower instructional systems development costs, increase the use of advanced instructional technology in military settings, and increase instructional efficiency in the military services" (Fletcher 1992, p. S3). This was to occur through specification of a "virtual device interface" that would mediate between a courseware application itself and the operating system of a target computer. In Europe, similar initiatives have been made, supported by the Commission of the European Community, primarily under the framework of the DELTA Project and with the goal of stimulating a common market for educational software products in Europe. One such large-scale initiative was "PETE" (Portable Educational Tools Environment). PETE was meant to provide integration among various tools for authoring, monitoring, tutoring, learning, and distribution of educational software products (Nicklin 1990).

In looking at worldwide trends, however, it does not appear that these sorts of initiatives have made an impact on the larger educational software market. Inroads that have been made toward portability over technical platforms are predominately influenced by a few large international companies that give no evidence of being motivated by educational efforts in their race to develop cross-platform market strategies.

Modularity and Architecture. A number of other projects have addressed the portability problem, not from the perspective of an additional layer of technical requirements to support different computer systems, but from a focus on more modular design of software packages themselves. Although many such projects took place in the 1980s (see, for example, Wilson and McCrum 1984), the principles they endorsed and the techniques they embodied are largely those of software engineering more generally, and thus do not need separate but parallel development specific to educational software.

Language Portability. Anticipating the technical issues involved in translating the language of the user interface of an educational software package, when the package is to be ported to a setting whose population requires a different language for user interpretation of the software, is a longstanding issue in educational software portability (see, for example, Trollip and Brown 1987) and in user-interface design more generally (see, for example, Nielsen 1990). Much work has gone on, and continues to go on, with respect to the problems of porting a product to a different language, particularly when the language uses a different character base. Sukaviriya and Moran discuss this for Asian languages (1990), and Hall and his colleagues (1993) summarize issues for non-Western scripts and languages more generally. Kearsley (1990) summarizes such experience with various guidelines:

- Avoid hard coding; define graphics, dialog boxes, color schemes, menu options, and all data as objects or variables and anticipate dynamic generation of windows, dialog boxes, and menus.
- Store all text strings as data files, not as part of the program itself.
- Anticipate the requirements of different character sets and the impact of different directions of text writing on all screen designs.

A recent case study that illustrates these issues involved the translation of an English-language educational software environment into Bulgarian and Catalan (Griffiths, Heppell, Millwood, and Mladenova 1994). The software involved, called "Work Rooms," was designed to provide a range of tools to young learners for painting, writing, simple database work, and mathematical problem solving. Each activity is represented to the users through the metaphor of a room in a house. The main screen shows the house with a wall removed and eight rooms available for choice. The rooms have names, in English, of "MacDoodle," "Write On," "Broken Text," "My Word," "My Data," "Broken Calculator," "Count Down," and "Home." Each room is visually represented as well as being labeled by words. The software was designed in HyperCard using compiled extensions to the HyperTalk programming language, and involves features such as context-sensitive balloon help, tool palettes, and sound. The package is described as "being distributed in large numbers worldwide in English and has stimulated delighted reactions from children, parents and teachers" (Griffiths et al. 1994, p. 9). For a number of motivations, including respect for cultural diversity and support for smaller cultures, the package has been translated into Catalan, Bulgarian, Danish, Norwegian, Russian, and Welsh.

In an analysis of the experiences encountered during the Catalan and Bulgarian translations of the user interface of the "Work Rooms" software, the authors note issues relating to how far to go in the borrowing of English for technical terms in the target language. The major world languages are served by the International Organization for Standardization, which, among other activities, aims to standardize equivalent technical terms in different languages, but the situation for lesser-used languages varies greatly. As an example, the term *bug* has an official translation in Catalan, but this official translation is not in common usage, and neither it nor the English original would be understood by children. Substituting the Catalan word for *error* would communicate the intent of the word, but destroy the visual pun of a graphic insect, which accompanied the "bug" error message in the English version and had been seen as a very positive and pleasant way to inform children that a technical problem was occurring with the program. Other experiences relating to screen design, software structure, and font technology are described; for example, the value of storing text associated with buttons in a text field that can be edited without interference with the button's function, and that can display non-Latin fonts.

Educational Issues

Just as progress has been made in anticipating and dealing with technical issues confronting educational software portability, there is also considerable insight into problems associated with educational aspects affecting portability. Six areas constituting "educational factors" were summarized by Collis and De Diana (1990):

- Educational need and relevance
- Curriculum fit
- Instructional approach
- Tone and style of educational interactions
- Classroom context in which the software will be used
- Teacher-related considerations.

In each of these areas, there is abundant evidence that a less-than-optimal match between local conditions and design decisions in a software package will result in teachers not using the software. This pertains to teachers not only in international portability contexts, but also to teachers within the original group for whom the software was made. For example, a recent analysis of university professors, all in the same country, all teaching a common, standard course in statistics, and all using the same textbook, found that the majority of the instructors failed to make use of educational software included with the textbook for practice purposes (Vernon 1993). The reasons for this lack of use did not include criticism of the software itself, but rather a range of items, including lack of motivation and difficulty in providing student access to the software for practice purposes. Thus, the educational need for the software was not strong enough, and the motivation for the instructor to deal with the organization of the software use was not great enough, to convince the instructor to bother.

Curriculum and Instructional Style. Vernon's example relates to a situation where the curriculum fit of the software was clear and where the instructional style embedded in the software was not a problem. In most portability situations, these two aspects are indeed problems and are major deterrents to software acceptability. As examples, a state-of-the-art overview of educational software portability in the European Community (Commission of the European Communities 1992) noted that member states differ in their opinions about whether there is any acceptable role for the computer in the primary classroom (p. 12).

Even when an area of study is common, and computer use within this area is not contentious in itself, the identification of a common topic within this area relevant to the teaching of the curriculum in different member states is still difficult to accomplish. For example, a decision was made by the Commission to fund a project involving educational experts from Italy, Spain, and Portugal on a common software package for use in geography teaching. "Great difficulty was experienced in finding an area of work relevant to the teaching of geography as it is practiced in all of the participating Member states" (p. 13). The result of the project was a database of primarily statistical information used with a dedicated program to run simulations for economic geography, but the program has had little diffusion because its storage requirements exceed the capacity of computers generally available in schools at present.

Candidates for Portability: The Case of the "Electronics Workbench." A general conclusion has been reached concerning the portability of educational software from an educational perspective, namely, that "the less structured or didactic the program the more usable it is in other systems" (Commission of the European Communities 1992, p. 13). The problem with this, however, is that products that have the characteristics of educational tools or exploration environments, and thus are most likely to be candidates for portability, are also the most complex for teachers to use. They often require the teacher to adapt his or her teaching practice and even philosophy in order to be integrated effectively into practice (Nagtegaal, Thomas, and Kabayashi 1990). Thus, the characteristics that increase their chance of educational portability from one perspective—that of avoiding portability problems related to the details of learning content—also decrease the programs' chances for use, in either original or destination context, because of lack of fit with the teacher's preferred teaching style and ability to integrate a complex technology into classroom practice.

To investigate this issue of optimal educational conditions for software portability, a multiyear study of a particular package, the "Electronics Workbench" (EWB), was recently concluded at the University of Twente in the Netherlands (Collis, Zhang, Stanchev, and Dong 1994). The software package "The Electronics Workbench" has been developed and is distributed and supported by Interactive Image Technologies Ltd. (IIT), 49 Bathurst Street, Toronto, Ontario, Canada, M5V 2P2. The package was originally developed for use in Ontario schools as an alternative or supplement to using electronic circuit board components and test equipment in laboratory environments for courses in which electronics are studied. The package, however, has come to be used in many other educational environments besides

Ontario secondary schools—different levels of education, different countries, and different organizational approaches to educational delivery. Thus, EWB was chosen as a good subject of analysis and research with respect to a better understanding of what makes an educational software package educationally portable.

A number of different investigations relating to EWB were carried out in 1991, 1992, and 1993 (see, among the more than 10 reports published relating to the overall EWB investigation, Collis, Zhang, Stanchev, and Dong 1994; Collis, Moonen, Wetterling, and Oliveira 1991; and Koenig and Collis 1992). These subprojects have included:

- A Dutch EWB study

- A Bulgarian EWB study

- A Chinese EWB study

- Contacts with other users of EWB in different countries

- Other analyses of EWB from various educational perspectives

- Literature reviews related to the use of laboratory simulation software for electronics instruction and the relationship of that literature to EWB and its portability.

All this activity has generated a number of insights into EWB's relative success as a portable educational software package. These success factors include:

- Its choice of a curriculum area (basic circuits) addressed in many different educational settings and contexts.

- The fact that the curriculum area has minimal cultural or social sensitivity and maximal educational-content similarity in countries throughout the world.

- The fact that the packages can be used for a variety of educational purposes such as compensating for lack of equipment or self-study, and also for classroom demonstrations.

- The design of the package itself, with its near-total reliance on visual aspects instead of text.

- The likelihood that teachers making use of the package (thus teachers of electronics) already have some computer-use skills or at least have not too much difficulty in handling the computer for simulation of electronic circuits.

- The cross-cultural acceptability of the sorts of interaction embedded in the software and the educational relevance of that interaction to the content being learned (i.e., to drag components across the screen to construct a circuit and then to attach a measuring instrument that shows the amount of current flowing through the circuit). (See Ely 1989, for an analysis of the importance of designing feedback and interaction in ways acceptable to the local culture.)

- The fact that the package is marketed separately and differently in different countries and often is introduced in combination with a teacher inservice opportunity or with locally made lesson materials to support its use.

Teacher Involvement. One way to increase the likelihood of teacher acceptance of educational software is to involve teachers in at least some aspects of the design and development process. In the five Nordic countries, teacher education has been an important part of a multiphase initiative to stimulate educational software use in schools. The Nordic Project long ago determined that portability of educational software among its member countries was important, and has set up a number of initiatives to stimulate this portability. One is the joint adoption of a common model for education software, the so-called *marketplace model*, based on the idea of educational software providing the learner with a "shopping center" sort of environment, in which he or she can move in and out of various areas or "stores" related to the exploration of a learning goal based on his or her learning needs (Bengtsson 1990). Using this marketplace model as a common framework, the Nordic Project has organized a number of different teacher-training initiatives in which teachers work on designs for new software packages, using the general marketplace approach. A number of the teacher-developed designs have been so successful that they have subsequently been fully developed, using the Nordic approach and dividing the labor of software development over specialized teams in the five Nordic countries. This teacher-originated approach has generated educational software accepted throughout the Nordic countries, a "cooperation which has saved each country quite a lot of money" (Vasström 1991).

Social and Cultural Factors

Cultural Constraints. Social and cultural factors play a central role in the likelihood that an educational software package will be used in a setting different from that in which it was created. It has long been known that school curriculum and learning materials are never neutral knowledge, but always the product of social legitimization and "cultural politics" (Apple 1992). Although some view the use of computing resources as becoming "a way of life, a manner of thinking" (Tchogovadze, 1989), and thus urge computer use in schools as a way to confront this reality, others are much more skeptical about the place of educational software from "outside." Murray-Lasso (1990), from Mexico, for example, feels that the lack of attention to the importance of culture is a major reason why educational software portability efforts between countries continue to fail. Murray-Lasso discusses 12 culture-related considerations and notes that cultural and national identity are so important to many countries that

> many feel that the elementary school educational system is the last bastion left to some countries for a measure of cultural independence and are very leery of losing it through an educational software invasion from advanced countries (p. 260).

Murray-Lasso applies his 12 cultural considerations to a particular portability case study, to predict whether an educational software package very popular in the United States would be a likely candidate for porting to Mexico. His answer is no, it would not be likely to succeed, because of violations of most of the 12 cultural constraints.

Sociopsychological Aspects. Those involved with technology transfer in education more broadly have long acknowledged the "not-invented-here" reaction to educational products coming from another country or even institution. This issue can be illustrated from the context of distance education, a context within which institutions must frequently make decisions about the suitability of learning materials developed elsewhere (Hershfield 1987).

Perhaps the chief barrier to the use of "other people's" distance education courses are the individual members of the faculty of the institution thinking of using instructional software that has been developed by another college or university. . . . Many faculty members are convinced that no course, whatever the qualifications and skills of its developers, could possibly substitute for locally prepared texts (p. 25).

Hershfield goes on to note cultural differences in the tone and style of learning materials coming from different countries, as further evidence to show that the "not-invented-here syndrome" has social and cultural motivations related more to the culture of the instructor than to educational considerations.

Cultural Norms and Their Effect on Decision Making. Many social scientists have analyzed the impact of culture on how decision making occurs in a country. Hofstede, in 1984, published an analysis of more than 50 countries relative to their differences on a number of cultural dimensions: in particular, individualism versus collectivism; large versus small power distance (*power distance* is the extent to which members of a society accept that power in institutions is distributed unequally); strong versus weak uncertainty avoidance (the need for rules to guide behavior); and masculinity versus femininity. Important to his conclusions is the thesis that an organization such as a school or ministry is very much embedded within its culture, and thus the way decisions are made (such as decisions about the acceptance of educational software coming from somewhere else) will very much differ in the different countries. In many countries, the decision about accepting educational software developed somewhere else will never come down to the teachers themselves; all decisions will be made by a few (males) with centralized power. In other, more individualist societies, persons lower in the power structure may be able to make decisions about using ported educational software, but as a consequence of this lack of centralization, the likelihood of broad-scale diffusion and substantial support for product adaptation is unlikely to occur.

Cultural Norms and Their Effect on Communication Style: Case Studies from Australia. As yet another way that sociocultural norms will affect the likelihood of portability of software in any particular setting, the impact of culture on communication style is well known (Knapp 1990). This relates not only to the meaning of words, but also to a wide variety of other communication aspects, such as conventions for signaling self-image, normal procedures for taking turns in speaking, preferred styles for expository writing and the presentation of arguments, and concepts of privacy. Each of these can affect the degree to which a software package is judged to be communicatively acceptable in a new setting.

There are some noteworthy examples of this sort of sensitivity being applied to the design of educational software packages for use with Aboriginal groups in Australia. Fleer (1989) describes how a careful observation of the way members of Aboriginal communities interact led to a design of an educational software package to reflect their communicative and cultural norms. Henderson and Putt (1993) go further, in that they attempt to shape an entire teacher-education program, to be offered at a distance to Aboriginal communities in Australia, in a way that takes into account the students' culture. The multimedia courseware in the program was developed to reflect the students' traditional ways of learning and interacting in their communities—through observation, rehearsal and practice, demonstration, obtaining immediate feedback, and private rehearsal of tasks rather than taking risks publicly. For example, students must not feel a sense of public shame; thus, audio feedback only accompanies correct answers. Students do not want a correct answer given to them after they make a mistake, as this would be taken as a lack of faith in one's intellectual abilities.

The degree to which such cultural styles and communication norms can affect the design of educational software is considerable. The likelihood that an educational software package made in one culture can be "retuned" to fit the cultural style of another setting rapidly decreases as the cultural differences between the two settings increase.

Organizational Influences on Educational Software Portability

The category of organizational influences is complex and often overlaps with sociocultural factors. For example, Ojo (1992), a Nigerian, analyzes organizational and sociocultural challenges for the adoption of information technology in Nigeria and notes the following as being of particular importance:

- A culture of lack of personal responsibility for organizational decisions, which manifests itself in a lack of concern for efficiency in the running of projects.

- A culture of preference for informality, whereby simple procedures for doing things become deliberately complicated and unclear to allow opportunities for personal gains.

- A culture for overpoliticized decision making, with the "obvious implication that an IT practitioner to some extent must be a shrewd politician and ready to make compromises, if he is to make a success of an IT application project" (p. 14).

- A culture of secrecy; "that one has knowledge which others do not have, is often considered a thing of pride" (p. 15).

- A culture of bureaucratic complexity, where artificial or real bottlenecks can occur to stall any project.

- An inadequate or wrongly motivated culture with respect to research, where "the society seems to prefer a trial and error approach, using ready-made tools like turnkey packages imported from developed countries" (p. 16).

- An inadequate policy culture, where policy makers "are more concerned with rhetorics rather than concrete formulation and adherence to such policies" (p. 18).

Such an analysis seems harsh, but can be substantiated from experience in many less-developed countries and situations. In such settings, careful planning for software porting is likely to be stymied regardless of how well a package is designed or could meet local needs.

International Projects for Software Portability: The EPES Case. The preceding description of the organizational culture in many less-developed countries makes for a pessimistic prediction about the success of educational software portability projects in those countries. However, other groupings of countries show more promising conditions for organizational support of educational software porting. The EPES Project (European Pool of Educational Software) is a major example (Aston and Dolden 1994; Gjørling 1994). Because this initiative is probably the most systematic and broad-scale activity to date with respect to stimulation of cross-border educational software portability, it is good to study it in detail. The goal of EPES is to promote and organize a pragmatic and effective exchange of educational software among producers in Europe. The project, influenced by previous initiatives in the Nordic countries, by the procedures of the International Council for Educational Media (ICEM), and by various earlier international projects in Europe investigating software portability, is an ambitious project that started in June 1992. The project was funded partly by the Commission of the European Community, partly by IBM Denmark A/S, and partly by the partners themselves. The partners in the first phase were the following countries: Belgium, Denmark, Finland, Germany, Greece, the Netherlands, Norway, Poland, Portugal, Spain, Sweden, and the United Kingdom. Each country had to be represented by a group in a position to produce and distribute educational software at a national level. Each representative was to bring to a Review Meeting four or five pieces of educational software from his or her country which could be candidates for the portability pool.

The Review Meeting took place on 11-14 May 1992, in Denmark. Each piece of software was demonstrated to a small group of reviewers, who filled out evaluation forms related to their prediction of suitability of the demonstrated package to the pool. The goal was to select 2 programs from each of the 12 participating countries for the pool; after various decision-making procedures (described in the Final Report of the Project, Späth 1994), two programs per country were in fact selected, all but two of which were for the secondary school level or higher. All countries then completed a standard contract, agreeing to a prespecified procedure for ownership and royalties of software in the pool that they wished to trade. Issues relating to copyright, taxes and customs, ISBNs, and publishing rights were addressed in a standard fashion. Following this, each of the 24 selected packages had then to be translated into an English version, along with their manuals, during the following two-month period.

The next meeting of the group was called the Translation Meeting and was held in Sweden from 27-30 July 1992. At this meeting, programmers responsible for each of the 24 programs were to be present (thus, at least two technical/programming specialists from each pool country) and had to bring along all tools and software necessary for an on-the-spot translation activity, along with source codes for their software, and their English versions of the software. Each country had already given a preliminary list of packages they wished to have translated from the pool for use in their own settings. The number of pool countries interested in a translation of a package ranged from 3 to 11 (with 11 countries interested in a local translation of a Spanish program of a workbench-type nature, "Laboratorio de Optica," for experiments with optics).

The main activity of the meeting was the exchange of technical advice on the further adaptation and translation of the software packages for localization to countries wishing to obtain a package from the pool. Problems relating to inhouse development tools were settled, and special problems relating to translation of the programs into Greek versions, because of the different characters needed for the language, were discussed. Among the technical issues discussed at this Translation Meeting were:

- Dealing with text external from the executable files
- Dealing with text external to the source-code files but embedded in the executable file at compilation
- Dealing with text and other resources embedded in the executable file but edited with a resource editor
- Dealing with nonsystem fonts (Aston and Dolden 1994).

Hardware incompatibility was not a problem in the EPES Project, because all software was required to work through MS-DOS or Windows running on IBM-compatible software. However, "most of the programs placed in the EPES did not feature portability in language and culture in their original design; this had been included as a 'bolt on' to the product developed for a more specific educational marketplace" (p. 4). On the basis of their involvement in this project, Aston and Dolden made the following conclusions relative to portability:

- Programs, albeit highly successful in their native country, that were based upon particular teaching styles presented barriers to adoption by other countries. The incompatibility between the underpinning pedagogy of some programs and teaching styles in another country highlighted the need for program developers to induce, at the planning stage, options for a wide range of modes of use (p. 6).

- Text displays should be dynamically assigned as the program is executed.

   —Probably the most important technical lesson to be learned from this project was that the development of future programs should not merely consider portability across different system platforms—the user interface and style of use should also incorporate maximum flexibility (p. 6).

- The cost of translating software can, in some cases, be small in comparison with the cost of developing and publishing curriculum support materials (p. 6).

After the Translation Meeting, countries made final decisions on which programs they wished to acquire from the pool, as well as, incidentally, other packages that partners became aware of at the meeting. As of March 1993, 22 of the 24 packages were contracted for, and a total of 135 national versions of EPES programs were finished or under final adaptation. Spain, Germany, Greece, and Poland contracted for 4 to 6 packages each; the rest of the participating countries obtained between 10 and 17 packages. The packages that were most successful as candidates for adaptation were:

- "Optica," from Spain, adapted by 10 countries; a workbench for optics instruction in physics courses.

- "Hefaistos," from Denmark, adapted by nine countries; a graphical database on volcanos and earthquakes.

- "Greenhouse Effect," from Norway, adapted by nine countries; a simulation of the greenhouse effect on the earth based on manipulation of gases in the atmosphere.

- "Probe," from Denmark, adapted by eight countries; a tool for processing and analyzing digital pictures from satellites, radar, and the like.

- "Draad," from the Netherlands, adapted by eight countries; an environment for the construction and study of three-dimensional figures.

- "ASD," from Poland, adapted by eight countries; demonstrations of six elementary algorithms working on different data structures for informatics instruction.

- "DiscMath," from Poland, adapted by eight countries; animated demonstrations of different algorithms implemented in pseudo-Pascal.

- "The Viking Village," from Sweden, adapted by eight countries (the only program for younger children among those most often chosen for adaptation); students make decisions about running a Viking village for at least three years.

This list is interesting, because it shows what kind of software is preferred, given maximal support for most of the other conditions affecting the portability of educational software, particularly the technical and organizational decisions. No information is yet available about the widespread use of the adapted programs in the participating countries, but 16 countries, including most of those participating in the first phase, have indicated interest in participating in a second round of activity (Gjørling 1994). However, as of May 1994, funding from the Commission had still not been obtained to support the travel and administrative costs associated with a second phase, nor was it clear if countries would consider the portability exercise valuable enough to finance their own costs.

EVOLUTION: WHAT NEXT FOR EDUCATIONAL SOFTWARE PORTABILITY?

As these case studies show, we have as a field gained considerable experience with educational software portability in the last decade. Projects such as EPES and the Nordic activities show that educational software can be designed to increase the likelihood of portability, or can be localized, *given adequate organizational support to provide an infrastructure for the activities and to bring together both exporters and importers of software.*

But, of course, all is not solved. Most students still have little or no experience using an educational software package ported from another country; most software developers have no commercially viable way to bring their products to widespread attention and adoption/ adaptation in other countries. What are major aspects of the educational software portability issue now, and what major new aspects are arising? Four aspects seem to be most relevant: technical advances in handling multiple languages; more reliance on visual communication and graphic user interfaces; implications of wide-area networking; and teachers' willingness to use educational software, whether ported or local. We close this review with some considerations of these aspects.

Handling Multiple Languages

Among the many technical developments in the computer world, one that should make considerable difference with respect to the portability of educational software is the speed and ease with which multiple-language environments can be developed and manipulated. Desktop publishing software has led the way in providing environments for many different language fonts and for combining different languages and scripts within documents. Moss (1989), for example, describes script systems and language-specific fonts that open the way to considerably easier handling of language, including in portability contexts. In addition, word processors are now commercially available that can simultaneously create "WYSIWYG" (what you see is what you get) documents in more than 20 languages. In addition to multilingual menus, these packages present all messages, dialog boxes, and online help in the language of the user's choice. Multilingual spelling checkers are available, as well as support for the differing keyboards for 31 languages.

In addition to improvements in handling scripts, maturing audio handling capabilities in computers are making new types of language environments possible which not only will increase the portability potential of the computer for language instruction and practice, but also will increase the value of the computer in general for language-related tasks. Thus, technological improvements will continue to reduce many of the previously enormous issues relating to the language-translation aspects of educational software. However, issues relating to the appropriate selection and use of language and to the translation of jargon and local references still continue to require human insight.

More Reliance on Visual Communication and
Graphical User Interfaces

Another trend in the general computer world is toward use of graphical user interfaces (GUI) and increased use of visualization in software. Windows and desktop GUI environments for major computer platforms have now become nearly industry standards; icons as representatives of objects, system resources, and problem states are also thus nearly standard; and objects such as menu bars, control buttons, and scroll-down windows are becoming universal. These developments in the commercial market will considerably influence and simplify some aspects of educational software translation (Barker 1993).

However, as with text translation, there are still many issues to consider with respect to the portability of visual communication, graphic user interfaces, icons, and other sorts of graphical interface components. Nielsen (1990) analyzes different types of icons, for example, and notes that "reference and arbitrary icons will do considerably worse than resemblance icons in internationalization." Graphic designers will have to be involved in future software translation teams, something for which there is a "total lack of tradition" (p. 240). Image acceptability, symbol interpretation, and color suitability also vary from country to country and require careful inventory before their assumed suitability for educational software can be claimed (Russo and Boor 1993). Field testing remains important. The learnability of signs, symbols, and icons, as well as user interface metaphors, are new considerations for predicting the portability success of highly graphic software products (Ossner 1990).

These references are representative of work occurring in the field of human-computer interaction (HCI): It is this field, rather than that of educational software design, that is actively contributing to the software internationalization knowledge base during the mid-1990s.

Implications of Wide-Area Networking

Perhaps the major new dimension to educational software portability is evolving through the escalating use of wide-area networking in society in general and also in education. Wide-area networking is opening up new possibilities for the distribution and sharing of software and other sorts of electronic learning materials. Gupta (1993), for example, notes that:

> An approach similar to that used in publishing cheap editions of books in developing countries could be used in producing cheap editions of popular software for developing countries. The cheaper editions could have documentation printed more cheaply in the developing countries and perhaps the packaging could be cheaper and carried out in the developing country itself. This should certainly be possible in countries where the markets are large enough and the volume of sales could justify local printing and packaging.

Gupta, an Indian, sent this message over the Internet; the message was received by hundreds of persons throughout the world, many of whom responded positively to the idea. Although such an approach does not jump over the sociocultural organizational problems described by Ojo in Nigeria (1992), it can go a long way toward bringing possibilities for educational software distribution to a broader group of persons, at least those in universities with access to the Internet. Internet protocols related to file transfer, anonymous FTP sites, and the use of Gopher and World Wide Web servers via the Internet system are rapidly bringing access to software to the desktops of potentially 20 million account holders; such distribution possibilities can radically change the nature and culture of educational software portability activities, away from high-budget commercial exercises toward more individual exchange of technically less complex software. "Little local programs" capable of license-free and technically easy dissemination over networks and through modems could regain a lease on life and reanimate aspects of educational software portability that were present in the early days of "quick and dirty" public domain software, but which have lost all credibility over the last two decades of increasingly professional software development processes.

Computational E-Mail. Even for those without full access to file transfer through wide-area networking, there are new possibilities for educational software dissemination if the software is simple enough. Borenstein (1992) discusses the potential impact of embedding software programs within electronic mail—what he calls "computational messages"—and notes that computational e-mail "promises to alleviate the problem of remote installation at separately-administered sites, the problem of getting users to 'buy in' to new applications, and the problem of extremely heterogeneous user environment" (p. 67). Although getting software into one's computer does not mean one will use it, or use it in educational settings, computation e-mail still offers great possibilities to remove many of the traditional frustrations of software portability activities.

Thus, the capacity to share software over a wide-area network may bring back a tolerance for the "small" educational software programs that fueled the enthusiasm of the field in the early days of computers in education, often because such programs were made by the enthusiast himself or herself. Such programs have long since disappeared from serious consideration as educational software; they were replaced by powerful packages built according to industrial standards, and requiring as a consequence extensive support even to install, let alone use. Perhaps there is a time again on the horizon for small, nonrobust, nonpowerful, but classroom-feasible programs, which are classroom-feasible because they are often made by teachers who have a good sense of what can be used in a typical class setting. These sorts of homemade programs are what are now available over educational bulletin board systems in many countries and suggest an interesting new (old) angle on software portability.

Supporting Multicultural Communication. The explosive growth of wide-area networking is bringing a new dimension into educational settings, that of communication across distances and even cultures. This may well bring a new and significantly important variation to the educational software portability situation; instead of the current methods for adapting a stand-alone program for use in different settings, portability partners may find it more useful to talk to each other via e-mail about possibilities for different types of software use in education, and thus better evaluate ahead of time the feasibility of portability activities. If portability efforts do begin, the ability to transmit various components of programs back and forth via wide-area networking can vastly simplify and lessen the cost of translation activities. Later, when document-sharing environments are more common, portability partners can work together, in real time, on common versions of the same software package, again offering major changes relative to the logistics and costs of translation activities.

Yet, merely reaching people through wide-area networking does not mean that one knows how to effectively communicate with them, or know what sort of learning materials are most appropriate for them. Educational specialists designing or adapting for portability will have to be even more sensitive to cultural and organizational norms and to communication than before, because they will now be directly in touch with a potential adaptor and must know how to appropriately and effectively engage in an online dialogue with him or her. These skills are complex, and may not be in the experience base of the persons engaged in software development projects. Nakakoji (1993) is an example of those starting to consider the implications of cross-cultural communication for user interfaces supporting online communication and sharing of resources (this is another case of work in which the internationalization of software comes from the human-computer interaction field rather than the educational-software design community).

And a Final Issue: Will Teachers Use Educational Software, With or Without Portability Considerations?

A final thought about advances and new issues relating to educational software portability is a sobering one. Assuming that we make it better and easier and cheaper and faster to get software into the hands of teachers—whether software localized from other countries or even developed in their own countries—will they use it after all? The evidence here, so far, is not too encouraging. Pettersson, Metallinos, Muffoletto, Shaw, and Takakuwa (1992) compared teachers' instructional use of a wide range of educational media in different countries and found computer use at the bottom or near-bottom of the list in most cases. In another international study, this time comparing 12 countries in their use of computers in schools, Pelgrum and Plomp (1993) found that the

> percentage of teachers using computers is quite low, and that the group of intensive computer using teachers, those who are using computers most of every week, will at best not exceed 15%. It is probably worse than that, as deeper analyses show that the percentage of teachers who integrate computers to a substantial extent among all teachers of the studied subject (mathematics, science, mother tongue) is only 3% (p. 330).

These low-usage figures can no longer be explained away by saying that teachers do not have access to computers and educational software. Veen (1994), for example, found that even giving teachers considerable technical and human support, and access to a wide range of software appropriate to their teaching areas, did not mean that the majority of the teachers made much use of it in their teaching practice. Veen interprets this as the lack of fit between the teacher's current view of appropriate methodology for his or her curriculum area (and his or her personal style of classroom management) and the demands imposed by trying to integrate educational computer use into a lesson. Ragsdale (1990) adds to the complexity when he notes that teachers, even when they do try to use computers with their students, often miss the "teachable moments" in the learning situation and instead expect the software to somehow be doing all the teaching. He reflects:

> There is a disillusionment with curriculum-based software. The question is: did you believe that it would work by itself? Did you believe that all you had to do was make the programs available and the students would learn? . . . I would say, we have to better emphasize the teachers' role. We're not creating programs which stand on their own (p. 2).

Are we making progress with educational software portability? Yes, in a number of ways. But the answer is not clear if progress is measured in more than technical aspects. The answer is not clear because it is not clear if we are making progress with educational software use in general, ported or not.

REFERENCES

Apple, M. W. (1992). The text and cultural politics. *Educational Researcher 21*(7), 419.

Aston, M., and Dolden, B. (1994). Logiciel sans frontières. *Computers & Education 22*(1/2), 18.

Ballini, D., and Poly, A. (1988). European methodology for the development of educational software programs. *Euryclée Info 3*, 310.

Barker, P. G. (1993). Pictorial communication. In *Nonvisual humancomputer interaction*, ed. D. Burger and J. C. Sperandio. (London: John Libby Eurotext Ltd.), 55–77.

Bengtsson, B. (1990). Portability of educational software: Reflections from a Scandinavian point of view. *Journal of Research on Computing in Education 23*(2), 161–72.

Borenstein, N. S. (1992). Computational mail as network infrastructure for computer-supported cooperative work. In *CSCW 92 Proceedings*, ed. J. Turner and R. Kraut (Toronto: ACM Press), 67–75.

Bork, Alfred. (1976). *Transferability of computer-based learning materials.* Unpublished paper, Physics Computer Development Project, University of California, Irvine, CA.

Collis, B., and De Diana, I. (1990). The portability of computer-related educational software resources: An overview of issues and directions. *Journal of Research on Computing in Education 23*(2), 147–59.

Collis, B., Moonen, J., Wetterling, J., and Oliveira, J. (1991). A model and an evaluation of a computer-based training simulator: The "Electronics Workbench." In *Proceedings of ICOMMET '91*, ed. T. Sakamoto (Tokyo: Japanese Association for Educational Technology), 223–25.

Collis, B., Zhang, J. P., Stanchev, I., and Dong, Z. C. (1994). Investigating cross-national education software portability: The case of electronic workbenches. *Educational Training and Technology International 31*(1), 44–58.

Commission of the European Communities. (1992). *New information technologies in education: The added value of Community measures.* Brussels: Task Force Human Resources, Education, Training and Youth.

De Diana, I., and Collis, B. (1990). The portability of computer-related educational software resources: Summary and directions for further research. *Journal of Research on Computing in Education 23*(2), 335–41.

DELTA OSIRIS. (1989). *Characteristics of interoperability environments.* Workpackage 2. Brussels: DELTA Office, Commission of the European Communities.

Ely, D. P. (1989). Protocols and processes for promoting interactive cross-cultural media transfer. *Educational Media International 26*(1), 6–12.

Fleer, M. (1989). Reflecting indigenous culture in educational software design. *Journal of Reading 32*(7), 611–19.

Fletcher, J. D. (1992). *Courseware portability.* IDA Paper P2648. Institute for Defense Analyses, 1801 N. Beauregard Street, Alexandria, VA 22311-1772.

Fyfe, A., and Fearn, S. (1990). *The portability of educational software in relation to the creation of a viable European market.* Enschede, the Netherlands: Educational Computing Consortium BV.

Gjørling, U. (1994). *Proposal, second round of the EPES Project.* Egå, Denmark: Orfeus [Skæring Skolevej 202, 8250 Egå].

Griffiths, D., Heppell, S., Millwood, R., and Mladenova, G. (1994). Translating software: What it means and what it costs for small cultures and large cultures. *Computers & Education 22*(1/2), 9–17.

Gupta, G. K. (1993, July 22). Message to Internet distribution list for IFIP WG 9.4. (wg9.4@luotsi.uku.fi)

Hall, P., Preece, J., Hudson, R., and Jin, L. (1993). Software localization. *IFIP Newsletter 1*(2), 10–11.

Henderson, L., and Putt, I. (1993). The Remote Area Teacher Program (RATEP): Cultural contextualization of distance education through interactive multimedia. *Distance Education 14*(3), 212–31.

Hershfield, A. F. (1987, July 8–10). *Distance education materials produced in other countries. To use or not to use? That is the question.* Paper prepared for the VI World Congress for Comparative Education, Caracas, Venezuela.

Hofstede, G. (1984). Cultural dimensions in management and planning. *Asia Pacific Journal of Management 17*(2), 112.

IFIP Working Conference. (1989). *Final report.* Reykjavik, Iceland: IFIP Working Group 3.5.

Kearsley, G. (1990). Designing educational software for international use. *Journal of Research on Computing in Education 23*(2), 242–50.

Knapp, K. (1990). Common Market–Common culture? *European Journal of Education 25*(1), 55–60.

Koenig, J., and Collis, B. (1992, May 7). *Learning how to sell software internationally: A case study of "The Electronics Workbench."* Invited presentation at the Seventh Canadian Symposium on Instructional Technology, Montreal.

McLean, R. (1989). EASI overview. *CALM Development Newsletter 5*(10), 3–7.

Michel, C. (1987). Educational radio and television: Their transfer to developing countries. In *Educational technology: Its creation, development and cross-cultural transfer,* ed. R. M. Thomas and V. N. Kobayashi (Oxford: Pergamon), 125–42.

Moss, S. (1989, July). Macintosh à la mode. *MacUser,* 46–51.

Murray-Lasso, M. (1990). Cultural and social constraints on portability. *Journal of Research on Computing in Education 23*(2), 252–71.

Nagtegaal, C. G. J., R. M. Thomas, and V. N. Kobayashi, Eds., (1990). The POCO Project: A response to the portability dilemma. *Journal of Research on Computing in Education 23*(2), 184–94.

Nakakoji, K. (1993). Cross-cultural considerations in designing human-computer interaction. *American Programmer 6*(10), 18–24.

Nicklin, P. (1990). *The concept of PETE and some preliminary user requirements.* Paper presented at the DELTA/EPOS Seminar, 22-23 January 1990, Madrid. Sponsored by DG XIII, Commision of the European Communities.

Nielsen, J., Ed. (1990). *Designing user interfaces for international use.* Amsterdam: Elsevier.

Ojo, S. O. (1992, March). *Challenges of sociocultural and organizational issues in IT applications in Nigeria.* Paper presented at the IFIP WG 9.4 Working Conference, Nairobi, Kenya.

Olimpo, G., Chioccariello, A., Tavella, M., and Trentin, G. (1992). On the concept of reusability in educational design. In *Learning technology in the European Communities,* ed. S. Cerri and J. Whiting (Dordrecht: Kluwer Academic Publishers), 535–48.

Oliveira, J. (1990). The economies of educational software portability. *Journal of Research on Computing in Education 23*(2), 318–34.

Ossner, J. (1990). Transnational symbols: The rule of pictograms and models in the learning process. In *Designing user-interfaces for international use,* ed. J. Nielsen (Amsterdam: Elsevier), 11–38.

Oualid, A. (1989). Problems of software development in developing countries. In *Information Processing '89,* ed. G. X. Ritter (Amsterdam: Elsevier), 1067–71.

Pelgrum, H., and Plomp, T. (1993). The worldwide use of computers: A description of main trends. *Computers & Education 20*(4), 323–32.

Pettersson, R., Metallinos, N., Muffoletto, R., Shaw, J., and Takakuwa, Y. (1992). The use of verbovisual information in teaching of geography: Views from teachers. In *Visual communication: Bridging across cultures,* ed. J. C. Baca, D. G. Beauchamp, and R. A. Braden (Blacksburg, VA: The International Visual Literacy Association), 211–21.

Ragsdale, R. (1990). Language selects and amplifies, may explain children's use of software. *CALM Development 6*(2), 1–7.

Ratcliff, B. (1987). *Software engineering principles and methods.* Oxford: Blackwell Scientific Publications.

Russo, P., and Boor, S. (1993, April). *How fluent is your interface? Designing for international users.* Paper presented at InterCHI '93, Boston, MA.

Späth, P. (1994). *EPES: European Pool of Educational Software. Final report.* Egå, Denmark: Orfeus [Skæring Skolevej 202, 8250 Egå].

Sukaviriya, P., and Moran, L. (1990). User interfaces for Asia. In *Designing user interfaces for international use,* ed. J. Nielsen (Amsterdam: Elsevier), 189–218.

Tchogovadze, G. G. (1989). Informatics and national cultures. In *Proceedings, International Congress Education and Informatics, Theme 5.2.* Paris: UNESCO.

Trollip, S. R., and Brown, G. (1987). Designing software for easy translation in other languages. *Journal of Computer-Based Instruction 14*(3), 119–23.

Vasström, U. (1991). *Nordic Committee on Educational Software and Technology: Activities and results until 1991.* Copenhagen, Denmark: Nordic Council of Ministers.

Veen, W. (1994). *Computer supported teachers: The role of the teacher in the implementation of computers in classroom practice.* Utrecht: University of Utrecht IVLOS.

Vernon, R. F. (1993). What really happens to complementary textbook software: A case study in software utilization. *Journal of Computer-Based Instruction 20*(2), 35–38.

Wilson, R. N., and McCrum, E. (1984). Use of modular design in the production of portable CAL software: A case study. *Computers & Education 8*(2), 229–37.

Wolansky, W. D., and Iyewarun, S. A. (1989). Effective transfer of technology in Third World countries: A systematic approach. *A.C.F.P. Journal 24*(3), 9–12.

Visualization and Effective Instruction

Jef Moonen
University of Twente
Enschede, The Netherlands

ABSTRACT

This paper reviews the potential relationship between visualization and effective instruction. Reference is made to the AIME concept introduced by Salomon, and it is concluded that research in this area should take into account aspects of costs, cost-effectiveness, and the motivation of the learner.

INTRODUCTION

Improving the quality of learning and instruction is a continuing objective of education and training. "Quality," however, can be described in many ways. One perspective is to focus on the effectiveness of the learning material for supporting the instruction.

As the traditional classroom and training situation is being expanded with technological features such as video, computer, and multimedia, there is considerable interest nowadays in the possibilities for using graphical user interfaces for electronic learning material to enhance visual communication. Presenting, transmitting, and processing information in visual, nontextual form is what we mean when we speak of visual communication. Nontextual symbols, pictures, graphs, images, and so on that convey information are called *visuals*.

The importance of visualization in electronic learning material is reflected in many authoring systems, as they offer more and more-varied possibilities for incorporating visuals in the courseware they produce. However, it remains difficult to derive guidelines for the integration of visual communication in courseware design. Improvement of courseware design methodology is therefore necessary, and research into the relationships between the types of courseware and the functions of visualization will be especially important to this endeavor.

In that context, there is a need for further development of theoretical principles of visual communication, especially with respect to the following questions:

- In what circumstances does the mind prefer the more complex, dynamic, lifelike image to the seemingly simpler verbal one?

- How do nontextual symbols, graphics, still pictures, and moving pictures contribute to visual communication?

- If visual literacy is the ability to understand, think, and create nonverbally, how should visual literacy be learned and taught?

- In what way will visual learning be of value in determining the (cost-)effectiveness of the learning process?

98

A special aspect is the inclusion of visual techniques in tools to handle nonverbal communication and in tools supporting the courseware design process. The latter is a logical consequence of what is going on in computer science itself, where two new styles of human-computer interaction have become popular: "programming through visual environments in which graphical elements play prominent roles alongside text, and iconic environments, in which users interact with the machine primarily by defining, pointing at, juxtaposing, overlapping, and otherwise manipulating postage-stamp size images commonly referred to as icons" (Glinert 1990, p. 1).

Answers to these questions about visual communication should help to better identify the advantages and disadvantages of the visualization of information in courseware and courseware design. These answers, in turn, lead to a new set of questions:

- What kinds of tools improve the process of visual communication in teaching and training?

- What kinds of tools improve the process of courseware design?

- What are the aspects and factors that determine the breakeven point of using visualization, in terms of cost-effectiveness of courseware design, development, and implementation?

- How does visualization improve the cultural portability of electronic learning material?

In addition, the evolution of human-computer interface technology will significantly change in the next decade, given the growing international research interest in virtual reality (Earnshaw, Gigante, and Jones 1993; Kalawsky 1993). As with any new technology, there are pedagogical questions to be addressed as methods of instruction are extended from being dominantly text-based to being multisensory-based. Additional questions such as the following are also important:

- How is learning in "virtual reality" different from that in a traditional educational environment?

- How are learning styles enhanced or changed by virtual reality?

- What kinds of research will be needed to assist instructional designers in developing effective virtual-reality learning environments?

RESULTS FROM RESEARCH

Because of the evolving technology, visual messages in different forms can now be presented much more easily than in the past. However, there are no consistent research results to support the hypothesis that the effectiveness of what is being delivered is increased by using visuals.

Print Material and Visuals

In considering the relationship of graphics to print materials, Fleming and Levie (1993) indicate, for instance, that "although the results of research on the effects of using graphics are neither consistent nor compelling, most authorities and professionals are convinced that in many circumstances graphics help readers (especially poor readers) to use and understand instructional text" (p. 41). They also say that "although research has failed to demonstrate conclusively that using pictures in courseware (in this context text-based material) is related to motivation, their instincts tell many designers that good pictures really do motivate learners" (p. 46).

In the context of message design variables, and with respect to the perception of pictures, Fleming and Levie present eight design guidelines. Their first and main guideline is that "pictures are usually more memorable than words, and are thus useful when information has to be remembered" (p. 86). However, their second guideline is that "pictures play many roles in instruction. It is therefore necessary to know precisely what a picture's function is intended to be before it is designed" (p. 86).

Graphic Design Principles and Interactive Systems

In their discussion of the design of effective visual presentations, Baecker and Buxton (1987) report that the application of graphic design principles to the medium of computer displays and interactive systems is not a trivial process. They suggest that "given the difficulty of the problem, good progress will probably be achieved through the multi-disciplinary collaboration of the technologist 'telling us what is possible,' the psychologist 'telling us what not to do,' and the designer 'suggesting what to do' " (pp. 300–301).

Cognitive Psychology and User-Interface Design

Gardiner and Christie (1987) investigate relevant areas of cognitive psychology in relation to user-interface design, and summarize their findings in 162 design guidelines. They discuss the relationship of the use of visual material and its impact on memory, and conclude, based on the dual-coding theory of Paivio, that "our ability to remember the appearance of novel, unorganized visual patterns over the short-term is extremely limited. On the other hand, our ability to remember the identity of a concrete item is better when it is presented as a picture than as a printed word" (p. 128). They further conclude that "ideally interfaces should be designed to be flexible enough to allow the users to vary the amount of information they have to deal with at any time, and, conversely, should not allow users to 'get away' with inadequate amounts of processing where the consequences of poor recall will be dire" (p. 157). More generally, Gardin and Christie summarize research findings in two principles:

> (a) The probability of recalling an item increases as a direct function of the depth of processing at which the item was encoded when put into memory. Depth of processing increases with the requirement to consider the meaning of an item and its relation to other items; (b) the probability of recalling an item increases as a direct function of the elaborateness of processing associated with its encoding into memory. Elaborateness of processing increases with the richness of the context information present at the time of the storage (p. 159).

These principles lead to the following design guideline:

Items which must be recalled from memory some time after being removed from the screen should be surrounded with supporting information to which they are related, and should be immersed in a visually rich environment (Design Guideline 125, p. 268).

Guidelines for the Design of Visuals for Information

Petterson (1989) presents practical guidelines for the design of visuals for information. He stresses that image variables should be considered in relation to content, graphic execution, context, and format. In the design and production of visuals for instruction, pictures must obviously contain the information they are intended to convey and must be relevant to the situation. However, Petterson reminds us that understanding a message in a visual is different in various cultures as well as in different socioeconomic groups. Lanzing (1993) has also done research in this area.

Relationship Between Verbal and Visual Messages

In addition, effective human-machine interaction requires an understanding of the relationships between verbal and visual messages, between characteristics of the learning material and the instructional process, and the instructional approach and learning styles. Verleur (1993) presents an interesting summary of research results in this context. Generally speaking, these results indicate that when audio and visuals are presented simultaneously, the visually presented information will be dominant (Jaspers 1991). Another conclusion is that presentations that focus on two senses or use two channels, including an iconic presentation and a linguistic approach (text or audio), are superior to a presentation using only one channel. The most powerful result of using multichannel presentation forms is their positive impact on the motivation of the learner.

Empirical Research

Although many guidelines appear in the literature for incorporating visuals into learning materials, most of these guidelines are based on theoretically driven research. Such research tends to seek out simple paradigms that appear to focus successfully on a single psychological process. However, it should be recognized that empirical research is also necessary, as factors such as individual skills and knowledge and the use of multisensory channels can make significant differences in performance and motivation. In other words, empirical research is needed to support general conclusions about the impact of visualization on the effectiveness of learning materials. In particular, a main focus for research is the investigation of circumstances under which visualization realizes a positive contribution to the quality of the instructional/learning process.

AIME: THE AMOUNT OF INVESTED MENTAL EFFORT

An interesting approach to the impact of television on learning was developed by Salomon (1984), who argued that when the structure of a communication is more or less congruent with one's past experience, that information is processed rather mindlessly. When, on the contrary, nonautomatic and effortful mental elaborations are necessary to capture the information, these lead to both depth and mindfulness. A measure to capture such efforts is called by Salomon "the amount of invested mental effort" (AIME).

Two other concepts affect the AIME exercised by an individual. The first is the learners' perception of the characteristics (PDC) of the task. The more demanding a PDC is, the more AIME will be expended. The second is the learners' perceived self-efficacy (PSE). According to Salomon: "The more efficacious learners perceive themselves to be, the more they are likely to invest sustained effort in a task and persist in doing so" (p. 649). Assuming that thorough and mindful coverage of information is characteristic of a better quality of instruction/learning, Salomon argues that such characteristics will be obtained when the instructional process stimulates an increase in AIME.

The main issue with respect to visualization therefore is not to investigate technical possibilities of new media to "maximize" the portion of visualization within an instructional program. Rather, the main issue is to match the visualization possibilities of the new media with the characteristics of the learners, to maximize their amount of invested mental effort.

DO MEDIA INFLUENCE LEARNING?

As we talk about visualization, it is not the medium but its presentation formats that are important. To better distinguish different aspects of media, Kozma (1991) defines them in terms of their technology, their symbol systems, and their processing capabilities.

The most common tendency is to talk about media in terms of their technology, that is, the mechanical and electronic aspects that determine their functioning and physical features. There are TVs, VCRs, CD-ROM players, slide projectors, and so on. The most interesting features of a medium, however, are its ability to present a range of symbols (for example, text, audio, visual), and its processing capabilities (for example, interactivity, search capabilities).

Questioning whether media will contribute to maximizing AIME through visualization clearly relates to the range of symbol systems the medium can present, and to its processing capabilities. It was emphasized earlier that empirical research should be done to determine in practice the impact of visualization on the effectiveness of the teaching/learning process. Given the different characteristics of media, this research should not concentrate on the technical possibilities of new and future media, nor on the comparison of one technical facility with another. On the contrary, research should be planned in relation to new symbol systems and/or new processing capabilities represented in new and future media. Unless a new medium creates such a new symbol system or a new processing capability, it has to be considered as belonging to a specific class of media capable of a certain kind of presentation and information transfer.

In that respect, for instance, a product presented through CD-I is not essentially different from a product presented through a computer program controlling an interactive videodisc. In terms of instructional effectiveness, there seems to be no reason why there should be a difference between these two media. However, there could be a significant difference in terms of their cost-effectiveness.

COSTS, COST-EFFECTIVENESS, AND MOTIVATION

Different media are not alike in terms of the costs involved—both costs for procurement and costs for the development of learning materials. Neither are they alike in terms of their potential to motivate the learner, or, to put it into a broader context, to stimulate the AIME of the learner.

When the expected instructional effects for two media are more or less comparable, then the cheaper medium is the most cost-effective.

Given the wealth of traditional and electronic media that are now available, and given the fact that many of these media have comparable features with respect to the symbol systems they can represent and comparable power in terms of their processing capabilities, the question of the cost-effectiveness of a medium is becoming most relevant.

Analysis of data in the context of cost-effectiveness very often leads to the understanding that potential effects (such as the instructional impact of a rise in the motivation or a change in the attitude of learners) are not (well) represented in the measurement of performance. Increased motivation of learners seems to be the most apparent effect.

CONCLUSION

Research with respect to visualization and media should concentrate on investigating relationships between symbol systems—in particular, visualization—and processing features, learner characteristics, and learning styles. In addition, both cost-effectiveness and motivation should be taken into consideration when investigating the instructional value of visualization.

REFERENCES

Baecker, R. M., and Buxton, W. A. S. (1987). *Readings in human-computer interaction.* San Mateo, CA: Morgan Kaufmann Publishers.

Earnshaw, R. A., Gigante, M. A., and Jones, H. (1993). *Virtual reality systems.* London: Academic Press.

Fleming, M., and Levie, W. H. (1993). *Instructional message design: Principles from the behavioral and cognitive sciences.* Englewood Cliffs, NJ: Educational Technology Publications.

Gardiner, M. M., and Christie, B. (1987). *Applying cognitive psychology to user-interface design.* Chichester, UK: John Wiley & Sons.

Glinert, E., ed. (1990). *Visual programming environments: Applications and issues.* Los Alamitos, CA: IEEE Computer Society Press.

Jaspers, F. (1991). The relationship sound-image. *International Journal of Instructional Media 18*(2), 161–74.

Kalawsky, R. S. (1993). *The science of virtual reality and virtual environments.* Wokingham, UK: Addison-Wesley.

Kozma, R. B. (1991). Learning with media. *Review of Educational Research 61*(2), 179–211.

Lanzing, J. W. A. (1993). *Visual aspects of the cultural portability of educational software: A literature analysis.* Unpublished report. Enschede, The Netherlands: University of Twente, Faculty of Educational Science and Technology.

Petterson, R. (1989). *Visuals for information: Research and practice.* Englewood Cliffs, NJ: Educational Technology Publications.

Salomon, G. (1984). Television is "easy" and print is "tough": The differential investment of mental effort in learning as a function of perceptions and attributions. *Journal of Educational Psychology 76*(4), 647–58.

Verleur, R. (1993). *The application of audiovisual material as a complement to printed instruction.* Unpublished report. Enschede, The Netherlands: University of Twente, Faculty of Educational Science and Technology.

Functions and Design of Video Components in Multimedia Applications

Pløn W. Verhagen
Department of Educational Instrumentation
Faculty of Educational Science and Technology
University of Twente

INTRODUCTION

Designers of interactive multimedia applications face the decision of whether the information to be presented should take the form of text, graphics, animation, video stills, moving video, sound, or any combination of the former. This paper focuses on design decisions with respect to the use of video segments, with or without sound. First, the functions and utilization patterns of video as a component of multimedia systems are presented. Next, research on audiovisual design is reviewed with respect to camera factors, audio factors, optical effects and special effects, and pacing and rhythm.

VIDEO FUNCTIONS

Video functions may be classified according to content-driven or logistic criteria, which both may be used to support decisions to select video as a component of an instructional application. Table 1 provides a list that is based on Verhagen (1992, 1993). The functions are:

- **Content-related use of photographic pictures or moving video** (showing people and objects). This function concerns the message-specific need for a certain mode of presentation (if I require a visual, audio will not do; and if I have to show motion, video has to be preferred over still pictures). In certain fields, such as medicine, biology, and geography, there are many content elements for which it is self-evident that certain kinds of visuals are needed. It has to be noted, however, that in many cases message characteristics are not unequivocally prescriptive with respect to communication mode. Visual referents in memory may, for instance, inhibit the need for pictures if they provide sufficient support for mental imagery in the context of verbal messages. Figure 1 shows that content-relatedness plays a role in several of the other listed video functions.

- **Depicting the invisible or the nonaccessible.** This function concerns presentation options that cannot exist without certain media techniques. Examples are slow motion, time-lapse photography, photography with invisible beams (like Röntgen or infrared photography), use of telescopes and microscopes, and animation. Here the "human size" with respect to perception in space and time is an important factor. Some experiences could not happen if events could not be speeded up, slowed down, scaled up, or scaled down to manageable proportions by use of media.

- **Logistic use.** Straightforward applications concern uses of media to solve problems of place, time, and identical repetition of messages. (In most cases, it is more feasible to show a slide of Vesuvius than to visit the volcano). Also substantial effort to develop an audiovisual program that contains a refined discourse about a certain subject is a one-time investment. (The program can be repeated infinitely with constant quality.) Logistic arguments apply also in the cases of several other functions, as represented in Table 1.

Table 1
Video Functions in Relation to Content or Logistics

Video functions:	Purpose: Content-related	Logistic
Content-related use of photographic pictures or moving video	*	
Depicting the invisible or the nonaccessible.	*	
Logistic use.		*
Cognitive help (visualizations as tools for thinking).	*	
Modelling of psychomotor skills.	*	*
Video feedback.	*	*
Providing observation materials.	*	*
Psychologically realistic simulation.		*
Video to present gifted teachers.		*
Video design for emotional involvement.	*	

- **Cognitive help** (visualizations as tools for thinking). Visualizations may offer new perspectives on knowledge or extend existing knowledge in the way that Bohr's atom model shaped conceptions about atomic structure. Bohr's model provided a way for insightful communication about the elementary decomposition of matter—a message for which visual media characteristics could be exploited successfully. Similar reasoning applies, for instance, to the insightful animations (with narration) that demonstrate the essence of the Lorenz transformation or Einstein's Special Theory of Relativity. In general, schematizing is the keyword here.

- **Modelling of psychomotor skills.** Video is, in many cases, an appropriate means to demonstrate motor behavior.

- **Video feedback.** Video may be used to record student behavior for feedback purposes. This may support the evaluation of psychomotor performances, feedback during microteaching sessions or interview training.

- **Providing observation materials.** Video registrations (of group discussions, of children playing, of animal behavior, etc.) may provide opportunities to train observation skills and to learn to analyze behavioral patterns.

- **Psychologically realistic simulation.** Social interaction may be simulated by having human models on—for instance—videodisc who react to decisions of students by talking directly to the students from the video screen. Well-known examples are video-based management games.

- **Video to present gifted teachers.** In fact a variant of logistic use, this video function provides the possibility to repeatedly enjoy the presentation of outstanding teachers who demonstrate their skill in handling subject matter.

- **Video design for emotional involvement.** In this case, aesthetic value, emotional value, and use of drama are at stake. Factors relating to pleasure, goodness, beauty, interest, and complexity can be identified as components of aesthetic value. These factors play a role in determining the attention of learners and their perception of the relevance of a learning task, which are components of their motivation. The depicted objects may have emotional qualities of their own. Wounded victims of war or hungry people of Africa can evoke emotional responses that may have an impact on certain types of learning. Responses such as anger, joy, curiosity, and desire for justice may also be stimulated by the appropriate use of drama. The filmic form of video offers excellent opportunities to exploit these possibilities. Recorded material thereby has the advantage of the carefully planned impact that results from skillful design and production.

BASIC APPROACHES FOR UTILIZATION

The previously mentioned video functions represent one set of variables to consider when designing practical applications. In addition, several basic utilization patterns may guide designers:

- **Text primacy** (symbolic first). Here, the basic question is: "Can printed material (text and pictures) do the job?" This starting point leads in many cases to cost-effective solutions. In cases where moving video is indispensable, this approach may be maintained by using barcode-controlled videodiscs as an adjunct to the written material. The approach is feasible for good readers with sufficient learning skills in the subject matter involved.

- **Visualization as starting point** (iconic first). Here, the basic question is: "Can we show what we mean?" This starting point leads in many cases to a look-and-tell format on the basis of video presentations. It results in concrete presentations that may very well suit rather concrete subject matter (or it may enlighten abstract subject matter by visualization). It is feasible for group instruction as well as for individual study, may help poor readers, and may involve students who are not very motivated to read.

- **Between-channel redundancy as reinforcement strategy.** Using two sensory channels increases the likelihood that messages will be received. This phenomenon may be used by developing educational materials in such a way that sight and sound are simultaneously used to present semantically overlapping information. The simplest (and most redundant) form is having a voice present texts that can be read from paper or from a computer screen at the same time. Striving for semantically overlapping information often leads to audiovisual presentations in which schematizing is frequently used to support abstract subject matter with appropriate images. Between-channel redundancy as a reinforcement strategy is appropriate for complex subject matter and/or poor learners, as long as the total amount of information does not exceed the information-processing capacities of the learners.

- **Orchestration for learning** (theater of life). This function uses video for emotional involvement. Creative communication solutions may attract and maintain attention, establishing learning situations that are entertaining, challenging, or have an emotional impact for other reasons. This technique is appropriate if motivation to learn is considered a problem; for instance, in distant learning situations where the delivery of instruction takes place by means of television and has to compete with other television channels.

- **Audiovisual archive as a starting point** (providing a computerized information environment). In this case the database capabilities of multimedia are exploited. This may be done for the purpose of knowledge acquisition in an educational setting, where personal development is paramount. Free navigation through the information space is here the starting point, even though the space available may be limited for didactic reasons to prevent novice learners from being overwhelmed by the difficulty level of encountered information, or from getting lost in the possibly vast amount of information contained in the system. In all cases, adequate help functions should be available. For experienced users, playing around in the information environment offers ways to extend and deepen knowledge by enriching existing schemata with new facts or new combinations of facts.

  Another application concerns problem solving on an individual basis, with the multimedia system as the main source of information. In that case, there are two more options: (1) the problem-solving activity is guided by the system (it is incorporated into a detailed planned teaching method); or (2) the system is an open information environment in which the user has to find his or her own way. The level of support by the system may be adjusted to the needs of the user, either automatically (with an online help system that detects ineffective conduct of the user), or on request (when the user decides to switch from the browse mode to "challenge me," "teach me," or "question me"). Further applications may take the form of interactive encyclopedias, interactive maintenance manuals, and the like.

- **Interactivity as the starting point.** This is the case when learning outcomes are desired for which it is considered necessary that practice, testing, and feedback be organized in interaction with the computer system. The main instruction functions are: *orienting* to the learning task (presenting subject matter, presenting content-specific ways of thinking, presenting new methods and techniques to operate on the subject matter, demonstrating working methods and problem-solving approaches); *practice* (providing opportunities to practice, providing feedback); *testing*; and *general feedback*. For the organization of multimedia applications to serve these instructional functions, common computer-based instruction formats may be used, such as drill-and-practice exercises, tutorials, and simulation, extended with the presentation richness of multimedia.

The video functions and the basic utilization patterns are not independent of each other. Table 2 shows how the different functions relate.

Table 2

Video Functions from Table 1 in Relation to Basic Utilization Patterns

Basic utilization patterns	Supported by the following video functions
Text primacy	• Limited supplementary use of content-related video
Visualization as starting point	• Content-related use of video • Depicting the invisible or the nonaccessible • Logistic use of video • Cognitive help • Modelling of psychomotor skills • Providing observation materials • Video design for emotional involvement
Between-channel redundancy as reinforcement strategy	• All functions with proper audio layers added
Orchestration for learning	• Video design for emotional involvement
Audiovisual archive as a starting point	• Content-related use of video • Depicting the invisible or the nonaccessible • Logistic use of video • Cognitive help • Modelling of psychomotor skills • Providing observation materials • Video to present gifted teachers
Interactivity as a starting point	• Modelling of psychomotor skills • Video feedback • Providing observation materials • Psychologically realistic simulations

The video functions and the basic utilization patterns form a limited set of factors to consider when selecting or developing multimedia applications. For instruction, proper handling of learning objectives, content analysis, and learner characteristics require thorough knowledge and skills with respect to the knowledge domain of the subject matter and of methods and theories of instruction, and knowledge and skills with respect to methods for multimedia design and production. These subjects are beyond the scope of the present chapter. This paper focuses instead on results from audiovisual research that relates to detailed design decisions for developing video presentations. This area is primarily concerned with the utilization patterns "visualization as starting point," "between-channel redundancy as rein-forcement strategy," and "orchestration for learning."

Much of the audiovisual research reported is carried out with linear video programs. The findings are, however, probably applicable to components for multimedia solutions, to a large extent.

RESULTS OF AUDIOVISUAL RESEARCH
ON PRESENTATION VARIABLES

Presentation variables are actually production variables that obtain their values during the production of video material. The following variables (derived from a list by Coldevin 1981, p. 87) are discussed: (1) camera factors (angle and shot); (2) setting; (3) audio factors; (4) special effects; and (5) pacing and rhythm. In addition, a brief passage is devoted to animation. The variables listed in Table 3 are shown with the production phase in which the pertinent design decisions are taken.

Camera Factors

As far as research is concerned, the effects of camera factors on learning seem to be limited, and results are often conflicting. Dwyer (1978, p. 168), for instance, refers to Roshal (1949) and McCoy (1955) to conclude that it is advisable to show a performance on the screen the way the learner would see it if he were doing the job himself. Coldevin (1981, p. 88), however, describes an experiment by Grant and Merrill (1963) which shows that, for relatively complex skills (and perhaps for most task-oriented productions), the viewing angle of the demonstrator should not be used; rather, the perspective of the student viewer who is watching the demonstration is better.

Research by Salomon (1974) seemed to show that certain camera factors—such as zooming-in—can positively supplant visual information that young viewers must fill in during cuts between shots. It has, however, been shown that this supplanting effect can be demonstrated by other means (Bovy 1983).

This effect is consistent with the fact that different authors often present different solutions to serve certain communication functions by camera factors. Zooming-in, for instance, is classified by Morrison (1979, p. 29) as a device for focusing attention, relating parts to a whole, emphasizing one aspect, and showing spatial relationships. All these functions can be accomplished by other means. Morrison himself says that the cut can be used to (re)focus attention and to relate parts to the whole.

But there seems to be no reason to exclude the use of cuts for emphasis and for showing spatial relationships. Moreover, for all these functions, the superimposition of optical markers can also be used (such as arrows, animation, encircling; see, for instance, Dwyer, 1978, p. 160). Lumsdaine and Sulzer (1951) had earlier shown the effectiveness of devices of this kind for directing perception in films. Boeckmann, Nessmann, and Petermandl (1988) confirmed this effect as part of an experiment in which subjects had to watch a video program with the task to notice objects and procedures that are forbidden in a professional kitchen for hygienic reasons. In the experimental version of the program, three things were made to stand out in a long shot by means of superimposed rings (flowers, cigarettes, and domestic animals). The results of that experiment show that: "The most impressive increase in recall was observed in the case of the point concerning flowers, these being difficult to see in the background of the picture (38% of the students who had seen the experimental version mentioned flowers in comparison with none of the students who had seen the original version)" (Boeckmann, Nessmann, and Petermandl 1988, p. 118).

Table 3
Selected Production Variables for Video Materials

Design decisions in production phase	Presentation variable	Purpose	Examples
Scripting and shooting	camera angle and shot	framing of objects to be depicted	close-up to focus attention, wide-angle shot to establish a visual context for a beginning scene, etc.
	audio (narration, live sound, and music)	supporting the visual layer or (in case of text) mainstream of factual information	narration to explain what the picture shows, live sound to demonstrate how a MIG-welding arc should sound, music to support a story-relevant mood.
Scripting and editing (postproduction)	optical effects/special effects	getting attention, relating scenes, symbolizing transitions in place or time	wiping to connect mutually supportive or opposing visual situations, lap dissolve to move to a scene in the past, fade out/fade in to suggest the passage of time, etc.
	pacing and rhythm	providing a presentation rate that gets and maintains thoughtful attention (by complying with the spectators' preferred state of cognitive pace)	shortening time by inserting only action-laden shots, edited for narrative continuity at an attention-demanding pace.
Scripting, shooting, editing	animation	attention-gaining and visualization	instructional visualizations without distracting details, focusing attention by animated pointing devices.

This supports the notion that camera factors do not have definite meanings that can be used as invariable building blocks in message design. Just like the ideas about editing that are put forward by Reisz and Millar (1981), the use of camera factors should be guided by the nature and order of the message components to be conveyed. Studying the effects of single shots seems not to be very useful in that respect. It is more that sequences of shots should establish adequate patterns to cover the scenes to be depicted. This is exactly what media handbooks offer to support the development of solutions for particular design problems. Arijon (1976), for instance, presents hundreds of model solutions for a wide range of camera problems, varying from staging straightforward two-person dialogues to staging complicated mass scenes or finding solutions in confined areas such as the interior of an aeroplane. It thus seems warranted to approach the treatment of the camera from the perspective of staging a message as a coherent series of shots. Consistent authorship may thereby lead to a style that establishes clarity and appeals to the audience. The following research results are consistent with this view:

- Low-angle shots can increase the perceived potency of a presenter, but the framing of these shots in the narrative structure then has to support this intention (Coldevin 1981, p. 88).

- In video programs, interest levels can be increased with medium close-ups or with close-up shots (Coldevin 1981, p. 88). Boeckmann, Nessmann, and Petermandl (1988, p. 110), however, concluded on the basis of their research that recall was not related to type of shot (close-ups, long shots, or intermediate shots).

These results illustrate that the function of the type of shot depends on the circumstances in which it is used. The camera treatment thus has to be regarded as a flexible component of audiovisual message design, whereby research-based rules to predict good results are weak or absent. Good results depend on the professionalism of responsible team members in a media project. Rules from practice, such as can be found in media handbooks, are nevertheless useful to support design decisions (see, for instance, Arijon 1976, or Millerson 1985).

Audio Factors

Audio factors are narration or dialogue (in the case of speaking characters), effects (the "natural" sounds of the setting depicted on the screen [effects may be recorded live or be produced artificially]), and music. For instruction, off-screen commentary is often used. According to Dwyer (1978, p. 169), the number of words per minute of film in the commentary has a definite effect on learning. He refers to Zuckermann (1949a) and Jaspen (1950a, 1950b) to conclude that care should be taken not to "pack" the sound track. Schmidt (1974, p. 332) found, in his analysis of the design of 20 outstanding instructional films, that the majority of these films had an average narration rate of 140 or fewer words per minute. Dwyer (1978) advises that:

> Too much or too little talking in words per minute of film has been found to detract from the teaching effectiveness of a film. The optimum word rate is about 100 words for each minute of film (p. 172).

The normal rate of speech ranges from 150 to 200 words per minute (Rossiter 1971). This leads to a rule of thumb that narration should normally take about two-thirds of the total presentation time of an instructional film.

Schmidt (1974, p. 332) also found that the majority of the outstanding instructional films he analyzed (1) did not use a style of narration that talked down or lectured to the audience; (2) did simplify the message as much as possible; and (3) used the active form of sentence structure. That "simplification of the message" was a factor most probably related to the fact that the analyzed films were not designed for specific audiences. Still, the message of Schmidt's observations is that narration should take the audience seriously; present in a clear, concise, and unambiguous way; and talk directly to the audience if the subject allows it.

About the other factors—sound effects and music—research results are very limited. Fleming and Levie derived one principle with respect to concept learning: that if a concept is basically temporal—such as rhythm, time, sequence, or frequency, or like poetry, music, or speech—then audition is appropriate (Fleming and Levie 1978, p. 48). Research about sound effects was not mentioned further by the authors reviewed. The informational and emotional nature of this kind of sound seems to be considered self-evident. Research about music in instructional audiovisual programs is scarce. When Coldevin (1981) prepared his review, he could refer to only one study (by Baggaley, Ferguson, and Brooks 1980). In that study different types of music for opening or closing a program were subjected to experimentation, with inconclusive results due to methodological problems (Coldevin 1981, p. 89). With respect to music, Jaspers (1991) reinforced the conclusions made by Zuckermann (1949b) that music has informational, emotional, and conceptual/integrative functions. Leitmotivs and other musical effects may help to structure a presentation and inform the listeners about what is going to happen. Tempo, modality, and rhythm may be used to evoke emotional responses. According to Jaspers, proper use of music may support instructional messages but—unless the topic is about music—there is no need to use it "when the purpose is transmission of referential information and cognitive information processing" (Jaspers 1991, p. 50). Music may, however, facilitate learning by giving students occasions for identifications and empathy. However, as Jaspers puts it: "Well-chosen music does not guarantee to create the supposed effect, but it is highly probable that ill-chosen music will do much harm to the learning process" (Jaspers 1991, p. 50).

Given the limited results from research, the main conclusion has to be that the treatment of sound effects and music has to rely on rules from practice. Inspiring ideas can, for instance, be found in Millerson (1985, pp. 353-62).

Optical Effects and Special Effects

The review by Dwyer (1978) as well as more recent research by Boeckmann, Nessmann, and Petermandl (1988) show that optical effects such as fades, wipes, and dissolves do not increase the instructional effectiveness of films or video programs over the use of straight cuts to connect subsequent shots. Ginsburg, Bartels, Kleingunther, and Droege (1988) found that with special effects, the situation may even be worse. Their experiments with a program containing highly abstract visual effects showed that these effects diminished recall. Most probably, the observation of Boeckmann, Nessmann, and Petermandl (1988) applies; that is, that formal elements such as fades or wipes that do not relate to the program content have no influence on recall. According to Ginsburg et al. (1988), special effects may even have negative effects on recall. Boeckmann et al. (1988) demonstrated that formal elements that played an explicit role in defining a message proved to influence recall. The conclusion seems to be that deliberate, content-related use of optical effects or special effects can be feasible, insofar as their function affects the quality of a message. As with use of the other presentation variables, the message design has to be content-driven. This is, however, not to deny that form influences content. The eventual meaning of a message is determined by the combination of what is depicted and the manner of its depiction. It may be stressed that, for instructional purposes, form and content should be balanced with the intention to reinforce the substance of the instructional message.

Pacing and Rhythm

Another question is how the pace of presentation in films or video programs has to be controlled to account for *cognitive pace*, that is, the rate of mental processing of incoming data. One principle is that: "The rate of development of a film should be slow enough to permit learners to grasp the material as it is shown (Jaspen 1950a; Ash and Jaspen 1953)" (Dwyer 1978, p. 168).

According to Dwyer, this means that the rate must be slow rather than fast. The outstanding instructional films that were analyzed by Schmidt (1974):

> Had a rate of development that was slow enough for the viewer to grasp the material as it was shown (p. 332) . . . had a slowing of the rate of development at points at which it is necessary for the viewer to change attention from one source of information to another (p. 332) . . . [and] had an average shot length of about 10 seconds (p. 334).

The 10 seconds are of the order of magnitude of the time that Simon (1974) has put forward as the time it takes to fix a chunk of information in long-term memory. The same 10 seconds seem also to be a candidate for a characteristic parameter in a study conducted by Leahy (1983), who investigated the relationship between visual realism and information-processing time in viewing projected visuals. His results, with respect to manipulating projection time to promote more efficient visual comprehension, did not yield clear advice. However, the fact that he found significant differences between projection times of 5 and 10 seconds and between 5 and 15 seconds, but not between 10 and 15 seconds, led him to believe that after 10 seconds a ceiling effect might have occurred. However, whether this means in general that a mean cutting rate of six shots per minute yields an adequate pace of an instructional film cannot be concluded.

Coldevin (1981) referred to a study by Schlater (1970) that showed that cutting rate should not be too slow:

> Schlater (1970) produced five videotapes in which the visual changes ranged from one every 30 seconds in the first treatment to nine per 30-second interval in treatment five. Three types of learning tests were administered: pictorial video (visual sketches), verbal video (verbal descriptions of pictorial information) and audio channel information. Testing results showed that verbal video comprehension increased directly with the increase in the rate of visual changes (levelling off at seven visuals per 30-second interval), but the opposite effect was noted in pictorial video recall. As might be expected, no significant differences were found between the treatments on recall of audio channel information (Coldevin 1981, p. 91).

It thus seems that, under most circumstances, a cutting rate that corresponds with a mean shot length of about 4.5 seconds may be feasible.

With respect to the audio channel, the narration rate that was discussed under "audio factors" also plays a role in pacing a program. The narration may drive the processing of visuals more when the two information channels correspond sufficiently (Grimes 1990). Clear research-based rules on how to proceed when deciding on cutting rate and narration-related pacing, however, do not exist.

SUMMARY AND CONCLUSIONS

The video components of multimedia applications may serve many different functions, such as providing content-motivated moving images, supporting mental imagery by visualizations, and stimulating personal (emotional) involvement with objects of study. The role of video will further be determined by the way in which the video is positioned in relation to the nonvideo components of the system. In that respect, video may be chosen as the primary form of presentation around which all the other components are organized. But the use of video components may also be limited to support text-based materials where the use of video seems inevitable, or as just one of the resources that users may encounter when browsing through a multimedia database. In all of these cases, the video components should be designed with sufficient clarity to fulfill their roles in the communication process. This paper reviewed research on production variables that should be properly controlled to accomplish video segments of sufficient impact. In sum, the results are as follows:

Camera Factors

Research on camera factors demonstrates that the function of type of shot depends on the circumstances in which it is used. The camera treatment must thus be regarded as a flexible component.

Research-based rules with respect to camera factors are very limited. A firm rule from practice is that for instruction the camera treatment should be content-driven. Each camera angle ought to be motivated by its function in the presentation.

Narration

Video commentary should take the audience seriously; be presented in a clear, concise, and unambiguous way; and talk directly to the audience if the subject permits.

Sound Effects and Music

Findings from research on the use of sound effects and music are very scarce. Here, too, the main conclusion has to be that the treatment of these variables must rely on rules from practice.

Optical Effects and Special Effects

Findings from research on the use of optical effects or special effects seem to show that deliberate, content-related use of such effects may augment the quality of a message.

Pacing

Clear research-based rules about proper cutting rate and narration-related pacing do not appear to exist. As with the other audiovisual design variables, the design decisions in this area are subject to professional judgment in each specific case.

Technical Qualities

Picture quality has to be such that the images can be appreciated without technical imperfections. This requirement can be met by using professional video formats and professional camera treatment and editing facilities to produce video materials.

Despite the research findings, and because of the limited direct applicability of these findings, it may be concluded that the judgment of an experienced producer and other experienced media personnel is indispensable in meeting professional standards. This puts media professionals in an important position, because of the fact that media design directs the impact of instructional messages. Control over media variables is essential to optimize instructional communication. This factor counts for economic advantages of media, for the motivational effects of media, and for media-specific didactics that extend the options for organizing instructional strategies in the sense of Reigeluth (1983, p. 18).

Now that multimedia developments stimulate the use of audiovisual components as parts of computer-based applications, sound rules and procedures are needed for the specific kind of audiovisual message design that comes with it. It is hoped that the research reported here, as well as subsequent research on (interactive) message design, will lead to more systematized knowledge to support design processes beyond the level of audiovisual craftsmanship.

REFERENCES

Arijon, D. (1976). *Grammar of the film language.* London: Focal Press.

Ash, P., and Jaspen, N. (1953). *The effects and interactions of rate of development, repetition, participation and room illumination on learning from a rear-projected film.* Technical Report, SDC-269-7-39. Port Washington, NY: Special Devices Center, Office of Naval Research.

Baggaley, J., Ferguson, M., and Brooks, P. (1980). *Psychology of the TV image.* Farnborough, UK: Saxon House.

Boeckmann, K., Nessmann, K., and Petermandl, M. (1988). Effects of formal features in educational video programmes on recall. *Journal of Educational Television 14*(2), 107–22.

Bovy, R. A. (1983, April). *Defining the psychologically active features of instructional treatments designed to facilitate cue attendance.* Paper presented at the Annual Meeting of the American Educational Research Association, Montreal, Canada.

Coldevin, G. O. (1981). Experimental research in television message design: Implications for ETV. *Programmed Learning and Educational Technology 18,* 87–99.

Dwyer, F. M. (1978). *Strategies for improving visual learning.* University Park, PA: State College, Pennsylvania State University, Learning Services Division.

Fleming, M., and Levie, W. H. (1978). *Instructional message design: Principles from the behavioral sciences.* Englewood Cliffs, NJ: Educational Technology Publications.

Ginsburg, H. J., Bartels, D., Kleingunther, R., and Droege, L. (1988). Cosmos revisited: Just how effective are special effects for instructional communication? *International Journal of Instructional Media 15*(4), 319–26.

Grant, T. S., and Merrill, I. R. (1963). Camera placement for recognition of complex behaviors. In *Television in Health Sciences Education* (Washington, DC: US Office of Education), ch. 6.

Grimes, T. (1990). Audio-video correspondence and its role in attention and memory. *Educational Technology, Research & Development 38*(3), 15–25.

Jaspen, N. (1950a). *Effects on training of experimental film variables, Study I: Verbalization, rate of development, nomenclature, errors, "how-it-works," repetition.* Technical Report SDC-269-7-17. Port Washington, NY: Special Devices Center, Office of Naval Research.

Jaspen, N. (1950b). *Effects on training of experimental film variables, Study II: Verbalization, "how-it-works," nomenclature, audience participation, and succinct treatment.* Technical Report SDC-269-7-11. Port Washington, NY: Special Devices Center, Office of Naval Research.

Jaspers, F. (1991). Music in audio-visual materials. *Journal of Educational Television 17*(1), 45–52.

Leahy, M. D. (1983). *The relationship among field dependence/field independence, visual realism, and information processing time in viewing projected visuals.* Unpublished doctoral dissertation, University of Connecticut.

Lumsdaine, A. A., and Sulzer, R. (1951). *The influence of simple animation techniques on the value of a training film.* Washington, DC: US Air Force Human Factors Research Lab.

McCoy, E. P. (1955). *An application of research findings to training film production.* Technical Report SDC-269-7-44. Port Washington, NY: Special Devices Center, Office of Naval Research.

Millerson, G. (1985). *The technique of television production.* London: Focal Press.

Morrison, G. R. (1979, April). *The design of instructional television programs.* Paper presented at the Annual Meeting of the American Educational Research Association, San Francisco.

Reigeluth, C. M. (1983). Instruction design: What is it and why is it? In *Instructional-design theories and models: An overview of their current status,* ed. C. M. Reigeluth (Hillsdale, NJ: Lawrence Erlbaum Associates), 3–36.

Reisz, K., and Millar, G. (1981). *The technique of film editing.* London: Focal Press.

Roshal, S. M. (1949). *Effects of learner representation in film-mediated perceptual motor learning.* Technical Report SDC-269-7-5. Port Washington, NY: Special Devices Center, Office of Naval Research.

Rossiter, C. M., Jr. (1971). Rate-of-presentation effects on recall of facts and of ideas and on generation of inferences. *AV Communication Review 19,* 313–24.

Salomon, G. (1974). Internalization of filmic schematic operation in interaction with learners' aptitudes. *Journal of Educational Psychology 66,* 499–511.

Schlater, R. (1970). Effect of speed of presentation on recall of television messages. *Journal of Broadcasting 14,* 207–14.

Schmidt, W. D. (1974). Analyzing the design of outstanding instructional films. *International Journal of Instructional Media 1*(4), 327–36.

Simon, H. A. (1974). How big is a chunk? *Science 183,* 482–88.

Verhagen, P. W. (1992). *Length of segments in interactive video programmes.* Unpublished doctoral dissertation. Enschede, The Netherlands: Faculty of Educational Science and Technology, University of Twente.

Verhagen, P. W. (1993, April 27-28). *Multi-media: Basic approaches for utilization.* Contribution to the COMETT training program EuroMedia Training: Entwicklung von Fernstudienmodellen im bereich Medizin und Gesundheitswesen für Anwender un Multiplikatoren, Magdeburg: Otto von Zernike Universität.

Zuckermann, J. V. (1949a). *Commentary variations: Level of verbalization, personal reference, and phase relations in instructional films on perceptual-motor tasks.* Technical Report SDC-269-7-4. Port Washington, NY: Special Devices Center, Office of Naval Research.

Zuckermann, J. V. (1949b). *Music in motion pictures: Review of literature with implications for instructional films.* Technical Report SDC-269-7-2. Port Washington, NY: Special Devices Center, Office of Naval Research.

A Mentoring Model for Technology Education for Teachers*

Charles A. MacArthur
University of Delaware

Virginia Pilato
Maryland State Department of Education

Mary Kercher
Prince Georges County Schools, Maryland

Dana Peterson
University of Maryland

David Malouf
U.S. Department of Education

Patricia Jamison
Prince Georges County Schools, Maryland

The effectiveness of microcomputers in school settings depends on how successfully teachers integrate computers with their educational goals and curricula (MacArthur and Malouf 1991; Winkler, Shavelson, Stasz, and Robyn 1985). Research indicates that teachers need both inservice education on specific technology applications and long-term support to integrate computers with the curriculum in meaningful ways (Goodson 1991; MacArthur and Malouf 1990; Woodhouse and Jones 1988). In their study of accomplished computer-using teachers, Sheingold and Hadley (1990) found that development of mastery in educational use of computers was a gradual process, requiring several years, and that "on-site support and colleagueship [were] critical ingredients to successful technology use."

One solution to providing the school-based collegial support needed to help teachers learn to integrate computers into their instruction is mentoring. Mentoring programs have been widely used to support beginning teachers (Huling-Austin 1990; Little 1990). Mentor teachers take on a wide range of roles in helping new teachers develop. They assist new teachers with procedures, coach them in instructional matters, advise them on classroom management, and provide emotional support when needed. Key features of the mentoring approach are that assistance is provided within the context of a personal relationship and is focused on the individual needs of the protégé. Mentoring programs have the potential to break down the isolation characteristic of the teaching profession and encourage collegial interaction and reflection (Feiman-Nemser and Parker 1992).

*The research and development reported in this article were supported by the U.S. Department of Education. However, it does not represent the policy of that agency and no endorsement is implied.

The Computer Mentor Program was designed to prepare experienced computer-using teachers to serve as mentors to other teachers in their school sites. The program was a collaborative effort of the University of Maryland and the Prince Georges County Public Schools. The goals of the program were to increase knowledge about educational applications of computers, to increase integration of computers into the curriculum for both protégés and mentors, and to establish collegial relationships within schools that would continue beyond the end of the formal mentoring program.

Several important features from the literature on mentoring were incorporated in the design of the program. First, mentors were selected based not only on experience with computers but also on recommendations about their teaching expertise and interpersonal skills. Second, mentors recruited protégés from their own schools to maximize opportunities for contact and the impact on educational practice in individual schools. Third, a formal structure and incentives for both mentors and protégés were established to enhance commitment to the mentoring program and provide recognition for their efforts. Finally, support from building administrators was sought to ensure that participants would have time to meet and support in implementing instructional changes.

THE STRUCTURE OF THE COMPUTER MENTOR PROGRAM

The Computer Mentor Program was designed to provide long-term, on-site support focused on teachers' individuals needs and the resources available at particular schools. The overall structure of the program included a course for mentors and a workshop for their protégés. Teachers with experience in using computers in their classes participated in a one-semester course that provided (1) guidance in how to serve as a mentor to other teachers, and (2) information on specific technology applications and local resources. These teachers selected as protégés one to five teachers in their schools who were interested in making better use of technology in their teaching. The mentoring relationship was structured through the use of individual plans developed between each mentor and protégé. Mentors and protégés met weekly for workshop sessions. Principals approved the participation of their staffs, agreed to provide meeting time for mentors and protégés and access to computers, and were encouraged to participate in planning the goals for staff development at their schools.

Course for Mentors

Ten to fifteen teachers selected as mentors each semester participated in a course entitled "Leadership in Computer Applications." The course was initially developed and co-taught by university and school district staff and later taught independently by school district staff. It was divided into two strands: mentoring and computer applications.

The mentoring strand included several themes or topics designed to help teachers understand the mentoring process and develop mentoring skills. These themes formed the basis for the videotape, *Mentoring: Issues and Concerns* (Computer Mentor Project 1992b), which consisted of six segments used to engage mentors in discussion of the mentoring process. The first segment, "What Is a Mentor?," introduced the concept of mentoring and explored various definitions of *mentor*. "Why Be a Mentor?" addressed the expectations and benefits for both mentor and protégé and demonstrated the reciprocity inherent in the mentor-protégé relationship. "What Do Mentors Do?" explained the kinds of staff development activities in which mentors have traditionally been involved and how their support helps further the careers of the teachers they mentor. Mentor characteristics and criteria used to select mentors were discussed in "What Does It Take to Be a Mentor?" A composite look at mentors and the act of mentoring was included in "What Works?" The final segment, "The Three R's of Mentoring," aimed to foster continuing growth as mentors by stimulating discussion about three critical aspects: repertoire, relationships, and reflection.

To stimulate reflection on the mentoring process, mentors were asked to write weekly response logs concerning the progress of their mentor-protégé sessions, their relationships with protégés, and their own development as computer mentors. The response logs stimulated discussions among the mentors about their concerns and successes and enabled the course instructor to follow the progress of each mentor-protégé team and to provide suggestions.

The mentoring strand was supported by a book of illustrative cases. The purpose of *Computer Mentoring: A Case Book* (Pilato, Peterson, Kercher, Malouf, MacArthur, and Jamison 1992) was to provide new mentors with a large array of experiences other computer mentors had had working with their protégés. The source of the vignettes contained in the book was the reflections written by previous mentors in their response logs. The case book was expanded and revised following each of the three years of the program.

The technology strand of the mentor course was designed to increase the mentors' knowledge of innovative and effective uses of technology and their awareness of technology resources in their own school district. Topics were selected collaboratively by the mentors and the instructors based on several sources of information. First, a needs assessment was completed by mentors and protégés at the beginning of the course (see discussion of the Computer Use Questionnaire in the evaluation section). Second, technology initiatives in the school district and state were considered. Finally, principals of participating teachers were consulted about goals and technology resources in their schools. Illustrative topics included the following: computer support for the writing process, telecommunications, multimedia applications, authoring software, integrated learning systems, troubleshooting hardware, writing fundable proposals, and assistive devices for students with disabilities.

Protégé Workshop

Each mentor worked with one to five protégés from his or her school. The mentoring relationship was structured through the use of individual mentoring plans developed collaboratively with each protégé. These plans included overall goals, specific objectives, and activities. These individual plans were the basis for awarding inservice credit to the protégés.

Mentors met weekly with their protégés to work on the objectives. In addition to these regular meetings, mentors were available informally, as they were located in the same schools as their protégés. In the last session of the mentoring course, mentoring-protégé teams presented their accomplishments during the semester.

Administrative Support

Support from principals was critical to the success of the program, which was designed to have an impact at the school level by teaming mentors and protégés within schools and by emphasizing individual goals and objectives for these teams. As instructional leaders, principals needed to be involved in determining goals and objectives for use of technology in their schools. Principals sometimes wished to integrate technology with particular aspects of the curriculum, or to use technology with particular groups of students. In addition, the support of the principal was important in securing time for the mentor-protégé meetings and adequate access to computers.

Major changes took place in schools where principals adopted an active role in the program. In one case, a principal initiated the involvement of his staff in the program. In that school, the computer laboratory aide position had been discontinued and the laboratory had fallen into disuse. Concerned about the lack of computer use by the teachers, this principal arranged for 5 teachers from the school with computer experience to participate as mentors and work with 17 protégés. The mentors modeled lessons, practiced troubleshooting, evaluated software with their protégés, and established new procedures for use of the laboratory. By the end of the year, the laboratory was in constant use and the teachers were asking for more computers.

PROGRAM EVALUATION

Participants

Summative evaluation data were collected for two semesters during the second year of the program (1991-1992) (MacArthur and Peterson 1992). All grade levels from preschool through high school and a wide range of subject areas, including special education, were represented among the 21 mentors and 54 protégés. Five of the mentors but only three of the protégés were male. Four of the mentors were computer teachers or coordinators; the rest were knowledgeable about computers but did not have any formal leadership role.

Measures

The evaluation drew on several different measures. First, course evaluations were completed by both mentors and protégés at the end of each semester. The evaluations covered both the technology and the mentoring aspects of the course. Mentors and protégés rated their overall learning and various components of the course on a five-point scale, and responded to open-ended questions about strengths and weaknesses.

Second, the Computer Use Questionnaire, completed at the beginning and end of each semester by both mentors and protégés, provided information on changes in technology knowledge and skills, and frequency and type of computer use. The questionnaire covered eight major categories: skills with (1) hardware, (2) computer-assisted instruction (CAI) software (e.g., simulations), and (3) tool software (e.g., word processing); skills in (4) management of computers in classrooms, (5) integration of computers into the curriculum, and (6) professional collaboration; and amount and type of computer use (7) with students and (8) for professional and personal purposes.

Third, protégés maintained logs of every instance in which they used computers for two weeks at the beginning and two weeks at the end of each semester. Finally, mentors wrote weekly in response logs.

Results

Mentor Course Evaluations. The results of the mentor course evaluations were highly positive. On the technology questions, all of the mentors in both semesters agreed or strongly agreed that the course had provided opportunities to learn more about educational software; 95 percent thought they had learned more about technology resources; and 85 percent agreed that they had increased their skill at integrating computers with instruction. About 75 percent thought that their overall technical skills had increased. Most (81 percent) of the mentors mentioned specific ways they had used the technical information gained in the course.

On the mentoring questions, all except one of the mentors agreed or strongly agreed that they had been successful as mentors and had learned a lot from the experience. With one or two exceptions, they agreed that the case book, individual mentoring plans, and response logs had been valuable. On the open-ended questions, many mentors commented that they had become more skilled and confident in sharing their knowledge and relating with peers. Several mentors thought they had become more sensitive to the needs of teachers who were not as familiar with technology. A few mentors noted that their technical skills had increased through teaching others. The only problem mentioned by more than one mentor was limited time for meeting with protégés.

Protégé Course Evaluations. The protégés were also highly positive in their evaluations of the program. Most of the protégés agreed or strongly agreed that the course had increased their technical skills (96 percent) and knowledge about integrating computers with instruction (85 percent). Most of them also agreed that they had learned more from their mentors than from traditional inservice courses (88 percent), and that the individual mentoring plans were useful in structuring the learning process (94 percent).

On the open-ended question about the disadvantages of the mentoring approach, a majority of the protégés commented on the importance of having the mentor available in the same school to answer questions and help out when needed. Almost half of the protégés mentioned the value of a supportive personal relationship with their mentor. About a third of the protégés mentioned the fact that the training met their needs because the mentor was familiar with the students and computer hardware and software in the school. The only comments about disadvantages referred to limitations of time for meetings.

Computer Use Questionnaire. Summary scores were developed for the eight categories covered by the questionnaire. Because the data were ordinal, the nonparametric Wilcoxon signed-ranks test (Siegel and Castellan 1988) was used to test the significance of changes from pretest to posttest.

Results for the protégés for both semesters indicate significant increases in knowledge and skill and in frequency of computer use. In all three technical areas (skills with hardware, CAI software, and tool software) and in frequency of use both with students and for professional/personal purposes, increases from pretest to posttest were highly significant ($p <.001$). Increases in skill in management of computers in classrooms and integration with the curriculum were smaller but still significant ($p <.01$). The only category in which significant change was not demonstrated was professional collaboration, which was not expected to increase among protégés.

Results for the mentors are discussed separately for the fall and spring semesters because the spring group had substantially more experience with computers. The fall mentors made significant gains ($p <.05$) in all areas except frequency of use with students. The largest gains ($p <.01$) were in skills with hardware and software tools and in professional collaboration. The spring group of mentors made significant gains in frequency of use with students, integration with the curriculum, and professional collaboration.

Computer Logs. The computer logs maintained by protégés confirm the questionnaire evidence of increases in frequency and type of computer use. In both semesters, the protégés reported significant increases (p <.05) in both the frequency of computer use and the variety of programs used. Median frequency of computer use increased from 0.4 to 7.5 instances per week for the fall group, and from 5.0 to 9.6 for the spring group. Median number of programs used increased from 0.4 to 3.9 for the fall group and from 2.1 to 3.3 for the spring group.

CONCLUSION

The Computer Mentor Program addressed the fact that teacher education is a critical factor in promoting the effective use of computers. Traditional inservice education, time-limited and decontextualized, cannot offer the on-site support that computer users require. To be effective, inservice methods must respond to the complexity of the process of adopting this new instructional technology. This teacher mentor model has proven to be highly appropriate in this area because of its ability to address a broad range of needs and to support an extended process of teacher development.

The program showed itself to be a cost-effective way to involve teachers in a technology education program that is sensitive to the individual needs of teachers and their students and works with the existing technology in their schools. The model for the Computer Mentor Program is quite straightforward and could easily be adopted by other school districts, with the mentor course offered by a local college or university or by a district's own staff development department.

Note: For those interested in implementing a similar program, the casebook (Pilato et al. 1992) and a course guide including sample syllabus, individual mentoring plan, handouts, and evaluation materials (Computer Mentor Project 1992a) are available through ERIC under the title *Mentoring: An Approach to Technology Education for Teachers, Executive Overview [and] Computer Mentoring Course Guide* (Charles A. MacArthur et al. 1993, 150pp.), ED 354 187.

REFERENCES

Computer Mentor Project. (1992a). *Computer mentoring course guide.* College Park, MD: University of Maryland, Department of Special Education. (Included in ED 364 187).

Computer Mentor Project. (1992b). *Mentoring: Issues and concerns.* [Videotape]. College Park, MD: University of Maryland, Department of Special Education.

Feiman-Nemser, S., and Parker, M. B. (1992). *Mentoring in context: A comparison of two U.S. programs for beginning teachers* (Special Report). East Lansing, MI: Michigan State University, National Center for Research on Teacher Learning.

Goodson, B., ed. (1991). *Teachers and technology: Staff development for tomorrow's schools.* Alexandria, VA: National School Board Association.

Huling-Austin, L. (1990). Teacher induction programs and internships. In *Handbook of research on teacher education,* ed. W. R. Houston (New York: Macmillan), 535–48.

Little, J. W. (1990). The mentoring phenomenon and the social organization of teaching. *Review of Research in Education 16,* 297–351.

MacArthur, C. A., and Malouf, D. B. (1990). Microcomputer use in educational programs for mildly handicapped students. *Preventing School Failure 34*(2), 39–44.

MacArthur, C. A., and Malouf, D. B. (1991). Teacher beliefs, plans and decisions about computer-based instruction. *Journal of Special Education 25,* 44–72.

MacArthur, C. A., and Peterson, D. (1992). *Evaluation of the computer mentor program (1991-1992)* (Technical Report No. 2). College Park, MD: University of Maryland, Institute for the Study of Exceptional Children and Youth.

Pilato, V. H., Peterson, D. B., Kercher, M. H., Malouf, D. B., MacArthur, C., and Jamison, P. (1992). *Computer mentoring: A case book.* College Park, MD: University of Maryland, Department of Special Education. (Included in ED 364 187).

Sheingold, K., and Hadley, M. (1990). *Accomplished teachers: Integrating computers into classroom practice.* New York: Center for Technology in Education, Bank Street College of Education.

Siegel, S., and Castellan, N. J. (1988). *Nonparametric statistics for the behavioral sciences.* New York: McGraw-Hill.

Winkler, J., Shavelson, R. J., Stasz, C., and Robyn, A. E. (1985). Pedagogically sound use of microcomputers in classroom instruction. *Journal of Educational Computing Research 1,* 285–93.

Woodhouse, D., and Jones, A. (1988). Professional development for effective use of computers in the classroom. *Evaluation and Program Planning 11*(4), 315–23.

Ignite Technology
Making the Difference with Staff Development

Dorothy "Gavin" Standish
Coordinator of Instructional Technology
Lake Forest School District
Dover, Delaware

ABSTRACT

Staff development in technology is one of the district's long-range planning goals. This report describes a program for formulating and implementing a staff development plan for technology. A staff development planning team was created which planned and implemented staff development programs for the district teachers. A one-group pretest-posttest design was used to evaluate the increased skill levels and improved positive attitudes toward the use of technology. The evaluation instrument was a survey designed by the staff development planning team. The comparison of the pre-and posttest responses of district teachers indicated improvement in skill levels and more positive attitudes toward the use of technology in education.

INTRODUCTION

Technology will revolutionize learning. Whether the reader believes this statement or not, it is an established fact that technology has become an integral part of discussions about teaching and learning. In reality, it is the teacher who will make the change in learning. Teachers must receive training to make technology the revolutionary instructional tool that it is touted to be.

The Lake Forest School District, like many in Delaware, has been involved in strategic planning. This planning has been accomplished by committees of community members, school board members, administrators, and staff. Three of the district's seven long-range plan goals deal with technology. The final goal, Goal 7, addresses the need for staff development. The district through its strategic planning has made a commitment to incorporating technology into the lives of its staff and students.

DESCRIPTION

Description of the Problem

Technology in the form of computers and software is being placed in classrooms throughout the Lake Forest School District. Many teachers receive this equipment with glee, but do not know how to use it. This situation leads to frustration for both the teachers and the students. Previous district staff development programs have been limited in scope and have not included follow-up instruction. Teachers have voiced a need for more instruction. Training must also address the specific needs of various grade levels and curricula.

Description of the District and Community

The Lake Forest School District stretches across Delaware from the Delaware Bay to the Maryland state line. The land is predominantly used for agriculture.

The three elementary schools, East, North, and South, dot the perimeter of the district. The students are promoted from the elementary schools to the middle school and finally to the centrally located high school.

Review of the Literature

"We bought *huge* quantities of the latest technology for the revolution but neglected to recruit and train the troops," states Tom Boe (1989, p. 39), the director of training programs at the Minnesota Educational Computing Corporation (MECC). This is the premise in "The Next Step for Educators and the Technology Industry: Investing in Teachers." Educational institutions purchase computers to improve student learning, improve thinking strategies, individualize instruction, create positive attitudes toward learning, and prepare students for the future technological world. The primary reason these goals have not been reached is lack of teacher training.

Boe agrees with the Office of Technology Assessment report, *Power On! New Tools for Teaching and Learning* (U.S. Congress 1988), that teachers must receive training and support before technology can be used effectively in the classroom. The first condition is training. Teachers are the key to educational change, and they need to see how computers can be of personal use to them. Second, teachers need a vision of technology and education. They must have time, expertise, resources, and structure to reevaluate learning with a focus on using technology. Then instructional change can happen. Next, innovation should be encouraged by administration and colleagues. Lastly, the necessary time and resources can be provided by giving teachers release time to attend classes and learn. Teachers also need access to technology during and after training to be able to practice and use what they have learned.

Rodgers and Bonja (1987) echoed the need for providing staff development in the use of computers "as a means to improve our education system" (p. 3). The National Task Force on Educational Technology (1986) recommended teacher training as one of the six major components in changing the educational system. The Task Force's report stated that teacher education is essential to the incorporation of educational technology in the classroom.

Are we ready for change? Boe challenges educators and the technology industry to confront the staff development issue. He recommends seven steps to long-term professional development:

1. Administrators must be supportive.

2. Teachers must be convinced of the need for the change.

3. Teachers need to be empowered in the decision-making process.

4. Teachers need to know that individual differences will be addressed.

5. Teachers should be shown that technology does support educational objectives.

6. Time to learn and practice must be available.

7. Resources and access to those resources must be made available.

An effective staff development program is possible with these elements in place.

Research conducted by Agnes A. Violenus (1989) found problems similar to those addressed in this study. The goals of the Violenus study were to increase teachers' use of technology and to vitalize student learning by using technology. Recommendations included expanded workshops and opportunities for teachers to observe other teachers or other professionals using technology as an instructional tool.

During a three-year evaluation, educators explored and identified applicable classroom applications for technology, designed staff development programs for the effective use of technology to meet curricular goals, and studied the effect of technology on learning and teaching (*Teaching and learning with technology: Evaluation report* 1991). The three years of ongoing staff development began with teaching strategies for basic keyboarding skills. Each year, two workshops were held on changing teacher and student roles and teaching styles. Monthly team meetings helped share ideas and progress. University staff was available for consultation.

Student achievement data were collected from observations, interviews, self-reports, and nationally normed test scores. Pretest-posttest comparisons indicated that computers were being used as tools to accomplish specific tasks, especially writing, instead of for playing games. Statistical analysis of test data indicated almost no difference after one year (grade 3), a small gain after the second year (grade 4), and a significant gain after the third year (grade 5) (*Teaching and learning report* 1991).

Staff development was evaluated by questionnaires and interviews. Teachers indicated that training is needed for successful classroom implementation of technology in the curriculum. The use of technology influenced the district's curriculum and its staff development program (*Teaching and learning report* 1991).

Evans and Elium (1982) noted that using the world of technology in developing staff training programs is becoming ever more paramount. In the future, teachers will no longer be experts in subject matter, due to the skyrocketing increase in the volume of knowledge. Teachers will need to use technology as a resource tool as well as an instructional tool. Technology has created a shift in the role of the professional educator. Although Evans and Elium's article is more than 10 years old, their vision of technology and education is even more true today than when the article was written.

The *Teaching and Learning with Technology: Evaluation Report* (1991) concluded that technology will not change a teacher. It is not a quick fix. Rather, it is a catalyst for dynamic change, provided that there is support for change. Technology can revitalize teachers and education.

Objectives of the Study

This study focused on increasing teacher use of technology, primarily computers, through increased staff development. The attitudinal changes toward the use of technology were also investigated.

Anticipated Outcome

Because the staff development classes were an after-school voluntary program, not all teachers participated. The enthusiasm and skills learned by participants in these classes were shared with colleagues. Sharing should create an increased use of and a more positive attitude toward the role of computers and technology in the classroom.

METHOD

Subjects

The entire district teaching staff was used in this study. Teachers' names and assignments were on the surveys so that direct comparisons could be made.

Apparatus

Two surveys were used. Both were designed by the technology staff development team. The first was given in November 1992; the second in May 1993. These surveys were considered a pretest and posttest for measurement purposes (Appendix A).

The surveys were designed to be used as both a needs assessment and a comparative tool. The staff development team felt that it was important to get as much input as possible from the staff members so that the staff development program would meet their needs. The comment section also provided the staff members with a method of presenting their suggestions and ideas.

PROCEDURE

The Staff Development Planning Team

A team was created of all interested district employees. This team functioned as a subcommittee of the district technology council. It met until both surveys and a draft of the technology staff development plan were completed. The team also selected the courses for the next year's technology inservice program.

This study was limited to the effects that staff development had on teacher skills and attitudes toward the use of technology.

The Staff Development Program

Staff Development Classes. The staff development team selected courses to be taught based on the staff development plan. These courses were approved by the school board and funded by the Director of Instructional Services. Course content was defined. Inservice credit was requested and granted from the Department of Public Instruction (DPI). Positions were posted according to the union contract. Instructors were hired by the school board. Facilities were selected and their use requested. Classes were announced to the staff and registration taken. Finally, the courses were taught. Participants evaluated each course at its conclusion. Inservice credit was awarded by DPI and approved by the district. There were two course cycles in the 1992–1993 year: Fall and Winter/Spring.

Mini Workshops. This new aspect of the staff development program began in the 1993 school year. Mini workshops were designed to meet the staff development needs of the teachers. They were one hour in length and held after school. There was approximately one per month in each building. The teachers in that building selected the topics.

Other Programs. Teachers were notified of other classes from numerous sources, such as the Teacher Center and Delaware Department of Instruction.

RESULTS

Design

Research Design. The one-group pretest-posttest design was used. The pretest and posttest were in the form of surveys taken of the staff members to identify their skills and attitudes toward the use of technology. A direct comparison of the surveys indicated changes in attitudes and skills.

Validity. The history of the teachers is as varied as the teaching staff in the five schools of the district. Individual incidents during the year would have affected the attitudes of the teachers. The instrument used was created by the staff development committee and was not field tested. There was a degree of mortality due to incomplete surveys that were not used in the tabulation of statistics. These issues are noted but not controlled.

Statistical Results

This research is based on 107 teacher surveys. A direct comparison of the teachers' confidence in the use of technology indicated that 66 teachers (62 percent of the teachers used in this study) had increased their confidence in the use of technology by an increase of 171 items. Chart 1 represents the sum of all the teachers' confidence scores, which equaled 1,266 in the fall and 1,413 in the spring. The confidence scores of 24 teachers remained the same and 17 indicated a decreased confidence level. This decrease may be attributed to increased knowledge of technology. This new understanding made teachers realize that they lacked confidence in the area.

Chart 1

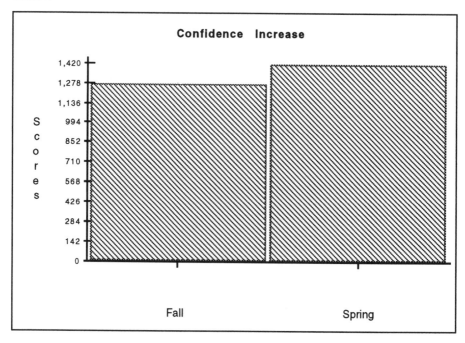

The 52 teachers who indicated an increased positive attitude toward technology plus the 9 who had already rated it at the top of the scale combine to make a total of 61 (57 percent) of the teachers with a very positive attitude toward the use of technology. The sum of all teachers' attitudes in the spring was 6,337 as compared to only 6,258 in the fall. Chart 2 visually indicates the positive change in the teachers' attitude toward the use of technology.

Chart 2

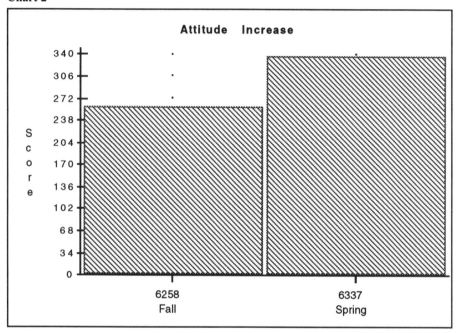

The survey results indicate that staff development had a positive effect on teachers' confidence in using technology as an instructional tool. Although many of the teachers did not directly participate in staff development courses, the enthusiasm of their colleagues and sharing of information resulted in increases in both areas. The survey results also indicate that the staff development program did, in fact, have a positive effect on teachers' attitudes toward the use of technology.

Other Results

An increased offering and participation in technology staff development courses indicated an increased interest. During the 1991-1992 school year, seven courses were offered. Twenty-two staff members participated, some taking more than one course.

In contrast, during the 1992-1993 school year, 16 classes were offered in Apple and PC platforms. Two courses, Introduction to Computers and Telecommunications, covered information that related to using all computer platforms. Six teachers were the instructors. Twenty-nine teachers participated, as well as a custodian, two paraprofessional librarians, fourteen paraprofessionals, and five secretaries. A total of 38.4 inservice credit hours was awarded. This is a 232 percent increase over the previous year. These figures do not include staff members who participated in classes but did not complete all sessions to receive inservice credit.

MECC district licenses for Apple software have been purchased for several years. There were 15 new programs available to teachers. Mini workshops demonstrated the use of these software programs. Two hundred forty-nine copies were made and distributed to the schools. Although records were not kept in previous years, comments from the teachers indicated that most of them would not have obtained or used this software if this program had not been available. The program increased the interest and the use of technology in the classroom as an instructional tool.

Implication of the Results

As projected, this study proved that technology staff development increased the use of computers and technology by the teachers in the district, as indicated by the increased confidence of the teachers in the use of computers and technology. It also increased positive attitudes of the teachers toward the use of technology as an instructional tool. With increased use by the teachers, the students also benefited by gaining increased use of technology.

Teachers indicated that they now have increased planning time because of the use of time-saving management computer software. The word processing and grade book programs have replaced many hours of work that were formerly tediously accomplished by hand. This has freed teachers to be more involved in instructional tasks rather than classroom management tasks.

Although this study concentrated on the use of technology by teachers, it can be generalized to all school staff. Participation in technology staff development courses by other staff members indicated an interest and positive attitudes. Further studies on these populations should show similar results.

Could similar programs in other school districts show similar gains? They should. Lake Forest teachers are not unique in their desire to provide the best education possible to their students. Dedicated teachers in all districts would gain confidence and skills in the use of technology if given an opportunity to participate in a staff development program in technology.

DISCUSSION

Impact

Staff development training increased the use of computers and other technology by teachers in the district. This decreased the time needed for management and increased the time available for instructional needs. With increased instructional time, student learning should increase. These results are implied but not proven or addressed in this study.

As teachers become more comfortable with the use of computers and technology, this equipment is being used more frequently as an instructional tool. Students have benefited. They have many more opportunities to learn to use technology for problem solving and creating materials, as well as drill and practice.

Implications

The value of staff development in the use of technology was proven by this study. The basic program was established in just one year. Advanced levels of training will have to be developed as teachers become more proficient and as the technology advances. Basic levels will always have to be available for new teachers and others jumping on the technology bandwagon. Funding will have to be increased as this program grows.

Further Application

The district staff development team will update the staff development plan annually to address the meteoric changes in technology. The results of the survey will indicate the changes and additions needed in the program. Inservice training may be added to the Inservice Day schedule.

REFERENCES

Boe, T. (1989). The next step for educators and the technology industry: Investing in teachers. *Educational Technology 29*(3), 39–44.

Evans, B., and Elium, M. D. (1982). Changing times: A challenge for educators. *Peabody Journal of Education 59*(2), 121–26.

National Task Force on Educational Technology. (1986, August). Transforming American education: Reducing the risk to the nation. A Report to the Secretary of Education, United States Department of Education. *T. H. E. Journal 15*(1), 58–67.

Rodgers, R. J., and Bonja, R. P. (1987, November). *Computer utilization training in staff development.* Paper presented at the National Conference of the National Council of States on Inservice Education, San Diego, CA. (ED 291 374).

Teaching and learning with technology. Evaluation report. (1991). Pontiac, MI: Oakland County Schools. (ED 339 362).

U.S. Congress, Office of Technology Assessment. (1988, September). *Power on! New tools for teaching and learning.* OTA-SET-379. Washington, DC: U.S. Government Printing Office.

Violenus, A. A. (1989). *Vitalizing instruction in the middle grades through staff development in technological methodology.* Practicum, Nova University. (ED 310 764).

APPENDIX A

Fall 1992 and Spring 1993 Surveys

ANNUAL TECHNOLOGY SURVEY

Name _____ Fall 1992
Position _____ School _____

Please check the item(s) that best describes you and your skills.
(Check as many as apply to you.)

Items that you can do with confidence:
__ Set a digital clock
__ Use a VCR
__ Use a camcorder
__ Program a VCR
__ Use a photocopier
__ Use a fax machine
__ Turn on a computer
__ Boot a program
__ Change programs (warm boot)
__ Load paper, change ribbon in printer
__ Use a printer
__ Use a computer with a hard drive
__ Use a mouse
__ Use a scanner
__ Use a CD-ROM drive & software
__ Use a Laserdisk player
__ Use an LCD player
__ Use a modem
__ Teach students to use computer
  programs
__ Format a blank disk
__ Copy a disk
__ Install a program on a hard drive
__ Use MS Windows
__ Use the Wand at the IRC
__ Use a word processing program
__ Use a print shop type program
__ Create a computer program

**I use computers/technology for
classroom management:**

__ yes __ no __ n/a

**How often do you use computers/ technology
at:**
LF_____Home _____
  __ Never   __ Occasionally
  __ Rarely   __ Frequently

**Rate your feelings about using technology/
computers:**

Using a scale of 1 to 5 with
1=Strongly Disagree, 5=Strongly Agree

__ Technology helps students learn
__ LF students should learn to use
  technology/computers

**LF should provide more instruction in the
use of technology/computers for:**
__ high school students (answer all 3)
__ middle school students
__ elementary school students
__ Technology saves time in my work
__ Technology makes my work easier
__ LF staff should be able to use technology
__ LF should provide more training in the
  use of computers/technology for staff
__ The district should purchase more
  computers/technology
__ Technology is NOT a waste of money
__ Technology is part of my daily life
  (TV, VCR, microwave, ATM (bank
  cards), grocery stores checkout,
  computer, etc.)
__ Technology will be used more in
  everyday life in the near future

Please turn over and complete the back page.

Your computer skill level:
__ Non-user
__ Novice (can turn it on & use 1 program)
__ Average (use several programs & printer)
__ Above Average (use many programs with many features)
__ Advanced (can make it do anything I want it to do)

Use computers/technology with students for:
__ Demonstrations
__ Desktop Publishing
__ Drill & Practice
__ Illustrations/graphics
__ Problem solving
__ Simulations
__ Telecommunications/modem
__ Whole class instruction
__ Word processing
__ Other

Type of Computer Used:
At LF

At home or other place

Any type of technology/computer training:

Comments:

What kind of staff development in technology/computers would you like LF to offer?

Credits in technology/computers earned this year not taught at LF?

Name of courses & who sponsored the course?

PURPOSE: The purpose of this survey is to measure the growth and needs of technology in the Lake Forest School District. The result will be used to plan an effective staff development program.

RETURN this survey to your principal by June 15.

Library Media Standards and Guidelines
A Survey of Resources for
K-12 Program Planning and Evaluation*

Gene L. Wilkinson
Department of Instructional Technology
University of Georgia

American public education is in a period of change. There is a strong movement for school reorganization and reform. Political pressures are building for the elimination of state mandates of program components and the return of local control over schools. There is a growing emphasis on learner outcomes as the measure of quality rather than resource inputs such as media programs. Rapid developments in telecommunications and information technology are changing the very nature of libraries. These changes should be reflected in school library media programs.

Media specialists need resources to assist them as they attempt to design programs to meet the needs of a rapidly changing school environment. A number of standards, assessment tools, and planning guidelines have been developed. Some, such as professional association guidelines, provide philosophical direction. Others, such as state and regional accrediting association standards, specify requirements that must be met in order to receive state funding or full transferability of credits from one school to another.

PROFESSIONAL ASSOCIATION GUIDELINES

There is a long tradition of leadership by the American Association of School Librarians (AASL) and the Association for Educational Communications and Technology (AECT) in the development of program standards and guidelines for media services and school libraries in the K–12 schools (see following listing). Starting with the 1920 secondary school and 1925 elementary school library standards, the National Educational Association (parent body of AECT) and the American Library Association (home of AASL) have been involved in defining standards for media resources within the public schools. From the concept of the unified media program promoted in the 1969 guidelines to the emphasis on learner outcomes and the instructional role of the media specialist in the current guidelines, these publications have had a major impact. Efforts have just been initiated to revise the 1988 guidelines to reflect the rapidly changing nature of information within society.

1988 *Information power: Guidelines for school library media programs.* American Association of School Librarians (AASL) and Association for Educational Communications and Technology (AECT). (Chicago: American Library Association, and Washington, DC: AECT). 185pp. ED 315 028.

---

*This study updates an earlier survey conducted by Wilkinson and reported in *Educational Media Yearbook 1983* (Libraries Unlimited, 1983).

1975 *Media programs: District and school.* American Association of School Librarians (ALA) and Association for Educational Communications and Technology (AECT). (Chicago: American Library Association, and Washington, DC: AECT). 128pp.

1969 *Standards for school media programs.* American Association of School Librarians (ALA) and Department of Audio-Visual Instruction (NEA). (Chicago: American Library Association, and Washington, DC: National Education Association). 44pp. ED 033 616.

1966 *Quantitative standards for audiovisual personnel, equipment, and materials in elementary, secondary, and higher education.* Department of Audio-Visual Instruction (NEA). (Washington, DC: National Education Association). 13pp. ED 024 277.

1960 *Standards for school library programs.* American Association of School Librarians. (Chicago: American Library Association).

1945 *School libraries for today and tomorrow: Functions and standards.* American Library Association. (Chicago: American Library Association).

1925 *Elementary school library standards.* National Education Association and American Library Association. (Chicago: American Library Association).

1920 *Standard library organization and equipment for secondary schools of different sizes.* National Education Association and North Central Association of Colleges and Secondary Schools. (Chicago: American Library Association).

SELECTED PLANNING AND EVALUATION INSTRUMENTS

A number of evaluation instruments and program planning procedures for school library media programs have been developed over the years. Some, such as the evaluation criteria and self-evaluation instruments developed by the National Study of School Evaluation (NSSE), have been developed for use with the regional accreditation associations. Current NSSE instruments deal primarily with library resources; however, the development of criteria and instruments related to educational technology is currently under way (Pershing and Molenda 1995). Other instruments, such as the AECT and Patrick references listed here, are built around the joint national guidelines for school media programs. Other evaluation tools are included in this listing because of interesting features, such as the flexibility for local needs of the Loertscher and Stroud instruments and the consensus-building techniques of the Liesener process.

Association for Educational Communications and Technology. (1980). *Evaluating media programs: District and school.* Washington, DC: Author. 77pp. ED 200 228.
   This evaluation instrument is designed for systematic data collection to assess the effectiveness of media programs at school and/or district levels. The instrument may provide internal and external evaluators with information for program improvement, program planning, or accreditation. It is suggested that such an instrument should be used as part of the informative evaluation process, and in conjunction with program objectives and goals or provided standards and guidelines. This instrument is organized into eight sections: (1) school

system profile, (2) media program goals and policies, (3) budget, (4) personnel, (5) operations and services, (6) collections, (7) facilities, and (8) student and staff opinionnaires. Each section contains the rationale, instructions for use, and the instrument.

Liesener, J. W. (1976). *A systematic process for planning media programs.* Chicago: American Library Association. 166pp.

Presents a comprehensive nine-step planning process for school media programs, which builds upon arriving at consensus among media center staff and clients served by the media program regarding the program's services and priorities. Presents a number of instruments to inventory current services, determine preferences for services, collect data on services, and allocate costs to service areas.

Loertscher, D. V., and Stroud, J. G. (1976). *PSES: Purdue self-evaluation system for school media centers: Elementary school catalog.* Littleton, CO: Hi Willow Research and Publishing. 23pp. ED 126 915.

Loertscher, D. V., and Stroud, J. G. (1976). *PSES: Purdue self-evaluation system for school media centers: Junior, senior high catalog.* Littleton, CO: Hi Willow Research and Publishing. 25pp. ED 126 914.

The elementary catalog lists 238 items that can be selected to develop individualized questionnaires for media staff, teachers, or students to rate accessibility services, awareness services, professional services, utilization services, planning services, acquisition services, production services, evaluation services, and activity services of elementary school media programs. The high school catalog lists 265 items that can be selected to rate junior or senior high media programs.

National Study of School Evaluation. (1984). *Secondary school evaluative criteria: A guide for school improvement.* Falls Church, VA: National Study of School Evaluation. 191pp.

National Study of School Evaluation. (1983). *K-12 school evaluative criteria: A guide for school improvement.* Falls Church, VA: National Study of School Evaluation. 211pp. ED 241 593.

National Study of School Evaluation. (1979). *Middle school/junior high school evaluative criteria: A guide for school improvement.* Falls Church, VA: National Study of School Evaluation. 194pp.

National Study of School Evaluation. (1973). *Elementary school evaluative criteria: A guide for school improvement.* Falls Church, VA: National Study of School Evaluation. 158pp.

These guidelines for conducting self-evaluations by individual schools and evaluation by a visiting committee have been developed by the National Study of School Evaluation for the use of regional accrediting associations. The guidelines are organized in several sections. The "manual" provides an overview of the evaluation process and explains how the illustrative materials may be used. Each of the evaluative criteria includes sections dealing with learning media services. These sections call for the team to look at principles of media services, a description of the learning media services, evaluation, plans for improvement, and a current status scale.

Patrick, R. B. (1989). Information power: The planning process. *School Library Media Quarterly 17*(2), 88a-j.

Defines planning and provides a rationale for planning library media programs within the context of joint AASL/AECT guidelines. Sets forth the steps involved in cooperatively planning the media program by media specialists, administrators, and teachers. Instruments to assess the awareness/attitudes/commitment, knowledge/skills (competencies), and resources (human/physical)/access of the three planning participants are presented, as is a program planning sheet.

CURRENT STATE STANDARDS AND GUIDELINES

Over the years, a number of surveys have been conducted of state program standards and guidelines for school library media programs. One of the most comprehensive was done by Milbrey L. Jones (1977) for the U.S. Department of Health, Education, and Welfare. More recent surveys by Wilkinson (1983) and Kuhlthau and Kunzel (1989) have not presented the depth of analysis of the Jones study. Other researchers have looked at specific aspects of media programs. *School Library Journal*, for example, publishes a biennial analysis of state certification requirements for school library media specialists (Perritt 1994). Hezel Associates (1994) have produced an in-depth, state-by-state analysis of telecommunications policies and developments, including statewide planning, networks, and higher-education use of telecommunications, as well as use within K–12 schools.

For this survey, an initial listing of state standards and guidelines was compiled from earlier listings in the *Educational Media and Technology Yearbook*, the *School Library Media Annual*, and other publications. State department personnel with primary responsibilities in the area of school library media programs within each of the 50 states and the District of Columbia were contacted by telephone to verify the accuracy and completeness of the published data and to request copies of the appropriate documents for physical review and annotation. Updated information was received from all 50 states and the District of Columbia. Copies of the various guideline publications were received from all but four of the surveyed agencies.

A number of trends can be observed in the responses to the survey. In the 1983 survey by Wilkinson, 43 guidelines published between 1972 and 1983 were reported. Only 22 of these guidelines have been updated since the publication of *Information Power* in 1988. Nine states indicate that they do not provide such guidelines. A number of states indicate that they recommend schools use *Information Power* in place of discontinued or outdated state guidelines when developing local media programs. A total of eight agencies indicated that their media program guidelines were in the process of revision.

The reduction in the number of up-to-date program planning guidelines reflects two major trends affecting the governance of K–12 public education: the movement toward an emphasis on learner outcomes that was evident in *Information Power*, and a movement toward local control and away from state-mandated program components. Thirty states in the survey indicated that they provide either mandated or voluntary information skills curriculum guidelines. A number of states, such as Arizona, Connecticut, and New York, indicated that the only state accreditation standards for media are in terms of learner outcomes. In many of the states, guidelines for media programs are provided primarily to assist local schools in achieving learner outcomes.

Alabama

Enriching education: Providing Information Power *for Alabama students (Bulletin 1992, No. 48).* Montgomery: Alabama State Department of Education, 1992. 51pp.

Describes the purpose and functions of library media programs within the context of *Information Power* and lists information skills objectives for grades one through twelve. Requirements are outlined for flexible scheduling; media specialist and paraprofessional; minimal collections for elementary, middle, and high schools; and facilities. A checklist and questionnaire for evaluation by school principals are included to be used in conjunction with *Accreditation standards for combined elementary and secondary schools* (Montgomery: Alabama State Department of Education, 1982). See also *Library Media Skill Curriculum Guide* (Montgomery: Alabama State Department of Education, 1982).

Alaska

Guidelines for Alaskan school library media programs. Juneau: Alaska Department of Education, draft 1992. 7pp.

A self-analysis checklist developed to evaluate progress of school library media programs toward accomplishment of guidelines in the areas of management and administration, personnel, collections, programs, services and accessibility, public and community relations, facilities, funding, and continuing education. Instructional goals of library media programs are provided in *Integration of Library Skills into the Language Arts Curriculum* (Juneau: Alaska Department of Education, 1988). See also *Library Media Standards for Alaska Schools* (Juneau: Alaska Association of School Librarians, 1990. 11pp.). Presents standards for staff, collections, budgets, equipment, space, and hours for six levels of school size.

Arizona

Currently Arizona has no accreditation or program requirements for school libraries. Library and information skill requirements for students, however, are built into state curriculum standards. See *Arizona Literature Essential Skills* (Phoenix: Arizona Department of Education, 1990. 47pp. ED 321 296); and *The Language Arts Essential Skills* (Phoenix: Arizona Department of Education, 1989. 100pp. ED 321 296).

Arkansas

Regulations regarding staff, expenditures, librarians, and libraries, as well as evaluation criteria related to librarians, libraries, and instructional materials, are provided in *Policies, Regulations, and Criteria for Accrediting Arkansas Elementary and Secondary Schools* (Little Rock: Arkansas Department of Education, 1993). See also *Guidelines for Planning School Facilities* (Little Rock: Arkansas Department of Education, 1975).

California

California does not provide state-level school library media program guidelines. The Department of Education has endorsed and recommends *Information Power* to the schools. Student skills in the location and processing of information are specified in *Guide and Criteria for Program Quality Review: Elementary or Middle School* (Sacramento: California Department of Education, 1994); and *Guide for Program Quality Review: High School* (Sacramento: California Department of Education, 1995, in press).

Colorado

Colorado Information Power: *Guidelines for school library media programs.* Denver: Colorado State Board of Education, 1989. 80pp.

Part I describes programs and services at the building level; district, area, and regional levels; and the state level. Information-processing skills and instructional consultation are incorporated in the services area. Part II provides guidelines for such resource components as physical facilities, audiovisual and computer equipment, collections, and automation/ technology, whereas Part III deals with management of media programs. Sample report forms and extensive needs assessment instruments related to information skills, consultation, physical facilities, and program management are included to serve as a basis for program planning and evaluation.

Connecticut

A guide to program development in learning resources and technology. Hartford: State of Connecticut Department of Education, 1991. 86pp.

Although media programs are not required for accreditation of schools in Connecticut, information skills are required for students, and these program development guides are provided to assist school systems in achieving such learning goals. In addition to a discussion of the role of learning resources and technology and the Connecticut common core of learning, sections deal with program development, instruction, communications technology, learning resources, program management, and copyright. See also *Challenge for Excellence: Connecticut's Comprehensive Plan for Elementary, Secondary, Vocational, Career and Adult Education 1991-1995* (Hartford: State of Connecticut Department of Education, 1990. 83pp. ED 357 478).

Delaware

Media programs for Delaware schools: Guidelines for program excellence. Dover: Delaware Department of Public Instruction, 1975. 36pp.

Contains sections dealing with personnel, scheduling and instruction, operations, access and delivery systems, and facilities. A revision of these guidelines, which were based on the 1975 joint standards, *Media Programs: District and School,* was in progress, with a targeted release date of June 1, 1995.

District of Columbia

The school media program in the District of Columbia: Guidelines for its operation. Washington, DC: Public Schools of the District of Columbia, 1976. 50pp.

Defines qualitative guidelines and quantitative levels for minimal, adequate, and innovative programs. A major revision of this publication is under consideration, but no timeline for completion has been established. Currently the school administration recommends the use of *Information Power* rather than the existing guidelines.

Florida

Florida school library media programs: A guide for excellence. Tallahassee: Florida Department of Education, 1978. 57pp.

Emphasis is on the development of qualitative principles for both building-level and district-level programs. Currently there are no plans to revise this publication. The Department of Education recommends the use of *Information Power* in place of the outdated state guidelines. See also *Information Skills for Florida Schools K–12* (Tallahassee: Florida Department of Education, 1984).

Georgia

Media specialist's handbook: You are the key. Atlanta: Georgia Department of Education, 1991. 99pp.

Consists of six major sections dealing with preparation and certification of media specialists; roles and responsibilities within media programs; standards and policies, including State Board policies, Georgia Accreditation Commission Standards, Southern Association standards, and related legal requirements; services and resources available to school media programs; media facilities; and professional organizations. Information access skills are integrated across the curriculum. Learner outcomes are specified in *Georgia's Quality Core Curriculum (K-12)* (Atlanta: Georgia Department of Education, 1989).

Hawaii

Guidelines for Hawaii school library instructional technology centers. Honolulu: State of Hawaii Department of Education, 1994.

A copy of this publication was not available for review at press time for the *Yearbook.* See also *Information Skills Continuum K-12* (Honolulu: State of Hawaii Department of Education, 1990). The information skills continuum is currently under revision.

Idaho

Managing school libraries in elementary and secondary schools. Boise: Idaho State Department of Education, 1986. 137pp.

In addition to general descriptions of school library programs, this publication contains chapters on district coordinators and processing centers, budgeting, teaching library and research skills, suggestions for facilities planners, book selection, weeding, copyright, and beginning a school library media program. See also *Accreditation Standards and Procedures for Idaho Elementary Schools* (Boise: State Department of Education, 1994–1995); *Accreditation Standards and Procedures for Idaho Middle and Junior High Schools* (Boise: State Department of Education, 1994–1995); and *Accreditation Standards and Procedures for Idaho Secondary Schools* (Boise: State Department of Education, 1994-1995).

Illinois

Recommended standards for educational library media programs in Illinois. Springfield: Illinois State Board of Education, 1986. 32pp.

Qualitative and three levels of quantitative standards are presented: practical standards that are achievable by every school system; normal growth beyond the basic level and toward the ideal; and a final level that reflects national guidelines. Presents an assessment guide for use in the evaluation of the school media program; describes district-level media services; and presents special considerations for low-enrollment school districts. The state is currently working on general school leadership guidelines which, when they are adopted, may replace this publication.

Indiana

Guidelines for Indiana school media programs. Indianapolis: Indiana Department of Public Instruction, 1978. 35pp.

Emphasis is on qualitative guidelines to expand on minimal quantitative levels. Includes sections on evaluation and the role of state agencies. Currently there are no plans to revise this publication. The Department of Public Instruction recommends the use of *Information Power* in place of the outdated state guidelines. See also *Survival Manual for Indiana School Media Personnel: A Quick Reference to School Library Media Related Information* (Indianapolis: Indiana Department of Public Instruction, 1986).

Iowa

Plan for progress in the library media center PK-12: A guide to planning for school library media programs and for district, AEAMC, and other support of those programs. Des Moines: Iowa Department of Education, 1992. 96pp. ED 351 012.

To assist educators in the development of quality library media programs, the roles and responsibilities of the program are defined and personnel needs of the program are considered, along with the necessary partnership of all school staff in program development. General goals and objectives for the integration of an information skills curriculum that is integrated with classroom instruction are presented. Budgets, collection development, student and faculty services, and facilities are reviewed along with related quantitative guidelines. Support services from other governmental agencies, cooperatives, online services, and networks are discussed. The document concludes with an extensive annotated bibliography of related resources.

Kansas

Guidelines for school library media programs in Kansas. Topeka: Kansas Association for School Librarians, 1980. 61pp. ED 190 068.

Discusses roles and responsibilities and presents qualitative guidelines for district and school library media programs, personnel, budgets and expenditures, collections, equipment and furniture, facilities, and program evaluation. Four levels of quantitative standards based on North Central Association standards and three versions of national association guidelines are presented. See also *Guidelines for Kansas Library Media Curriculum Standards (Draft)* (Topeka: Kansas State Department of Education, 1994. 13pp.).

Kentucky

ON-LINE 2: Essentials of a model library media program. Frankfort: Kentucky Department
  of Education, 1995. 71pp.

The initial section discusses the role of media programs and library media specialists
within the school reform movement. The second major section deals with information literacy
and briefly with collaboration within media skills instruction. Extensive appendices deal with
everything from library media specialist evaluation forms, resources, and facilities, to an
extended discussion of libraries of the future. In keeping with the trends discussed in the
document, in addition to normal hard copy, it is available in an electronic format on the
Internet (http//www.kbe.state.ky.us).

Louisiana

*Standards and guidelines for library media programs in Louisiana schools (Bulletin 1134,
  revised).* Baton Rouge: Louisiana State Department of Education, 1990. 73pp.

Defines the mission of the library media program; outlines the cooperation and support
needed by successful media programs from administrators, faculty, and other groups; and
discusses guidelines for personnel, collections, management, budgets, and facilities of media
programs. Basic and advanced levels for collections are presented, as well as the objectives
and learner skills represented in the information-processing curriculum. Appendices include
a self-assessment checklist that lists a number of program characteristics and supporting
documentation within the six major areas of philosophy, instruction, resources and resource
services, facilities, program evaluation, and school district support.

Maine

Maine school library media programs. Augusta: Maine Educational Media Association and
  Maine State Library, 1992. 27pp.

Provides direction and a set of guidelines to assist schools in program planning, design,
management, and evaluation in relation to the library facility and library instruction requirements of Maine's 1984 Education Reform Act. Sections deal with personnel, facilities and
equipment, collections, the role of the school media program in the curriculum, and an
information skills philosophy. Currently the guidelines are being updated to more effectively
deal with newer forms of technology.

Maryland

Standards for school library media programs in Maryland. Baltimore: Maryland State
  Department of Education, 1986. 22pp. ED 275 341.

Presents standards to improve, support, and encourage school library media programs
based on a statement of purpose which defines the unified school library media program as
essential to effective education for an information-based society. Presents a series of criteria
statements following each standard to help school personnel in determining appropriate
ratings. See also *The Library Media Program: A Maryland Curricular Framework* (Baltimore: Maryland State Department of Education, 1991. 51pp. ED 342 404), which presents
goals, subgoals, and a general framework for the design and development of the library
and information skills curriculum. See also *Learning Outcomes in Library Media Skills*

(Baltimore: Maryland State Department of Education, 1992. 47pp. ED 349 005), which identifies learning outcomes across the areas of mathematics, reading, writing, science, and social studies.

Massachusetts

Standards for school library media centers in the Commonwealth of Massachusetts. Three
    Rivers: Massachusetts School Library Media Association, 1988. 31pp.
      Provides a rationale for the school library media center and discusses the direct and indirect roles of the library media specialist and support staff. Relations with school library media programs beyond the building level are explored. Minimal, advanced, and exemplary quantitative standards are presented for personnel, collections, technology, and budgets, and general considerations for space and furnishings for media facilities are described. The document is currently under revision, and no timeline for completion has been announced.

Michigan

Guidelines for library media programs in Michigan schools. Lansing: Library Media Program
    Advisory Committee, Michigan Department of Education, 1994. 4pp.
      Briefly presents a blueprint for school library media centers to implement the State Board of Education's *Model Core Curriculum Outcomes.* Presents qualitative guidelines regarding staffing, information networking, facilities, evaluation, and budgeting of media programs. See also *Information Processing Skills: Scope and Sequence Planning and Integration Matrix* and *Information Processing Skills: Developing Sample Lesson Plans, and Sample Lesson Plans A-G* (Lansing: Library Media Program Advisory Committee, Michigan Department of Education, 1994. 13pp). This dual publication presents 46 specific information-processing skills within eight broad areas and places awareness, practice, mastery, or reinforcement of the skills over four grade-level groupings.

Minnesota

Minimum and long-range goals for media programs. St. Paul: Media and Technology Unit,
    Minnesota Department of Education, 1983.
      A copy of this publication was not available for review at press time for the *Yearbook.* See also *Model Learner Outcomes for Educational Media and Technology* (St. Paul: Minnesota Department of Education, 1989. 78pp. ED 336 070). Covers values, philosophy, goals, and learner outcomes. Outcomes are presented on a matrix encouraging integration of a broad range of technology into library media programs and curriculum. See also *Model Learner Outcomes for Information Technology Education: Curriculum Integration Guide* (St. Paul: Minnesota Department of Education, 1991. 46pp. ED 336 069).

Mississippi

    The Mississippi Department of Education does not provide general program guidelines for media programs. Accreditation requirements related to budgets, staffing, and services of school library media programs are detailed in *Accreditation Requirements of the State Board of Education, 11th Edition, Revised (Bulletin 171)* (Jackson: Mississippi Department of Education, 1994. 93pp.).

Missouri

Learning resources: A guide for learning resources programs and services. Jefferson City: Missouri State Department of Elementary and Secondary Education, 1975. 160pp.

Provides qualitative guidelines and describes procedures for schools that wish to assess and improve their media programs beyond minimal state levels. Areas covered include administration of the learning resources program; services for students, teachers, administrators, and the instructional and inservice programs; learning resources; local production; equipment; facilities; instructional design; assessment and evaluation; and future directions. A revision of this publication is currently under way, with a projected completion date of fall 1995. See also *Guidelines for Performance Based Evaluation: Teachers, Counselors, Librarians* (Jefferson City: Missouri State Department of Elementary and Secondary Education, 1991. 73pp. ED 337 853).

Montana

Although general guidelines for school library media programs are not provided by Montana, minimal state accreditation standards are described in *Montana School Accreditation: Standards and Procedures Manual* (Helena: Montana Office of Public Instruction, 1988). Voluntary information skills curriculum guidelines are provided in *The Montana Library and Information Skills Model Curriculum Guide* (Helena: Montana Office of Public Instruction, 1993. 101pp.).

Nebraska

The Nebraska guide for establishing, developing, evaluating school library media programs. 5th edition. Lincoln: Nebraska State Department of Education, 1994.

A copy of this publication was not available for review at press time for the *Yearbook*. Earlier editions of the guide, which was developed by the Nebraska Educational Media Association, contained extensive sets of analysis forms and questionnaires to be used in media program planning and evaluation. Areas reviewed included the school system profile and budget, services, staffing, physical facilities, and collections. Included were opinion questionnaires for both students and faculty.

Nevada

Information Power *Nevada.* Carson City: Nevada Department of Education, 1995.

This publication, which replaces the earlier *Media Standards for Nevada Schools* (1986), was not available for review at press time for the *Yearbook*. It was scheduled for release in March 1995. The earlier standards presented conceptual statements and quantitative standards for such program components as staffing, collections, facilities, selection, and equipment.

New Hampshire

Applying results-planning concepts in educational media services. 2nd edition. Concord: New Hampshire State Department of Education, 1983. 82pp.

Uses student learning results as the basis for initiating and revising media programs. In a three-phase process, the ideal desired learner results and the characteristics of programs in schools that develop such learner results are defined; the resources and instructional activities of the current status of the school's media program are identified and evaluated; and a plan to achieve the ideal media program from the current status is developed. See also *Minimum Standards for Elementary School Programs* (NH Code of Administrative Rules, part ed. 308).

New Jersey

Guidelines for school library media programs in New Jersey: A planning tool. Trenton: New Jersey Department of Education, School and College Media Services Section, 1992. 92pp.

Designed for use in conjunction with *Information Power,* these guidelines are designed to assist school districts and individual schools in realizing the potential of their library media programs. The philosophy and partnerships of successful programs are defined. Sections of the planning guide deal with program, staff, resources, facilities, and communication. Each section follows the same organization: definitions, goals, objectives, practical considerations, steps for implementation, and evaluation. See also *Library Media Center Study and Research Skills Instructional Program K-12* (Trenton: Educational Media Association of New Jersey and the Library Development Bureau, New Jersey State Library, Department of Education, 1985, 8pp.).

New Mexico

State standards for library media programs. Santa Fe: New Mexico State Department of Education, 1987.

A copy of this publication was not available for review at press time for the *Yearbook.* A revision is in process, but no timeline for completion has been established.

New York

Currently New York has no general program guidelines for school library media programs. Library and information skill requirements for students, however, are built into state curriculum standards, such as *The Elementary Library Media Skills Curriculum: Grades K-6* (Albany: Bureau of Curriculum Development, New York State Department of Education, 1980. 367pp. ED 205 199); and *Secondary Library Media and Information Skills Syllabus: Grades 7-12. Part I: Scope and Sequence* (Albany: Bureau of Curriculum Development, New York State Department of Education, 1988. 55pp. ED 318 486).

North Carolina

Learning connections: Guidelines for media and technology programs. Raleigh: North Carolina Department of Public Instruction, 1992. 302pp. ED 344 576.

Aligned closely with *Information Power,* these guidelines seek to demonstrate the changing roles of the media coordinator and other media and technology professionals in a dynamic school culture. Designed for computer teachers and coordinators, supervisors, facilitators, media and technology directors, and school administrators, as well as the more traditional media specialists, the guidelines for such program components as program services, planning and assessment, resources, budget, facilities, personnel, and system-level services have been expanded to reflect newer technologies and electronic formats. See also

Teacher Handbook: Information Skills and Computer Skills Curriculum K-12 (Raleigh: North Carolina Department of Public Instruction, 1992. 196pp.).

North Dakota

Guidelines for North Dakota school library media centers. Bismarck: North Dakota Library Association, Public Library Planning Committee, 1985.

A copy of this publication was not available for review at press time for the *Yearbook*. Accreditation standards for elementary and K-12 school media services are defined in *Accreditation Standards* (Bismarck: North Dakota Department of Public Instruction, 1991).

Ohio

Quality library services, K-12. Columbus: Ohio State Department of Education, 1985, 112pp. ED 274 355.

Provides a rationale for integration of the school library into the total educational program of the school. Describes the service dimensions and essential components of effective K–12 library programs. A practical guide for planning a district library media program is presented. Emerging trends and developments in library science and educational technology are discussed. Qualitative accreditation standards for the state of Ohio, which will likely eliminate the need for this document, are scheduled to be completed during the summer of 1995. See also *A Self-Appraisal Checklist for Library/Media Programs in Ohio (K-12)* (Columbus: Ohio State Department of Education, 1982, 20pp.).

Oklahoma

Guidelines for library media programs in Oklahoma. Oklahoma City: Oklahoma State Department of Education, 1991. 92pp.

Designed to be practical and useful for administrators, teachers, and school library media personnel, as all aspects of an effective program are assessed, goals are established, and plans are made for achieving them. Fundamental considerations in the design of facilities and in the selection and evaluation of personnel are examined. Three levels of quantitative guidelines for resources and equipment are defined. Looks at the media specialist as a manager, a teacher, an information specialist, and an instructional consultant. A revision of the *Guidelines* is currently in process. See also *Priority Academic Student Skills: A Core Curriculum for Our Children's Future* (Oklahoma City: Oklahoma State Department of Education, 1993. 169pp. ED 371 993).

Oregon

Media program guide. Salem: Oregon Department of Education, 1979. 105pp.

Looks at the school library media program as both an instructional program and a support program, with emphasis on the support aspect. Includes guidelines and extensive assessment questionnaires for both roles. See also *Library Information Skills Guide for Oregon Schools, K-12* (Salem: Oregon Department of Education, 1987. 105pp. ED 291 388). This program of library information skills instruction was the result of cooperative planning by library media specialists and classroom teachers.

Pennsylvania

Pennsylvania guidelines for school library media programs. Harrisburg: Pennsylvania Department of Education, 1989. 84pp.

Reviews information skills, program and staff evaluation, facilities, collections, and budgets. These guidelines were being revised, with a targeted release date in spring 1995. See also *Integrating Information-Management Skills into Content Areas* (Harrisburg: Pennsylvania Department of Education, 1987); and *Pennsylvania Online: A Curriculum Guide for School Library Media Centers* (Harrisburg: Pennsylvania Department of Education, 1990, 110pp. ED 324 009).

Rhode Island

Standards for school libraries in the state of Rhode Island. Providence: State Department of Education, 1995.

This publication was still under development at press time for the *Yearbook,* with a projected release date of fall 1995.

South Carolina

Guidelines for school library media centers. Columbia: South Carolina Department of Education, 1986. 13pp. ED 281 531.

Designed to be used in conjunction with the *Defined Minimum Program for South Carolina School Districts,* these guidelines were developed as part of an effort to evaluate the statewide library media program and make recommendations for improvement. Major sections review goals for media programs, media center personnel, facilities, resources, program, and finances. This publication was under revision, with a targeted completion date of fall 1995.

South Dakota

South Dakota's planning guide for building school library media programs. Revised edition. Pierre: State Department of Education, 1980. 26pp.

Defines three levels of goals for program evaluation and planning. Basic is level two of state accreditation, better is level one, and advanced is the North Central Association accreditation standards. See also *Information Skills for South Dakota Students* (Pierre: South Dakota State Library, 1986. 42pp. ED 285 605). Current reports are that the state of South Dakota is in the process of dropping all state-mandated standards and program guidelines in favor of full local control over schools.

Tennessee

Library media handbook. Nashville: Tennessee Department of Education, 1978. 49pp.

Presents an extension of state minimum standards in the areas of management and operation of library media programs, services of the program, collections, facilities, and program evaluation. See also *Rules, Regulations, and Minimum Standards for the Governance of Public schools in the State of Tennessee* (Nashville: Tennessee Department of Education, 1992); and *Information Skills for Tennessee* (Nashville: Tennessee Department of Education, 1985).

Texas

The library media center: A force for student excellence. Austin: Texas Education Agency, 1993. 93pp. ED 366 345.

Describes the service role of the library media program and presents qualitative guidelines for the media center staff; resources at the campus, district, and regional levels; facilities; and finances. Examines the role of the media center within the curriculum. A final chapter looks at the role of technology within library media programs. A series of appendices present policy statements and specific quantitative standards. See also *Planning the Library Media Facility for the 1990s and Beyond* (Austin: Texas Education Agency, 1991. 92pp.), and *Library/Information Skills for Quality Education* (Austin: Texas Education Agency, 1987. 65pp. ED 281 558). The curriculum guide is currently being revised to reflect newer developments in information technology.

Utah

Utah's school library media programs: Empowering students to function effectively in an information world. Salt Lake City: Utah State Office of Education, 1991. 53pp. ED 339 352.

Presents a report on how school library media centers and programs can prepare students to function effectively in an increasingly technological and information-oriented society in competition with international peers. Describes the functions and components of effective library media programs. Appendices present the standards and learning objectives of the library media skills core for levels K–6, and a sample of how library media skills are infused into the language arts core for levels 7–12. Includes examples of job descriptions for both certified and noncertified personnel and quantitative standards of the Northwest Association of Schools and Colleges. See also *Elementary and Secondary Core Curriculum Standards. Levels K-12. Library Media* (Salt Lake City: Utah State Office of Education, 1991. 48pp. ED 371 720).

Vermont

A 1981 set of general guidelines for media programs within Vermont schools is no longer available from the Vermont Department of Education. Accreditation requirements related to student performance of skills in locating and using a variety of materials and information services, and the budgets, staffing, and services of school library media programs needed to develop such skills, are detailed in *Revised Standards for Approving Vermont's Public Schools* (Montpelier: State of Vermont Department of Education, 1991, 41pp.).

Virginia

The state of Virginia does not provide local guidelines for library media programs within the state's public schools. Student learning requirements related to information processing are currently being developed for adoption by the Department of Education. Specific state requirements for media program services, staff, and facilities are provided in *Standards and Regulations for Public Schools in Virginia* (Richmond: Virginia Department of Education, 1992). See also *Standards of Learning Objectives for Virginia Public Schools* (Richmond: Virginia Department of Education, adoption anticipated in 1995).

Washington

Information Power *for Washington: Guidelines for school library media programs.* Olympia: Washington Library Media Association and Office of Superintendent of Public Instruction, 1991. 82pp. ED 337 174.

This document is designed to explain and elaborate upon the minimum accreditation standards and guidelines established by the State Board of Education for school library media programs in Washington. Sections deal with definitions of library media programs and roles within such programs, instruction in information skills and services of the program, staff, resources and budgets, facilities, outside support for school programs, and program evaluation. Each section starts with the appropriate standards statement, which is then followed by discussion. See also *Information Skills Curriculum Guide: Process, Scope, and Sequence* (Olympia: Washington Library Media Association, Supervisors' Subcommittee on Information Skills, 1988. 46pp. ED 288 554).

West Virginia

Although state accreditation standards specify that students have access to libraries or technology centers, the nature of these facilities is not defined. Standards for student performance in the area of information skills are specified in *Performance Based Accreditation System. Policy 2320* (Charleston: West Virginia Board of Education, 1992. 19pp.). These standards are used in conjunction with *Training Manual and Handbook for On-Site Review* (Charleston: Office of Accreditation and Recognition, West Virginia Board of Education, 1992. 74pp.), which documents the requirements for meeting the standards.

Wisconsin

School library media programs: A resource and planning guide. Bulletin No. 7368. Madison: Wisconsin Department of Public Instruction, 1987. 89pp. ED 286 529.

These guidelines are intended to be used by school boards, administrators, teachers, and curriculum leaders, as well as media specialists and other educators, to ensure that the school library media program is an integral part of the school's instructional program. See also *Matrix for Curriculum Planning in Library Media and Information Skills Education. Bulletin No. 9288* (Madison: Wisconsin Department of Public Instruction, 1989. 41pp. ED 308 870). The matrix organizes more than 900 competencies and skills extracted from teaching guides for language arts, mathematics, reading, science, and social studies.

Wyoming

Guidelines for Wyoming school library/media programs. Cheyenne: Wyoming State Department of Education, 1981. 12pp.

These guidelines for program evaluation and planning are out of print and are no longer being distributed by the department. The intent is that library and information-processing skills will be addressed in student learning objectives that are currently under development by the Department of Education and have yet to be adopted or implemented.

REFERENCES

Hezel Associates. (1994). *Educational telecommunications: The state-by-state analysis 1994.* Syracuse, NY: Hezel Associates.

Jones, M. L. (1977). *Survey of school media standards.* Washington, DC: U.S. Department of Health, Education, and Welfare. ED 148 380.

Kuhlthau, C., and Kunzel, B. L. (1989). State guidelines/standards for school library media programs. In *School library media annual 1989: Volume 7,* ed. J. B. Smith (Englewood, CO: Libraries Unlimited), 78–83.

Perritt, P. H. (1994). School library media certification requirements: 1994 update. *School Library Journal 40*(6), 32–51.

Pershing, J., and Molenda, M. (1995, February). *NSSE evaluation criteria for educational technology in K-12 schools.* Paper presented at the national convention of the Association for Educational Communications and Technology, Anaheim, CA.

Wilkinson, G. L. (1983). Media program standards and guidelines: A survey and review. In *Educational media yearbook 1983,* ed. J. W. Brown and S. N. Brown (Littleton, CO: Libraries Unlimited), 76–89.

Telephone Lines in the Classroom*

Larry W. Lucas
Texas Center for Educational Technology
University of North Texas

This ERIC Digest discusses the results of a survey on the installation and use of telephone lines in K–12 classrooms. A summary of the observations, comments, and opinions from teachers and educational administrators from around the world, as well as references to conference presentations and printed articles about the subject, is included.

INTRODUCTION

In June 1994, a Texas Center for Educational Technology (TCET) "customer" (a teacher in a Texas public school) requested information/documentation that could persuade the school district administration, the school board, and the community that telephones in K–12 classrooms are necessary. Since TCET did not have information on file concerning the use of telephones and telephone lines in education, the request for information was forwarded to educators worldwide via the Internet. Several educational listservs and conference groups on the Internet posted a request for comments, observations, and opinions from educators having experience with telephones in the classroom. TCET received responses to the information request from large and small schools (public and private). Geographically, responses came from school districts all across the United States and from Australia. Although reports included a few cautions and negative observations, the vast majority of comments were resoundingly positive favoring the installation of telephone lines in classrooms.

Respondents agreed overwhelmingly that in an age of information and communications, it is essential to equip K–12 classrooms with modern communications tools, including telephone lines. Students and teachers need to learn how to use communications tools to gather information to support learning in various curricula.

The survey indicated that telephone lines are used in classrooms in predominately two ways: voice communications and computer communications (telecommunications and telecomputing). A couple of respondents mentioned the use of phone lines for the exchange of FAX messages.

*Larry W. Lucas is Technical Specialist at the Texas Center for Educational Technology at the University of North Texas, Denton, Texas.

ERIC Digests are in the public domain and may be freely reproduced.

This digest was prepared with funding from the Office of Educational Research and Improvement, U.S. Department of Education, contract no. RR93002009. The opinions expressed in this report do not necessarily reflect the positions or policies of OERI or the Department of Education.

VOICE COMMUNICATIONS

As expected, most respondents indicated that improved parent/teacher communication was the primary advantage of voice communications. Many also reported improved intra-campus and inter-campus communications. Telephone installations improved office-to-classroom communications in many schools. With classroom telephones it was not necessary to disrupt the whole class with an announcement over the PA for a student to come to the office. The office can contact the teacher by phone and the teacher can quietly tell the student to go to the office.

Ken Phillips, Principal at Taylor Elementary School in Cleveland, Tennessee, installed a key electronic telephone system as a flexible, versatile solution to the need for an intercom system. Three telephone lines come into the school. The phone rings only in the office. If a call for a teacher is determined to be important enough, it is transferred to the teacher's phone. The system can also be an intercom and can even be used to pipe background music into the classrooms.

Many respondents found that a telephone in the classroom helped considerably with discipline management. John Eye, Media Generalist/Computer Coordinator in Round Lake, Minnesota, stated, "I observed a teacher walk a disruptive student right up to the phone to call home, explain the situation, and discuss a solution." Some school districts have also reported a considerable decrease in absenteeism because of phones in the classroom.

According to Nancy Martin, Principal at Monroe High School in Monroe, Washington, one of the pluses of phones in the classroom is "more immediate access from the classroom to the main office in cases of emergency (medically fragile students or accidents for example)." In a related scenario, some schools include phones as a key part of security.

Many reported an increase in teachers' morale (teachers are finally being treated like the professionals that they are). Apparent increases in efficiency and productivity have accompanied increases in morale. Quoting Leeanne Needham, Technology Specialist with the Issaquah School District in Issaquah, Washington, "What a difference the phone made! We were much more productive as educators. The most beneficial part was the improvement of teacher/parent communication."

In an article in *Education Technology News* (February 16, 1993), Lockwood Elementary School (Montana) reported that having telephones in the classrooms improved student morale. When students complete outstanding work, they are encouraged to call their parents and relate the good news.

In some high schools with classroom telephone installations, the teachers put information in their voice mail about homework and assignments for the week, easily retrievable from a student's home. This has resulted in considerable improvement in communication between teachers, students, and parents. Announcements for sports and other events are sometimes posted on voice mail.

At some schools, students use classroom telephones to obtain local research information and to contact content experts. These activities enhance learning and add current knowledge to many curricula.

In the Reader Exchange column of *Learning94* (August, 1994), Beverly Blackman Dornburg of Bill Brown Elementary in Spring Branch, Texas, reported that she used a speaker phone in her classroom to let her students communicate with their pen pals in Australia. Similarly, Lockwood Elementary School teachers had their students talk long distance with President Clinton during the presidential campaign to get, first hand, his position on various issues. Students also talked with an executive of Taco Bell to obtain information about the corporation's new automatic taco-making machine.

Gellerman (1994) discusses many applications of various telephone systems that are now in K–12 schools. Major uses include: (1) making important school information available to the community, (2) allowing connection to electronic grade book programs, (3) ability to check on a student's progress (homework hotlines), (4) obtaining test schedules via voice mail, and (5) checking attendance records. A few high schools have installed telephone registration similar to that used at many universities.

Potential negatives of having telephones in classrooms include abuse of the communications tool by teachers and/or students. Proper use of the system needs to be part of orientation for students and teachers. A phone ringing in the classroom can be disruptive, but probably no more so than the teacher from across the hall coming in to borrow something. Most of the schools are preventing this by answering all calls in the office. Calls are then forwarded to the classroom only when the teacher has a free period or if the call is an emergency.

COMPUTER COMMUNICATIONS

Computer communications via telephone lines (telecomputing) allow teachers and students access to information for conducting research in almost any area of the K–12 curriculum. It opens connections to content experts from around the world via e-mail, e-mail lists, and newsgroups, and allows for the exchange of document and data files. Survey respondents reported that the best way to connect classrooms to the Internet (and other information highways) is to establish a local area network (LAN), a computer network throughout the school. Once the LAN is in place, equip it with a communications server that allows any computer on the network to connect to the outside world.

The negatives of telecomputing are few but include the fact that the telephone line is not the best connection (access) to the Internet, although it is the most economical. The worst negative might be the "garbage" that is accessible through the Internet. Some means will need to be established to control what information students access. Flanders (1994) discusses various aspects of this issue.

FAX

Yet another mode of communication via telephone lines is the fax machine. In his response to TCET's request for information, Gary Bowers of Region X Education Service Center in Richardson, Texas, reported that Lawrence Livermore Laboratories in Livermore, California, faxes answers to questions from middle school students in the Livermore area.

Gellerman (1994) also reports that some schools will now fax course information, enrollment forms, and student grade reports.

PRIMARY DETERRENT TO INSTALLATION

For many school districts, the principal hindrance to installing telephones or telephone outlets in classrooms appears to be the cost. Many districts have found ways to minimize the expense, however. Several schools have four or five lines coming into the school that are connected to a key telephone system or a PBX system from which lines are run to each classroom. Other schools have found different ways to split one line into four or five to similarly cut down the cost of phone bills yet provide the classrooms with this essential communications tool.

In a presentation at TelEd '93, Fergus (1993) revealed one sizable school district's solution for putting phone lines in classrooms. The Des Moines Public School District chose to install its own telephone system to serve the entire district. Although it was a large financial investment in the beginning, money was saved in the long run, and there is a telephone in each classroom. The district phone system was installed in 1985. They are currently wiring 8 schools per year and should have all 60 schools in the district wired and telephones in all classrooms by the end of 1995.

REFERENCES

Fergus, T. (1993, November). Fewer dollars vs. more service. *Proceedings of TelEd 1993* (pp. 307–9). Eugene, OR: International Society for Technology in Education. ED 366 334.

Flanders, B. (1994). A delicate balance. *School Library Journal 40*(10), 32–35.

Gellerman, E. (1994). Telephone technology increases communication across the board. *T.H.E. Journal 21*(10), 14–20.

Reader exchange column. (1994, August). *Learning94 23*(1), 6.

Staff. (1993, February 16). Phones help encourage parent involvement in Montana school. *Education Technology News,* 5.

Copyright Issues for the Electronic Age*

Janis H. Bruwelheide
College of Education, Health, and Human Development
Montana State University

In the 1990s, the term *digital age* is commonplace. Computers allow us to translate text and visual information into digital format and give us the ability to create and share new information seamlessly. This digest will focus on a variety of issues confronting copyright law in the digital age.

CURRENT COPYRIGHT LAW

Because information is now so freely available, particularly in electronic form, does that mean we are free to use that information in any way we want? Current copyright law was adopted in 1976 and went into effect in 1978. It is difficult to imagine how the authors of the 1976 Copyright Act could have foreseen so many new technologies. However, they did attempt to cover all of the bases by using language that was intended to be somewhat elastic in section 102(a) of the law:

> *Copyright protection subsists . . . in original works of authorship fixed in any tangible medium of expression, now known or later developed, from which they can be perceived, reproduced, or otherwise communicated, either directly or with the aid of a machine or device.*

POSSIBLE LEGISLATIVE CHANGES

A current report by the U.S. Department of Commerce, commonly referred to as the "green report," has set forth some preliminary recommendations for dealing with digital information. The green report was published in July 1994, and hearings were held in the fall of 1994. A final report, the "white report," expected in May 1995, may result in proposed legislative changes to the copyright law.

Several areas of special interest to educators are included in the report. One is the discussion of a definition of *multimedia*. The report has suggested that "mixed" or "multiple"

*Janis Bruwelheide is a professor in the College of Education, Health, and Human Development at Montana State University.

ERIC Digests are in the public domain and may be freely reproduced.

This digest was prepared with funding from the Office of Educational Research and Improvement, U.S. Department of Education, contract no. RR93002009. The opinions expressed in this report do not necessarily reflect the positions of policies of OERI or the Department of Education.

157

media is a more accurate term, and better describes the variety of rights that need to be acquired. A second area being addressed is "transmission." An additional right of transmission may be added to the existing rights of copyright owners. The terms *transmit* and *transmission* may be added to existing definitions in section 106, rights of copyright owners. Section 106(3) might be modified to include distribution "by transmission." The definition of *transmit* may be expanded to include reproductions of a work as well as performances and displays. In addition to proposed changes in section 106, the definition of *publication* may be expanded to include "by transmission," in addition to physical copies.

Another area needing clarification, according to the green report, is section 108 of the law, which addresses library exemptions. For example, the legal implications of "browsing" through electronic documents, scanning, uploading, and document transfer may be of concern to copyright holders. The American Association of Publishers has issued a strong statement against digitizing without licensing. Professional organizations such as the American Library Association and the Association of Research Libraries have taken a strong pro-user stance.

Until guidelines and clarification are developed for digital information, it would be prudent to be cautious—especially about digitizing. However, educators must also realize that there are exemptions provided in the existing law which should be exercised.

Questions and Answers About Existing Copyright Law

Q: What is copyright?

A: Copyright is a statutory privilege extended to creators of works fixed in a tangible medium of expression.

Q: What are the rights of a copyright owner?

A: Copyright involves five separate rights (section 106):

1. The right to reproduce or copy the work;
2. The right to prepare derivative works;
3. The right to distribute copies of the work to the public;
4. In the case of audiovisual works, the right to perform the work publicly;
5. In the case of literary, musical, dramatic and choreographic works, pantomimes and pictorial, graphic or sculptural works, the right to display the work publicly.

These exclusive rights may be transferred by the copyright owner as individual rights or as a "bundle of rights."

Q: What is meant by fair use (section 107)?

A: Four factors are to be considered in determining whether or not a particular use of a copyrighted work is fair:

1. Purpose and character of the use, including whether such use is of a commercial nature or is for nonprofit educational purposes;
2. Nature of the copyrighted work;
3. Amount and substantiality of the portion used in relation to the work as a whole; and
4. Effect of the use upon potential market for or value of the work.

Q: What is meant by the "classroom exemption"?

A: This exemption (section 110) refers to performance or display of copyrighted works in a classroom setting. The language in the law reads:

> . . . *performance or display of a work by instructors or pupils in the course of face-to-face teaching activities of a nonprofit educational institution, in a classroom or similar place devoted to instruction, unless, in the case of a motion picture or other audiovisual work, the performance, or the display of individual images, is given by means of a copy that was not lawfully made . . . and that the person responsible for the performance knew or had reason to believe it was not lawfully made . . . [is not an infringement].*

Q: Is a work without a copyright notice considered to be in the public domain?

A: No, not if it was published after March 1, 1989. There is a lack of awareness among educators concerning an important change for copyright notice which occurred at that time. As of March 1, 1989, placement of a copyright notice on works became optional when the United States joined the Berne Convention. Placement of notice is certainly recommended; it is very difficult to locate a copyright owner when the notice is absent. However, just because the notice is absent, we cannot assume that anything published since March 1, 1989, is in the public domain unless specifically told so. Now we assume, unless the works are specifically in the public domain or meet a few other criteria, that a work is copyrighted when it is fixed in a tangible medium. Of course, this includes postings on electronic bulletin boards, Internet messages, etc., unless told it may be reposted.

Q: May a library scan and store its reserve works into a database to reproduce copies on demand or store them on a network for students to access electronically?

A: Not in all cases. If approval is obtained, original works by instructors such as syllabi, sample tests, etc., could be scanned and stored. However, course readings could not be stored without permission, licensing, or royalty fees.

Q: May a library circulate computer software to patrons?

A: Yes. However, as of 1990, the following notice must be permanently attached to the disk or permanent packaging for the software (notice the length!):

> **Notice:** *Warning of Copyright Restrictions—The copyright law of the United States (Title 17, United States Code) governs the reproduction, distribution, adaptation, public performance, and public display of copyrighted material. Under certain conditions specified in law, nonprofit libraries are authorized to lend, lease, or rent copies of computer programs to patrons on a nonprofit basis and for nonprofit purposes. Any person who makes an unauthorized copy or adaptation of the computer program, or redistributes the loan copy, or publicly performs or displays the computer program, except as permitted by Title 17 of the United States code, may be liable for copyright infringement. This institution reserves the right to refuse to fulfill a loan request if, in its judgment, fulfillment of the request would lead to violation of the copyright law.*

This notice must be attached by means of a label in permanent fashion to the disk(s) or the box, reel, cartridge, cassette, or other container used as a permanent receptacle for the copy of the program. A font size must be used which is legible, comprehensible, and readily apparent to the user of the program.

BIBLIOGRAPHY

An act for the general revision of the copyright law, Title 17 of the United States Code, and for other purposes (PL 94553, 19 Oct. 1976), 90. *United States Statutes at Large*, pp. 2541–2602.

Association of American Publishers. (1994). *An AAP position paper on scanning.* Washington, DC: Author.

Bennett, S. (1994, November). The copyright challenge: Strengthening the public interest in the digital age. *Library Journal 119*(19), 34-37. EJ 493 395.

Brinson, J. D. (1994). *Multimedia law handbook: A practical guide for developers & publishers.* Menlo Park, CA: Ladera Press.

Bruwelheide, J. H. (1995). *The copyright primer for librarians & educators.* Chicago: American Library Association.

Bruwelheide, J. H. (1994). *Suggestions for multimedia educators. Multimedia and learning: A technology leadership network special report.* Alexandria, VA: National School Boards Association.

Jensen, M. B. (1993). Is the library without walls on a collision course with the 1976 copyright act? *Law Library Journal 85*, 619–41.

Lyman, P. (1995, January/February). Copyright and fair use in the digital age: A Q & A with Peter Lyman. *Educom Review 30*(1), 32–35. IR 529 999; EJ number pending.

Nimmer, M. B. (1978). *Nimmer on Copyright.* New York: Bender Publications.

U.S. Department of Commerce. (1994). *Intellectual property and the national information infrastructure: A preliminary draft of the report of the working group on intellectual property rights.* Washington, DC: Author.

Valauskas, E. J. (1992, August). Copyright: Know your electronic rights. *Library Journal 117*(13), 40–43. EJ 450 79.

Part Four
Leadership Profiles

Introduction

One of the annual features of the *Yearbook* has been the biographies of educational media and technology leaders. There is no formal survey or popularity contest to determine the persons for whom the biographies will be written. If there is any question about the names selected, they should be addressed to the Senior Editor, who makes the final selections.

The individuals who are featured each year are usually still active in the field. They have sometimes held offices or written important works that withstand the test of time. They have often been directly responsible for mentoring individuals who have themselves become recognized for their contributions. An attempt is made to consider leaders who reflect the diversity of people in the field who have made important impressions on the development of educational media and technology.

This year's profiles reflect two individuals whose contributions are quite different. Robert Morgan, a psychologist who saw the potential of educational technology through his early association with programmed instruction, has made a stellar professional reputation in the United States through his leadership at Florida State University. His contributions go well beyond the North American shores to many African, Latin American, and Southeast Asian countries. His biography is ably written by Robert Branson, a colleague and friend.

The other biography is for L. Paul Saettler, the historian of the field. His two books on the history of instructional and educational technology are standard resources in almost every graduate academic program in the field. As the first doctoral candidate to finish a Ph.D. under James D. Finn, he has seen the field grow and been an integral part of its diffusion. The Senior Editor considers it a privilege to be the author of the biography.

Robert Marion Morgan

Robert K. Branson
Professor
Florida State University

Robert M. Morgan is the Director of Florida State University's Learning Systems Institute and a professor in the Department of Educational Research, having joined that department as its head in 1968. He served in that role during the formative years of 1968–1974 and set the direction that was to move this previously obscure department into international prominence. Bob earned his bachelor's degree at Oklahoma State University in 1955 and his master's in 1956; both degrees were in psychology. His doctorate in experimental psychology from Ohio State University was awarded in 1958, and his dissertation on human learning was directed by Professor Delos D. Wickens.

Like his longtime friend and colleague Robert M. Gagné, Morgan was significantly influenced by the teachings of Paul M. Fitts, a professor of engineering psychology and human factors at Ohio State and Michigan. He credits Gagné for his understanding of how research can improve education.

During the period 1958–1961, when he was at the University of New Mexico, Morgan conducted classified research on nuclear weapon fail-safe mechanisms at the Sandia National Laboratory. Having combined the intellectually stimulating fields of human factors engineering and learning psychology, he co-founded a venture firm to develop research-based training materials and programmed learning texts.

By then well grounded in the nuances of the education and training business in the United States, he accepted a key position with the Educational Systems Division of Litton Industries in 1965 to design the curriculum, instructional system, and media support for the Parks Job Corps Center in California, during President Johnson's War on Poverty. Morgan's creative work at Parks led to his early promotion to head all of Litton's Educational Materials Development programs.

Due to his success in Litton's Job Corps and instructional materials development programs, he was drafted by then Associate Commissioner of Education, R. Lewis Bright, to join the U.S. Office of Education's (USOE) Bureau of Research in Washington, DC, to initiate major national programs to introduce the systems approach to public education. He credits the late Lou Bright with inspiring him to believe that it was possible to make major systemic changes in the education world. Morgan enjoyed the reputation of being a demanding, focused public servant who knew exactly how to tweak the bureaucracy for maximum effectiveness. His first national initiative was "ES'70: Educational Systems for the Seventies."

The ES'70 Initiative was a collaborative effort of the USOE and some 17 school districts across the country. Their mission was to introduce systems thinking and practices into operation in public education. Well ahead of its time in concept, ES'70 sought to provide a mechanism whereby all students would graduate from high school with criterion competencies in traditional subjects and skills to make them attractive to employers. ES'70 was the first to integrate basic skills instruction into the context of career preparation.

Unfortunately, ES'70 lacked sufficient firepower to penetrate the armor of the divided basic and vocational education communities. The country suffered a tragedy in losing ES'70 in that post-Sputnik era when true innovation was really needed. However, it provided Morgan with a wealth of experience that again proved Nietzsche's wisdom: "Those trials that do not kill us make us stronger." His newly gained strength enhanced his ability and commitment to produce his masterpiece: the redesign of Korean public education.

In 1968, at the height of visibility for the ES'70 program, Morgan accepted an offer to fulfill a longtime ambition, that of returning to the faculty at a first-rate university. Florida State University (FSU) President Stanley Marshall invited Bob to become the head of the Department of Educational Research and Testing at FSU. Few academicians in those times could have guessed that Florida State was soon to become the world leader in instructional systems. Understandably, Tallahassee, a town of 30,000 permanent residents, did not attract new residents easily. Marshall was convincing, though. He said to Morgan, "Oh, by the way, if you take the job, I will release four additional full professor lines for you to recruit anyone you want. Don't let salary be a consideration in those you select." That was apparently the last time in academic history that a major university president has made such a statement and backed it up with the necessary resources.

As a longtime personal friend and professional colleague, Morgan telephoned me in California from Washington, DC, to tell me of the offer. My reaction was similar to that of many others: Why would anyone want to move to Tallahassee? One wouldn't ever *want to*, but one *would* to join the colleagues Morgan chose.

Before arriving on the campus in the fall of 1968, Bob began communicating with colleagues he was to select for the university's new thrust. The first to accept was Leslie J. Briggs, Director of the Palo Alto office of the American Institutes for Research, a major research and development group in education and training. Next, he chose Thorwald Esbensen, the innovative Associate Superintendent from Duluth, to be a bridge to public education. In September, he called again to tell me of his next ambitious scheme, that of recruiting Bob Gagné away from Berkeley. Although I was skeptical, 30 days later Gagné committed to join the FSU faculty in the fall of 1969. Others who were at Florida State during Morgan's tenure as department head include Duncan Hansen, Bob Tennyson, Roger Kaufman, Walter Dick, an impressive list of graduate students, and the author.

During 1969, the U.S. Agency for International Development (USAID) approached Morgan to provide technical assistance to the Korean Ministry of Education. His name had been brought to the attention of USAID through the Washington networks. That contact initiated 25 years of innovative and effective work in some three dozen developing countries around the world. He credits Bascom Story of USAID with teaching him how to apply professional knowledge effectively in Third World countries.

Morgan soon went to Korea as head of an interdisciplinary team for USAID to conduct a sector analysis of education and formulate a plan to effect major improvements. The Koreans had just rejected a plan offered by a consortium of midwest educators to build more schools and hire more teachers—fruitless suggestions that the Korean government could not afford.

During that period, Morgan's team of researchers drafted the first complete national systems analysis of education. Using the talents of economists, teacher trainers, systems designers, educational administrators, cost-benefit analysts, and others, this pioneering team recommended fundamental systemic changes in Korea's educational design, development, and delivery. The most appealing and significant result of the study was that, through systems analysis and design, it enabled the Koreans to include more than one million children for whom there were then no schools. All of this was to be accomplished within the available and predictable budget.

The report was a bombshell in Korea. Virtually overnight, the Prime Minister decided to begin the work and demanded immediate action. Unfortunately, a small group of senior and influential Korean educators were enraged by the decision and protested to the Prime Minister that the United States wouldn't use such methods in its own schools and that Koreans shouldn't be their guinea pigs. However, since Korea was then a strong democracy, the Prime Minister's decision represented a consensus. He insisted that Morgan personally supervise the start-up effort and invited him to live in Korea during that critical period. With unprecedented speed and efficiency, USAID funded the project in 30 days. It was during that intense period that Morgan became friends and professional colleagues with Young Dug Lee, now Prime Minister of Korea, and then the first director of the Korean Educational Development Institute (KEDI).

Although one can find other stories of successful programs in the literature, the Korean project served to produce two ingenious outcomes: that of redesigning Korean public education, and, more importantly, that of becoming the prime instance of a generic systems model that could be applied in a variety of contexts. I will speak more directly to this latter point later.

Morgan's experience base and intellectual schemata were growing at a fast pace. He had been so close to a significant breakthrough before, only to have critical, but previously unknown, variables block complete implementation. Based on his human factors work, where order-of-magnitude improvements are routine, he knew that substantial gains were possible by applying the same principles and logic to education. The successful Korean program is distinguished by three major features: first, the total involvement of all stakeholders in program design; second, the adherence to the integrity of system design principles; and third, the building of institutional support in the form of KEDI, now considered by many scholars to be the best educational research and development organization in the world.

It took eight years to rebuild the Korean educational system. Eight years of hard, mission-driven, intelligent, and committed work by a large number of professionals. Two independent evaluations reported outstanding results: first, the system educated one million additional children (a 15 percent increase) at a cost that was well within the normal cost growth; and second, the system produced a 25 percent (an effect size of over one standard deviation based on about 225,000 students) across-the-board increase in student achievement, the largest reported increase to date in a total education system.

Following the successful completion of the Korean program, USAID and other international agencies awarded FSU's Learning Systems Institute contracts and grants totaling more than $130 million to apply the same systems principles in other developing nations. Morgan has spent the majority of his professional life to date struggling to create major educational improvements in the developing world. Nations benefiting include: Namibia, Zambia, Indonesia, Nepal, Somalia, and Zimbabwe, and others in Asia and Latin America.

Having served as the major professor to many graduate students, he has graduated more than 40 Ph.D.s from all over the world. In collaboration with the National Society for Performance and Instruction (NSPI), he co-founded the journal *Performance Improvement Quarterly*, which has been published at the Center for Educational Technology since 1989; its predecessor was the *Journal of Instructional Development* from 1982 to 1988.

His personal life was equally touched. One of his more brilliant acts was to seek the hand of Constance Claus, of Albuquerque, in 1960. After a dazzling courtship, involving many exotic trips and excursions, Bob and Connie were married in Las Vegas on January 1, 1962. Their daughter, Melayne, received her Ph.D. in economics from Yale in 1994, and their son, Steve, a systems engineer, designs computer systems for communications companies.

In the early 1960s, Bob applied his systems skills to New Mexico politics. He quickly moved to his party's short list to be nominated for governor. Having personally witnessed the New Mexico politics of the day, I believe that he had an excellent chance of election to that office. His decision not to run was unfortunate for the citizens of the state, but it did allow him to continue as president of General Programmed Teaching Corporation (GPTC). As president of GPTC, he believed that markets in California would be more receptive to new and innovative approaches to training and teaching. He moved the company to Palo Alto in 1964, then delegated U.S. operations and personally opened a branch office in Vienna, Austria. In 1965, he accepted an offer from the majority shareholders to buy GPTC.

Throughout his career, he has chosen action instead of authorship and to do critical work himself rather than to rely on reading the reports of others. As a consequence, only an intimate coterie of scholars have had access to his work. It is my hope that this brief biographical sketch will put his contribution in proper perspective.

Paul Saettler
The Historian of Educational Technology

Donald P. Ely
Professor of Education
Syracuse University

Whenever the word *history* is mentioned in the context of educational technology, the name of Paul Saettler almost always follows. If there is a historian of this relatively young field, Paul Saettler is the prime candidate. As recently as 1992, the same time as emeritus status was conferred by California State University at Sacramento, he received a special award from the Association for Educational Communications and Technology (AECT) for "a contribution to the classic literature of the field for his *Evolution of American Educational Technology.*"

This was not the first time that a Saettler book received an award. *A History of Instructional Technology* (1968) was selected as one of the outstanding publications in education that year. To understand the background of these works, it is necessary to go back to Paul's graduate study. His dissertation on the history of educational technology fulfilled the requirements for the first Ph.D. in the Department of Instructional Technology at the University of Southern California in 1953 under the legendary leader James D. Finn. (It was the only four-volume dissertation ever seen by the author of this biographical sketch.) Interest in the history of the field was not, however, a lifelong preoccupation. To fully understand Saettler's contributions to the field of education, it is necessary to know about some of his earlier (and later) experiences, as well as to review his curriculum vitae.

Born in Olney, Texas, in 1921 and spending most of his teenage years in California, Louis Paul Saettler seemed destined (at least by his own choices) to spend a professional life in endeavors related to communications media. His Ph.D. in Instructional Technology (1953) and Master's in Telecommunications (1949) at the University of Southern California were preceded by undergraduate study in psychology at California State University, Fresno, in 1946. While serving as an elementary school teacher in Santa Barbara County, he became increasingly interested in radio and became a Program Director for KRJM, Santa Maria. He returned to the classroom, this time as a secondary school teacher in Menlo Park, and shortly thereafter was employed by NBC as a newscaster and editor. This background led to a lecturer's assignment in the Department of Communication at the University of California at Los Angeles and Director of Training Material Development at Northrop Aircraft, Inc. just as he finished his Ph.D. In 1955 he began his 37-year teaching career at California State University, Sacramento.

Always in demand as a teacher, Paul Saettler taught summers and offered short-term courses at the University of Washington, New York University, Harvard University, Concordia University (Canada), and the Federal University of Rio Grande du Sul (Brazil), and served as a Senior Fulbright Scholar to Lebanon. He has taught at California State Universities at Chico, Davis, and San Francisco. International assignments have taken him to Great Britain and the Federal Republic of Germany. Of special note was his two-year assignment as Special Advisor in Educational Technology to the Brazilian Ministry of Education.

The hidden dimension of Paul Saettler's professional life is the time he spent as a radio announcer, newscaster, producer, and writer. He worked his way through undergraduate school as a radio employee. During World War II, he spent 3-1/2 years overseas in the U.S. Signal Corps, serving in the North African and Italian theaters as a radio newscaster with Armed Forces Radio Service. After the war, he was a free-lance radio scriptwriter for the major networks, specializing in radio mystery plays. One of his first published works was the *Radio Writing Handbook* (1950). As television came along, Paul was the first program director of KUSC, one of the first educational television stations in the United States. At the same time, he was news editor for NBC in Hollywood and worked closely with Chet Huntley. His deep involvement with the communications media almost captured his professional commitment, but he became increasingly interested in the field of educational technology and decided that he wanted to spend his professional life in that field.

At this point in many biographies, the author states that "The rest is history." For Paul Saettler, the rest *is* history—history of a 20th-century field that was emerging even as he was undergoing his own professional development; history of a field that was testing its wings, exploring its borders, and trying to establish professional credibility. To accomplish the professional recognition and credibility that the early pioneers so earnestly sought, a history of the field was the sine qua non for legitimacy. Paul Saettler validated the claim with his 1968 *History*. The 1990 *Evolution* book confirmed once again that the field does indeed have purpose and roots. Saettler has conducted a one-person documentation project. His histories have been acknowledged to be *the* source for authentic origins of ideas, trends, terms, and movements.

During his retirement, Paul Saettler continues to teach, consult, and write. He is currently a member of the adjunct faculty at Saybrook Institute Graduate School and Research Center, and he is writing a definitive biography of Maria Montessori based on his extensive collection of documents and notes obtained from interviews with her son, Mario. In Paul's case, retirement means working on projects in which he has strong interests.

This germane and genuine gentleman is generous with his credits to those who influenced his professional and personal life: F. Dean McClusky, an early mentor to whom the 1968 book was dedicated; James D. Finn, his doctoral advisor and dissertation chair who wrote the preface to the book; and even to this author, who has been supportive of his work over the years. He is married to Dian Saettler, who has been a coworker, travel companion, and, as a gourmet cook, a contributor to the joy of life which they both share.

BIBLIOGRAPHY

Saettler, P. (1968). *A History of Instructional Technology*. New York: McGraw-Hill.

Saettler, P. (1990). *The Evolution of American Educational Technology*. Englewood, CO: Libraries Unlimited.

Part Five
The Year in Review

Introduction

There is one less major professional association this year. After almost 25 years, the Association for the Development of Computer-based Instructional Systems (ADCIS) is no longer in business. The 20th edition of the *Yearbook* announced that the annual meeting would be held in conjunction with the Association for Educational Communications and Technology (AECT) convention in 1995. The AECT convention was held in Anaheim, California, but there was no ADCIS presence, and word of its demise permeated hallway conversations.

It is always sad to see a professional association disappear, especially during a time of increasing activity in the field. ADCIS will be missed and so will its highly respected journal, *The Journal of Computer-Based Instruction (JCBI)*. One might expect that the emergence of other organizations with purposes similar to those of ADCIS contributed to the dissolution. A look at the calendar of meetings and conferences addressing "computer-based instruction" (or some derivative of the term) would give the impression that professional education interests are still strong in this area. Many of the activities of ADCIS will, no doubt, be assumed by other organizations, and the increased number of publications that report research and development activities in educational computing will compensate, to some degree, for the absence of *JCBI*.

Other organizations and associations continue to serve special populations. The current status of these groups is reported here with 1996 conference dates, new publications, and, in most cases, current officers.

AECT
Association for Educational Communications and Technology

Established in 1923, the Association for Educational Communications and Technology is an international professional association dedicated to the improvement of instruction through the utilization of media and technology. The mission of the association is to provide leadership in educational communications and technology by linking professionals holding a common interest in the use of education technology and its application to the learning process. In the past few years, convention topics have focused on hypermedia, teleconferencing, and converging technologies, and AECT cosponsored the teleconference, "Teaching and Technology: A Critical Link," which addressed issues on the restructuring of public schools and the role of technology. AECT also honors outstanding individuals or groups making significant contributions to the field of educational communications and technology or to the association. (See the separate listing for full information on these awards.)

MEMBERSHIP

AECT members include instructional technologists; media or library specialists; university professors and researchers; industrial/business training specialists; religious educators; government media personnel; school, school district, and state department of education media program administrators and specialists; educational/training media producers; and numerous others whose professional work requires improvement of media and technology in education and training. AECT members also work in the armed forces, in public libraries, in museums, and in other information agencies of many different kinds, including those related to the emerging fields of computer technology.

MEMBERSHIP SERVICES

AECT serves as a central clearinghouse and communications center for its members. The association maintains TechCentral, a national electronic mail network and bulletin board service. Through its various committees and task forces, it compiles data and prepares recommendations to form the basis of guidelines, standards, research, and information summaries on numerous topics and problems of interest to the membership. AECT professional staff members report on government activities of concern to the membership and provide current data on laws and pending legislation relating to the educational media/technology field. AECT also maintains the ECT Foundation, through which it offers a limited number of financial grants to further the association's work. Archives are maintained at the University of Maryland.

CONFERENCES

The 1995 Annual Convention and International Computing and Instructional Technology Exposition (InCITE) was held February 8-12 in Anaheim, CA. The 1996 Convention and Exposition will be held February 14-18 in Indianapolis, IN.

PUBLICATIONS

AECT maintains an active publication program which includes *TechTrends for Leaders in Education and Training* (6/yr., free with membership); *Educational Technology Research & Development* (4/yr.); various division publications; and a number of books and videotapes, including the following recent titles: *Distance Education: A Review of the Literature* (1994); *Quality Management for Educational Technology Services* (1994); *Compressed Video: Operations and Applications, 2nd ed.* (1995); *Getting Started in Instructional Technology Research* (1995); *Degree Curricula in Educational Communications and Technology, 5th ed.* (1995); *Adoptable Copyright Policy: Copyright Policy and Manuals Designed for Adoption by Schools, Colleges and Universities* (1992); *A Copyright Primer, 2nd ed.* (1994); *Library Copyright Guide* (1992); *Appraising Audiovisual Media: A Guide for Attorneys, Trust Officers, Insurance Professionals, and Archivists in Appraising Films, Video, Photographs, Recordings, and Other Audiovisual Assets* (1993); *The 1992-93 Educational Software Preview Guide* (1992); *Educational Technology: A Review of the Research* (1992); *Evaluating Computer Integration in the Elementary School: A Step by Step Guide* (1990); *Focus on Reform: State Initiatives in Educational Technology* (1992); *Graduate Curricula in Educational Communications and Technology: A Descriptive Directory, 4th ed.* (1992); *Videographing the Pictorial Sequence: AECT Presidents' Library Vol. II* (1991); *Teaching and Learning through Technology, the Star Schools Videotape* (one VHS tape, 1989); *TQM for Media Managers* (1994); *Instructional Technology: The Definition and Domains of the Field* (1994).

AFFILIATED ORGANIZATIONS

Because of similarity of interests, a number of organizations have chosen to affiliate with AECT. These include the Association for MultiImage (AMI); Association for Special Education Technology (ASET); Community College Association for Instruction and Technology (CCAIT); Consortium of University Film Centers (CUFC); Federal Educational Technology Association (FETA); Health Science Communications Association (HeSCA); International Association for Learning Laboratories (IALL); International Visual Literacy Association (IVLA); Minorities in Media (MIMS); National Association of Regional Media Centers (NARMC); National Instructional Television Fixed Service Association (NIA/ITFS); New England Educational Media Association; Northwest College and University Council for the Management of Educational Technology; Southeastern Regional Media Leadership Council (SRMLC); and State University of New York Educational Communications Center.

Two additional organizations are also related to the Association for Educational Communications and Technology: the AECT Archives and the AECT ECT Foundation.

AECT DIVISIONS

AECT has 11 divisions: Division of Educational Media Management (DEMM); Division of Interactive Systems and Computers (DISC); Division of Instructional Development (DID); Division of Learning and Performance Environments (DLPE); Division of School Media Specialists (DSMS); Division of Telecommunications (DOT); Industrial Training and Education Division (ITED); International Division (INTL); Media Design and Production Division (MDPD); Research and Theory Division (RTD); Systemic Change in Education (CHANGE).

CURRENT OFFICERS/MEMBERS OF THE AECT BOARD OF DIRECTORS

Stanley D. Zenor, Executive Director; Lynn Milet, President; Bill Burns, President-Elect; David Graf, Secretary-Treasurer; and David Tiedemann, Mary Adrion, Roberts Braden, Joaquin Holloway, Robin Taylor-Roth, Charles White, Victoria DeFields, and Joan Wallin, Board Members.

Further information is available from AECT, 1025 Vermont Avenue NW, Suite 820, Washington, DC 20005. (202) 347-7834. Fax (202) 347-7839.

AMTEC
Association for Media and Technology in Education in Canada
L'Association des Media et de la Technologie en Education au Canada

PURPOSE

Canada's national association for educational media and technology professionals, AMTEC is a forum concerned with the impact of media and technology on teaching, learning, and society. As an organization, AMTEC provides national leadership through annual conferences, publications, workshops, media festival awards, ongoing reaction to media and technology issues at the international, national, provincial, and local levels, and linkages with other organizations with similar interests.

MEMBERSHIP

AMTEC's membership is geographically dispersed and professionally diversified. Membership stretches from St. John's, Newfoundland, to Victoria, British Columbia, and from Inuvik, Northwest Territories, to Niagara Falls, Ontario. Members include teachers, consultants, broadcasters, media managers, photographers, librarians/information specialists, educational technology specialists, instructional designers/trainers, technology specialists, artists, and producers/distributors. They represent all sectors of the educational media and technology fields: elementary and secondary schools, colleges, institutes of technology, universities, provincial governments, school boards, military services, health services libraries, and private corporations.

ACTIVITIES

Workshops. AMTEC offers workshops in cooperation with other agencies and associations based on AMTEC members' needs, in addition to the in-depth workshops at the AMTEC annual conference.

Annual Conference. The AMTEC annual conference provides opportunities to meet delegates from across the nation and to attend sessions on the latest issues and developments in such areas as copyright law, instructional design, distance education, library standards, media production, broadcasting and educational technology, media utilization, and visual literacy. AMTEC 95 was held in May 1995, in Guelph, ON; AMTEC 96 will be held in Victoria, BC, in May 1996, and AMTEC 97 in Saskatoon, SK.

Awards. AMTEC annually recognizes outstanding individual achievement and leadership in the field through the EMPDAC (Educational Media Producers and Distributors Association of Canada) Achievement Award, the AMTEC Leadership Award, and the Telesat Educational Telecommunications Award. In addition, AMTEC acts as the correspondent for the Commonwealth Relations Trust Bursary for educational broadcasters. This annual bursary provides a three-month study tour of educational broadcasting in the United Kingdom.

Annual Media Festival. AMTEC conducts a national showcase for educational media and technology productions. Awards are presented annually at the AMTEC conference in recognition of outstanding achievement in areas such as television, radio, film, slide, and computer software.

Reaction to Issues. AMTEC provides opportunities for members to contribute to educational media and technology issues and their solutions. The association frequently communicates with other associations and levels of government to resolve issues of concern to the membership.

PUBLICATIONS

- *The Canadian Journal of Educational Communications (CJEC)*, a quarterly covering the latest in research, application, and periodical literature. It also publishes reviews on significant books and films and critiques on computer programs.

- *Media News*, a quarterly newsletter that covers the news in the field, including helpful tips, future conferences, comments on current projects, and information about AMTEC members and the AMTEC Board.

- *Membership Directory*, which expands the professional network of members.

In addition, occasional publications are produced to assist members in keeping abreast in the field. These include directories, guidelines, and monographs. AMTEC also operates a mailserv on the Internet.

CURRENT OFFICERS

The AMTEC Board of Directors includes the association's President, Allen LeBlanc; Past President, Ross Mutton; President-Elect, Gary Karlsen; Secretary/Treasurer, Lillian Carefoot; and three Directors, Genevieve Gallant, Bob Christie, and Danielle Fortosky. Additional information may be obtained from AMTEC, 3-1750 The Queensway, Suite 1318, Etobicoke, ON, Canada M9C 5H5; Attn. Ms. Lillian Carefoot, Secretary/Treasurer.

ISTE
International Society for Technology in Education

PURPOSE

The International Society for Technology in Education is a nonprofit professional society of educators. Its goals include the improvement of education through the appropriate use of computer-related technology and the fostering of active partnerships between businesses and educators involved in this field. The majority of ISTE's efforts are aimed at precollege education and teacher preparation.

MEMBERSHIP

ISTE members are teachers, administrators, computer coordinators, curriculum coordinators, teacher educators, information resource managers, and educational technological specialists. Approximately 85 percent of the 10,000-person membership is in the United States, 10 percent is in Canada, and the remainder is scattered throughout nearly 100 other countries.

ACTIVITIES

ISTE works to achieve its mission through its publication program, which includes 12 periodicals as well as a wide range of books and courseware, cosponsorship or sponsorship of a variety of conferences and workshops, and its extensive network of regional affiliates, a Private Sector Council, a distance education program, and membership in NCATE (National Council for the Accreditation of Teacher Education).

PUBLICATIONS

Periodical publications include membership periodicals: *Learning and Leading with Technology: The ISTE Journal of Educational Technology Practice and Policy* (formerly *The Computing Teacher* (8/yr.); the *Journal of Research on Computing in Education* (quarterly); and *ISTE Update: People, Events, and News in Education Technology* (newsletter, 8/yr.). Quarterly periodicals for special-interest groups include: *Logo Exchange*, for the SIG Logo; the *Journal of Computing in Teacher Education*, for the Teacher Educators SIG; *HyperNEXUS*, for the Hyper/Multi-Media SIG; the *Journal of Computer Science Education*, for the Computer Science SIG; *T.I.E. News*, for the Telecommunications SIG; and *SIGTC Connections*, for the Technology Coordinator SIG. Other periodicals include the *Microsoft Works in Education*, a quarterly for users of Microsoft Works; and *CAELL Journal* (Computer Assisted English Language Learning Journal), quarterly for teachers of English, foreign languages, and adult literacy.

ISTE also publishes a variety of books and courseware.

CONFERENCES

ISTE is the administrative house for the National Educational Computing Conference (NECC). NECC'95 was held in Baltimore in June 1995; NECC'96 will be held in Minneapolis, MN, June 9-13, 1996. ISTE also ran the fourth International Symposium on Telecommunications in Education (TelEd) on November 30-December 3, 1995, in Ft. Lauderdale, FL.

CURRENT OFFICERS

The current ISTE Board includes Peggy Kelly, President; David Brittain, President-Elect; Lajeane Thomas, Past President; Connie Stout, Secretary; Barry Pitsch, Treasurer; Dennis Bybee, Associate Executive Officer; David Moursund, Executive Officer; Sheila Cory; Terrie Gray; Terry Killion; Don Knezek; Paul O'Driscoll; Lynne Schrum; Carla Schutte; and Gwen Solomon.

For further information, contact Maia Howes, ISTE Executive Secretary, at 1787 Agate Street, Eugene, OR 97403-1923. (503) 346-2414. Fax (503) 346-5890. Internet iste@oregon. uoregon.edu.

IVLA
International Visual Literacy Association

PURPOSE

IVLA, Inc., a nonprofit international association, was established in 1968 to provide a multidisciplinary forum for the exploration, presentation, and discussion of all aspects of visual communication and their applications through visual images, visual literacy, and literacies in general. The association serves as the organizational bond for professionals from many diverse disciplines who are creating and sustaining the study of the nature of visual experiences and literacies and their cognitive and affective bases, and who are developing new means for the evaluation of learning through visual methods. It also encourages the funding of creative visual literacy projects, programs, and research, and promotes and evaluates projects intended to increase the use of visuals in education and communications.

MEMBERSHIP

IVLA members represent a diverse group of disciplines, including fine and graphic artists, photographers, researchers, scientists, filmmakers, television producers, graphic and computer-graphic designers, phototherapists, business communication professionals, school administrators, classroom teachers, visual studies theorists and practitioners, educational technologists, photojournalists, print and electronic journalists, and visual anthropologists.

MEMBER SERVICES

Members of IVLA benefit from opportunities to interact with other professionals whose ideas may be challenging or reinforcing. Such opportunities are provided by the annual conference, information exchanges, research programs, workshops, seminars, presentation opportunities as an affiliate of the Association for Educational Communications and Technology (AECT), and access to the Visual Literacy Collection located at Arizona State University.

PUBLICATIONS

IVLA publishes two periodicals: the *Journal of Visual Literacy* (2 per year) and the *Review*, a visual literacy newsletter. It also publishes an annual book of selected conference readings.

CONFERENCES

The 1995 conference was held in Chicago, IL, October 18-22. The theme was "Eyes on the Future: Converging Images, Ideas, and Instruction." The 1996 conference is scheduled to be held in Cheyenne, WY, October 2-6, 1996.

CURRENT OFFICERS

Landra Rezabek, President; Nancy Knupfer, President-Elect; Ron Sutton, Immediate Past President; Ann Marie Barry, Robert Griffin, and Rune Pettersson, Vice Presidents; Alice D. Walker, Executive Treasurer; and Beth Wiegmann, Recording Secretary.

Further information may be obtained from Alice D. Walker, Treasurer, Virginia Tech, Educational Technologies-LRC, Old Security Building, Blacksburg, VA 24061-0232. (703) 231-8992. E-mail alice.walker@vt.edu.

NSPI
National Society for Performance
and Instruction

NSPI is an international association dedicated to increasing productivity in the workplace through the application of performance and instructional technologies. Founded in 1962, the society promotes the improvement of human performance among governmental, legislative, business, corporate, and educational leaders, and through the national media.

MEMBERSHIP

The 5,500 members of NSPI are located throughout the United States, Canada, and 33 other countries. Members include performance technologists, training directors, human resource managers, instructional technologists, change agents, human factors practitioners, and organizational development consultants. They work in a variety of settings, including business, industry, universities, governmental agencies, health services, banks, and the armed forces.

SERVICES TO NSPI MEMBERS

NSPI offers its members opportunities to grow professionally and personally, to meet and know leaders in the field and learn about new things before they are published for the world at large, to make themselves known in the field, and to pick up new ideas on how to deal with their own political and technical challenges on the job. Membership benefits include subscriptions to *Performance & Instruction* and *News & Notes*; the *Annual Membership Directory*; participation in the annual conference and exposition; access to a variety of resources and individuals to help improve professional skills and marketability; a variety of insurance programs at group rates; leadership opportunities through participation in special projects, 12 major committees, and task forces, or serving as national or chapter officers; an executive referral service; and discounts on publications, advertising, conference registration and recordings, and other society services.

CONFERENCES

Annual Conference and Expo: Atlanta, GA, March 27-31, 1995; Dallas, TX, April 15-19, 1996; Anaheim, CA, April 14-18, 1997; and Chicago, IL, March 23-28, 1998.

PUBLICATIONS

NSPI publications include *Performance & Instruction Journal* (10/yr.); *Performance Improvement Quarterly*; *News & Notes* (10/yr.); and the *Annual Membership Directory*.

CURRENT OFFICERS

William Coscarelli, President; Carol Valen, President-Elect; Mark Greene, Vice President–Chapter Development; Noel Villacorta, Vice President–Conferences; Darryl Sink, Vice President–Finance; C. J. Wallington, Vice President–Publications; Clay Carr, Vice President–Research and Development.

Annual dues: active member, $125; student, $40. Further information is available from NSPI, 1300 L Street NW, Suite 1250, Washington, DC 20005. (202) 408-7969. Fax (202) 408-7972.

SALT
Society for Applied Learning Technology

PURPOSE

The Society for Applied Learning Technology (SALT) is a nonprofit professional membership organization that was founded in 1972. Membership in the society is oriented to professionals whose work requires knowledge and communication in the field of instructional technology. The society provides members a means to enhance their knowledge and job performance by participation in society-sponsored meetings, through subscriptions to society-sponsored publications, by association with other professionals at conferences sponsored by the society, and through membership in special-interest groups and special society-sponsored initiatives and projects.

The society sponsors conferences that are educational in nature and cover a wide range of application areas, such as interactive videodisc in education and training, development of interactive instructional materials, CD-ROM applications in education and training, interactive instruction delivery, and learning technology in the health care sciences. These conferences provide attendees with an opportunity to become familiar with the latest technical information on application possibilities, on technologies, and on methodologies for implementation. In addition, they provide an opportunity for interaction with other professional and managerial individuals in the field.

The society also offers members discounts on society-sponsored journals, conference registration fees, and publications.

PUBLICATIONS

- *Journal of Interactive Instruction Development*. This established quarterly journal meets the needs of instructional systems developers and designers by providing important perspectives on emerging technologies and design technologies.

- *Journal of Medical Education Technologies*. Now in its third year of publication, this exciting journal helps keep readers abreast of developments utilizing technology-based learning systems to train health care professionals and educate students involved in the various health care disciplines.

- *Journal of Educational Technology Systems*. This quarterly publication deals with systems in which technology and education interface, and is designed to inform educators who are interested in making optimum use of technology.

- *Journal of Instruction Delivery Systems*. Published quarterly, this journal covers interactive multimedia applications. It is devoted to enhancing productivity through appropriate applications of technology in education, training, and job performance.

CONFERENCES

Conferences for 1995 were held in Kissimmee, FL, February 22-24, "Orlando Multi-media '95"; Arlington, VA, February 22-24, "Interactive Multimedia '95." Conferences in 1996 will be held in Kissimmee, FL, August 23-25, "Orlando Multimedia '96"; Arlington, VA, "Interactive Multimedia '96."

CURRENT OFFICERS

Dr. Nathaniel Macon, Chairman; Raymond G. Fox, President; Dr. Stanley Winkler, Vice President; and Dr. Carl R. Vest, Secretary/Treasurer.

Further information is available from the Society for Applied Learning Technology, 50 Culpeper Street, Warrenton, VA 22186. (540) 347-0055. Fax (540) 349-3169.

Part Six
Organizations and Associations in North America

Introduction

This part of *EMTY* includes annotated entries for several hundred associations and organizations headquartered in North America whose interests are in some manner significant to the fields of instructional technology/educational media, library and information science, communication, computer technology, training/management in business/industry, publishing, and others. They are organized into two general geographic areas: the United States and Canada. The section on the United States includes a classified list with headings designed to be useful in finding subject leads to the alphabetical list. Readers who know only the acronym for an association or organization of interest may refer to the index to obtain its full name.

It was not deemed necessary to include a classified list for Canada because the overall number of organizations listed is considerably smaller than for the United States.

All organizations listed in part 6 were sent a copy of the entry describing the organization that appeared in *EMTY 1994*. Respondents were invited to update and edit these entries, with the proviso that, if no response was received, the entry would be omitted from *EMTY 1995-96*. However, information on organizations from which a response was received for the 1994 edition are included in this list with an asterisk to indicate that the information is a year old. Organizations for which no response has been received since before 1993 have been omitted. Any organization that has had a name change since the 1993 edition is listed under the new name; a note referring the user to the new name appears under the former name. If information was received that an organization had ceased operations, a note to this effect appears under the organization name in the alphabetical listing.

The reader is reminded that changes in communications and media are frequent and extensive and that the information in this directory is as accurate as possible at the time of publication.

United States

Adult, Continuing, Distance Education
(ALA) Reference and Adult Services Division
(RASD)
(ALA Round Table) Continuing Library
Education Network and Exchange
(CLENE)
Association for Continuing Higher Educa-
tion (ACHE)
Association for Educational Communica-
tions and Technology (AECT)
ERIC Clearinghouse on Adult, Career, and
Vocational Education (CE)
National Education Telecommunications
Organization & Education Satellite
Company (NETO/EDSAT)
National University Continuing Education
Association (NUCEA)
Network for Continuing Medical Education
(NCME)
Superintendent of Documents

**Audio (Records, Audiocassettes and Tapes,
Telephone, Radio); Listening**
American Women in Radio and Television
(AWRT)
Clearinghouse on Development Communication
Corporation for Public Broadcasting (CPB)
Federal Communications Commission (FCC)
Recording for the Blind
Recording Industry Association of America,
Inc. (RIAA)

Audiovisual (General)
Association for Educational Communica-
tions and Technology (AECT)
(AECT) Division of Educational Media
Management (DEMM)
(AECT) Division of School Media Specialists
(DSMS)
Association of AudioVisual Technicians
(AAVT)
HOPE Reports
National Audiovisual Center

Censorship
Freedom of Information Center (FOI)

Children-, Youth-Related Organizations
(ALA) Association for Library Service to
Children (ALSC)
(ALA) Young Adult Library Services Asso-
ciation (YALSA)
Association for Childhood Education Inter-
national (ACEI)
Children's Television International, Inc.
Close Up Foundation
Council for Exceptional Children (CEC)
(CEC) Technology and Media Division
(TAM)
ERIC Clearinghouse on Elementary and
Early Childhood Education (PS)
ERIC Clearinghouse on Disabilities and
Gifted Education (EC)
National Association for the Education of
Young Children (NAEYC)
National PTA

Communication
Clearinghouse on Development Communication
ERIC Clearinghouse on Information &
Technology (IR)
ERIC Clearinghouse on Languages and
Linguistics (FL)
ERIC Clearinghouse on Reading, English, and
Communication (CS)
Freedom of Information Center (FOI)
International Association of Business Com-
municators (IABC)
National Council of the Churches of Christ—
Communication Unit
Speech Communication Association (SCA)

Community Resources
Teachers and Writers Collaborative (T&W)

**Computers, Computer Software, Computer
Hardware**
(AECT) Division of Interactive Systems
and Computers (DISC)
International Society for Technology in Educa-
tion (ISTE) (formerly International
Council for Computers in Education)

MECC (Minnesota Educational Computing Corporation)
OCLC (Online Computer Library Center)
Society for Computer Simulation (SCS)
SOFTSWAP
SpecialNet

Copyright
Copyright Clearance Center (CCC)
International Copyright Information Center (INCINC)

Databases; Networks
ERIC (Educational Resources Information Center) (See separate entries for the various clearinghouses.)
ERIC Document Reproduction Service (EDRS)
ERIC Processing and Reference Facility
SpecialNet

Education (General)
American Association of School Administrators (AASA)
American Montessori Society (AMS)
American Society of Educators (ASE)
Association for Childhood Education International (ACEI)
(AECT) Minorities in Media (MIM)
Association for Experiential Education (AEE)
Center for Instructional Research and Curriculum Evaluation
Council for Basic Education
Education Development Center, Inc.
ERIC Clearinghouse on Counseling and Student Services (CG)
ERIC Clearinghouse on Educational Management (EA)
ERIC Clearinghouse on Elementary and Early Childhood Education (PS)
ERIC Clearinghouse on Disabilities and Gifted Education (EC)
ERIC Clearinghouse on Rural Education and Small Schools (RC)
ERIC Clearinghouse for Science, Mathematics, and Environmental Education (SE)

ERIC Clearinghouse for Social Studies/Social Science Education (ERIC/ChESS)
ERIC Clearinghouse on Teaching and Teacher Education (SP)
ERIC Clearinghouse on Urban Education (UD)
National Association of Secondary School Principals (NASSP)
National Association of State Boards of Education (NASBE)
National Association of State Educational Media Professionals (NASTEMP)
National Association of State Textbook Administrators (NASTA)
National Center for Appropriate Technology (NCAT)
National Clearinghouse for Bilingual Education
National Council for Accreditation of Teacher Education (NCATE)
National Endowment for the Humanities (NEH)
National Science Foundation (NSF)
National Science Teachers Association (NSTA)

Education (Higher)
American Association of Community Colleges (AACC)
American Association of State Colleges and Universities
Association for Continuing Higher Education (ACHE)
Association of Teacher Educators (ATE)
(AECT) Community College Association for Instruction and Technology (CCAIT)
(AECT) Northwest College and University Council for the Management of Educational Technology
Association for Library and Information Science Education (ALISE)
Consortium of College and University Media Centers
ERIC Clearinghouse for Community Colleges (JC)
ERIC Clearinghouse on Higher Education (HE)

Equipment (Manufacturing, Maintenance, Testing, Operating)

(ALA) Library and Information Technology Association (LITA)

American National Standards Institute (ANSI)

Association of AudioVisual Technicians (AAVT)

EPIE Institute

ERIC Clearinghouse on Assessment and Evaluation (TM)

ITA (formerly International Tape/Disc Association [ITA])

National School Supply and Equipment Association (NSSEA)

Society of Cable Television Engineers (SCTE)

ERIC-Related

ACCESS ERIC

Adjunct ERIC Clearinghouse for Art Education (ADJ/AR)

Adjunct ERIC Clearinghouse for ESL Literacy Education (ADJ/LE)

Adjunct ERIC Clearinghouse for Law Related Education (ADJ/LR)

Adjunct ERIC Clearinghouse for the Test Collection (ADJ/TC)

Adjunct ERIC Clearinghouse for United States-Japan Studies (ADJ/JS)

Adjunct ERIC Clearinghouse on Chapter 1 (Compensatory Education) (ADJ/Chapter 1)

Adjunct ERIC Clearinghouse on Clinical Schools (ADJ/CL)

Adjunct ERIC Clearinghouse on Consumer Education (ADJ/CN)

ERIC (Educational Resources Information Center)

ERIC Clearinghouse on Adult, Career, and Vocational Education (CE)

ERIC Clearinghouse on Assessment and Evaluation (TM)

ERIC Clearinghouse for Community Colleges (JC)

ERIC Clearinghouse on Counseling and Student Services (CG)

ERIC Clearinghouse on Educational Management (EA)

ERIC Clearinghouse on Elementary and Early Childhood Education (PS)

ERIC Clearinghouse on Disabilities and Gifted Education (EC)

ERIC Clearinghouse on Higher Education (HE)

ERIC Clearinghouse on Information & Technology (IR)

ERIC Clearinghouse on Languages and Linguistics (FL)

ERIC Clearinghouse on Reading, English, and Communication Skills (CS)

ERIC Clearinghouse on Rural Education and Small Schools (RC)

ERIC Clearinghouse for Science, Mathematics, and Environmental Education (SE)

ERIC Clearinghouse for Social Studies/Social Science Education (SO)

ERIC Clearinghouse on Teaching and Teacher Education (SP)

ERIC Clearinghouse on Urban Education (UD)

ERIC Document Reproduction Service (EDRS)

ERIC Processing and Reference Facility

Films—Educational/Instructional/ Documentary

Anthropology Film Center (AFC)

Association of Independent Video and Filmmakers/Foundation for Independent Video and Film (AIVF/FIVF)

Children's Television International, Inc.

CINE Information

Council on International Non-theatrical Events

Film Advisory Board (FAB)

Film Arts Foundation (FAF)

Film/Video Arts, Inc.

National Aeronautics and Space Administration (NASA)

National Alliance for Media Arts and Culture (NAMAC)

National Audiovisual Center (NAC)

National Film Board of Canada (NFBC)

National Information Center for Educational Media (NICEM)

Pacific Film Archive (PFA)

PCR: Films and Video in the Behavioral Sciences

University Film and Video Association

Films—Theatrical (Film Study, Criticism, Production)

Academy of Motion Picture Arts and Sciences (AMPAS)

American Society of Cinematographers

Film Advisory Board (FAB)

Film Arts Foundation (FAF)

Hollywood Film Archive

National Film Information Service (offered by AMPAS)

The New York Festivals (formerly International Film and TV Festival of New York)

Films—Training

(AECT) Industrial Training and Education Division (ITED)

Association of Independent Video and Film-makers/Foundation for Independent Video and Film (AIVF/FIVF)

Council on International Non-theatrical Events

Great Plains National ITV Library (GPN)

National Audiovisual Center (NAC)

National Film Board of Canada (NFBC)

Training Media Association

Futures

Institute for the Future (IFTF)

Office of Technology Assessment (OTA)

World Future Society (WFS)

Games, Toys, Drama, Play, Simulation, Puppetry

Puppeteers of America

Society for Computer Simulation (SCS)

Graphics

International Graphic Arts Education Association (IGAEA)

Health-Related Organizations

American Foundation for the Blind (AFB)

Health Science Communications Association (HeSCA)

Lister Hill National Center for Biomedical Communications of the National Library of Medicine

Medical Library Association (MLA)

National Association for Visually Handicapped (NAVH)

Network for Continuing Medical Education (NCME)

Information Science

International Information Management Congress (IMC)

Instructional Technology/Design/ Development

Agency for Instructional Technology (AIT)

Association for Educational Communications and Technology (AECT)

(AECT) Community College Association for Instruction and Technology (CCAIT)

(AECT) Division of Educational Media Management (DEMM)

(AECT) Division of Instructional Development (DID)

National Society for Performance and Instruction (NSPI)

Office of Technology Assessment (OTA)

Professors of Instructional Design and Technology (PIDT)

Society for Applied Learning Technology (SALT)

International Education

(AECT) International Division (INTL)

(AECT) International Visual Literacy Association, Inc. (IVLA)

East-West Center

Program of Cultural Studies (East-West Center)

Libraries—Academic, Research

American Library Association (ALA)

(ALA) Association of College and Research Libraries (ACRL)

ERIC Clearinghouse on Information & Technology (IR)

Libraries—Public

American Library Association (ALA)

(ALA) Association for Library Service to Children (ALSC)

(ALA) Audiovisual Committee (of the Public Library Association)

(ALA) Library Administration and Management Association (LAMA)

(ALA) Library and Information Technology Association (LITA)

(ALA) Public Library Association (PLA)

(ALA) Reference and Adult Services Division (RASD)

(ALA) Technology in Public Libraries Committee (of the Public Libraries Association)

(ALA) Young Adult Library Services Association (YALSA)

ERIC Clearinghouse on Information & Technology (IR)

Libraries—Special

American Library Association (ALA)

(ALA) Association for Library Service to Children (ALSC)

(ALA) Association of Specialized and Cooperative Library Agencies (ASCLA)

ERIC Clearinghouse on Information & Technology (IR)

Medical Library Association (MLA)

Special Libraries Association (SLA)

Theater Library Association

Libraries and Media Centers—General, School

American Library Association (ALA)

(ALA) American Association of School Librarians (AASL)

(ALA) American Library Trustee Association (ALTA)

(ALA) Association for Library Collections and Technical Services (ALCTS)

(ALA) Association for Library Service to Children (ALSC)

(ALA Round Table) Continuing Library Education Network and Exchange (CLENE)

Association for Educational Communications and Technology (AECT)

(AECT) Division of School Media Specialists (DSMS)

(AECT) National Association of Regional Media Centers (NARMC)

Catholic Library Association (CLA)

Consortium of College and University Media Centers

Council of National Library and Information Associations

ERIC Clearinghouse on Information & Technology (IR)

International Association of School Librarianship (IASL)

Library of Congress

National Alliance for Media Arts and Culture (NAMAC)

National Commission on Libraries and Information Science (NCLIS)

National Council of Teachers of English (NCTE), Commission on Media

On-Line Audiovisual Catalogers (OLAC)

Southeastern Regional Media Leadership Council (SRMLC)

Microforms; Micrographics

See ERIC-related entries.

Museums; Archives

(AECT) Archives

Association of Systematics Collections

George Eastman House (formerly International Museum of Photography at George Eastman House)

Hollywood Film Archive

Museum Computer Network, Inc. (MCN)

Museum of Modern Art

National Gallery of Art (NGA)

National Public Broadcasting Archives (NPBA)

Pacific Film Archive (PFA)

Smithsonian Institution

Photography

George Eastman House (formerly International Museum of Photography at George Eastman House)

International Center of Photography (ICP)

National Press Photographers Association, Inc. (NPPA)

Photographic Society of America (PSA)

Society for Imaging Science and Technology (IS&T)

Society for Photographic Education (SPE)
Society of Photo Technologists (SPT)

Print—Books
American Library Association (ALA)
Association for Educational Communications and Technology (AECT)
Smithsonian Institution

Production (Media)
American Society of Cinematographers (ASC)
Association for Educational Communications and Technology (AECT)
(AECT) Media Design and Production Division (MDPD)
Association of Independent Video and Film-makers/Foundation for Independent Video and Film (AIVF/FIVF)
Film Arts Foundation (FAF)

Publishing
Magazine Publishers of America (MPA)
National Association of State Textbook Administrators (NASTA)

Religious Education
Catholic Library Association (CLA)
National Religious Broadcasters (NRB)

Research
American Educational Research Association (AERA)
Appalachia Educational Laboratory, Inc. (AEL)
(AECT) ECT Foundation
(AECT) Research and Theory Division (RTD)
Center for Advanced Visual Studies (CAVS)
Center for Technology in Education (CTE)
Center for Instructional Research and Curriculum Evaluation
Clearinghouse on Development Communication
Council for Educational Development and Research (CEDaR)
Education Development Center, Inc.
ERIC Clearinghouses. See ERIC-related entries.

Far West Laboratory for Educational Research and Development (FWL)
HOPE Reports
Institute for Development of Educational Activities, Inc. (IDEA)
Institute for Research on Teaching
Mid-continent Regional Educational Laboratory (McREL)
National Center for Improving Science Education
National Center for Research in Mathematical Sciences Education
National Center for Science Teaching and Learning
National Technology Center (NTC)
The NETWORK
North Central Regional Educational Laboratory (NCREL)
Northwest Regional Educational Laboratory (NWREL)
Office of Technology Assessment (OTA)
Pacific Regional Educational Laboratory (PREL)
Regional Laboratory for Educational Improvement of the Northeast and Islands
Research for Better Schools, Inc.
SouthEastern Regional Vision for Education (SERVE)
Southwest Educational Development Laboratory (SEDL)

Selection, Collections, Processing (Materials)
National Information Center for Educational Media (NICEM)

Special Education
American Foundation for the Blind (AFB)
(CEC) Council for Exceptional Children, Technology and Media Division (TAM)
Council for Exceptional Children (CEC)
ERIC Clearinghouse on Disabilities and Gifted Education (EC)
National Association for Visually Handicapped (NAVH)
National Center to Improve Practice (NCIP)
National Technology Center (NTC)

Training

American Management Association (AMA)

American Society for Training and Development (ASTD)

Association for Educational Communications and Technology (AECT)

(AECT) Federal Educational Technology Association (FETA)

(AECT) Industrial Training and Education Division (ITED)

ERIC Clearinghouse on Adult, Career, and Vocational Education (CE)

National Society for Performance and Instruction (NSPI)

Training Media Association

Video (Cassette, Broadcast, Cable, Satellite, Videodisc, Videotex)

Agency for Instructional Technology (AIT)

American Women in Radio and Television (AWRT)

Association for Educational Communications and Technology (AECT)

(AECT) Division of Telecommunications (DOT)

(AECT) National ITFS Association (NIA/ITFS)

Association of Independent Video and Filmmakers/Foundation for Independent Video and Film (AIVF/FIVF)

Cable in the Classroom

Central Educational Network (CEN)

Children's Television International, Inc.

Close Up Foundation

Community College Satellite Network

Corporation for Public Broadcasting (CPB)

Federal Communications Commission (FCC)

Great Plains National ITV Library (GPN)

International Telecommunications Satellite Organization (INTELSAT)

International Teleconferencing Association (ITCA)

International Television Association (ITVA)

ITA (formerly International Tape/Disc Association [ITA])

National Aeronautics and Space Administration (NASA)

National Association of Broadcasters (NAB)

National Cable Television Institute (NCTI)

National Education Telecommunications Organization & Education Satellite Company (NETO/EDSAT)

National Federation of Community Broadcasters (NFCB)

National Telemedia Council, Inc. (NTC)

PBS Adult Learning Service (ALS)

PBS ENCORE

PBS VIDEO

Public Broadcasting Service (PBS)

Society of Cable Television Engineers (SCTE)

Society of Motion Picture and Television Engineers (SMPTE)

University Film and Video Association (UFVA)

ALPHABETICAL LIST

Academy of Motion Picture Arts and Sciences (AMPAS). 8949 Wilshire Blvd., Beverly Hills, CA 90211. (310) 247-3000. Fax (310) 859-9351. Bruce Davis, Exec. Dir. An honorary organization composed of outstanding individuals in all phases of motion pictures. Seeks to advance the arts and sciences of motion picture technology and artistry. Presents annual film awards; offers artist-in-residence programs; operates reference library and National Film Information Service. *Membership*: 5,300. *Publications: Annual Index to Motion Picture Credits*; *Academy Players Directory*.

*Agency for Instructional Technology (AIT). Box A, Bloomington, IN 47402-0120. (812) 339-2203. Fax (812) 333-4218. Michael F. Sullivan, Exec. Dir., Mardell Raney, Editor-in-Chief. AIT is a nonprofit U.S.-Canadian organization established in 1962 to strengthen education through technology. The Agency provides leadership and service through the development, acquisition, and distribution of technology-based instructional materials. AIT pioneered the consortium process to develop instructional series that meet learners' needs. It has cooperatively produced more than 32 series since 1970. Today, major funding comes from state and provincial departments of education, federal and private institutions, corporate sponsors, and other partners. *Publications: TECHNOS: Quarterly for Education and Technology* is the journal of the Agency for Instructional Technology. It is a forum for the discussion of ideas about the use of technology in education, with a focus on reform. A think piece for decision makers, *TECHNOS Quarterly* focuses on the policy and pedagogical implications of the electronic revolution. ISSN 1060-5649. $20/yr. (four issues). AIT also publishes two product catalogs, one for audiovisual and one for broadcast customers. Materials include video programming, interactive videodiscs, computer software, and supporting print. Its series are broadcast on six continents, reaching nearly 34 million students in North American classrooms each year. Catalogs are available free on request.

American Association of Community Colleges (AACC). One Dupont Cir. NW, Suite 410, Washington, DC 20036. (202) 728-0200. Fax (202) 833-2467. David Pierce, Pres. AACC serves the nation's 1,211 community, technical, and junior colleges through advocacy, professional development, publications, and national networking. The annual convention draws more than 4,000 mid- and top-level administrators of two-year colleges. Staff and presidents offer expertise in all areas of education. Sixteen councils and six commissions address all areas of education. AACC also operates the Community College Satellite Network, providing programming and assistance to colleges. *Membership:* 1,110 institutional, 16 international, 3 foundation, 65 corporate, 75 individual, and 80 educational associate members. *Dues:* Vary for each category. *Meetings:* Annual Convention, April 22-25, 1995, Minneapolis, MN, "New Thinking for a New Century." *Publications: Community College Journal* (bi-mo.); *Community College Times* (bi-weekly newspaper); *College Times*; Community College Press (books and monographs).

*(AACC) Community College Satellite Network (CCSN). One Dupont Cir. NW, Suite 410, Washington, DC 20036. (202) 728-0200. Fax (202) 833-2467. Monica W. Pilkey, Dir. An affiliate of AACC, CCSN provides leadership and facilitates distance education, teleconferencing, and satellite training to the nation's community colleges. CCSN offers discounted teleconferences, free program resources, and general informational assistance in telecommunications. It also coordinates community college satellite downlinks nationally for teleconference users and producers. CCSN meets with its members at various industry trade shows and is very active in the AACC annual convention held each spring. *Membership:* 170 educational institutions. *Dues:* Vary by enrollment numbers. *Publications: Schedule of Programming,* 2/yr., contains listings of live and taped teleconferences for training and staff development; several other publications (free catalog available).

*American Association of State Colleges and Universities (AASCU). One Dupont Cir. NW, Suite 700, Washington, DC 20036-1192. (202) 293-7070. Fax (202) 296-5819. James B. Appleberry, Pres. Membership is open to regionally accredited institutions of higher education, and those in the process of securing accreditation, that offer programs leading to the degree of bachelor, master, or doctor, and that are wholly or partially state-supported and state-controlled. Organized and operated exclusively for educational, scientific, and literary purposes, its particular purposes are to improve higher education within its member institutions through cooperative planning, studies, and research on common educational problems and the development of a more unified program of action among its members; and to provide other needed and worthwhile educational services to the colleges and universities it may represent. *Membership:* 375 institutions (university), 28 system, and 7 associate members. *Dues:* Based on current student enrollment at institution. *Publications: MEMO: To the President; The Center Associate; Office of Federal Program Reports; Office of Federal Program Deadlines.* (Catalogs of books and other publications available upon request.)

*American Educational Research Association (AERA). 1230 17th St. NW, Washington, DC 20036. (202) 223-9485. Fax (202) 775-1824. William J. Russell, Exec. Dir. AERA is an international professional organization with the primary goal of advancing educational research and its practical application. Its members include educators; administrators; directors of research, testing, or evaluation in federal, state, and local agencies; counselors; evaluators; graduate students; and behavioral scientists. The broad range of disciplines represented includes education, psychology. statistics, sociology, history, economics, philosophy, anthropology, and political science. *Membership:* 20,000. *Dues:* Vary by category—voting, active, student, and international affiliate. *Meetings:* 1994 Annual Convention, April 4-8, New Orleans, LA; 1995 Convention, April 17-21, San Francisco, CA. *Publications: Educational Researcher; American Educational Research Journal; Journal of Educational Statistics; Educational Evaluation and Policy Analysis; Review of Research in Education; Review of Educational Research.*

*American Foundation for the Blind (AFB). 15 West 16th St., New York, NY 10011. (212) 620-2000; (800) AFB-LINE. Carl R. Augusto, Pres. and Exec. Dir.; Liz Greco, Dir. of Communications. AFB is a leading national resource for people who are blind or visually impaired, the organizations that serve them, and the general public. A nonprofit organization founded in 1921 and recognized as Helen Keller's cause in the United States, AFB has as its mission to enable persons who are blind or visually impaired to achieve equality of access and opportunity that will ensure freedom of choice in their lives. AFB is headquartered in New York City with regional centers in Chicago, Dallas, San Francisco, and Washington, DC. *Meeting:* The Josephine L. Taylor Leadership Institute, March 1994, Washington, DC, "The Future of Uniquely Designed Services (Education, Rehabilitation, etc.) for People Who Are Blind or Visually Impaired." *Publications: AFBnews; Journal of Visual Impairment & Blindness.*

*American Library Association (ALA). 50 E. Huron St., Chicago, IL 60611. (312) 944-6780. Fax (312) 440-9374. Peggy Sullivan, Exec. Dir. The ALA is the oldest and largest national library association. Its 55,000 members represent all types of libraries—state, public, school, and academic, as well as special libraries serving persons in government, commerce, the armed services, hospitals, prisons, and other institutions. Chief advocate of achievement and maintenance of high-quality library information services through protection of the right to read, educating librarians, improving services, and making information widely accessible. *Membership:* 55,000. *Dues:* Basic dues $38 first year, $75 renewing members. *Meetings:* 1994: Midwinter Meeting, February 5-10, Los Angeles; Annual Conference, June 23-30, 1994, Miami. Theme for both meetings, "Customer Service, the Heart of the Library." 1995: Midwinter Meeting, January 20-26, Cincinnati; Annual Conference, June 22-29, Chicago. *Publications: American Libraries*; *Booklist*; *Choice*; *Book Links*.

(ALA) American Association of School Librarians (AASL). 50 E. Huron St., Chicago, IL 60611. (312) 280-4386. Fax (312) 664-7459. Ann Carlson Weeks, Exec. Dir. Interested in the general improvement and extension of school library media services for children and youth. Activities and projects of the association are divided among 55 committees and 3 sections. *Membership*: 7,690. *Dues:* Membership in ALA (1st yr., $38; 2d yr., $57; 3d and subsequent yrs., $75) plus $40; retired memberships and student membership rates available. *Meetings*: National Conference, April 1-6, 1997, Portland, OR. *Publications*: *School Library Media Quarterly* (journal, q.); *Hotline Connections* (newsletter, 4/yr.).

*(ALA) American Library Trustee Association (ALTA). 50 E. Huron St., Chicago, IL 60611. (312) 280-2160. Fax (312) 280-3257. Susan Roman, Exec. Dir. Interested in the development of effective library service for people in all types of communities and libraries. Members, as policymakers, are concerned with organizational patterns of service, the development of competent personnel, the provision of adequate financing, the passage of suitable legislation and the encouragement of citizen support for libraries. *Membership:* 1,710. *Dues:* $40 plus membership in ALA. *Publications: ALTA Newsletter*; professional monographs and pamphlets.

(ALA) Association for Library Collections and Technical Services (ALCTS). 50 E. Huron St., Chicago, IL 60611. (312) 944-6780. Karen Muller, Exec. Dir; Robert P. Holley, Pres., July 1994-June 1995. Dedicated to acquisition, identification, cataloging, classification, and preservation of library materials, the development and coordination of the country's library resources, and aspects of selection and evaluation involved in acquiring and developing library materials and resources. Sections include Acquisitions, Cataloging and Classification, Collection Management and Development, Preservation and Reformatting, and Serials. *Membership:* 5,946. *Dues:* $45 plus membership in ALA. *Meetings:* Annual conference and midwinter meeting with ALA. *Publications: Library Resources & Technical Services* (q.); *ALCTS Newsletter* (6/yr.); *ALCTS Network News (AV 2)*, electronic newsletter issued irregularly.

(ALA) Association for Library Service to Children (ALSC). 50 E. Huron St., Chicago, IL 60611. (312) 280-2163. (800) 545-2433. Fax (312) 280-3257. Susan Roman, Exec. Dir. Interested in the improvement and extension of library services for children in all types of libraries, evaluation and selection of book and nonbook library materials, and improvement of techniques of library services for children from preschool through the eighth grade or junior high school age. Annual conference and midwinter meeting with the ALA. Committee membership open to ALSC members. *Membership:* 3,600. *Dues:* $35 plus membership in ALA. *Meetings:* ALA Midwinter Meeting, February 3-9, 1995, Philadelphia, PA; ALA Annual Conference June 22-29, 1995, Chicago, IL. *Publications: Journal of Youth Services in Libraries* (q.); *ALSC Newsletter* (q.).

(ALA) Association of College and Research Libraries (ACRL). 50 E. Huron St., Chicago, IL 60611-2795. (312) 280-3248. Fax (312) 280-2520. E-mail Althea. Jenkins@ala.org. Althea H. Jenkins, Exec. Dir. Represents academic librarians and is dedicated to enhancing the ability of academic library and information professionals to serve the information needs of the higher education community in research, teaching, and learning. Has available library standards for colleges, universities, and two-year institutions. Publishes statistics on academic libraries. Committees include Academic Library Statistics, Academic Status, Colleagues Committee, Copyright, Government Relations, Image Enhancement, Intellectual Freedom, International Relations, Media Resources, Professional Education, Professional Liaison, Publications, Social and Ethnic Diversity, Research, and Standards and Accreditation. Free list of materials available. The association administers 13 different awards, most of which are given annually. *Membership:* 10,000. *Dues:* $35 (in addition to ALA membership). *Meetings:* 1995 National Conference, March 24-April 1, Pittsburgh, "Continuity and Transformation: The Promise of Confluence." *Publications: College & Research Libraries* (6/yr.); *College & Research Libraries News* (11/yr.); *Rare Books and Manuscripts Librarianship* (2/yr.); 11 section newsletters; *Choice* (11/yr.); *CLIP Notes* (current issues are #17-20). Recent titles include: *Discovering Librarians: Profiles of a Profession*; *Academic Status: Statements and Resources*; *ACRL University Library Statistics, 1992-93*; *Guide to Searching the Bibliographic Utilities for Conference Proceedings*.

(ALA) Association of Specialized and Cooperative Library Agencies (ASCLA). 50 E. Huron St., Chicago, IL 60611. (800) 545-2433, ext. 4399. Fax (312) 944-8085. Cathleen Bourdon, Exec. Dir. Represents state library agencies, multitype library cooperatives, and libraries serving special clienteles to promote the development of coordinated library services with equal access to information and material for all persons. The activities and programs of the association are carried out by 21 committees, 3 sections, and various discussion groups. Write for free checklist of materials. *Membership:* 1,300. *Dues:* (in addition to ALA membership) $30 for personal members, $50 for organizations, $500 for state library agencies. *Meetings:* Midwinter: 1995, Philadelphia, PA, February 3-9; 1996, San Antonio, TX, January 19-25; 1997, Washington, DC, February 14-20. Annual Conferences: 1995, Chicago, IL, June 22-29; 1996, Orlando, FL, June 20-27; 1997, San Francisco, CA, June 26-July 3. *Publications: Interface* (q.). Recent titles include: *The Americans with Disabilities Act: Its Impact on Libraries*; *Deafness: An Annotated Bibliography and Guide to Basic Materials*; *Library Standards for Adult Correctional Institutions 1992*.

(ALA) Library Administration and Management Association (LAMA). 50 E. Huron St., Chicago, IL 60611. (312) 280-5038. Karen Muller, Exec. Dir.; Donald E. Riggs. Pres., July 1994-June 1995. Provides an organizational framework for encouraging the study of administrative theory, for improving the practice of administration in libraries, and for identifying and fostering administrative skills. Toward these ends, the association is responsible for all elements of general administration that are common to more than one type of library. These may include: Buildings and Equipment Section (BES); Fundraising & Financial Development Section (FRFDS); Library Organization & Management Section (LOMS); Personnel Administration Section (PAS); Public Relation Section (PRS); Systems & Services Section (SASS); Statistic Section (SS). *Membership:* 5,131. *Dues:* $35 (in addition to ALA membership); $15 library school students. *Publication: Library Administration & Management* (q.).

*(ALA) Library and Information Technology Association (LITA). 50 E. Huron St., Chicago, IL 60611. (312) 280-4270; (voice) (800) 545-2433, ext. 4270. Fax (312) 280-3257. Linda J. Knutson, Exec. Dir. Concerned with library automation, the information sciences, and the design, development, and implementation of automated systems in those fields, including systems development, electronic data processing, mechanized information retrieval, operations research, standards development, telecommunications, video communications, networks and collaborative efforts, management techniques, information technology, optical technology, artificial intelligence and expert systems, and other related aspects of audiovisual activities and hardware applications. *Membership:* 5,800. *Dues:* $35 plus membership in ALA, $15 for library school students, $25 first year, new members. *Publications: Information Technology and Libraries*; *LITA Newsletter.*

(ALA) Public Library Association (PLA). 50 E. Huron St., Chicago, IL 60611. (312) 280-5PLA. Fax (312) 280-5029. E-mail U22540@UICVM.UIC.EDU. George M. Needham, Exec. Dir.; Judith Drescher, Pres., 1994-95; LaDonna Kienitz, Pres., 1995-96. Concerned with the development, effectiveness, and financial support of public libraries. Speaks for the profession and seeks to enrich the professional competence and opportunities of public libraries. Sections include Adult Lifelong Learning, Community Information, Metropolitan Libraries, Public Library Systems, Small and Medium-sized Libraries, Public Policy for Public Libraries, and Marketing of Public Library Services. *Membership:* 7,800. *Dues:* $50, open to all ALA members. *Meetings:* National Conference, March 26-30, 1996, Portland, OR. "Access for All: The Public Library Promise." *Publication: Public Libraries* (bi-mo.).

> **(ALA) Audiovisual Committee (of the Public Library Association)**. 50 E. Huron St., Chicago, IL 60611. (312) 280-5752. James E. Massey, Chair. Promotes use of audiovisual materials in public libraries.

> **(ALA) Technology in Public Libraries Committee (of the Public Library Association)**. 50 E. Huron St., Chicago, IL 60611. (312) 280-5752. William Ptacek, Chair. Collects and disseminates information on technology applications in public libraries.

(ALA) Reference and Adult Services Division (RASD). 50 E. Huron St., Chicago, IL 60611. (800) 545-2433, ext. 4395. Fax (312) 944-8085. Cathleen Bourdon, Exec. Dir. Responsible for stimulating and supporting in every type of library the delivery of reference information services to all groups and of general library services and materials to adults. *Membership:* 5,500. *Dues:* $35 plus membership in ALA. *Publications: RQ* (q.); *RASD Update*; others.

(ALA) Young Adult Library Services Association (YALSA) (formerly Young Adult Services Division). 50 E. Huron St., Chicago, IL 60611. (312) 280-4390. Fax (312) 664-7459. Linda Waddle, Deputy Exec. Dir.; Jennifer Jung Gallant, Pres. Seeks to advocate, promote, strengthen service to young adults as part of the continuum of total library services, and assumes responsibility within the ALA to evaluate and select books and nonbook media, and to interpret and make recommendations regarding their use with young adults. Committees include Best Books for Young Adults, Recommended Books for the Reluctant Young Adult Reader, Media Selection and Usage, Publishers' Liaison, and Selected Films for Young Adults. *Membership:* 2,223. *Dues:*

$40 (in addition to ALA membership), $15 for students. *Publication: Journal of Youth Services in Libraries* (q.).

(ALA) Continuing Library Education Network and Exchange Round Table (CLENERT). 50 E. Huron St., Chicago, IL 60611. (312) 280-4278. Kenna J. Forsythe, Pres.; Duncan F. Smith, Pres.-Elect. Seeks to provide access to quality continuing education opportunities for librarians and information scientists and to create an awareness of the need for such education in helping individuals in the field to respond to societal and technological changes. *Membership:* 350. *Dues:* Open to all ALA members; individual members $15, $50 for organizations. *Publications: CLENExchange* (q.), available to nonmembers by subscription at $20/yr. U.S. zip, $25 non-U.S. zip.

American Management Association (AMA). 135 W. 50th St., New York, NY 10020-1201. (212) 586-8100. Fax (212) 903-8168. David Fagiano, Pres. and CEO. Founded in 1923, the AMA provides educational forums worldwide where members and their colleagues learn superior, practical business skills and explore best practices of world-class organizations through interaction with each other and expert faculty practitioners. Its publishing program provides tools individuals use to extend learning beyond the classroom in a process of life-long professional growth and development through education. The AMA operates eight management centers and offices in the United States and, through AMA/International, in Brussels, Belgium, and Tokyo, Japan; it also has affiliated centers in Toronto, Canada, and Mexico City, Mexico. AMA offers conferences, seminars, and membership briefings where there is an interchange of information, ideas, and experiences in a wide variety of management topics. AMA publishes approximately 60 books per year, as well as numerous surveys and management briefings. *Publications* (periodicals): *Management Review* (membership); *Compensation & Benefits Review*; *CompFlash*; *Organizational Dynamics*; *HR Focus*; *The President*; *Small Business Reports*; *Supervisory Management*; *Supervisory Sense*; and *Trainer's Workshop*. Other services offered by AMA include AMA Video; Extension Institute (self-study programs in both print and audio formats); Operation Enterprise (young adult program); AMA On-Site (seminars delivered at site of the company's choice); AMA by Satellite (videoconferences); the Information Resources Center (for AMA members only); a management information and library service; and five AMA bookstores. It also cooperates with management associations around the world through correspondent association agreements.

*American Montessori Society (AMS). 150 5th Ave., New York, NY 10011. (212) 924-3209. Fax (212) 727-2254. Michael N. Eanes, Natl. Dir. Dedicated to promoting better education for all children through teaching strategies consistent with the Montessori system. Membership is composed of schools in the private and public sectors employing this method, as well as individuals. It serves as a resource center and clearinghouse for information and data on Montessori, affiliates teacher training programs in different parts of the country, and conducts a consultation service and accreditation program for school members. Sponsors three regional and one national educational conference per year and four professional development symposia under the auspices of the AMS Teachers' Section. *Dues:* Teachers, schoolheads, $37/yr.; parents, $29/yr.; institutions, from $235/yr. and up. *Meetings* (selected): 34th Annual Conference, April 22-24, 1994, Dearborn, MI; 8th Annual Teacher's Section Touring Symposium for Teachers and Parents, April 30-May 1, 1994, Minneapolis, MN; Summer Regional Symposium, August 19-21, 1994, Breckenridge, CO. *Publications: AMS Montessori LIFE* (q.); *Schoolheads* (newsletter); *Montessori in Contemporary American Culture*; *Authentic American Montessori School*; *The Montessori School Management Guide*; occasional papers.

*American National Standards Institute (ANSI). 11 W. 42d St., New York, NY 10036. (212) 642-4900. Fax (212) 398-0023. Sergio Mazza, Pres.; Anthony R. O'Neill, Chairman of the Board. ANSI is the coordinator of the U.S. voluntary standards system, approves American National Standards, and represents the United States in the International Organization for Standardization (ISO) and the International Electrotechnical Commission (IEC). The Institute does not write standards or codes, but coordinates those developed through an open consensus process by the approximately 1,300 national and international companies, 30 government agencies, 20 institutional members, and 250 professional, technical, trade, labor, and consumer organizations that compose its membership. *Meetings:* 1994 Annual Public Conference, March 3-4, Washington, DC, "Accessing Global Markets through Standardization." *Publications: Catalog of Standards* (annual) lists more than 8,000 standards for all topic areas; *ANSI Reporter* (mo.), newsletter of the national and international standards community; *Standards Action* (bi-weekly), listing of status of revisions on standards in the United States, international community, Europe, and other foreign national bodies.

American Society for Training and Development (ASTD). 1640 King St., Box 1443, Alexandria, VA 22313. (703) 683-8100. Fax (703) 683-8103. Curtis E. Plott, Pres. and CEO. Leading professional organization for individuals engaged in employee training and education in business, industry, government, and related fields. Members include managers, program developers, instructors, consultants, counselors, suppliers, and academics. The purpose of its extensive professional publishing program is to build an essential body of knowledge for advancing the competence of training and development practitioners in the field. Many special-interest subgroups relating to industries or job functions are included in the organization. *Membership:* 55,000 National and Chapter members. *Dues:* $150/yr., national. *Meetings:* International Conference, June 4-8, 1995, Dallas, TX; Technical and Skills Training Conference, September 13-18, 1995, Philadelphia, PA. *Publications: Training and Development Magazine; Technical & Skills Training Magazine; Info-Line; ASTD Video Directories; ASTD Directory of Academic Programs in T&D/HRD; Training and Development Handbook; Technical & Skills Training Handbook.* Quarterly publications: *National Report on Human Resources; Washington Policy Report.* ASTD also has recognized professional areas, networks, and industry groups, most of which produce newsletters.

*American Society of Cinematographers (ASC). 1782 N. Orange Dr., Hollywood, CA 90028. (213) 969-4333. Fax (213) 876-4973. Fax (213) 882-6391. Victor J. Kemper, Pres. ASC is an educational, cultural, and professional organization. Membership is by invitation to those who are actively engaged as directors of photography and have demonstrated outstanding ability. *Membership:* 271, including active, active retired, associates, and honorary members. *Meeting:* Annual ASC Awards, February 27, 1994, Beverly Hills, CA. *Publications: American Cinematographer Video Manual; American Cinematographer Film Manual* (7th ed.); *Anton Wilson's Cinema Workshop* (4th ed.); *The Cinema of Adventure, Romance, & Terror; The Light on Her Face;* and *American Cinematographers Magazine.*

*American Society of Educators (ASE). 1429 Walnut St., Philadelphia, PA 19102. (215) 563-3501. Fax (215) 563-1588. Diane Falten, Mng. Ed. A multifaceted professional organization that serves the nation's teachers by providing information and evaluation of media resources and technologies for effective classroom use. *Membership:* 41,000. *Dues:* $29/yr., $47/yr. foreign. *Publications: Media and Methods; School Executive.*

*American Women in Radio and Television (AWRT). 1650 Tyson Blvd., Suite 200, McLean, VA 22102-3915. (703) 506-3290. Fax (703) 506-3266. Ellen Teplitz, Mgr. of Association Services. Terri Dickerson-Jones, Exec. Dir. Organization of professionals in the electronic media, including owners, managers, administrators, and those in creative positions in broadcasting, satellite, cable, advertising, and public relations. The objectives are to work worldwide to improve the quality of radio and television; to promote the entry, development, and advancement of women in the electronic media and allied fields; to serve as a medium of communication and idea exchange; and to become involved in community concerns. Organized in 1951. Student memberships available. *Membership:* 40 chapters. *Dues:* $125/yr. *Publications: News and Views*; *Resource Directory*; *Careers in the Electronic Media*; *Sexual Harassment* (pamphlet).

*Anthropology Film Center (AFC). Box 493-87504, 1626 Canyon Rd., Santa Fe, NM 87501. (505) 983-4127. Carroll Williams, Dir. Offers the Documentary Film Program, a 30-week full-time course in 16mm film production and theory and summer workshops. Also provides consultation, research, 16mm film equipment sales and rental, facilities rental, occasional seminars and workshops, and a specialized library. *Publications: An Ixil Calendrical Divination* (16mm color film); *First Impressions of Ixil Culture* (16mm color film).

*Appalachia Educational Laboratory, Inc. (AEL). 1031 Quarrier St., P.O. Box 1348, Charleston, WV 25325. (304) 347-0400. (800) 624-9120 (outside WV). (800) 344-6646 (in WV). Terry L. Eidell, Exec. Dir. One of 10 Office of Educational Research and Improvement (OERI) regional educational laboratories designed to help educators and policymakers solve educational problems in their schools. Using the best available information and the experience and expertise of professionals, AEL seeks to identify solutions to education problems, tries new approaches, furnishes research results, and provides training to teachers and administrators. AEL serves Kentucky, Tennessee, Virginia, and West Virginia.

*Association for Childhood Education International (ACEI). 11501 Georgia Ave., No. 315, Wheaton, MD 20902. (301) 942-2443. Fax (301) 942-3012. Lucy Prete Martin, Ed. and Dir. of Publications. Concerned with children from infancy through early adolescence. ACEI publications reflect careful research, broad-based views, and consideration of a wide range of issues affecting children. Many are media-related in nature. The journal (*Childhood Education*) is essential for teachers, teachers-in-training, teacher educators, day care workers, administrators, and parents. Articles focus on child development and emphasize practical application. Regular departments include book reviews (child and adult); reviews of films, pamphlets, and software; research; and classroom idea-sparkers. Articles address timely concerns. Five issues are published yearly, including a theme issue devoted to critical concerns. *Membership:* 14,000. *Dues:* $45/yr. *Publications: Childhood Education* (official journal) with *ACEI Exchange* (insert newsletter); *Journal of Research in Childhood Education*; professional division newsletters (*Focus on Infancy, Focus on Early Childhood*, and *Focus on Later Childhood/Early Adolescence*); *Developmental Continuity Across Preschool and Primary Grades: Implications for Teachers*; *Developmentally Appropriate Middle Level Schools*; *Common Bonds: Antibias Teaching in a Diverse Society*; *Childhood 1892-1992*; *Infants and Toddlers with Special Needs and Their Families* (position paper); and pamphlets.

Association for Continuing Higher Education (ACHE). Continuing Education, Trident Technical College, P.O. Box 118067, CE-P, Charleston, SC 29423-8067. (803) 722-5546. Fax (803) 722-5520. Wayne Whelan, contact person. The Association for Continuing Higher Education is an institution-based organization of colleges, universities, and individuals dedicated to the promotion of lifelong learning and excellence in continuing higher education. ACHE encourages professional networks, research, and exchange of information for its members and advocates continuing higher education as a means of enhancing and improving society. *Membership:* 1,622 individuals in 674 institutions. *Dues:* $60/yr. professionals, $240/yr. institutional. *Meetings:* 1995 Annual Meeting, Kansas City. MO, October 8-10. "Redefining the Continuing Education Classroom." 1996 Annual Meeting, Palm Desert, CA. *Publications: Journal of Continuing Higher Education* (3/yr.); *Five Minutes with Ache* (newsletter, 10/yr.); *Proceedings* (annual).

Association for Educational Communications and Technology (AECT). 1025 Vermont Ave. NW, Suite 820, Washington, DC 20005. (202) 347-7834. Fax (202) 347-7839. Stanley Zenor, Exec. Dir; Lynn Milet, Pres. AECT is an international professional association concerned with the improvement of learning and instruction through media and technology. It serves as a central clearinghouse and communications center for its members, who include instructional technologists; media or library specialists; religious educators; government media personnel; school, school district, and state department of education media program administrators and specialists; and educational/training media producers. AECT members also work in the armed forces, in public libraries, in museums, and in other information agencies of many different kinds, including those related to the emerging fields of computer technology. *Membership:* 4,500, plus 9,000 additional subscribers, 11 divisions, 15 national affiliates, 46 state and territorial affiliates, and more than 30 national committees and task forces. *Dues:* $75/yr. regular, $35/yr. student and retired. *Meetings:* 1995 Annual Convention and InCITE Exposition, February 8-12, Anaheim, CA; 1996 Annual Convention and InCITE Exposition, February 14-18 in Indianapolis, IN. *Publications: TechTrends* (6/yr., free with membership; $36/yr. nonmembers); *Report to Members* (6/yr., newsletter); *Educational Technology Research and Development* (q., $40/yr. member; $55/yr. nonmembers); various division publications; several books; videotapes.

Because of similarity of interests, the following organizations have chosen to affiliate with the Association for Educational Communications and Technology. (As many as possible have been polled for inclusion in *EMTY*.)

- Community College Association for Instruction and Technology (CCAIT)
- Consortium of College and University Media Centers (CCUMC)
- Federal Educational Technology Association (FETA)
- Health Sciences Communications Association (HeSCA)
- International Association for Learning Laboratories (IALL)
- International Visual Literacy Association, Inc. (IVLA)
- Minorities in Media (MIM)
- National Association of Regional Media Centers (NARMC)
- National Instructional Television Fixed Service Association (NIA/ITFS)
- New England Educational Media Association (NEEMA)
- Northwest College and University Council for the Management of Educational Technology (NW/MET)
- Southeastern Regional Media Leadership Council (SRMLC)

Two additional organizations are also related to the Association for Educational Communications and Technology:

- AECT Archives
- AECT ECT Foundation

Association for Educational Communications and Technology (AECT) Divisions:

(AECT) Division of Educational Media Management (DEMM). 1025 Vermont Ave. NW, Suite 820, Washington, DC 20005. (202) 347-7834. Connie Bakker, Pres. Seeks to develop an information exchange network and to share information about common problems, solutions, and program descriptions of educational media management. Develops programs that increase the effectiveness of media managers; initiates and implements a public relations program to educate the public and administrative bodies as to the use, value, and need for educational media management; and fosters programs that will help carry out media management responsibilities effectively. *Membership:* 780. *Dues:* One division membership included in the basic AECT membership; additional division memberships $10/yr. *Publication: Media Management Journal.*

(AECT) Division of Instructional Development (DID). 1025 Vermont Ave. NW, Suite 820, Washington, DC 20005. (202) 347-7834. Tillman Ragan, Pres. DID is composed of individuals from business, government, and academic settings concerned with the systematic design of instruction and the development of solutions to performance problems. Members' interests include the study, evaluation, and refinement of design processes; the creation of new models of instructional development; the invention and improvement of techniques for managing the development of instruction; the development and application of professional ID competencies; the promotion of academic programs for preparation of ID professionals; and the dissemination of research and development work in ID. *Membership:* 726. *Dues:* One division membership included in the basic AECT membership; additional division memberships $10/yr. *Publications: DID Newsletter;* occasional papers.

(AECT) Division of Interactive Systems and Computers (DISC). 1025 Vermont Ave. NW, Suite 820, Washington, DC 20005. (202) 347-7834. Franz Frederick, Pres. Concerned with the generation, access, organization, storage, and delivery of all forms of information used in the processes of education and training. DISC promotes the networking of its members to facilitate sharing of expertise and interests. *Membership:* 883. *Dues:* One division membership included in the basic AECT membership; additional division memberships $10/yr. *Publication:* Newsletter.

(AECT) Division of Learning and Performance Environments (DLPE). 1025 Vermont Ave. NW, Suite 820, Washington, DC 20005. (202) 347-7834. Cynthia Leshin, Pres. Seeks to provide continuing education and leadership in the field of learning and human performance using computer-based technologies. The Division is composed of individuals from business, academic settings, and government who are looking for a forum for sophisticated discussions of the issues they face. Member interests include scholarly research, the application of theory to practice, design, development, evaluation, assessment, and implementation of learning and performance support systems for adults. *Membership:* New division; data not provided. *Dues:* One division membership included in the basic AECT membership; additional division memberships $10/yr.

(AECT) Division of School Media Specialists (DSMS). 1025 Vermont Ave. NW, Suite 820, Washington, DC 20005. (202) 347-7834. Helen M. DeWell, Pres. DSMS promotes communication among school media personnel who share a common concern in the development, implementation, and evaluation of school media programs; and strives to increase learning and improve instruction in the school setting through the utilization of educational media and technology. *Membership:* 902. *Dues:* One division membership included in the basic AECT membership; additional division memberships $10/yr. *Publication:* Newsletter.

(AECT) Division of Telecommunications (DOT). 1025 Vermont Ave. NW, Suite 820, Washington, DC 20005. (202) 347-7834. Candis Isberner, Pres. Seeks to improve education through use of television and radio, video and audio recordings, and autotutorial devices and media. Aims to improve the design, production, evaluation, and use of telecommunications materials and equipment; to upgrade competencies of personnel engaged in the field; to investigate and report promising innovative practices and technological developments; to promote studies, experiments, and demonstrations; and to support research in telecommunications. Future plans call for working to establish a national entity representing instructional television. *Membership:* 607. *Dues:* One division membership included in the basic AECT membership; additional division memberships $10/yr. *Publication:* Newsletter.

(AECT) Industrial Training and Education Division (ITED). 1025 Vermont Ave. NW, Suite 820, Washington, DC 20005. (202) 347-7834. Andrew Yeaman, Pres. Seeks to promote the sensitive and sensible use of media and techniques to improve the quality of education and training; to provide a professional program that demonstrates the state of the art of educational technology as a part of the AECT convention; to improve communications to ensure the maximum use of educational techniques and media that can give demonstrable, objective evidence of effectiveness. *Membership:* 273. *Dues:* One division membership included in the basic AECT membership; additional division memberships $10/yr. *Publication:* Newsletter.

(AECT) International Division (INTL). 1025 Vermont Ave. NW, Suite 820, Washington, DC 20005. (202) 347-7834. John G. Hedberg, Pres. Seeks to improve international communications concerning existing methods of design; to pretest, use, produce, evaluate, and establish an approach through which these methods may be improved and adapted for maximum use and effectiveness; to develop a roster of qualified international leaders with experience and competence in the varied geographic and technical areas; and to encourage research in the application of communication processes to support present and future international social and economic development. *Membership:* 295. *Dues:* One division membership included in the basic AECT membership; additional division memberships $10/yr. *Publication:* Newsletter.

(AECT) Media Design and Production Division (MDPD). 1025 Vermont Ave. NW, Suite 820, Washington, DC 20005. (202) 347-7834. Keith Danielson, Pres. Seeks to provide formal, organized procedures for promoting and facilitating interaction between commercial and noncommercial, nontheatrical filmmakers, and to provide a communications link for filmmakers with persons of similar interests. Also seeks to provide a connecting link between creative and technical professionals of the audiovisual industry.

Advances the informational film producer's profession by providing scholarships and apprenticeships to experimenters and students and by providing a forum for discussion of local, national, and universal issues. Recognizes and presents awards for outstanding films produced and for contributions to the state of the art. *Membership:* 318. *Dues:* One division membership included in the basic AECT membership; additional division memberships $10/yr. *Publication:* Newsletter.

(AECT) Research and Theory Division (RTD). 1025 Vermont Ave. NW, Suite 820, Washington, DC 20005. (202) 3477834. Gary R. Morrison, Pres. Seeks to improve the design, execution, utilization, and evaluation of educational technology research; to improve the qualifications and effectiveness of personnel engaged in educational technology research; to advise the educational practitioner as to use of the research results; to improve research design, techniques, evaluation, and dissemination; to promote both applied and theoretical research on the systematic use of educational technology in the improvement of instruction; and to encourage the use of multiple research paradigms in examining issues related to technology in education. *Membership:* 452. *Dues:* One division membership included in the basic AECT membership; additional division memberships $10/yr. *Publication:* Newsletter.

(AECT) Systemic Change Division (CHANGE). 1025 Vermont Ave. NW, Suite 820, Washington, DC 20005. (202) 347-7834. Alison Carr, Pres. Serves those who are interested in systemic change in a wide variety of settings, including public and private schools. Fosters the belief that systemic change is necessary in educational settings for meeting learners' needs and for dramatically improving the quality of education. *Membership:* New division; data not provided. *Dues:* One division membership included in the basic AECT membership; additional division memberships $10/yr. *Publication:* Newsletter.

Association for Educational Communications and Technology (AECT) Affiliate Organizations:

(AECT) Community College Association for Instruction and Technology (CCAIT). John Wood Community College, Quincy, IL 62301. (217) 224-6500, ext. 4512. Fax (217) 224-4208. John Gebhart, Pres. A national association of community and junior college educators interested in the discovery and dissemination of information about problems and processes of teaching, media, and technology in community and junior colleges. Facilitates member exchange of data, reports, proceedings, personnel, and other resources; sponsors AECT convention sessions and social activities. *Membership:* 200. *Dues:* $10. *Meeting:* February 1996, Indianapolis, IN. *Publications:* Regular newsletter; irregular topical papers.

(AECT) Federal Educational Technology Association (FETA). FETA Membership, Sara Shick, FETA, P.O. Box 3412, McLean, VA 22103-3412. (703) 406-3040 (Clear Spring, Inc.). George H. Stevens, Pres. FETA is dedicated to the improvement of education and training through research, communication, and practice. It encourages and welcomes members from all government agencies, federal, state, and local; from business and industry; and from all educational institutions and organizations. FETA encourages interaction among members to improve the quality of education and training in any arena, but with specific emphasis on government-related applications. *Meetings:* Meets in conjunction with AECT InCITE and concurrently with SALT's Washington meeting in August. *Publication:* Newsletter (occasional).

(AECT) Health Sciences Communications Association (HeSCA). See separate listing.

(AECT) International Visual Literacy Association, Inc. (IVLA). Virginia Tech, Educational Technologies-LRC, Old Security Building, Blacksburg, VA 24061-0232. Alice D. Walker, Treas. Provides a multidisciplinary forum for the exploration of modes of visual communication and their application through the concept of visual literacy; promotes development of visual literacy and serves as a bond between the diverse organizations and groups working in that field. *Dues:* $40 regular; $20 student. *Meeting:* Chicago, IL, October 18-22, 1995, "Eyes on the Future: Converging Images, Ideas, and Instruction." Publications: *Journal of Visual Literacy*; *Readings from Annual Conferences.*

(AECT) Minorities in Media (MIM). Arizona State University, 146 Payne Hall, Tempe, AZ 85287-0111. (602) 965-1832. Dr. Benjamin Kinard, Pres. Seeks to encourage the effective use of educational media in the teaching/learning process; provide leadership opportunities in advancing the use of technology as an integral part of the learning process; provide a vehicle through which minorities might influence the use of media in institutions; develop an information exchange network to share information common to minorities in media; study, evaluate, and refine the educational technology process as it relates to the education of minorities; and encourage and improve the production of materials for the education of minorities. *Membership:* 100. *Dues:* $10. *Publication:* Annual newsletter.

(AECT) National Association of Regional Media Centers (NARMC). NARMC, 1314 Hines Ave., San Antonio, TX 78206-1816. Joseph P. Price, Pres. Seeks to foster the exchange of ideas and information among educational communications specialists responsible for the administration of regional media centers, through workshops, seminars, and national meetings. Studies the feasibility of developing joint programs that could increase the effectiveness and efficiency of regional media services. Disseminates information on successful practices and research studies conducted by regional media centers. Member institutions serve more than 20 million students. *Membership:* 285 regional centers (institutions), 70 corporations. *Dues:* $55 institutions, $250 corporations. *Meetings:* National Conference, affiliated with AECT National Conference, Anaheim, CA, February 8-12, 1995. Theme: "Information Technology—Expanding Frontiers." *Publications: N.A.R.M.C.—Highlights*; *N.A.R.M.C.— 'etin*; *Annual Membership Report*; *Biannual Survey Report of Regional Media Centers.*

(AECT) National ITFS Association (NIA). National ITFS Association, Box #1130, 3421 M Street, NW, Washington, DC 20007. Theodore Steinke, Chair, Bd. of Dirs.; Dr. Daniel Niemeyer, Pres. Established in 1978, NIA/ITFS is a nonprofit, professional organization of Instructional Television Fixed Service (ITFS) licensees, applicants, and others interested in ITFS broadcasting. The goals of the association are to gather and exchange information about ITFS, to gather data on utilization of ITFS, and to act as a conduit for those seeking ITFS information or assistance. The NIA represents ITFS interests to the FCC, technical consultants, and equipment manufacturers. The association provides its members with a quarterly newsletter and an FCC regulation update as well as information on excess capacity leasing and license and application data. *Meeting:* Meets with AECT and InCITE. *Publications: National ITFS Association Newsletter* (q.); FCC regulation update.

(AECT) Northwest College and University Council for the Management of Educational Technology (NW/MET). Listserv NW-MET@williamette.edu. Membership queries can be sent to mmorandi@williamette.edu. Charlene Clark, NW/MET Secretary, Intercollegiate Center for Nursing Education, W. 2917 Ft. George Wright Drive, Spokane, WA 99204. William Odell, Eastern Washington University, 1994-95 Dir.; Kees Hof, Langara College, Vancouver, BC, 1995-96 Dir. The first regional group representing institutions of higher education in Alberta, Alaska, British Columbia, Idaho, Montana, Oregon, Saskatchewan, and Washington to receive affiliate status in AECT. Membership is restricted to media managers with campus-wide responsibilities for educational technical services in the membership region. Corresponding membership is available to those who work outside the membership region. An annual conference and business meeting are held the last weekend of October each year, rotating throughout the region. Current issues under consideration include managing emerging telecommunication technologies, copyright, accreditation, and certification. Organizational goals include identifying the unique status problems of media managers in higher education and improving the quality of the major publication. *Membership:* approx. 85. *Dues:* $35. *Publications:* Two annual newsletters and a single *NW/MET Journal.*

Southeastern Regional Media Leadership Council (SRMLC). P.O. Box 3508, 1415 Amherst St., Winchester, VA 22601. (703) 662-3888, Ext. 140. Fax (703) 722-2788. Betty Hutsler, Dir. The purpose of the SRMLC is to strengthen the role of the individual state AECT affiliates with the Southeastern region; to seek positive change in the nature and status of instructional technology as it exists within the Southeast; to provide opportunities for the training and development of leadership for both the region and the individual affiliates; and to provide opportunities for the exchange of information and experience among those who attend the conference.

Other AECT-Related Organizations:

***(AECT) Archives.** University of Maryland at College Park, Hornbake Library, College Park, MD 20742. Thomas Connors, Archivist, National Public Broadcasting Archives. (301) 405-9988. Fax (301) 314-9419. A collection of media, manuscripts, and related materials representing important developments in visual and audiovisual education and in instructional/educational technology. The collection is housed as part of the National Public Broadcasting Archives. Maintained by the University of Maryland at College Park in cooperation with AECT. Open to researchers and scholars.

(AECT) ECT Foundation. c/o AECT, 1025 Vermont Ave. NW, Suite 820, Washington, DC 20005. Hans-Erik Wennberg, Pres. The ECT Foundation is a nonprofit organization whose purposes are charitable and educational in nature. Its operation is based on the conviction that improvement of instruction can be accomplished, in part, by the continued investigation and application of new systems for learning and by periodic assessment of current techniques for the communication of information. In addition to awarding scholarships, internships, and fellowships, the foundation develops and conducts leadership training programs for emerging professional leaders.

Association for Experiential Education (AEE). 2885 Aurora Ave., #28, Boulder, CO 80303-2252. (303) 440-8844. (303) 440-9581. Barbara A. "Babs" Baker, Exec. Dir. AEE is a not-for-profit international professional organization with roots in adventure education, committed to the development, practice, and evaluation of experiential learning in all settings.

Our vision is to be a leading international organization for the development and application of experiential education principles and methodologies. Our intent is to create a just and compassionate world by transforming education and promoting positive social change. *Membership:* More than 2,000 members in over 20 countries. Membership consists of individuals and organizations with affiliations in education, recreation, outdoor adventure, youth service, mental health, physical education, management, development training, corrections, programming for people with disabilities, and environmental education. *Dues:* $50-$250/yr. Types of membership are individual, family, corporate/organizational. *Meetings:* 23rd International Conference, November 9-12, 1995, Lake Geneva, WI; Northwest Region Conference, March 24-26, 1995, Sun Mountain Lodge, WA; Southeast Region Conference, April 7-9, 1995, Montreat Center, Black Mountain, NC. *Publications: Jobs Clearinghouse; The Journal of Experiential Education; Adventure Therapy; Therapeutic Applications of Adventure Programming; The Theory of Experiential Education; Experiential Learning in Schools and Higher Education; Ethical Issues in Experiential Education; Book of Metaphors, Volume II;* directories of programs and membership directory.

Association for Library and Information Science Education (ALISE). Penney DePas, CAE, Exec. Dir. 4101 Lake Boone Tr., Suite 201, Raleigh, NC 27607-4916. Seeks to advance education for library and information science and produces annual *Library and Information Science Education Statistical Report.* Open to professional schools offering graduate programs in library and information science; personal memberships open to educators employed in such institutions; other memberships available to interested individuals. *Membership:* 650 individuals, 85 institutions. *Dues:* institutional, $250 full; $150 associate; $75 international; personal, $60 full-time; $25 part-time, student, retired. *Publications: Journal of Education for Library and Information Science;* directory; *Library and Information Science Education Statistical Report.*

*Association of Independent Video and Filmmakers/Foundation for Independent Video and Film (AIVF/FIVF). 625 Broadway, 9th Floor, New York, NY 10012. (212) 473-3400. Fax (212) 677-8732. Ruby Lerner, Exec. Dir. The national trade association for independent video and filmmakers, representing their needs and goals to industry, government, and the public. Programs include domestic and foreign festival liaison for independents, screenings and seminars, insurance for members and groups, and information and referral services. Recent activities include monitoring status of independent work on public television, advocacy for cable access, and lobbying for modifications in copyright law. *Dues:* $45 individuals, $75 libraries, $100 nonprofit organizations, $150 business/industry, $25 students. *Publications: The Independent Film and Video Monthly; The AIVF Guide to International Film and Video Festivals; The AIVF Guide to Film and Video Distributors; The Next Step: Distributing Independent Films and Videos; Alternative Visions: Distributing Independent Media in a Home Video World; Directory of Film and Video Production Resources in Latin America and the Caribbean.*

Association of Systematics Collections (ASC). 730 11th St. NW, 2d Floor, Washington, DC 20001. (202) 347-2850. Fax (202) 347-0072. K. Elaine Hoagland, Exec. Dir. Fosters the care, management, and improvement of biological collections and promotes their utilization. Institutional members include private, free-standing museums, botanical gardens, zoos, college and university museums, and public institutions, including state biological surveys, agricultural research centers, the Smithsonian Institution, and the U.S. National Biological Survey. The ASC also represents affiliate societies, keeps members informed about funding and legislative issues, and provides technical consulting for such subjects as collection permits, care of collections, and taxonomic expertise. *Membership:* 82 institutions, 22 societies, 1,200 newsletter subscribers. *Dues:* Depend on the size of collections. *Publications: ASC Newsletter* (for members and nonmember subscribers, bi-mo.); *Guidelines for Institutional Policies and Planning in Natural History Collections; Biogeography of the Tropical Pacific; Collections of Frozen Tissues; Guidelines for Institutional Database Policies.*

Cable in the Classroom. 1900 N. Beauregard St., Suite 108, Alexandria, VA 22311. (703) 845-1400. Fax (703) 845-1409. Dr. Bobbi L. Kamil, Exec. Dir. Cable in the Classroom is the cable industry's $300 million public service initiative to enrich education. It provides free cable connections to over 65,000 schools (approximately two-thirds of all public and private schools K–12), reaching over 75 percent of all U.S. students with commercial-free, quality educational programming. It also provides curriculum-related suport materials for its programming and conducts Teacher Training and Media Literacy workshops throughout the country. *Membership:* Cable in the Classroom is a consortium of more than 74 multiple system operators, over 6,200 local cable companies, and 28 national cable programming networks. *Publications: "Delivering the Future": Cable and Education Partnerships for the Information Age* (Dr. Bobbi Kamil); *Cable in the Classroom Magazine* (mo.).

Catholic Library Association (CLA). St. Joseph's Central High School, 22 Maplewood Ave., Pittsfield, MA 01201. (413) 447-9121. Sr. Jean R. Dostley, SFJ, Pres. and Exec. Dir. Provides educational programs, services, and publications for Catholic libraries and librarians. *Membership:* approx. 1,000. *Dues:* $45 individuals; special rates for students and retirees. *Meetings:* Meetings are held in conjunction with the National Catholic Education Association: April 11-14, 1995, Cincinnati, OH; 1996, April 2-5, Philadelphia, PA; 1997, March 25-28, Minneapolis, MN. *Publications: Catholic Library World* (q.); *Catholic Periodical and Literature Index* (q. with annual cumulations).

*Center for Children and Technology. Education Development Center, Inc., 96 Morton St., New York, NY 10014. (212) 222-6700. Dr. Jan Hawkins, Dir. One of 25 university-based national education and development centers supported by the Office of Educational Research and Improvement (OERI) in the U.S. Office of Education to help strengthen student learning in the United States. These centers conduct research on topics that will help policy makers, practitioners, and parents meet the national education goals by the year 2000. In addition to addressing specific topics, most of these centers focus on children at risk. Many are also cooperating with other universities, and many work with elementary and secondary schools. All have been directed by OERI to make sure the information they produce reaches parents, teachers, and others who can use it to make meaningful changes in America's schools.

*Central Educational Network (CEN). 1400 E. Touhy, Suite 260, Des Plaines, IL 60018-3305. (708) 390-8700. Fax (708) 390-9435. James A. Fellows, Pres. Provides general audience and instructional television programming and ITV services. *Membership:* PTV stations and educational agencies.

Children's Television International (CTI)/GLAD Productions, Inc. 14512 Lee Road, Chantilly, VA 22021. (703) 502-3006; (800) CTI-GLAD (284-4523). Ray Gladfelter, Pres.; Susan Johnson, Dir. of Marketing and Customer Services. An educational organization that develops, produces, and distributes a wide variety of color television programming and television-related materials as a resource to aid children's social, cultural, and intellectual development. Program areas cover language arts, science, social studies, history, and art for home, school, and college viewing. *Publications: The History Game: A Teacher's Guide;* other teacher's guides for instructional television series; and a complimentary catalog for educational videos. A retail location to promote educational programming to the general public, which will open in 1995, will feature CTI material and *Reading Rainbow*.

CINE Information. 215 W. 90th St., New York, NY 10024. (212) 877-3999. Barbara Margolis, Exec. Dir. CINE Information is a nonprofit educational organization established to develop sound methods and tools for the more effective use of film by community groups and educational programmers. It produces and distributes materials about film and videotape use and produces films on topics of social and cultural importance. Newest releases include an Academy Award nominee for Best Documentary feature in *Adam Clayton Powell*, which was also broadcast on PBS's *The American Experience* series, and American Film Festival winner, *Are We Winning, Mommy? America and the Cold War*. *Mommy* was also featured at the Berlin, Toronto, Chicago, and Park City, Utah, Film Festivals. *Publication: In Focus: A Guide to Using Films*, by Linda Blackaby, Dan Georgakas, and Barbara Margolis, a complete step-by-step handbook for film and videotape users, with detailed discussions of how to use film and tape in educational, cultural, and fundraising activities.

*Clearinghouse on Development Communication. 1815 N. Fort Myer Dr., 6th Floor, Arlington, VA 22209. (703) 527-5546. Fax (703) 527-4661. Valerie Lamont, Acting Dir. A center for materials and information on applications of communication technology to development problems. Operated by the Institute for International Research and funded by the Bureau for Research and Development of the U.S. Agency for International Development. Visitors and written requests for information are welcome, and an electronic bulletin board, CDCNET, is available to individuals with computer communications software and modems. *Dues:* Subscription, $10. *Publications: Development Communication Report* (q.); other special reports, information packages, project profiles, books, bulletins, and videotapes.

Close Up Foundation. 44 Canal Center Plaza, Alexandria, VA 22314. (703) 706-3300; (800) 765-3131. Fax (703) 706-0002. Stephen A. Janger, Pres. A nonprofit, nonpartisan civic education organization promoting informed citizen participation in public policy and community service. Programs reach more than a million participants a year. *Publications: Current Issues*; *The Bill of Rights: A User's Guide*; *Perspectives*; *International Relations*; *The American Economy*; documentary videotapes on domestic and foreign policy issues. Close Up brings 24,000 secondary and middle school students and teachers and older Americans each year to Washington for week-long government studies programs, and produces television programs on the C-SPAN cable network for secondary school and home audiences.

Consortium of College and University Media Centers. 121 Pearson Hall-MRC, Iowa State University, Ames, IA 50011. (515) 294-1811. Fax (515) 294-8089. Don Rieck, Exec. Dir. A professional group of higher education media personnel whose purpose is to improve education and training through the effective use of educational media. Assists educational and training users in making films, video, and educational media more accessible. Fosters cooperative planning among university media centers. Gathers and disseminates information on improved procedures and new developments in instructional technology and media center management. *Membership:* 400. *Dues:* $160/yr. constituents; $60 active; $160 sustaining (commercial); $25 students; $100 associates. *Publications: Leader* (newsletter to members); *University and College Media Review* (journal).

*Copyright Clearance Center, Inc. (CCC). 222 Rosewood Dr., Danvers, MA 01923. (508) 750-8400. Fax (508) 750-4744. Joseph S. Alen, Pres. and CEO. An organization through which corporations, academic and research libraries, information brokers, government agencies, copyshops, bookstores, and other users of copyrighted information may obtain authorizations and pay royalties for photocopying these materials in excess of exemptions contained in the U.S. Copyright Act of 1976. In addition to offering a Transactional Reporting Service (TRS), CCC also offers the Annual Authorization Service (AAS), an annual-license program serving photocopy permission needs of large U.S. corporations, and the Academic Permissions Service (APS), which provides photocopy authorizations in academic settings, specifically for authorizing anthologies and coursepacks. *Membership:* over 2,000 users, over 8,500 foreign and domestic publishers, 1.5 million publications. *Dues:* Vary. *Publications: COPI: Catalog of Publisher Information* (2/yr., $42 issue, $84/yr.); *CopyFacts: The Guide to Rights Holders, Titles, and Fees for the APS* (2/yr., $40 issue, $80/yr.).

*Corporation for Public Broadcasting (CPB). 901 E St. NW, Washington, DC 20004. (202) 879-9800. Richard W. Carlson, Pres. and CEO. A private, nonprofit corporation authorized by the Public Broadcasting Act of 1967 to develop noncommercial television and radio services for the American people, while insulating public broadcasting from political pressure or influence. CPB supports station operations and funds radio and television programs for national distribution. CPB sets national policy that will most effectively make noncommercial radio and television and other telecommunications services available to all citizens. *Publications: CPB Report* (bi-weekly, 3 yrs. for $25); *Annual Report*; *CPB Public Broadcasting Directory* ($15).

Council for Basic Education. 1319 F St. NW, Suite 900, Washington, DC 20004-1152. (202) 347-4171. Fax (202) 347-5047. Christopher T. Cross, Pres. CBE's mission is to strengthen teaching and learning of the basic subjects—English, history, government, geography, mathematics, the sciences, foreign languages, and the arts—in order to develop the capacity for lifelong learning and foster responsible citizenship. CBE advocates this goal by publishing analytical periodicals and administering practical operational programs as examples to strengthen content in curriculum and teaching at the pre-college level. The Council also sponsors independent summer study fellowship programs for teachers in the humanities, arts, and sciences, and is currently involved in offering program assistance to school districts who are setting curriculum standards in academic subjects consonant with Goals 2000. *Membership:* 4,000. *Dues:* $100 Friends; $40 members; $25/yr. subscribers. *Publications: Basic Education* (monthly periodical on educational issues); *Perspective* (quarterly that treats current educational issues in depth).

*Council for Educational Development and Research (CEDaR). 2000 L St. NW, Suite 601, Washington, DC 20036. (202) 223-1593. Dena G. Stoner, Exec. Dir. Members are educational research and development institutions. Aims to advance the level of programmatic, institutionally based educational research and development and to demonstrate the importance of research and development in improving education. Provides a forum for professional personnel in member institutions. Coordinates national dissemination program. Other activities include research, development, evaluation, dissemination, and technical assistance on educational issues. *Membership:* 15. *Publication: R&D Preview.*

*Council for Exceptional Children (CEC). 1920 Association Dr., Reston, VA 22091. (703) 620-3660. Fax (703) 264-9494. Jeptha Greer, Exec. Dir. A membership organization providing information to teachers, administrators, and others concerned with the education of handicapped and gifted children. Maintains a library and database on literature on special education; prepares books, monographs, digests, films, filmstrips, cassettes, and journals; sponsors annual convention and conferences on special education; provides on-site and regional training on various topics and at varying levels; provides information and assistance to lawmakers on education of the handicapped and gifted; coordinates a political action network on the rights of exceptional persons. *Membership:* 55,000. *Dues:* Professionals, $60-80, depending on state of residence; students, $26-26.50, depending on state of residence. *Publications: Exceptional Children*; *Teaching Exceptional Children*; *Exceptional Child Educational Resources*; numerous other professional publications dealing with the education of handicapped and gifted children.

> ***(CEC) Technology and Media Division (TAM)**. Council for Exceptional Children, 1920 Association Dr., Reston, VA 22091. (703) 620-3660. The Technology and Media Division (TAM) of the Council for Exceptional Children (CEC) encourages the development of new applications, technologies, and media for use as daily living tools by special populations. This information is disseminated through professional meetings, training programs, and publications. TAM members receive four issues annually of the *Journal of Special Education Technology* containing articles on specific technology programs and applications, and five issues of the TAM newsletter, providing news of current research, developments, products, conferences, and special programs information. *Membership:* 1,500. *Dues:* $10 in addition to CEC membership.

*Council of National Library and Information Associations. 1700 18th St. NW, Suite B-1, Washington, DC 20009. (718) 990-6735. Fax (718) 380-0353. Marie F. Melton, R.S.M., Secy/Treas. The council is a forum for discussion of many issues of concern to library and information associations. *Membership:* 21 associations. *Dues:* Inquire. *Meetings:* Councils meet in May and December in New York City.

Council on International Non-theatrical Events CINE). 1001 Connecticut Ave. NW, Suite 638, Washington, DC 20036. (202) 785-1136. Fax (202) 785-4114. Richard Calkins, Exec. Dir. Coordinates the selection and placement of U.S. documentary, television, short subject, and didactic films in more than 200 overseas film festivals annually. A Golden Eagle Certificate is awarded to each professional film considered most suitable to represent the United States in international competition. A CINE Eagle Certificate is awarded to winning adult amateur-, youth-, and university student-made films. Prizes and certificates won at overseas festivals are presented by embassy representatives at an annual awards luncheon. Deadlines for receipt of entry forms are 1 February and 1 August. *Meeting:* Annual CINE Showcase and Awards, March 2-3, 1995, Washington, DC. *Publications: CINE Annual Yearbook of Film and Video Awards*; *Worldwide Directory of Film and Video Festivals and Events* (annual); *CINE News* (q.).

*East-West Center. 1777 East-West Rd., Honolulu, HI 96848. (808) 944-7666. Fax (808) 944-7333. E-mail culture@ewc. Geoffrey M. White, Dir. The U.S. Congress established the East-West Center in 1960 to foster mutual understanding and cooperation among the governments and peoples of the Asia-Pacific region, including the United States. Principal funding for the center comes from the U.S. government, with additional support provided by private agencies, individuals, and corporations, and more than 20 Asian and Pacific governments. The Program for Cultural Studies pursues research on areas of public policy interest such as education, media, family, religion, the arts, and human rights in which cultural values, identities, and histories become matters of voiced concern. Program research focuses particularly on ways in which culture enters the public sphere and impacts on national integration and international relations, taking into account the increasingly powerful role of film, video, and other mass media in shaping perceptions of culture, gender, and nationality. *Publication: East-West Film Journal.*

*Education Development Center, Inc. 55 Chapel St., Newton, MA 02160. (617) 969-7100. Fax (617) 244-3436. Janet Whitla, Pres. Seeks to improve education at all levels, in the United States and abroad, through curriculum development, institutional development, and services to the school and the community. Produces filmstrips and videocassettes, primarily in connection with curriculum development and teacher training. *Publications: Annual Report*; *EDC News* (newsletter, 2/yr.).

Educational Film Library Association. See listing for American Film and Video Association (AFVA).

Eisenhower National Clearinghouse for Mathematics and Science Education. 1929 Kenny Road, Columbus,OH 43210-1079. (614) 292-7784. Fax (614) 292-2066. E-mail info@enc.org. Dr. Len Simutis, Dir. The Eisenhower National Clearinghouse for Mathematics and Science Education (ENC) is located at The Ohio State University and funded by the U.S. Department of Education's Office of Educational Research and Improvement (OERI). ENC provides K-12 teachers and other educators a central source of information on mathematics and science curriculum materials, particularly those which support education reform. Among ENC's products and services are an online *Catalog of Curriculum Materials* available through a toll-free number and via Internet; 12 demonstration sites located throughout the nation; and a variety of publications, including the *Guidebook to Excellence*, which lists federal resources in mathematics and science education by region. In 1995, ENC will produce CD-ROMs that will include curriculum resources and the full *Catalog of Curriculum Materials*. *Membership:* Users include K-23 teachers, other educators, policy makers, and parents. *Publications: ENC Update* (newsletter); *ENC Focus* (print catalog on selected topics); *ENC Online* (brochure); *Guidebook to Excellence* (federal programs in mathematics and science education). *ENC's Catalog of Curriculum Materials* is available online through a toll-free number (1-800-ENC-4448) or via Internet at enc.org.

EPIE Institute (Educational Products Information Exchange). 103 W. Montauk Highway, Hampton Bays, NY 11946. (516) 728-9100. Fax (516) 728-9228. E-mail komoski@bnlc16.bnl.gov. P. Kenneth Komoski, Exec. Dir. Involved primarily in assessing educational materials and providing product descriptions/citations of virtually all educational software. All of EPIE's services, including its Curriculum Alignment Services for Educators, are available to schools and state agencies as well as individuals. *Publications: The Educational Software Selector (T.E.S.S.)* (annual); *The Educational Software Selector Database: TESS*, available to members of the States Consortium for Improving Software Selection.

ERIC (Educational Resources Information Center). Office of Educational Research and Improvement (OERI), U.S. Department of Education, 555 New Jersey Ave. NW, Washington, DC 20208-5720. (202) 219-2289. Fax (202) 219-1817. Internet eric@inet.ed.gov. Pat Coulter, Acting Dir. ERIC is a nationwide information network that provides access to the English-language education literature. The ERIC system consists of 16 Clearinghouses, 8 Adjunct Clearinghouses, and system support components that include the ERIC Processing and Reference Facility, ACCESS ERIC, and the ERIC Document Reproduction Service (EDRS). ERIC actively solicits papers, conference proceedings, literature reviews, and curriculum materials from researchers, practitioners, educational associations and institutions, and federal, state, and local agencies. These materials, along with articles from nearly 800 different journals, are indexed and abstracted for entry into the ERIC database. The ERIC database—the largest education database in the world—now contains approximately 800,000 records of documents and journal articles. Users can access the ERIC database online, on CD-ROM, or through print and microfiche indexes. ERIC microfiche collections, which contain the full text of most

ERIC documents, are available for public use at nearly 900 locations worldwide. Reprints of ERIC documents, on microfiche or in paper copy, can also be ordered from EDRS. A list of the ERIC Clearinghouses, together with full addresses, telephone numbers, and brief scope notes describing the areas they cover, follows here. *Dues:* None. *Publications: Resources in Education*; *Current Index to Journals in Education.*

ERIC Clearinghouse for Community Colleges (JC) (formerly Junior Colleges). University of California at Los Angeles (UCLA), 3051 Moore Hall, 405 Hilgard Ave., Los Angeles, CA 90024-1521. (310) 825-3931; (800) 832-8256. Fax (310) 206-8095. Internet eeh3rie@mvs.oac.ucla.edu. Arthur M. Cohen, Dir. Development, administration, and evaluation of two-year public and private community and junior colleges, technical institutes, and two-year branch university campuses. Two-year college students, faculty, staff, curricula, programs, support services, libraries, and community services. Linkages between two-year colleges and business/industrial/community organizations. Articulation of two-year colleges with secondary and four-year postsecondary institutions.

ERIC Clearinghouse for Social Studies/Social Science Education (SO). Indiana University, Social Studies Development Center, 2805 E. Tenth St., Suite 120, Bloomington, IN 47408-2698. (812) 855-3838; (800) 266-3815. Fax (812) 855-0455. Internet ericso@ucs.indiana.edu or ericso@indiana. John Patrick, Dir. All aspects of social studies and social science education, including values education (and the social aspects of environmental education and sex education), international education, comparative education, and cross-cultural studies in all subject areas (K-12). Ethnic heritage, gender equity, aging, and social bias/discrimination topics. Also covered are music, art, and architecture as related to the fine arts. Includes input from the Adjunct ERIC Clearinghouses for U.S.-Japan Studies and on Art Education and Law-Related Education.

ERIC Clearinghouse on Adult, Career, and Vocational Education (CE). Ohio State University, Center on Education and Training for Employment, 1900 Kenny Rd., Columbus, OH 43210-1090. (614) 292-4353; (800) 848-4815. Fax (614) 292-1260. Internet ericacve@magnus.acs.ohio-state.edu. Susan Imel, Dir. All levels of adult and continuing education from basic literacy training through professional skill upgrading. The focus is upon factors contributing to the purposeful learning of adults in a variety of situations usually related to adult roles (e.g., occupation, family, leisure time, citizenship, organizational relationships, retirement, and so forth). Includes input from the Adjunct ERIC Clearinghouse on Consumer Education.

ERIC Clearinghouse on Assessment and Evaluation (TM) (formerly Tests, Measurement and Evaluation). Catholic University of America, 210 O'Boyle Hall, Washington, DC 20064-4035. (202) 319-5120; (800) 464-3742. Fax (202) 319-6692. Internet eric_ae@cua.edu. Lawrence M. Rudner, Dir. All aspects of tests and other measurement devices. The design and methodology of research, measurement, and evaluation. The evaluation of programs and projects. The application of tests, measurement, and evaluation devices/instrumentation in education projects and programs.

ERIC Clearinghouse on Counseling and Student Services (CG) (formerly Counseling and Personnel Services). University of North Carolina at Greensboro, School of Education, Greensboro, NC 27412-5001. (910) 334-4114; (800) 414-9769. Fax (910) 334-4116. Internet ericcass@iris.uncg.edu. Garry R. Walz, Dir. Preparation, practice, and supervision of counselors at all educational levels and in all settings. Theoretical development of counseling and guidance, including the nature of relevant human characteristics. Use and results of personnel practices and procedures. Group process (counseling, therapy, dynamics) and case work.

ERIC Clearinghouse on Disabilities and Gifted Education (EC) (formerly Handicapped and Gifted Children). Council for Exceptional Children (CEC), 1920 Association Dr., Reston, VA 22091-1589. (703) 264-9474; (800) 328-0272. Fax (703) 264-9494. Internet ericce@inet.ed.gov. Sheila Mingo, Dir. All aspects of the education and development of persons (of all ages) who have disabilities or who are gifted, including the delivery of all types of education-related services to these groups. Includes prevention, identification and assessment, intervention, and enrichment for these groups in both regular and special education settings.

ERIC Clearinghouse on Educational Management (EA). University of Oregon, 1787 Agate St., Eugene, OR 97403-5207. (503) 346-5043; (800) 438-8841. Fax (503) 346-2334. Internet ppiele@oregon.uoregon.edu. Philip K. Piele, Dir. All aspects of the governance, leadership, administration, and structure of public and private educational organizations at the elementary and secondary levels, including the provision of physical facilities for their operation.

ERIC Clearinghouse on Elementary and Early Childhood Education (PS). University of Illinois, 805 W. Pennsylvania Ave., Urbana, IL 61801-4897. (217) 333-1386; (800) 583-4135. Fax (217) 333-3767. Internet ericeece@ux1.cso.uiuc.edu. Lilian G. Katz, Dir. All aspects of the physical, cognitive, social, educational, and cultural development of children, from birth through early adolescence. Among the topics covered are: prenatal and infant development and care; parent education; home and school relationships; learning theory research and practice related to children's development; preparation of early childhood teachers and caregivers; and educational programs and community services for children.

ERIC Clearinghouse on Higher Education (HE). George Washington University, One Dupont Cir. NW, Suite 630, Washington, DC 20036-1183. (202) 296-2597; (800) 773-3742. Fax (202) 296-8379. Internet eriche@inet.ed.gov. Jonathan D. Fife, Dir. All aspects of the conditions, programs, and problems at colleges and universities providing higher education (i.e., four-year degrees and beyond). This includes: governance and management; planning; finance; interinstitutional arrangements; business or industry programs leading to a degree; institutional research at the college/university level; federal programs; legal issues and legislation; professional education (e.g., medicine, law, etc.) and professional continuing education.

ERIC Clearinghouse on Information & Technology (IR) (formerly Information Resources). Syracuse University, 4-194 Center for Science and Technology, Syracuse, NY 13244-4100. (315) 443-3640; (800) 464-9107. Fax (315) 443-5448. Internet eric@ericir.syr.edu. AskERIC (question-answering service via Internet) askeric@ericir.syr.edu. Michael B. Eisenberg, Dir. Educational technology and library and information science at all academic levels and with all populations, including the preparation of professionals. The media and devices of educational communication as they pertain to teaching and learning (in both conventional and distance education settings). The operation and management of libraries and information services. All aspects of information management and information technology related to education.

ERIC Clearinghouse on Languages and Linguistics (FL). Center for Applied Linguistics, 1118 22d St. NW, Washington, DC 20037-0037. (202) 429-9292. Fax (202) 659-5641. Internet eric@cal.org. Charles Stansfield, Dir. Languages and language sciences. All aspects of second language instruction and learning in all commonly and uncommonly taught languages, including English as a second language. Bilingualism and bilingual education. Cultural education in the context of second language learning, including intercultural communication, study abroad, and international educational exchange. All areas of linguistics, including theoretical and applied linguistics, sociolinguistics, and psycholinguistics. Includes input from Adjunct ERIC Clearinghouse on Literacy Education for Limited-English-Proficient Adults.

ERIC Clearinghouse on Reading, English, and Communication (CS) (formerly Reading and Communication Skills). Indiana University, Smith Research Center, Suite 150, 2805 E. 10th St., Bloomington, IN 47408-2698. (812) 855-5847; (800) 759-4723. Fax (812) 855-4220. Internet ericcs@ucs.indiana.edu. Carl B. Smith, Dir. Reading and writing, English (as a first language), and communications skills (verbal and nonverbal), kindergarten through college. Includes family or intergenerational literacy. Research and instructional development in reading, writing, speaking, and listening. Identification, diagnosis, and remediation of reading problems. Speech communication (including forensics), mass communication (including journalism), interpersonal and small group interaction, oral interpretation, rhetorical and communication theory, and theater/drama. Preparation of instructional staff and related personnel in all the above areas.

ERIC Clearinghouse on Rural Education and Small Schools (RC). Appalachia Educational Laboratory (AEL), 1031 Quarrier St., P.O. Box 1348, Charleston, WV 25325-1348. (304) 347-0465; (800) 624-9120. Fax (304) 347-0487. Internet u56d9@wvnvm. wvnet.edu. Craig Howley, Dir. Curriculum and instructional programs and research/evaluation efforts that address the education of students in rural schools or districts, small schools wherever located, and schools of districts wherever located that serve American Indian and Alaskan natives, Mexican Americans, and migrants, or that have programs related to outdoor education. Includes the cultural, ethnic, linguistic, economic, and social conditions that affect these educational institutions and groups. Preparation programs, including related services, that train education professionals to work in such contexts.

ERIC Clearinghouse on Science, Mathematics, and Environmental Education (SE). Ohio State University, 1929 Kenny Road, Columbus, OH 43210-1080. (614) 292-6717; (800) 276-0462. Fax (614) 292-0263. Internet ericse@osu.edu. David L. Haury, Dir. Science, mathematics, engineering/technology, and environmental education at all levels. The following topics when focused on any of the above broad scope areas: applications of learning theory; curriculum and instructional materials; teachers and teacher education; educational programs and projects; research and evaluative studies; applications of educational technology and media.

ERIC Clearinghouse on Teaching and Teacher Education (SP) (formerly Teacher Education). American Association of Colleges for Teacher Education (AACTE), One Dupont Cir. NW, Suite 610, Washington, DC 20036-1186. (202) 293-2450; (800) 822-9229. Fax (202) 457-8095. Internet ericsp@inet.ed.gov. Mary E. Dilworth, Dir. School personnel at all levels. Teacher recruitment, selection, licensing, certification, training, preservice and inservice preparation, evaluation, retention, and retirement.

The theory, philosophy, and practice of teaching. Organization, administration, finance, and legal issues relating to teacher education programs and institutions. All aspects of health, physical, recreation, and dance education. Includes input from the Adjunct ERIC Clearinghouse on Clinical Schools.

ERIC Clearinghouse on Urban Education (UD). Teachers College, Columbia University, Institute for Urban and Minority Education, Main Hall, Rm. 303, Box 40, 525 W. 120th St., New York, NY 10027-9998. (212) 678-3433; (800) 601-4868. Fax (212) 678-4048. Internet eric-cue@columbia.edu. Erwin Flaxman, Dir. The educational characteristics and experiences of the diverse racial, ethnic, social class, and linguistic populations in urban (and suburban) schools. Curriculum and instruction of students from these populations and the organization of their schools. The relationship of urban schools to their communities. The social and economic conditions that affect the education of urban populations, with particular attention to factors that place urban students at risk educationally, and ways that public and private sector policies can improve these conditions.

ACCESS ERIC. Aspen Systems Corp., 1600 Research Blvd., Rockville, MD 20850-3172; 1-800-LET-ERIC [538-3742]. Fax (301) 251-5767. Internet acceric@inet.ed.gov. Beverly Swanson, ERIC Project Dir. Toll-free service provides access to the information and services available through the ERIC system. Staff will answer questions as well as refer callers to education sources. ACCESS ERIC also produces several publications and reference and referral databases that provide information about both the ERIC system and current education-related issues and research. *Publications: A Pocket Guide to ERIC*; *All About ERIC*; *The ERIC Review*; the Conclusion Brochure series; *Catalog of ERIC Clearinghouse Publications*; *ERIC Calendar of Education-Related Conferences*; *ERIC User's Interchange*; *Directory of ERIC Information Service Centers*. *Databases*: ERIC Digests Online (EDO); Education-Related Information Centers; ERIC Information Service Providers; ERIC Calendar of Education-Related Conferences. (The databases are available through GTE Education Services on a subscription basis.)

Adjunct ERIC Clearinghouse for Art Education. Indiana University, Social Studies Development Center, 2805 East 10th St., Suite 120, Bloomington, IN 47408-2373. (812) 855-3838. Fax (812) 855-0455. Internet clarkgl@ucs.indiana.edu; hubbard@ucs.indiana.edu; zimmerm@ucs.indiana.edu. Gilbert Clark, Guy Hubbard, and Enid Zimmerman, Co-Directors. Adjunct to the ERIC Clearinghouse on Social Studies/Social Science Education.

Adjunct ERIC Clearinghouse for Consumer Education (ADJ/CN). National Institute for Consumer Education, 207 Rackham Bldg., West Cir. Dr., Eastern Michigan University, Ypsilanti, MI 48197-2237. (313) 487-2292. Fax (313) 487-7153. Internet cse_banniste@emuvax.emich.edu. Rosella Bannister, Dir. Adjunct to the ERIC Clearinghouse on Adult, Career, and Vocational Education.

Adjunct ERIC Clearinghouse for ESL Literacy Education (ADJ/LE). National Clearinghouse for Literacy Education, Center for Applied Linguistics (CAL), 1118 22d St. NW, Washington, DC 20037-0037. (202) 429-9292, Ext. 200. Fax (202) 659-5641. Internet ncle@cal.org. Joy Peyton, Dir. Adjunct to the ERIC Clearinghouse on Languages and Linguistics.

Adjunct ERIC Clearinghouse for Law-Related Education (ADJ/LR). Indiana University, Social Studies Development Center, 2805 East 10th St., Suite 120, Bloomington, IN 47408-2373. (812) 855-3838. Fax (812) 855-0455. Internet patrick@ucs.indiana.edu; rleming@ucs.indiana.edu. John Patrick and Robert Leming, Co-Directors. Adjunct to the ErIC Clearinghouse on Social Studies/ Social Sciences Education.

Adjunct ERIC Clearinghouse for the Test Collection (ADJ/TC). Educational Testing Service (ETS), ETS Test Collection, Rosedale and Carter Roads. Princeton, NJ 08541. (609) 734-5737. Fax (609) 683-7186. Internet mhalpern@rosedale.org. Marilyn Halpern, Mgr., Library, Text Collection. Adjunct to the ERIC Clearinghouse on Assessment and Evaluation.

Adjunct ERIC Clearinghouse for United States-Japan Studies (ADJ/JS). Indiana University, Social Studies Development Center, 2805 E. 10th St., Suite 120, Bloomington, IN 47408-2373. (812) 855-3838. Fax (812) 855-0455. C. Frederick Risingerr, Dir. Adjunct to the ERIC Clearinghouse on Social Studies/Social Science Education.

Adjunct ERIC Clearinghouse on Chapter 1 (Compensatory Education) (ADJ/CHP1). Chapter 1 Technical Assistance Center, PRC Inc., 2601 Fortune Cir. E., One Park Fletcher Bldg., Suite 300-A, Indianapolis, IN 46241-2237. (317) 244-8160; (800) 456-2380. Fax (317) 244-7386. Sheila M. Short, Coord. Adjunct to the ERIC Clearinghouse on Urban Education.

Adjunct ERIC Clearinghouse on Clinical Schools (ADJ/CL). American Association of Colleges for Teacher Education, One Dupont Cir. NW, Suite 610, Washington, DC 20036-1186. (202) 293-2450; (800) 8229229. Fax (202) 457-8095. Internet iabdalha@inet.ed.gov. Ismat Abdal-Haqq, Coord. Adjunct to the ERIC Clearinghouse on Adult, Career, and Vocational Education.

ERIC Document Reproduction Service (EDRS). 7420 Fullerton Rd., Suite 110, Springfield, VA 22153-2852. (703) 440-1400; (800) 443-ERIC (3742). Fax (703) 440-1408. Internet edrs@gwuvm.gwu.edu. Peter M. Dagutis, Dir. Operates the document delivery arm of the ERIC system. Furnishes microfiche and/or paper copies of most ERIC documents. Address purchase orders to the preceding address. Fax order and delivery service available.

ERIC Processing and Reference Facility. 1301 Piccard Dr., Suite 300, Rockville, MD 20850-4305. (301) 258-5500; (800) 799-ERIC (3742). Fax (301) 948-3695. Internet ericfac@inet.ed.gov. Ted Brandhorst, Dir. A centralized information processing facility serving all components of the ERIC network, under policy direction of Central ERIC. Services provided include acquisitions, editing, receiving and dispatch, document control and analysis, lexicography, computer processing, file maintenance, and database management. Receives and edits abstracts from 16 ERIC Clearinghouses for publication in *Resources in Education* (*RIE*); updates and maintains the *Thesaurus of ERIC Descriptors*. Publications: *Resources in Education*; *Source Directory*; *Report Number Index*; *Clearinghouse Number/ED Number Cross Reference Listing*; *Title Index*; *ERIC Processing Manual*; numerous other listings and indexes.

*Far West Laboratory for Educational Research and Development (FWL). 730 Harrison St., San Francisco, CA 94107-1242. (415) 565-3000. Fax (415) 565-3012. Dr. Dean Nafziger, Exec. Dir. Far West Laboratory for Educational Research and Development serves the four-state region of Arizona, California, Nevada, and Utah, working with educators at all levels to plan and carry out school improvements. The mission of FWL is to challenge and enable educational organizations and their communities to create and sustain improved learning and development opportunities for their children, youth, and adults. To accomplish its mission, FWL directs resources toward: advancing knowledge; developing products and programs for teachers and learners; providing assistance to educational agencies; communicating with outside audiences to remain informed and to inform others about the results of research, development, and exemplary practice; and creating an environment in which diverse educational and societal issues can be addressed and resolved. Far West Laboratory maintains a reference library.

*Federal Communications Commission (FCC). 1919 M St. NW, Washington, DC 20554. Patti Grace Smith, Deputy Dir. of Policy/Public Information and Reference Services. The FCC is a federal government agency regulating interstate and international communications by radio, television, wire, satellite, and cable in the United States and its territories and possessions. It allocates frequencies and channels for different types of communication activities, issues amateur and commercial radio operators' licenses, and regulates rates of many types of interstate communication services. Public Service Division: Consumer Assistance Branch (202) 632-7000. Fax (202) 632-0274. TT (202) 632-6999. Public Policy Planning Branch (202) 632-0244. Martha Contee, Chief, Public Service Div. (PSD). *Publications:* Fact Sheets, Information Bulletins, and Public Notices pertaining to FCC-regulated services.

*Film Advisory Board (FAB). 1727-1/2 Sycamore, Hollywood, CA 90028. (213) 874-3644. Fax (213) 969-0635. Elayne Blythe, Pres. Previews and evaluates films and film-type presentations in all formats, makes recommendations for improved family entertainment fare, and presents awards of excellence to outstanding motion pictures, television programs, videos, and audiotapes, and for innovations in these industries. Technical awards are also presented, as are awards for outstanding contributions to the entertainment industry and for the most promising newcomers. Awards of excellence are presented for videocassettes; the FAB Award Winner Seal is featured worldwide on many of the family and child videocassettes for Prism, RCA Columbia, Rhino, Turner, Fox, and others. Supplies film list to many national organizations encouraging them to support FAB award-winning products. *Membership:* 450. *Dues:* $40/yr. *Publication: Film Advisory Board Newsletter,* monthly film list distributed to studios, libraries, churches, public relations firms, youth groups, PTAs, clubs, and colleges. Now rating home videos with Film Advisory Board (FAB) Rating System, the only official rating system other than the MPAA. *FAB Rating Categories:* C=Children (ages 10 and under); F=Family (all ages); *PD=Parental Discretion; **PD-M=Parental Discretion-Mature (ages 13 and over). Categories replaced as of March 1, 1993: *M=Mature and ** VM=Very Mature. FAB's system was the first to use content descriptions with its rating categories.

Film Arts Foundation (FAF). 346 9th St., 2d Floor, San Francisco, CA 94103. (415) 552-8760. Fax (415) 552-0882. Gail Silva, Dir. Service organization designed to support and promote independent film and video production. Services include low-cost 16mm and Super-8 editing facility, festivals file, resource library, group legal plan, association health options, seminars, workshops, annual film and video festival, grants program, monthly publication, work-in-progress screenings, proposal and distribution consultation, nonprofit sponsorship of selected film and video projects, and advocacy for independent film and video. *Membership:* 2,800 plus. *Dues:* $35. *Meetings:* International Film Financing Conference (IFFCON '95), January 13-15, 1995, San Francisco, CA. *Publications: Release Print*; *AEIOU (Alternative Exhibition Information of the Universe)*; *Media Catalog* (over 200 titles of independent media projects completed with FAF's nonprofit fiscal sponsorship).

*Film/Video Arts, Inc. 817 Broadway, New York, NY 10003. (212) 673-9361. Fax (212) 475-3467. Karen Helmerson, Deputy Dir. Film/Video Arts is a nonprofit media arts center dedicated to the advancement of emerging and established media artists of diverse backgrounds. F/VA provides support services that include low-cost production equipment and facilities, education and training, exhibition, and grant and employment opportunities. F/VA offers scholarship assistance to women, African-Americans, Latinos, Asians, and Native Americans. *Dues:* $40/individuals, $60/nonprofit organizations (Oct. 1-Sept. 30).

*Freedom of Information Center (FOI). 20 Walter William Hall, University of Missouri, Columbia, MO 65211. (314) 882-4856. Kathleen Edwards, Center Mgr. Collects and indexes material on actions by government, media, and society affecting the flow of information at international, national, state, and local levels. The center answers questions on the federal FOI Act, censorship issues, access to government at all levels, privacy, ethics, bar-press guidelines, and First Amendment issues. *Publications:* Back issues of FOI publications available for purchase.

*George Eastman House (formerly International Museum of Photography at George Eastman House). 900 East Ave., Rochester, NY 14607. (716) 271-3361. Fax (716) 271-3970. James L. Enyeart, Dir. World-renowned museum of photography and cinematography established to preserve, collect, and exhibit photographic art and technology, film materials, and related literature. Services include archives, traveling exhibitions, research library center for the conservation of photographic materials, and photographic print service. Educational programs, films, symposia, and internship stipends offered. *Dues:* $40 libraries; $50 families; $40 individuals; $25 students or senior citizens; $75 Contributors; $125 Sustainers; $250 Patrons; $500 Benefactors; $1,000 George Eastman Society. *Publications: IMAGE*; *Microfiche Index to Collections*; *Newsletter*; *Annual Report: The George Eastman House and Gardens*; *Masterpieces of Photography from the George Eastman House Collections*; and exhibition catalogues.

The George Lucas Educational Foundation. P.O. Box 3494, San Rafael, CA 94912. (415) 662-1600. Fax (415) 662-1605. E-mail edutopia@glef.org; America Online edutopia; gopher glef.org; URL http://glef.org. The Foundation was formed to create a vision of a technology-rich effective educational system. We are producing a dramatic movie that depicts this vision and a resource document that provides examples of programs, resources, policies, experts, etc. that support and reinforce what will be seen in the movie. We are trying to help change public policy and look at education as an investment in the future. The target audience is elected officials, corporate executives, community and opinion leaders, media, and parents. We hope to give educators useful tools as they work to change teaching and learning. Subscribers to the newsletter, *EDUTOPIA*, include educators, parents, the media, elected officials, corporate executives, community and opinion leaders. The work in which we are involved is targeted at the same diverse audience. The George Lucas Educational Foundation is a private operating foundation; it is not a grant-making organization. *Publication: EDUTOPIA* (bi-annual newsletter).

*Great Plains National ITV Library (GPN). PO Box 80669, Lincoln, NE 68501-0669. (402) 472-2007; (800) 228-4630. Fax (402) 472-1785. Lee Rockwell, Dir. Acquires, produces, promotes, and distributes educational video series and singles. Offers more than 200 videotape (videocassette) courses and related teacher utilization materials. Available for purchase or, in some instances, lease. Also distributes instructional videodiscs and CD-ROMs. *Publications: GPN Educational Video Catalog* (annual); *GPNewsletter* (q.); periodic brochures.

*Health Sciences Communications Association (HeSCA). 6728 Old McLean Village Dr., McLean, VA 22101. (703) 556-9324. Fax (703) 556-8729. Cheryl Kilday, Assoc. Dir. HeSCA is an international nonprofit organization dedicated to the promotion and sharing of ideas, skills, resources, and techniques to enhance communication and education in the health sciences. HeSCA is actively supported by leading medical and veterinary schools, hospitals, medical associations, and businesses. *Membership:* 350. *Dues:* $90 individual; $135 institutional ($90 additional institutional dues); $55 retirees; $70 students; $1,000 sustaining; all include subscriptions to the journal and newsletter). *Meeting:* World Congress on Biomedical Communications, June 18-23, 1994, Orlando, FL. *Publications: Journal of Biocommunications; Feedback* (newsletter); *Patient Education Sourcebook Vol. II; 1993 Media Festivals and LRC Catalogue.*

Hollywood Film Archive. 8344 Melrose Ave., Hollywood, CA 90069. (213) 933-3345. D. Richard Baer, Dir. Archival organization for information about feature films produced worldwide, from the early silents to the present. Offers comprehensive movie reference works for sale, including *Variety Film Reviews* (1907-1994) and the *American Film Institute Catalogs* (1911-20, 1921-30, 1931-40, 1961-70), as well as the *Film Superlist* (1894-1939, 1940-1949, 1950-1959) volumes, which provide information both on copyrights and on motion pictures in the public domain, and *Harrison's Reports and Film Reviews* (1919-1962). *Publications:* Reference books.

HOPE Reports, Inc. 58 Carverdale Dr., Rochester, NY 14618-4004. (716) 442-1310. Fax (716) 442-1725. Thomas W. Hope, Pres., Chair, and CEO; Mabeth S. Hope, Vice Pres. Supplies statistics, marketing information, trends, forecasts, and salary and media studies to the visual communications industries in printed reports, in custom studies, or by consulting, or by telephone. Clients/users in the United States and abroad include manufacturers, dealers, producers, and media users in business, government, health sciences, education, and community agencies. *Publications: Hope Reports AV Events Calendar* (annual); *Hope Reports Industry Quarterly; Contract Production for the '90s; Video Post-Production; Media Market Trends; Educational Media Trends through the 1990's; LCD Panels and Projectors; Overhead Projection System; Presentation Slides; Producer & Video Post Wages & Salaries; Noncommercial AV Wages & Salaries; Corporate Media Salaries; Digital Photography: Pictures of Tomorrow.*

*Institute for Development of Educational Activities, Inc. (IDEA). 259 Regency Ridge, Dayton, OH 45459. (513) 434-6969. Fax (513) 434-5203. Action-oriented research and development organization, originating from the Charles F. Kettering Foundation, established to assist the educational community in bridging the gap that separates research and innovation from actual practice in the schools. Goal is to design and test new responses to improve education and to create arrangements that support local application. Main activities include: developing new and improved processes, systems, and materials; training local facilitators to use the change processes; providing information and services about improved methods and materials.

Sponsors an annual fellowship program for administrators and conducts seminars for school administrators and teachers.

*Institute for Research on Teaching. College of Education, MSU, East Lansing, MI 48824. (517) 355-1737. E-mail penny@msu.bitnet. Penelope Peterson and Jere Brophy, Co-Dirs. Funded primarily by the U.S. Department of Education and Michigan State University; conducts research on the continuing problems of practice encountered by teaching professionals, the teaching of subject matter disciplines in elementary schools (through the Center for the Learning and Teaching of Elementary Subjects), and publishes numerous materials detailing this research. *Publications:* Research series; occasional papers; annual catalog.

*Institute for the Future (IFTF). 2744 Sand Hill Rd., Menlo Park, CA 94025-7020. (415) 854-6322. Fax (415) 854-7850. J. Ian Morrison, Pres. Works with organizations to plan their long-term futures. Helps them to evaluate the external environment and take advantage of the opportunities offered by new technologies. Founded in 1968, IFTF has emerged as a leader in action-oriented research for business, industry, and governments, having worked with more than 300 organizations. Typical projects include environmental scanning, strategic planning assistance, policy analyses, and market outlooks and evaluations for new products and next-generation technologies. The success of the organization is based on several unique strengths, including a pragmatic futures orientation, studies of emerging technologies, networking of ideas and people, and use of scenarios to identify and analyze issues and options. *Publications:* List available from IFTF free of charge.

Institute of Culture and Communication. See listing for Program of Cultural Studies.

International Association of Business Communicators (IABC). One Hallidie Plaza, Suite 600, San Francisco, CA 94102. (415) 433-3400. Fax (415) 362-8762. David Paulus, Pres. and CEO. IABC is the worldwide association for the communication and public relations profession. It is founded on the principle that the better an organization communicates with all its audiences, the more successful and effective it will be in meeting its objectives. IABC is dedicated to fostering communication excellence, contributing more effectively to organizations' goals worldwide, and being a model of communication effectiveness. *Membership:* 11,000 plus. *Dues:* $180 in addition to local and regional dues. *Meetings:* 1995, June 11-14, Toronto, ON; 1996, June 16-19, Dallas, TX. *Publication: Communication World.*

International Association of School Librarianship (IASL). Box 19586, Kalamazoo, MI 49019. (616) 343-5728. Dr. Jean E. Lowrie, Exec. Secy. Seeks to encourage development of school libraries and library programs throughout the world, to promote professional preparation of school librarians and continuing education programs, to achieve collaboration among school libraries of the world, and to facilitate loans and exchanges in the field. *Membership:* 900 plus. *Dues:* $25/yr. personal and institution for North America, Western Europe, Japan, and Australia; $15/yr. for all other countries; $30-$100/yr. associations (based on membership). *Meetings:* July 17-22, 1995, Worcester, UK. *Publications: IASL Newsletter* (q.); *Annual Proceedings*; *Connections: School Library Associations and Contact People Worldwide*; *Indicators of Quality for School Library Media Programs*; *Books and Borrowers*; *School Libraries Worldwide*; *Conference Proceedings Index 1972-1984.*

International Center of Photography (ICP). 1130 Fifth Ave., New York, NY 10128. (212) 860-1777. Fax (212) 360-6490. ICP Midtown, 1133 Avenue of the Americas, New York, NY 10036. (212) 768-4680. Fax (212) 768-4688. Willis Hartshorn, Dir.; Phyllis Levine, Dir. of Public Information. A comprehensive photographic institution whose exhibitions, publications, collections, and educational programs embrace all aspects of photography from aesthetics to technique; from the 18th century to the present; from master photographers to newly emerging talents; from photojournalism to the avant garde. Changing exhibitions, lectures, seminars, workshops, museum shops, and screening rooms make ICP a complete photographic resource. *Membership:* 7,000. *Dues:* $50 individual membership, $60 double membership, $125 Supporting Patron, $250 Photography Circle, $500 Silver Card Patron, $1,000 Gold Card Patron; corporate memberships available. *Meetings:* ICP Infinity Awards, May 1995. *Publications: A Singular Elegance: The Photographs of Baron Adolph de Meyer; Talking Pictures: People Speak about the Photographs That Speak to Them; Library of Photography; Encyclopedia of Photography—Master Photographs from PFA Collection; Man Ray in Fashion; Quarterly Program Guide; Quarterly Exhibition Schedule.*

International Copyright Information Center (INCINC). c/o Association of American Publishers, 1718 Connecticut Ave. NW, 7th Floor, Washington, DC 20009-1148. (202) 232-3335. Fax (202) 745-0694. MCI mail aapdc. Carol A. Risher, Dir. Assists developing nations in their efforts to secure permission to translate and/or reprint copyrighted works published in the United States.

International Council for Computers in Education (ICCE). See listing for International Society for Technology in Education (ISTE).

International Film and TV Festival of New York. See listing for The New York Festivals.

***International Graphic Arts Education Association (IGAEA).** 4615 Forbes Ave., Pittsburgh, PA 15213-3796. (412) 621-6941. Lenore D. Collins, Pres. (401) 456-8703. Fax (401) 456-8379. An organization of professionals in graphic arts education and industry, dedicated to promoting effective methodology in teaching, relevant educational research and efficient dissemination of information concerning graphic arts, graphic communications, and related fields. To achieve these goals, the IGAEA sponsors conferences, publications, and industry liaison programs. The association has recently revised its mission and now includes and invites not only graphic arts educators but teachers of graphic design, technology education, journalism, photography, and any other field relating to visual/graphic communications and imaging technology. *Membership:* approx. 700. *Dues:* $20 regular; $12 associate (retired); $5 student; $10 library; $50-$200 sustaining members based on number of employees. *Meetings:* 1995, August 6-11, Warrensburg, MO. *Publications: Visual Communications Journal; Research and Resource Reports.*

International Information Management Congress (IMC). 1650 38th St., 205W, Boulder, CO 80301. (303) 440-7085. Fax (303) 440-7234. John A. Lacy, Pres. and CEO. Promote understanding and cooperation among organizations of the world engaged in furthering the progress and application of document-based information systems. Provide an international clearinghouse for information and advancement in systems and technology. Conduct conferences and exhibitions for the exchange of information. Provide document-based information through the publication of the *IMC Journal.* Encourage and assist in the establishment and use of document-based standards. *Membership:* 30 associations, 70 sustaining company members. *Dues:* $85/yr. affiliates (any individual with an interest in the document-based information systems field); $200 associate (any association or society with common goals within the industry); $350-$5100/yr. sustaining (any corporate organization with a common interest in the industry; includes major computer companies, major photographic companies, and numerous smaller specialized companies). *Meetings:* 1995, June 12-15, Amsterdam, The Netherlands, "IMC Document Imaging '95"; 1995, November 7-9, Seoul, Korea, "MC

Document Imaging '95"; 1996, June 3-6, Paris, France, "IMC Document Imaging '96." *Publication: IMC Journal* (bi-mo.).

International Museum of Photography at George Eastman House. See listing for George Eastman House.

International Society for Technology in Education (ISTE) (formerly International Council for Computers in Education [ICCE]). 1787 Agate St., Eugene, OR 97403-1923. (503) 346-4414. Fax (503) 346-5890. Internet iste@oregon.uoregon.edu. David Moursund, CEO; Maia S. Howes, Exec. Secy. The largest nonprofit professional organization dedicated to the improvement of all levels of education through the use of computer-based technology. Technology-using educators from all over the world rely on ISTE for information, inspiration, ideas, and updates on the latest electronic information systems available to the educational community. ISTE is a prominent information center and source of leadership to communicate and collaborate with educational professionals, policy makers, and other organizations world-wide. *Membership:* 12,000 individual members, 75 organizational affiliates, 25 Private Sector Council members. *Dues:* $55 individuals, $215 all-inclusive memberships (U.S.); $420 institutions; $1,500 to $5,000, Private Sector Council members. *Meeting:* 1995 National Educational Computing Conference (NECC '95), June 17-19, Baltimore, MD, "Emerging Technologies—Lifelong Learning." *Publications: Learning and Leading with Technology: The ISTE Journal of Educational Technology Practice and Policy* (formerly *The Computing Teacher*) (8/yr.); *The Update Newsletter* (7/yr.); *The Journal of Research on Computing in Education* (q.); guides to instructional uses of computers at the precollege level and in teacher training, about 80 books, and a range of distance education courses that carry graduate-level credit.

International Tape/Disc Association. See listing for ITA.

*International Telecommunications Satellite Organization (INTELSAT). 3400 International Dr. NW, Washington, DC 20008. (202) 944-7500. Fax (202) 944-7890. Irving Goldstein, Dir. Gen. and CEO; Tony A. Trujillo, Mgr., Public and External Relations. Dedicated to the design, development, construction, establishment, operation, and maintenance of the global telecommunications satellite system that currently provides most of the world's international overseas telecommunications links and virtually all live international television services. *Membership:* 128 countries. *Publications: INTELSAT News* (q.); *INTELSAT Annual Report.*

International Teleconferencing Association (ITCA). 1650 Tysons Blvd., Suite 200, McLean, VA 22102. (703) 506-3280. Fax (703) 506-3266. Fax on demand (800) 891-8633. E-mail dasitca@aol.com. Tom Gibson, Executive Dir.; Christie Scott, Mgr., Publications and Programming. ITCA, an international nonprofit association, is dedicated to the growth and development of teleconferencing as a profession and an industry. ITCA provides programs and services which foster the professional development of its members; champions teleconferencing and related technologies as primary communications tools; recognizes and promotes broader applications and the development of teleconferencing and related technologies; and serves as the authoritative resource for information and research on teleconferencing and related technologies. *Membership:* ITCA represents over 1,900 teleconferencing professionals throughout the world. ITCA members use teleconferencing, manage business television and teleconferencing networks, design the technology, sell products and services, advise customers and vendors, conduct research, teach courses via teleconference, and teach about teleconferencing. They represent such diverse industry segments as health care, aerospace, government, pharmaceutical, education, insurance, finance and banking, telecommunications, and manufacturing. *Dues:* $2,000 gold sustaining; $1,000 sustaining; $500 organizational; $250 small business; $100 individual; and $30 student.

Meetings: Annual trade show and convention: ITCA '96, May 21-24, Washington, DC (for more information, call (703) 506-3283). *Publications: ITCA Connections Newsletter* (mo.); *Videoconferencing Room Directory; Member Directory; Yearbook; Classroom of the Future; Teleconferencing in State Government Guide; Teleconferencing Success Stories.*

ITA (formerly International Tape/Disc Association [ITA]). 505 Eighth Ave., New York, NY 10018. (212) 643-0620. Fax (212) 643-0624. Charles Van Horn, Exec. V.P.; Charles Riotto, Exec. Dir. of Operations. An international association providing a forum for the exchange of management information on global trends and innovations which drive the magnetic/optical recording media and associated industries. Members include magnetic and optical recording media manufacturers, rights holders to video programs, recording and playback equipment manufacturers, and audio and video duplicators/replicators. For more than 24 years, ITA has provided vital information and educational services throughout the magnetic and optical recording media industries. By promoting a greater awareness of marketing, merchandising, and technical developments, the association serves all areas of the entertainment, information, and delivery systems industries. *Membership:* 450 corporations. *Dues:* Corporate membership dues based on sales volume. *Meetings:* 25th Annual Seminar, March 8-12, 1995, Rancho Mirage, CA; REPLItech Europe, April 4-6, 1995, Vienna, Austria; REPLItech International, June 13-15, 1995, Santa Clara, CA; REPLItech Asia, October 24-26, 1995, Singapore. (REPLItech is a seminar and trade show aimed at duplicators and replicators of magnetic and optical media.) *Publications: ITA Membership Newsletter; Seminar Proceedings; 1995 International Source Directory.*

ITVA (International Television Association). 6311 N. O'Connor Rd., Suite 230, Irving, TX 75039. (214) 869-1112. Fax (214) 869-2980. Fred M. Wehrli, Exec. Dir. Founded in 1968, ITVA's mission is to advance the video profession, to serve the needs and interests of its members, and to promote the growth and quality of video and related media. Association members are video professionals working in or serving the corporate, governmental, institutional, or educational markets. ITVA provides professional development opportunities through local, regional, and national workshops, video festivals, and publications. The networking opportunities available to members are another principal benefit. ITVA welcomes anyone who is interested in professional video and is seeking to widen his/her horizons either through career development or networking. ITVA offers its members discounts on major medical insurance, production/liability insurance; hotel, car rental, and long distance telephone discounts; and a MasterCard program. The association is also a member of the Small Business Legislative Council. *Membership:* 9,000, 77 commercial member companies. *Dues:* $150 individuals; $425 organizational (includes 3 individuals); $1,500 commercial sustaining; $625 commercial associate. *Meetings:* 1995, Annual International Conference, June 13-17, Dallas, TX, "Transformations"; 1996, Annual International Conference, June 11-15, Philadelphia, PA (both meetings are in conjunction with INFOCOMM International). *Publications: ITN (International Television News)* (6/yr.); *Membership Directory* (annual); *Handbook of Treatments; It's a Business First . . . and a Creative Outlet Second; Handbook of Forms; How To Survive Being Laid Off; Employment Tax Procedures: Classification of Workers Within the Television Commercial Production and Professional Video Communication Industries; A Report on the IRS Guidelines Classifying Workers in the Video Industry.*

Library of Congress. James Madison Bldg., 101 Independence Ave. SE, Washington, DC 20540. (202) 707-5000. Fax (202) 707-1389. Contact the National Reference Service, (202) 707-5522. The Library of Congress is the major source of research and information for the Congress. In its role as the national library, it catalogs and classifies library materials in some 470 languages, distributes the data in both printed and electronic form, and makes its vast collections available through interlibrary loan and on-site to anyone over high school age. It contains the world's largest television and film archive, acquiring materials through gift, purchase, and copyright deposit. The collections of the Motion Picture, Broadcasting, and Recorded Sound Division include 994,188 moving images and 2,118,881 recordings. Bibliographic data in the computerized Library of Congress Information System is now available for online searching over the Internet. The Internet address for telnet (connecting) to LOCIS is locis.loc.gov. The numeric address is 140.147.254.3. In 1993, the library had 900,000 readers and visitors and performed 1,400,000 direct reference services. *Publications:* Listed in *Library of Congress Publications in Print* (free from Office Systems Services).

Lister Hill National Center for Biomedical Communications. National Library of Medicine, 8600 Rockville Pike, Bethesda, MD 20894. (301) 496-4441. Fax (301) 402-0118. Harold M. Schoolman, M.D., Acting Dir. The center conducts research and development programs in three major categories: Computer and Information Science; Biomedical Image and Communications Engineering; and Educational Technology Development. Major efforts of the center include its involvement with the Unified Medical Language System (UMLS) project; research and development in the use of expert systems to embody the factual and procedural knowledge of human experts; research in the use of electronic technologies to distribute biomedical information not represented in text and in the storage and transmission of x-ray images over the Internet; and the development and demonstration of new educational technologies, including the use of microcomputer technology with videodisc-based images, for training health care professionals. A Learning Center for Interactive Technology serves as a focus for displaying new and effective applications of educational technologies to faculties and staff of health sciences educational institutions and other visitors, and health professions educators are assisted in the use of such technologies through training, demonstrations, and consultations.

Magazine Publishers of America (MPA). 919 Third Ave., 22nd Floor, New York, NY 10022. (212) 872-3700. Fax (212) 888-4217. Donald D. Kummerfeld, Pres. MPA is the trade association of the consumer magazine industry. MPA promotes the greater and more effective use of magazine advertising, with ad campaigns in the trade press and in MPA member magazines, presentations to advertisers and their ad agencies, and magazine days in cities around the United States. MPA runs educational seminars, conducts surveys of its members on a variety of topics, represents the magazine industry in Washington, D.C., maintains an extensive library on magazine publishing, and carries on other activities. *Membership:* 230 publishers representing more than 1,200 magazines. *Meetings:* American Magazine Conferences: 1995, November 5-9, Boca Raton, FL; 1996, October 13-16, Southampton Princess, Bermuda. *Publications: Newsletter of Consumer Marketing; Newsletter of Research; Newsletter of International Publishing; Magazine; Washington Newsletter.*

*MECC (Minnesota Educational Computing Corporation). 6160 Summit Dr. N., Minneapolis, MN 55430-4003. (612) 569-1500; (800) 685-MECC. Fax (612) 569-1551. Dale LaFrenz, Pres.; Dean Kephart, Dir., Marketing Communications. MECC is the leading producer of K-12 educational software in the United States and an emerging player in the rapidly growing home market. For the past 20 years, MECC has provided children and young adults with high-quality educational software that helps them develop a lifelong love of learning. More than 80 million MECC products have been sold to homes and schools since MECC was established in 1973. MECC creates learning opportunities that are fun and provides teachers and parents with products that use technology to enhance learning. MECC products take a child-centered approach, celebrating the uniqueness of individual children and cultivating their talents. MECC software helps children to combine learning with imagination. In addition to software products, MECC offers emerging technology products and an annual international conference. MECC currently offers 150 MAC/DOS/Apple titles to schools for instructional use. The 24 MAC and 20 DOS titles included in the offering lead the industry in quantity and quality. In the home market, MECC offers 10 fun-loving titles on both the DOS and MAC platforms. The company takes great pride in its flagship product, *The Oregon Trail,* which is found in the hands of more kids than any other education product produced. Now *Amazon Trail, DynoPark Tycoon, My Own Stories,* and *Odell Down Under* are carrying on the tradition of excellence.

Medical Library Association (MLA). 6 N. Michigan Ave., Suite 300, Chicago, IL 60602. (312) 419-9094. Fax (312) 419-8950. Fred W. Roper, Pres.; Carla J. Funk, Exec. Dir. MLA is a professional organization of 5,000 individuals and institutions in the health sciences information field, dedicated to fostering medical and allied scientific libraries, promoting professional excellence and leadership of its members, and exchanging medical literature among its members. *Membership:* 3,743 individuals, 1,281 institutions. *Dues:* $65-$110 individuals, $25 students; $175-$410 institutional dues depend on number of periodical subscriptions. *Meeting:* 1995, May 5-11, Washington, DC, "Health Information for the Global Village." *Publications: MLA News* (newsletter, 10/yr.); *Bulletin of the Medical Library Association* (q.); monographs.

Mid-continent Regional Educational Laboratory (McREL). Denver Office: 2550 S. Parker Rd., Suite 500, Aurora, CO 80014. (303) 337-0990. Kansas City Office: 4709 Belleview Ave., Kansas City, MO 64112. (816) 756-2401. C. L. Hutchins, Exec. Dir. One of 10 Office of Educational Research and Improvement (OERI) regional educational laboratories designed to help educators and policymakers solve educational problems in their schools. Using the best available information and the experience and expertise of professionals, McREL seeks to identify solutions to education problems, tries new approaches, furnishes research results, and provides training to teachers and administrators. McREL serves Colorado, Kansas, Nebraska, Missouri, Wyoming, North Dakota, and South Dakota. An affiliate organization, McREL Institute, works nationwide and markets curriculum products and training.

*Museum Computer Network (MCN). 8720 Georgia Ave., Suite 501, Silver Spring, MD 20910. (301) 585-4413. Fax (301) 495-0810. Michele Devine, Admin. Diane Zorich, Pres. As a not-for-profit professional association, membership in MCN means access to professionals committed to using computer technology to achieve the cultural aims of museums. Members include novices and experts, museum professionals, and vendors and consultants, working in application areas from collections management to administrative computing. Activities include an annual conference, educational workshops, advisory services, special projects, and publication of a quarterly newsletter. *Membership dues:* Sponsor $250; vendor $150; institution $100; individual $50. *Meeting:* Annual Conference, August 28-September 3, 1994, Washington, DC. *Publications: Spectra* (newsletter); *CMI.* Subscription to *Spectra* is available to libraries only for $60 plus $10 surcharge for delivery.

*Museum of Modern Art, Circulating Film and Video Library. 11 W. 53d St., New York, NY 10019. (212) 708-9530. Fax (212) 708-9531. William Sloan, Libr. Sponsors film study programs and provides film rentals and sales. *Publications: Circulating Film and Video Catalog Vols. 1 and 2.*

National Aeronautics and Space Administration (NASA). NASA Headquarters, Code FET, Washington, DC 20546. (202) 358-1540. Fax (202) 358-3048. E-mail mphelps@hr.hq.nasa.gov. Dr. Malcolm V. Phelps, Chief, Technology and Evaluation Branch. Frank C. Owens, Dir., Education

Division. From elementary through postgraduate school, NASA's educational programs are designed to capture students' interests in science, mathematics, and technology at an early age; to channel more students into science, engineering, and technology career paths; and to enhance the knowledge, skills, and experiences of teachers and university faculty. NASA's educational programs include NASA Spacelink (an electronic information system); videoconferences (60-minute interactive staff development videoconferences to be delivered to schools via satellite); and NASA Television (informational and educational television programming). Additional information is available from the Education Division at NASA Headquarters and counterpart offices at the nine NASA field centers. Over 180,000 educators make copies of Teacher Resource Center Network materials each year, and thousands of teachers participate in interactive video teleconferencing, use Spacelink, and watch NASA Television. Additional information may be obtained from Spacelink (spacelink.msfc.nasa.gov).

*National Alliance for Media Arts and Culture (NAMAC). 655 13th St., Suite 201, Oakland, CA 94612. (510) 451-2717. Fax (510) 451-2715. Julian Low, Dir. A nonprofit organization dedicated to increasing public understanding of and support for the field of media arts in the United States. Members include media centers, cable access centers, universities, and media artists, as well as other individuals and organizations providing services for production, education, exhibition, distribution, and preservation of video, film, audio, and intermedia. NAMAC's information services are available to the general public, arts and nonarts organizations, businesses, corporations, foundations, government agencies, schools, and universities. *Membership:* 200 organizations, 150 individuals. *Dues:* Institutional ranges from $50 to $250/yr. depending on annual budget; $30/yr. individual. *Publications: Media Arts Information Network*; *NAMAC Directory* (published biennially, available for $25 to nonmembers).

National Association for the Education of Young Children (NAEYC). 1509 16th St. NW, Washington, DC 20036-1426. (202) 232-8777; (800) 424-2460. Fax (202) 328-1846. Marilyn M. Smith, Exec. Dir.; Pat Spahr, contact person. Dedicated to improving the quality core and education provided to young children (birth-8 years). *Membership:* Nearly 90,000. *Dues:* $25. *Meeting:* 1995 Annual Conference, November 29-December 2, Washington, DC. *Publications: Young Children* (journal); more than 60 books, posters, videos, and brochures.

National Association for Visually Handicapped (NAVH). 22 W. 21st St., 6th Floor, New York, NY 10010. (212) 889-3141. Fax (212) 727-2931. Lorraine H. Marchi, Founder/Exec. Dir.; Eva Cohen, Asst. to Exec. Dir. (or) 3201 Balboa St., San Francisco, CA 94121. (415) 221-3201. Serves the partially sighted (not totally blind). Offers informational literature for the layperson and the professional, most in large print. Newsletters for adults—*Seeing Clearly*—and for children—*In Focus*—are published at irregular intervals and distributed free throughout the English-speaking world. Maintains a loan library of large-print books. Provides counseling and guidance for the visually impaired and their families and the professionals and paraprofessionals who work with them. *Membership:* 12,000. *Dues:* Full membership $40/yr. for individuals. *Publications: Visual Aids and Informational Material Catalog*; *Large Print Loan Library*; two newsletters; informational pamphlets on topics ranging from *Diseases of the Macula* to knitting and crochet instructions.

*National Association of Secondary School Principals (NASSP). 1904 Association Dr., Reston, VA 22091. (703) 860-0200. Fax (703) 476-5432. Robert Mahaffey, Dir., Publications and Marketing. Provides a national voice for secondary education, supports promising and successful educational practices, conducts research, examines issues, and represents secondary education at the federal level. *Membership:* 40,000. *Publications: NASSP Bulletin*; *NASSP*

NewsLeader; *Curriculum Report*; *Legal Memorandum*; *Schools in the Middle*; *TIPS for Principals*; *AP Special*; *Practitioner and Leadership Magazine*.

*National Association of State Boards of Education (NASBE). 1012 Cameron St., Alexandria, VA 22314. (703) 684-4000. Fax (703) 836-2313. Brenda Lilienthal Welburn, Exec. Dir.; Andrew Stamp, contact person. Studies problems and improves communication among members, exchanges information, provides educational programs and activities, and serves as a liaison with other educators' groups. *Membership:* 650. *Publications: The State Board Connection* (member newsletter, 4/yr.); *Issues in Brief* (4/yr.); guides for policymakers and practitioners; task force reports.

National Association of State Textbook Administrators (NASTA). Textbook Adoptions, Indiana Department of Education, Room 229 State House, Indianapolis, IN 46209. (317) 232-9127. Fax (317) 232-9121. Linda Dierstein, Pres. NASTA's purposes are (1) to foster a spirit of mutual helpfulness in adoption, purchase, and distribution of instructional materials; (2) to arrange for study and review of textbook specifications; (3) to authorize special surveys, tests, and studies; and (4) to initiate action leading to better quality instructional materials. Services provided include a working knowledge of text construction, monitoring lowest prices, sharing adoption information, identifying trouble spots, and discussions in the industry. The members of NASTA meet to discuss the textbook adoption process and to improve the quality of the instructional materials used in the elementary, middle, and high schools. NASTA is not affiliated with any parent organization and has no permanent address. Meetings are conducted with the American Association of Publishers and the Book Manufacturers' Institute. *Membership:* The textbook administrator from each of the 23 states that adopts textbooks at the state level. *Dues:* $25/yr. individual. *Meetings:* February 18-21, 1995, Santa Fe, NM; July 22-26, 1995, New Orleans, LA.

*National Audiovisual Center (NAC). National Archives and Records Administration, 8700 Edgeworth Dr., Capitol Heights, MD 20743. (301) 763-1896; (800) 788-6282. Fax (301) 763-6025. George Ziener, Dir. Central information and distribution source for more than 8,000 audiovisual programs produced by or for the U.S. government. Materials are made available for sale or rent on a self-sustaining basis, at the lowest price possible. *Publications: Media Resource Catalog* (1991), listing 600 of the latest and most popular programs, is available free. Also available free are specific subject listings such as science, history, medicine, and safety and health. There is a free quarterly update that lists significant additions to the collection. A computer bulletin board has been available for information searches and production orders since late 1993.

*National Cable Television Institute (NCTI). 801 West Mineral Ave., Littleton, CO 80120-4501. (303) 797-9393. Fax (303) 797-9394. Byron K. Leech, Pres.; Don Oden, Dir. of Admissions. The largest independent provider of cable television training in the world. The Institute "partners" with cable television companies to provide a fully managed training program. Offers a five-level career path that leads employees through self-study in all technical areas of the cable television system. NCTI also offers training in new and specialized technologies for the broadband telecommunications professional. An NCTI Certificate of Graduation is recognized throughout the cable television industry as a symbol of technical achievement and competence. Call, fax, or write for a *free* Training Kit.

*The National Center for Improving Science Education. 2000 L St. NW, Suite 603, Washington, DC 20036. (202) 467-0652. Fax (202) 467-0659. BITNET sentar@-gwuvm.gwu.edu. Senta A. Raizen, Dir./300 Brickstone Square, Suite 900, Andover, MA

01810. (508) 470-1080. (508) 475-9220. Internet janeta@neirl.org. Janet Anglis, Dir. of Communications. A division of The NETWORK, Inc. (a nonprofit organization dedicated to educational reform) that works to promote changes in state and local policies and practices in science curriculum, teaching, and assessment through research and development, evaluation, technical assistance, and dissemination. *Publications: Science and Technology Education for the Elementary Years: Frameworks for Curriculum and Instruction; Developing and Supporting Teachers for Elementary School Science Education; Assessment in Elementary School Science Education; Getting Started in Science: A Blueprint Elementary School Science Education; Building Scientific Literacy: Blueprint for the Middle Years; Science and Technology Education for the Middle Years: Frameworks for Curriculum and Instruction; Assessment in Science Education: The Middle Years; Developing and Supporting Teachers for Science Education in the Middle Years; Elementary School Science for the 90s; The High Stakes of High School Science; Future of Science in Elementary Schools: Educating Prospective Teachers.* Publications catalog is available from The NETWORK on request.

National Center for Research in Mathematical Sciences Education (NCRMSE). Wisconsin Center for Education Research, School of Education, University of Wisconsin-Madison, 1025 West Johnson St., Madison, WI 53706. (608) 263-4285. Fax (608) 263-3406. E-mail romberg@ums.macc.wisc.edu. Dr. Thomas A. Romberg, Dir. One of 25 university-based national education and development centers supported by the Office of Educational Research and Improvement (OERI) in the U.S. Department of Education to help strengthen student learning in the United States. The mission of this Center is to provide a research base for the reform of school mathematics. The changes needed in the teaching and learning of mathematics in the United States are a consequence of several factors: development of new technologies; changes in mathematics itself; new knowledge about teachers, learning, teaching, and schools as institutions; and renewed calls for equity in learning mathematics regardless of race, class, gender, or ethnicity. To accomplish its mission, the 5-year-old Center has created national networks of scholars who will collaborate on the identification of reform goals as they develop a long-range research plan designed to improve mathematics in U.S. schools. *The Curriculum and Evaluation Standards for School Mathematics* (1989) and the *Professional Standards for Teaching Mathematics* (1992), published by the National Council of Teachers of Mathematics, provide a foundation for Center research. The Center is organized around seven working groups. The working groups involve more than 300 scholars, classroom teachers, and Ph.D. students in research on teaching and learning in K-12 mathematics. *Meetings:* Numerous meetings are scheduled at AERA and NCTM conferences to present research findings. Members of working groups meet one or two times annually to review and critique their research. *Publications: NCRMSE Research Review: The Teaching and Learning of Mathematics* (quarterly newsletter), and numerous books, chapters, articles, and working papers. A 43-page bibliography of publications is available.

National Center for Science Teaching and Learning (NCSTL). Ohio State University, 1929 Kenny Road, Columbus, OH 43210. (614) 292-3339. Fax (614) 292-1595. E-mail ncstl@magnus.acs.ohio-state.edu. Dr. Arthur L. White, Dir.; Michael Aiello, Prog. Dir., contact person. Since 1990, as part of a national effort to reform our country's science education system, with the goal of making science, mathematics, and technology education one of America's highest priorities, Ohio State has housed the NCSTL. Funded by the Office of Educational Research and Improvement of the U.S. Department of Education, the Center supports improvements in science teaching and learning by initiating, promoting, and facilitating research and disseminating the research findings to all those with an interest in science education. The NCSTL studies the impact of non-curricular factors in science teaching and learning in America's schools by collaborating with teachers in the classroom to enhance the science learning experience. These factors include social and cultural influences on science teaching and learning such as language; public expectations and societal incentives including the role of partnerships for fostering science teaching and learning; economic, political, and administrative forces at play in the science teaching and learning endeavor including reform processes; the influences of educational technology on the teaching and learning of science with emphases on instruction and assessment environments; examination of the relationship of science learning to other content areas with particular focus on mathematics; and models for evaluation and assessment. The Center also has a sizable evaluation component which looks at the overall operation of the NCSTL and also participates in projects related to authentic and alternate assessment. The underlying philosophy of the Center is that science educators alone should not, and indeed cannot, define science education. Science teaching and learning research must be a product of a diverse group of individuals including educators, scientists, researchers, policy makers, business and community leaders, parents, and students. In accordance with this philosophy, the Center encourages the participation of and promotes discourse among individuals from these groups. The NCSTL networks that have already been established include faculty, administration, business, and governmental persons within the University, across the state of Ohio, nationally, and internationally. More than 50 individuals in five Colleges at The Ohio State University (Agriculture, Education, Engineering, Mathematical and Physical Sciences, and Medicine) participate in Center projects. The Center has also established on-going collaborative relationships with Clark-Atlanta University (GA), the University of California at Santa Cruz, East Carolina University (NC), the Southeastern Regional Vision for Education (NC), the University of Michigan, the Far West Laboratory for Educational Research and Development (CA), the University of California at Riverside, the Coalition of Essential Schools at Brown University (RI), the AIMS Education Foundation (CA), and Florida Atlantic University. Users include educators, parents, researchers, education agencies, students, policy makers, and the general public. *Publications: COGNOSOS* (q.); *NSF/SSMA Wingspread Conference: A Network for Integrated Science and Mathematics Teaching and Learning. Conference Plenary Papers*; *Advanced Technologies as Educational Tools in Science*; *Integration of Science and Mathematics: What Parents Can Do*; *A Review of Educational Technology in Science Assessment.*

*National Clearinghouse for Bilingual Education (NCBE). The George Washington University, 1118 22d St. NW, Washington, DC 20037. (202) 467-0867; (800) 321-NCBE. Joel Gomez, Dir. NCBE is funded by the U.S. Department of Education, Office of Bilingual Education and Minority Languages Affairs, to provide information on the education of limited-English-proficient students to practitioners, administrators, researchers, policymakers, and parents. NCBE collects and disseminates information on print resources, software and courseware, video resources, and organizations. Provides computerized access to bulletin board, bibliographic database, and resources databases. *Publications: FORUM* (bi-mo. newsletter); *Focus* (occasional papers); program information guides.

National Center to Improve Practice (NCIP). Education Development Center, 55 Chapel St., Newton, MA 02160. (617) 969-4529. (800) 225-4276 ext 2422. NCIP is a collaborative project between the Education Development Center, Inc., and WGBH Educational Foundation (Boston's Public Television Station). The mission of NCIP is to promote change within local schools and districts so that practitioners will effectively use technology, media, and materials (TMM) to improve educational outcomes for students with disabilities. NCIP's evolving approach is grounded in the belief that change at the local level is facilitated by change agents who are able to provide stakeholders (administrators, practitioners, parents) with the knowledge, resources, and training they need to embrace and implement innovative uses of TMM. Services include issuing Practice Packages of print and video materials organized around curricular themes three times within the academic year; NCIP InfoNet (electronic bulletin boards and a resource library); videoconferences; technical assistance; conference workshops; and training institutes.

National Commission on Libraries and Information Science (NCLIS). 1110 Vermont Ave. NW, Suite 820, Washington, DC 20005-3522. (202) 606-9200. Fax (202) 606-9203. E-mail py_nclis@inet.ed.gov. Peter R. Young, Exec. Dir. A permanent independent agency of the U.S. government charged with advising the executive and legislative branches on national library and information policies and plans. The commission reports directly to the White House and the Congress on the implementation of national policy; conducts studies, surveys, and analyses of the nation's library and information needs; appraises the inadequacies and deficiencies of current resources and services; promotes research and development activities; conducts hearings and issues publications as appropriate; and develops overall plans for meeting national library and information needs and for the coordination of activities at the federal, state, and local levels. *Membership:* 15 commissioners, 14 appointed by the president and confirmed by the Senate; ex-officio, the Librarian of Congress. *Publication: Annual Report.*

*National Council for Accreditation of Teacher Education (NCATE). 2010 Massachusetts Ave. NW, Suite 200, Washington, DC 20036. (202) 466-7496. Fax (202) 296-6620. Arthur E. Wise, Pres. A consortium of professional organizations that establishes standards of quality and accredits professional education units in schools, colleges, and departments of education. Interested in the self-regulation and improvement of standards in the field of teacher education. *Membership:* 500 colleges and universities, 26 educational organizations. *Publications: Standards, Procedures and Policies for the Accreditation of Professional Education Units; Teacher Education: A Guide to NCATE-Accredited Colleges and Universities; Quality Teaching* (newsletter, 3/yr.).

National Council of Teachers of English (NCTE), Commission on Media. 1111 W. Kenyon Rd., Urbana, IL 61801-1096. (217) 328-0977. Fax (217) 328-9645. Miles Myers, Exec. Dir.; Carole Cox, Commission Dir. An advisory body that identifies key issues in teaching of media. Reviews current projects and recommends new directions and personnel to undertake them, monitors NCTE publications on media, and suggests program ideas for the annual convention. *Membership:* 68,000 individual, 125,000 subscribers. *Dues:* $40 individual. *Publications: English Journal* (8/yr.); *College English* (8/yr.); *Language Arts* (8/yr.); *English Education* (q.); *Research in the Teaching of English* (q.); *Teaching English in the Two-Year College* (q.); *College Composition and Communication* (q.); *English Leadership Quarterly* (q.); *Quarterly Review of Doublespeak* (q).

*National Council of the Churches of Christ in the U.S.A. Communication Dept., 475 Riverside Dr., New York, NY 10115. (212) 870-2574. Fax (212) 870-2030. Rev. Dr. J. Martin Bailey, Dir. Ecumenical arena for cooperative work of Protestant and Orthodox denominations and agencies in broadcasting, film, cable, and print media. Offers advocacy to government and industry structures on media services. Services provided include liaison to network television and radio programming; film sales and rentals; distribution of information about syndicated religious programming; syndication of some programming; cable television and emerging technologies information services; news and information regarding work of the National Council of Churches, related denominations, and agencies. Works closely with other faith groups in Interfaith Broadcasting Commission. Online communication via Ecunet/NCCLink. *Membership:* 32 denominations. *Publication: EcuLink.*

National Education Telecommunications Organization & Education Satellite Company (NETO/EDSAT). 1735 I Street NW, Suite 601, Washington, DC 20006. (202) 293-4211; (800) 220-1235. Fax (202) 293-4210. Shelly Weinstein, Pres. and CEO. NETO/EDSAT is a not-for-profit organization bringing together the users and providers of telecommunications to deliver education, instruction, and training in America's classrooms, colleges, workplaces, and other distance education centers. NETO/EDSAT facilitates and collaborates with key stakeholders in the education and telecommunications fields. Programs and services include research and education, outreach, seminars and conferences, and satellite services and scheduling. The NETO/EDSAT mission is to help create an integrated nationwide multitechnology infrastructure, a dedicated satellite that links space and existing secondary access roads—i.e., telephone and cable—over which teaching and education resources are delivered and shared in a user friendly format with students, teachers, workers, and individuals. "A transparent I-95." A modern-day "learning place" for the rural, urban, migrant, suburban, disadvantaged, and youths-at-risk which provides equal and affordable access to and utilization of educational resources, and teaching and learning tools. A U.S. technologically integrated telecommunications system which transports educational resources to all children and adults regardless of the wealth and geography of their community. *Membership:* Members include school districts, colleges, universities, state agencies, public/private educational consortia, libraries, and other distance education providers. *Publications: NETO/EDSAT "UPDATE"* (newsletter, q.); *Analysis of a Proposal for an Education Satellite, EDSAT Institute.*

*National Endowment for the Humanities (NEH). 1100 Pennsylvania Ave. NW, Rm. 420, Washington, DC 20506. (202) 608-8278. James Dougherty, Asst. Dir., Media Program. Independent federal grant-making agency that supports research and educational programs grounded in the disciplines of the humanities. The Media Program supports film and radio programs in the humanities for public audiences, including children and adults. *Publication: Humanities Projects in Media* (guidelines).

*National Federation of Community Broadcasters (NFCB). 666 11th St. NW, Suite 805, Washington, DC 20001. (202) 393-2355. Lynn Chadwick, Pres. NFCB represents its members in public policy development at the national level and provides a wide range of practical services. *Membership:* 90 stations, 100 (assoc.) stations and production groups. *Dues:* Based on income, from $75 to $500 for associates; $400 to $2,500 for participants. *Publications: Legal Handbook; Audio Craft* (1989 edition); *Community Radio News; NFCB's Guide to Political Broadcasting for Public Radio Stations; NFCB's Guide to Volunteer Management.*

National Film Board of Canada (NFBC). 1251 Avenue of the Americas, 6th Floor, New York, NY 10020. (212) 596-1770. Fax (212) 595-1779. E-mail gsem78a@prodigy.com. John Sirabella, U.S. Marketing Mgr./Nontheatrical Rep. Established in 1939, the NFBC's main objective is to produce and distribute high-quality audiovisual materials for educational, cultural, and social purposes.

National Film Information Service (offered by the Academy of Motion Picture Arts and Sciences). 8949 Wilshire Blvd., Beverly Hills, CA 90211-1972. (310) 247-3000. The purpose of this organization is to provide an information service on film. The service is fee-based and all inquiries must be accompanied by a self-addressed stamped envelope.

National Gallery of Art (NGA). Department of Education Resources: Art Information and Extension Programs, Washington, DC 20565. (202) 842-6273. Ruth R. Perlin, Head. This department of NGA is responsible for the production and distribution of educational audiovisual programs, including interactive technologies. Materials available (all loaned free to schools, community organizations, and individuals) range from films, videocassettes, and color slide programs to videodiscs. A free catalog of programs is available upon request. Two videodiscs on the gallery's collection are available for long-term loan. *Publication: Extension Programs Catalogue.*

National Information Center for Educational Media (NICEM). P.O. Box 40130, Albuquerque, NM 87196. (505) 265-3591; (800) 926-8328. E-mail tnaccessi@technet.nm.org. Marjorie M. K. Hlava, Pres., Access Innovations, Inc.; Patrick Sauer, Mng. Dir., NICEM; C. J. Donnelly, Marketing. In conjunction with the Library of Congress, NICEM is a centralized facility that collects, catalogs, and disseminates information about nonbook materials of many different kinds. Its mission is to build and expand the database to provide current and archival information about nonbook educational materials; to apply modern techniques of information dissemination that meet user needs; and to provide a comprehensive, centralized nonbook database used for catalogs, indexes, multimedia publications, special search services, machine-readable tapes, and online access. NICEM services include NICEM EZ (user-defined searches of the database, fee set at editorial time rate, one-day turnaround) and AVxpress ("Document" delivery of any media title [in print] found in NICEM or in any other listing of media material, in cooperation with Dynamic Information in Burlingame, CA). The NICEM masterfile is also available on DIALOG File 46, via CompuServe as the Knowledge Index, and on CD-ROM (AVOnline via SilverPlatter); (NICEM AVmarc via BiblioFile). A 45,000 unit subset of NICEM titles is carried on the Human Resource Information Network, via National Standards Association. *Clients, Users:* College and university media centers, school districts, BOCES, libraries, corporate researchers, students, and filmmakers. Non-membership organization—no charge to catalog. *Publications: Film & Video Finder, 4th ed., 1994-95; Index to AV Producers & Distributors, 9th ed., 1994-95; Audiocassette & CD Finder, 1995.*

National Press Photographers Association, Inc. (NPPA). 3200 Croasdaile Dr., Suite 306, Durham, NC 27705. (919) 383-7246. Fax (919) 383-7261. Charles Cooper, Exec. Dir. An organization of professional news photographers who participate in and promote photojournalism in publications and through television and film. Sponsors workshops and contests; maintains a tape library and collections of slides in the field. *Membership:* 11,000. *Dues:* $55 professional, $30 student. *Meetings:* 50th Anniversary Celebration and Convention, June 28-July 2, 1995, Washington, DC. *Publications: News Photographer*; membership directory; *Best of Photojournalism Books.*

National PTA. 330 N. Wabash, Suite 2100, Chicago, IL 60611. (312) 670-6782. Fax (312) 670-6783. Kathryn Whitfill, Pres.; Patty Yoxall, Public Relations Mgr. Advocates for the education, health, safety, and well-being of children and teens. Provides parenting education and leadership training to PTA volunteers. *Membership:* 6.8 million. *Dues:* Varies by local unit. *Sample Publications: PTA Today* (magazine); *What's Happening in Washington* (legislative newsletters); numerous brochures for parents, such as *Help Your Child Get the Most Out of Homework* and *How to Talk to Your Children and Teens about AIDS.* Catalog available.

*National Public Broadcasting Archives (NPBA). Hornbake Library, University of Maryland at College Park, College Park, MD 20742. (301) 405-9255. Thomas Connors, Archivist. NPBA brings together the archival record of the major entities of noncommercial broadcasting in the United States. NPBA's collections include the archives of the Corporation for Public Broadcasting (CPB), the Public Broadcasting Service (PBS), and National Public Radio (NPR). Other organizations represented include the Midwest Program for Airborne Television

Instruction (MPATI), the Public Service Satellite Consortium (PSSC), America's Public Television Stations (APTS), and the Joint Council for Educational Telecommunications (JCET). NPBA also makes available the personal papers of many individuals who have made significant contributions to public broadcasting, and its reference library contains basic studies of the broadcasting industry, rare pamphlets, and journals on relevant topics, plus up-to-date clippings from the PBS press clipping service. NPBA also collects and maintains a selected audio and video program record of public broadcasting's national production and support centers and of local stations. Oral history tapes and transcripts from the NPR Oral History Project are also available at the archives. The archives are open to the public from 9 am to 5 pm, Monday through Friday. Research in NPBA collections should be arranged by prior appointment. For further information, call (301) 405-9988.

*National Religious Broadcasters (NRB). 7839 Ashton Ave., Manassas, VA 22110. (703) 330-7000. Fax (703) 330-7100. E. Brandt Gustavson, Pres. NRB essentially has two goals: (1) to ensure that religious broadcasters have access to the radio and television airwaves, and (2) to encourage broadcasters to observe a high standard of excellence in their programming and station management for the clear presentation of the gospel. Holds national and regional conventions. *Membership:* 800 organizational stations, program producers, agencies, and individuals. *Dues:* Based on income. *Meetings:* 1994, 51st Annual Convention, January 29-February 1, Washington, DC; 1995, 52nd Annual Convention, February 11-14, Nashville, TN. *Publications: Religious Broadcasting Magazine* (mo.); *Annual Directory of Religious Media*; *Religious Broadcasting Resources Library Brochure*; *Religious Broadcasting Cassette Catalog.*

National School Supply and Equipment Association (NSSEA). 8300 Colesville Rd., Suite 250, Silver Spring, MD 20910. (301) 495-0240. Fax (301) 495-3330. Tim Holt, Exec. V.P. A service organization of 1,200 manufacturers, distributors, retailers, and independent manufacturers' representatives of school supplies, equipment, and instructional materials. Seeks to maintain open communications between manufacturers and dealers in the school market, to find solutions to problems affecting schools, and to encourage the development of new ideas and products for educational progress. *Meetings:* Ed Expo '95, March 16-19, Dallas, TX; 79th Annual NSSEA Fall Show (members only), November 2-5, Las Vegas, NV. *Publications: Tidings*; *Annual Membership Directory.*

*National Science Foundation (NSF). 4201 Wilson Blvd., Arlington, VA 22230. (703) 306-1234. Michael Fluharty, Chief, Media Relations and Public Affairs. Primary purposes of this agency of the federal government are to increase the nation's base of scientific knowledge; encourage research in areas that can lead to improvements in economic growth, productivity, and environmental quality; promote international cooperation through science; and develop and help implement science education programs to aid the nation in meeting the challenges of contemporary life. Grants go chiefly to universities and research organizations. Applicants should refer to the *NSF Guide to Programs*. Scientific material and media reviews are available to help the public learn about NSF-supported programs. Information is also electronically disseminated through STIS at no cost but the users' long-distance phone charges. For start-up assistance contact via e-mail: stis-request@NSF.gov (Internet) or stis-req@NSF (BITNET), or phone: (703) 306-0214 (voice mail).

National Science Teachers Association (NSTA). 1840 Wilson Blvd., Arlington, VA 22201. (703) 243-7100. Fax (703) 243-7177. E-mail alex.mondale@nsta.org. Bill Aldridge, Exec. Dir. A national nonprofit association of science teachers ranging from kindergarten through university level. NSTA conducts one national and three regional conventions and provides numerous programs and services, including awards and scholarships, inservice teacher workshops, professional certification, a major curriculum reform effort, and more. It has position statements on many issues, such as teacher preparation, laboratory science, and the use of animals in the classroom. It is involved in cooperative working relationships in a variety of projects with educational organizations, government agencies, and private industries. *Membership:* 50,000. *Dues:* $52/yr. individual or institutional (includes one journal and other benefits). *Meetings:* 1995: National, March 23-26, Philadelphia, PA; Area, October 19-21, Seattle, WA; November 16-18, Baltimore, MD; December 14-16, San Antonio, TX. 1996: National, March 28-31, St. Louis, MO. *Publications: Science and Children* (8/yr., journal for elementary teachers); *Science Scope* (8/yr., journal for middle-level teachers); *The Science Teacher* (9/yr., for high school teachers); *Journal of College Science Teaching* (6/yr., journal for college teachers); *NSTA Reports!* (6/yr., newspaper for K-college teachers, free to all NSTA members); *Quantum* (magazine for physics and math high school students); books (free catalog available).

National Society for Performance and Instruction (NSPI). 1300 L St. NW, Suite 1250, Washington, DC 20005. (202) 408-7969. Fax (202) 408-7972. Paul Tremper, Exec. Dir. NSPI is an international association dedicated to increasing productivity in the workplace through the application of performance and instructional technologies. Founded in 1962, its members are located throughout the United States, Canada, and 30 other countries. The society offers an awards program recognizing excellence in the field. The Annual Conference and Expo are held in the spring. *Membership:* 5,000. *Dues:* $125, active members; $40, students and retirees. *Meetings:* 1995 Conference & Expo, March 27-31, Atlanta, GA; 1996, April 15-19, Dallas, TX; 1997, April 14-18, Anaheim, CA; 1998, March 23-28, Chicago, IL. *Publications: Performance & Instruction Journal* (10/yr.); *Performance Improvement Quarterly*; *News & Notes* (newsletter, 10/yr.); *Annual Membership Directory.*

*National Technology Center. American Foundation for the Blind, 15 W. 16th St., New York, NY 10011. (212) 620-2080. Evaluations Laboratory: (212) 620-2051. Fax (212) 620-2137. Elliot M. Schreier, Dir. The center has three components: National Technology Information System, Evaluations Laboratory, and Research and Development Laboratory. Provides a resource for blind and visually impaired persons and professionals in education, rehabilitation, and employment; their families; and rehabilitation professionals, educators, researchers, manufacturers, and employers. The NTC also develops products to enhance education, employment, mobility, and independent living opportunities for blind and visually impaired people worldwide.

*National Telemedia Council Inc. (NTC). 120 E. Wilson St., Madison, WI 53703. (608) 257-7712. Fax (608) 257-7714. Dr. Marti Tomas, Pres.; Marieli Rowe, Exec. Dir. The NTC is a national not-for-profit organization dedicated to promoting media literacy, or critical television viewing skills, for children and youth. This is done primarily through work with teachers, parents, and caregivers. NTC activities include the development of the Media Literacy Clearinghouse and Center; the Teacher Idea Exchange (T.I.E.); national conferences and regional and local workshops; Sponsor Recognition Awards for companies and corporate entities for their support of programs deemed to be outstanding; the Jessie McCanse Award for individual contribution to media literacy. *Dues:* $30 basic membership; $50 contributing; $100 patron. *Publications: Telemedium* (newsletter, q.); *Telemedium UPDATE.*

National University Continuing Education Association (NUCEA). One Dupont Cir. NW, Suite 615, Washington, DC 20036. (202) 659-3130. Fax (202) 785-0374. Edward Simpson, Pres. 1995-96; Kay J. Kohl, Exec. Dir.; Susan Goewey, Dir. of Pubs.; J. Noah Brown, Dir.

of Govt. Relations & Public Affairs. An association of public and private institutions concerned with making continuing education available to all population segments and to promoting excellence in the continuing higher education community. NUCEA has an annual national conference and several professional development seminars throughout the year, and many institutional members offer university and college film rental library services. *Membership:* 425 institutions; 2,000 professionals. *Dues:* Vary according to membership category. *Publications:* Monthly newsletter; quarterly occasional papers; scholarly journal; *Independent Study Catalog; The Electronic University. A Guide to Distance Learning Programs; Guide to Certificate Programs at American Colleges and Universities;* NUCEA-ACE/Oryx Continuing Higher Education book series; *Lifelong Learning Trends* (a statistical factbook on continuing higher education); organizational issues series; membership directory; other publications relevant to the field.

The NETWORK, Inc. 300 Brickstone Square, Suite 900, Andover, MA 01810. (508) 470-1080. Fax (508) 475-9220. Internet suem@neirl.org. Sue Martin, Pub. Mgr. A research and service organization providing training, research and evaluation, technical assistance, and materials to schools, educational organizations, and private sector firms with educational interests. *Publications: Portrait of Our Mothers: Using Oral History in the Classroom; Juggling Lessons: A Curriculum for Women Who Go to School, Work, and Care for Their Families; An Action Guide for School Improvement; Making Change for School Improvement: A Simulation Game; Report on National Dissemination Efforts: Volumes I-X; The Effective Writing Teacher; Cumulative Writing Folder; Developing Writing and Thinking Skills Across the Curriculum: A Practical Program for Schools; Five Types of Writing Assignments.* Publications catalog is available upon request.

Network for Continuing Medical Education (NCME). One Harmon Plaza, 7th Floor, Secaucus, NJ 07094. (201) 867-3550. Fax (201) 867-2491. Produces and distributes videocassettes to hospitals for physicians' continuing education. Programs are developed for physicians in the practice of General Medicine, Anesthesiology, Emergency Medicine, Gastroenterology, and Surgery. Physicians who view all the programs can earn up to 25 hours of Category 1 (AMA) credit and up to 20 hours of Prescribed (AAFP) credit each year. *Membership:* More than 1,100 hospitals provide NCME programs to their physicians. *Dues:* Subscription fees: VHS-$1,920/yr. Sixty-minute videocassettes are distributed to hospital subscribers every three weeks.

*The New York Festivals (formerly the International Film and TV Festival of New York). Admin. offices: 780 King St., Chappaqua, NY 10514. (914) 238-4481. Bilha Goldberg, Vice Pres. An annual competitive festival for industrial and educational film and video productions, filmstrips and slide programs, multi-image business theater and interactive multimedia presentations, and television programs. Entry fees begin at $100. First entry deadline is August 1.

North Central Regional Educational Laboratory (NCREL). 1900 Spring Rd., Suite 300, Oak Brook, IL 60521-1480. (708) 571-4700; (800) 356-2735. Fax (708) 571-4716. E-mail info@ncrel.org. Jan Bakker, Resource Center Dir. NCREL's work is guided by a focus on comprehensive and systemic school restructuring that is research-based and learner-centered. One of 10 Office of Educational Research and Improvement (OERI) regional educational laboratories, NCREL disseminates information about effective programs, develops educational products, holds conferences, provides technical assistance, and conducts research and evaluation. In addition to conventional print publications, NCREL uses computer networks, videoconferencing via satellite, and video and audio formats to reach its diverse audiences.

NCREL operates the Midwest Consortium for Mathematics and Science Education which works to advance systemic change in mathematics and science education. Persons living in Illinois, Indiana, Iowa, Michigan, Minnesota, Ohio, and Wisconsin are encouraged to call NCREL Resource Center with any education-related questions. *Publications: Clipboard* (q.); a catalog of print, video, and other media products is available by calling the main number.

Northwest Regional Educational Laboratory (NWREL). 101 SW Main St., Suite 500, Portland, OR 97204. (503) 275-9500. Fax (503) 275-9489. Robert R. Rath, Exec. Dir. One of 10 Office of Educational Research and Improvement (OERI) regional educational laboratories, NWREL works with schools and communities to improve educational outcomes for children, youth, and adults. NWREL provides leadership, expertise, and services based on the results of research and development. NWREL serves Alaska, Idaho, Oregon, Montana, and Washington. *Membership:* 817. *Dues:* None. *Publication: Northwest Report* (newsletter).

OCLC Online Computer Library Center, Inc. 6565 Frantz Rd., Dublin, OH 43017-3395. (614) 764-6000. Fax (614) 764-6096. Internet nita_dean@oclc.org. K. Wayne Smith, Pres. and CEO. Nita Dean, Mgr., Public Relations. A nonprofit membership organization that engages in computer library service and research and makes available computer-based processes, products, and services for libraries, other educational organizations, and library users. From its facility in Dublin, Ohio, OCLC operates an international computer network that libraries use to catalog books, order custom-printed catalog cards and machine-readable records for local catalogs, arrange interlibrary loans, and maintain location information on library materials. OCLC also provides online and offline reference products and services for the electronic delivery of information. More than 19,000 libraries contribute to and/or use information in the OCLC Online Union Catalog. *Publications: OCLC Newsletter* (6/yr.); *OCLC Reference News* (6/yr.); *Annual Report; Annual Review of Research.*

Office of Technology Assessment (OTA). U.S. Congress, Washington, DC 20510-8025. (202) 228-6938. Fax (202) 228-6293. E-mail kfulton@ota.gov. Kathleen Fulton, Proj. Dir. (contact for education). (Education in now part of the Education and Human Resources Program, Denise Dougherty, Dir.) Established by Congress to study, report on, and assess the significance and probable impact of new technological developments on U.S. society and to advise Congress on public policy implications and options. Recent assessments focusing on technology and education issues include *Elementary and Secondary Education for Science and Engineering, A Technical Memorandum* (1989); *Higher Education for Science and Engineering, A Background Paper* (1989); *Linking for Learning: A New Course for Education* (1989); *Critical Connections: Communication for the Future* (1990); *Computer Software and Intellectual Property, A Background Paper* (1990); the assessment, *Power On! New Tools for Teaching & Learning* (1988), includes an interim staff paper on "Trends and Status of Computers in Schools: Use in Chapter 1 Programs and Use with Limited English Proficient Students" (March 1987); *Testing and Assessment in Vocational Education; Risks to Students in School* (January 1995); *Teachers and Technology* (February 1995); *Technology and Work-Based Learning* (Spring 1996). *Publications:* For a list, contact the publishing office at (202) 224-8996.

On-line Audiovisual Catalogers (OLAC). c/o Columbia University Health Sciences Library, 701 West 168th St., New York, NY 10032. (212) 305-1406. Fax (212) 234-0595. Johanne LaGrange, Treas. Formed as an outgrowth of the ALA conference, OLAC seeks to permit members to exchange ideas and information, and to interact with other agencies that influence audiovisual cataloging practices. *Membership:* 725. *Dues:* Available for single or multiple years, ranges from $10 to $27 individual, $16 to $45 institutional. *Publication: OLAC Newsletter.*

Pacific Film Archive (PFA). University Art Museum, 2625 Durant Ave., Berkeley, CA 94720-2250. (510) 642-1437 (library); (510) 642-1412 (general). Fax (510) 642-4889. Edith Kramer, Dir. and Curator of Film; Nancy Goldman, Head, PFA Library and Film Study Center. Sponsors the exhibition, study, and preservation of classic, international, documentary, animated, and avant-garde films. Provides on-site research screenings of films in its collection of over 6,000 titles. Provides access to its collections of books, periodicals, stills, and posters (all materials are noncirculating). Offers UAM members and University of California, Berkeley, affiliates reference and research services to locate film and video distributors, credits, stock footage, etc. Library hours are 1pm-5pm weekdays. *Membership:* Through parent organization, the University Art Museum. *Dues:* $40 individual and nonprofit departments of institutions. *Publication: UAM/PFA Calendar* (6/yr.).

*Pacific Regional Educational Laboratory (PREL). 828 Fort Street Mall #500, Honolulu, HI 96813-4321. (808) 532-1900. John W. Kofel, Exec. Dir. One of 10 Office of Educational Research and Improvement (OERI) regional educational laboratories designed to help educators and policymakers solve educational problems in their schools. Using the best available information and the experience and expertise of professionals, PREL seeks to identify solutions to education problems, tries new approaches, furnishes research results, and provides training to teachers and administrators. PREL serves American Samoa, Commonwealth of the Northern Mariana Islands, Federated States of Micronesia, Guam, Hawaii, Republic of the Marshall Islands, and Republic of Palau.

PCR: Films and Video in the Behavioral Sciences. Special Services Bldg., Pennsylvania State University, University Park, PA 16802. (814) 863-3102; purchasing info, (800) 826-0132. Fax (814) 863-2574. E-mail tjm@psulias.psu.edu. Thomas McKenna, Mng. Ed. Collects and makes available to professionals 16mm films and video in the behavioral sciences judged to be useful for university teaching and research. A free catalog of the films in PCR is available. The PCR catalog now contains some 1,400 films in the behavioral sciences (psychology, psychiatry, anthropology, animal behavior, sociology, teaching and learning, and folklife). Some 7,000 professionals now use PCR services. Films and tapes are available on loan for a rental charge. Many films may also be purchased. Films may be submitted for international distribution. Contact the managing editor through PCR.

*Photographic Society of America (PSA). 3000 United Founders Blvd., Suite 103, Oklahoma City, OK 73102. (405) 843-1437. Terry S. Stull, Operations Mgr. A nonprofit organization for the development of the arts and sciences of photography and for the furtherance of public appreciation of photographic skills. Its members, largely amateurs, consist of individuals, camera clubs, and other photographic organizations. Divisions include color slide, motion picture, nature, photojournalism, travel, pictorial print, stereo, and techniques. Sponsors national, regional, and local meetings, clinics, and contests. Request dues information from preceding address. *Meetings:* 1994, International Conference, Colorado Springs, CO; 1995, International Conference, Williamsburg, VA. *Publication: PSA Journal.*

*Professors of Instructional Design and Technology (PIDT). Center for Media and Teaching Resources, Indiana University, Bloomington, IN 47405-5901. (812) 855-2854. Fax (812) 855-8404. Dr. Thomas M. Schwen, contact person. An organization designed to encourage and facilitate the exchange of information among members of the instructional design and technology academic and corporate communities. Also serves to promote excellence in academic programs in instructional design and technology and to encourage research and inquiry that will benefit the field while providing leadership in the public and private sectors in its application and practice. Membership consists of faculty employed in higher education institutions whose primary responsibilities are teaching and research in this area; their corporate counterparts; and other persons interested in the goals and activities of the PIDT. *Membership:* 300. *Dues:* None.

Program of Cultural Studies. East-West Center, 1777 East-West Rd., Honolulu, HI 96848. (808) 944-7666. Geoffrey M. White, Dir. A program of the East-West Center, which was established by the U.S. Congress "to promote better relations and understanding among the nations of Asia, the Pacific and the United States through cooperative study, training and research." The Program for Cultural Studies pursues research and dialogue on the evolving significance of culture and ideologies of culture in the Asia-Pacific region. Program research focuses particularly on ways that culture enters the public sphere and impacts on national integration and international relations. In the age of electronic communication, film, video, and other mass media play an increasingly powerful role in shaping perceptions of culture, gender, and nationality.

Public Broadcasting Service (PBS). 1320 Braddock Pl., Alexandria, VA 22314-1698. (703) 739-5000. National distributor of public television programming, obtaining all programs from member stations, American independent producers, or foreign sources. PBS also offers educational services for teachers, students, and parents including: PTV, The Ready to Learn Service on PBS; Going the Distance; PBS MATHLINE; PBS ONLINE; and PBS Learning Link. Owned and operated by local public television organizations through annual membership fees. PBS services include program acquisition, distribution, and scheduling; development and fundraising support; and engineering and technical development. Of special interest are: the PBS Adult Learning Service, which offers telecourses through college/public television station partnerships; PBS K-12 Learning Services, providing learning resources for elementary and secondary school teachers and students; and PBS VIDEO, which offers videotapes of PBS programs for rent or sale to educational institutions. PBS is governed by a board of directors elected by PBS members for three-year terms. *Membership:* 198 organizations operating 346 stations.

> ***PBS Adult Learning Service (ALS)**. 1320 Braddock Pl., Alexandria, VA 22314-1698. (800) 257-2578. Fax (703) 739-8495. Will Philipp, Dir. Contact ALS Customer Service. The mission of ALS is to help colleges, universities, and public television stations increase learning opportunities for distance learners; enrich classroom instruction; update faculty; train administrators, management, and staff; and provide other educational services for local communities. A pioneer in the widespread use of video and print packages incorporated into curricula and offered for credit by local colleges, ALS began broadcasting telecourses in 1981. Since that time, over 2 million students have earned college credit through telecourses offered in partnership with more than two-thirds of the nation's colleges and universities. In 1988, ALS established the Adult Learning Satellite Service (ALSS) to provide colleges, universities, businesses, hospitals, and other organizations with a broad range of educational programming via direct satellite. *Membership:* 500-plus colleges, universities, hospitals, government agencies, and Fortune 500 businesses are now ALSS Associates. Organizations that are not Associates can still acquire ALS programming, but at higher fees. *Dues:* $1,500/yr.; multisite and consortia rates are available. *Publications: ALSS Programming Line-Up* (catalog of available programming, 3/yr.); *The Agenda* (news magazine about issues

of interest to distance learning and adult learning administrators); and *Changing the Face of Higher Education* (an overview of ALS services).

PBS ENCORE. 1320 Braddock Pl., Alexandria, VA 22314. (703) 739-5225. Bonnie Green, Prog. Assoc. Distributes PBS programs with extant broadcast rights to public television stations. *Publication: PBS Encore A to Z Listing.*

PBS VIDEO. 1320 Braddock Pl., Alexandria, VA 22314. (703) 739-5380; (800) 344-3337. Fax (703) 739-5269. Jon Cecil, Dir., PBS VIDEO Marketing. Markets and distributes PBS television programs for sale on videocassette or videodisc to colleges, public libraries, schools, governments, and other organizations and institutions. *Publications: PBS VIDEO Catalog*; *PBS VIDEO Check It Out*; and *PBS Video News*.

*Puppeteers of America. 5 Cricklewood Path, Pasadena, CA 91107. (818) 797-5748. Gayle Schulter, Membership Officer. Founded in 1937 to promote and develop the art of puppetry. It has a large collection of films and videotapes for rent in its audiovisual library and offers books, plays, and related items from the Puppetry Store. Puppeteers is a national resource center that offers workshops, exhibits, a puppetry exchange, and regional festivals. *Membership:* 2,200. *Dues:* Various classes of membership, which range from $15 to $50. *Meetings:* 1994 National Festival, July 13-17, St. Paul, MN; 1995 National Festival, July 23-29, Bryn Mawr, PA. *Publications:* Annual directory; bi-monthly newsletter; quarterly journals.

*Recording for the Blind (RFB). 20 Roszel Rd., Princeton, NJ 08540. (609) 452-0606. Fax (609) 987-8116. Ritchie L. Geisel, Pres. and CEO; Laurie Facciarosso, Public Inf. Officer. RFB is a national, nonprofit organization, providing recorded textbooks, library services, and other educational resources to people who cannot read standard print because of a visual, physical, or perceptual disability. It is supported by volunteers and contributions from individuals, corporations, and foundations. RFB services include a lending library with master tapes of 80,000 titles for students from grade 5 through graduate school; recordings of educational books not available in other accessible formats (about 3,000 are recorded each year by volunteers); bibliographic and subject reference services with lists of search results available in large print, braille, or recorded formats; books on computer diskettes for purchase (more than 400 titles are available); and a fee-based service that produces printed materials in accessible formats for commercial interests, government agencies, and nonprofit organizations seeking to comply with the Americans with Disabilities Act. *Dues:* RFB consumers pay a one-time registration fee of $37.50 which entitles them to a lifetime of borrowing privileges. *Publications: RFB Issues* (for service providers); *RFB Impact* (for donors); *RFB News Cassette* (for consumers).

*Recording Industry Association of America, Inc. (RIAA). 1020 19th St. NW, Suite 200, Washington, DC 20036. (202) 775-0101. Fax (202) 775-7253. Jason S. Berman, Pres.; Tim Sites, Vice Pres. Communications (contact person). Compiles and disseminates U.S. industry shipment statistics by units and wholesale/retail dollar equivalents; establishes industry technical standards; conducts audits for certification of gold and platinum records and video awards; acts as the public information arm on behalf of the U.S. recording industry; provides antipiracy intelligence to law enforcement agencies; presents an RIAA cultural award for contributions to cultural activities in the United States; and acts as a resource center for recording industry research projects. *Membership:* 200 sound recording manufacturers. *Publications: RIAA Annual Report*; *Inside RIAA* (newsletter); press releases.

The Regional Laboratory for Educational Improvement of the Northeast and Islands. 300 Brickstone Square, Suite 950, Andover, MA 01810. (508) 470-0098. Fax (508) 475-9220. Internet janeta@neirl.org. Janet Angelis, Dir. of Communications. One of 10 regional educational laboratories funded in part by the U.S. Department of Education's Office of Educational Research and Improvement (OERI). The laboratory works to achieve educational improvement by linking schools and classrooms in the Northeast and Islands region (New England, New York, Puerto Rico, and the Virgin Islands) with R&D-based knowledge and confirmed practical experience, complementing and multiplying the activities and accomplishments of existing organizations. *Membership:* Open to individuals, schools, or other organizations committed to improving education. *Meetings:* The Designing Learner Centered Schools Annual Conference, November 1994; Multiage Conference, March 1994; Regional Alliance for Mathematics and Science Education Reform Annual Conference, March 1994. *Publications: Kindle the Spark: An Action Guide Committed to the Success of Every Child; Continuing to Learn: A Guidebook for Teacher Development; Education by Charter: Restructuring School Districts; Building Bridges of Learning and Understanding: A Collection of Classroom Activities on Puerto Rican Culture; Managing Change in Rural Schools: An Action Guide; Mentoring: A Resource and Training Guide for Educators; Work in Progress: Restructuring Ten Maine Schools; CaMaPe: An Organizational and Educational Systems Approach to Secondary School Development; Building Systems for Professional Growth: An Action Guide; The Copernican Plan: Restructuring the American High School; The DeWitt Wallace-Reader's Digest Fund Study Conference: Developing a Framework for the Continual Professional Development of Administrators in the Northeast.* Publications catalog is available upon request.

*Research for Better Schools, Inc. (RBS). 444 North Third St., Philadelphia, PA 19123-4107. John E. Hopkins, Exec. Dir. One of 10 Office of Educational Research and Improvement (OERI) regional educational laboratories designed to help educators and policymakers solve educational problems in their schools. Using the best available information and the experience and expertise of professionals, RBS seeks to identify solutions to education problems, tries new approaches, furnishes research results, and provides training to teachers and administrators. RBS serves Delaware, Maryland, New Jersey, Pennsylvania, and the District of Columbia.

*Smithsonian Institution. 1000 Jefferson Drive SW, Washington, DC 20560. (202) 357-2700. Fax (202) 786-2515. Robert McCormick Adams, Secy. An independent trust instrumentality of the United States that conducts scientific, cultural, and scholarly research; administers the national collections; and performs other educational public service functions, all supported by Congress, trusts, gifts, and grants. Includes 16 museums, including the National Museum of Natural History, the National Museum of American History, the National Air and Space Museum, and the National Zoological Park. Museums are free and open daily except December 25. The Smithsonian Institution Traveling Exhibition Service (SITES) organizes exhibitions on art, history, and science and circulates them across the country and abroad. *Membership:* Smithsonian Associates (Resident and National Air and Space). *Dues:* Vary. *Publications: Smithsonian; Air & Space/Smithsonian; The Torch* (staff newsletter, mo.); *Research Reports* (semitechnical, q.); *Smithsonian Runner* (for and about American Indians and Smithsonian-related activities, 6/yr.); Smithsonian Institution Press Publications, 470 L'Enfant Plaza, Suite 7100, Washington, DC 20560.

Society for Applied Learning Technology (SALT). 50 Culpeper St., Warrenton, VA 22186. (540) 347-0055. Fax (540) 349 3169. Raymond G. Fox, Pres. The society is a nonprofit, professional membership organization that was founded in 1972. Membership in the society is oriented to professionals whose work requires knowledge and communication in the field of instructional technology. The society provides members a means to enhance their knowledge and job performance by participation in society-sponsored meetings, through subscription to society-sponsored publications, by association with other professionals at conferences sponsored by the society, and through membership in special interest groups and special society-sponsored initiatives/projects. In addition, the society offers members discounts on society-sponsored journals, conferences, and publications. *Membership:* 900. *Dues:* $45. *Meetings:* 1995, "Orlando Multimedia '95," February 22-24, Kissimmee, FL; "Interactive Multimedia '95," August 23-25, Arlington, VA. 1996, "Orlando Multimedia '96," Kissimmee, FL; "Interactive Multimedia '96, "Arlington, VA. *Publications: Journal of Educational Technology Systems; Journal of Instruction Delivery Systems; Journal of Interactive Instructional Development; Journal of Medical Education Technologies.* Send for list of books.

*Society for Computer Simulation (SCS). P.O. Box 17900, San Diego, CA 92177-7900. (619) 277-3888. Fax (619) 277-3930. Bill Gallagher, Exec. Dir. Founded in 1952, SCS is a professional-level technical society devoted to the art and science of modeling and simulation. Its purpose is to advance the understanding, appreciation, and use of all types of computer models for studying the behavior of actual or hypothesized systems of all kinds. Sponsors standards and local, regional, and national technical meetings and conferences, such as Eastern & Western Simulation Multiconferences, Summer Computer Simulation Conference, Winter Simulation Conference, International Simulation Technology Conference (SIMTEC), National Educational Computing Conference (NECC), and others. *Membership:* 1,900. *Dues:* $60. *Publications: Simulation* (mo.); Simulation series (q.); *Transactions of SCS* (q.). Additional office in Ghent, Belgium.

Society for Photographic Education (SPE). P.O. Box 222116, Dallas, TX 75222-2116. (817) 273-2845. Fax (817) 273-2846. M. L. Hutchins, Exec. Dir. An association of college and university teachers of photography, museum photographic curators, writers, and publishers. Promotes higher standards of photographic education. *Membership:* 1,700. *Dues:* $55. *Meetings:* March 1995, Atlanta; March 21-24, 1996, Los Angeles, CA. *Publications: Exposure;* newsletter.

*Society of Cable Television Engineers (SCTE). 669 Exton Commons, Exton, PA 19341. (215) 363-6888. Fax (215) 363-5898. William W. Riker, Pres. SCTE is dedicated to the technical training and further education of members. A nonprofit membership organization for persons engaged in engineering, construction, installation, technical direction, management, or administration of cable television and broadband communication technologies. Also eligible for membership are students in communications, educators, government and regulatory agency employees, and affiliated trade associations. *Membership:* 11,000. *Dues:* $40/yr. *Publication: The Interval.*

*Society of Photo Technologists (SPT). 6535 S. Dayton, Suite 2000, Englewood, CO 80111. (303) 799-1632. Karen A. Hone, contact person. An organization of photographic equipment repair technicians, which improves and maintains communications between manufacturers and independent repair technicians. *Membership:* 1,000. *Dues:* $60-$250. *Publications: SPT Journal; SPT Parts and Services Directory; SPT Newsletter; SPT Manuals—Training and Manufacturer's Tours.*

Society of Photographic Engineering. See listing for Society for Imaging Science and Technology (IS&T).

*SOFTSWAP. 1210 Marina Village Pkwy #100, Alameda, CA 94501. (510) 814-6630. Fax (510) 814-0195. Gloria Gibson, contact person. Part of CUE, Inc., a nonprofit organization that promotes the use of technology in the classroom, SOFTSWAP is an inexpensive yet high-quality library of many teacher-developed and commercial educational programs for use in Apple, IBM, and MAC computers. These copyrighted programs are organized onto disks that are sold for a nominal charge, with permission to copy. *Membership:* Approx. 7,000 (CUE, Inc.). *Dues:* $25/yr. *Meetings:* 1994, May 5-7, Palm Springs, CA, "Technology of Education: Mosaic of the Future"; October 27-29, Santa Clara, CA. *Publication: CUE Newsletter,* 6/yr.

SouthEastern Regional Vision for Education (SERVE). P.O. Box 5367, Greensboro, NC 27435-3277. (910) 334-3211; (800) 755-3277. Fax (910) 334-3268. E-mail jglobe@serve.org. Dr. Roy H. Forbes, Exec. Dir. SERVE's mission is to promote and support the continuous improvement of educational opportunities for all learners in the Southeast. This federally funded education laboratory is a coalition of business leaders, governors, policy makers, and educators who are seeking systemic, lasting improvement in education in Alabama, Florida, Georgia, Mississippi, North Carolina, and South Carolina. It has six offices, one each in Alabama, Florida, Mississippi, and South Carolina, as well as the North Carolina office listed here. Products and services offered by SERVE include SERVE-LINE, a computerized communication system; a free information and retrieval service; Sharing Success, a program to identify successful programs in the area; free and low-cost publications and videotapes designed to give educators practical information and the latest research on common issues and problems; field services and technical assistance; conferences and teleconferences; research and development project on practical issues related to school-based educational improvement; policy analysis and improvement; and toll-free numbers to call for information and assistance. *Meetings:* For dates and topics of Conferences and Workshops, contact Jan Crotts, (910) 334-3211. *Publications: Reengineering High Schools for Student Success; Schools for the 21st Century: New Roles for Teachers and Principals* (rev. ed.); *Designing Teacher Evaluation Systems That Promote Professional Growth; Learning by Serving: 2,000 Ideas for Service-Learning Projects; Sharing Success: Promising Service-Learning Programs; Future Plans* (Videotape, Discussion Guide, and Pamphlet); *Future Plans Planning Guides; Reducing Baby Bottle Tooth Decay: A SERVE Research Brief.*

Southwest Educational Development Laboratory (SEDL). 211 East Seventh St., Austin, TX 78701. (512) 476-6861. Fax (512) 476-2286. Internet jpollard@sedl.org. Preston C. Kronkosky, Exec. Dir.; Joyce Pollard, Dir. Institutional Communications & Policy Services. One of 10 Office of Educational Research and Improvement (OERI) regional educational laboratories designed to help educators and policymakers solve educational problems in their schools. Using the best available information and the experience and expertise of professionals, SEDL seeks to identify solutions to education problems, tries new approaches, furnishes research results, and provides training to teachers and administrators. SEDL serves Arkansas, Louisiana, New Mexico, Oklahoma, and Texas. *Publications:* SEDL publishes *SEDLETTER* for general distribution and a range of topic-specific publications related to educational change, policy, mathematics, and science. It also maintains a gopher and a MOSAIC interface to the Internet.

*Special Libraries Association (SLA). 1700 18th St. NW, Washington, DC 20009-2508. (202) 234-4700. Fax (202) 265-9317. David R. Bender, Exec. Dir. SLA is an international professional organization of more than 14,000 librarians, information managers, and brokers serving business, research, government, universities, media, museums, and institutions that use or produce specialized information. Founded in 1909, the goal of the association is to advance the leadership role of special librarians in the information society. SLA encourages its members to increase their professional competencies and performance by offering continuing education courses, workshops, and middle management and executive management courses. *Membership:* 14,000 plus. *Dues:* $75 individual. *Meeting:* 1994 Annual Conference, June 11-16, Atlanta, GA. *Publications: SpeciaList* (mo. newsletter); *Special Libraries* (q.); bibliographic aids in library and information services.

*SpecialNet. Part of GTE Educational Network Services. 1090 Vermont Ave. NW, Suite 800, Washington, DC 20005. (202) 408-7021; (800) 659-3000. Fax (202) 628-8216. Mike McLean, contact person. A computerized, fee-charging information database emphasizing special education resources.

Speech Communication Association (SCA). 5105 Backlick Rd., Bldg. E, Annandale, VA 22003. (703) 750-0533. James L. Gaudino, Exec. Dir. A voluntary society organized to promote study, criticism, research, teaching, and application of principles of communication, particularly of speech communication. *Membership:* 7,000. *Dues:* $75. *Publications: Spectra Newsletter* (mo.); *Quarterly Journal of Speech*; *Communication Monographs*; *Communication Education*; *Critical Studies in Mass Communication*; *Journal of Applied Communication Research*; *Text and Performance Quarterly*; *Speech Communication Teacher*; *Index to Journals in Communication Studies through 1990*; *Speech Communication Directory of SCA and the Regional Speech Communication Organizations* (CSSA, ECA, SSCA, WSCA). For additional publications, request brochure.

*Teachers and Writers Collaborative (T&W). 5 Union Square W., New York, NY 10003. (212) 691-6590. Nancy Larson Shapiro, Dir. Sends writers and other artists into New York public schools to work with teachers and students on writing and art projects. Hosts seminars, workshops, and lectures. Publishes a magazine and books on teaching writing, featuring creative work from across the United States and beyond. *Dues:* $35/yr. basic membership. *Publications: Teachers & Writers* (magazine, 5/yr.); *The Story in History*; *The T&W Handbook of Poetic Forms*; *The T&W Guide to Walt Whitman*; *Personal Fiction Writing*; *Blazing Pencils*; *Like It Was: A Complete Guide to Writing Oral History*; *Origins*; *Moving Windows: Evaluating the Poetry Children Write*; *Poetic Forms: 10 Audio Programs*. Request free publications catalog for list of titles.

Theater Library Association (TLA). 111 Amsterdam Ave., Rm. 513, New York, NY 10023. (212) 870-1670. Richard M. Buck, Secy./Treas. Seeks to further the interests of collecting, preserving, and using theater, cinema, and performing arts materials in libraries, museums, and private collections. *Membership:* 500. *Dues:* $20 individual, $25 institutional. *Publications: Broadside* (q.); *Performing Arts Resources* (membership annual).

Training Media Association. 198 Thomas Johnson Dr., Suite 206, Frederick, MD 21702. (301) 662-4268. Robert A. Gehrke, Exec. Dir. An organization dedicated to the protection of film and videotape copyright and copyright education. *Membership:* 85 voting members and associate members. *Dues:* Based on number of employees. *Meetings:* Senior Management Seminar, February 25-26, 1995, Scottsdale, AZ; Annual Membership Meeting, June 4, 1995, Dallas, TX. *Publication: Previews* (newsletter).

World Future Society (WFS). 7910 Woodmont Ave., Suite 450, Bethesda, MD 20814. (301) 656-8274. Edward Cornish, Pres. Organization of individuals interested in the study of future trends and possibilities. *Membership:* 30,000. *Dues:* For information, please write to preceding address. *Meetings:* 1995 Annual Meeting, July 19-20, Atlanta, GA. *Publications: The Futurist: A Journal of Forecasts, Trends and Ideas About the Future*; *Futures Research Quarterly*; *Future Survey*. The society's bookstore offers audio- and videotapes, books, and other items.

Canada

This section on Canada includes information on ten Canadian organizations whose principal interests lie in the general fields of education, educational media, instructional technology, and library and information science. Organizations listed in the 1994 *EMTY* were contacted for updated information and changes have been made accordingly.

ACCESS NETWORK. 3720 76 Ave., Edmonton, AB T6B 2N9, Canada. (403) 440-7777. Fax (403) 440-8899. Malcolm Knox, Gen. Mgr., contact person; Sherrell Steele, Dir., Development and Production. ACCESS NETWORK is the registered trade name of the Alberta Educational Communications Corporation, which was established in 1973 to consolidate a variety of educational media services developing at that time in the province. ACCESS NETWORK acquires, develops, produces, and distributes curriculum-related video and audio programs and print support to Alberta schools. Intended primarily for use in Alberta classrooms, ACCESS NETWORK productions are also available for national and international distribution. In 1985, the corporation launched a province-wide educational television service, which is available by cable, satellite, and off-air transmitters to 85 percent of Alberta's population.

*Association for Media and Technology in Education in Canada (AMTEC). 3-1750 The Queensway, Suite 1818, Etobicoke, ON M9C 5H5, Canada. Allen LeBlanc, Pres.; Lillian Carefoot, Secy. Promotes applications of educational technology in improving education and the public welfare. Fosters cooperation and interaction; seeks to improve professional qualifications of media practitioners; organizes and conducts media and technology meetings, seminars, and annual conferences; stimulates and publishes research in media and technology. *Membership:* 550. *Dues:* $80.25 individual, $32.10 student and retiree. *Meeting:* 1994 Annual Conference, AMTEC '94, June 12-15, Lethbridge, AB, "Winds of Change." *Publications: Canadian Journal of Educational Communication* (q.); *Media News* (q.); *Membership Directory* (with membership).

*Canadian Book Publishers' Council (CBPC). 250 Merton St., Suite 203, Toronto, ON M4S 1B1 Canada. (416) 322-7011. Fax (416) 322-6999. Jacqueline Hushion, Exec. Dir. CBPC members publish and distribute an extensive list of Canadian and imported learning materials in a complete range of formats from traditional textbook and ancillary materials to CDs and interactive video. The primary markets for CBPS members are schools, universities and colleges, bookstores, and libraries. CBPC also provides exhibits throughout the year and works through a number of subcommittees and groups within the organization to promote effective book publishing. *Membership:* 48 companies, educational institutions, or government agencies that publish books as an important facet of their work.

Canadian Broadcasting Corporation (CBC)/Société Radio-Canada (SRC). 1500 Bronson Ave., Box 8478, Ottawa, ON K1G 3J5, Canada. (613) 738-6784. Fax (613) 738-6742. Anthony S. Manera, Pres. and CEO; Charlotte O'Dea, Senior Dir. of Corporate Communications and Public Affairs. The CBC is a publicly owned corporation established in 1936 by an Act of the Canadian Parliament to provide a national broadcasting service in Canada in the two official languages. CBC services include English and French television networks; English and French AM Mono and FM Stereo radio networks virtually free of commercial advertising; CBC North, which serves Canada's North by providing radio and television programs in English, French, and eight native languages; Newsworld, a 24-hour national satellite to cable English-language news and information service funded entirely by cable subscription and commercial advertising revenues; and Radio Canada International, a shortwave radio service that broadcasts in seven languages and is managed by CBC and financed by External Affairs. The CBC is financed mainly by public funds voted annually by Parliament.

Canadian Education Association/Association canadienne d'éducation (CEA). 252 Bloor St. W., Suite 8-200, Toronto, ON M5S 1V5, Canada. (416) 924-7721. Fax (416) 924-3188. Robert E. Blair, Exec. Dir.; Suzanne Tanguay, Communications Officer. The Canadian equivalent of the U.S. National Education Association. *Membership:* 400 individual, 43 associate, 100 school board. *Dues:* $90 individual, $380 associate, 10 cents per pupil for school board. *Meetings:* September 19-22, 1995, Winnepeg, Man. *Publications: CEA Handbook; Education Canada* (q.); *CEA Newsletter* (9/yr.); *Violence in the Schools; Criteria for Admission to Faculties of Education in Canada: What You Need to Know; First Nations and Schools: Triumphs and Struggles; The Canadian Education Association: The First 100 Years 1891-1991; The Multi-Grade Classroom: Myth and Reality; French Immersion Today; Heritage Language Programs in Canadian School Boards.*

*Canadian Film Institute (CFI). 2 Daly, Ottawa, ON K1N 6E2, Canada. (613) 232-6727. Fax (613) 232-6315. Serge Losique, Exec. Dir.; Brian Wilson, Dir., Non-Theatrical Services. Established in 1935, the Institute promotes the study of film and television as cultural and educational forces in Canada. It distributes over 6,000 films and videos on the sciences and the visual and performing arts through the Canadian Film Institute Film Library. *Publications: Canadian Film* (series of monographs); *Northern Lights* (programmer's guide to the Festival of Festivals Retrospective); *Switching on to the Environment* (critical guide).

Canadian Library Association. 200 Elgin St., Suite 602, Ottawa, ON K2P IL5, Canada. (613) 232-9625. Fax (613) 563-9895. E-mail ai077@freenet.carleton.ca. Patricia Cavill, Pres.; Karen Adams, Exec. Dir. The mission of the Canadian Library Association is to provide leadership in the promotion, development, and support of library and information services in Canada for the benefit of Association members, the profession, and Canadian society. In the spirit of this mission, CLA aims to engage the active, creative participation of library staff, trustees, and governing bodies in the development and management of high quality Canadian library service; to assert and support the right of all Canadians to the freedom to read and to free universal access to a wide variety of library materials and services; to promote librarianship and to enlighten all levels of government as to the significant role that libraries play in educating and socializing the Canadian people; and to link libraries, librarians, trustees, and others across the country for the purpose of providing a unified nationwide voice in matters of critical concern. *Membership:* 3,200 individual, 850 institutional. *Dues:* Range from $50 to $1,600. *Meetings:* 1995 Annual Conference, June 15-18, Calgary, AB; 1996 Annual Conference, June 6-9, Halifax, NS. *Publications: Feliciter* (member newsletter, 10/yr.); *CM: A Reviewing Journal of Canadian Materials for Young People.*

Canadian Museums Association/Association des musées canadiens (CMA/AMC). 280 Metcalfe St., Suite 400, Ottawa, ON K2P 1R7, Canada. (613) 567-0099. Fax (613) 233-5438. John G. McAvity, Exec. Dir. The Canadian Museums Association is a nonprofit corporation and registered charity dedicated to advancing public museums and museum works in Canada, promoting the welfare and better administration of museums, and fostering a continuing improvement in the qualifications and practices of museum professionals. *Membership:* 2,000. *Publications: Museogramme* (bi-mo. newsletter); *Muse* (q. journal). Canada's only national, bilingual, scholarly magazine devoted to museums, it contains museum-based photography, feature articles, commentary, and practical information; *The Official Directory of Canadian Museums and Related Institutions* (1993-94 edition) lists all museums in Canada plus information on government departments, agencies, and provincial and regional museum associations.

National Film Board of Canada (NFBC). 1251 Avenue of the Americas, 16th Floor, New York, NY 10020. (212) 596-1770. Fax (212) 595-1779. E-mail gsem78a@prodigy.com. John Sirabella, U.S. Marketing Mgr./Nontheatrical Rep. Established in 1939, the NFBC's main objective is to produce and distribute high-quality audiovisual materials for educational, cultural, and social purposes.

Ontario Film Association, Inc. (also known as the Association for the Advancement of Visual Media/L'association pour l'avancement des médias visuels). 3-1750 The Queensway, Suite 1341, Etobicoke, ON M9C 5H5, Canada. (416) 761-6056. Margaret Nix., Exec. Dir. A nonprofit organization whose primary objective is to promote the sharing of ideas and information about film and video through seminars, workshops, screenings, and publications. Sponsors the annual Grierson Documentary Seminar on film and video, and the Annual Showcase of film and video, a marketplace for buyers. *Membership:* 181. *Dues:* $120 regular and commercial, $180 extended. *Publication: Visual Media/Médias Visuels* (5/yr.).

Part Seven
Graduate Programs

Doctoral Programs in Instructional Technology

This directory presents information on 46 doctoral (Ph.D. and Ed.D.) programs in instructional technology, educational communications/technology, media services, and closely allied programs in 25 states. Notification of the closing of one program is also included. Information in this section for 25 of the programs was obtained from, and updated by, the institutional deans, chairs, or their representatives, in response to an inquiry questionnaire mailed to them during the fall of 1994. Updated information was requested with the proviso that, if no reply was received, information provided for the 1994 edition would be used; programs for which no information has been received since 1993 or before would be dropped. Nineteen programs for which the information was updated for the 1994 edition but no response was forthcoming for this edition are indicated by an asterisk (*).

Entries provide as much of the following information as was provided by respondents: (1) name and address of the institution; (2) chairperson or other individual in charge of the doctoral program; (3) types of degrees offered and specializations, including information on positions for which candidates are prepared; (4) special features of the degree program; (5) admission requirements, including minimal grade point average; (6) number of full-time and part-time faculty; (7) number of full-time and part-time students; (8) types of financial assistance available; and (9) the number of doctoral degrees awarded in 1994.

Directors of advanced professional programs for instructional technology/media specialists should find this information useful as a means of comparing their own offerings and requirements with those of institutions offering comparable programs. This listing should also assist individuals seeking a school at which to pursue advanced graduate studies in locating institutions that best suit their interests and requirements.

Additional information on the programs listed, including instructions on applying for admission, may be obtained by contacting individual program coordinators. General or graduate catalogs usually are furnished for a minimal charge; specific program information normally is sent at no charge.

In endeavoring to provide complete listings, we are greatly indebted to those individuals who responded to our requests for information. Although considerable effort has been expended to ensure completeness of the listings, there may be institutions within the United States or its territories that now have programs or that have been omitted. Readers are encouraged to furnish new information to the publisher who, in turn, will follow up for the next edition of *EMTY*.

Institutions in this section are listed alphabetically by state.

ALABAMA

*Alabama State University. Library Education Media, School of Education, P.O. Box 271, Montgomery, AL 36195. (205) 293-4107. Fax (205) 241-7192. Katie R. Bell, Ph.D. Coord., Library Education Media, School of Education. *Specializations:* M.Ed., AA Certification, and Ed.S., preparation for K-12 school media programs. *Degree Requirements:* 36 semester hours; thesis required for Ed.S.; 300-clock-hour practicum (100 each in elementary, high school, and other library settings). *Faculty:* 2 part-time. *Students:* 1 full-time; 21 part-time. *Financial Assistance:* Assistantships available for full-time students. *Doctoral Degrees Awarded 1 July 1992-30 June 1993:* 2.

*University of Alabama. School of Library and Information Studies, The University of Alabama, Box 87052, Tuscaloosa, AL 35487-0252. (205) 348-1523. Fax (205) 348-3746. J. Gordon Coleman, Jr., Asst. Dean and Assoc. Prof., Doctoral Program, School of Library and Information Studies. *Specializations:* Ph.D. in Librarianship with specializations in library management, information studies, youth services, library media studies, historical studies. *Features:* Program is designed to fit the needs of the student using the resources of the entire university. Students may prepare for careers in teaching and research in colleges and universities or for innovative practice in the profession. *Admission Requirements:* Master's in library science, instructional technology, or equivalent; Miller Analogies score of 55 or GRE score of 1,650; 3.5 graduate GPA. *Faculty:* 10 full-time; 1 part-time. *Students:* 4 full-time; 12 part-time. *Financial Assistance:* Fellowships, assistantships, scholarships. *Doctorates Awarded 1992-93:* 3 (program began 1988; intentionally small).

CALIFORNIA

United States International University. School of Education, 10455 Pomerado Rd., San Diego, CA 92131-1799. (619) 635-4715. Fax (619) 635-4714. E-mail feifer@sanac.usiu.edu. Richard Feifer, contact person. *Specializations:* Ed.D. in Technology and Learning offers three specializations: Designing Technology for Learning, Planning Technology for Learning, and Technology Leadership for Learning. Completely revamped program begun in fall of 1994. *Features:* Interactive multimedia, cognitive approach to integrating technology and learning. *Admission Requirements:* Master's degree, English proficiency, interview, GPA greater than 3.0 and GRE score of at least 1900 or GPA greater than 2.0 and MAT score of at least 115. *Minimum Degree Requirements:* 88 graduate quarter units, dissertation. *Faculty:* 2 full-time; 4 part-time. *Students:* Master's, 32 full-time, 12 part-time; Doctoral, 6 full-time, 1 part-time. *Financial Assistance:* graduate assistantships, grants, student loans, scholarships. *Degrees Awarded 1994:* Ed.D., 1; master's, 42.

*University of California at Los Angeles. Graduate School of Education, 405 Hilgard Ave., Los Angeles, CA 90024-1521. (310) 825-8326; (310) 825-1838. Fax (310) 206-6293. Aimee Dorr, Prof. of Education, Learning and Instruction Specialization, Div. of Educational Psychology, Graduate School of Education. *Specializations:* Offers Ph.D. and Ed.D. programs. Ph.D. program prepares graduates for research, teaching educational technology, and consultancies in the development of instructional materials. Ed.D. program prepares graduates for leadership roles in the development of instructional materials and educational technologies. *Features:* The program addresses the design and utilization principles and processes underlying all effective applications of instructional technologies and their products. Television, microcomputer-based, and multimedia systems are encouraged. *Admission Requirements:* Superior academic record, combined GRE score of 1,000 or better. For the Ed.D. program, two or more years of relevant field experience is desirable. *Faculty:* 4 full-time; 2 part-time. *Students:* 10-15 in M.A., Ph.D., and Ed.D. programs. *Financial Assistance:* Fellowships, loans, and resident advisors. *Doctorates Awarded 1993:* Data not reported.

University of Southern California. 702C W.P.H., School of Education, Los Angeles, CA 90089-0031. (213) 740-3476. Fax (213) 746-8142. Dr. Edward J. Kazlauskas, Prof., Prog. Chair, Instructional Technology. *Specializations:* M.A., Ph.D., Ed.D. to prepare individuals to teach instructional technology; manage educational media/training programs in business or industry, research and development organizations, and higher educational institutions; perform research in instructional technology and media; and deal with computer-driven technology. Satellite Ed.D. program in Silicon Valley in northern California. *Features:* Special emphasis upon instructional design, systems analysis, and computer-based training. *Admission Requirements:* A bachelor's degree and satisfactory performance (combined score of 1,000) on the GRE aptitude test. *Faculty:* 5 full-time; 1 part-time. *Students:* 5 full-time; 41 part-time. *Financial Assistance:* Part-time work available (instructional technology-related) in the Los Angeles area and on the university campus.

COLORADO

University of Colorado at Denver. School of Education, Campus Box 106, P.O. Box 173364, Denver, CO 80217-3364. (303) 556-2962. Fax (303) 556-4479. R. Scott Grabinger, Program Leader of Instructional Technology in the Division of Technology and Special Services. *Specializations:* Ph.D. in instructional technology, in instructional development, and/or instructional computing for use in business/industry and higher education. *Features:* Courses in management and consulting, emphasizing instructional development, interactive video technologies, evaluation, and internship opportunities in a variety of agencies. *Admission Requirements:* Satisfactory GPA, GRE, writing/publication background, letters of recommendation, transcripts, and application form. *Faculty:* 5 full-time; 4 part-time. *Students:* 2 full-time; 16 part-time. *Financial Assistance:* Assistantships, grants, student loans, scholarships. *Doctorates Awarded 1994:* 4.

University of Northern Colorado. College of Education, Greeley, CO 80639. (303) 351-2687. Fax (303) 351-2312. E-mail caffarel@edtech.univnorthco.edu. Edward P. Caffarella, Prof., Chair, Educational Technology, Division of Research, Evaluation, and Development. *Specializations:* Ph.D. in Educational Technology with emphasis areas in instructional development/design, interactive technology, and technology integration. *Features:* Graduates are prepared for careers as instructional technologists, course designers, trainers, instructional developers, media specialists, and human resource managers. *Admission Requirements:* GPA of 3.2, three letters of recommendation, congruency between applicant's statement of career goals and program goals, GRE combined test score of 1,650, and interview with faculty. *Faculty:* 5 full-time; 2 part-time. *Students:* 16 full-time, 28 part-time. *Financial Assistance:* Assistantships, grants, student loans, scholarships. *Doctorates Awarded 1994:* 4.

CONNECTICUT

*University of Connecticut. U-64, Storrs, CT 06269-2064. (203) 486-0181. Fax 486-0210. E-mail sbrown@UConnvm.UConn.edu, or myoung@UConnvm.UConn.edu. Scott W. Brown, Chair; Michael Young, contact person. *Specializations:* The emphasis in Educational Technology is a specialization within the Program of Cognition and Instruction, in the

Department of Educational Psychology. *Features:* The emphasis in Educational Technology is a unique program at UConn. It is co-sponsored by the Department of Educational Psychology in the School of Education and the Psychology Department in the College of Liberal Arts and Sciences. The emphasis in Educational Technology within the Cognition and Instruction Program seeks to provide students with knowledge of theory and applications regarding the use of advanced technology to enhance learning and thinking. The Ed. Tech. emphasis provides suggested courses, and opportunities for internships and independent study experiences that are directed toward an understanding of both the effects of technology on cognition and instruction, and the enhancement of thinking and learning with technology. Facilities include the UCEML computer lab featuring Mac and IBM networks and a multimedia development center. The School of Education also features a multimedia classroom/auditorium renovated in 1993 for Mac and IBM computer displays and peripherals, including videodisc, CD-ROM, interactive videotape, and fiber connections to our broadcast studio. Faculty research interests include interactive videodisc for anchored instruction and situated learning, telecommunications for cognitive apprenticeship, technology-mediated interactivity for generative learning, and in cooperation with the National Research Center for Gifted and Talented (a collaboration with Yale and the U. of Georgia, housed at UConn), research on the use of technology to enhance cooperative learning and the development of gifted performance in all students. *Admission Requirements:* Admission to the graduate school at UConn, GRE test completion or other evidence of success at the graduate level. Previous experience in a related area of technology, education, or training is a plus. *Faculty:* The program in Cognition and Instruction has 5 full-time faculty; 2 full-time faculty administer the emphasis in Educational Technology. *Students:* Data not reported. *Financial Assistance:* Graduate assistantships, research fellowships, teaching assistantships, and federal and minority scholarships are available competitively. *Doctorates Awarded 1992-93:* 2.

FLORIDA

Florida State University. Instructional Systems Program, Department of Educational Research, College of Education, 305 Stone Bldg., Tallahassee, FL 32306. (904) 644-8785. Fax (904) 644-8776. Marcy P. Driscott, Prof. *Specializations:* Ph.D. degree in instructional systems with specializations for persons planning to work in academia, business, industry, government, or military; Specialist Degree. *Features:* Core courses include systems and materials development, analysis of media, project management, psychological foundations, current trends in instructional design, and research and statistics. Internships are also required. *Admission Requirements:* Total score of 1,000 on the verbal and quantitative sections of the GRE, or a GPA of 3.0 for the last two years of undergraduate study; international students, TOEFL score of 550. *Faculty:* 6 full-time; 5 part-time. *Students:* 40. *Financial Assistance:* Some graduate research assistantships on faculty grants and contracts; university fellowships. *Doctorates Awarded 1994:* 2.

Nova Southeastern University. Fischler Center for the Advancement of Education, 3301 College Ave., Fort Lauderdale, FL 33314. (800) 986-3223. Fax (305) 476-4764. Johanne Peck, M.S. and Ed.S. Programs for Teachers. *Specializations:* M.S. and Ed.S. in Educational Media. *Minimum Degree Requirements:* M.S., 36 semester hours including a practicum; Ed.S. 36 semester hours beyond the master's, including a practicum. *Faculty:* 2 full-time; 5 part-time. *Students:* 38. *Financial Assistance:* NDSL; Federal Stafford Loan, Unsubsidized Federal Stafford Loan, SLS. *Doctorates Awarded 1994:* Data not reported.

*University of Florida. College of Education, Gainesville, FL 32611. (904) 392-0705, ext. 600; (904) 392-0705. Fax (904) 392-9193. Lee Mullally, Assoc. Prof., Chair, Educational Media and Instructional Design Program, College of Education. *Specializations:* Ph.D. and Ed.D. programs that stress theory, research, training, teaching, evaluation, and instructional development. *Admission Requirements:* A composite score of at least 1,000 on the GRE, an undergraduate GPA of 3.0 minimum and a graduate GPA of 3.5 minimum, and three letters of recommendation. *Faculty:* 2 full-time. *Students:* 15 full- and part-time. *Financial Assistance:* A few scholarships through the Graduate School. *Doctorates Awarded 1992-93:* 2.

GEORGIA

*Georgia State University. College of Education, Atlanta, GA 30303-3083. (404) 651-2510. Fax (404) 651-2546. Francis D. Atkinson, Coord., Instructional Technology Programs, Dept. of Curriculum and Instruction. *Specializations:* Ph.D. in Instructional Technology. *Admission Requirements:* Three letters of recommendation, handwritten and autobiographical sketch, admission tests, and acceptance by department. *Faculty:* 2 full-time; 6 part-time. *Students:* 3 full-time; 12 part-time. *Financial Assistance:* Assistantships, paid internships, student loans and grants. *Doctorates Awarded 1991-92:* 0.

University of Georgia. College of Education, 607 Aderhold Hall, Athens, GA 30602-7144. (706) 542-3810. Fax (706) 542-4032. E-mail kgustafs@moe.coe.uga.edu. Kent L. Gustafson, Prof. and Chair, Dept. of Instructional Technology. *Specializations:* M.Ed, Ed.S., Ed.D, and Ph.D. for leadership positions as specialists in instructional design and development. The program offers advanced study for individuals with previous preparation in instructional media and technology, as well as a preparation for personnel in other professional fields requiring a specialty in instructional systems/instructional technology. Representative career fields for graduates include designing/developing/evaluating new courses, tutorial programs, and instructional materials in a number of different settings; military/industrial training; medical/dental/nursing professional schools; allied health agencies; teacher education/staff development centers; state/local school systems; higher education/teaching/research; and publishers/producers of instructional products (textbooks, workbooks, films, etc.). *Features:* Minor areas of study available in a variety of other departments. Personalized programs are planned around a common core of courses; practica, internships, and/or clinical experiences. Research activities include special assignments, applied projects, and task forces, as well as thesis and dissertation studies. *Admission Requirements:* Application to graduate school, satisfactory GRE score, other criteria as outlined in Graduate School Bulletin. *Faculty:* 11 full-time. *Students:* 40 full-time. *Financial Assistance:* Graduate assistantships available. *Doctorates Awarded 1994:* Data not reported.

ILLINOIS

Northern Illinois University. College of Education, DeKalb, IL 60115. (815) 753-0464. Fax (815) 753-9371. Dr. Gary L. McConeghy, Chair, Instructional Technology, College of Education—LEPS. *Specializations:* Ed.D. in Instructional Technology, emphasizing instructional design and development, computer education, media administration, production, and preparation for careers in business, industry, and higher education. *Features:* Considerable flexibility in course selection, including advanced seminars, internships, individual study, and research. Program is highly individualized. A total of 60 courses offered by several departments, including Library Science, Radio/Television/Film, Art, Journalism, Educational

Psychology, and Research and Evaluation. *Admission Requirements:* 2.75 undergraduate GPA, 3.5 M.S. GPA; combined score of 1,000 on GRE; a writing sample; and three references. *Faculty:* 8 full-time; 3 part-time. *Students:* 88 part-time. *Financial Assistance:* Assistantships available at times in various departments. *Doctorates Awarded 1994:* 4.

Northwestern University. Institute for Learning Sciences, 1890 Maple Ave., Evanston, IL 60201. (708) 467-1332. Fax (708) 491-5258. E-mail tina@ils.nwu.edu. Roy D. Pea, Chair, Learning Sciences Ph.D. Program. Tina Turnbull, Grad. Prog. Coord., contact person. *Specializations:* Ph.D. in the Learning Sciences with three flexible tracks: teaching-learning environments; cognitive aspects of learning; and the design and development of effective computational and multimedia architectures for learning and teaching. *Features:* An integrated body of coursework and apprenticing activities is designed for all students, regardless of specialization, to develop their facility with theory and methods through laboratory work, field experiences, studies in nonlaboratory settings, participation in ongoing research and development projects, and independent research guided by faculty mentors. *Admission Requirements:* Data not reported. *Degree Requirements:* seven quarter core courses in the learning sciences; three or more methods courses; three advanced topic courses; participation in a variety of research laboratories and activities; a written preliminary examination; publication-quality predissertation paper reporting research conducted under the supervision of a faculty member; an oral qualifying examination; and a dissertation demonstrating original and significant research. *Faculty:* 22. *Students:* Data not reported. *Financial Assistance:* Students are eligible for competitively awarded multiyear funding. *Doctorates Awarded 1994:* Data not reported.

Southern Illinois University at Carbondale. Department of Curriculum and Instruction, Carbondale, IL 62901-4610. (618) 536-2441. Fax (618) 453-4244. Internet ga4051@siucvmb.siu.edu. Sharon Shrock, Coord., Instructional Technology/Development. *Specializations:* Ph.D. in education including specialization in instructional technology. *Features:* All specializations are oriented to multiple education settings. *Admission Requirements:* 3.25 GPA or better; Miller Analogies Test or GRE score; letters of recommendation; and a writing sample. *Faculty:* 6 full-time; 2 part-time. *Students:* 25. *Financial Assistance:* Assistantships, scholarships. *Doctorates Awarded 1994:* 2.

*University of Illinois at Urbana-Champaign. College of Education, Champaign, IL 61820. (217) 244-3391. Fax (217) 244-4572. Graduate Programs Office, Dept. of Curriculum and Instruction, College of Education. *Specializations:* Ph.D., Ed.D. programs (including advanced certificate program) with emphasis in the following areas: preparation of university research faculty, materials/training designers, computer resources managers, and continuing professional teacher training. *Features:* Programs designed to accommodate individuals with diverse background preparations. *Admission Requirements:* Master's degree, 4.0 out of 5.0 GPA, GRE at least 50th percentile in two of Verbal, Quantitative, and Analytic; a sample of scholarly writing in English; TOEFL scores, including scores on Test of Written English and Test of Spoken English for non-English-speaking students. *Faculty:* 8 full- and part-time. *Students:* 20 full- and part-time. *Financial Assistance:* Fellowships for very highly academically talented; assistantships for 20-25 percent; some tuition fee waivers. *Doctorates Awarded 1992-93:* 5.

*University of Illinois at Urbana-Champaign. Department of Educational Psychology, 210 Education Bldg., 1310 S. 6th St., Champaign, IL 61820. (217) 333-2245. Fax (217) 244-7620. E-mail cwest@uiuc.edu. Charles K. West, Prof., Div. of Learning and Instruction, Dept. of Educational Psychology. *Specializations:* Ph.D. in educational psychology with emphasis in instructional psychology, instructional design, and educational computing. *Features:* Individually tailored program. Strongly research-oriented with emphasis on applications of cognitive science to instruction. *Admission Requirements:* Excellent academic record, high GRE scores, and strong letters of recommendation. *Faculty:* 17. *Students:* 35. *Financial Assistance:* Scholarships, research assistantships, and teaching assistantships available. *Doctorates Awarded 1992-93:* 7.

INDIANA

Indiana University. School of Education, W. W. Wright Education Bldg., Bloomington, IN 47405-1006. (812) 855-1791. Fax (812) 855-3044. Thomas Schwen, Chair, Dept. of Instructional Systems Technology. *Specializations:* Offers Ph.D. and Ed.D. degrees with four program focus areas: Foundations; Instructional Analysis, Design, and Development; Instructional Development and Production; and Implementation and Management. *Features:* Requires computer skills as a prerequisite and makes technology utilization an integral part of the curriculum; eliminates the separation of the various media formats; and establishes a series of courses of increasing complexity integrating production and development. The latest in technical capabilities have been incorporated in the new Center for Excellence in Education, including teaching, photographic, computer, and science laboratories, a 14-station multimedia laboratory, and television studios. *Admission Requirements:* Data not reported. *Degree Requirements:* Ed.D., 60 post-bachelor's degree credit hours including nine credit hours in inquiry; portfolio examination; and dissertation (may be project based). Ph.D., 90 post-bachelor's degree credit hours of which 27 hours of credit must be in inquiry; publication; portfolio examination; participation in a research colloquium; and research-based dissertation. *Faculty:* 6 full-time; 3 part-time. *Students:* Data not reported. *Financial Assistance:* Data not reported. *Doctorates Awarded 1994:* Data not reported.

Purdue University. School of Education, W. Lafayette, IN 47907-1442. (317) 494-5673. Fax (317) 496-1622. James D. Russell, Prof. of Educational Computing and Instructional Development, Dept. of Curriculum and Instruction. *Specializations:* Ph.D. programs in instructional research and development or educational computing. *Admission Requirements:* GPA of 3.0 or better, three recommendations, scores totaling 1,000 or more on the GRE, statement of personal goals. *Faculty:* 6 full-time. *Students:* 12 full-time; 31 part-time. *Financial Assistance:* Assistantships and fellowships. *Doctorates Awarded 1994:* 8.

IOWA

Iowa State University. College of Education, Ames, IA 50011. (515) 294-6840. Fax (515) 294-9284. E-mail mrs@iastate.edu. Michael Simonson, Prof., Curriculum and Instruction Dept., College of Education. *Specializations:* Ph.D. in education with emphasis in instructional computing, instructional design, and technology research. *Features:* Practicum experiences related to professional objectives, supervised study and research projects tied to long-term studies within the program, development and implementation of new techniques, teaching strategies, and operational procedures in instructional resources centers and computer labs. *Admission Requirements:* Top half of undergraduate class, autobiography, three letters of recommendation, GRE general test scores. *Faculty:* 3 full-time; 3 part-time. *Students:* 21 full-time; 20 part-time. *Financial Assistance:* 10 assistantships. *Doctorates Awarded 1993-94:* 6.

*University of Iowa. College of Education, Iowa City, IA 52242. (319) 335-5577. Fax (319) 335-5386. Lowell Schoer, Prof., Psychological and Quantitative Foundations, College of Education. *Specializations:* Ed.D. and M.A. with specializations in Classroom Instruction, Computer Applications, Instructional Development, Media Production, and Training and Human Resource Development. *Features:* Flexibility in planning to fit individual needs, backgrounds, and career goals. The program is interdisciplinary, involving courses within divisions of the College of Education, as well as in the schools of Business, Library Science, Radio and Television, Linguistics, and Psychology. *Admission Requirements:* A composite score of at least 1,000 on GRE (verbal and quantitative) and a 3.2 GPA on all previous graduate work for regular admission. (Conditional admission may be granted.) Teaching or relevant experience may be helpful. *Minimum Degree Requirements:* 60 semester hours of approved coursework—16 in core, 18 in specialization, 6 outside College of Education, 6 in a project, the rest in electives. *Faculty:* 4 full-time; 3 part-time. *Students:* 90 full- and part-time. *Financial Assistance:* Special assistantships (in the College of Education) for which students in any College of Education program may compete. Application deadlines for the special assistantships is 1 February. *Doctorates Awarded 1992-93:* Data not reported.

KANSAS

Emporia State University. School of Library and Information Management, 1200 Commercial, P.O. Box 4025, Emporia, KS 66801. (316) 341-5203. Fax (316) 341-5233. E-mail vowell@esuvm.bitnet. Faye N. Vowell, Dean, School of Library and Information Management. *Specializations:* Ph.D. in Library and Information Management; Master's of Library Science (ALA accredited program). *Features:* The MLS program is also available in Colorado, Oregon, North Dakota, and New Mexico. Video courses are being developed. *Admission Requirements:* Selective admissions process for M.L.S. and Ph.D. based on a combination of admission criteria, including (but not limited to): minimum GRE or TOEFL score; personal interview; GPA; statement of goals and references. Please request admission packet for specific criteria. *Minimum Degree Requirements:* Total of 83-97 semester hours depending on the number of hours received for an M.L.S. *Faculty:* 12 full-time; 35 part-time. *Students:* 100 full-time; 500 part-time in all sites. *Financial Assistance:* Assistantships, grants, student loans, scholarships. *Doctoral Degrees Awarded in 1994:* Data not reported.

*Kansas State University. College of Education, Manhattan, KS 66506-5301. (913) 532-5904. Fax (913) 532-7304. John Parmley, Chair, Secondary Education. *Specializations:* Ph.D. and Ed.D. programs in Instructional Design, other specializations in development. *Faculty:* 3. *Students:* 15. *Financial Assistance:* Data not available. *Doctorates Awarded 1992-93:* 6.

MARYLAND

*The Johns Hopkins University. Center for Technology in Education, Division of Education, Baltimore, MD 21218. (410) 646-3000. Fax (410) 646-2310. Sarah McPherson, Coord., M.S. Technology for Educators, Ed.D. Technology for Special Education, Div. of Education. *Specialization:* M.S. in Technology for Educators, Ed.D. in Technology for Special Education.

University of Maryland. College of Library and Information Services, College Park, MD 20742-4345. (301) 405-2038. Fax (301) 314-9145. Ann Prentice, Dean and Prog. Chair, College of Library and Information Services. *Specializations:* Ph.D. in Library Science and

Educational Technology/Instructional Communication. *Features:* Program is broadly conceived and interdisciplinary in nature, using the resources of the entire campus. The student and the advisor design a program of study and research to fit the student's background, interests, and professional objectives. Students prepare for careers in teaching and research in information science and librarianship and elect concentrations including educational technology/instructional communication. *Admission Requirements:* Baccalaureate degree (the majority enter with master's degrees in library science, educational technology, or other relevant disciplines), GRE general tests, three letters of recommendation, and a statement of purpose. Interviews required when feasible. *Faculty:* 15 full-time; 8 part-time. *Students:* 9 full-time; 8 part-time. *Financial Assistance:* Assistantships, grants, student loans, scholarships. *Doctorates Awarded in 1994:* 2.

MASSACHUSETTS

Boston University. School of Education, 605 Commonwealth Ave., Boston, MA 02215-1605. (617) 353-3519. Fax (617) 353-3924. David B. Whittier, Acting Dir., Program in Educational Media and Technology. *Specializations:* Ed.D. specializing in instructional design/development for developing and teaching academic programs in instructional technology in community colleges and universities; or specialization in such application areas as business and industrial training, biomedical communication, or international development projects. Program specializations in instructional development, media production and design, and multimedia design and development for education and training. Students participate in mandatory research sequence and may elect courses in other university schools and colleges. *Features:* Doctoral students have a great deal of flexibility in program planning and are encouraged to plan programs that build on prior education and experience that lead to specific career goals; there is strong faculty participation in this process. *Admission Requirements:* Three letters of recommendation, Miller Analogies Test or GRE test score(s), undergraduate and graduate transcripts, completed application form with statement of goals. Minimum GPA is 2.7 with Miller Analogies Test score of 50. *Degree Requirements:* 60 credit hours, comprehensive exam., dissertation. *Faculty:* 1 full-time; 11 part-time. *Students:* 46. *Financial Assistance:* Some assistantships and fellowships. *Doctorates Awarded 1994:* Data not reported.

MICHIGAN

*University of Michigan. Educational Studies, Ann Arbor, MI 48109-1259. (313) 763-0612. Fax (313) 763-1229. Patricia Baggett, Assoc. Prof., Dept. of Educational Studies. *Specializations:* Ph.D. sequences in Educational Technology and Science Education, Educational Technology and Mathematics Education, and Educational Technology and Literacy. *Minimum Degree Requirements:* 60 credit hours beyond B.A. (trimester). *Faculty:* 1 full-time, 7 part-time. *Students:* Data not reported. *Doctoral Degrees Awarded 1992-93:* 0 (new program). See also listing in Educational Computing Programs.

Wayne State University. College of Education, Detroit, MI 48202. (313) 577-1728. Fax (313) 577-1693. Rita C. Richey, Prof., Program Coord., Instructional Technology Programs, Div. of Administrative and Organizational Studies, College of Education. *Specializations:* Ed.D. and Ph.D. programs to prepare individuals for leadership in business, industry, health care, and the K-12 school setting as instructional design and development specialists; media or learning resources managers or consultants; specialists in instructional video; and computer-assisted instruction and multimedia specialists. *Features:* Guided experiences in instructional design and development activities in business and industry are available. *Admission Requirements:* Master's, GPA of 3.5, GRE, and Miller Analogies Test, strong professional recommendations, and an interview. *Faculty:* 5 full-time; 5 part-time. *Students:* 135 at the doctoral level. *Financial Assistance:* Contract industrial internships, university scholarships. *Doctorates Awarded 1993-94:* 10.

MISSOURI

*University of Missouri-Columbia. College of Education, 212 Townsend Hall, Columbia, MO 65211. (314) 882-3832. Fax (314) 884-5455. E-mail wedmanjf@missou1.missouri.edu. John F. Wedman, Assoc. Prof., Educational Technology Program, Curriculum and Instruction Dept., College of Education. *Specializations:* Ph.D. in Instructional Theory and Practice. The program emphasizes learning and instructional design, electronic performance support systems (including multimedia development), and change processes. *Features:* Program includes a major in Instructional Theory and Practice with two support areas (i.e., Educational Psychology and Computer Science), research tools, and R&D apprenticeship experiences. The program is rapidly expanding, providing the cornerstone for improving mathematics, science, and technical education. These areas have been identified for enhancement and supported with an annual R&D budget of over $150,000. *Admission Requirements:* Graduate GPA above 3.2 and a combined score of 1,500 or better on the GRE; letters of recommendation; and a statement of purpose. *Faculty:* 3 full-time, 4 part-time, plus selected faculty in related fields. *Students:* 16. *Financial Assistance:* Graduate assistantships with tuition waivers; numerous academic scholarships ranging from $200 to $10,000. *Doctorates Awarded 1993:* 3.

NEW JERSEY

Rutgers-The State University of New Jersey. The Graduate School, New Brunswick, NJ 08903. (908) 932-7447. Fax (908) 932-6916. Lea P. Stewart, Prof., Dir., Ph.D. Program in Communication, Information, and Library Studies, The Graduate School. *Specializations:* Ph.D. programs in communication; information systems, structures, and users; information and communication policy and technology; and library and information services. *Features:* Program provides doctoral-level coursework for students seeking theoretical and research skills for scholarly and professional leadership in the information and communication fields. *Admission Requirements:* Typically, students should have completed a master's degree in information studies, communication, library science, or related field. The undergraduate GPA should be 3.0 or better. The GRE is required; TOEFL is also required for foreign applicants whose native language is not English. *Faculty:* 43 full- and part-time. *Students:* 104 full- and part-time. *Financial Assistance:* Assistantships and Title II-B fellowships. *Doctorates Awarded 1993-94:* 4.

NEW YORK

New York University. School of Education, New York, NY 10003. (212) 998-5520. Fax (212) 995-4041. Francine Shuchat Shaw, Assoc. Prof., Dir., Educational Communication and Technology Program; Donald T. Payne, Assoc. Prof., Doctoral Advisor, Educational Communication and Technology Program, 239 Greene St., Suite 300, School of Education. *Specializations:*

Ph.D., Ed.D. in education for the preparation of individuals to perform as instructional media designers, developers, and producers in education, business and industry, health and medicine, community services, government, and other fields; to coordinate media communications programs in educational television centers, museums, schools, corporations, health and medicine, and community organizations; to serve as directors and supervisors in audiovisual programs in all settings listed; and to teach in educational communications and instructional technology programs in higher education, including instructional television, microcomputers, multimedia, and telecommunications. *Features:* Emphasizes theoretical foundations, in particular a cognitive perspective of learning and instruction and their implications for designing media-based learning environments; participation in special research and production projects in multi-image, television, microcomputers, and computer-based interactive multimedia systems. *Admission Requirements:* Combined score of 1,000 minimum on GRE, responses to essay questions and interview related to academic and/or professional preparation and career goals. *Degree Requirements:* 54 semester hours including specialization, foundations, research, content seminar, and elective coursework; candidacy papers; dissertation; and English Essay Examination. *Faculty:* 2 full-time; 10 part-time. *Students:* 14 full-time; 30 part-time. *Financial Assistance:* Graduate and research assistantships, student loans, scholarships, and work-study programs. *Doctorates Awarded 1994:* 3.

State University of New York at Buffalo. Graduate School of Education, Buffalo, NY 14214. (716) 636-3164. Fax (716) 645-2481. Taher A. Razik, Prof. of Education, Dept. of Educational Organization, Administration and Policy, 480 Baldy Hall. *Specializations:* Ph.D., Ed.D., and Ed.M. in instructional design systems and management. Emphasis is on the systems approach, communication, and computer-assisted instruction and model building, with a specific focus on the efficient implementation of media in instruction. *Features:* The program is geared to instructional development, systems analysis, systems design and management in educational and noneducational organizations; research is oriented to the analysis of communication and information theory. Laboratories are available to facilitate student and faculty research projects in educational and/or training settings. Specifically, the knowledges and skills are categorized as follows: planning and designing; delivery systems and managing; and evaluating. *Admission Requirements:* Satisfactory scores on the Miller Analogies Test and/or GRE, minimum 3.0 GPA, sample of student writing, and personal interview. *Faculty:* 3 full-time; 3 part-time. *Students:* 18 full- and part-time. *Financial Assistance:* Some graduate assistantships and various fellowships (apply by March 10). *Doctorates Awarded 1993-94:* 5.

Syracuse University. School of Education, Syracuse, NY 13244-2340. (315) 443-3703. Fax (315) 443-5732. Philip L. Doughty, Prof., Chair, Instructional Design, Development, and Evaluation Program, School of Education. *Specializations:* Ph.D. and Ed.D. degree programs for instructional design of programs and materials, educational evaluation, human issues in instructional development, media production (including computers and videodisc), and educational research and theory (learning theory, application of theory, and educational and media research). Graduates are prepared to serve as curriculum developers, instructional developers, program and product evaluators, researchers, resource center administrators, communications coordinators, trainers in human resource development, and higher education instructors. *Features:* Field work and internships, special topics and special issues seminar, student- and faculty-initiated minicourses, seminars and guest lecturers, faculty-student formulation of department policies, and multiple international perspectives. *Admission Requirements:* A master's degree from an accredited institution and GRE (V, Q & A) scores. *Faculty:* 5 full-time; 4 part-time. *Students:* 46 full-time; 24 part-time. *Financial Assistance:* Some fellowships, scholarships, and graduate assistantships entailing either research or administrative duties in instructional technology. *Doctorates Awarded 1994:* 8.

OHIO

*The Ohio State University. College of Education, Columbus, OH 43210. (614) 292-4872. Fax (614) 292-7900. Robert Lawson, Dept. of Educational Policy and Leadership, College of Education. *Specializations:* Ph.D. in Instructional and Interactive Technologies, within the program area of Instructional Design and Technology, for the preparation of individuals to perform research and to teach in higher education, administer comprehensive media services, or engage in research, production, and development of leadership functions in higher education and related educational agencies. *Features:* Interdisciplinary work in other departments (journalism, communications, radio and television, computer and information science); individual design of doctoral programs according to candidate's background, experience, and goals; and internships provided on campus in business and industry and in schools; integrated school media laboratory, microcomputer, and videodisc laboratories. *Admission Requirements:* Admission to graduate school and specific program area in the College of Education, GRE general test (Ph.D. only), minimum 2.7 GPA, and satisfactory academic and professional recommendations. *Faculty:* 5 full-time; 1 part-time. *Students:* 11 full-time, 3 part-time. *Financial Assistance:* Some assistantships. *Doctorates Awarded 1992-93:* 6.

*University of Toledo. College of Education and Allied Professions, Toledo, OH 43606-3390. (419) 537-3846. Fax (419) 537-3853. Amos C. Patterson, Prof., Dir. of Academic Programs, College of Education and Allied Professions. *Specializations:* Ph.D. and Ed.D. *Features:* Research and theory in the areas of instructional design, development, evaluation, computers, video, and training and human resources development. Emphasis is in the empirical study of systematic processes in instructional technology. Residency requirement of one year or three full-time summer quarters, depending on Ph.D. or Ed.D. option. Option of one or two minor areas of study to be included in total program hours. *Admission Requirements:* GRE score of 1,000, combined totals, Miller Analogies Test at or above 50th percentile, three letters of recommendation, official transcripts of undergraduate and graduate work, and autobiographical details. *Faculty:* 7 full-time, 2 part-time. *Students:* 10 full-time; 16 part-time. *Financial Assistance:* Graduate assistantships for research and teaching, Board of Trustee scholarships and grants (tuition only). *Doctorates Awarded 1992-93:* 2.

OKLAHOMA

*University of Oklahoma. Department of Educational Psychology, 820 Van Vleet Oval, Norman, OK 73019-0260. (405) 325-5974. Fax (405) 325-3242. Raymond B. Miller, Prog. Area Coord., Dept. of Educational Psychology. *Specializations:* Ph.D. in instructional psychology and technology. *Features:* The program is built around a core of learning and cognition, instructional design, and research methods. Students' programs are tailored to their professional goals within the areas of emphasis within instructional psychology and technology, e.g., instructional design, computer applications, management of technology programs. *Admission Requirements:* A minimum of 3.25 GPA in all graduate work or 3.0 in the last 60 hours of undergraduate work, GRE scores, three letters of recommendation. *Faculty:* 10 full-time; 2 part-time. *Financial Assistance:* Assistantships, out-of-state fee waivers, graduate scholarships (both general and targeted minorities). *Doctorates Awarded 1992-93:* 1.

PENNSYLVANIA

Pennsylvania State University. 270 Chambers Bldg., University Park, PA 16802. (814) 865-0473. Fax (814) 865-0128. E-mail jonassen@psu.edu. D. Jonassen, Prof. in Charge. *Specializations:* Ph.D. and Ed.D. in Instructional Systems. Current teaching emphases are on corporate training, emerging technologies, and educational systems design. Research interests include hypermedia/multimedia, visual learning, educational reform, emerging technologies, and constructivist learning. *Features:* A common thread throughout all programs is that candidates have basic competencies in the understanding of human learning; instructional design, development, and evaluation; and research procedures. Practical experience is available in mediated independent learning, research, instructional development, computerbased education, and dissemination projects. *Admission Requirements:* GRE, TOEFL, transcript, three letters of recommendation, writing sample, vita/resume, and letter of application detailing reasoning. *Degree Requirements:* Candidacy exam, courses, residency, comprehensives, dissertation. *Faculty:* 9 full-time; 2 part-time. *Students:* 20 full-time; 40 part-time at the doctoral level. *Financial Assistance:* Two assistantships and internships and assistantships on grants, contracts, and projects. *Doctorates Awarded 1994:* Data not reported.

University of Pittsburgh. School of Education, Pittsburgh, PA 15260. (412) 612-7254. Fax (412) 648-7081. E-mail bseels+@pitt.edu. Barbara Seels, Assoc. Prof., Prog. Coord., Program in Instructional Design and Technology, Dept. of Instruction and Learning, School of Education. *Specializations:* Ed.D. and M.Ed. programs for the preparation of instructional technologists with skills in designing, developing, using, evaluating, and managing processes and resources for learning. Certification option for instructional technologists available. *Features:* Program prepares people for positions in which they can effect educational change through instructional technology. Program includes three competency areas: instructional design, technological delivery systems, and communications research. *Admissions Requirements:* Submission of written statement of applicant's professional goals, three letters of recommendation, demonstration of English proficiency, satisfactory GPA, sample of professional writing, GRE, and personal interviews. *Faculty:* 3 full-time. *Students:* 39 at the doctoral level. *Financial Assistance:* Tuition scholarships and assistantships may be available. *Doctorates Awarded 1994:* 6.

TENNESSEE

University of Tennessee Knoxville. College of Education, Education in Sciences, Mathematics, Research, and Technology Unit, 319 Claxton Addition, Knoxville, TN 37996-3400. (615) 974-4222 or (615) 974-3103. Dr. Al Grant, Coord., Instructional Media and Technology Program. *Specializations:* M.S. in Ed., Ed.D., and Ed.S. under Education in Sciences, Mathematics, Research, and Technology; Ph.D. under the College of Education, concentration in Instructional Media and Technology, Ed.D. in Curriculum and Instruction, concentration in Instructional Media and Technology. *Features:* Coursework in media management, advanced software production, utilization, research, theory, psychology, instructional computing, television, and instructional development. Coursework will also meet the requirements for state certification as Instructional Materials Supervisor in the public schools of Tennessee. *Admission Requirements:* Send for the Graduate Catalog, The University of Tennessee. *Media Faculty:* 1 full-time, with additional assistance from Curriculum and Instruction and university faculty. *Students:* 2 part-time at the doctoral level. *Doctorates Awarded 1994:* 1.

TEXAS

The University of Texas. College of Education, Austin, TX 78712. (512) 471-5211. Fax (512) 471-4607. DeLayne Hudspeth, Assoc. Prof., Area Coord., Instructional Technology, Dept. of Curriculum and Instruction, College of Education. *Specializations:* Ph.D. program emphasizes research, design, and development of instructional systems and communications technology. *Features:* The program is interdisciplinary in nature, although certain competencies are required of all students. Programs of study and dissertation research are based on individual needs and career goals. Learning resources include a model LRC; computer labs and classrooms, a color television studio, interactive multimedia lab, and access to a photo and graphics lab. *Admission Requirements:* Minimum 3.25 GPA and a score of at least 1200 on the GRE. *Faculty:* 4 full-time; 2 part-time. Many courses are offered cooperatively by other departments, including Radio-TV Film, Computer Science, and Educational Psychology. *Students:* 31. *Financial Assistance:* Assistantships may be available to develop instructional materials, teach undergraduate computer literacy, and assist with research projects. There are also some paid internships. *Doctorates Awarded 1994:* 11.

UTAH

*Brigham Young University. Department of Instructional Science, 201 MCKB, BYU, Provo, UT 84602. (801) 378-7072. Fax (801) 378-4017. E-mail paul_merrill@byu.edu. Paul F. Merrill, Prof., Chair. *Specializations:* M.S. and Ph.D. degrees are offered in instructional science and technology. In the Ph.D. program, students may specialize in instructional design, research and evaluation, instructional psychology, literacy education, or second language acquisition. *Features:* Course offerings include principles of learning, instructional design, assessing learning outcomes, evaluation in education, empirical inquiry in education, project and instructional resource management, quantitative reasoning, microcomputer materials production, naturalistic inquiry, and more. Students are required to participate in internships and projects related to development, evaluation, measurement, and research. *Admission Requirements:* General university requirements plus GRE entrance examination. Applications will not be considered without GRE scores. *Faculty:* 10 full-time. *Students:* 59. *Financial Assistance:* Internships and tuition waivers. *Doctorates Awarded 1992-93:* 1. Students agree to live by the BYU Honor Code.

Utah State University. College of Education, Logan, UT 84322-2830. (801) 797-2694. Fax (801) 797-2693. Don C. Smellie, Prof., Chair, Dept. of Instructional Technology, College of Education. *Specializations:* Ph.D. in Educational Technology. Offered for individuals seeking to become professionally involved in instructional development in corporate education, public schools, community colleges, and universities. Teaching and research in higher education is another career avenue for graduates of the program. *Features:* The doctoral program is built on a strong master's and specialist's program in instructional technology. All doctoral students complete a core with the remainder of the course selection individualized, based upon career goals. *Admission Requirements:* 3.0 GPA, successful teaching experience or its equivalent, a verbal and quantitative score at the 40th percentile on the GRE, and three written recommendations. *Faculty:* 9 full-time; 7 part-time. *Students:* 120 M.S./M.Ed. candidates; 5 Ed.S. candidates; 24 Ph.D. candidates. *Financial Assistance:* Approximately 18 to 26 assistantships (apply by June 1). *Doctorates Awarded 1993-94:* 3.

VIRGINIA

*University of Virginia. Curry School of Education, Ruffner Hall, Charlottesville, VA 22903. (804) 924-7471. Fax (804) 924-7987. John B. Bunch, Assoc. Prof., Coord. Instructional Technology Program, Dept. of Educational Studies. *Specializations:* Ed.D. or Ph.D. degrees offered with focal areas in media production, interactive multimedia, and K-12 educational technologies. For specific degree requirements, write to the address above or refer to the UVA *Graduate Record. Faculty:* 3 full-time. *Doctorates Awarded 1992-93:* 3.

Virginia Polytechnic Institute and State University. College of Education, Blacksburg, VA 24061-0313. (703) 231-5598. Fax (703) 231-9075. Terry M. Wildman, Prog. Area Leader, Instructional Systems Development, Curriculum and Instruction. *Specializations:* Ed.D. and Ph.D. in Instructional Technology. Preparation for education, business, and industry. *Features:* Areas of emphasis are instructional design, educational computing, evaluation, and media management. Facilities include 70 computer lab microcomputers (IBM, Macintosh), interactive video, speech synthesis, and telecommunications. *Admission Requirements:* 3.3 GPA for master's degree, interview, three letters of recommendation, transcripts of previous academic work. *Faculty:* 8 full-time; 5 part-time. *Students:* 30 full-time; 8 part-time at the doctoral level. *Financial Assistance:* 10 assistantships, tuition scholarships, and contracts with other agencies. *Doctorates Awarded 1994:* Data not reported.

WASHINGTON

University of Washington. College of Education, Seattle, WA 98195. (206) 543-6636. Fax (206) 543-8439. E-mail stkerr@u.washington.edu. Stephen T. Kerr, Prof. of Education, College of Education. *Specializations:* Ph.D. and Ed.D. for individuals in business, industry, higher education, public schools, and organizations concerned with education or communication (broadly defined). *Features:* Emphasis on instructional design as a process of making decisions about the shape of instruction; additional focus on research and development in such areas as message design (especially graphics and diagrams); electronic information systems; interactive instruction via videodisc, videotex, and computers. *Admission Requirements:* GRE scores, letters of reference, transcripts, personal statement, master's degree or equivalent in field appropriate to the specialization, 3.5 GPA in master's program, two years of successful professional experience and/or experience related to program goals. *Faculty:* 2 full-time; 3 part-time. *Students:* 12 full-time; 32 part-time. *Financial Assistance:* Assistantships awarded competitively and on basis of program needs; other assistantships available depending on grant activity in any given year. *Doctorates Awarded 1992-93:* 3.

WISCONSIN

*University of Wisconsin-Madison. School of Education, Madison, WI 53706. (608) 263-4670. Michael Streibel, Prof., Dept. of Curriculum and Instruction, School of Education. *Specializations:* Ph.D. programs to prepare college and university faculty. *Features:* The program is coordinated with media operations of the university. Traditional instructional technology courses are processed through a social, cultural, and historical frame of reference. Current curriculum emphasizes communication, perception, and cognitive theories, critical cultural studies, and theories of textual analysis and instructional development. Strength in small-format video production and computers. *Admission Requirements:* Previous experience in instructional technology preferred, previous teaching experience, minimum 3.0 GPA on last 60 undergraduate credits, acceptable scores on GRE for Ph.D., and a minimum 3.0 GPA on all graduate work. (Note: Exceptions may be made on some of these requirements if all others are acceptable.) *Faculty:* 3 full-time; 1 part-time. *Students:* 23. *Financial Assistance:* A few stipends of approximately $1,000 a month for 20 hours of work per week; other media jobs are also available.

Master's Degree and Six-Year Programs
in Instructional Technology

During the fall semester of 1994, an inquiry-questionnaire was sent to the program chairs or their representatives for the 147 programs listed in the 1994 yearbook. Responses were received from 75 of the programs, two of which notified us that the programs had been discontinued. Information that was updated in 1994 is also included in this edition for 28 additional programs, which are indicated by an asterisk (*) before the name of the institution. We would like to express our appreciation of the many responses that were received, and for more current information on programs from which no response was received that was supplied by Jenny K. Johnson in *Degree Curricula in Educational Communications and Technology: A Descriptive Directory*, Fifth Edition (AECT, 1995). In several cases, programs for which no information has been received since 1993 or before have been updated to some extent with information from other sources; 10 have been dropped from this listing. Entries for several programs that have not been listed previously are indicated by two asterisks (**).

Each entry in the directory contains as much of the following information as was available to us: (1) name and mailing address of the institution; (2) name, academic rank, and title of program head or the name of a contact person; (3) name of the administrative unit offering the program; (4) minimum degree requirements; (5) number of full-time and part-time faculty; and (6) number of students who graduated with master's degrees from the program in 1994 or during the one-year period between 1 July 1993 and 30 June 1994. The availability of six-year specialist/certificate programs in instructional technology and related media is indicated where appropriate following the description of the master's program.

Several institutions appear in both this list and the list of graduate programs in educational computing, either because their computer technology programs are offered separately from the educational/instructional technology programs, or because they are separate components of the overall educational technology program.

To ensure completeness of this directory, considerable effort has been expended. However, readers who know of either new programs or omissions are encouraged to provide information to the publisher who, in turn, will follow up on them for the next edition of *EMTY*. Information on any programs that have been discontinued would also be most welcome.

Individuals who are interested in any of these graduate programs are encouraged to make direct contact with the head of the program to obtain the most recent information available.

Institutions in this section are arranged alphabetically by state.

ALABAMA

*Alabama State University. College of Education, 915 South Jackson, Montgomery, AL 36195. (205) 293-4107. Fax (205) 241-7192. Katie R. Bell, Master's Prog. Coord., Instructional Support Services. *Specializations:* M.Ed., AA Certification, and Ed.S., preparation for K-12 school media programs. *Degree Requirements:* 36 semester hours; thesis required for Ed.S.; 300-clock-hour practicum (100 each in elementary, high school, and other library settings); research project required for M.Ed. and AA Certification. *Faculty:* 2 part-time. *Students:* 1 full-time; 21 part-time. *Financial Assistance:* Assistantships available for full-time students. *Master's Degrees Awarded 1 July 1992-30 June 1993:* 5. An advanced certificate program is available (see Specializations).

Auburn University. Educational Foundations, Leadership, and Technology, 2084 Haley Center, Auburn, AL 36849. (205) 844-4291. Fax (205) 844-5785. Susan H. Bannon, Coord., Educational Media. *Specializations:* School Library Media Specialist Certification, Instructional Design Specialist. The Instructional Design program has a concentration in computers and interactive technologies. *Degree Requirements:* School Library Media: 48 quarter hours minimum with 32 qtr. hrs. in educational media required; 8 qtr. hrs. in educational media prerequisites. Instructional Design: 48 qtr. hrs. minimum. *Faculty:* 18 full-time; 5 part-time. *Students:* 6 full-time; 40 part-time. *Financial Assistance:* Graduate assistantships. *Master's degrees awarded in 1994:* 12. The school also offers a sixth-year program only for school library media specialist.

Jacksonville State University. Instructional Media Division, Jacksonville, AL 36265. (205) 782-5011. Martha Merrill, Coord., Dept. of Educational Resources, Instructional Media Div. *Specializations:* M.S. in Education with emphasis on instructional media. *Minimum Degree Requirements:* 33 semester hours including 24 in library media; thesis optional. *Faculty:* 2 full- and part-time. *Students:* 30 full- and part-time. *Master's Degrees Awarded 1994:* Data not reported.

*University of Alabama. Graduate School of Library Serv., P.O. Box 870252, Tuscaloosa, AL 35487-0252. (205) 348-4610. Fax (205) 348-3746. Philip M. Turner, Dean, School of Library and Information Studies. *Specializations:* M.L.S., Ed.S., M.F.A., Ph.D. *Minimum Degree Requirements:* M.L.S., 36 semester hours, no thesis; Ed.S., 30 semester hours, no thesis; M.F.A., 48 semester hours, creative project; Ph.D., 48 semester hours, dissertation. *Faculty:* 11 full-time; 3 part-time. *Students:* 120 full-time; 100 part-time. *Financial Assistance:* 21 graduate assistantships. *Master's Degrees Awarded 1 July 1992-30 June 1993:* 64. The school also offers a six-year specialist degree program in instructional technology.

*University of South Alabama. College of Education, UCommons 3108, Mobile, AL 36688. (205) 380-2861. Fax (205) 380-2758. E-mail rdaughen@jaguar1.usouthal.edu. Dr. Richard Daughenbaugh, Masters Prog. Coord., Dept. of Behavioral Studies and Educational Technology. *Specializations:* M.Ed. program in Educational Media for state school library media certification; M.S. program in Instructional Design for employment in business, industry, the military, etc.; the Ed.S. in Educational Media leads to higher certification in library media. *Minimum Degree Requirements:* 58 quarter hours including 42 in media; thesis optional. *Faculty:* 3 full- and part-time. *Students:* 51 full- and part-time. *Financial Assistance:* Assistantships. *Master's Degrees Awarded 1 July 1992-30 June 1993:* Data not reported. The school also offers a six-year specialist degree program in Instructional Technology for the improvement of teaching.

ARIZONA

Arizona State University. Educational Media and Computers, Education, Box 870111, Tempe, AZ 85287-0111. (602) 965-7192. Fax (602) 965-7058. E-mail aogbb@asuvm.inre.asu.edu. Gary G. Bitter, Coord., Educational Media and Computers. *Specialization:* Master's degree. Course in Instructional Media Design offered via distance education (CD-ROM/Internet, 3 semester hours credit). The program has Internet Home Page. *Admission Requirements:* Bachelor's degree; TOEFL, 550 min. score; GRE, 500 min.; Miller Analogy Test, 45 min. *Minimum Degree Requirements:* 33 semester hours, including 21 hours educational media and computers, 9 hours education, 3 hours outside program, 3-hour practicum/internship required, comprehensive exam required. *Faculty:* 7 full-time; 6 part-time. *Students:* 121 full-time; 32 part-time. *Financial Assistance:* Assistantships, grants, student loans. *Master's Degrees Awarded 1994:* 46.

Arizona State University. Learning and Instructional Technology, FPE-0611, ASU, Tempe, AZ 85287-0611. (602) 965-3384. Fax (602) 965-0300. E-mail icnla@asuvm.inre.asu.edu. Nancy Archer, Admissions Secy., contact person. *Specializations:* M.A. in Learning, M.Ed. in Instructional Technology. *Minimum Degree Requirements:* 30 semester hours; comprehensive exam required; M.A. requires thesis. *Faculty:* 5. *Students:* 40. *Financial Assistance:* Graduate assistantships available for qualified applicants. *Master's Degrees Awarded 1994:* 10.

*University of Arizona. School of Library Science. 1515 E. First St., Tucson, AZ 85719. (602) 621-3565. Fax (602) 621-3279. C. D. Hurt, Prof. and Dir., School of Library Science. *Specialization:* Master's degree. *Minimum Degree Requirements:* 36 graduate semester hours including 12 hours of core courses and a computer proficiency requirement; comprehensive required; thesis optional. *Faculty:* 7. *Master's Degrees Awarded 1992 Calendar Year:* 74.

ARKANSAS

*Arkansas Tech University. Instructional Technology, 308 Crabaugh, Russellville, AR 72801. (501) 968-0434. Fax (501) 964-0811. Connie Zimmer, Asst. Prof., Coord., Master of Instructional Technology. *Specializations:* M.Ed. in Instructional Technology, six-year program. *Features:* Program includes Library Media Education, Training Program, Media Production, Computer Education, and Technology Coordinator. *Minimum Degree Requirements:* 36 credit hours for M.Ed., thesis optional, practicum available. *Faculty:* 1 full-time, 3 part-time. *Students:* 2 full-time, 50 part-time. *Financial Assistance:* Graduate assistantships available. *Master's Degrees Awarded 1 July 1992-30 June 1993:* 10. ATU is located off I-40 between Little Rock and Fort Smith, AR, in what is known as the Arkansas River Valley.

University of Central Arkansas. Educational Media/Library Science Department, Campus Box 4918, Conway, AR 72035. (501) 450-5463. Fax (501) 450-5468. Selvin W. Royal, Prof., Chair, Applied Academic Technologies. *Specializations:* M.S. Educational Media/Library Science: Track 1—School Library Media, Track 2—Public Information Agencies, Track 3—Media Information Studies. *Minimum Degree Requirements:* 36 semester hours, optional thesis, practicum (for Track 1), professional research paper. *Faculty:* 5 full-time; 3 part-time. Students: 8 full-time; 25 part-time. *Financial Assistance:* 3 to 4 graduate assistantships each year. *Master's Degrees Awarded 1994:* 25. Advanced certificate program is available for Track 1 to a Master's School Library Media Specialist.

CALIFORNIA

*California State University-Los Angeles. Division of Educational Foundations, Los Angeles, CA 90032-8143. (213) 343-4330. Fax (213) 343-4318. E-mail psemrau@atss.cal-statela.edu. Dr. Penelope Semrau, Prog. Coord. *Specialization:* M.A. in Education in Instructional Technology or Computer Education. *Minimum Degree Requirements:* 45 quarter hours; thesis optional and worth 7 credits, alternative is a project. *Admission Requirements:* B.A. or B.S., 2.75 GPA, TOEFL minimum score of 550. *Faculty:* 6 full-time. *Students:* 30. *Financial Assistance*: Contact Student Financial Services Office at (213) 343-3240 for information. *Master's Degrees Awarded 1993:* 20.

California State University-San Bernardino. 5500 University Parkway, San Bernardino, CA 92407. (909) 880-5677. (909) 880-7011. Fax (909) 880-7010. E-mail rsantiag@wiley.csusb.edu. Dr. Rowena Santiago, Prog. Coord. *Specializations:* M.A. The program has two emphases: video production and computer application. These emphases allow students to choose courses related to the design and creation of video products or courses involving lab and network operation of advanced microcomputer applications. The program does not require teaching credential certification. *Admission Requirements:* Bachelor's degree, appropriate work experience, GPA of 3.0 or higher, completion of introductory computer course and expository writing course. *Minimum Degree Requirements:* 48 units including a master's project (33 units completed in residence); GPA of 3.0 (B), grades of "C" (2) or better in all courses. *Faculty:* 4 full-time; 1 part-time. *Students:* 65 full- and part-time, 49 of which have been classified. *Financial Assistance:* Contact Office of Graduate Studies. *Master's Degrees Awarded 1994:* Data not reported. Advanced certificate programs in Computer Technology and in Educational Technology are available.

*San Diego State University. Educational Technology, San Diego, CA 92182-0311. (619) 594-6718. Fax (619) 594-6376. E-mail harrison@ucsuvax.sdsu.edu. Dr. Patrick Harrison, Prof., Chair, Dept. of Educational Technology. *Specialization:* Master's degree in Educational Technology with specializations in Computers in Education, Workforce Education and Lifelong Learning. *Minimum Degree Requirements:* 36 semester hours including 6 prerequisite hours, GRE combined total 950 Verbal and Quantitative scores. *Faculty:* 6 full-time. *Students:* 110. *Financial Assistance:* Graduate Assistantships. *Master's Degrees Awarded 1993:* 40. The Educational Technology Department participates in a College of Education joint doctoral program with The Claremont Graduate School.

*San Francisco State University. School of Education, Department of Instructional Technology, 1600 Holloway Ave., San Francisco, CA 94132. (415) 338-1509. Fax (415) 338-0510. E-mail michaels@sfsuvax1.edu. Dr. Eugene Michaels, Chair & Prof. *Specializations:* Master's degree with emphasis on Training and Designing Development, Instructional Computing, and Instructional and Interactive Video. *Minimum Degree Requirements:* 30 semester hours, field study thesis or project required. *Faculty:* 3 full-time; 4-7 part-time. *Students:* 160. *Master's Degrees Awarded 1 July 1992-30 June 1993:* Data not reported. The school also offers an 18-unit Graduate Certificate in Training Systems Development, which can be incorporated into the master's program.

United States International University. School of Education, 10455 Pomerado Rd., San Diego, CA 92131-1799. (619) 635-4715. Fax (619) 635-4714. E-mail feifer@sanac.usiu.edu. Richard Feifer, School of Education. *Specialization:* Master's in Designing Technology for Learning, Planning Technology for Learning, Technology Leadership for Learning. *Features:*

Interactive multimedia, cognitive approach to integrating technology and learning. Completely revamped program begun in the fall of 1994; for additional information, see the listing for the doctoral program. *Faculty:* 2 full-time; 4 part-time. *Students:* (at the master's level) 32 full-time, 12 part-time. *Financial Aid:* Internships, grants, scholarships, student loans. *Master's Degrees Awarded 1994:* 42.

*University of California-Los Angeles. Dept. of Education, 405 Hilgard Ave., Los Angeles, CA 90024-1521. (310) 825-1838. Fax (310) 206-6293. E-mail ilt3jid@mvs.oac.ucla.edu. Aimee Dorr, Prof., Learning and Instruction Specialization, Div. of Educational Psychology. *Specialization:* M.A. in Education only. *Minimum Degree Requirements:* 36 quarter units, pass written comprehensive exam or complete research thesis. *Faculty:* 4 full-time; 2 part-time. *Students:* 10-15 in M.A., Ph.D., and Ed.D. programs. *Financial Assistance:* Fellowships, loans, resident advisors. *Master's Degrees Awarded 1993:* 3.

University of Southern California. Instructional Technology, Division of Curriculum and Instruction, Los Angeles, CA 90007-0031. (213) 740-3476. Fax (213) 746-8142. Ed Kazlauskas, Prof., Chair, Dept. of Curriculum and Teaching, School of Education. *Specialization:* Master's degree. *Minimum Degree Requirements:* 31 semester hours, thesis optional. *Faculty:* 5 full-time; 1 part-time. *Students:* 1 full-time; 9 part-time. *Master's Degrees Awarded 1994:* 29.

COLORADO

University of Colorado-Denver. School of Education, Denver, CO 80217-3364. (303) 556-2962. Fax (303) 556-4479. R. Scott Grabinger, Program Leader, Instructional Technology, Division of Technology and Special Services. *Specialization:* Master's degree. *Minimum Degree Requirements:* For several tracks, including instructional computing, corporate training and development, library/media and instructional technology, 36 semester hours including comprehensive; project or internship required. *Faculty:* 5 full-time; 4 part-time. *Master's Degrees Awarded 1994:* 30.

University of Northern Colorado. College of Education, Greeley, CO 80639. (303) 351-2687. Fax (303) 351-2312. E-mail caffarel@edtech.univnorthco.edu. Edward F. Caffarella, Prof., College of Education. *Specializations:* M.A. in Educational Technology; M.A. in Educational Media. *Minimum Admission Requirements:* Bachelor's degree; undergraduate GPA of at least 3.0; GRE minimum score 1500 combined. *Minimum Degree Requirements:* 36 semester hours; comprehensive exam. *Faculty:* 5 full-time; 2 part-time. *Students:* (at the master's level) 8 full-time; 85 part-time. *Financial Assistance:* Graduate assistantships, grants, scholarships, and student loans. *Master's Degrees Awarded 1994:* 41. Ph.D. program is also offered.

CONNECTICUT

Central Connecticut State University. 1615 Stanley St., New Britain, CT 06050. (203) 832-2130. Fax (203) 832-2109. Roger Zeiger, Chair, Dept. of Educational Technology and Media. *Specializations:* M.S. in Education, Educational Media. Curriculum emphases include media management, materials production, librarianship, and computer technologies. *Minimum Admission Requirements:* Bachelor's degree; undergraduate GPA of at least 2.5. *Minimum Degree Requirements:* 33-36 semester hours; optional thesis worth 3 credits, or comprehensive exam or project. *Faculty:* 2 full-time; 6 part-time. *Students:* Data not reported. *Financial Assistance:* Data not reported. *Master's Degrees Awarded 1994:* Data not reported.

Fairfield University. Media Center, N. Benson Road, Fairfield, CT 06430. (203) 254-4000. Fax (203) 254-4087. Dr. Ibrahim M. Hefzallah, Prof., Co-Dir. of Media/Educational Technology Program; Dr. John Schurdak, Assoc. Prof., Co-Dir., Computers in Education/Educational Technology Program. *Specializations:* M.A. in Media/Educational Technology with emphasis on theory, practice, and new instructional developments in computers in education, multimedia, and satellite communications. *Admission Requirements:* Bachelor's degree from an accredited institution with a minimum 2.67 GPA. *Minimum Degree Requirements:* 33 credits with an average grade of B. *Faculty:* 1 full-time; 5 part-time. *Students:* 4 full-time; 60 part-time. *Financial Assistance:* Assistantships, student loans, scholarships. *Master's Degrees Awarded 1994:* Data not reported. A Certificate of Advanced Studies in Media/Educational Technology is available, which includes instructional development, television production, and media management; customized course of study also available.

Southern Connecticut State University. School of Library Science and Instructional Technology, 501 Crescent St., New Haven, CT 06515. (203) 392-5781. Fax (203) 392-5780. E-mail libscienceit@csu.ctstateu.edu. Nancy Disbrow, Chair, Library Science/Instructional Technology. *Specializations:* M.S. in Instructional Technology; Sixth-Year Professional Diploma Library-Information Studies (student may select area of specialization in instructional technology). *Minimum Degree Requirements:* For instructional technology only, 30 semester hours including 21 in media with comprehensive examination; 36 hours without examination. For sixth year: 30 credit hours with 6 credit hours of core requirements, 9-15 credit hours in specialization. *Faculty:* 1 full-time. *Students:* 37 full- and part-time in M.S./IT program. *Financial Assistance:* Graduate assistantship: salary $1,800 per semester; assistants pay tuition and a general university fee sufficient to defray cost of student accident insurance. *Master's Degrees Awarded 1994:* 4. The school also offers a Professional Diploma in Library Information Studies; students may select instructional technology as area of specialization.

DISTRICT OF COLUMBIA

Gallaudet University. School of Education, 800 Florida Ave. NE, Washington, DC 20002-3625. (202) 651-5535 (voice or TDD). Fax (202) 651-5710. E-mail renomeland@gallua.bit-net. Ronald E. Nomeland, Prof., Chair, Dept. of Educational Technology. *Specializations:* M.S. in Special Education/Deafness with specialization in Educational Computing, Instructional Design, and Media Product Development. *Features:* Combines educational technology skills with study in special education and deafness to prepare graduates for positions in programs serving deaf and other disabled learners as well as in regular education programs, or in government and industry. *Minimum Degree Requirements:* 36 semester hours, including 26 in educational media and a comprehensive exam; optional practicum. *Faculty:* 3 full-time; 1 part-time. *Students:* 15. *Financial Assistance:* Partial tuition waiver; graduate assistantships. *Master's Degrees Awarded 1994:* 8.

George Washington University. School of Education and Human Development, Washington, DC 20052. Dr. William Lynch, Educational Technology Leadership Program. Program is offered through Mind Extension University, ME/U Education Center. Contact Student Advisors at (800) 777-MIND. *Specialization:* M.A. in Education and Human Development with a major in Educational Technology Leadership. *Features:* The 36-hour degree program is available via cable television, satellite, and/or videotape to students across North America and in other locations. The degree is awarded by George Washington University (GWU). Students may work directly with ME/U or GWU to enroll. Student advisors at ME/U handle inquiries about the program, send out enrollment forms and applications, process book orders, and set up students on an electronic bulletin board system. *Minimum Degree Requirements:* 36 credit hours, of which 24 hours are required 3-hour courses. Required courses include Managing Computer Applications, Applying Educational Media and Technology, Design and Implementation of Educational Software, Policy-Making for Public Education, and Quantitative Research Methods. *Faculty:* Courses are taught by faculty at GWU. *Students:* Data not reported. *Financial Assistance:* For information, contact the Office of Student Financial Assistance, George Washington University, Washington, DC 20052. Some cable systems that carry ME/U offer local scholarships. *Master's Degrees Awarded 1994:* New program.

FLORIDA

Florida State University. Department of Educational Research, College of Education, Stone Bldg., Tallahassee, FL 32306. (904) 644-8785. Fax (904) 644-8776. E-mail driscoll@cet.fsu.edu. Marcy P. Driscoll, Prof. and Prog. Leader, Instructional Systems Prog. *Specialization:* M.S. in Instructional Systems and Specialist Degree. *Minimum Degree Requirements:* 36 semester hours; 2-4-hour internship required; written comprehensive exam. *Faculty:* 6 full-time; 5 part-time. *Students:* 49 (at the master's level). *Financial Assistance:* Some graduate research assistantships on faculty grants and contracts; university fellowships for high GRE students. *Master's Degrees Awarded 1994:* 17. A specialist degree program is now being offered for students with or without the M.S. in Instructional Systems.

Nova Southeastern University. Fischler Center for the Advancement of Education, 3301 College Ave., Fort Lauderdale, FL 33314. (800) 986-3223. Fax (305) 476-4764. Johanne Peck, M.S. and Ed.D. Programs for Teachers. *Specializations:* M.S. and Ed.S. in Educational Media. *Minimum Degree Requirements:* 36 semester hours, including a practicum experience. *Faculty:* 2 full-time; 5 part-time. *Students:* (total) 38. *Financial Aid:* NDSL; Federal Stafford Loan, unsubsidized Federal Stafford Loan, SLS. *Master's Degrees Awarded 1994:* Data not reported.

University of Central Florida. College of Education, ED Room 318, UCF, Orlando, FL 32816. (407) 823-2153. Fax (407) 823-5135. Richard Cornell/Gary Orwig, Instructional Systems; Judy Lee, Educational Media; Donna Baumbach, Educational Technology. *Specializations:* M.A. Instructional Technology/Instructional Systems, 39-42 semester hours; M.Ed. Instructional Technology/Educational Media, 39-45 semester hours; M.A. Instructional Technology/Educational Technology, 39-45 semester hours; practicum required in all three programs; thesis, research project, or substitute additional coursework. *Students:* 99 Instructional Systems; 37 Educational Media; 10 full-time, 126 part-time. *Faculty:* 3 full-time; 5 part-time. *Financial Assistance:* Graduate assistantships in department and college awarded competitively; numerous paid internships; limited number of doctoral fellowships. *Master's Degrees Awarded 1994:* 25. A doctorate in C&I with an emphasis on Instructional Technology is offered. Board of Regents permission granted to conduct feasibility study for new free-standing Ph.D. in Instructional Technology.

*University of Florida. Educational Media and Instructional Design, Gainesville, FL 32611. (904) 392-0705. Fax (904) 392-9193. Lee J. Mullally, Assoc. Prof. and Prog. Leader, Educational Media and Instructional Design. *Specialization:* Master's degree. *Minimum Degree Requirements:* 36 semester hours including 24 in educational media and instructional design; thesis optional. *Faculty:* 2 full-time. *Students:* 20 full- and part-time. *Master's Degrees Awarded 1 July 1992-30 June 1993:* 6. The Education Specialist Program is an advanced degree program and has the same requirements for admission as the Ph.D. and Ed.D. programs.

*University of South Florida. School of Library and Information Science, Tampa, FL 33620. (813) 974-3520. Fax (813) 974-6840. Kathleen de la Peña McCook, Prof., Dir., School of Library and Information Science. *Specialization:* Master's degree. *Minimum Degree Requirements:* 36 semester hours, thesis optional. *Faculty:* 7 full-time; 5 part-time. *Master's Degrees Awarded 1991-92:* 106.

GEORGIA

Georgia State University. Middle-Secondary Education and Instructional Technology, Atlanta, GA 30303-3083. (404) 651-2510. Fax (404) 651-2546. E-mail mstfda@gsusgi2.gsu.edu. Dr. Francis D. Atkinson. *Specialization:* Master of Library Science. *Admission Requirements:* Bachelor's degree; undergraduate GPA of at least 2.5; Miller Analogy Test score 44 or GRE minimum score 800; TOEFL Exam minimum score 550. *Degree Requirements:* 60 quarter hours. *Faculty:* 4 full-time. *Students:* Data not reported. *Financial Assistance:* Data not reported. *Master's Degrees Awarded 1994:* Data not reported.

*Georgia Southern University. College of Education, Statesboro, GA 30460. (912) 681-5307. Fax (912) 681-5093. Jack A. Bennett, Prof., Dept. of Educational Leadership, Technology, and Research. *Specialization:* M.Ed. *Minimum Degree Requirements:* 60 quarter credit hours, including a varying number of hours of media for individual students. *Financial Assistance:* See graduate catalog for general financial aid information. *Faculty:* 3 full-time. *Master's Degrees Awarded 1992-93:* Data not reported. The school also offers a six-year specialist degree program.

University of Georgia. College of Education, 607 Aderhold Hall, Athens, GA 30602-7144. (706) 542-3810. Fax (706) 542-4032. E-mail kgustafs@moe.coe.uga.edu. Kent L. Gustafson, Prof. and Chair, Dept. of Instructional Technology, College of Education. *Specializations:* Master's degree in Instructional Technology; master's degree in Computer-Based Education. *Minimum Degree Requirements:* 60 or more quarter hours in each master's degree; both have an oral examination and/or portfolio presentation. *Faculty:* 11 full-time. *Students:* 20 full-time; 120 part-time. *Financial Assistance:* Limited assistance. *Master's Degrees Awarded 1994:* Data not reported. The school also offers a 45-hour, six-year specialist degree program in instructional technology and a doctoral program.

Valdosta State University. School of Education, 1500 N. Patterson St., Valdosta, GA 31698. (912) 333-5927. Fax (912) 333-7167. E-mail cprice@grits.valdosta.peachnet.edu. Catherine B. Price, Assoc. Prof., Dept. of Instructional Technology. *Specializations:* Master's degree with two tracks: Library/Media or Technology Applications. The program has a strong emphasis on technology. *Minimum Degree Requirements:* 65 quarter credits. *Faculty:* 4 full-time; 2 part-time. *Students:* 14 full-time; 70 part-time. *Financial Assistance:* Variety, including graduate assistantships. *Master's Degrees Awarded 1994:* 15. A six-year program is pending approval.

West Georgia College. Department of Media Education, Education Center, Carrollton, GA 30118. (404) 836-6558. Fax (404) 836-6729. E-mail bmckenzi@sun.cc.westga.edu. Dr.

Barbara K. McKenzie, Assoc. Prof., Dir., Center for Technological Development and Implementation. *Specializations:* M.Ed. with specializations in Media and Technology and add-on certification for students with master's degrees in other disciplines. The program strongly emphasizes technology in the schools. *Admission Requirements:* For M.Ed.—800 GRE; minimum 550 NTE Core Exam; undergraduate GPA of 2.5 is necessary. For Ed.S.—900 GRE or minimum of 575 on NTE and graduate GPA of 3.25. *Minimum Degree Requirements:* 60 quarter hours minimum. *Faculty:* 3 full-time. *Students:* 8 full-time; 120 part-time. *Financial Assistance:* One graduate assistantship for the department. *Master's Degrees Awarded 1994:* 15 M.Ed., 6 Ed.S. The school also offers a six-year Ed.S. program in media and a six-year program in Instructional Technology is pending.

HAWAII

*University of Hawaii-Manoa. Educational Technology Department, 1776 University Ave., Honolulu, HI 96822. (808) 956-7671. Fax (808) 956-3905. E-mail geoffrey@uhunixuhcc. hawaii.edu. Geoffrey Z. Kucera, Prof., Chair, Educational Technology Dept. *Specializations:* M.Ed. in Educational Technology with specialization in Instructional Development and in Computer Technology. *Minimum Degree Requirements:* 39 semester hours (27 in educational technology, 3 in practicum, 3 in internship, 6 in electives), thesis and non-thesis available. *Faculty:* 4 full-time; 3 part-time. *Students:* 4 full-time; 12 part-time. *Financial Assistance:* Consideration given to meritorious second-year students for tuition waivers and scholarship applications. *Master's Degrees Awarded 1 July 1992-30 June 1993:* 6.

IDAHO

Boise State University. Division of Continuing Education-IPT, 1910 University Drive, Boise, ID 83725. (208) 385-4457; (800) 824-7017 ext. 4457. Fax (208) 385-3346. E-mail aitfenne@idbsu.idbsu.edu. Dr. David Cox, IPT Program Dir.; Jo Ann Fenner, IPT Program Developer and distance program contact person; Linda Burnett, IPT Office Coordinator and on-campus contact person. *Specialization:* M.S. in Instructional & Performance Technology available in a traditional campus setting or via computer conferencing to students located anywhere on the North American continent. The program is fully accredited by the Northwest Association of Schools and Colleges and is the recipient of an NUCEA award for Outstanding Credit Program offered by distance education methods. *Special Features:* Leading experts in learning styles, evaluation, and leadership principles serve as adjunct faculty in the program via computer and modem from their various remote locations. *Admission Requirements:* An undergraduate degree, a minimum GPA of 2.75, a minimum score of 50 on the Miller Analogy Text, a one-to-two page essay describing why you want to pursue this program and how it will contribute to your personal and professional development, and a resume of personal qualifications and work experience. *Minimum Degree Requirements:* 33 semester hours in instructional and performance technology and related coursework; project/thesis available for on-campus program and an oral comprehensive exam required for distance program (included in 33 credit hours). *Faculty:* 2 full-time; 5 part-time. *Students:* Approx. 125. *Financial Assistance:* DANTES provides funding to some military personnel; low-interest student loans are available to those who are eligible; and graduate assistantships for on-campus enrollees. *Master's Degrees Awarded 1994:* 30. (A total of 61 degrees have been awarded since the program's first graduates in 1989.)

ILLINOIS

Chicago State University. Department of Library Science and Communications Media, Chicago, IL 60628. (312) 995-2278; (312) 995-2503. Fax (312) 995-2473. Janice Bolt, Prof., Chair, Dept. of Library Science and Communications Media. *Specialization:* Master's degree in School Media. Program has been approved by NCATE: AECT/AASL through accreditation of University College of Education; State of Illinois Entitlement Program. *Minimum Admission Requirements:* Teacher's certification or a Bachelor's in Education; any B.A. or B.S. *Minimum Degree Requirements:* 36 semester hours; thesis optional. *Faculty:* 3 full-time; 2 part-time. *Students:* 48 part-time. *Financial Assistance:* Assistantships. *Master's Degrees Awarded 1994:* 21.

Eastern Illinois University. Rm. 213 Buzzard Bldg., Charleston, IL 61920. (213) 581-5931. Dr. John T. North, Dept. of Information Services and Technology. *Specialization:* M.S. in Information Service and Technology. *Admission Requirements:* Bachelor's degree; undergraduate GPA of at least 2.5; Miller Analogy Test score 50; GRE minimum score 1000; TOEFL Exam score 550. *Minimum Degree Requirements:* 32 semester credits; optional thesis worth 3 credits. *Faculty:* 3 full-time; 1 part-time. *Students:* Data not reported. *Financial Assistance:* Data not reported. *Master's Degrees Awarded 1994:* Data not reported.

Governors State University. College of Arts and Sciences, University Park, IL 60466. (708) 534-4082. Fax (708) 534-7895. Michael Stelnicki, Prof., Human Performance and Training, College of Arts and Sciences. *Specializations:* M.A. in Communication with HP&T major. *Features:* Emphasizes three professional areas—Instructional Design, Performance Analysis, and Design Logistics. *Minimum Degree Requirements:* 36 credit hours (trimester), all in instructional and performance technology; internship/advanced field project required. Metropolitan Chicago area based. *Faculty:* 2 full-time. *Students:* 40 part-time. *Master's Degrees Awarded 1994:* 9.

Northern Illinois University. Instructional Technology Faculty, LEPS Department, DeKalb, IL 60115. (815) 753-0464. Fax (815) 753-9371. Dr. Gary L. McConeghy, Chair, Instructional Technology. *Specializations:* M.S.Ed. in Instructional Technology with specializations in Instructional Design, Microcomputers, or Media Administration. *Minimum Degree Requirements:* 39 semester hours, practicum and internship highly recommended. *Faculty:* 8 full-time; 3 part-time. *Students:* 106 part-time. *Financial Assistance:* Assistantships available at times in various departments. *Master's Degrees Awarded 1994:* 32.

Rosary College. Graduate School of Library and Information Science, River Forest, IL 60305. (708) 524-6850. Fax (708) 524-6657. Michael E. D. Koenig, Dean. *Specialization:* Master of Library and Information Science. *Minimum Degree Requirements:* 36 semester hours. A particularly relevant area of concentration is the School Library Media Program which, upon completion of the degree and with required education courses and supervised internships, meets the requirements for an Illinois Media Specialist (K-12) Certificate. *Faculty:* 11 full-time; 22 part-time. *Students:* 474 (217 FTE). *Financial Assistance:* Yes. *Master's Degrees Awarded 1 July 1993-30 June 1994:* 150. The school also offers post-master's certificate programs in Law Librarianship, Library Administration, and Technical Services, and several joint-degree programs.

Southern Illinois University at Carbondale. Dept. of Curriculum and Instruction, College of Education, Carbondale, IL 62901-4610. (618) 536-2441. Fax (618) 453-1646. E-mail ga4051@siucvmb.siu.edu. Sharon Shrock, Coord., Instructional Technology/Development.

Specializations: M.S. in Education; specializations in Instructional Development and Computer-Based Instruction. *Features:* The ID program emphasizes nonschool (primarily corporate) learning environments. *Minimum Degree Requirements:* 32 semester hours plus thesis or 36 credit hours without thesis. *Faculty:* 6 full-time; 2 part-time. *Students:* 56 full- and part-time. *Financial Assistance:* Some graduate assistantships and scholarships available to qualified students. *Master's Degrees Awarded 1994:* 10.

*Southern Illinois University at Edwardsville. Instructional Technology Program, School of Education, Edwardsville, IL 62026-1125. (618) 692-3277. Fax (618) 692-3359. Dr. Charles E. Nelson, Dir., Dept. of Educational Leadership. *Specialization:* M.S. in Education with concentrations in Library/Media Specialist or Instructional Systems Design Specialist. *Minimum Degree Requirements:* 36 semester hours; thesis optional. *Faculty:* 6 part-time. *Master's Degrees Awarded 1992-93:* 18.

*University of Illinois at Urbana-Champaign. College of Education, 1310 S. Sixth St., Champaign, IL 61820-6925. (217) 333-0964. Fax (217) 333-5847. E-mail fcoombs@ux1. cso.uiuc.edu. Fred S. Coombs, Assoc. Dean. *Specializations:* M.Sc., M.A., or M.Ed. *Minimum Degree Requirements:* 32 semester hours with emphasis on Theory and Design of Interactive Instructional Systems, Educational Psychology, and Educational Policy Studies. *Faculty:* 15. *Students:* 20. *Financial Assistance:* Fellowships for very highly academically talented; assistantships for about 10-15 percent; some tuition waivers. *Master's Degrees Awarded 1 July 1992-30 June 1993:* 15. The school also offers a six-year specialist degree program in Instructional Technology.

*University of Illinois at Urbana-Champaign. Department of Educational Psychology, 210 Education Bldg., 1310 S. Sixth St., Champaign, IL 61820. (217) 333-2245. Fax (217) 244-7620. E-mail cwest@uiuc.edu. Charles K. West, Prof., Div. of Learning and Instruction, Dept. of Educational Psychology. *Specializations:* M.A., M.S., and Ed.M. with emphasis in instructional psychology, instructional design, and educational computing. *Minimum Degree Requirements:* 8 units for Ed.M., 6 units and thesis for M.A. or M.S. *Faculty:* 17. *Students:* 11. *Financial Assistance:* Scholarships, research assistantships, and teaching assistantships available. *Master's Degrees Awarded 1993:* 0.

Western Illinois University. Media and Educational Technology, 37 Horrabin Hall, Macomb, IL 61455. (309) 298-1952. Fax (309) 298-2222. E-mail bo-barker@bgu.edu. Bruce O. Barker, Chair, Dept. of Media and Educational Technology. *Specialization:* Master's degree in Instructional Technology & Telecommunication. New program is now offered with emphasis in distance education, telecommunications, and instructional technology. *Minimum Degree Requirements:* 32 semester hours, thesis or practicum. *Faculty:* 6. *Students:* 12. *Financial Assistance:* Graduate and research assistantships, internships, residence hall assistants, veterans' benefits, and loans and part-time employment. *Master's Degrees Awarded 1994:* Second year of operation, no graduates yet.

INDIANA

Indiana State University. Media Technology, Terre Haute, IN 47809. (812) 237-2937. Fax (812) 237-4348. Dr. James E. Thompson, Prog. Coord., Dept. of Curriculum, Instruction, and Media Technology. *Specializations:* Master's degree; six-year Specialist Degree program in Instructional Technology. *Minimum Degree Requirements:* 32 semester hours, including 18 in media; thesis optional. *Faculty:* 5 full-time. *Students:* 15 full-time; 10 part-time. *Financial*

Assistance: Assistantships, fellowships. *Master's Awarded Degrees in 1994:* Data not reported. A six-year program is available.

Indiana University. School of Education, W. W. Wright Education Bldg., Bloomington, IN 47405-1006. (812) 855-1791. Fax (812) 855-3044. Thomas Schwen, Chair, Dept. of Instructional Systems Technology. *Specializations:* Offers M.S. degree designed for individuals seeking to be practitioners in the field of instructional technology. *Features:* Requires computer skills as a prerequisite and makes technology utilization an integral part of the curriculum; eliminates the separation of the various media formats; and establishes a series of courses of increasing complexity integrating production and development. The latest in technical capabilities have been incorporated in the new Center for Excellence in Education, including teaching, photographic, computer, and science laboratories, a 14-station multimedia laboratory, and television studios. *Admission Requirements:* Bachelor's degree from an accredited institution. *Degree Requirements:* 40 credit-hour (minimum) including 16 credits in required courses; colloquia; an instructional product or master's thesis; and 12 credits in outside electives. *Faculty:* 6 full-time; 3 part-time. *Students:* Data not reported. *Financial Assistance:* Data not reported. *Masters Degrees Awarded 1994:* Data not reported. For information on the Ed.D. and Ph.D. programs, see the Doctoral listing.

Purdue University. School of Education, W. Lafayette, IN 47907-1442. (317) 494-5673. Fax (317) 496-1622. James Russell, Prof., Educational Computing and Instructional Development, Dept. of Curriculum and Instruction. *Specializations:* Master's degree, Educational Specialist, and Ph.D. in Educational Computing and Instructional Development. Master's program started in 1982 and specialist and doctoral in 1985. *Admission Requirements:* GPA of 3.0 or better; 3 letters of recommendation; statement of personal goals; total score of 1,000 or more on GRE for Ph.D. admission. *Minimum Degree Requirements:* Master's—36 semester hours (15 in computer or instructional development, 9 in education, 12 unspecified); thesis optional. Specialist—60-65 semester hours (15-18 in computer or instructional development, 30-35 in education; thesis, internship, and practicum required). *Faculty:* 6 full-time. *Students:* 10 full-time; 20 part-time. *Financial Assistance:* Assistantships and fellowships. *Master's Degrees Awarded 1994:* 14.

IOWA

Iowa State University. College of Education, Ames, IA 50011. (515) 294-6840. Fax (515) 294-9284. E-mail mrs@iastate.edu. Michael Simonson, Prof. and Coord., Curriculum and Instructional Technology (including media and computers). *Specialization:* M.S. in Curriculum and Instructional Technology. *Minimum Degree Requirements:* 30 semester hours; thesis required. *Faculty:* 3 full-time; 3 part-time. *Students:* 20 full-time; 20 part-time. *Financial Assistance:* 10 assistantships available. *Master's Degrees Awarded 1994:* 6.

***University of Iowa**. College of Education, Iowa City, IA 52242. Dr. Lowell Schoer, Coord., Instructional Design and Technology Program. *Specialization:* M.A. with concentrations in Classroom Instruction, Computer Applications, Instructional Development, Media Production, and Training and Human Resource Development. *Minimum Degree Requirements:* 35 semester hours of approved coursework (16 in core, 12 in specialization, 7 in electives). *Faculty:* 7. *Students:* 100 plus. *Financial Assistance:* Teaching, research, and production assistantships. *Master's Degrees Awarded 1993:* 15. A six-year program is available.

**University of Northern Iowa. Educational Technology Program, Cedar Falls, IA 50614-0606. (319) 273-3250. Fax (319) 273-6997. E-mail smaldinos@uni.edu. Sharon Smaldino, contact person. *Specialization:* M.A. in Education. *Admission Requirements:* Bachelor's degree; undergraduate GPA of at least 3.0 of 4; TOEFL Exam minimum score 500. *Minimum Degree Requirements:* 38 semester credits; optional thesis worth 6 credits or alternate research paper of project; comprehensive exam. *Faculty:* 2 full-time; 6 part-time. *Students:* Data not reported. *Financial Assistance:* Data not reported. *Master's Degrees Awarded 1994:* Data not reported.

KANSAS

Emporia State University. School of Library and Information Management, 1200 Commercial, P.O. Box 4025, Emporia, KS 66801. (316) 341-5203. Fax (316) 341-5233. E-mail vowell@esuvm.bitnet. Faye N. Vowell, Dean, School of Library and Information Management. *Specialization:* Ph.D. in Library and Information Management; Master's of Library Science (ALA accredited program). *Features:* The MLS program is also available in Colorado, Oregon, North Dakota, and New Mexico. Video courses are being developed. *Admission Requirements:* Selective admissions process for M.L.S. and Ph.D. based on a combination of admission criteria, including (but not limited to): minimum GRE or TOEFL score; personal interview; GPA; statement of goals and references. Please request admission packet for specific criteria. *Minimum Degree Requirements:* 42 semester hours, comprehensive examination. *Faculty:* 12 full-time; 35 part-time. *Students:* 100 full-time; 500 part-time in all sites. *Financial Assistance:* Assistantships, grants, student loans, scholarships. *Master's Degrees Awarded 1994:* 169. The school also offers a School Library Certification program, which includes 27 hours of the MLS program.

*Kansas State University. College of Education, 363 Bluemont Hall, Manhattan, KS 66506. (913) 532-5525. Fax (913) 532-7304. John Parmley, Chair, Secondary Education. *Specialization:* Master's degree in Instructional Design or Instructional Development. *Minimum Degree Requirements:* 30 semester hours, including 21 in media; thesis optional. *Faculty:* 3. *Students:* 25. *Financial Assistance:* Assistantships. *Master's Degrees Awarded 1993:* Data not reported.

KENTUCKY

University of Louisville. School of Education, Louisville, KY 40292. (502) 588-0609. Fax (502) 852-1416. E-mail crrude@ulkyvm.louisville.edu. Carolyn Rude-Parkins, contact person, Occupational Training and Development. *Specialization:* M.Ed., Occupational Education Training and Development with Instructional Technology track. The program focuses on training and development for a business/industry audience; technology courses are appropriate for business or school audiences. *Minimum Degree Requirements:* 30 semester hours; thesis optional. *Faculty:* 5. *Students:* Data not reported. *Financial Assistance:* Graduate assistantships in the school. *Master's Degrees Awarded 1994:* Data not reported.

LOUISIANA

Louisiana State University. School of Library and Information Science, Baton Rouge, LA 70803. (504) 388-3158. Fax (504) 388-4581. Bert R. Boyce, Dean, Prof., School of Library and Information Science. *Specializations:* M.L.I.S., C.L.I.S. (post-master's certificate), Louisiana School Library Certification. *Minimum Degree Requirements:* M.L.I.S., 37 hours; comprehensive examination; one semester full-time residence; completion of degree program in five years. *Faculty:* 10 full-time. *Students:* 84 full-time; 83 part-time. *Financial Assistance:* A large number of graduate assistantships are available to qualified students. *Master's Degrees Awarded 1994:* 81. An advanced certificate program is available.

McNeese State University. Burton College of Education, Dept. of Administration, Supervision, and Educational Technology, P.O. Box 91815, Lake Charles, LA 70609-1815. (318) 475-5421. Fax (318) 475-5467. E-mail vdronet@mcneese.edu. Dr. Virgie M. Dronet. *Specialization:* M.Ed. in Educational Technology with concentrations in educational technology, computer education, and instructional technology. *Minimum Degree Requirements:* 30 semester hours for educational technology or instructional technology, 36 hours for computer education. *Faculty:* 2 full-time; 5 part-time. *Students:* 24. *Financial Assistance:* 4 graduate assistantships per year (teaching and lab). *Master's Degrees Awarded 1994:* Data not reported. Advanced certificate programs are offered in Computer Literacy and Computer Education.

MARYLAND

*The Johns Hopkins University. 2500 E. Northern Parkway, Baltimore, MD 21214. (410) 516-0006. Fax (410) 646-2310. E-mail jnunn@jhunix.hcs.jhu.edu. Dr. Jacqueline A. Nunn, Center for Technology in Education. *Specialization:* M.S. in Education with concentration in Technology. *Admission Requirements:* Bachelor's degree. *Minimum Degree Requirements:* 36 semester hours, 8 required courses in computer-related technology and media, with remaining courses being electives in other education areas. *Faculty:* 2 full-time; 8 part-time. *Master's Degrees Awarded 1993:* 12.

*Towson State University. College of Education, Hawkins Hall Rm. 206, Towson, MD 21204. (410) 830-2194. Fax (410) 830-2733. E-mail rosecransg@toe.towson.edu. Dr. Gary W. Rosecrans, Assoc. Prof., General Education Dept. *Specializations:* M.S. in Instructional Development or Educational Media. *Minimum Degree Requirements:* 36 graduate semester hours without thesis; 33 graduate semester credits with thesis. *Faculty:* 5 full-time, 2 adjunct. *Financial Assistance:* Graduate assistantships, work-study, scholarships. *Master's Degrees Awarded 1993:* 12.

University of Maryland. College of Library and Information Services, 4105 Hornbake Library Bldg., South Wing, College Park, MD 20742-4345. (301) 405-2033. Fax (301) 314-9145. Ann E. Prentice, Dean and Prog. Chair. *Specialization:* Master's of Library Science, including specialization in school library media; Doctorate in Library and Information Services. *Minimum Degree Requirements:* 36 semester hours for MLS; thesis option. *Faculty:* 15 full-time; 8 part-time. *Students:* 110 full-time, 130 part-time, M.L.S. *Master's Degrees Awarded 1994:* 120.

University of Maryland, Baltimore County (UMBC). Department of Education, 5401 Wilkens Ave., Baltimore, MD 21228. (410) 455-2310. Fax (410) 455-3986. Dr. William R. Johnson, Dir., Grad. Progs. in Education. *Specializations:* Master's degrees in School Instructional Systems, Post-Baccalaureate Teacher Certification, English as a Second Language, Training in Business and Industry. *Admissions Requirements:* 3.0 or higher GPA in undergraduate degree; GRE. *Minimum Degree Requirements:* 36 semester hours, including 18 in systems development for each program; an internship is required. *Faculty:* 13 full-time; 10 part-time. *Students:* 66 full-time; 216 part-time. *Financial Assistance:* Assistantships, scholarships. *Master's Degrees Awarded 1994:* 66.

Western Maryland College. Department of Education, Main St., Westminster, MD 21157. (410) 857-2507. Fax (410) 857-2515. Dr. Ramona N. Kerby, Coord., School Library Media Program, Dept. of Education. *Specializations:* M.S. in School Library Media. *Minimum Degree Requirements:* 34 credit hours, including 19 in media and 6 in education; comprehensive examination. *Faculty:* 1 full-time; 7 part-time. *Students:* 120 full- and part-time. *Master's Degrees Awarded 1994:* 15.

MASSACHUSETTS

Boston University. School of Education, 605 Commonwealth Ave., Boston, MA 02215. (617) 353-3519. Fax (617) 353-3924. David Whittier, Acting Dir., Program in Educational Media and Technology. *Specialization:* Master's degree. *Minimum Degree Requirements:* 36 semester hours; thesis optional. *Faculty:* 1 full-time; 11 part-time. *Students:* 20. *Master's Degrees Awarded 1994:* Data not reported. The school also offers a six-year specialist degree program Certificate of Advanced Graduate Specialization (C.A.G.S.) in Instructional Technology and a corporate training program. For general graduate admissions information, call the Graduate Admissions Office at (617) 353-4237.

*Bridgewater State College. Library Media Program, Room 211, Maxwell Library Bldg., Bridgewater, MA 02325. (508) 697-1370. Fax (508) 697-1729. Richard Neubauer, Coord., Dept. of Media and Librarianship. *Specialization:* M.Ed. in Educational Technology. *Minimum Degree Requirements:* 33 semester hours; comprehensive exam. *Faculty:* 2 full-time, 6 part-time. *Students:* 58 in degree program, 30 non-degree. *Financial Assistance:* Graduate assistantships, graduate internships. *Master's Degrees Awarded 1993:* 11. The school also offers a Certificate of Advanced Graduate Study in Educational Leadership. This is a fully integrated program of library science, technology, and teacher education that focuses on "cutting edge" technology.

*Harvard University. Appian Way, Cambridge, MA 02138. (617) 495-3541. Fax (617) 495-3626. Gerald S. Lesser, Prof, Dept. of Human Management. *Specialization:* M.Ed. in Technology in Education. *Admission Requirements:* Bachelor's degree; Miller Analogy Test score or GRE score or TOEFL Exam minimum score 600; 3 recommendations. *Minimum Degree Requirements:* 32 semester credits. *Faculty:* 3 full-time and 4 part-time. *Students:* Approx. 30. *Financial Assistance:* Within the school's policy. *Master's Degrees Awarded 1992:* 30. An advanced certificate program is available.

*Simmons College. Graduate School of Library and Information Science, 300 The Fenway, Boston, MA 02115-5898. (617) 521-2800. Fax (617) 521-3192. E-mail jmatarazzo@vmsvaxsimmons.edu. Dr. James M. Matarazzo, Dean. *Specializations:* M.S. *Features:* The program prepares individuals for a variety of careers, technology/media emphasis being only one. There are special programs for Unified Media Specialist and Archives Management with strengths in information science/systems, media management, etc. *Minimum Degree Requirements:* 36 semester hours; thesis or research paper and comprehensive exam required. *Faculty:* 13 full-time. *Students:* 66 full-time; 374 part-time. *Financial Assistance:* Grants and scholarships are available. *Master's Degrees Awarded 1993:* Data not reported. A Doctor of Arts in Administration is also offered.

University of Massachusetts-Boston. Graduate College of Education, 100 Morrissey Blvd., Boston, MA 02125. (617) 287-7622 or 287-5980. Fax (617) 265-7173. Canice H. McGarry, Instructional Design Prog. *Specialization:* M.Ed. in Instructional Design; Graduate Certificate in Educational Technology (Fall 1995). *Minimum Degree Requirements:* 36 semester hours; thesis or project required. *Faculty:* 1 full-time; 9 part-time. *Students:* 8 full-time; 80 part-time. *Financial Assistance:* Graduate assistantships providing tuition plus stipend. *Master's Degrees Awarded 1994:* 24.

MICHIGAN

**Eastern Michigan University. 234 Boone Hall, Ypsilanti, MI 48197. (313) 487-3260. Fax (313) 484-6471. Bert Greene, Prof., Coord. Dept. of Teacher Education. *Specialization:* M.A. in Educational Psychology with concentration in Educational Technology. *Admission Requirements:* Bachelor's degree; undergraduate GPA of at least 2.75 or Miller Analogy Test score; TOEFL Exam minimum score 500. *Minimum Degree Requirements:* 30 semester hour credits; optional thesis worth 6 credits. *Faculty:* 8 full-time. *Students:* Data not reported. *Financial Assistance:* Data not reported. *Master's Degrees Awarded 1994:* Data not reported.

**Michigan State University. School of Education, 346 Erickson, East Lansing, MI 48824. (517) 353-9272. Fax (517) 349-8852. E-mail normbell@msu.edu. Dr. Norman T. Bell, Counseling, Educational Psychology, and Special Education. *Specialization:* M.A. in Educational Communications and Technology. *Admission Requirements:* Bachelor's degree; TOEFL Exam minimum score 80. *Minimum Degree Requirements:* 45 quarter credits; optional thesis worth 10 credits. *Faculty:* 10 full-time. *Students:* Data not reported. *Financial Assistance:* Data not reported. *Master's Degrees Awarded 1994:* Data not reported.

*University of Michigan. School of Education, 610 East University, Ann Arbor, MI 48109-1259. (313) 763-4664. Fax (313) 763-4663. E-mail carl.berger@umich.edu. Dr. Carl Berger, Dir., Instructional Technology Development, Curriculum and Teaching. *Specialization:* M.A. in Educational Communications and Technology. *Minimum Degree Requirements:* 30 credit hours (semester). *Faculty:* 5 full-time; 1 part-time. *Master's Degrees Awarded 1993:* 4.

Wayne State University. College of Education, Detroit, MI 48202. (313) 577-1728. Fax (313) 577-1693. Instructional Technology Prog., Div. of Administrative and Organizational Studies. Rita Richey, Prof. and Prog. Coord. *Specialization:* Master's degrees in Business and Human Services Training, K-12 Educational Technology. *Minimum Degree Requirements:* 36 semester hours, including required project; internship recommended. *Faculty:* 5 full-time; 5 part-time. *Students:* 400 full- and part-time. *Master's Degrees Awarded 1993-94:* 48. The school also offers a six-year specialist degree program in Instructional Technology.

MINNESOTA

*Mankato State University. MSU Box 20, P.O. Box 8400, Mankato, MN 56001-8400. (507) 389-5210. Fax (507) 389-5751. E-mail frb2@vax1.mankato.msus.edu. Frank Birmingham, Prof., Chair, Dept. of Library Media Education. *Specialization:* M.S. in Library Media Education. *Minimum Degree Requirements:* 51 quarter hours, including 27 in media. *Faculty:* 4 full-time. *Master's Degrees Awarded 1993:* 20. The school also offers a six-year specialist degree program in Library Media Education.

**Mankato State University. MSU Box 20, P.O. Box 8400, Mankato, MN 56001-8400. (507) 389-1965. Fax (507) 389-5751. E-mail pengelly@vax1.mankato.msus.edu. Kenneth C. Pengelly, Assoc. Prof., Dept. of Library Media Education. *Specialization:* M.S. in Technology in Education. *Admission Requirements:* Bachelor's degree; undergraduate GPA of at least 3.0; GRE minimum score 1350; TOEFL Exam score 500. *Minimum Degree Requirements:* 51 quarter credits; comprehensive exam. *Faculty:* 4 full-time. *Students:* Data not reported. *Financial Assistance:* Data not reported. *Master's Degrees Awarded 1994:* Data not reported.

St. Cloud State University. College of Education, St. Cloud, MN 56301-4498. (612) 255-2022. Fax (612) 255-4778. E-mail jberling@tigger.stcloud.msus.edu. John G. Berling, Prof., Dir., Center for Information Media. *Specializations:* Master's degrees in Information Technologies, Educational Media, and Human Resources Development/Training. *Minimum Degree Requirements:* 51 quarter hours with thesis; 54 quarter hours, Plan B; 57 quarter hours, portfolio; 200-hour practicum is required for media generalist licensure—coursework applies to Educational Media master's program. *Faculty:* 7 full-time. *Students:* 170 full-time. *Financial Assistance:* Assistantships, scholarships. *Master's Degrees Awarded 1994:* 20. The school also offers a 45-quarter-credit, six-year specialist degree.

*University of Minnesota. 130 Peik Hall, 159 Pillsbury Dr. SE, Minneapolis, MN 55455. (612) 625-0534. Fax (612) 624-8277. E-mail simon@maroon.tc.umn.edu. Simon Hoodge, Dept. of Curriculum and Instruction. *Specializations:* M.Ed. or M.A. in Educational Communications and Technology. *Admission Requirements:* Bachelor's degree; undergraduate GPA of at least 3.0; Miller Analogy Test score for M.A. only; TOEFL Exam minimum score 550. *Degree Requirements:* 45 quarter hours; thesis worth 4 credits required for M.A. only. *Faculty:* 5 full-time. *Students:* Data not reported. *Financial Assistance:* Data not reported. *Master's Degrees Awarded 1994:* Data not reported.

MISSISSIPPI

*University of Southern Mississippi. School of Library and Information Science, Box 5146, Hattiesburg, MS 39406-5146. (601) 266-4228. Fax (601) 266-5723. Joy M. Greiner, Assoc. Prof., Dir., School of Library and Information Science. *Specialization:* Master's degree; dual master's in Library Science and History. *Minimum Degree Requirements:* 38 semester hours, comprehensive required. *Faculty:* 6. *Students:* Data not reported. *Master's Degrees Awarded 1993:* 44.

MISSOURI

*University of Missouri-Columbia. 212 Townsend Hall, University of Missouri-Columbia, Columbia, MO 65201. (314) 882-3828. Fax (314) 884-5455. E-mail wedmanjf@mizzou1.missouri.edu. John Wedman, Assoc. Prof., Coord., Educational Technology Prog., Curriculum and Instruction Dept., College of Education. *Specialization:* Master's degree emphasizing instructional design, development, and evaluation. The program is rapidly moving into the areas of performance support systems and multimedia design, production, and application. *Admission Requirements:* Bachelor's degree; Miller Analogy Test score. *Minimum Degree Requirements:* 32 semester hours including 16 hours of upper-level graduate work. *Faculty:* 3 full-time; 4 part-time. *Students:* 15. *Financial Assistance:* Graduate assistantships with tuition waivers; numerous academic scholarships. *Master's Degrees Awarded 1993:* 8. An Education Specialist degree program is also available.

Webster University. Instructional Technology, St. Louis, MO 63119. Fax (314) 968-7118. Paul Steinmann, Assoc. Dean and Dir., Graduate Studies and Instructional Technology. *Specialization:* Master's degree. *Minimum Degree Requirements:* 33 semester hours, including 24 in media; internship required. State Certification in Media Technology is a program option; six-year program not available. *Faculty:* 4. *Students:* 6 full-time; 18 part-time. *Financial Assistance:* Partial scholarships, government loans, and limited state aid. *Master's Degrees Awarded 1994:* 7.

MONTANA

University of Montana. School of Education, Missoula, MT 59812. (406) 243-5785. Fax (406) 243-4908. E-mail cjlott@selway.umt.edu. Dr. Carolyn Lott, Asst. Prof. of Library/Media. *Specializations:* Master's degree; K-12 School Library Media specialization. *Admission Requirements:* Letters of recommendation, application, 2.5 GPA cum. *Minimum Degree Requirements:* 36 semester credit hours, 28 in library media; thesis optional. *Faculty:* 2 full-time; 1 part-time. *Students:* 10 full-time; 5 part-time. *Financial Assistance:* Assistantships; contact the University of Montana Financial Aid Office. *Master's Degrees Awarded 1994:* 36 (all emphases). The school has a School Library Media Certification endorsement program at the undergraduate/graduate levels.

NEBRASKA

*University of Nebraska at Kearney. Kearney, NE 68849. (308) 234-8513. Fax (308) 234-8157. E-mail fredrickson@platte.unk.edu. Dr. Scott Fredrickson, Dir. of Instructional Technology. *Specializations:* M.S. in Instructional Technology, M.S. in Educational Media/Specialist in Educational Media. *Minimum Degree Requirements:* Information not reported. *Faculty:* 4 full-time; 6 part-time. *Students:* 45. *Master's Degrees Awarded 1993:* Approx. 17.

*University of Nebraska-Lincoln. 118 Henflik, Lincoln, NE 68588-0355. (402) 472-2231. Fax (402) 472-8317. E-mail dbrooks@popmail.unl.edu. Dr. David Brooks, Center for Curriculum and Instruction. *Specializations:* M.A. or M.Ed. *Admission Requirements:* Bachelor's degree in education; undergraduate GPA of 3.0; Miller Analogy Test score. *Minimum Degree Requirements:* 36 semester credits; optional thesis worth 6 credits; comprehensive exam. *Faculty:* 4 full-time. *Students:* Data not reported. *Financial Assistance:* Data not reported. *Master's Degrees Awarded 1994:* Data not reported.

University of Nebraska-Omaha. Department of Teacher Education, College of Education, Kayser Hall 208D, Omaha, NE 68182. (402) 554-2211. Fax (402) 554-3491. Verne Haselwood, Prof., Educational Media Prog. in Teacher Education. *Specializations:* M.S. in Education, M.A. in Education, both with Educational Media concentration. *Minimum Degree Requirements:* 36 semester hours, including 24 in media; practicum required; thesis optional. *Faculty:* 2 full-time; 3 part-time. *Students:* 12 full-time; 55 part-time. *Financial Assistance:* Contact Financial Aid Office. *Master's Degrees Awarded 1994:* Data not reported. The school also offers an advanced certificate program in Educational Administration and Supervision.

NEVADA

University of Nevada. College of Education, Reno, NV 89557. (702) 784-4961. Fax (702) 784-4526. Dr. LaMont Johnson, Chair, Dept. of Curriculum and Instruction. *Specializations:* M.A. or M.Ed. *Admission Requirements:* Bachelor's degree; undergraduate GPA of at least 2.75; GRE minimum score 750. *Minimum Degree Requirements:* 36 semester credits; optional thesis worth 6 credits; comprehensive exam. *Faculty:* 2 full-time. *Students:* Data not reported. *Financial Assistance:* Data not reported. *Master's Degrees Awarded 1994:* Data not reported.

NEW JERSEY

Glassboro State College. See listing for Rowan College of New Jersey.

Montclair State College. Department of Reading and Educational Media, Upper Montclair, NJ 07043. Robert R. Ruezinsky, Dir. of Media and Technology. *Specializations:* No degree program exists. Two certification programs, A.M.S. and E.M.S, exist on the graduate level. *Minimum Degree Requirements:* 18-21 semester hours of media and technology are required for the A.M.S. program and 30-33 hours for the E.M.S. program. *Faculty:* Includes 5 administrators and 1 adjunct, teaching on an overload basis. *Students:* Data not reported. *Certificates Awarded 1994:* Data not reported.

*Rowan College of New Jersey. School and Public Librarianship, Glassboro, NJ 08028. (609) 256-4755. Fax (609) 256-4918. E-mail pauly@saturn.rowan.edu. Regina Pauly, Asst. Prof., Dept. of Secondary Education. *Specialization:* M.A. *Minimum Degree Requirements:* 39 semester hours, including required thesis project. *Faculty:* 1 full-time; 3 part-time. *Master's Degrees Awarded 1993:* 11. A six-year program is available.

Rutgers-The State University of New Jersey. School of Communication, Information and Library Studies, New Brunswick, NJ 08903. (908) 932-9717. Fax (908) 932-6916. Dr. Betty J. Turock, Chair, Dept. of Library and Information Studies. *Specializations:* M.L.S. degree with specializations in Information Retrieval, Technical and Automated Services, Reference, School Media Services, Youth Services, Management and Policy Issues, Generalist Studies. A new course on Multimedia Structure, Organization, Access, and Production is being offered. *Minimum Degree Requirements:* 36 semester hours, in which the hours for media vary for individual students; practicum of 150 hours. *Faculty:* 7 full-time; 6 adjuncts. *Students:* 98 full-time; 253 part-time. *Financial Assistance:* Scholarships, fellowships, and graduate assistantships available. *Master's Degrees Awarded 1994:* 131. The school also offers a six-year specialist certificate program.

William Paterson College. School of Education, 300 Pompton Rd., Wayne, NJ 07470. (201) 595-2140. Fax (201) 595-2585. Dr. Amy G. Job, Librarian, Assoc. Prof., Coord., Prog. in Library/Media, Curriculum and Instruction Dept. *Specializations:* M.Ed. for Educational Media Specialist, Associate Media Specialist. *Minimum Degree Requirements:* 33 semester hours, including research projects and practicum. *Faculty:* 6 full-time; 2 part-time. *Students:* 30 part-time. *Financial Assistance:* Limited. *Master's Degrees Awarded 1994:* 6.

NEW YORK

**Columbia University-Teachers College. Teachers College, Box 8, 525 W. 120th St., New York, NY 10027. (212) 678-3773. Fax (212) 678-4048. E-mail hb50@columbia.edu. Howard Budin, Coord., Dept. of Communications, Computing and Technology. *Specializations:* M.A. or M.Ed. *Admission Requirements:* Bachelor's degree; TOEFL Exam score. *Minimum Degree Requirements:* 32 credits (semester) for M.A., 60 credits for M.Ed.; master's project; comprehensive exam. *Faculty:* 4 full-time. *Students:* Data not reported. *Financial Assistance:* Data not reported. *Master's Degrees Awarded 1994:* Data not reported.

*Fordham University. Communications Department, Bronx, NY 10458. Edward A. Wachtel, Assoc. Prof. and Chair; James A. Capo, Assoc. Prof., Dir. of Graduate Studies, Communications Dept. *Specialization:* Master's degree. *Minimum Degree Requirements:* 30 semester hours; internship or thesis required. *Faculty:* 9. *Students:* 31. *Financial Assistance:* Scholarships and assistantships. *Master's Degrees Awarded 1993:* 8.

Ithaca College. School of Communications, Ithaca, NY 14850. (607) 274-1025. Fax (607) 274-1664. E-mail herndon@ithaca.edu. Sandra L. Herndon, Prof., Chair, Graduate Corporate Communications; Roy H. Park, School of Communications. *Specialization:* M.S. in Corporate Communications. *Minimum Degree Requirements:* 36 semester hours; required seminar. *Faculty:* 8 full-time. *Students:* Approx. 25 full-time, 15 part-time. *Financial Assistance:* Full- and part-time research/lab assistantships. *Master's Degrees Awarded 1993:* 25.

New York Institute of Technology. School of Education-Instructional Technology, Wheatley Rd., Old Westbury, NY 11568. (Also 1855 Broadway, New York, NY 10023.) (516) 686-7777. Fax (212) 626-7206. Helen Greene, Dean, School of Education. (516) 686-7936. Davenport Plumer, Chair, Depts. of Instructional Technology and Elementary Education. (Courses are offered at three campuses and several off-campus sites in Metropolitan New York.) *Specializations:* Master's degree in Instructional Technology for Teachers; Master's Degree in Instructional Technology for Trainers; Computers in Education Certificate (18-credits); Distance Learning Certificate (18-credits). *Features:* Technology integration in virtually all courses; instruction delivered via computer with teleconferencing and interactive two-way audio/two-way video. *Admission Requirements:* Bachelor's degree from accredited college with 2.85 cumulative average; candidates for the master's degree for teachers must be provisionally certified. *Minimum Degree Requirements:* 36 credits with 3.0 GPA for master's degree; 18 credits with 3.0 GPA for certificates. *Faculty:* 9 full-time; 15 part-time. *Students:* 11 full-time; 438 part-time. *Financial Assistance:* Graduate assistantships, institutional and alumni scholarships, student loans. *Master's Degrees Awarded 1994:* 54.

New York University. School of Education, 239 Greene St., Suite 300, New York, NY 10003. (212) 998-5520. Fax (212) 995-4041. Francine Shuchat Shaw, Assoc. Prof. and Dir., Prog. in Educational Communication and Technology. *Specialization:* M.A. in Education with program emphasis on design and production, application and evaluation of materials and environments for all instructional technologies. *Admission Requirements:* School application, minimum 3.0 undergraduate GPA, essay, and reference letters. *Minimum Degree Requirements:* 36 semester hours including final master's project and English Essay Examination. *Faculty:* 2 full-time; 10 part-time. *Students:* Data not reported. *Financial Assistance:* Graduate and research assistantships, student loans, scholarships, and work-study programs. *Master's Degrees Awarded 1994:* 17. The school also offers a post-M.A. 30-point Certificate of Advanced Study in Education.

*New York University-Tisch School of the Arts. Interactive Telecommunications Program, 721 Broadway, New York, NY 10003. (212) 998-1880. Fax (212) 998-1898. Red Burns, Prof., Chair, The Interactive Telecommunications Program/Institute of Film and Television. *Specialization:* Master's degree. *Minimum Degree Requirements:* 60 semester hours (15 courses at 4 credit hours each; program is 2 years for full-time students), including 5-6 required courses and thesis. *Faculty:* 3 full-time, 32 adjunct. *Students:* 150. *Financial Assistance:* Graduate assistantships. *Master's Degrees Awarded 1993:* Data not reported.

St. John's University. Division of Library and Information Science, 8000 Utopia Parkway, Jamaica, NY 11439. (718) 990-6200. Fax (718) 380-0353. E-mail bensonj@sjuvm.bitnet. James Benson, Dir., Div. of Library and Information Science. *Specializations:* M.L.S. with specializations in School Media, Public, Academic, Law, Health/Medicine, Business, Archives. Double degree programs: Pharmacy and M.L.S., Government and Politics and M.L.S. *Minimum Degree Requirements:* 36 semester hours; comprehensive; practicum (school media required). *Faculty:* 5 full-time; 14 part-time; 2 full-time vacancies. *Students:* 30 full-time; 100 part-time. *Financial Assistance:* Seven assistantships and five fellowships. *Master's Degrees Awarded 1994:* 62. The school also offers a 24-credit Advanced Certificate program.

State University College of Arts and Science. School of Education, 204 Satterlee Hall, Potsdam, NY 13676. (315) 267-2527. (315) 267-2771. E-mail lichtnc@snypotvx.bitnet. Norman Licht, Coord., Instructional Technology and Media Management; Dr. Charles Mlynarczyk, Chair, Education Department. *Specializations:* Master of Science in Education with concentration in Instructional Technology and Media Management. *Minimum Degree Requirements:* 33 semester hours. *Faculty:* 7. *Master's Degrees Awarded 1994:* 35.

State University of New York at Albany. School of Education, 1400 Washington Ave., Albany, NY 12222. (518) 442-5032. Fax (518) 442-5008. E-mail swan@cnsunix.albany.edu. Karen Swan (ED114A), contact person. *Specialization:* Master's degree in Curriculum Theory and Instructional Technology with concentrations in Curriculum Theory, Instructional Design, Program Evaluation, Language in Education, and Teaching and Learning of Academic Disciplines. *Minimum Degree Requirements:* 30 semester hours at the graduate level, including at least 3 credits (1 course) each in curriculum development, instruction, technology, and research; at least 6 credits in the foundations of education; and 12 credits in the student's chosen area of specialization as developed with his/her advisor. *Faculty:* 5 full-time. *Students:* 119 full-time. *Financial Assistance:* Assistantships, loans. *Master's Degrees Awarded 1994:* 27.

State University of New York at Buffalo. Graduate School of Education, 480 Baldy Hall, Amherst, NY 14260. (716) 645-3164. Fax (716) 645-4281. Taher A. Razik, Prof., Instructional Design and Management, Dept. of Educational Organization, Administration, and Policy. *Specialization:* M.Ed. in Instructional Design and Management. *Minimum Degree Requirements:* 32 semester hours, including 21 hours in Instructional Design and Management; thesis or project required. *Faculty:* 3. *Students:* 10. *Financial Assistance:* Some graduate assistantships are available. *Master's Degrees Awarded 1994:* Data not reported.

State University of New York at Buffalo. School of Information and Library Studies, Buffalo, NY 14260. (716) 645-2411. Fax (716) 645-3775. E-mail wakefld@aixl.ucok.edu. George S. Bobinski, Dean. This program has been discontinued.

Syracuse University. School of Education, Syracuse, NY 13244-2340. (315) 443-3703. Fax (315) 443-5732. Philip Doughty, Prof., Chair, Instructional Design, Development and Evaluation Prog. *Specializations:* M.S. degree programs for Instructional Design of programs and materials,

Educational Evaluation, human issues in Instructional Development, Media Production (including computers and videodisc), and Educational Research and Theory (learning theory, application of theory, and educational and media research). Graduates are prepared to serve as curriculum developers, instructional developers, program and product evaluators, researchers, resource center administrators, communications coordinators, trainers in human resource development, and higher education instructors. *Features:* Field work and internships, special topics and special issues seminar, student- and faculty-initiated minicourses, seminars and guest lecturers, faculty-student formulation of department policies, and multiple international perspectives. *Minimum Degree Requirements:* 30 semester hours; comprehensive and intensive examinations required. *Faculty:* 5 full-time; 4 part-time. *Students:* 19 full-time; 27 part-time. *Financial Assistance:* Some fellowships, scholarships, and graduate assistantships entailing either research or administrative duties in instructional technology. *Master's Degrees Awarded 1994:* 14. The school also offers an advanced certificate program.

NORTH CAROLINA

Appalachian State University. Department of Library Science and Educational Foundations, Boone, NC 28608. (704) 262-2243. E-mail tashnerjh@alf.appstate.edu. John H. Tashner, Prof., Coord., Dept. of Library Science and Educational Foundations, College of Education. *Specialization:* Master's degree. *Features:* IMPACT NC (business/university/public school) partnership offers unusual opportunities. *Minimum Degree Requirements:* 36 semester hours, including 15 in Computer Education; thesis optional. *Faculty:* 2. *Students:* 8 full-time; 15 part-time. *Financial Assistance:* Assistantships, grants, student loans. *Master's Degrees Awarded 1994:* 1.

East Carolina University. Department of Library Studies and Educational Technology, Greenville, NC 27858-4353. (919) 328-6621. Fax (919) 328-4368. E-mail lsauld@ecuvm. cis.ecu.edu. Lawrence Auld, Assoc. Prof., Chair. *Specializations*: Master of Library Science; Certificate of Advanced Study (Library Science); Master of Arts in Education (Instructional TechnologyComputers). *Features:* M.L.S. graduates are eligible for North Carolina School Media Coordinator certification; C.A.S. graduates are eligible for North Carolina School Media Supervisor certification; M.A.Ed. graduates are eligible for North Carolina Instructional Technology-Computers certification. *Admission Requirements:* M.L.S. and M.A.Ed., bachelor's degree; C.A.S., M.L.S. or equivalent degree. *Minimum Degree Requirements:* M.L.S., 38 semester hours; M.A.Ed., 36 semester hours; C.A.S., 30 semester hours. *Faculty:* 9 full-time. *Students:* 5 full-time; 70 part-time. *Financial Assistance:* Assistantships. *Master's Degrees Awarded 1994:* 20.

North Carolina Central University. School of Education, 238 Farrison-Newton Communications Bldg., Durham, NC 27707. (919) 560-6218. Dr. Marvin E. Duncan, Prof., Dir., Graduate Prog. in Educational Technology. *Specialization:* M.A. with special emphasis on Instructional Development/Design. *Minimum Degree Requirements:* 33 semester hours, including 21 in Educational Technology; thesis or project required unless student has already written a thesis or project for another master's program. *Features:* The master's program in educational technology is designed to prepare graduates to serve as information and communication technologists in a variety of professional ventures, among which are institutions of higher education (college resource centers); business; industry; and professional schools, such as medicine, law, dentistry, and nursing. The program is also designed to develop in students the theory, practical experience, and techniques necessary to analyze, develop, utilize, manage, and evaluate the process and resources for learning and manage an instructional resources center. Many of our students teach in two- and four-year colleges. *Faculty:* 3 full-time; 1 part-time. *Students:* 25 full-time; 40 part-time. *Financial Assistance:* Assistantships and grants available. *Master's Degrees Awarded 1994:* Data not reported.

University of North Carolina. School of Education (CB#3500), Chapel Hill, NC 27599. (919) 962-5372. Fax (919) 962-1538. Ralph E. Wileman, Prof., Chair, Educational Media and Instructional Design. *Specialization:* M.Ed. in Educational Media and Instructional Design. *Features:* Skills based program; at least one practicum for each candidate; good placement record. *Admission Requirements:* 1000 minimum on Verbal/Quantitative GRE; 3.0 undergraduate GPA; 3 letters of recommendation. *Minimum Degree Requirements:* 36 semester hours; comprehensive examination. *Faculty:* 2 full-time; 1 part-time. *Students:* 16 full-time; 1 part-time. *Financial Assistance:* Assistantships; student loans. *Master's Degrees Awarded 1994:* 10.

OHIO

**Kent State University. 405 White Hall, Kent, OH 44242. (216) 672-2256. Fax (216) 672-3407. E-mail aevans@kentvh.kent.edu. Dr. Alan Evans, Coord., Instructional Technology Program. *Specializations:* M.Ed. or M.A. *Admission Requirements:* Bachelor's degree in education with educational media specialist certificate; undergraduate GPA of at least 2.75; GRE minimum score. *Minimum Degree Requirements:* 34 credits (semester); thesis required for M.A. but not for M.Ed. *Faculty:* 4 full-time. *Students:* Data not reported. *Financial Assistance:* Data not reported. *Master's Degrees Awarded 1994:* Data not reported.

**Miami University. Room 301, McGuffey Hall, Oxford, OH 45056. (513) 529-6443. Fax (513) 529-4931. Dr. Robert Shearer, Coord., Dept. of Teacher Education. *Specialization:* M.Ed. Arts. *Admission Requirements:* Bachelor's degree in education; undergraduate GPA of at least 2.75; TOEFL Exam score. *Minimum Degree Requirements:* 30 credits (semester); optional thesis worth 6-12 credits. *Faculty:* 4 full-time; 1 part-time. *Students:* Data not reported. *Financial Assistance:* Data not reported. *Master's Degrees Awarded 1994:* Data not reported.

*The Ohio State University. College of the Arts, Department of Art Education, 340 Hopkins Hall, 128 North Oval Mall, Columbus, OH 43210. (614) 292-0259. Fax (614) 292-4401. E-mail scott+@osu.edu. Dr. Tony Scott, Prog. Coord., Prog. in Electronic Media in Art Education. *Specializations:* Ph.D. and M.A. in Art Education with specializations in the teaching and learning of computer graphics and computer-mediated art; multimedia production and its curricular implications; electronic networking in the arts; multicultural aspects of computing; hypermedia applications for teaching and art education research; and the application of computing to arts administration, galleries, and museums. *Faculty:* 3 full-time in specialty; 19 in department. *Students:* 15 full-time in specialty. *Financial Assistance:* Graduate teaching associate positions that carry tuition and fee waivers and pay a monthly stipend; various fellowship programs for applicants with high GRE scores. *Master's Degrees Awarded 1993:* 3 directly related to program.

*Ohio State University. Instructional Design and Technology Program, 29 West Woodruff Ave., Columbus,OH 43210. (614) 292-4872. (614) 292-7900. E-mail jbelland@magus.acs.ohio-state.edu. John C. Belland, Prof., Coord., Dept. of Educational Policy and Leadership. *Specialization:* M.A. *Admission Requirements:* Bachelor's degree; undergraduate GPA of at least 2.7; TOEFL Exam minimum score 550. *Minimum Degree Requirements:* 50 quarter hours; optional thesis worth at least 5 credits; comprehensive exam. *Faculty:* 8 full-time. *Students:* Data not reported. *Financial Assistance:* Data not reported. *Master's Degrees Awarded 1994:* Data not reported.

Ohio University. School of Curriculum and Instruction, 248 McCracken Hall, Athens, OH 45701-2979.(614) 593-4457. Fax (614) 593-0177. *Specialization:* M.Ed. in Media Management. *Admission Requirements:* Bachelor's degree; undergraduate GPA of at least 2.5; Miller Analogy Test score 35; GRE minimum test score 420 verbal, 400 quant.; TOEFL Exam minimum score 550; three letters of recommendation. *Minimum Degree Requirements:* 54 quarter credits; optional thesis worth 2-10 credits or alternative seminar and paper. Students may earn two graduate degrees simultaneously in education and in any other field. *Faculty:* 3 full-time; 3 part-time. *Students:* 24 full-time; 5 part-time. *Financial Assistance:* Data not reported. *Master's Degrees Awarded 1992:* 3.

University of Cincinnati. College of Education, 401 Teachers College, ML002, Cincinnati, OH 45221-0002. (513) 556-3577. Randall Nichols and Janet Bohren, Div. of Teacher Education. *Specialization:* M.A. or Ed.D. in Curriculum and Instruction with an emphasis on instructional design and technology. *Minimum Degree Requirements:* 54 quarter hours; written examination; thesis or research project. *Faculty:* 2 full-time. *Students:* 20 full-time. *Financial Assistance:* Scholarships, assistantships, grants. *Master's Degrees Awarded 1994:* 8.

*University of Toledo. SM 352. Toledo, OH 43606. (419) 537-2471. Fax (419) 537-7719. E-mail dmyers@uoft02.utoledo.edu. Dennis C. Myers, Prof., Dept. of Curriculum and Educational Technology. *Specializations:* M.Ed. in Educational Media. *Admission Requirements:* Bachelor's degree; undergraduate GPA of at least 2.7; GRE score; TOEFL Exam score. *Minimum Degree Requirements:* 48 quarter hours; optional thesis worth 4 credits. *Faculty:* 6 full-time. *Students:* 13 full-time; 14 part-time. *Financial Assistance:* Graduate assistantships for research and teaching. Board of Trustee scholarships and grants (tuition only). *Master's Degrees Awarded 1992:* Data not reported.

*Wright State University. College of Education and Human Services, 244 Millett Hall, Dayton, OH 45435. (513) 873-2509 or (513) 873-2182. Fax (513) 873-3301. Dr. Bonnie K. Mathies, Chair, Dept. of Educational Technology, Vocational Education and Allied Programs. *Specializations:* M.Ed. in Educational Media or Computer Education, or for Media Supervisor or Computer Coordinator; M.A. in Educational Media or Computer Education. *Minimum Degree Requirements:* M.Ed. requires a comprehensive examination that, for this department, is the completion of a portfolio and videotaped presentation to the faculty; the M.A. incorporates a 9-hour thesis; students are eligible for Supervisor's Certificate after completion of C&S; Computer Coordinator or C&S; Media Supervision programs. *Faculty:* 2 full-time; 13 part-time, adjuncts, and other university full-time faculty and staff. *Students:* 61 part-time (not including Computer Education students). *Financial Assistance:* Graduate assistantships available, including three positions in the College's Educational Resource Center; limited number of small graduate scholarships. *Master's Degrees Awarded 1 July 1992-30 June 1993:* 8.

OKLAHOMA

Southwestern Oklahoma State University. School of Education, 100 Campus Drive, Weatherford, OK 73096. (405) 772-6611. Fax (405) 772-5447. Lessley Price, Assoc. Prof., Coord. of Library/Media Prog. *Specialization:* M.Ed. in Library/Media Education. *Admission Requirements:* GPA of at least 2.5 on 4.0 scale; copy of GRE or GMAT scores; letter of recommendation; GPA x 150 + GRE = 1100. *Minimum Degree Requirements:* 32 semester hours, including 24 in library/media. *Faculty:* 1 full-time; 4 part-time. *Students:* Data not reported. *Master's Degrees Awarded 1994:* 16.

*University of Oklahoma. 321 Collings Hall, Education, Norman, OK 73019. (405) 325-5974. Fax (405) 325-6655. E-mail db5244@uokhvsa. Dr. Raymond B. Miller, Coord., Instructional Psychology/Technology Prog. *Specializations:* M.Ed. in Educational Technology as a Generalist or with emphasis on Computer Applications or Instructional Design; dual degree in Library Science and Educational Technology. *Minimum Degree Requirements:* 32 semester hours for the Generalist and Computer Applications options; 39 hours for the Instructional Design program; 60 hours for the dual degree; comprehensive examination required for all programs. *Faculty:* 10 full-time; 2 part-time. *Students:* 43 full- and part-time. *Financial Assistance:* Assistantships; out-of-state fee waivers; general and targeted minorities graduate scholarships. *Master's Degrees Awarded 1 July 1992-30 June 1993:* 6.

OREGON

*Portland State University. School of Education, P.O. Box 751, Portland, OR 97207. (503) 725-4656. Fax (503) 725-5599. Paul Gregorio, Asst. Prof., Program in Educational Media/Librarianship. *Specializations:* M.A. or M.S. in Educational Media. *Minimum Degree Requirements:* 45 quarter hours, including 42 in media; thesis optional. *Faculty:* 3 full-time; 4 part-time. *Master's Degrees Awarded 1993:* 35.

*Western Oregon State College. Ed. 202L, Monmouth, OR 97361. (503) 838-8471. Fax (503) 838-8474. E-mail forcier@fsa.wosc.osshe.edu. Richard C. Forcier, Prof., Dept. of Secondary Education. *Specialization:* M.S. in Educational/Information Technology. *Features:* Offers advanced courses in Library Management, Media Production, Instructional Systems, Instructional Development, and Computer Technology. Some specialization in distance delivery of instruction and computer-interactive video instruction. *Minimum Degree Requirements:* 45 quarter hours, including 36 in media; thesis optional. *Faculty:* 3 full-time; 4 part-time. *Students:* 3 full-time; 210 part-time. *Master's Degrees Awarded 1 July 1992-30 June 1993:* 12.

PENNSYLVANIA

**Bloomsburg University. 1212 MCHS, Bloomsburg, PA 17815. (717) 389-4506. Fax (717) 389-4943. E-mail bail@husky.bloomu.edu. Dr. Harold J. Bailey, Institute for Interactive Technologies. *Specialization:* M.S. with emphasis on computer technologies. *Admission Requirements:* Bachelor's degree; undergraduate GPA of at least 2.5; Miller Analogy Test score; GRE score; TOEFL Exam score 570. *Minimum Degree Requirements:* 36 semester credits; optional thesis worth 6 credits. *Faculty:* 3 full-time; 1 part-time. *Students:* Data not reported. *Financial Assistance:* Data not reported. *Master's Degrees Awarded 1994:* Data not reported.

**Clarion University of Pennsylvania. Becker Hall, Clarion, PA 16214. (814) 226-2328. Fax (814) 226-2444. Carmen S. Felicetti, Chair, Dept. of Communications. *Specialization:* M.S. in Communication. *Admission Requirements:* Bachelor's degree; undergraduate GPA of at least 2.75; Miller Analogy Test score. *Minimum Degree Requirements:* 36 semester credit with minimum GPA of 3.0; optional thesis worth 6 credits. *Faculty:* 9 full-time. *Students:* Data not reported. *Financial Assistance:* Data not reported. *Master's Degrees Awarded 1994:* Data not reported.

*Drexel University. College of Information Studies, Philadelphia, PA 19104. (215) 895-2474. Fax (215) 895-2494. Richard H. Lytle, Prof. and Dean, College of Information Studies. *Specialization:* M.S. and M.S.I.S. degrees. *Minimum Degree Requirements:* 48 quarter hours taken primarily from six functional groupings: Technology of Information Systems; Principles of Information Systems; Information Organizations; Collection Management; Information Resources and Services; and Research. *Faculty:* 18. *Students:* 331. *Master's Degrees Awarded 1993:* 87 M.S. and 3 M.S.I.S.

*Lehigh University. Lehigh University College of Education, Bethlehem, PA 18015. (215) 758-3231. Fax (215) 758-5323. Leroy J. Tuscher, Prof., Coord., Educational Technology Program. *Specialization:* Master's degree with emphasis in Interactive Digital Multimedia for Teaching and Learning. *Minimum Degree Requirements:* 30 semester hours, including 9 in media; thesis optional. *Faculty:* 3 full-time; 2 part-time. *Financial Assistance:* University graduate and research assistantships, graduate student support as participants in R&D projects. *Master's Degrees Awarded 1992-93:* 15.

Pennsylvania State University. Division of Adult Education and Instructional Systems, 27D Chambers Bldg., University Park, PA 16802. (814) 865-0473. Fax (814) 865-0128. D. D. Jonassen, Prof. in Charge, Instructional Systems Prog. *Specializations:* M.Ed., M.S. in Instructional Systems. *Minimum Degree Requirements:* 33 semester hours, including either a thesis or project paper. *Faculty:* 9 full-time; 2 affiliate; 2 part-time. *Students:* Approx. 160. *Financial Assistance:* Some assistantships, graduate fellowships, student aid loans. *Master's Degrees Awarded 1994:* Data not reported.

*Rosemont College. Rosemont College Graduate Studies, 1400 Montgomery Ave., Rosemont, PA 19010-1699. (610) 526-2982; (800) 531-9431 outside 610 area code. Fax (610) 525-2930. E-mail rosemont@villum.bitnet. Dr. Robert J. Siegfried, Dir. *Specializations:* M.Ed. in Technology in Education, Certificate in Advanced Graduate Study in Technology in Education for those who already hold a master's degree. *Minimum Degree Requirements:* Completion of 12 units (36 credits) and comprehensive exam. *Students:* Approx. 110. *Financial Assistance:* Graduate assistantships, internships, Stafford student loans, and Supplemental Loans to Students. *Master's Degrees Awarded 1993:* 19.

Shippensburg University. Dept. of Communications and Journalism, 1871 Old Main Drive, Shippensburg, PA 17257-2292. (717) 532-1521. Fax (717) 532-1273. Dr. C. Lynne Nash, Dept. Chair. *Specialization:* Master's degree with specializations in public relations, radio/television, communication theory, press and public affairs. *Admission Requirements:* 2.5 GPA. *Minimum Degree Requirements:* Completion of between 30 and 33 credits plus a thesis or a professional project or a comprehensive examination. *Faculty:* 9 full-time; 1 half-time; 3 adjunct. *Students:* 15 full-time; 15 part-time. *Financial Assistance:* Assistantships, grants, student loans, scholarships. *Master's Degrees Awarded 1994:* 5.

University of Pittsburgh. Instructional Design and Technology, School of Education, Pittsburgh, PA 15260. (412) 612-7254. Fax (412) 648-7081. E-mail bseels+@pitt.edu. Barbara Seels, Assoc. Prof., Coord., Program in Instructional Design and Technology, Dept. of Instruction and Learning. *Specialization:* Ed.D. and M.Ed. programs for the preparation of instructional technologists with skills in designing, developing, using, evaluating, and managing processes and resources for learning. Certificate option for instructional technologists available. *Features:* Program prepares people for positions in which they can effect educational change through instructional technology. Program includes three competency areas: instructional design, technological delivery systems, and communications research. *Minimum Degree Requirements:* 36 trimester hours, including 18 in instructional technology, 9 in core courses, and 9 in electives; comprehensive examination. *Faculty:* 3 full-time. *Students:* 72 master's, 33 doctoral. *Financial Assistance:* Assistantships and grants are available. *Master's Degrees Awarded 1994:* 9. The school also offers a 39-credit specialist certification program.

RHODE ISLAND

The University of Rhode Island. Graduate School of Library and Information Studies, Rodman Hall, Kingston, RI 02881-0815. (401) 792-2947. Fax (401) 792-4395. Elizabeth Futas, Prof. and Dir. *Specializations:* M.L.I.S. degree. Offers accredited master's degree with specialties in Archives, Law, Health Sciences, Rare Books, and Youth Services Librarianship. *Minimum Degree Requirements:* 42 semester-credit program offered in Rhode Island and regionally in Boston and Amherst, MA, and Durham, NH. *Faculty:* 7 full-time; 20 adjunct. *Students:* 27 full-time; abt. 222 part-time. *Financial Assistance:* Graduate assistantships, some scholarship aid, student loans. *Master's Degrees Awarded 1994:* 72.

SOUTH CAROLINA

*University of South Carolina. Educational Psychology Department, Columbia, SC 29208. (803) 777-6609. Dr. Margaret Gredler, Prof., Chair, Educational Psychology Dept. *Specialization:* Master's degree. *Minimum Degree Requirements:* 33 semester hours, including 3 each in administration, curriculum, and research, 9 in production, and 3 in instructional theory; no thesis required. *Faculty:* 3. *Students:* 5. *Master's Degrees Awarded 1993:* 1.

*Winthrop University. Division of Leadership, Counseling and Media, Rock Hill, SC 29733. (803) 323-2136 or 2151. Dr. George H. Robinson, Coord., Educational Media Prog., School of Education. *Specialization:* M.Ed. in Educational Media. *Features:* Students completing this program qualify for certification as a school library media specialist in South Carolina and most other states. *Minimum Degree Requirements:* 36-45 semester hours, including 15-33 in media, depending on media courses a student has had prior to this program; no thesis. *Faculty:* 2 full-time; 5 part-time. *Students:* 4 full-time; 34 part-time. *Financial Assistance:* Graduate assistantships of $1,500 per semester plus tuition. *Master's Degrees Awarded 1 July 1992-30 June 1993:* 11.

TENNESSEE

East Tennessee State University. College of Education, Box 70684, Johnson City, TN 37614-0684. (615) 929-5848. Fax (615) 929-5746. E-mail millerr@eduserv.east_tenn_st.edu.

Dr. Rudy Miller, Prof., Dir. Media Services, Dept. of Curriculum and Instruction. *Specializations:* M.Ed. in Instructional Media (Library), M.Ed. in Instructional Technology. *Minimum Degree Requirements:* 39 semester hours, including 18 hours in instructional technology. *Faculty:* 2 full-time. *Students:* 38 part-time. *Financial Assistance:* Scholarships, aid for handicapped. *Master's Degrees Awarded 1994:* 8. A six-year program is under development.

Middle Tennessee State University. Department of Educational Leadership, Murfreesboro, TN 37132. (615) 898-2855. Dr. Nancy Keese, Prof. and Chair, Dept. of Educational Leadership. *Specialization:* Master's degree. *Minimum Degree Requirements:* 33 semester hours, including 15 in media; no thesis required. *Faculty:* 1 full-time; 4 part-time. *Students:* 2 full-time; 25 part-time. *Financial Assistance:* Assistantships. *Master's Degrees Awarded 1994:* 10.

University of Tennessee-Knoxville. College of Education, Knoxville, TN 37996-3400. (615) 974-4222 or (615) 974-3103. Dr. Alfred D. Grant, Coord., Graduate Media Prog., Dept. of Education in Science, Mathematics, Research, and Technology. *Specialization:* M.S. in Education, concentration in Instructional Media and Technology. *Minimum Degree Requirements:* 33 semester hours, thesis optional. *Faculty:* 1. *Students:* 1 full-time; 2 part-time at the master's level. *Master's Degrees Awarded 1994:* 2. The Department of Curriculum and Instruction also offers a six-year specialist degree program in Curriculum and Instruction with a concentration in Instructional Media and Technology.

TEXAS

East Texas State University. Department of Secondary and Higher Education, East Texas Station, Commerce, TX 75429-3011. (903) 886-5607. Fax (903) 886-5603. E-mail mundayb@tenet.edu. Dr. Robert S. Munday, Prof., Head, Dept. of Secondary and Higher Education. *Specialization:* Master's degree in Learning Technology and Information Systems with emphasis on Educational Micro Computing, Educational Media and Technology, and Library and Information Science. *Admission Requirements:* 700 GRE. *Minimum Degree Requirements:* 30 semester hours with thesis, 36 without thesis. M.Ed. (Educational Computing), 30 hours in ed. tech.; M.S. (Educational Media and Technology), 21 hours in ed. tech.; M.S. (Library and Information Science), 15 hours in library/information science, 12 hours in ed. tech. *Faculty:* 3 full-time; 5 part-time. *Students:* 30 full-time; 150 part-time. *Financial Assistance:* Graduate assistantships in teaching, graduate assistantships in research, scholarships, federal aid program. *Master's Degrees Awarded 1994:* 20. A six-year program is available.

*Texas A&M University. College of Education, College Station, TX 77843-4232. (409) 845-8383. Fax (409) 845-9663. E-mail zellner@tamu.edu. Ronald D. Zellner, Coord., Dept. of Curriculum & Instruction. *Specialization:* M.Ed. in Educational Technology. *Admission Requirements:* Bachelor's degree; GRE minimum score 800; TOEFL Exam minimum score 550. *Minimum Degree Requirements:* 37 semester credits; oral exam. *Faculty:* 6 full-time; 1 part-time. *Students:* Data not reported. *Financial Assistance:* Teaching assistantships available. *Master's Degrees Awarded 1992:* 12.

*Texas Tech University. College of Education, Box 41071, Lubbock, TX 79409. (806) 742-2393. Fax (806) 742-2179. E-mail bprice@tenet.edu. Dr. Robert Price, Assoc. Prof., Dir., Instructional Technology Prog. *Specializations:* Master's degree with emphasis in Educational

Computing or Learning Resources. *Minimum Degree Requirements:* 39 semester hours; no thesis. *Faculty:* 3 full-time; 2 part-time. *Master's Degrees Awarded 1992-93:* 12.

*University of North Texas. College of Education, Box 13857, Denton, TX 76203-3857. (817) 565-3790. Fax (817) 565-2185. Dr. Jon I. Young, Chair, Dept. of Computer Education and Cognitive Systems, College of Education. *Specialization:* M.S. in Computer Education and Cognitive Systems. *Minimum Degree Requirements:* 36 semester hours, including 27 hours in Instructional Technology and Computer Education; comprehensive exam. *Faculty:* 8. *Master's Degrees Awarded 1992-93:* 35.

University of Texas-Austin. College of Education, Austin, TX 78712. (512) 471-5211. DeLayne Hudspeth, Assoc. Prof., Coord., Area of Instructional Technology, Dept. of Curriculum and Instruction, College of Education. *Specialization:* Master's degree. *Admission Requirements:* 3.25 GPA and a score of at least 1,200 on the GRE. *Minimum Degree Requirements:* 30-36 semester hours minimum depending on selection of program; 18 in Instructional Technology plus research course; thesis optional. A 6-hour minor is required outside the department. *Faculty:* 4 full-time; 2 part-time. *Master's Degrees Awarded 1994:* 18.

*The University of Texas-Southwestern Medical Center at Dallas. 5325 Harry Hines Blvd., Dallas, TX 75235-9065. (214) 648-2258. Fax (214) 648-8805. Perrie N. Adams, Acting Chair, Dept. of Biomedical Communications. *Specializations:* M.A. in Biomedical Communications with an emphasis in media development and instructional design. *Minimum Degree Requirements:* 36 semester hours; thesis required. *Faculty:* 1 full-time; 8 part-time. *Students:* Program limited to 6 full-time students each year. *Financial Assistance:* Student assistantships available when budget permits. *Master's Degrees Awarded 1993:* 4.

UTAH

*Brigham Young University. Department of Educational Psychology, 201 MCKB, Provo, UT 84602. (801) 378-2746. Fax (801) 378-4017. E-mail paul_merrill@byu.edu. Paul F. Merrill, Prof., Chair. *Specializations:* M.S. and Ph.D. degrees in instructional science and technology. In the M.S. program, students may specialize in instructional design and production, computers in education, or research and evaluation. *Minimum Degree Requirements:* 6 semester hours of prerequisite credit in technical writing and A/V production; 14 hrs. of core credit in instructional design, statistics, assessing learning outcomes, computer applications, and evaluation; 3 credit hrs. of internship; 9 hrs. of specialization; and 6 hrs. of project or thesis. *Admission Requirements:* General university requirements, plus GRE entrance examination. Application will not be considered without GRE scores. *Faculty:* 10 full-time. *Students:* 30 M.S., 59 Ph.D. *Financial Assistance:* Internships and tuition waivers. *Other:* Students agree to live by the BYU Honor Code. *Master's Degrees Awarded 1993:* 5.

Utah State University. Department of Instructional Technology, Logan, UT 84322-2830. (801) 797-2694. Fax (801) 797-2693. Dr. Don C. Smellie, Prof., Head, Dept. of Instructional Technology. *Specializations:* M.S. and Ed.S. with concentrations in the areas of Instructional Development, Interactive Learning, Educational Technology, and Information Technology/School Library Media Administration. *Features:* Programs in Information Technology/School Library Media Administration and Master Resource Teacher/Educational Technology are also delivered via an electronic distance education system. *Admission Requirements:* 3.0 GPA, successful teaching experience or its equivalent, a verbal and quantitative score at the 40th percentile on the GRE, three written recommendations. *Minimum Degree Requirements:* M.S.—60 quarter hours, including 45 in media; thesis or project option. Ed.S.—45 quarter hours if M.S. is in the field, 60 hours if it is not. *Faculty:* 9 full-time; 7 part-time. *Students:* 52 full-time; 68 part-time (in graduate program). *Financial Assistance:* Fellowships and assistantships. *Master's Degrees Awarded 1994:* Data not reported.

VIRGINIA

*Radford University. Educational Studies Department, College of Education, P.O. Box 6959, Radford, VA 24142. (703) 831-5302. Fax (703) 831-6053. Dr. Richard A. Buck, Human Services Dept. *Specialization:* M.S. in Educational Media. *Minimum Degree Requirements:* 33 semester hours; thesis optional; practicum required. *Faculty:* 3 full-time; 2 part-time. *Students:* 4 full-time; 29 part-time. *Financial Assistance:* Graduate assistantships available. *Master's Degrees Awarded 1 July 1992-30 June 1993:* 7.

*University of Virginia. Curry School of Education, Ruffner Hall, Charlottesville, VA 22903. (804) 924-0834. Fax (804) 924-7987. E-mail jbb2s@curry.edschool.virginia.edu. Dr. John D. Bunch, Assoc. Prof., Coord., Instructional Technology Prog., Dept. of Educational Studies. *Specializations:* M.Ed., Ed.S. (Educational Specialist), Ph.D. and Ed.D. degrees offered, with focal areas in Media Production, Interactive Multimedia, and K-12 Educational Technologies. *Minimum Degree Requirements:* For specific degree requirements, write to the address above or refer to the UVA *Graduate Record*. *Faculty:* 3 full-time. *Degrees Awarded 1 July 1992-30 June 1993:* 4 master's, 2 Ed. Specialist, 3 doctoral.

*Virginia Commonwealth University. Division of Teacher Education, Richmond, VA 23284-2020. (804) 828-1945. Fax (804) 828-1323. E-mail sjohnson@edunet.soe.vcu.edu. Dr. Sheary D. Johnson, Asst. Prof., Core Coord. of Instructional Technology, Dept. of Teacher Education. *Specialization:* Master's Degree in Curriculum and Instruction with a specialization in Library Media. *Minimum Degree Requirements:* 36 semester hours; internship (field experience); externship (project or research study); comprehensive examination. *Faculty:* 2 full-time. *Students:* 40 part-time. *Financial Assistance:* Graduate assistantship in School of Education. *Master's Degrees Awarded 1 July 1992-30 July 1993:* 4.

Virginia Polytechnic Institute and State University (Virginia Tech). College of Education, Blacksburg, VA 24061-0313. (703) 231-5598. Fax (703) 231-9075. Terry M. Wildman, Prof., Prog. Area Leader, Instructional Systems Development, Curriculum and Instruction. *Specializations:* M.S. in Instructional Technology, with emphasis on Training and Development, Educational Computing, Evaluation, and Media Management. *Features:* Facilities include 70-computer laboratory (IBM, Macintosh), interactive video, speech synthesis, telecommunications. *Minimum Degree Requirements:* 30 semester hours, including 15 in Instructional Technology; thesis optional. *Faculty:* 8 full-time; 5 part-time. *Students:* 8 full-time; 15 part-time. *Financial Assistance:* Assistantships are sometimes available, as well as opportunities with other agencies. *Master's Degrees Awarded 1994:* Data not reported. An advanced certificate program is available.

Virginia State University. School of Liberal Arts & Education, Petersburg, VA 23806. (804) 524-5937. Vykuntapathi Thota, Acting Chair and Prog. Dir., Dept. of Educational Leadership. *Specializations:* M.S., M.Ed. in Educational Media and Technology. *Features:* Video Conferencing Center and PLATO Laboratory, internship in ABC and NBC channels. *Minimum Degree Requirements:* 30 semester hours plus thesis for M.S.; 33 semester hours plus project for M.Ed.; comprehensive examination. *Faculty:* 1 full-time; 2 part-time. *Students:* 5

full-time; 41 part-time. *Financial Assistance:* Scholarships through the School of Graduate Studies. *Master's Degrees Awarded 1994:* 5.

WASHINGTON

University of Washington. Department of Education, Seattle, WA 98195. (206) 543-6636. Fax (206) 543-8439. E-mail stkerr@u.washington.edu. Stephen T. Kerr, Prof. of Education, Prog. in Educational Communication and Technology, School of Education. *Specialization:* Master's degree. *Minimum Degree Requirements:* 45 quarter hours, including 24 in media; thesis optional. *Faculty:* 2 full-time. *Master's Degrees Awarded 1994:* 10.

Western Washington University. Woodring College of Education, Bellingham, WA 98225-9087. (206) 676-3381. Tony Jongejan, Assoc. Prof., Instructional Technology Prog., Dept. of Educational Administration and Foundations. *Specializations:* M.Ed. for Curriculum and Instruction, with emphasis in Instructional Technology, elementary and secondary programs; Adult Education; Master's Degree with emphasis on Instructional Design and Multimedia Development for education and industry persons; and Learning Resources (Library Science) for K-12 school librarians only. *Minimum Degree Requirements:* 48-52 quarter hours (24-28 hours in instructional technology, 24 hours in education-related courses, thesis required; internship and practicum possible. *Financial Assistance:* Standard financial assistance for graduate students, some special assistance for minority graduate students. *Faculty:* 4 full-time; 8 part-time. *Students:* 5 full-time, 18 part-time. *Master's Degrees Awarded 1994:* Data not reported.

WISCONSIN

*University of Wisconsin-La Crosse. Educational Media Program, Rm. 109, Morris Hall, La Crosse, WI 54601. (608) 785-8121. Fax (608) 785-8119. Dr. Russell Phillips, Dir., Educational Media Prog., College of Education. *Specializations:* M.S. in Educational Media with specializations in Initial Instructional Library Specialist, License 901; Instructional Library Media Specialist, License 902 (39 credits); Instructional Technology Specialist, License 903; or Instructional Library Media Supervisor (contact director). *Minimum Degree Requirements:* 30 semester hours, including 15 in media; no thesis. *Faculty:* 2 full-time; 4 part-time. *Students:* 21. *Financial Assistance:* Guaranteed student loans, graduate assistantships. *Master's Degrees Awarded 1993:* 11.

*University of Wisconsin-Madison. School of Education, 225 North Mills St., Madison, WI 53706. (608) 263-4670. Fax (608) 263-9992. Michael Streibel, Prof., Dept. of Curriculum and Instruction. *Specializations:* Ph.D. programs to prepare college and university faculty; master's degree. *Faculty:* 3 full-time; 1 part-time. *Students:* 23 Ph.D., 27 M.S. *Financial Assistance:* A few stipends of approximately $1,000/mo. for 20 hours of work per week; other media jobs are also available. *Master's Degrees Awarded 1993:* Data not reported. For additional information, see listing in Doctoral Programs.

*University of Wisconsin-Oshkosh. College of Education and Human Services, 800 Algoma Blvd., Oshkosh, WI 54901-8666. (414) 424-1490. Richard R. Hammes, Prof., Chair, Dept. of Human Services and Professional Leadership. *Specialization:* M.S. in Educational Leadership with special emphasis in Library/Media. *Minimum Degree Requirements:* 36 semester hours; thesis optional. *Faculty:* 7. *Students:* Approx. 30. *Financial Assistance:* Limited graduate assistantships. *Master's Degrees Awarded 1993:* 8.

University of Wisconsin-Stout. Menomonie, WI 54751. (715) 232-1202. Fax (715) 232-1441. E-mail hartzr@uwstout.edu. Dr. Roger L. Hartz, Prog. Dir., Media Technology Prog. This program has been discontinued.

WYOMING

**University of Wyoming. Div. of Life Long Learning and Instruction, College of Education, Box 3374, Laramie, WY 82071-3374. (307) 766-3608. Fax (307) 766-6668. E-mail johncoc@uwyo.edu. Dr. John Cochenour, Head, Dept. of Instructional Technology. *Specialization:* M.S. in Instructional Technology. *Admission Requirements:* Bachelor's degree; undergraduate GPA of at least 3.0; GRE minimum score 900; TOEFL Exam score 25. *Minimum Degree Requirements:* 36 semester credits; required thesis or project paper worth 4 credits. *Faculty:* 3 full-time; 1 part-time. *Students:* Data not reported. *Financial Assistance:* Data not reported. *Master's Degrees Awarded 1994:* Data not reported.

Graduate Programs in Educational Computing

When the directory of graduate programs in educational computing first appeared in the *1986 EMTY*, there were 50 programs. This year's listing consists of 43 such programs in 23 states, down from the 1993 total of 71 programs in 31 states, the District of Columbia, and the Virgin Islands. The information in this section has been revised and updates the information assembled in *EMTY 1994*. Individuals who are considering graduate study in educational computing should contact the institution of their choice for current information. It should be noted that some programs that appear in this listing also appear in the listings of master's and six-year programs and doctoral programs.

Copies of the entries from the 1994 *EMTY* were sent to the programs with a request for updated information and/or corrections, with the proviso that, if no response was received and the information in the 1994 edition was not current, the entry would be dropped. Programs from which a response was received in 1993 but not in 1994 are indicated with an asterisk (*). It should be noted that not all of the information in these descriptions is necessarily correct for the current year.

We would like to express our appreciation to the 21 program administrators who complied with our request for the 1994 edition. Of the remaining programs, 23 had been updated in the 1994 edition; 11 have been dropped for lack of response since 1993 or before. Our special thanks go to those who notified us of the status of programs that have been discontinued.

Data in this section include as much of the following information as was provided to us: the name of the institution and the program, telephone and fax numbers, e-mail addresses, a contact person, the degree(s) offered, admission requirements, minimum requirements for each degree, the number of faculty, the number of students currently enrolled, information on financial assistance, and the number of degrees awarded.

This section is arranged alphabetically by state and name of institution.

ARIZONA

Arizona State University. Educational Media and Computers, Box 870111, Tempe, AZ 85287-0111. Dr. Gary Bitter, Coord., Educational Media and Computers. (602) 965-7192. Fax (602) 965-7058. E-mail aogbb@asuvm.inre.asu.edu. *Specializations:* M.A. and Ph.D. in Educational Media and Computers. Master's program started in 1971 and doctorate started in 1976. *Features:* A three semester hour course in Instructional Media Design is offered via CD-ROM/Internet (Internet access is through Home Page). *Minimum Degree Requirements:* Master's—33 semester hours (21 hours in educational media and computers, 9 hours in education, 3 hours outside education); thesis not required; internship, comprehensive exam, and practicum required. Doctorate—93 semester hours (24 hours in educational media and computers, 57 hours in education, 12 hours outside education); thesis, internship, and practicum required. *Admission Requirements:* MAT/TOEFL. *Faculty:* 7 full-time; 6 part-time. *Students:* M.A., 121 full-time; 32 part-time. Ph.D., 17 full-time; 8 part-time. *Financial*

Assistance: Graduate assistantships, grants, student loans. *Degrees Awarded 1994:* M.A., 46; Ph.D., 3.

CALIFORNIA

California State University-Dominguez Hills. 1000 E. VIctoria St., Carson, CA 90747. (310) 516-3524. Fax (310) 516-3518. E-mail pdesberg@dhva20.csudh.edu. Peter Desberg, Prof., Coord., Computer-Based Education Program. *Specializations:* M.A. and Certificate in Computer-Based Education. *Admission Requirements:* 2.75 GPA. *Minimum Degree Requirements:* 30 semester hours including a master's project; 15 hours for the certificate. *Faculty:* 2 full-time; 2 part-time. *Students:* 50 full-time; 40 part-time. *Degrees Awarded 1994:* M.A., 20. An advanced certificate program is available.

CONNECTICUT

Fairfield University. Graduate School of Education and Allied Professions, Fairfield, CT 06430. (203) 254-4000, ext. 2697. Fax (203) 254-4087. Dr. Ibrahim Hefzallah, Prof. of Educational Technology; Dr. John J. Schurdak, Assoc. Prof., Co-Directors, Computers in Education/Educational Technology Program. *Specializations:* M.A. in two tracks: (1) Computers in Education, or (2) Media/Educational Technology (for school media specialists, see listing of Master's Programs). *Features:* Emphasis on theory, practice, and new instructional developments in computers in education, multimedia, and satellite communications. *Admission Requirements:* Bachelor's degree from an accredited institution, minimum 2.67 GPA. *Minimum Degree Requirements:* 33 semester credits, average B grade. *Faculty:* 1 full-time; 5 part-time. *Students:* 4 full-time; 60 part-time. *Financial Assistance:* Graduate assistantships, scholarships, student loans. *Degrees Awarded 1994:* Data not reported.

FLORIDA

*Barry University. School of Education, 11300 N.E. Second Ave., Miami Shores, FL 33161. (305) 899-3608. Fax (305) 899-3630. E-mail levine@buvax.barry.edu. Sister Evelyn Piche, Dean, School of Education, and Joel S. Levine, Assoc. Prof. and Dir. of Computer Education Programs. *Specializations:* Master's and Education Specialist degrees in (1) Computer Science Education and (2) Computer Applications in Education. *Minimum Degree Requirements:* Master's degree—36 semester credit hours including Directed Research; Education Specialist degree—36 semester hours including Directed Research and Seminar on Computer-Based Technology in Education. *Faculty:* 5 full-time; 18 part-time. *Students:* 95. *Financial Assistance:* Assistantships, discounts to educators. *Master's Degrees Awarded 1 July 1992-30 June 1993:* 52.

*Florida Institute of Technology. Science Education Department, 150 University Blvd., Melbourne, FL 32901-6988. (407) 768-8000, ext. 8126. Fax (407) 768-8000 ext. 7598. E-mail fronk@sci-ed.fit.edu. Dr. Robert Fronk, Dept. Head. *Specialization:* Master's degree options in Computer Education and in Instructional Technology; Ph.D. degree options in Computer Education and in Instructional Technology. *Admission Requirements:* GPA 3.0 for regular admission; 2.75 for provisional admission. *Minimum Degree Requirements:* Master's—48 quarter hours (18 in computer, 18 in education, 12 outside education); no thesis or internship required; practicum required. *Faculty:* 6 full-time. *Students:* 10 full-time; 9 part-time. *Financial*

Assistance: Graduate student assistantships (full tuition plus stipend) available. *Degrees Awarded in 1993:* Master's, 5; Ph.D., 3.

*Jacksonville University. Department of Education, 2800 University Blvd. N., Jacksonville, FL 32211. (904) 744-3950. Dr. Daryle C. May, Dir., Teacher Education and M.A.T. Prog. *Specialization:* M.A. in Teaching in Computer Education. Master's program started in 1983. *Minimum Degree Requirements:* 36 semester hours (21 hours in computer, 15 hours in education, 0 hours outside education); no thesis, internship, or practicum required; comprehensive exam required. *Faculty:* 5 full-time; 2 part-time. *Students:* 10. *Financial Assistance:* 40 percent scholarship to all local teachers. *Degrees Awarded 1993:* Master's, 10.

GEORGIA

*Georgia State University. MSEIT Dept., Atlanta, GA 30303. (404) 651-2510. Fax (404) 651-2546. Dr. Skip Atkinson, Prof. *Specializations:* M.A. and Ph.D. in Instructional Technology. *Minimum Degree Requirements:* Master's—60 quarter hours (25 hours in computers, 35 hours in education); thesis required; no internship or practicum is required. Doctorate—90 quarter hours (35 hours in computers, 40 hours in education, 15 hours outside education); thesis required; no internship or practicum is required. *Faculty:* 3. *Students:* 50. *Degrees Awarded 1993:* M.A., 12; Ph.D., 5.

University of Georgia. College of Education, Athens, GA 30602-7144. (706) 542-3810. Fax (706) 542-4072. E-mail kgustafs@moe.coe.uga.edu. Dr. Kent L.Gustafson, Prof. and Chair, Dept. of Instructional Technology. *Specialization:* M.Ed. in Computer-Based Education. *Minimum Degree Requirements:* 60 quarter credit hours (25 hours in computers, 10 hours in education, 25 hours not specified [55 hours with applied project]); thesis not required; internship and practicum optional. *Faculty:* 11 full-time. *Students:* 16. *Degrees Awarded 1994:* Data not reported.

HAWAII

*University of Hawaii-Manoa. Educational Technology Department, 1776 University Ave., Honolulu, HI 96822. (808) 956-7671. Fax (808) 956-3905. Dr. Geoffrey Z. Kucera, Prof. and Chair, Educational Technology Dept. *Specializations:* M.Ed. in Educational Technology. Specialization in Computer Technology has three options: (a) Computer-Based Learning, (b) Courseware Development, and (c) Information Center Management. Program began in 1983. *Admission Requirements:* GPA 3.0, GRE min. 50th percentile standing. *Minimum Degree Requirements:* 39 semester credit hours (27 in computing, 6 in instructional design, 6 electives); thesis available; practicum and internship required. *Faculty:* 4 full-time; 3 part-time. *Students:* 5 full-time. *Degrees Awarded 1993:* M.Ed., 6.

ILLINOIS

Concordia University. 7400 Augusta, River Forest, IL 60305-1499. (708) 209-3023. Fax (708) 209-3176. Dr. Manfred Boos, Chair, Mathematics/Computer Science Education Dept. *Specialization:* M.A. in Mathematics Education/Computer Science Education. Master's program started in 1987. *Admission Requirements:* GPA 2.85 or above, 2.25 to 2.85 provision status; bachelor's degree from regionally accredited institution; two letters of recommendation; GRE required in cases of inadequate evidence of academic proficiency. *Minimum Degree Requirements:* 48 quarter hours; no thesis, internship, or practicum required. *Faculty:* 6 full-time; 7 part-time. *Students:* 3 full-time; 43 part-time. *Financial Assistance:* A number of graduate assistantships; Stafford Student loans and Supplement Loan for Students. *Degrees Awarded 1994:* M.A., 8.

*Governors State University. College of Education, University Park, IL 60466. (708) 534-4380. Fax (708) 534-8451. E-mail j_meyer@acs.gsu.bgu.edu. Dr. John Meyer, University Prof. *Specialization:* M.A. in Education (with Computer Education as specialization). Master's program started in 1986. *Minimum Degree Requirements:* 36-39 semester hours (15 hours in computer, 21-24 hours in education, 0 hours outside education); thesis/project and practicum required; internship not required. *Faculty:* 2 full-time; 7 part-time. *Students:* 46. *Degrees Awarded 1993:* M.A., 11.

Northern Illinois University. Instructional Technology Faculty, LEPS Department, DeKalb, IL 60115. (815) 753-0464. Fax (815) 753-9371. Dr. Gary L. McConeghy, Chair, Instructional Technology Faculty. *Specialization:* M.S.Ed. in Instructional Technology with a concentration in Microcomputers in School-Based Settings. Master's program started in 1968. *Admission Requirements:* GPA 2.75; GRE 800 combined scores; two references. *Minimum Degree Requirements:* 39 hours (27 hours in technology, 9 hours in education, 0 hours outside education); no thesis, internship, or practicum is required. *Faculty:* 8 full-time; 3 part-time. *Students:* 106 part-time. *Financial Assistance:* Some assistantships available at various departments on campus. *Degrees Awarded 1994:* M.S.Ed., 32. See also the listing of Master's Programs.

INDIANA

Purdue University. School of Education, Department of Curriculum and Instruction, West Lafayette, IN 47907-1442. (317) 494-5673. Fax (317) 494-0587. Dr. James Russell, Prof., Educational Computing and Instructional Development. *Specializations:* M.S., Ed.S., and Ph.D. in Educational Computing and Instructional Development. Master's program started in 1982 and specialist and doctoral in 1985. *Admission Requirements:* GPA of 3.0 or better; three letters of recommendation; statement of personal goals; total score of 1,000 or more on GRE for Ph.D. admission. *Minimum Degree Requirements:* Master's—36 semester hours (15 in computer or instructional development, 9 in education, 12 unspecified); thesis optional. Specialist—60-65 semester hours (15-18 in computer or instructional development, 30-35 in education); thesis, internship, and practicum required. Doctorate—90 semester hours (15-18 in computer or instructional development, 42-45 in education); thesis, internship, and practicum required. *Faculty:* 6 full-time. *Students:* M.S./Ed.S., 10 full-time, 20 part-time; Ph.D., 12 full-time, 31 part-time. *Financial Assistance:* Assistantships and fellowships. *Degrees Awarded 1994:* Ph.D., 8; master's, 14. See also listings in Doctoral and Master's Programs.

IOWA

Dubuque Tri-College Department of Education (a consortium of Clarke College, The University of Dubuque, and Loras College). Graduate Studies, 1550 Clarke Drive, Dubuque, IA 52001. (319) 588-6331. Fax (319) 588-6789. Robert Adams, Clarke College, (319) 588-6416. *Specializations:* M.A. in Technology and Education. *Admission Requirements:* Minimum GPA 2.5 on 4.0 scale; GRE (verbal and quantitative) or Miller Analogies Test;

application form and $25 application fee; and two letters of recommendation. *Minimum Degree Requirements:* 25 semester hours in computer courses, 12 hours in education. *Faculty:* 1 full-time; 1-2 part-time. *Students:* master's, 11 part-time. *Financial Assistance:* Scholarships, student loans. *Degrees Awarded 1994:* master's, 0 (newly revised program).

Iowa State University. College of Education, Ames, IA 50011. (515) 294-6840. E-mail mrs@iastate.edu. Dr. Michael R. Simonson, Prof. *Specializations:* M.S., M.Ed., and Ph.D. in Curriculum and Instructional Technology with specializations in Instructional Computing, Instructional Design, and Distance Education. Master's and doctoral programs started in 1967. Participates in Clova Distance Education Alliance: Clova Star Schools Project. *Admission Requirements:* M.S. and M.Ed., three letters; top half of undergraduate class; autobiography. Ph.D., the same plus GRE. *Minimum Degree Requirements:* Master's—30 semester hours; thesis required; no internship or practicum is required. Doctorate—78 semester hours, thesis required; no internship or practicum is required. *Faculty:* 3 full-time; 5 part-time. *Students:* 20 full-time; 20 part-time. *Financial Assistance:* 10 assistantships. *Degrees Awarded 1994:* Data not reported.

*Teikyo Marycrest University. Department of Computer Science and Mathematics, 1607 W. 12th St., Davenport, IA 52804. (319) 326-9252. Fax (319) 326-9250. Mark McGinn, Dept. Head. *Specialization:* M.S. in Computer Science. *Admission Requirements:* Bachelor's degree in Computer Science from an accredited institution, or complete all preparatory courses *and* have a working knowledge of an assembly language, Pascal, and at least one other high-level programming language. *Minimum Degree Requirements:* 27 graduate semester hours plus 6 hours thesis; 36 graduate semester hours non-thesis. *Faculty:* 5 full time. *Students:* Data not available. *Degrees Awarded in 1993:* M.S., 5.

KANSAS

Kansas State University. Educational Computing, Design, and Telecommunications, 363 Bluemont Hall, Manhattan, KS 66506. (913) 532-7686. Fax (913) 532-7304. E-mail dmcgrath@ksuvm.bitnet. Dr. Diane McGrath, contact person. *Specializations:* M.S. in Secondary Education with an emphasis in Educational Computing; Ph.D. and Ed.D. in Curriculum & Instruction with an emphasis in Educational Computing, Design, and Telecommunications. Master's program started in 1982; doctoral in 1987. *Admission Requirements:* M.S.—B average in undergraduate work; one programming language; TOEFL score of 590 or above. Ph.D./Ed.D.—B average in undergraduate and graduate work; one programming language, GRE or MAT; three letters of recommendation. *Minimum Degree Requirements:* M.S.—30 semester hours (minimum of 12 in Educational Computing); thesis, internship, or practicum not required, but all three are possible. Ph.D.—90 semester hours (minimum of 21 hours in Educational Computing, Design, and Telecommunications or related area approved by committee; 30 hours for dissertation research); thesis required; internship and practicum not required but available. Ed.D.—94 semester hours (minimum of 18 hours in Educational Computing or related area approved by committee; 16 hours for dissertation research; 12 hours of internship); thesis required. *Faculty:* 2.5 full-time. *Students:* 35 M.S., 35 doctoral. *Financial Assistance:* Some assistantships available. *Degrees Awarded 1994:* Ph.D., 3; M.S., 7.

MARYLAND

*The Johns Hopkins University. 2500 E. Northern Parkway, Baltimore, MD 21214. (410) 516-0006. Fax (410) 646-2310. E-mail jnunn@jhunix.hcs.jhu.edu. Dr. Jacqueline A. Nunn, Center for Technology in Education. *Specialization:* M.S. in Education with a concentration in Technology. *Minimum Degree Requirements:* 36 semester hours, 8 required courses in computer-related technology and media, with remaining courses being electives in other education areas. *Faculty:* 2 full-time; 8 part-time. *Degrees Awarded 1993:* M.S., 12.

MASSACHUSETTS

*Fitchburg State College. Division of Graduate and Continuing Education, 10 Pearl St., Fitchburg, MA 01420-2697. (508) 665-3260. Fax (508) 665-3043. Dr. Elena Kyle, Communications/Media Dept. *Specialization:* M.S. in Communications/Media Management. *Admission Requirements:* Bachelor's degree; undergraduate GPA of at least 2.5; Miller Analogy Test score. *Minimum Degree Requirements:* 36 semester credits; required thesis worth 6 credits. *Faculty:* 4 part-time. *Students:* Data not reported. *Financial Assistance:* Data not reported. *Master's Degrees Awarded 1994:* Data not reported.

Lesley College. 29 Everett St., Cambridge, MA 02138-2790. (617) 349-8419. Dr. Nancy Roberts, Prof. of Education. *Specializations:* M.A. in Computers in Education; C.A.G.S. in Computers in Education; Ph.D in Education with a Computers in Education major. Master's program started in 1980. Master's degree program is offered off-campus at 22 sites in 10 states; contact Professional Outreach Associates [(800) 843-4808] for information. *Minimum Degree Requirements:* Master's—33 semester hours in computers (number of hours in education and outside education not specified); integrative final project in lieu of thesis; no internship or practicum is required. Specialist—36 semester hours (hours in computers, education, and outside education not specified); thesis, internship, practicum not specified. Ph.D. requirements available on request. *Faculty:* 5 full-time; 90 part-time on the master's and specialist levels. *Students:* 440 on master's level; 5 on specialist level. *Degrees Awarded 1994:* Data not reported.

*University of Massachusetts-Lowell. College of Education, One University Ave., Lowell, MA 01854. (508) 934-4621. Fax (508) 934-3005. E-mail lebaronj@woods.uml.edu. Dr. John LeBaron, Assoc. Prof., College of Education. *Specializations:* M.Ed. in Curriculum and Instruction; C.A.G.S. in Curriculum and Instruction; Ed.D. in Leadership in Schooling. (Note: Technology and Learning Environments is a component of each of the programs.) Master's, specialist, and doctoral programs started in 1984. *Admission Requirements:* M.Ed.— undergraduate degree from accredited college or university with a minimum GPA of 2.75 on a 4.0 scale; Miller Analogies Test or GRE. C.A.G.S. and Ed.D.—master's degree from an accredited college or university with a minimum GPA of 3.00 on a 4.0 scale; Miller Analogies Test or GRE. *Minimum Degree Requirements:* Master's—33 semester hours (hours in computers, education, and outside education not specified); no thesis or internship is required; practicum required. Doctorate—60 semester hours beyond master's plus dissertation (hours in computers, education, and outside education not specified); thesis, residency, and comprehensive examination required. *Faculty:* 20 full-time; 16 part-time. *Students:* (professional education graduate programs) 121 full-time; 362 part-time. *Financial Assistance:* Limited assistantships available. *Degrees Awarded 1993:* Doctoral, 11; master's and CAGS, 138.

MICHIGAN

*University of Michigan. Educational Studies, Ann Arbor, MI 48109. (313) 763-0612. Fax (313) 763-1229. Patricia Baggett, Assoc. Prof. *Specialization:* Master's degree in Computers in Education. *Minimum Degree Requirements:* 30 trimester credit hours. *Faculty:* 1 full-time; 7 part-time. *Students:* Data not reported. *Degrees Awarded in 1993:* Master's, 4.

MINNESOTA

*University of Minnesota. 130 Peik Hall, 159 Pillsbury Dr. SE, Minneapolis, MN 55455. (612) 625-0534. Fax (612) 624-8277. simon@maroon.tc.umn.edu. Simon Hoodge, Dept. of Curriculum and Instruction. *Specialization:* M.Ed. or M.A. *Admission Requirements:* Bachelor's degree; undergraduate GPA of at least 3.0; Miller Analogy Test score for M.A. only; TOEFL Exam minimum score 550. *Minimum Degree Requirements:* 45 quarter hours; thesis worth 4 credits required for M.A. *Faculty:* 5 full-time. *Students:* Data not reported. *Financial Assistance:* Data not reported. *Master's Degrees Awarded 1994:* Data not reported.

MISSOURI

*Fontbonne College. 6800 Wydown Blvd., St. Louis, MO 63105. (314) 862-3456. Dr. Mary K. Abkemeier, Master of Science in Computer Education. *Specializations:* M.S. in Computer Education. Master's program started in 1986. *Admission Requirements:* B.S. from accredited school; three letters of recommendation; GPA 2.5 or master's degree. *Minimum Degree Requirements:* 33 semester hours. *Faculty:* 3 full-time; 7 part-time. *Students:* 110 part-time. *Financial Assistance:* Title II funding for St. Louis City full-time school teachers. *Degrees Awarded 1993:* M.S., 14.

*Northwest Missouri State University. Department of Computer Science, 800 University Ave., Maryville, MO 64468-6001. (816) 562-1600. Fax (816) 562-1484. E-mail 0100205@northwest.missouri.edu. Dr. Phillip J. Heeler, Chair, Dept. of Computer Science. *Specializations:* M.S. in School Computer Studies; M.S.Ed. in Educational Uses of Computers; M.S.Ed. in Using Computers in Specific Disciplines. *Admission Requirements:* GRE General Exam, writing samples. *Minimum Degree Requirements:* 32 semester hours for each of the three master's degree programs. The first includes 26 credit hours of core computer courses; the second includes 14 credit hours of core computer courses and 12 hours of educational courses; and the third requires 7 hours of core computer courses, 12 hours of education courses, and 7 hours in technology-related areas. *Faculty:* 7 full-time; 1 part-time. *Students:* 10. *Financial Assistance:* Graduate assistant appointments. *Degrees Awarded 1993:* Master's, 10.

NEW YORK

*Buffalo State College. 1300 Elmwood Ave., Buffalo, NY 14222-1095. (716) 878-4923. Dr. Thomas G. Kinsey, Coord. of M.S. in Education in Educational Computing. *Specializations:* M.S. in Ed. in Educational Computing. Master's program started in 1988. *Minimum Degree Requirements:* 33 semester hours (18 hours in computers, 12-15 hours in education, 0 hours outside education); thesis or project required; no internship or practicum is required. *Faculty:* 10 part-time. *Students:* 75. *Degrees Awarded 1993:* Master's, 11.

*Iona College. 715 North Ave. NW, New Rochelle, NY 10801. (914) 633-2578. Robert Schiaffino, Asst. Prof. and Coord., Educational Computing Prog. *Specializations:* M.S. in Educational Computing. Master's program started in 1982. *Admission Requirements:* GPA 3.0 or better. *Minimum Degree Requirements:* 36 hours—trimester basis ("all hours listed in educational computing"). *Faculty:* 6 full-time; 8 part-time. *Students:* Data not reported. *Financial Assistance:* Federal student loan programs, veterans' benefits, various scholarships, graduate assistantships, work-study programs. *Degrees Awarded 1993:* M.S., 10.

Pace University. Department of Educational Administration, 1 Martine Ave., White Plains, NY 10606. (914) 422-4198. Fax (914) 422-4311. Dr. Lawrence Roder, Chair. *Specialization:* M.S. in Curriculum and Instruction with a concentration in Computers and Education. Master's program started in 1986. *Admission Requirements:* GPA 3.0; interview; application. *Minimum Degree Requirements:* 33 semester hours (15 hours in computers, 18 hours in educational administration). *Faculty:* 2 full-time; 12 part-time. *Students:* 60. *Financial Assistance:* Assistance is available. *Degrees Awarded June 1992-June 1994:* M.S., 75.

State University College of Arts and Science at Potsdam. 204 Satterlee Hall, Potsdam, NY 13676. (315) 267-2527. Fax (315) 267-2771. E-mail lichtnc@snypotvx.bitnet. Dr. Norman Licht, Prof. of Education. *Specializations:* M.S. in Education, Instructional Technology, and Media Management with Educational Computing concentration. Master's program started in 1981. *Minimum Degree Requirements:* 33 semester hours (15 hours in computers, 18 hours in education, 0 hours outside education); thesis not required; internship or practicum required. *Faculty:* 6 full-time; 4 part-time. *Students:* 135. *Degrees Awarded 1994:* M.S., 37.

*State University of New York at Stony Brook. Department of Technology and Society, 210 Old Engineering Bldg., Stony Brook, NY 11794-2250. (516) 632-8763. Fax (516) 632-8205. E-mail dferguson@ccmail.sunysb.edu. David L. Ferguson, Assoc. Prof. *Specializations:* M.S. in Technology and Systems Management with concentration in Educational Computing. *Admission Requirements:* Bachelor's degree; undergraduate GPA of at least 2.75; GRE score 500; TOEFL Exam minimum score 550. *Minimum Degree Requirements:* 30 semester hours; required master's project worth 3 credits. *Faculty:* 10 full-time. *Students:* 20. *Financial Assistance:* Teaching or research assistantships. *Degrees Awarded 1993:* M.S., 10.

NORTH CAROLINA

Appalachian State University. Department of Library Science and Educational Foundations, Boone, NC 28608. (704) 262-2243. E-mail tashnerjh@alf.appstate.edu. Dr. John H. Tashner. *Specialization:* M.A. in Educational Media (Instructional Technology-Computers). Master's program started in 1986. *Features:* IMPACT NC (Business/University/Public School) Partnership offers unusual opportunities. *Minimum Degree Requirements:* 36 semester hours; thesis optional; internship required. *Admission Requirements:* Selective. *Faculty:* 2 full-time; 1 part-time. *Students:* M.A., 8 full-time; 15 part-time. *Financial Assistance:* Assistantships, grants, student loans. *Degrees Awarded 1994:* M.A., 1.

North Carolina State University. Department of Curriculum and Instruction, P.O. Box 7801, Raleigh, NC 27695-7801. (919) 515-1779. E-mail esvasu@unity.ncsu.edu. Dr. Ellen Vasu, Assoc. Prof., Dept. of Curriculum and Instruction. *Specializations:* M.Ed. and M.S. in Instructional Technology-Computers (program track within one master's in Curriculum and Instruction). Master's program started in 1986. *Minimum Degree Requirements:* 36 semester hours; thesis optional; practicum required. *Faculty:* Data not reported. *Students:* M.Ed., 10 part-time; doctoral, 6 part-time. *Financial Assistance:* Data not reported. *Degrees Awarded 1994:* Data not reported.

*Western Carolina University. Cullowhee, NC 28723. (704) 227-7415. Dr. Don Chalker, Head, Dept. of Administration, Curriculum and Instruction. *Specializations:* M.A.Ed. in Supervision, with concentration in Educational Technology-Computers. Master's program started in 1987. *Minimum Degree Requirements:* 41 semester hours (18 hours in computers, 20 hours in education, 3 hours outside education); internship required. *Faculty:* 25-plus full-time. *Students:* 13.

NORTH DAKOTA

*Minot State University. 500 University Ave. W., Minot, ND 58707. (701) 857-3817. Fax (701) 839-6933. Dr. James Croonquist, Dean, Graduate School. *Specializations:* M.S. in Audiology, M.S. in Education of the Deaf, M.S. in Elementary Education, M.S. in Learning Disabilities, M.S. in Special Education, M.S. in Speech-Language Pathology, M.A.T. in Mathematics, M.S. in Criminal Justice, M.A.T. in Science, M.M.E. in Music, M.S. in School Psychology. Master's program started in 1964. *Admission Requirements:* Application with $20 fee, three letters of recommendation, 300-word autobiography, transcripts. *Minimum Degree Requirements:* 45 quarter hours (hours in computers, education, and outside education vary according to program). *Faculty:* 84 full-time; 26 part-time. *Students:* 142. *Financial Assistance:* Loans, teaching assistantships, research assistantships, tuition waivers, scholarships. *Degrees Awarded 1993:* Master's, 65.

OHIO

*Wright State University. College of Education and Human Services, 244 Millett Hall, Dayton, OH 45435. (513) 873-2509 or (513) 873-2182. Fax (513) 873-3301. Dr. Bonnie K. Mathies, Chair, Dept. of Educational Technology, Vocational Education, and Allied Programs. *Specializations:* M.Ed. in Computer Education; M.Ed. for Computer Coordinator; M.A. in Computer Education. Master's programs started in 1985. *Admission Requirements:* 2.7 GPA for regular admission; GRE or Miller Analogies Test. *Minimum Degree Requirements:* 48 quarter hours (hours in computers, education, and outside education not specified); thesis required for M.A. degree only; comprehensive examination in the form of the completion of a portfolio and a videotaped presentation to the faculty for M.Ed.; eligible for Supervisor's Certificate after completion of C&S; Computer Coordinator program. *Faculty:* 2 full-time; 9 part-time adjuncts and other university full-time faculty and staff. *Students:* 2 full-time; 31 part-time. *Financial Assistance:* Graduate assistantships available, including three positions in the College's Educational Resource Center; limited number of small graduate scholarships. *Degrees Awarded 1993:* M.A. and M.Ed., 11.

OKLAHOMA

The University of Oklahoma. Department of Educational Psychology, 820 Van Vleet Oval, Norman, OK 73019. (405) 325-1521. Fax (405) 325-3242. E-mail tragan@aardvark.ucs. uoknor.edu. Dr. Tillman J. Ragan, Prof. *Specialization:* M.Ed. in Educational Technology with Computer Applications emphasis. For additional options in Educational Technology, see the listing for Master's Programs. *Admission Requirements:* 3.0 GPA over last 60 hours of undergraduate work or at least 12 credit hours of graduate work with a 3.0 GPA from an accredited college or university. *Minimum Degree Requirements:* 32 semester hours (12 hours in computers, 21 hours in instructional technology [including computers 12]); internship required. *Faculty:* 10 full-time; 2 part-time. *Students:* 5 full-time; 18 part-time. *Financial Assistance:* Assistantships; out-of-state fee waivers; graduate scholarships (both general and targeted minorities). *Degrees Awarded 1 July 1993-30 June 1994:* M.Ed., 8.

TEXAS

East Texas State University. Department of Secondary and Higher Education, East Texas Station, Commerce, TX 75429-3011. (903) 886-5607. Fax (903) 886-5603. E-mail mundayb@tenet.edu. Dr. Robert S. Munday, Prof., Head, Dept. of Secondary and Higher Education. *Specialization:* Master's degree in Learning Technology and Information Systems with emphasis on Educational Micro Computing, Educational Media and Technology, and Library and Information Science. *Admission Requirements:* 700 GRE. *Minimum Degree Requirements:* 30 semester hours with thesis, 36 without thesis. M.Ed. (Educational Computing), 30 hours in ed. tech.; M.S. (Educational Media and Technology), 21 hours in ed. tech.; M.S. (Library and Information Science), 15 hours in library/information science, 12 hours in ed. tech. *Faculty:* 3 full-time; 5 part-time. *Students:* 30 full-time; 150 part-time. *Financial Assistance:* Graduate assistantships in teaching, graduate assistantships in research, scholarships, federal aid program. *Master's Degrees Awarded 1994:* 20. A six-year program is available.

Texas Tech University. College of Education, Box 41071, TTU, Lubbock, TX 79409. (806) 742-2362. Fax (806) 742-2179. Dr. Robert Price, Dir., Instructional Technology. *Specializations:* M.Ed. in Instructional Technology (Educational Computing emphasis); Ed.D. in Instructional Technology. Master's program started in 1981; doctoral in 1982. *Features:* Program is NCATE accredited and follows ISTE and AECT guidelines. *Admission Requirements:* M.Ed., GRE score of 850 and GPA of 3.0 on last 30 hours of undergraduate program; Ed.D., GRE score of 1050; GPA of 3.0 on last 30 hours. *Minimum Degree Requirements:* Master's—39 hours (24 hours in computing, 15 hours in education or outside education); practicum required. Doctorate—87 hours (45 hours in educational technology, 18 hours in education, 15 hours in resource area or minor); practicum required. *Faculty:* 3 full-time; 1 part-time. *Students:* Approximately 30 FTE. *Financial Assistance:* Teaching and research assistantships available ($7,500/9 months). *Degrees Awarded 1994:* Ed.D., 2; M.Ed., 5.

VIRGINIA

*George Mason University. Center for Interactive Educational Technology, Mail Stop 4B3, 4400 University Dr., Fairfax, VA 22030-4444. (703) 993-2052. Fax (703) 993-2013. Dr. Charles S. White, Coord. of Instructional Technology Academic Programs. *Specializations:* M.Ed. in Instructional Technology with tracks in Instructional Design and Development, School-Based Technology Coordinator, Instructional Applications of Technology, Computer Science Educator; M.Ed. in Special Education Technology (S.E.T.); Ph.D. with specialization in Instructional Technology or Special Education Technology. Master's program started in 1983 and doctoral in 1984. *Admission Requirements:* Teaching or training experience; introductory programming course or equivalent; introductory course in educational technology or equivalent. *Minimum Degree Requirements:* M.Ed. in Instructional Technology, 36 hours;

practicum/internship/project required. M.Ed. in Special Education Technology, 36-42 hours. Ph.D., 56-62 hours beyond master's degree for either specialization. *Faculty:* 5 full-time; 5 part-time. *Students:* M.Ed.-I.T.—6 full-time; 36 part-time. M.Ed.-S.E.T.—10 full-time; 8 part-time. Ph.D.—10 part-time. *Financial Assistance:* Assistantships and tuition waivers available for full-time (9 credits) graduate students. *Degrees Awarded 1 July 1992-30 June 1993:* M.Ed.-I.T., 10; M.Ed.-S.E.T., 7; Ph.D., 3.

Hampton University. School of Liberal Arts and Education, 301 A Phenix Hall, Hampton, VA 23668. (804) 727-5751. Fax (804) 727-5084. Dr. JoAnn W. Haysbert, Prof. and Coord. of Graduate Programs in Education. This program will be phased out in 1996.

Virginia Polytechnic Institute and State University. Instructional Systems Development, College of Education, War Memorial Hall, Blacksburg, VA 24061-0313. (703) 231-5598. Fax (703) 231-9075. Terry M. Wildman, Prof., Prog. Area Leader, Instructional Systems Development, Curriculum and Instruction. *Specializations:* Ed.D. and Ph.D. programs in Instructional Technology. *Features:* Areas of emphasis are Instructional Design, Educational Computing, Evaluation, Media Management, Speech Synthesis, and Telecommunications. *Admission Requirements:* 3.3 GPA for master's degree; three letters of recommendation; transcripts of previous academic work. *Faculty:* 8 full-time; 5 part-time. *Students:* 6 full-time; 6 part-time. *Financial Assistance:* 10 assistantships; tuition scholarships; contracts with other agencies. *Degrees Awarded 1994:* Data not reported.

WASHINGTON

Eastern Washington University. Department Computer Science, Cheney, WA 99004-2495. (509) 359-7092. Fax (509) 359-2215. Internet dhorner@ewu.edu. Dr. Donald R. Horner, Prof. of Computer Science. *Specializations:* M.Ed. in Computer Education (elementary); M.Ed. in Computer Education (secondary); M.S. in Computer Education (Interdisciplinary). Master's program started in 1983. *Admission Requirements:* GRE, at least 3.0 GPA for last 90 quarter credits (60 semester credits). *Minimum Degree Requirements:* M.S., 52 quarter hours (30 hours in computers, 0 hours in education, 15 hours outside education—not specifically computer science; the hours do not total to 52 because of freedom to choose where Methods of Research is taken, where 12 credits of supporting courses are taken, and where additional electives are taken); thesis not required (a research project with formal report is required, although it need not be a thesis in format); internship and/or practicum not required. M.S., 52 quarter hours divided between computer science and another science or mathematics; one area is primary and includes a research project; the second area generally requires fewer hours than the primary. M.Ed., 48 quarter hours minimum (24 hours in computer science, 16 hours in education, 8 hours outside education). Most projects involve the use of high-level authoring systems to develop educational products. *Faculty:* 3 full-time. *Students:* About 35. *Financial Assistance:* Some research and teaching fellowships; financial assistance. *Degrees Awarded 1 July 1993-30 June 1994:* M.S. and M.Ed., 4.

Western Washington University. Woodring College of Education, Bellingham, WA 98225. (206) 650-3090. Fax (206) 650-6526. E-mail tonyj@henson.cc.wwu.edu. Dr. Tony Jongejan, Assoc. Prof. of Education. *Specializations:* M.Ed. in Instructional Technology with Elementary, Secondary, Administrative, or Adult Education emphasis. *Features:* Emphasis on interactive multimedia development. *Admission Requirements:* Graduate Record Examination; 3.0 GPA on last 45 credits; transcript of all college work; letters of recommendation. *Minimum Degree Requirements:* 48-52 quarter hours (24-48 hours in instructional technology,

24 hours in education); field project or thesis required. *Faculty:* 4 full-time; 8 part-time. *Students:* 5 full-time; 15 part-time. *Financial Assistance:* Work study, graduate assistantships, student loans. *Degrees Awarded 1994:* M.Ed., 12.

WISCONSIN

Edgewood College. Department of Education, 855 Woodrow St., Madison, WI 53711-1997. (608) 257-4861, ext. 2293. Fax (608) 257-1455. Internet schmied@edgewood.edu. Dr. Joseph E. Schmiedicke, Chair, Dept. of Education. *Specializations:* M.A. in Education with emphasis on Educational Computing and Educational Technology. Master's program started in 1987. *Features:* Classes conducted in laboratory setting with emphasis on applications and software. *Admission Requirements:* 2.75/4.0 GPA. *Minimum Degree Requirements:* 36 semester hours. *Faculty:* 2 full-time; 3 part-time. *Students:* 2 full-time; 130 part-time. *Financial Assistance:* Grants, student loans. *Degrees Awarded 1994:* M.A., 12.

Scholarships, Fellowships, and Awards

In the instructional technology/media-related fields, various scholarships, fellowships, and awards have been established. Many of these are available to those who either are or will be pursuing advanced degrees at the master's, six-year specialist, or doctoral levels.

Because various colleges, universities, professional organizations, and governmental agencies offer scholarships, fellowships, and awards and may wish to have them included in this section, it would be greatly appreciated if those aware of such financial awards would contact either the editors or the publisher for inclusion of such entries in the next edition of *EMTY*.

We are greatly indebted to the staff members of the Association for Educational Communications and Technology (AECT) for assisting with this section.

Information is furnished in the following sequence:

- Overview of AECT and ECT Foundation Awards

- AECT Awards

- ECT Foundation Awards

AECT AND ECT FOUNDATION AWARDS

The Association for Educational Communications and Technology recognizes and rewards the outstanding achievement of its members and associates through a program that provides for three major annual awards—Achievement, Special Service, and Distinguished Service—and through the ECT Foundation, which provides awards in the areas of leadership, scholarship, and research.

AECT encourages members and associates to apply for these awards, and to disseminate information about the awards to professional colleagues. Specific information about each award is available from the AECT national office. The annual deadline for submitting most award applications is October 15.

All ECT Foundation and AECT awards are presented during the AECT National Convention and InCITE Exposition.

For additional information on all awards, please contact:

AECT Awards Program
1025 Vermont Ave. NW
Suite 820
Washington, DC 20005
(202) 347-7834
Fax: (202) 347-7839
E-mail: aect@aect.org

AECT Service Awards

The Association for Educational Communications and Technology (AECT) provides for three annual awards:

Special Service Award: Granted to a person who has shown notable service to AECT as a whole or to one of its programs or divisions (nominee must have been a member of AECT for at least 10 years and must not be currently an AECT officer, board member, or member of the Awards Committee).

Distinguished Service Award: Granted to a person who has shown outstanding leadership in advancing the theory and/or practice of educational communications and technology over a substantial period of time (nominee need not be an AECT member but must not have received this award previously).

Annual Achievement Award: Honors the individual who during the past year has made the most significant contribution to the advancement of educational communications and technology (nominee need not be a member of AECT, and the award can be given to the same person more than once).

ECT Foundation Awards

The ECT Foundation, a nonprofit organization that carries out the purposes of AECT that are charitable and educational in nature, coordinates the following awards:

AECT National Convention Internship Program: Provides complimentary registration and housing at the annual conference plus a cash award for full-time graduate students (applicants must be a member of AECT and enrolled in a recognized program in educational communications and technology).

Richard B. Lewis Memorial Award: Presented to the outstanding school district media utilization program along with a cash award (awarded to either a public or private school having media utilization programs in place).

AECT Leadership Development Grant: Supports innovative leadership development activities undertaken by affiliates, divisions, or regions with one cash grant. (Special consideration will be given to proposals that demonstrate a commitment to leadership development, that propose programs unique to the applicant's organization, and that include activities of potential benefit to other AECT programs.)

AECT Memorial Scholarship Award: Donations given in memory of specific past leaders of the field provide a scholarship fund that gives annual cash grants to AECT members enrolled in educational technology graduate studies. Two scholarships will be awarded to graduate students enrolled in a master's or specialist's program to fund graduate study or research.

Dean and Sybil McClusky Research Award: Recognizes the year's outstanding doctoral thesis proposal that has been approved by the student's university and offers two cash awards to defray the research expenses.

Robert deKieffer International Fellowship Award: Recognizes a professional in educational communications and technology, at any level, from a foreign country who has demonstrated leadership in the field with a $200 cash prize and a plaque. The recipient must be a member of AECT who normally resides outside of the United States.

James W. Brown Publication Award: Recognizes the outstanding publication in the field of educational technology in any media format during the past year with a cash award (excluded from consideration are doctoral, master's, or other types of dissertations prepared in fulfillment of degree program requirements).

ECT Qualitative Research Award: Provides $1,000 for the best original, unpublished qualitative research investigation in the field of educational communications and technology by an individual. Qualitative theories and methods may be applied from areas such as cultural anthropology, history, social psychology, and sociology. In addition, the winner will receive the opportunity to present the paper at the AECT National Convention.

ETR&D Young Scholar Award: Recognizes a fresh, creative approach to research and theory in educational technology by a young scholar (applicant must be an individual who does not hold a doctorate degree or who has received a doctorate degree within the past five years).

Robert M. Gagné Instructional Development Research Award: Recognizes the most significant contribution by a graduate student to the body of knowledge on which instructional development is based with a cash prize (the research must have been done in the past three years while the candidate was enrolled as a graduate student).

McJulien Minority Scholarship Award: Recognizes a minority graduate student enrolled in an educational communications and technology program at the master's or doctoral level by providing a $500 cash grant plus a plaque. The recipient must be an AECT member.

Carl F. and Viola V. Mahnke Film Production Award: Honors excellence in message design with a $200 cash award for film, video, CD-ROM, or diskette product created by undergraduate or graduate students who are AECT members. Products must have been completed within a two-year period prior to the competition.

ECT Mentor Endowment Scholarship: One scholarship of $3,000 will be awarded to a graduate student in educational communications and technology for continued studies in the field. The scholarship may be used to assist the recipient to further his or her education at the doctoral level at any accredited college or university in the United States or Canada. Recipient must be a member of AECT and accepted in or enrolled in a graduate-level program.

ECT Mentor Endowment Professional Development Grant: Two professional development grants of $2,000. One grant is given in honor of the past presidents of AECT. The grants are intended for use by professionals in the field of educational communications and technology for the purpose of enhancing professional growth and leadership in a manner other than formal graduate study at a college or university. Applicants must be members of AECT and employed in some area of the field of educational communications and technology.

AECT Special Service Award

Qualifications

- Award is granted to a person who has shown notable service to AECT. This service may be to the organization as a whole, one of its programs, or one of its divisions.
- Nominee currently must be a member of AECT and have at least 10 years of service to AECT.

Disqualifications

- Recipient may not now be serving as an elected officer of AECT nor as a member of the board of directors.
- Nominee must not be currently serving as a member of the AECT Awards Committee.

Nomination

Nominations are judged and selected on the basis of an outstanding contribution to a division, committee, commission, or program of AECT but not to an affiliate organization. Please provide as much information as you can.

- Write in 100 words or less why you think nominee should receive this award. Include a description of nominee's contribution.
- What year did nominee join AECT?

AECT Distinguished Service Award

Qualifications

- Award is granted to a person who has shown outstanding leadership in advancing the theory and/or practice of educational communications and technology over a substantial period of time.
- The nominee need not be a member of AECT.
- Award may be given posthumously.

Disqualifications

- Nominee must not have received this award previously.
- Nominee must not be currently serving as a member of the AECT Awards Committee.

Nomination

Nominations are judged primarily on the distinction or magnitude of the nominee's leadership in advancing the field rather than the association.

Categories

The following categories suggest areas in which the nominee may have rendered distinguished service to the field. The nominee may not be represented in these areas. Use those that apply or add others.

- Leadership • Research/Theory • Development/Production • Publication

- Major Contribution to Education Outside the United States

AECT Annual Achievement Award

Qualifications

- Recipient may be an individual or a group.

- The AAA honors the individual who during the past year has made the most significant contribution to the advancement of educational communications and technology.

- The nominee need not be a member of AECT.

- The contribution being honored should be publicly visible—a specific thing or event.

- It must be timely—taking place within approximately the past year.

- Award can be given to the same person more than once.

Nomination

The nature of this award precludes the use of a single checklist or set of categories for nomination. The nomination and selection are inherently subjective. You are asked simply to present a succinct argument in favor of your nominee. Your statement ought to answer the following questions:

- What is the specific achievement being honored?

- What impact has this achievement had, or is likely to have, on the field?

- How is the nominee connected with the achievement?

ECT Foundation
1996 AECT National Convention
Internship Program

Awards: Five students will be chosen as convention interns. The winners will receive complimentary convention registration, complimentary housing, and a $200 cash award. There will also be a limited number of division interns. The interns will be expected to arrive at the convention on the day before the convention and to stay until the close of the convention. (Applicants are encouraged to request financial support for transportation and on-site expenses from their institutions or state affiliate organizations.)

Program
Activities: Each intern will be expected to participate fully in a coordinated program of activities. These activities include private seminars with selected association and professional leaders in the field, observation of the AECT governance and program committees, and behind-the-scenes views of the convention itself. Each intern will also be responsible for specific convention-related assignments, which will require approximately 15 hours of time during the convention. A former intern, who is now a member of the AECT Leadership Development Committee, will serve as the program coordinator.

Eligibility: To qualify for consideration, an applicant must be a full-time student throughout the current academic year in a recognized graduate program in educational communications and technology, and must be a member of AECT. (Applicant may join AECT when applying for the award.)

Application
Process: To apply for the internship program, qualified graduate students must complete and return an application form and must submit two letters of recommendation.

ECT Foundation
1996 Richard B. Lewis Memorial Award

Award:
$750, provided by the Richard B. Lewis Memorial Fund for "Outstanding School District Media Utilization," is awarded to the winner.

Selection
Process:
The winner will be selected by a unified committee appointed from the divisions of Educational Media Management (DEMM) and School Media Specialists (DSMS) of the Association for Educational Communications and Technology, and the National Association of Regional Media Centers (NARMC).

Selection
Criteria:
- Evidence of strong media utilization as gathered from:

  1. special utilization studies conducted by or for the school district;

  2. specific instances of good utilization as described in writing by school district or other personnel.

- Evidence of having provided in the school district budget means of implementing good utilization programs in its schools and of the degree to which AECT/ALA media standards are met for services, equipment, and personnel.

- Assessment of applicant's statements as to how the $750 (if awarded) would be spent, such as for:

  1. attending national, regional, or state conferences or workshops related to media utilization;

  2. selecting media specialist(s) to attend advanced training programs;

  3. buying software or hardware needed to improve media utilization programs;

  4. other purposes (indicating especially creative approaches).

- Recognition by an AECT state, regional, or national affiliate organization or representative, or from a National Association of Regional Media Centers state or regional representative:

  1. through prior recognition or awards;

  2. through a recommendation.

Eligibility:
All school districts, public and private, having media utilization programs in place, and conforming to the preceding criteria, are eligible.

Other:
The winning district will receive a plaque as part of this award.

ECT Foundation
1996 AECT Leadership Development Grant

Grants:

One grant of $500 is provided by the ECT Foundation and administered by the AECT Leadership Development Committee. The grant is awarded to assist an AECT affiliate, an AECT division, or an AECT regional organization to undertake leadership development activities that will improve the participant's skills as a leader in the professional organization or in educational technology.

Selection:

The grant award will be recommended by the Leadership Committee's Subcommittee on Leadership Development Grants.

Selection
Criteria:

All AECT state affiliates, divisions, and regional organizations are eligible for these competitive grants. An application from a previous grant recipient will not be considered unless a summary report has been submitted to the Leadership Development Committee and the AECT national office. Organizations that have not received a grant in the past are particularly invited to apply. Funds must be intended for some unique aspect or function not previously undertaken. Proposals that demonstrate a commitment to leadership development, that propose programs that are unique to the applicant's organization, and that include activities or products of potential benefit to other AECT programs will be given special consideration.

Awards:

The awards will be presented during the AECT National Convention and InCITE Exposition.

ECT Foundation
1996 AECT Memorial Scholarships

Awards: Two scholarships of $1,000 each will be awarded to graduate students or public school teachers in educational communications/technology to fund graduate study or research. The scholarships may be used to assist the recipients to further their education in a summer session or academic year of graduate study at any accredited college or university in the United States or Canada. Programs of study may be at the master's or educational specialist level.

Eligibility: All recipients must be members of AECT.

Selection
Criteria: Selections will be based on the following:

1. scholarship;

2. experience related to the field of educational media, communications, or technology, such as employment, field experience, course work, assistantships, publications, etc.;

3. service to the field through AECT activities and membership in other related professional organizations;

4. three letters of recommendation from persons familiar with the candidate's professional qualifications and leadership potential;

5. the candidate's own knowledge of key issues and opportunities facing the educational communications/technology field today, with respect to the candidate's own goals.

**ECT Foundation
1996 Dean and Sybil McClusky
Research Award**

Award: $1,000 is available to honor two outstanding doctoral research proposals in
                    educational technology, as selected by a jury of researchers from AECT's
                    Research and Theory Division. Each winner will be awarded $500.

Guidelines
for Preparing
and Submitting
Papers: Submitted proposals may follow acceptable formats of individual schools but
                    must include at least:

                    1. The definition of the problem, including a statement of significance;

                    2. A review of pertinent literature;

                    3. Research hypothesis to be examined;

                    4. Research design and procedures, including statistical techniques.

                    Applicants are encouraged to review pages 157-61 of Stephen Isaac and
                    William B. Michaels, *Handbook in Research and Evaluation*, Robert R.
                    Knapp, San Diego, CA, 1971.

Eligibility: Applicants must be presently enrolled in a doctoral program in educational
                    technology and have obtained committee acceptance of their proposal. The
                    winner will be expected to sign a statement that the proposed doctoral study
                    will be completed in accordance with the sponsoring university's graduate
                    school policies (including any time limitations) or be required to return the
                    funds received.

ECT Foundation
1996 Robert deKieffer
International Fellowship Award

Purpose:	To recognize, annually, a professional in educational communications and technology at any level from a foreign country who has demonstrated leadership in the field.
Award:	$200 and a plaque will be presented to the recipient at the AECT National Convention.
Selection:	The Awards Committee of the International Division of the Association for Educational Communications and Technology (AECT) is responsible for the selection of the recipient of this award.
Selection Criteria:	The following criteria will be used in the selection process:

1. The recipient will be a professional in educational communications and technology at any level.

2. The recipient will be a member of AECT.

3. The recipient normally resides outside of the United States.

4. The recipient will meet at least one of the following criteria:

   (a) has conducted a major project or been involved in the advancement of educational communication and technology outside of the United States;

   (b) is recognized as a leader in the field based on his/her teaching, research, or service records;

   (c) has been active and is instrumental in forging a professional tie in educational communications and technology between the United States and one or more foreign countries.

ECT Foundation
1996 James W. Brown Publication Award

Award: $500 cash award will be given to the author or authors of an outstanding publication in the field of educational technology.

Eligibility: Nominated items are not restricted to books or print; they may be in any media format (film, video, broadcast program, book, etc.). Any nonperiodic publication in the field of educational technology is eligible if it bears a publication date of 1994 or 1995.

Guidelines
for
Nominations: Nominations are solicited from all possible sources: AECT members, media-related publishers and producers, authors themselves, the AECT nonperiodic publications committee, and others.

Criteria: Nominated publications shall be judged on the basis of:

1. Significance of the item's content for the field of media/instructional technology, as defined in the *Definition of Educational Technology*, published by AECT in 1977, or in any subset of the publication.

2. Professional quality of the item.

3. Potential impact of the item's content on the field of media/instructional technology, as defined in the *Definition of Educational Technology*.

4. Technical quality of the item.

ECT Foundation
1996 Qualitative Research Award

Award:

The ECT Foundation announces the creation of an annual award for the best qualitative research in educational communications and technology. This award is open to qualitative studies of all instructional areas including training. In addition to the $1,000 prize, the winner will receive a certificate of achievement and the opportunity to present a paper at the AECT National Convention. Qualitative theories and research methods may be applied from disciplines including, but not limited to, anthropology, art criticism, philosophy, and sociology. This award supports the independent thinking of individual scholars, and is not for collaboration. Upon notice from the review committee, the Chair of the Award has the authority to split the annual prize fund and make more than one award.

Applications:

Applications must include:

1. Cover letter: Indicate whether applicant requests ECT *sponsorship* for a planned project or a project under way, or *recognition* of a completed project.

2. Brief vita, one or two pages indicating:
   - Education: Degrees awarded, dates, and institutions
   - Employment history
   - Representative publications and/or productions
   - Achievements
   - Membership in professional societies

3. Abstract: Outline of a qualitative project in one page or less of double-spaced text.

4. Project narrative: Describe the qualitative project. It may be a *plan* for work to be completed, an *interim* report of work in progress, a *final* report, or a *synopsis* of a final report. This description may range from 15 to 20 pages of double-spaced text, including references. It should be prepared in accordance with a current style manual such as *Chicago* or those published by the APA or MLA.

   - Identify clearly the *qualitative foundations* of the project by describing the theoretical base, the research issue, research strategy, and the results (if any at this time). Emphasize the importance of the project in developing understanding of educational communications and technology in a social or cultural context. It is to the applicant's advantage to show that the project has been approved by another agency, recently published, or accepted for publication.
   - Justify *sponsorship* by ECT Foundation for *planned projects* and *projects under way*. Include a plan of action, assessment of its feasibility, time line, and budget if resources are needed.
   - Justify *recognition* by ECT Foundation of *completed projects* by giving evidence of completion, a description of the project, and interpretation of the findings.

ECT Foundation
1996 ETR&D Young Scholar Award

Award:

$250 will be presented to the winner during the AECT National Convention. Additionally, the winning paper will be published in *ETR&D*, the refereed scholarly research journal published by the Association for Educational Communications and Technology (AECT).

For:

The best paper discussing a theoretical construct that could guide research and/or development in educational technology.

Eligibility:

An individual who does not hold a doctorate degree or who received a doctorate not more than five years ago as of November 5, 1995.

Guidelines
for Preparing
and Submitting
Papers:

The paper must be an original unpublished work dealing with research and theory in educational technology. It must deal with a theoretical construct, analyses of related research, and original recommendations for future research and/or development. The paper may not be a report of a specific research study or development project. It must be 20-30 pages long, excluding the references, and must conform to the *American Psychological Association Style Manual*, 3rd ed.

Selection
of
Winner:

The selection of the winning paper will be the responsibility of the editor and editorial board of *ETR&D*. Only the best paper judged worthy of the award will win. (There may not be a recipient of this award every year.)

ECT Foundation
1996 Robert M. Gagné Award for Graduate Student
Research in Instructional Development

Purpose: To provide recognition and financial assistance for outstanding research by a graduate student in the field of instructional development.

Award: $500 is awarded for the most significant contribution to the body of knowledge upon which instructional development is based. The Gagné Award competition is sponsored by the Association for Educational Communications and Technology (AECT) and its Division of Instructional Development. A jury of scholars will select the winning contribution. The award will be presented to the recipient during the AECT National Convention.

Eligibility: The work must have been completed after December 31, 1992, while the award candidate was enrolled as a graduate student.

Nomination
Procedure: You may nominate any individual (including yourself) for the Gagné Award.

ECT Foundation
1996 McJulien Minority
Graduate Scholarship Award

Award: The Wes McJulien Minority Graduate Scholarship Award has been estab-
           lished in memory of his son, Patrick D. McJulien. The award shall consist
           of $500 plus a plaque for the selected minority student, to be presented at
           the AECT National Convention.

Purpose: To recognize, annually, a minority graduate student in educational commu-
           nications and technology.

Selection: Minorities in Media (MIM), an AECT national affiliate, shall be responsible
           for the selection of the award recipient.

Selection
Criteria: The following criteria will be used in the selection process:

           1. The recipient must be a full-time graduate student enrolled in a
              degree-granting program in educational technology at the master's,
              educational specialist, or doctoral level.

           2. The recipient must have a "B" average or better to apply for this
              award.

           3. The recipient must be an AECT member.

           4. The recipient must obtain three letters of reference.

ECT Foundation
1996 Carl F. and Viola V. Mahnke
Film Production Award

Award: $200 will be awarded to honor a film or video product that demonstrates excellence in message design and production for educational purposes. In addition, certificates of merit will be awarded to entries with outstanding qualities worthy of recognition. In the event that no entry demonstrates excellence, in the opinion of the judges, no award will be given.

Eligibility: Eligibility is limited to film, video, or video programs incorporated into multimedia products. The program must have a predominant educational objective in the judges' opinion. The submission must be produced by undergraduate or graduate students. Faculty and professional mentoring is acceptable; however, **all** production work must be done by the person(s) submitting the program. The winners must be members of AECT. Only entries completed within a two-year period prior to the competition will qualify.

Formats: All entries must be either on film, videotape, CD-ROM, or diskette. Film entries are limtied to 16mm. Video entries can either be $\frac{1}{2}$-inch VHS or $\frac{3}{4}$-inch U-matic. CD-ROM entries must work on the following platform:

- CPU: Intel 486SX/33 MHz minimum (66 MHz recommended)
- RAM: 4 MB minimum (8 MB recommended)
- Operating System: Windows 3.1
- CD-ROM Drive: Double spin (triple spin recommended)
- Monitor: VGA 640 X 480, 256 colors
- Sound Card: 8-bit Sound Blaster or compatible (16-bit recommended)
- Speakers: Amplified (shielded) speakers
- User Input: Keyboard and mouse

Video programs submitted on diskette must meet the following guidelines:

- Run on either Macintosh or PC platform
- Be a "runtime" or executable file to enable judges to view the video program without the application
- Created in multimedia authoring package (for example, Authorware, HyperCard, HyperStudio, MacroMind Director, and others)

Judging: All entries will be judged by a panel of judges from the AECT Media Design and Production Division during the AECT National Convention.

Entry Fee: Entrants must include an entry fee of $10 per program, made payable to MDPD-AECT. For programs consisting of more than one film or videocassette, CD-ROM, or diskette, each must be submitted separately. An entry form must be completed for each entry. The entry form may be duplicated if necessary.

ECT Foundation
1996 ECT Mentor Endowment Scholarship

Award: One scholarship of $3,000.

Purpose: This scholarship is intended for use by a graduate student in educational communications and technology to pursue studies in this field. The scholarship may be used to assist the recipient in enrolling in graduate study during an academic year or a summer session in any accredited college or university in the United States or Canada. Graduate study must be at the doctoral level.

Eligibility: Applicants must be members of AECT and accepted in or enrolled in a graduate-level program as outlined above.

Selection
Criteria: Selections will be based upon:

- Scholarship;

- Leadership potential;

- Experience related to the field of educational communications and technology, such as employment, field experience, course work, assistantships, presentations, publications;

- Three letters of recommendation from persons familiar with the candidate's professional qualifications and leadership potential.

ECT Foundation
1996 Mentor Endowment Professional
Development Grants

Award: Two professional development grants of $2,000. One grant is given in honor of the past presidents of AECT.

Purpose: These grants are intended for use by professionals in the field of educational communications and technology for the purpose of enhancing professional growth and leadership in a manner other than formal graduate study at a college or university. Appropriate uses of these grants may include, but are not limited to, participation in a workshop or conference, development of a new skill, involvement in a special project, or acquisition of materials, hardware, publications, or other resources.

Eligibility: Applicants must be members of AECT and employed in some area of the field of educational communications and technology.

Selection
Criteria: Selection of the ECT Mentor Endowment Professional Development Grants will be based on the following:

1. The quality of the Professional Development Plan proposed in the application and the appropriateness of that plan to the goals of the Mentor Grant Program.

2. Leadership potential.

3. Experience in the field of educational communications and technology such as employment, field experience, and professional involvement.

4. Three letters of recommendation from persons familiar with the candidate's professional qualifications and leadership potential.

Part Eight
Mediagraphy
Print and Nonprint Resources

Introduction

CONTENTS

This resource list includes media-related journals, books, ERIC documents and journal articles, and nonprint media resources of interest to practitioners, researchers, students, and others concerned with educational technology and educational media. Emphasis in this section is on *currency*; the vast majority of books cited here were published in 1994 or 1995. ERIC documents and journal articles were all *announced* in the ERIC database in 1994, but many of them were issued in the latter half of the previous year and bear a 1993 publication date. Media-related journals include those listed in past issues of *EMTY* and new entries in the field. The computer software, CD-ROMs, online resources, and videos listed are also recent products.

SELECTION

Items were selected for the Mediagraphy in several ways. The ERIC (Educational Resources Information Center) Database was the source for ERIC document and journal article citations. Most of these entries are from a subset of the database selected by the directors of the ERIC Clearinghouse on Information Resources as being the year's most important database entries for this field. Media-related journals were either retained on the list or added to the list when they met one or more of the following criteria: were from a reputable publisher; had a broad circulation; were covered by indexing services; were peer reviewed; and filled a gap in the literature. Journal data were verified using *Ulrich's International Periodicals Directory 1994-95*. In keeping with the title and original purpose of this section, we have included listings for a sampling of the wealth of current nonbook media products that are now becoming available. They include CD-ROMs, computer software, courseware, online products and resources, and videotapes. Currency is still a major factor—for example, online services not only provide additional ways of accessing information already available in standard printed formats, they also provide information that has been updated since the publication of the most recent printed version. All of the materials listed are produced by organizations that are well established in the field. Finally, the complete contents of the Mediagraphy were reviewed by the editors of *EMTY 1995-1996*.

OBTAINING RESOURCES

Media-Related Periodicals and Books. Publisher, price, and ordering/subscription address are listed wherever available.

ERIC Documents. ERIC documents can be read in microfiche at any library holding an ERIC microfiche collection. The identification number beginning with ED (for example, ED 332 677) is used to find the document in the collection. ERIC documents can also be ordered from the ERIC Document Reproduction Service. Prices charged depend upon format chosen (microfiche or paper copy), length of the document, and method of shipping. Online orders, fax orders, and expedited delivery are available.

To find the closest library with an ERIC microfiche collection, contact:

ACCESS ERIC
1600 Research Blvd.
Rockville, MD 20850-3172
1-800-LET-ERIC (538-3742)
Internet: acceric@gwuvm.gwu.edu

To order ERIC documents, contact:

ERIC Document Reproduction Service (EDRS)
7420 Fullerton Rd., Suite 110
Springfield, VA 22153-2852
voice: 1-800-443-ERIC (443-3742), 1-703-440-1400
fax: 703-440-1408
Internet: edrs@gwuvm.gwu.edu

Journal Articles. Journal articles can be obtained in one of the following ways: (1) from a library subscribing to the title; (2) through interlibrary loan; (3) through the purchase of a back issue from the journal publisher; or (4) from an article reprint service. Articles noted as being available from the UMI (University Microfilms International) reprint service can be ordered using their ERIC identification numbers (numbers beginning with EJ, such as EJ 421 772).

University Microfilms International (UMI)
Article Clearinghouse
300 North Zeeb Rd.
Ann Arbor, MI 48106
1-800-521-0600 ext. 2786 (toll-free in U.S. and Canada)
313-761-4700 ext. 2786 (outside U.S. and Canada)

ARRANGEMENT

Mediagraphy entries are classified according to major subject emphasis under the following headings:

- Artificial Intelligence and Robotics
- CD-ROM
- Computer-Assisted Instruction

- Databases and Online Searching

- Distance Education

- Educational Research

- Educational Technology

- Electronic Publishing

- Information Science and Technology

- Instructional Design and Training

- Libraries and Media Centers

- Media Technologies

- Simulation and Virtual Reality

- Telecommunications and Networking

Mediagraphy

ARTIFICIAL INTELLIGENCE AND ROBOTICS

Media-Related Periodicals

Intelligent Tutoring Media. Information Today, Inc. (formerly Learned Information), 143 Old Marlton Pike, Medford, NJ 08055. q.; $125. Concerned with the packaging and communication of knowledge using advanced information technologies. Studies the impact of artificial intelligence, hypertext, interactive video, mass storage devices, and telecommunications networks.

International Journal of Robotics Research. MIT Press, 55 Hayward St., Cambridge, MA 02142. bi-mo.; $80 indiv. (foreign $102); $185 inst. (foreign $199); $50 students and retired (foreign $72). Interdisciplinary approach to the study of robotics for researchers, scientists, and students.

Journal of Artificial Intelligence in Education. Association for Advancement of Computing in Education, Box 2966, Charlottesville, VA 22902-2966. q.; $65 indiv., $93 inst. and libraries. International journal publishes articles on how intelligent computer technologies can be used in education to enhance learning and teaching. Reports on research and developments, integration, and applications of artificial intelligence in education.

Knowledge-Based Systems. Butterworth-Heinemann Ltd., Turpin Transactions, Ltd., Distribution Centre, Blackhorse Rd., Letchworth, Herts SG6 1HN, England. q.; £165. Interdisciplinary and applications-oriented journal on fifth-generation computing, expert systems, and knowledge-based methods in system design.

Minds and Machines. Kluwer Academic Publishers, Box 358, Accord Station, Hingham, MA 02018-0358. q.; $221.50. Discusses issues concerning machines and mentality, artificial intelligence, epistemology, simulation, and modeling.

Books

Mellar, Harvey, Bliss, Joan, Boohan, Richard, Ogborn, Jon, and Tompsett, Chris, eds. (1994). **Learning with artificial worlds: Computer based modelling in the curriculum.** The Falmer Press, Taylor & Francis Inc., 1900 Frost Rd., Suite 101, Bristol, PA 19007. 244pp. $85 (case); $29 (paper). Focuses on modelling in education and providing children with computer tools to enable them to create their own worlds, to express their own representations of their world, and also to explore other people's representations.

ERIC Documents

Vitale, Michael R., and Romance, Nancy. (1993, April). **Developing applications of artificial intelligence technology to provide consultative support in the use of research methodology by practitioners.** Paper presented at the American Educational Research Association, Atlanta, GA, April 12-16, 1993. 20pp. ED 366 306. Discusses methodological strategies and issues that underlie the development of artificial intelligence software that has been proven in industry and the general concept of an expert system in the context of increasing the accessibility of expert assistance to research practitioners.

Journal Articles

Baker, Michael. (1994). A model for negotiation in teaching-learning dialogues. **Journal of Artificial Intelligence in Education, 5**(2), 199-254. EJ 491 455. (Available UMI). Describes a model for negotiation based on an analysis of teaching-learning dialogues and discusses the relevance of dialogue analysis and modelling for artificial intelligence research.

Kearsley, Greg. (1993). Intelligent agents and instructional systems: Implications of a new paradigm. **Journal of Artificial Intelligence in Education, 4**(4), 295-304. EJ 476 363. (Available UMI). Examines the relationship between intelligent agents (i.e., computer programs that carry out tasks for users) and intelligent tutoring systems; suggests implications for instructional theory and practice; and discusses a new paradigm for instruction based on the concept of shared abilities and cooperative learning between humans and computers.

Roesler, Marina, and Hawkins, Donald T. (1994, July). Intelligent agents: Software servants for an electronic information world (and more!). **Online, 18**(4), 18-32. EJ 488 257. (Available UMI). Discusses the concept and characteristics of artificial intelligence software for information retrieval, news filtering, clerical support, personal shopping, and investment counseling.

White, Frank. (1994, Summer). The user interface of expert systems: What recent research tells us. **Library Software Review, 13**(2), 91-98. EJ 493 300. (Available UMI). Discussion of expert systems and how they can be used focuses on recent research and empirically validated interface features.

CD-ROM

Media-Related Periodicals

CD-ROM Databases. Worldwide Videotex, Box 3273, Boynton Beach, FL 33424-3273. mo.; $150 U.S., $190 elsewhere. Descriptive listing of all databases being marketed on CD-ROM with vendor and system information.

CD-ROM Professional. Pemberton Press, Inc., 462 Danbury Rd., Wilton, CT 06897. bi-mo.; $55 indiv. and school libraries, U.S. (foreign $90); $98 inst. (foreign $133). Assists publishers, librarians, and other information professionals in the selection, evaluation, purchase, and operation of CD-ROM systems and titles.

CD-ROM World (formerly **CD-ROM Librarian**). Meckler Publishing Corp., 11 Ferry Lane W., Westport, CT 06880-5808. 10/yr.; $29. Articles and reviews for CD-ROM users.

Books

Hogan, Kathleen, and Shelton, James, eds. (1995). **CD-ROM Finder.** 6th Edition 1995. Information Today, Inc. (formerly Learned Information, Inc.), 143 Old Marlton Pike, Medford, NJ 08055-8750. 520pp. $69.50. This new and expanded edition provides information on more than 2,000 CD-ROM titles covering such topics as business, technology, library systems, medicine, science, education, and law. Information provided includes product content, hardware/software requirements, and market data.

LaGuardia, Cheryl. (1994). **The CD-ROM primer: The ABC's of CD-ROM.** Neil-Schuman, Publishers, 100 Varick St., New York, NY 10013. 250pp. $39.95. This crash course for the beginner covers assessing needs, designing the workstation, selecting and collecting CDs, using a network, what CDs will and won't do for you, and keeping up with the technology.

ERIC Documents

Poulton, Bruce R. (1994). **The Workplace Literacy Project (WLS). Phase II. Final performance report.** Winston-Salem, NC: Forsyth Technical Community College; Raleigh, NC: North Carolina State University. 193pp. ED 369 930. Describes a national demonstration program in which North Carolina State University, Forsythe Technical Community College, and Sara Lee Knit Products Company (SLKP) participated as partners. The program included the development of a nine-module curriculum for textile workers and its conversion to 50 hours of CD-ROM courseware.

Journal Articles

Bowers, Richard A. (1994). Welcome to the second computer revolution: A beginner's guide to CD-ROM. **CD-ROM Professional, 7**(1), 20-32. EJ 478 072. (Available UMI). Describes CD-ROM technologies and how to access them.

Truett, Carol. (1994). New technologies in reference services for school libraries: How their use has changed the teaching of library and research skills in North Carolina. **Reference Librarian, 44**, 123-44. EJ 488 280. Discusses the results of a survey of school librarians in

North Carolina conducted to determine the extent of CD-ROM and videodisc use and how these technologies are changing the teaching of library, information, and research skills.

Wolfe, Janet L. (1994). Special considerations for networking multimedia CD-ROM titles. **CD-ROM Professional, 7**(1), 55-57. EJ 478 073. (Available UMI). Discussion of issues to be considered when networking multimedia CD-ROMs covers CD-ROM networking software; licensing concerns; configurations of CD-ROM servers; data caching; SCSI devices; CD-ROM drives; workstation configurations; and system setup troubleshooting tips.

COMPUTER-ASSISTED INSTRUCTION

Media-Related Periodicals

Apple Library Users Group Newsletter. Apple Computer, 10381 Bandley Dr., Cupertino, CA 95014. 4/yr.; free. For people interested in using Apple and Macintosh computers in libraries and information centers.

BYTE. Box 550, Hightstown, NJ 08520-9886. mo.; $29.95 ($34.95 Canada and Mexico; $50 elsewhere). Current articles on microcomputers provide technical information as well as information on applications and products for business and professional users.

CALICO Journal. Computer Assisted Language and Instruction Consortium, 014 Language Building, Box 90267, Duke University, Durham, NC 27708-0267. q.; $35 indiv., $65 inst., $125 corporations. Provides information on the applications of technology in teaching and learning languages.

Compute. Compute Publications, Inc., Box 3245, Harlan, IA 51537-3041. mo.; $19.94. Specifically designed for users of IBM PC, Tandy, and compatible machines at home, at work, and in the school.

Computer Book Review. 735 Ekekela Place, Honolulu, HI 96817. 6/yr.; $30. Reviews books on computers and computer-related subjects.

Computers and Education. Elsevier Science, 660 White Plains Rd., Tarrytown, NY 10591-5153. 8/yr.; $605. Presents technical papers covering a broad range of subjects for users of analog, digital, and hybrid computers in all aspects of higher education.

Computers and the Humanities. Kluwer Academic Publishers, Box 358, Accord Station, Hingham, MA 02018-0358. bi-mo.; $225. Contains papers on computer-aided studies, applications, automation, and computer-assisted instruction.

Computers in Human Behavior. Elsevier Science, 660 White Plains Rd., Tarrytown, NY 10591-5153. q.; £232 ($355 U.S.). Addresses the psychological impact of computer use on individuals, groups, and society.

Computers in the Schools. Haworth Press, 10 Alice St., Binghamton, NY 13904. q.; $34 indiv., $75 inst., $115 libraries. Features articles that combine theory and practical applications of small computers in schools for educators and school administrators.

Dr. Dobb's Journal. M&T Publishing, Inc., 411 Boreal Ave., Suite 100, San Mateo, CA 94402-3516. mo.; $29.97 U.S.; $45 Mexico and Canada; $70 elsewhere. Articles on the latest in operating systems, programming languages, algorithms, hardware design and architecture, data structures, and telecommunications; in-depth hardware and software reviews.

Education Technology News. Business Publishers, Inc., 951 Pershing Dr., Silver Spring, MD 20910-4464. bi-w.; $286. For teachers and those interested in educational uses of computers in the classroom. Feature articles on applications and educational software.

Electronic Learning. P.O. Box 3024, Southeast, PA 19398. 8/yr.; $23.95. Features articles on applications and advances of technology in education for K-12 and college educators and administrators.

Home Office Computing. Scholastic, Inc., Box 51344, Boulder, CO 80321-1344. mo.; $19.97 (foreign $27.97). For professionals who use computers and do business at home.

InfoWorld. InfoWorld Publishing, 155 Bovet Rd., Suite 800, San Mateo, CA 94402. w.; $130. News and reviews of PC hardware, software, peripherals, and networking.

Interpersonal Computing and Technology: An Electronic Journal for the 21st Century. Electronic journal published by the Center for Teaching and Technology, Academic Computer Center, Georgetown University, Washington, DC 20057, with support from the Center for Academic Computing, The Pennsylvania State University, University Park, PA 16802. Articles may be retrieved from: (1) GOPHER: GUVM.CCF.GEORGETOWN.EDU or (2) LISTSERV: LISTSERV@GUVN.BITnet.

Journal of Computer Assisted Learning. Blackwell Scientific Publications Ltd., Osney Mead, Oxford OX2 0EL, England. q.; £26.50 indiv. Europe, $44 elsewhere; £109 inst. Europe, $179 elsewhere. Articles and research on the use of computer-assisted learning.

Journal of Educational Computing Research. Baywood Publishing Co., 26 Austin Ave., Box 337, Amityville, NY 11701. 8/yr. (2 vols., 4 each); $95 indiv., $173 inst. Presents original research papers, critical analyses, reports on research in progress, design and development studies, article reviews, and grant award listings.

Journal of Research on Computing in Teacher Education (formerly **Journal of Research on Computing in Education**). International Society for Technology in Education, University of Oregon, 1787 Agate St., Eugene, OR 97403-1923. q.; $65 U.S. nonmembers (foreign $750), $30 members (foreign $40). Provides reports on original research and detailed system and project evaluations.

Learning and Leading with Technology. The ISTE Journal of Educational Technology Practice and Policy (formerly **Computing Teacher**). International Society for Technology in Education, University of Oregon, 1787 Agate St., Eugene, OR 97403-1923. 8/yr.; $52 nonmembers, $46 members, $23 student members. Articles and columns on language arts, Logo, science, mathematics, telecommunications, equity, and international connections for K-12 teachers.

MacWorld. MacWorld Communications, Box 54529, Boulder, CO 80322-4529. mo.; $30. Describes hardware, software, tutorials, and applications for users of the Macintosh microcomputer.

Microcomputer Index. Information Today, Inc. (formerly Learned Information, Inc.), 143 Old Marlton Pike, Medford, NJ 08055-8750. bi-mo.; $159. Abstracts of literature on the use of microcomputers in business, education, and the home.

Microcomputer Industry Update. Industry Market Reports, Inc., Box 681, Los Altos, CA 94023. mo.; $295. Abstracts of product announcements and reviews of interest appearing in weekly trade press.

PC Magazine: The Independent Guide to IBM-Standard Personal Computing. Ziff-Davis Publishing Co., Box 54093, Boulder, CO 80322. bi-w.; $44.97. Comparative reviews of computer hardware and general business software programs.

PC Week. Ziff-Davis Publishing Co., 10 Presidents Landing, Medford, MA 02155-5146. w.; $160, free to qualified personnel. Provides current information on the IBM PC, including hardware, software, industry news, business strategies, and reviews of hardware and software.

PC World. PC World Communications, Inc., Box 55029, Boulder, CO 80322-5029. mo.; $29.90 U.S., $49.90 Canada and Mexico, $75.90 elsewhere. Presents articles on applications and columns containing news, systems information, product announcements, and hardware updates.

Social Science Computer Review. Duke University Press, Box 90660, Durham, NC 27708-0660. q.; $48 indiv. (foreign $67); $86 inst. (foreign $86); $24 students (foreign $32). Features include software reviews, new product announcements, and tutorials for beginners.

Software Digest Ratings Report. National Software Testing Laboratories, Plymouth Corporate Center, Box 1000, Plymouth Meeting, PA 19462. mo.; $450. For IBM personal computer users. Each issue reports the ratings for one category of IBM PC software, based on multiple-user tests.

Software Magazine. Sentry Publishing Co., Inc., 1900 W. Park Dr., Westborough, MA 01581. mo.; $65 U.S., $75 Canada, $125 elsewhere (free to qualified personnel). Provides information on software and industry developments for business and professional users, and announces new software packages.

Software Reviews on File. Facts on File, 460 Park Ave. S., New York, NY 10016. mo.; $210. Condensed software reviews from more than 150 publications. Features software for all major microcomputer systems and programming languages for library, school, home, and business use.

Books

Abrams, Arnie H. (1995). **Educator's guide to Macintosh applications.** Allyn & Bacon, Dept. 894, 160 Gould St., Needham Heights, MA 02194-2315. 400pp. $28. Provides a practical, step-by-step tutorial to the basics of popular Macintosh applications for teachers and future teachers as they plan presentations, maintain grade books, help pupils publish their own storybooks, and carry out other classroom activities.

Beaver, John F. (1994). **Problem solving across the curriculum—Improving students' problem-solving skills using off-computer & on-computer activities.** International Society for Technology in Education, 1787 Agate St., Eugene, OR 97403-1923. 352pp. $25.15 members; $27.95 nonmembers. This guide presents extensively tested problem-solving activities drawn from various subject areas for grades 3-8. Many activities are on reproducible masters and provide practice in a variety of problem-solving strategies. Computer activities cover public domain programs, several integrated programs, and commercially available problem-solving software.

Beekman, George. (1994). **Computer currents—Navigating tomorrow's technology.** Benjamin-Cummings Publishing Co. Orders to: Addison Wesley Order Dept., 7 Jacob Way, Reading, MA 01867. 350pp. $33.95. This book is intended for use in computer literacy courses at the high school or college level. The first of three sections, on using computers, looks at word processing, calculating, visualizing, and simulating; database applications; and telecommunications and networking. The second section, on mastering computers, covers graphics, hypermedia, and multimedia; systems design and development; and artificial intelligence. The final section discusses the impact of technology on society, including computer security and piracy.

Dockterman, David. (1993). **Great teaching in the one computer classroom.** Tom Snyder Productions, Inc., 80 Coolidge Hill Rd., Watertown, MA 02172-2817. Approx. 50 pp. $19.95, or free bonus gift with every order, including the 30-day free loan for the *One computer classroom* video (see the Video listings in this section). Practical guide to technology in the classroom shows how a single computer can help ease administrative burdens, enliven classroom presentations, spark discussions, and foster cooperative learning and critical thinking.

Geisert, Paul G., and Futrell, Mynga K. (1995). **Teachers, computers, and curriculum.** Second edition. Allyn & Bacon, Dept. 894, 160 Gould St., Needham Heights, MA 02194-2315. 384pp. $42. Designed to help teachers incorporate microcomputers into their teaching, this text focuses on applications of computers for quality teaching and learning and how and when to use them.

Keegan, Mark. (1995). **Scenario educational software: Design and development of discovery learning.** Educational Technology Publications, 700 Palisade Ave., Englewood Cliffs, NJ 07632. 378pp. $39.95. This handbook presents research from education, psychology, and physiology to show the strengths of discovery-based educational environments, as well as when and why didactic methods should be used. It then shows how to create the discovery-based "scenario" and the interactive software and multimedia; optimize feedback, challenge, and the duration of the scenario; and evaluate the software.

Kurshan, Barbara, Kohl, Herbert, and Kahn, Ted M. (1994). **Exploring Creative Writer — Imaginative and fun computer activities.** Addison-Wesley Publishing Co., 7 Jacob Way, Reading, MA 01867. 136pp. $14.95. Activities for pupils in grades 3-8 at home or at school to use Microsoft's *Creative Writer* to run an office, publish a newsletter, organize a club, create an illustrated family history, play with words, and write poetry and stories. Provides tips, techniques, and shortcuts for using both the Macintosh and Windows versions of the software.

Lee, William W., and Mamone, Robert A. (1995). **The computer based training handbook: Assessment, design, development, evaluation.** Educational Technology Publications, 700 Palisade Ave., Englewood Cliffs, NJ 07632. 312pp. $37.95. This handbook is a complete, systematic guide to the design and development of computer-based training (CBT) lessons and courses for use in business, industry, and other training environments. It treats all aspects of analysis, design, development, and evaluation.

Maran, Richard. (1994). **Computers simplified.** (Category PCs/Windows.) IDG Books, 155 Bovet Rd., Suite 310, San Mateo, CA 94402. 128pp. $14.99. Designed to demystify technical jargon and explain computer basics with a maximum number of pictures and minimum text, this book covers the basic computer, input/output devices, microprocessors, storage devices, portable computers, operating systems, application software, and networking.

Milheim, William D., ed. (1994). **Authoring-systems software for computer-based training.** Educational Technology Publications, 700 Palisade Ave., Englewood Cliffs, NJ 07632. 200pp. $37.95. This book compares and contrasts eight leading authoring systems on the market for applicability to their own courseware projects. Case study material and chapters on the use of authoring systems and concurrent authoring are included.

Squires, David, and McDougall, Anne. (1994). **Choosing and using educational software: A teacher's guide.** Taylor and Francis, Inc., 1900 Frost Rd., Suite 101, Bristol, PA 19007. 161pp. $27. This book proposes a new approach for selecting educational software, which is based on the mutual interaction of the perspectives of the student, the teacher, and the software designer. Closely associated with software use, this approach emphasizes educational considerations such as classroom interaction, theories of learning, and curriculum issues. Forms and guidelines for various kinds of evaluation are appended.

ERIC Documents

Brummelhuis, Alfons ten. (1994, April). **What do students know about computers and where did they learn it? Results from an international comparative survey.** Paper presented at the American Educational Research Association, New Orleans, LA, April 4-8, 1994. 15pp. ED 374 774. Conducted to determine if there are cross-national factors that account for students' computer know-how, this study collected and analyzed data from seven different countries on student attitudes, computer use at home, and scores on the Functional Information Technology Test (FITT).

ChanLin, Lih-Juan. (1994, April 25). **A theoretical analysis of learning with graphics— Implications for computer graphics design.** 22pp. ED 370 526. Reviews the literature pertinent to learning with graphics, including the dual coding theory, the level of processing theory, the area of motivation and attention, and knowledge from cognitive science.

Chubb, Beverly. (1994, February). **Using a mnemonic approach to teach fourth graders to use a computer keyboard.** Practicum report, Master of Science, Nova University. 123pp. ED 370 537. Investigated the effectiveness of the combination of four approaches to teaching fourth-grade students to use a computer keyboard: a mnemonic approach to teach the entire alphabet keyboard in one lesson; age-appropriate drills and games; a project for reinforcement of the mnemonic lesson; and a computer program for practice.

Gavora, Mark, and Hannafin, Michael. (1993, April). **Interaction strategies and emerging technologies.** 67pp. ED 363 276. Describes and critically analyzes the traditional operational and functional perspectives on interaction and computer technology, examines dimensions of interactions, and presents a framework for the design of interaction strategies.

Hooper, Simon, and others. (1994). **Persistence and small group interaction.** Paper presented at the National Convention of the Association for Educational Communications and Technology, Research and Theory Division, Nashville, TN, February 16-20, 1994. 11pp. ED 373 720. Studied the effects of persistence on the ability of 138 sixth-grade students to interact and learn in cooperative learning groups and assessed the effect of collaboration on their attitudes toward their partners.

Lai, Yee-Rong, and Waugh, Michael L. (1994, April). **From information searching to learning: A comparison of contrasting hypertextual menu designs for computer-based instructional documents.** Paper presented at the American Educational Research Association, New Orleans, LA, April 4-8, 1994. 25pp. ED 374 770. Examined the influence of three different combinations of document structures and menu designs on users' attitude, performance, and learning in five different search tasks.

Mills, Steven C., and Ragan, Tillman J. (1994). **Adapting instruction to individual learner differences: A research paradigm for computer-based instruction.** Paper presented at the National Convention of the Association for Educational Communications and Technology, Research and Theory Division, Nashville, TN, February 16-20, 1994. 23pp. ED 373 740. Examines a research paradigm that is particularly suited to experimentation-related computer-based instruction and integrated learning systems.

Nieveen, Nienke, and others. (1994, April). **Exploration of computer assisted curriculum development.** Paper presented at the American Educational Research Association (New Orleans, LA, April 4-8, 1994). 17pp. ED 374 775. Describes the early steps and findings of a long-term project being conducted collaboratively by the University of Twente (Netherlands) Faculty of Educational Science and Technology and the Dutch National Institute for Curriculum Development to explore the potentially supportive role of the computer in improving the quality and efficiency of curriculum development activities.

Stephenson, Stanley D. (1992, March). **The effects of student-instructor interaction on achievement in a dyad computer-based training environment. Interim technical paper for period June 1991-August 1991.** Air Force Human Resources Directorate, Brooks AFB, TX. Armstrong Lab. Technical Training Research Div. and Southwest Texas State Univ., San Marcos, TX, Dept. of Computer Information Systems and Administrative Sciences. 17pp. ED 364 245. Studied the impact of interaction between the student and the instructor when 41 college-level business statistics students worked computer-based training in pairs.

Williams, Gertrude Rebecca. (1993, July). **Efficacy of computer assisted instruction in the areas of math application and reading comprehension.** 28pp. ED 371 752. Investigated whether a computer-assisted instruction (CAI) program increased the reading and math standardized test scores for 54 selected sixth-grade high-risk students in a rural school district in Alabama.

Journal Articles

Aarntzen, Diana. (1993, November). Audio in courseware: Design knowledge issues. **Educational and Training Technology International, 30**(4), 354-66. EJ 476 342. (Available UMI). Considers issues to be addressed when incorporating audio in courseware design.

Becker, Henry Jay. (1994, Spring). How our best computer-using teachers differ from other teachers: Implications for realizing the potential of computers in schools. **Journal of Research on Computing in Education, 26**(3), 291-321. EJ 491 498. (Available UMI). Reports on a national survey of 516 third- through twelfth-grade teachers of academic subjects, of whom 45 were identified as being exemplary computer-using teachers. Four factors in the teaching environment made exemplary computer users more likely to be present: collegiality among users, school support for using computers for consequential activities, resources allocated to staff development and computer coordination, and smaller class sizes. Certain common factors in teachers' backgrounds were also found to be related to the probability of their being named exemplary users.

Bejar, Isaac I., and Braun, Henry I. (1994). On the synergy between assessment and instruction: Early lessons from computer-based simulations. **Machine-Mediated Learning, 4**(1), 5-25. EJ 485 244. Argues that synergy between computer-based instruction and automated assessment is possible because of the common needs in assessment and instruction; outlines a framework for characterizing performance; and examines procedures developed as part of an ongoing project to develop fully automated scoring of architectural design for a licensing exam.

Biraimah, Karen. (1993, June). The non-neutrality of educational computer software. **Computers and Education, 20**(4), 283-90. EJ 472 967. (Available UMI). Discusses bias in educational computer software by using examples of database programs to illustrate their cultural selection and amplification functions.

Brown, Christine, and others. (1994). Metacognition as a basis for learning support software. **Performance Improvement Quarterly, 7**(2), 3-26. EJ 481 871. Considers metacognition as a basis for software used in computer-assisted instruction.

Brummelhuis, Alfons ten, and Plomp, Tjeerd. (1994, May). Computers in primary and secondary education: The interest of an individual teacher or a school policy? **Computers and Education, 22**(4), 291-99. EJ 488 252. (Available UMI). Examines the growth of computer usage in Dutch primary and secondary schools from 1989-1992 based on statistics from the international "Computers in Education" study.

Carlson, Randal D. (1993-94). Computer adaptive testing: A shift in the evaluation paradigm. **Journal of Educational Technology Systems, 22**(3), 213-24. EJ 483 730. Reviews the development and use of mass testing procedures for evaluating large groups of relatively homogeneous individuals and suggests computer adaptive testing as an alternative to conventional testing.

Cates, Ward Mitchell. (1994). Estimating the time required to produce computer-based instructional lessons: Descriptive analyses of the production data of novice instructional developers. **Journal of Educational Computing Research, 10**(1), 29-40. EJ 481 860. Discussion of the time needed to create computer-based instruction focuses on descriptive analyses of production data gathered from novice instructional designers and novice authors who used a commercial authoring system to produce computer-based lessons.

Cousins, J. Bradley, and Ross, John A. (1993, Fall). Improving higher order thinking skills by teaching "with" the computer: A comparative study. **Journal of Research on Computing in Education, 26**(1), 94-115. EJ 479 799. (Available UMI). Describes a study that used experimental and control groups to investigate the potential of the computer to improve high school students' correlational reasoning skills.

Dennis, Verl E. (1994, Winter). How interactive instruction saves time. **Journal of Instruction Delivery Systems, 8**(1), 25-28. EJ 481 915. (Available UMI). Discusses interactive instruction methods using computer-based instruction (CBI), computer-based training (CBT), and interactive video (CD-I, DVI, and IVD.)

Ely, Donald P. (1993, September). Computers in schools and universities in the United States of America. **Educational Technology, 33**(9), 53-57. EJ 471 110. (Available UMI). Describes four aspects of computer technology in education in the United States: (1) the number of computers available to students and teachers; (2) where the computers are located and how they are used; (3) the impact of computer use; and (4) hypotheses concerning nonuse, limited use, and inappropriate use.

Goforth, Dave. (1994). Learner control = decision making + information: A model and meta-analysis. **Journal of Educational Computing Research, 11**(1), 1-26. EJ 489 805. Presents a meta-analysis of research concerning the effectiveness of learner control in tutorial computer-assisted instruction based on a model of control as decision making plus information.

Hannafin, Michael J., and others. (1994, October). Learning in open-ended environments: Assumptions, methods, and implications. **Educational Technology, 34**(8), 48-55. EJ 491 541. (Available UMI). Examines assumptions inherent in open-ended learning; describes features of open-ended learning environments; and discusses implications for research, development, and implementation of open-ended learning systems.

Hazari, Sunil I., and Reaves, Rita R. (1994, April). Student preferences toward microcomputer user interfaces. **Computers and Education, 22**(3), 225-29. EJ 481 844. (Available UMI). Describes a study that was conducted to determine undergraduate students' preferences toward graphical user interface versus command line interface during computer-assisted instruction.

Holzberg, Carol S. (1994, April). Technology in special education. **Technology and Learning, 14**(7), 18-21. EJ 481 960. (Available UMI). Presents examples of the use of technology to motivate, teach, and empower children with physical and cognitive disabilities.

Perkins, David N., and Unger, Chris. (1994). A new look in representations for mathematics and science learning. **Instructional Science, 22**(1), 1-37. EJ 489 740. (Available UMI). Discusses how visual analogies aid students' understanding of math and science with emphasis on new types of representations that use computers.

Reinen, Ingeborg Janssen, and Plomp, Tjeerd. (1993, June). Some gender issues in educational computer use: Results of an international comparative survey. **Computers and Education, 20**(4), 353-65. EJ 472 973. (Available UMI). Discussion of the results of an international survey of computer use in education focuses on three areas: (1) the degree to which female role models are offered to girls; (2) ways school policies take gender equity issues into account; and (3) the extent to which gender equity issues are dealt with in the curriculum.

Ross, Steven M., and others. (1994, Winter). Preferences for different CBI text screen designs based on the density level and realism of the lesson content viewed. **Computers in Human Behavior, 10**(4), 593-603. EJ 493 289. (Available UMI). Reports on a study of college student preferences for learning from computer-based instruction screen designs representing four levels of screen density, varied by the type of stimulus material and number of frames presented from a single lesson.

Shifflett, Bethany, and others. (1993). Computing needs among college educators. **Computers in the Schools, 9**(4), 107-17. EJ 486 815. Reports on a survey of California State University system faculty to examine the extent to which they utilized computers professionally and to determine their computing resource needs.

Steeples, Christine. (1993, June). A computer-mediated learning environment for adult learners: Supporting collaboration and self-direction. **Journal of Educational Multimedia and Hypermedia, 2**(4), 443-54. EJ 481 781. (Available UMI). Explores how computer-mediated systems may support the professional development of adults by providing environments that allow individual needs and purposes to be met and experience and understanding to be shared.

Tennyson, Robert D. (1994). The big wrench versus integrated approaches: The great media debate. **Educational Technology Research and Development, 42**(3), 15-28. EJ 493 372. (Available UMI). Compares seven positions on media influences on learning that were presented in a previous journal issue; discusses the conflict between advocates of a given approach versus integrated approaches to the solving of complex problems; and presents a model that links cognitive processes to computer-based prescriptions for improvements in learning.

Tessmer, Martin, and Jonassen, David. (1994, August). Evaluating computer-based training for repurposing to multimedia: A case study. **Performance and Instruction, 33**(7), 3-8. EJ 489 825. (Available UMI). Describes criteria developed to determine which of three existing computer-based training lessons could be repurposed into a multimedia format.

Vasu, Michael L., and Vasu, Ellen Storey. (1993, August). Computer usage in research methods courses in the social sciences and education: A conceptual framework. **Collegiate Microcomputer, 11**(3), 177-82. EJ 471 078. (Available UMI). Explores various aspects of a conceptual framework for integrating computing into social sciences and education courses.

Weiss, Elaine. (1994, February). Is your CBT people-literate? **Performance and Instruction, 33**(2), 3-6. EJ 481 868. (Available UMI). Discusses how to design effective user interfaces for computer-based training (CBT) programs and describes four types of interfaces: presentation, conversation, navigation, and explanation.

Computer Software

Curriculum connections. (1994). EDuQuest, The IBM Educational Systems Co., P.O. Box 2150, Atlanta, GA 30055. $19,302. Some components are available separately. Call EDuQuest, 1-800-426-4338, for additional information. This complete computer-based instructional management package supports individual state curriculum standards for grades K-6 language arts and math. It is designed to enable teachers and administrators to determine how well special competencies and skills are being achieved by students on a daily basis, and to assist teachers in taking corrective action if students fail to achieve mastery of learning outcomes. The program supports EDuQuest's *Teaching and Learning with Computers*, a model designed to integrate computers and courseware into the classroom.

Courseware

Desberg, Peter, and Fisher, Farah. (1995). **Teaching with technology.** Allyn & Bacon, Dept. 894, 160 Gould St., Needham Heights, MA 02194-2315. 4 Macintosh disks. $26.67. Published on disk rather than paper, this introductory-level text presents materials usually covered in computers-in-education courses in a totally interactive format.

Videos

The new literacy. Films for the Humanities & Sciences, P.O. Box 2053, Princeton, NJ 08543-2053. 26 min., color. Purchase $89.95. This look at how computers are changing the face of American education examines some of the practical applications of computer technology in the classroom and their effect on both teachers and students.

The one computer classroom video. (1994). Tom Snyder Productions, 80 Coolidge Hill Rd., Watertown, MA 02172-2817. 30 min. Free 30-day loan. This interactive video for teachers and workshop presenters includes a complete video outline to help structure staff development workshops; an exploration of five categories of classroom computer use; information on and strategies for integrating the computer into the curriculum; the Video Discussion Generator; and a technology planning guide. See the Books section for *Great teaching in the one computer classroom.*

DATABASES AND ONLINE SEARCHING

Media-Related Periodicals

CompuServe. 5000 Arlington Centre Blvd., Columbus, OH 43220. mo.; $30. Gives current information on fundamentals of micro-based communications, computer and information industry news, coverage of CompuServe services, commentary, and computer product reviews.

Data Sources. Ziff-Davis Publishing Co., One Park Ave., New York, NY 10016. 2/yr.; $440. Comprehensive guide to the information-processing industry. Covers equipment, software, services, and systems, and includes profiles of 10,000 companies.

Database. Online, Inc. 462 Danbury Rd., Wilton, CT 06897. bi-mo.; $99 U.S. and Canada, $121 Mexico, $134 foreign airmail. Features articles on topics of interest to online database users; includes database search aids.

Document Delivery World (formerly **Database Searcher**). Meckler Publishing, 11 Ferry Lane W., Westport, CT 06880-5808. mo.; $98. Covers news of changes and developments in the online industry; related news; new products and publications; conference and meeting announcements.

Gale Directory of Databases (formerly **Directory of Online Databases**). Gale Research Inc., 835 Penobscot Building, Detroit, MI 48226. q.; set $280; vol. 1, $199; vol. 2, $119. Contains information on database selection and database descriptions, including producers and their addresses.

Information Today. Information Today, Inc. (formerly Learned Information, Inc.), 143 Old Marlton Pike, Medford, NJ 08055. 11/yr.; $39.95. Newspaper for users and producers of electronic information services. Articles and news about the industry, calendar of events, and product information.

Journal of Database Management (formerly **Journal of Database Administration**). Idea Group Publishing, 4811 Jonestown Rd., Suite 230, Harrisburg, PA 17109-1751. q.; $60 indiv., $105 inst. Provides state-of-the-art research to those who design, develop, and administer DBMS-based information systems.

Link-Up. Information Today, Inc. (formerly Learned Information, Inc.), 143 Old Marlton Pike, Medford, NJ 08055. bi-mo.; $25 U.S., $48 elsewhere. Newsmagazine for communications covers hardware, software, communications services, and search methods.

Online. Online, Inc., 462 Danbury Rd., Wilton, CT 06897. 6/yr.; $99 U.S. and Canada, $121 Mexico, $134 foreign airmail. For online information system users. Articles cover a variety of online applications for general and business use.

Online and CD-ROM Review (formerly **Online Review**). Information Today, Inc. (formerly Learned Information, Inc.), 143 Old Marlton Pike, Medford, NJ 08055-8750. bi-mo.; $99. An international journal of online information systems featuring articles on using and managing online and optical information systems, training and educating online users, developing search aids, and creating and marketing databases.

Resource Sharing and Information Networks. Haworth Press, 10 Alice St., Binghamton, NY 13904. semi-ann.; $35 indiv., $90 inst. A forum for ideas on the basic theoretical and practical problems faced by planners, practitioners, and users of network services.

ERIC Documents

Leader, Lars F., and Klein, James D. (1994). **The effects of search tool and cognitive style on performance in hypermedia database searches.** Paper presented at the National Convention of the Association for Educational Communications and Technology, Research and Theory Division, Nashville, TN, February 16-20, 1994. 14pp. ED 373 729. This study investigated the effects of interface tools and learner cognitive styles on performance in searches for information within a hypermedia database by 75 students in a university English as a Second Language (ESL) program.

Standards for data exchange and case management information systems in support of comprehensive school-linked services. Version 2.0. (1994, March 28). Far West Laboratory for Educational Research and Development, San Francisco, CA; Youth Law Center, San Francisco, CA; California Interagency Data Collaboration. 209pp. ED 372 748. Provides guidance for local comprehensive integrated school-linked services sites and software vendors in developing and implementing case management information systems for the exchange and management of client data.

Journal Articles

Germain, Jack M. (1994, January-February). ERIC goes Internet. **Online Access, 9**(1), 50-60. EJ 477 954. Description of the ERIC database covers suggested uses for teachers, students, parents, and researchers; information available in ERIC; how to access ERIC, including through the Internet; the AskERIC service, which is available through the Internet; and steps for searching the database.

CD-ROMS

Information directory of electronic resources. (1994). SilverPlatter Information, Inc., 100 River Ridge Dr., Norwood, MA 02062-5026. For subscription price information, contact the producer. This CD-ROM contains information about the titles in SilverPlatter's collection of more than 150 electronic information products. (More than 50 new titles were added this year.) Also on the CD-ROM are SPIRS, SilverPlatter Information Retrieval Systems software, and a subset of the ERIC database. This electronic directory is thoroughly indexed to facilitate the location of new and/or appropriate resources and will be updated every six months.

International ERIC. (1994). Dialog Information Services, Inc., 3460 Hillview Ave., Palo Alto, CA 94304. For subscription price information, contact the producer. Dialog OnDisc International ERIC combines three international, educational research databases on a single disc: Australian Education Index (AEI), British Education Index (BEI), and Canadian Education Index (CEI). Each database provides extensive coverage of educational research in, and relating to, its country. International ERIC provides information on just about every aspect of education from a wide variety of sources, and an on-screen thesaurus is available for each database to assist in locating relevant terms.

DISTANCE EDUCATION

Media-Related Periodicals

American Journal of Distance Education. Pennsylvania State University, School of Education, 403 S. Allen St., Suite 206, University Park, PA 16801-5202. 3/yr.; $30 regular; $55 personal; $6 shipping and handling Canada, Mexico, and South America, $15 elsewhere. Focuses on the professional trainer, adult educator, college teacher, and others interested in the latest developments in methods and systems for delivering education to adults.

Appropriate Technology. Intermediate Technology Publications, Ltd., 103-105 Southampton Row, London, WC1B 4HH, England. q.; $27 indiv., $37 inst. Articles on less technologically advanced, but more environmentally sustainable, solutions to problems in developing countries.

Development Communication Report. Clearinghouse on Development Communication, 1815 N. Ft. Myer Dr., Suite 600, Arlington, VA 22209. q.; $10 (free to readers in developing countries). Applications of communications technology to international development problems such as agriculture, health, and nutrition.

Distance Education. University College of Southern Queensland Publications, Darling Heights, Toowoomba, Queensland 4350, Australia. semi-ann.; $A48 in Australia; $65 airmail overseas. Papers on the history, politics, and administration of distance education.

Journal of Distance Education. Canadian Association for Distance Education, 151 Slater St., Ottawa, ON K1P 5N1, Canada. (Text in English, French) 2/yr.; $40. Aims to promote and encourage scholarly work of empirical and theoretical nature relating to distance education in Canada and throughout the world.

Open Learning. Longman Group UK Ltd., Westgate House, 6th floor, The High, Harlow, Essex CM20 1YR, England. 3/yr.; £37 (U.K.), £38 Europe, $73 U.S., single copy £13 U.K., $27 overseas. Academic, scholarly publication on any aspects of open and distance learning anywhere in the world. Includes issues for debate and research notes.

Open Praxis (formerly **International Council for Distance Education Bulletin**). International Council for Distance Education, National Extension College, 18 Brookside Ave., Cambridge C82 2HN, England. 2/yr.; $65 individual membership; $50 libraries. Reports on activities and programs of the ICDE.

Research in Distance Education. Centre for Distance Education, Athabasca University, Box 1000, Athabasca, AB T0G 2R0, Canada. irreg.; free. A forum for the discussion of issues surrounding the process of conducting research within the field of distance education.

Books

Kember, David. (1995). **Open learning courses for adults: A model of student progress.** Educational Technology Publications, 700 Palisade Ave., Englewood Cliffs, NJ 07632. 378pp. $37.95. This book develops a comprehensive conceptual model of distance education and open learning, with special emphasis on courses taken by part-time adult learners. The model is explained and illustrated with case studies and interview quotations from students in a wide range of courses.

Mood, Terry Ann. (1995). **Distance education: An annotated bibliography.** Libraries Unlimited, P.O. Box 6633, Englewood, CO 80155-6633. 200pp. $27.50. Evaluative comments on usefulness and audience are provided for the approximately 300 books listed. Emphasis is on books printed in the last five years, and seven subject areas are covered: history, philosophy, administration, teacher-related issues, student-related issues, special groups, and international issues.

Schlosser, Charles, and Anderson, Mary. (1994). **Distance education: A review of the literature.** Association for Educational Communications and Technology, 1025 Vermont Ave. NW, Washington, DC 20005-3547. 64pp. $10 AECT members; $15 nonmembers. This brief yet comprehensive overview of the literature on distance education addresses a definition of distance education; major distance education theories; and history of the field and current operational issues. A selected bibliography is included.

ERIC Documents

Goodwin, Bonny N., and others. (1993, November). **Perceptions and attitudes of faculty and students in two distance learning modes of delivery: Online computer and telecourse.** Paper presented at the Symposium for the Marketing of Higher Education, Orlando, FL, November, 1993. 14pp. ED 371 708. A study was conducted to discover the perceptions and attitudes of students and faculty toward their experiences with two distance learning programs: an online computer program at the University of Phoenix, AZ, and a telecourse program offered by Coastline Community College, CA.

Jones, Judy I., and Simonson, Michael. (1993, January). **Distance education: A cost analysis.** Paper presented at the Association for Educational Communications and Technology, New Orleans, LA, January 13-17, 1993. 59pp. ED 362 171. The costs of three types of transmission technology in distance education—fiber optics, microwave, and compressed video—are compared and the costs for equipping and installing a distance education classroom are estimated.

Kinyanjui, Peter, and Morton, Augusta. (1992, November). **The role of teleconferencing in support of distance education: The case for developing countries.** Paper presented at the International Conference on Distance Education, Bangkok, Thailand, November 8-13, 1992. 18pp. ED 366 296. Explores issues involved in establishing and supporting distance education in developing countries, with emphasis on the role of teleconferencing in support of distance learners.

Moulton, Jeanne. (1994, January). **Interactive radio instruction: Broadening the definition. LearnTech Case Study Series No. 1.** Education Development Center, Inc., Newton, MA. 45pp. ED 371 715. Reviews use of interactive radio instruction as a low-cost means of improving the academic achievement of primary school students, and describes the Radio Mathematics Project in Nicaragua, which was initiated in 1974, and subsequent programs developed by the Learning Technologies for Basic Education (LearnTech) Project.

Wagner, Ellen D. (1993, January). **Evaluating distance learning projects: An approach for cross-project comparisons.** Western Interstate Commission for Higher Education, Boulder, CO. Paper presented at the Association for Educational Communications and Technology, New Orleans, LA, January 13-17, 1993. 32pp. ED 363 273. Describes the methodology developed for the Western Cooperative for Educational Telecommunications' evaluation of seven "New Pathways to a Degree" projects funded by the Annenberg/CPB Project.

Journal Articles

Brush, Thomas, and others. (1993, November). Developing a collaborative performance support system for practicing teachers. **Educational Technology, 33**(11), 39-45. EJ 473 081. (Available UMI). Describes a performance support system that was developed at Indiana University to assist in the delivery of a distance education inservice teacher training program through course presentations, monitoring practicum activities, and promoting collaboration among teachers.

Butterworth, Christine, and Edwards, Richard. (1993, November). Accrediting prior learning at a distance. **Open Learning, 8**(3), 36-43. EJ 474 656. (Available UMI). Discusses the Assessment of Prior Learning (APL) and describes a pilot project at the Open University (United Kingdom) that introduced credit for APL in one course.

Cutright, Patricia J., and Girrard, Kenneth. (1993). Applying innovative technology to the needs of the distant learner. **Library Hi Tech, 11**(4), 67-74. EJ 476 241. (Available UMI). Describes the Eastern Oregon Information Network (EOIN), which was developed to provide off-campus students with dial-in remote access to CD-ROM indexes, an interlibrary loan network module, and an electronic mail system.

Dede, Chris, and others. (1993, November-December). Trends and forecasts. **EDUCOM Review, 28**(6), 35-38. EJ 476 199. (Available UMI). Presents trends and future possibilities in the areas of distance education; handheld wireless information delivery devices; computer applications; academic and administrative computing; electronic communications; and the national information infrastructure.

Fulford, Catherine P., and Zhang, Shuqiang. (1993). Perceptions of interaction: The critical predictor in distance education. **American Journal of Distance Education, 7**(3), 8-21. EJ 477 992. Describes a study of elementary school teachers that examined learner perceptions of interaction—both personal and overall—and satisfaction in an inservice education course delivered by interactive television.

Garland, Maureen R. (1993). Student perceptions of the situational, institutional, dispositional and epistemological barriers to persistence. **Distance Education, 14**(2), 181-98. EJ 481 782. (Available UMI). Discusses situational, institutional, dispositional, and epistemological factors that lead to attrition from adult distance learning courses.

Garrison, D. R. (1993). A cognitive constructivist view of distance education: An analysis of teaching-learning assumptions. **Distance Education, 4**(2), 199-211. EJ 481 783. (Available UMI). Cognitive constructivist learning theory is used to clarify current and emerging assumptions regarding teaching and learning at a distance.

Hillman, Daniel C. A., and others. (1994). Learner-interface interaction in distance education: An extension of contemporary models and strategies for practitioners. **American Journal of Distance Education, 8**(2), 30-42. EJ 489 841. Argues that treatments of the concept of interaction in distance education based on Moore's (1989) discussion of interaction are inadequate; presents a concept of learner-interface interaction; and recommends instructional design strategies that will facilitate students' acquisition of the skills needed to participate effectively in the electronic classroom.

Jones, Ann, and Petre, Marian. (1994, January-February). Computer-based practical work at a distance: A case study. **Computers and Education, 22**(1-2), 27-37. EJ 479 720. (Available UMI). Reports the results of a case study of home computing use in an Open University (Great Britain) multimedia course.

LeBaron, John F., and Bragg, Charles A. (1994). Practicing what we preach: Creating distance education models to prepare teachers for the twenty-first century. **American Journal of Distance Education, 8**(1), 5-19. EJ 483 692. Discusses the advantages of including distance education strategies in preservice teacher education to help prepare for future needs.

Tait, Alan. (1993). Systems, values and dissent: Quality assurance for open and distance learning. **Distance Education, 14**(2), 303-14. EJ 481 786. (Available UMI). Examines the development of quality assurance in higher education delivered through open and distance learning.

Wagner, Ellen D. (1994). In support of a functional definition of interaction. **American Journal of Distance Education, 8**(2), 6-29. EJ 489 840. Discusses several systems models of interaction in distance education and relates them to the contexts of instructional delivery, instructional design, instructional theory, and learning theory in order to establish conceptual parameters for the function of interaction.

EDUCATIONAL RESEARCH

Media-Related Periodicals

American Educational Research Journal. American Educational Research Association, 1230 17th St., NW, Washington, DC 20036-3078. q.; $37 indiv., $46 inst. Reports on original research, both empirical and theoretical, and brief synopses of research.

Current Index to Journals in Education (CIJE). Oryx Press, 4041 N. Central at Indian School Rd., Phoenix, AZ 85012-3397. mo.; $245; semi-ann. cumulations $245; combination $457. A guide to articles published in some 830 education and education-related journals. Includes complete bibliographic information, annotations, and indexes. Semiannual cumulations available. Contents are produced by the ERIC (Educational Resources Information Center) system, Office of Educational Research and Improvement, U.S. Department of Education.

Education Index. H. W. Wilson, 950 University Ave., Bronx, NY 10452. mo. (except July and August); variable costs. Author-subject index to educational publications in the English language. Cumulated quarterly and annually.

Educational Research. ITPS Ltd., Cheritan House, Andover, Hants SP10 5BE, England. 3/yr.; £28 indiv. (foreign £33); £62 inst. (foreign £72). Reports on current educational research, evaluation, and applications.

Educational Researcher. American Educational Research Association, 1230 17th St., NW, Washington, DC 20036-3078. 9/yr.; $37 indiv., $46 inst. Contains news and features of general significance in educational research.

Research in Science & Technological Education. Carfax Publishing Co., P.O. Box 25, Abington, Oxfordshire OX14 3UE England. 2/yr.; $109 indiv., $308 inst. Publication of original research in the science and technological fields. Includes articles on psychological, sociological, economic, and organizational aspects.

Resources in Education (RIE). Superintendent of Documents, U.S. Government Printing Office, P.O. Box 371954, Pittsburgh, PA 15250-7954. mo.; $73 U.S, $91.25 elsewhere; cumulative semi-ann. indexes, $30 U.S., $37.50 elsewhere. Announcement of research reports and other documents in education, including abstracts and indexes by subject, author, and institution. Contents produced by the ERIC (Educational Resources Information Center) system, Office of Educational Research and Improvement, U.S. Department of Education.

Books

Ross, Steven M., and Morrison, Gary R. (1995). **Getting started in instructional technology research.** Association for Educational Communications and Technology, 1025 Vermont Ave. NW, Suite 820, Washington, DC 20005. 31pp. $7.95 AECT members; $9.95 nonmembers. Designed to motivate new professionals to start an active and productive research program and to help experienced professionals to refine their research skills, this guide presents a summary of the ideas and experiences of two reviewers and editors related to doing research in the field.

ERIC Documents

Aust, Ronald, and Padmanabhan, Sandra. (1994). **Empowering teachers with technology: An agenda for research and development.** Paper presented at the National Convention of the Association for Educational Communications and Technology, Research and Theory Division, Nashville, TN, February 16-20, 1994. 16pp. ED 373 700. A review of 847 articles in the major research journals of the Association for Educational Communication and Technology (AECT) from 1953-1993 found that few articles provided specific explanations of how educational technology can be integrated into school structures and/or identified specific needs and corresponding educational technology solutions for empowering teachers.

Field initiated studies program: Abstracts of funded projects, 1993. (1994, Spring). Office of Educational Research and Improvement (ED), Washington, DC. Office of Research. 18pp. ED 370 609. Provides information on 11 research projects funded in 1993 as part of the Field-Initiated Studies program of the U.S. Department of Education.

Hanson, LuEtt. (1993, January). **Perceptions of between-channel redundancy in television messages.** Paper presented at the Annual Conference of the International Visual Literacy Association, Pittsburgh, PA, September 30-October 4, 1992. 11pp. ED 363 301. (Available only as microfiche). Describes a study that used a videotape of 15 short (5- to 20-second) programs with various compositions of audio/visual redundancy to compare researchers' descriptions of audio/video combinations with those of audience members and television producers and discover common grounds of understanding among those groups.

Klein, James D., and others. (1993, January). **Effects of cooperative learning and incentive on motivation and performance.** Paper presented at the Association for Educational Communications and Technology, New Orleans, LA, January 13-17, 1993. 10pp. ED 362 174. Describes an exploration of the effects of cooperative learning and type of reward on the performance and continuing motivation of undergraduate education majors as part of a study designed to investigate how cooperative groups can be implemented with media originally designed for individual learning.

Lenze, James S. (1993, January). **Learner generated versus instructor induced visual imagery.** Paper presented at the Annual Conference of the International Visual Literacy Association, Pittsburgh, PA, September 30-October 4, 1992. 15pp. ED 363 326. Reviews the concepts of imagery, mathemagenic behaviors, and generative imagery; discusses the learner's use of visual imagery; and explores studies examining the relationship between mathemagenic behavior and instructionally induced imagery.

Wagner, Ellen D. (1993, April). **New directions for American education: Implications for continuing educators.** Western Interstate Commission for Higher Education, Boulder, CO. Paper presented at the National University Continuing Education Association, Nashville, TN, April 17, 1993. 10pp. ED 363 275. Identifies issues and trends currently affecting the enterprise of education, with emphasis on how they relate to continuing education.

Journal Articles

Cook, Donald A. (1993, October). Behaviorism evolves. **Educational Technology, 33**(10), 62-77. EJ 472 983. (Available UMI). Reviews basic ideas presented in this special issue on the evolution of behaviorism.

Lankford, J. Scott, and others. (1994, Winter). Computerized versus standard personality measures: Equivalency, computer anxiety, and gender differences. **Computers in Human Behavior, 10**(4), 497-510. EJ 493 287. (Available UMI). Reports on a study of the association between computer anxiety and measures of positive and negative affect when using computerized versus standard administration, including gender differences and the association between computer anxiety and computerized personality tests.

Yeaman, Andrew R. J. (1994, February). Deconstructing modern educational technology. **Educational Technology, 34**(2), 15-24. EJ 478 103. (Available UMI). Discusses modern educational technology, including postmodernism; deconstruction; the Shannon-Weaver Model for telecommunication apparatus and the epistemology of educational technology; the systems approach; and possible demands of postmodern educational technology.

EDUCATIONAL TECHNOLOGY

Media-Related Periodicals

British Journal of Educational Technology. National Council for Educational Technology, Millburn Rd., Science Park, Coventry CV4 7JJ, England. 3/yr.; £60 U.K., £70 overseas airmail; personal subscriptions £32 U.K., £42 overseas. Published by the National Council for Educational Technology, this journal includes articles on education and training, especially theory, applications, and development of educational technology and communications.

Canadian Journal of Educational Communication. Association of Media and Technology in Education in Canada, AMTEC-CJEC Subscription, 3-1750 The Queensway, Suite 1318, Etobicoke, ON, M9C 5H5, Canada. 3/yr.; $45. Articles, research reports, and literature reviews on all areas of educational communication and technology.

Educational and Training Technology International. Kogan Page Ltd., Distribution Centre, Blackhorse Rd., Letchworth, Herts, SG6 1HN, England. q.; £52 U.K., $98 U.S., and North, Central, and South America. Journal of the Association for Educational and Training Technology emphasizes developing trends in and the efficient use of educational technology.

Educational Technology. Educational Technology Publications, Inc., 700 Palisade Ave., Englewood Cliffs, NJ 07632. mo.; $119 U.S. (foreign $139), $12 single copy. Covers telecommunications, computer-aided instruction, information retrieval, educational television, and electronic media in the classroom.

Educational Technology Abstracts. Carfax Publishing Co., P.O. Box 25, Abington, Oxfordshire OX14 3UE, England. 6/yr.; $175 indiv., $407 inst. An international publication of abstracts of recently published material in the field of educational and training technology.

Educational Technology Research and Development. Association for Educational Communications and Technology, 1025 Vermont Ave., NW, Suite 820, Washington, DC 20005-3516. q.; $45 U.S. (foreign $53), $12 single copy. Focuses on research and instructional development in the field of educational technology.

Journal of Instruction Delivery Systems. Learning Technology Institute, 50 Culpeper St., Warrenton, VA 22186. q.; $60 indiv., $75 inst., add $15 postage for countries outside North America. Devoted to the issues and applications of technology to enhance productivity in education, training, and job performance.

Journal of Technology and Teacher Education. Association for the Advancement of Computing in Education (AACE), P.O. Box 2966, Charlottesville, VA 22902. q.; $65 indiv. U.S. (foreign $80), $83 inst. U.S. (foreign $103). Serves as an international forum to report research and applications of technology in preservice, inservice, and graduate teacher education.

Science Communication (formerly **Knowledge: Creation, Diffusion, Utilization**). Sage Publications, Inc., 2455 Teller Rd., Thousand Oaks, CA 91320. q.; $51 indiv., $141 inst. (In California, add 7.25%.) An international, interdisciplinary journal examining the nature of expertise and the translation of knowledge into practice and policy.

Technology and Learning. Peter Li Education Group, 330 Progress Rd., Dayton, OH 45449. 8/yr.; $24. Publishes features, reviews, news, and announcements of educational activities and opportunities in programming, software development, and hardware configurations.

TECHNOS. Agency for Instructional Technology, Box A, 1111 W. 17th St., Bloomington, IN 47402-0120. q.; $20 indiv., $16 libr. (foreign $24). A forum for discussion of ideas about the use of technology in education, with a focus on reform.

Tech Trends. Association for Educational Communications and Technology, 1025 Vermont Ave., NW, Suite 820, Washington, DC 20005-3516. 6/yr.; $36 U.S., $40 elsewhere, $4 single copy. Features authoritative, practical articles about technology and its integration into the learning environment.

T.H.E. Journal (Technological Horizons in Education). T.H.E., 150 El Camino Real, Suite 112, Tustin, CA 92680-3670. 11/yr.; $29 (free to qualified educators). For educators of all levels. Focuses on a specific topic for each issue, as well as technological innovations as they apply to education.

Books

Anglin, Gary, ed. (1995). **Instructional technology: Past, present, and future.** 2nd edition. Libraries Unlimited, P.O. Box 6633, Englewood, CO 80155-6633. 432pp. $39. This comprehensive view of the field has been updated to cover such current topics as educational and instructional systems development, postmodernism and instructional technology, interactive technologies, the Internet and higher education, qualitative research, and instructional technology and attitude change.

Brock, Patricia Ann. (1994). **Educational technology in the classroom.** Educational Technology Publications, 700 Palisade Ave., Englewood Cliffs, NJ 07632. 250pp. $34.95. Written for the nonspecialist in educational technology, this guide uses a question-answer format to provide information on computer fundamentals, including microcomputer hardware and software; computer-mediated communications and facsimile; online databases and electronic bulletin board systems; educational radio and instructional television; compact disc technology; videodisc technology; desktop computer music; and multimedia, hypermedia, and beyond. Numerous reference sources are also provided.

Brody, Philip J. (1995). **Technology planning and management handbook: A guide for school district educational technology leaders.** Educational Technology Publications, 700 Palisade Ave., Englewood Cliffs, NJ 07632. 180pp. $34.95. Written for practitioners, this book provides practical guidance for administrators of school district educational technology programs. It includes potential solutions to problems common to virtually all school districts, two dozen "reality checks," and sixteen worksheets for use in the field.

The electronic school: Innovative uses of technology in education. (1994). National School Boards Association, 1680 Duke St., Alexandria, VA 22314-3493. 56pp. $10. Case studies demonstrate how educators are using technology to produce positive results in K-12 classrooms and school offices nationwide. Feature stories cover the issues surrounding technology in schools, including telecommunications, online networking, wireless technology, virtual reality, digital yearbooks, and school technology purchasing cooperatives. Names and telephone numbers for obtaining more information are included.

Ely, Donald P., and Minor, Barbara B., eds. (1994). **Educational media and technology yearbook, 1994. Volume 20.** Libraries Unlimited, Inc., P.O. Box 6633, Englewood, CO 80155-6633. 409pp. $60. Provides media and instructional technology professionals with an up-to-date, single-source overview and assessment of the field of educational technology. Covers trends, issues, and current developments, and provides leadership profiles and annotated listings of the organizations, agencies, and colleges and universities that serve the field.

Havelock, Ronald G. (1995). **The change agent's guide. Second edition.** Educational Technology Publications, 700 Palisade Ave., Englewood Cliffs, NJ 07632. 270pp. $37.95. A comprehensive guide to the process of social systems change, this revised and updated guide begins with case histories of change agents in action. The book then covers "The Stages of Planned Change," followed by a detailed review of the change literature, and concludes with a discussion of the role of the change agent and his or her team.

Johnson, Jenny K., ed. (1995). **Degree curricula in educational communications and technology. A descriptive directory.** 5th edition. 456pp. $24 AECT members; $36 nonmembers. Formerly *Graduate curricula in educational communications and technology*, this directory has been updated and expanded to include undergraduate programs. Information provided on individual programs includes courses, program duration, graduation requirements, and faculty. A 3.5" MS-DOS database disk is included.

Means, Barbara, ed. (1994). **Technology and education reform: The reality behind the promise.** Jossey-Bass, 350 Sansome St., San Francisco, CA 94104-1310. 232pp. $28.95. The eight papers in this book show how the introduction of such new educational technologies as multimedia systems, networks, video, and microcomputers can support and further the efforts of school reform. Papers were prepared by leading researchers as part of the National Study of Technology and Education Reform, sponsored by the Office of Educational Research and Improvement (OERI).

Moore, David M. (Mike), and Dwyer, Francis M., eds. (1994). **Visual literacy: A spectrum of visual learning.** Educational Technology Publications, 700 Palisade Ave., Englewood Cliffs, NJ 07632. 450pp. $39.95. The 22 articles presented in this compilation include discussions of the theoretical foundations of visual learning, defining visual literacy, use of visuals in various settings, design considerations, interpretation of visuals, and a research paradigm.

Reigeluth, Charles M., and Garfinkle, Robert J., eds. (1994). **Systemic change in education.** Educational Technology Publications, 700 Palisade Ave., Englewood Cliffs, NJ 07632. 184pp. $34.95. Articles in this book are presented in four sections, preceded by an introduction by Charles M. Reigeluth that addresses the questions of what systemic change is and why it is needed in education. Section 1 describes some theoretical frameworks that can be used to begin thinking systemically about educational change, and Section 2 describes models that flesh out the theoretical articles. Key components that are likely to make up a new paradigm of education for the information age are explored in Section 3, and Section 4 provides some examples of systemic change efforts.

Seels, Barbara, and Richey, Rita C. (1994). **Instructional technology: The definition and domains of the field.** Association for Educational Communications and Technology, 1025 Vermont Ave. NW, Washington, DC 20005. 192pp. $25.95 AECT members; $30.95 non-members. This book builds upon new developments in theory and practice that have evolved with the technology employed by the field. Chapters address an analysis of the definition, the domains of the field, sources of influence on instructional technology, and the practice of instructional technology.

Simonson, Michael, ed. (1994). **Research proceedings: 1994 AECT national convention.** Association for Educational Communications and Technology, 1025 Vermont Ave., NW, Suite 820, Washington, DC 20005-3547. 1,100+pp. $45 AECT members; $60 nonmembers. The 16th annual collection of research papers from AECT's 1994 convention in Nashville, TN, includes research on multimedia instruction, embedded training environments, compressed video, intelligent tutoring, and effects of various technologies on learning. Also available as ERIC document no. ED 373 774; individual papers, ED 373 775-784.

Simonson, Michael, ed. (1995). **Research proceedings: 1995 AECT national convention.** Association for Educational Communications and Technology, 1025 Vermont Ave., NW, Suite 820, Washington, DC 20005-3547. Approx. 1,100pp. $45 AECT members; $60 nonmembers. The 17th annual collection of research papers from AECT's 1995 convention in Anaheim, CA, includes research on multimedia instruction, embedded training environments, compressed video, intelligent tutoring, and effects of various technologies on learning.

Wilson, Brent G., Teslow, James L., Cyr, Thomas A., and Hamilton, Roger. (1994). **Technology making a difference: The Peakview Elementary School Study.** Information Resources Publications, 4-194 Center for Science and Technology, Syracuse University, Syracuse, NY 13244-4100. 220pp. $15 plus $2 shipping and handling. This case study examines the impact of technology on a school that has installed a network that includes multi-age student groupings, cross-functional teaching teams, and cooperative learning strategies. The report not only documents a recognizable move to innovative teaching methods that promote small-group instruction, coaching, increased interactive strategies, and the integration of visual media, but also models ways to measure the impact of technology on a school that extend beyond the media comparison studies of two decades ago.

ERIC Documents

Greene, Perry E., and others. (1993). **Tarnished silver: Technology images as history.** Paper presented at the Annual Conference of the International Visual Literacy Association, Rochester, NY, October 13-17, 1993. 9pp. ED 370 552. This paper discusses the development of a sociocultural and local, context-sensitive base for guidance in selection and evaluation of instructional media, with emphasis on 16mm educational film.

Ismail, M. I., and Al-Turkait, A. A. (1993). **Excellence center for high technology transfer.** 131pp. ED 367 307. The 15 chapters in this monograph introduce the assured system that results in excellency in services and expectations from technology transfer, focusing on simple techniques of potential interest for community and public interest.

Kantor, Ronald J., and others. (1993, April). **Extending the impact of classroom-based technology: The Satellite Challenge Series.** Paper presented at the American Educational Research Association, Atlanta, GA, April 12-16, 1993. 15pp. ED 364 205. The Jasper Challenge Series of Vanderbilt University (TN) has been used in conjunction with the university's videodisc problem-solving series, "The Adventures of Jasper Woodbury," to provide a teleconference-based performance arena that allows students and teachers to assess the degree to which they are learning to solve the kinds of problems that the Jasper series emphasizes. These Special Multimedia Arenas for Refining Thinking (SMART) challenges are described, and the challenge-based assessment model that has been developed is explored.

Lloyd, R. Scott. (1993, January). **An introduction to educational holography.** Paper presented at the Annual Conference of the International Visual Literacy Association, Pittsburgh, PA, September 30-October 4, 1992. 10pp. ED 363 327. Argues that holograms, which can be used as educational tools to explain information visually to everyone, are not limited to recording images from original objects, but may be used to synthesize views of anything that can be represented graphically. Potential applications of this technology in visual literacy are discussed.

Means, Barbara, and others. (1993). **Using technology to support education reform.** Education Development Center, Inc., Newton, MA; SRI International, Menlo Park, CA. 118pp. ED 364 220. Report prepared for the Office of Educational Research and Improvement in the U.S. Department of Education presents a model of school reform; describes how technology can support the kind of student learning described in the model and as defined by education reformers; and describes ways in which technology can support teacher efforts to promote student learning. A review of the literature on the effects of technology on student learning outcomes and discussion of issues involved in implementing technology-supported educational reform conclude the report.

Mergendoller, John R., and others. (1994, January). **The Utah Educational Technology Initiative: Evaluation update.** Beryl Buck Institute for Education, Novato, CA. 17pp. ED 370 534. Provides an overview of the Utah Educational Technology Initiative (ETI); descriptions of previous evaluation reports; and findings from the three-year course of this evaluation in the following areas: ETI impact on student achievement and motivation; ETI impact on student access to technology; the nature of student computer use; teacher computer utilization; efforts to support technology use; program implementation and outreach; teacher competence with educational technology; and ETI at colleges of education. Three remaining challenges are also presented.

Wilson, Brent G., and others. (1993, January). **Evaluating the impact of technology at Peakview Elementary School: The full report.** 207pp. ED 366 288. This case study focuses on the impact of technology in the Peakview Elementary School (CO), which, in order to implement organizational and teaching strategies advocated by the school restructuring reform movement, installed more than 80 networked computers and related technology. Data were gathered at the beginning and end of the 1991-92 school year via written surveys and interviews with teachers and students. Peakview was also compared with three other elementary schools. Findings are reported in the following areas: (1) use of technology; (2) impact on teaching; (3) implementation factors; (4) teacher attitudes; and (5) student achievement.

Journal Articles

Banathy, Bela H. (1994, January). Writing the new script of education: Introduction to special issue on educational systems design. **Educational Technology, 34**(1), 7-10. EJ 477 960. (Available UMI). Provides an overview of this special issue on educational systems design and summarizes the articles included.

Beishuizen, J. J., and Moonen, J. (1993, July-September). Technology-enriched schools: Co-operation between teachers and researchers. **Computers and Education, 21**(1-2), 51-59. EJ 473 111. (Available UMI). Discussion of the Dutch Technology-Enriched School (TES) project highlights teacher involvement, development versus controlled research, characteristics of the TES project, and the progressive broadening implementation strategy (i.e., implementing computers in education).

Clark, Richard E. (1994). Media and method. **Educational Technology Research and Development, 42**(3), 7-10. EJ 493 370. (Available UMI). Discusses the question of whether instructional methods are replaceable or interchangeable, covering the influence of external events on learning and cognitive processes, media variables, linking instructional design to research on learning from instruction, and construct validity. An example of adequate instructional design and media development is included.

Cradler, John. (1994, Spring-Summer). School-based technology use planning. **Educational IRM Quarterly, 3**(3-4), 12-16. EJ 488 366. Describes how to conduct systematic planning for technology use and the components of an effective technology use plan based on a comprehensive study of school-based technology.

Koumi, Jack. (1994, January). Media comparison and deployment: A practitioner's view. **British Journal of Educational Technology, 25**(1), 41-57. EJ 486 807. (Available UMI). Proposes a framework to help course developers design criteria for optimal media deployment and compares the merits of radio, television, audio, video, and print with computer-based media vis-à-vis six types of media characteristics.

Kozma, Robert B. (1994). Will media influence learning? Reframing the debate. **Educational Technology Research and Development, 42**(2), 7-19. EJ 488 323. (Available UMI). Argues that the capabilities of media as they interact with the cognitive and social processes by which knowledge is constructed must be considered. This approach is examined within the context of two major media-based projects.

Laurillard, Diana. (1993). Balancing the media. **Journal of Educational Television, 19**(2), 81-93. EJ 471 141. Discusses an analytical framework to assist in the selection of educational technology that will support the learning process, including print, video, computer-based tutorial, and teacher-student discussion. Use of multimedia in the British Open University is described.

Muffoletto, Robert. (1994, February). Technology and restructuring education: Constructing a context. **Educational Technology, 34**(2), 24-28. EJ 478 104. (Available UMI). Considers educational change, school restructuring, and the role of technology, including instructional technology and a history of educational reform and national goals and guidelines.

Phelps, Malcolm V. (1994). The federal role in educational technology. **Educational Media and Technology Yearbook, 20**, 142-50. EJ 491 614. (Available UMI). Describes the Educational Technologies Working Group of the Federal Coordinating Council for Science, Engineering and Technology, which is charged with identifying technology-related activities that promise to improve science, mathematics, engineering, and technology education; developing resident expertise; and sharing information. Milestones to measure federal progress in using educational technology are discussed.

Richey, Rita C., and Seels, Barbara. (1994). Defining a field: A case study of the development of the 1994 *Definition of Instructional Technology*. **Educational Media and Technology Yearbook, 20**, 2-17. EJ 491 599. (Available UMI). Documents the process used to construct the definition of the field of instructional technology, including a chronology of the development and the key factors that influenced the construction process.

Russell, James D., and others. (1994, April). Improving technology implementation in grades 5-12 with the ASSURE model. **T.H.E. Journal, 21**(9), 66-70. EJ 481 965. (Available UMI). Presents the ASSURE (Analyze learners, State objectives, Select media and materials, Utilize media/materials, Require participation, Evaluate and revise) model, an approach for training professional staff on implementing technology in schools. Design and implementation of workshops for school staff are described, and a sidebar outlines a six-day workshop schedule.

Spotts, Thomas H., and Bowman, Mary Ann. (1993, December). Increasing faculty use of instructional technology: Barriers and incentives. **Educational Media International, 30**(4), 199-204. EJ 488 307. (Available UMI). Examines factors influencing use of technology by faculty members at an American university.

Ullmer, Eldon J. (1994). Media and learning: Are there two kinds of truth? **Educational Technology Research and Development, 42**(1), 21-32. EJ 483 758. (Available UMI). Examines the methods of conventional instructional media research to gauge their sufficiency; gives examples of complex media effects; identifies three emerging media application paradigms; and offers an alternative values framework for guiding research on the effects of modern interactive technologies in complex learning environments.

Vooijs, Marcel W., and van der Voort, Tom H. A. (1993). Teaching children to evaluate television violence critically: The impact of a Dutch schools television project. **Journal of Educational Television, 19**(3), 139-52. EJ 478 068. Describes a study conducted in Dutch primary schools to alter the cognitive effects that television violence can have on 10- to 12-year-olds by encouraging them to critically evaluate the portrayal of violence.

Videos

Instructional technology review and update. (1994). Institute for Academic Technology, 2525 Meridian Parkway, Suite 400, Durham, NC 27713. 2.5 hours. $395 individual; $325 in series. This satellite broadcast videotape discusses and provides technical demonstrations of instructional technology from the basics to the cutting edge. The other two videotapes in the series are *Reengineering Distributed Learning Environments* and *Libraries: Today's Issues, Tomorrow's Challenges.*

Learning by doing: Lessons from the field. (1994). WMHT Home Video, P.O. Box 17, Schenectady, NY 12301. 30 min. $19.95 plus New York state sales tax and $4 shipping and handling. This case study looks at new ways of teaching and learning at the Ithaca Alternative Community School (ACS) in Ithaca, New York. ACS has long been a model for the principles and objectives of *A New Compact for Learning*. Originally broadcast on April 5, 1994, on PBS.

ELECTRONIC PUBLISHING

Media-Related Periodicals

Desktop Communications. International Desktop Communications, Ltd., 342 Madison Ave., Suite 622, New York, NY 10173-0002. bi-mo.; $24. Helps small business, corporate, and individual computer users to design and implement innovative and effective newsletters, reports, presentations, and other business communications.

Electronic Publishing: Origination, Dissemination, and Design. John Wiley & Sons, Ltd., Baffins Lane, Chichester, W. Sussex, PO19 1UD, England. q.; $275. Covers structured editors, authoring tools, hypermedia, document bases, electronic documents over networks, and text integration.

Publish! PC World Communications, Inc., Box 51967, Boulder, CO 80322-5415. mo.; $23.95. A how-to magazine for desktop publishing.

Books

Azarmsa, Reza. (1993, 1994). **Educator's handbook to desktop publishing using Aldus® PageMaker®.** Libraries Unlimited, P.O. Box 6633. Englewood, CO 80155-6633. Mac edition: 231pp., $24. IBM-compatible edition: 231pp., $23.50. (Each edition includes a disk.) This comprehensive introduction to desktop publishing provides all the information needed to produce high-quality documents with Aldus PageMaker versions 4.0-5.0.

Journal Articles

Broering, Naomi C., and Lilienfield, Lawrence S. (1994). Electronic textbook in human physiology. **Library Hi Tech, 12**(1), 49-54. EJ 478 033. (Available UMI). Describes the development of an electronic textbook in human physiology at the Georgetown University Medical Center Library, which was designed to enhance learning and visualization through a prototype knowledge base of core instructional materials stored in digital format on Macintosh computers.

Siegel, Martin A., and Sousa, Gerald A. (1994, September). Inventing the virtual textbook: Changing the nature of schooling. **Educational Technology, 34**(7), 49-54. EJ 489 817. (Available UMI). Discussion of the educational effectiveness of textbooks; focuses on a model of a virtual textbook that relies on hypermedia.

INFORMATION SCIENCE AND TECHNOLOGY

Media-Related Periodicals

Bulletin of the American Society for Information Science. ASIS, 8720 Georgia Ave., Suite 501, Silver Spring, MD 20910-3602. bi-mo.; $60 North America, $70 elsewhere, $10 single copy. Newsmagazine concentrating on issues affecting the information field; management reports; opinion; and news of people and events in ASIS and the information community.

Canadian Journal of Information and Library Science/Revue canadienne des sciences de l'information et de bibliothèconomie. CAIS, University of Toronto Press, Journals Dept., 5201 Dufferin St., Downsview, ON M3H 5T8, Canada. q.; nonmembers $95 Canada, $110 elsewhere. Published by the Canadian Association for Information Science to contribute to the advancement of library and information science in Canada.

Datamation. Cahners Publishing Co., 44 Cook St., Denver, CO 80206. 24/yr.; $75 indiv., $47 libr.; $110 Canada, Mexico; $195 Japan, Australia, New Zealand; $165 elsewhere. Covers semi-technical news and views on hardware, software, and databases, for data- and information-processing professionals.

Information Processing and Management. Elsevier Science, 660 White Plains Rd., Tarry-town, NY 10591-5153. £341; $525 U.S. An international journal covering data processing, database building, and retrieval.

Information Retrieval and Library Automation. Lomond Publications, Inc., Box 88, Mt. Airy, MD 21771. mo.; $66 U.S. (foreign $79.50). News, articles, and announcements on new techniques, equipment, and software in information services.

Information Services & Use. Elsevier Science Publishers, Box 10558, Burke, VA 22009-0558. 4/yr.; $214. An international journal for those in the information management field. Includes online and offline systems, library automation, micrographics, videotex, and telecommunications.

The Information Society. Taylor and Francis, 1900 Frost Rd., Suite 101, Bristol, PA 19007. q.; $43 indiv., $86 inst. Provides a forum for discussion of the world of information, including transborder data flow, regulatory issues, and the impact of the information industry.

Information Technology and Libraries. American Library Association, Library and Information Technology Association, 50 E. Huron St., Chicago, IL 60611-2795. q.; $45 U.S. nonmembers, $50 Canada and Mexico, $55 elsewhere. Articles on library automation, communication technology, cable systems, computerized information processing, and video technologies.

Journal of the American Society for Information Science. Subscription Department, 605 3rd Ave., New York, NY 10158-0012. 10/yr.; $550 U.S. nonmembers, $650 Canada and Mexico, $687.50 elsewhere. Publishes research articles in the area of information science.

Journal of Documentation. Aslib, Association for Information Management, Publications Dept., Information House, 20-24 Old St., London EC1V 9AP, England. q.; £60 members, £90 ($180) nonmembers. Describes how technical, scientific, and other specialized knowledge is recorded, organized, and disseminated.

Books

Maxian, Bruce, ed. (1994). **Proceedings of the 57th Annual Meeting of the American Society for Information Science, October 17-20, 1994, Alexandria, VA. Volume 31.** Information Today, Inc. (formerly Learned Information, Inc.), 143 Old Marlton Pike, Medford, NJ 08055-8750. 128pp. $29.50. The theme of the meeting was "The Economics of Information." The first of three parts, Contributed Papers, presents 10 papers on topics ranging from the value of information to cost-efficiency of document delivery, the costs of interlibrary cooperation, and the teaching of economics of information in professional programs. The second part contains reports/presentations from sessions of Special Interest Groups, and the third contains two Sig Session papers. Author and subject indexes are also provided. Sessions on Hot Topics, special sessions on copyright and access to public documents, and Theme Sessions are not included.

Mendrinos, Roxanne. (1994). **Building information literacy using high technology: A guide for schools and libraries.** Libraries Unlimited, P.O. Box 6633, Englewood, CO 80155-6633. 185pp. $25, $30 outside North America. This guide to using the high-tech tools of online databases, telecommunications, and CD-ROM technology in the educational environment provides step-by-step procedures for going online and gives guidelines for using CD-ROM and networking. It also contains field-tested curriculum applications, classroom and inservice teaching strategies, case studies of successful library media specialist/teacher partnerships, and actual units of interdisciplinary instruction for both the secondary school and graduate library science levels.

Proceedings of the 15th National Online Meeting, May 10-12, 1994. (1994). Information Today, Inc. (formerly Learned Information), 143 Old Marlton Pike, Medford, NJ 08055-8750. 464pp. $55. Fifty-eight papers by experts from all facets of the electronic information field.

Williams, Martha E., ed. (1994). **Annual Review of Information and Science Technology, volume 29—1994 (ARIST).** Information Today, Inc. (formerly Learned Information, Inc.), 143 Old Marlton Pike, Medford, NJ 08055-8750. $76 for members of the American Society for Information Science, $95 for nonmembers. A literary source of ideas, trends, and references that offers a comprehensive view of information science technology. The nine topics covered in this edition fit into the fundamental structure of planning information systems and services, basic techniques and technologies, applications, and the profession.

ERIC Documents

Booker, Di, ed. (1993). **Information literacy: The Australian agenda. Proceedings of a conference conducted by the University of South Australia Library (Adelaide, Australia, December 2-4, 1992).** University of South Australia, Underdale. 193pp. ED 365 336. The aims of this conference were to promote information literacy as a means of personal and national advancement in today's information-dependent society; to emphasize information literacy as an essential competency for lifelong learning; to ensure that all delegates understand information literacy and its importance for the economic and social well-being of their community; to develop cross-sectoral cooperation in promoting information literacy; to establish a broad-based national coalition for information literacy; and to identify the agenda for change needed across education and information sectors to raise the level of information literacy.

Strategic Information Technology Plan. State of Washington. (1993, January). Washington State Department of Information Services, Olympia. Policy and Regulation Division. 39pp. ED 365 297. The Strategic Information Technology Plan of Washington is intended to create a new framework for communication and collaboration to bring together agency technology planning with the achievement of statewide information technology goals and strategies. It provides a point of reference for the agency strategic plans, agency performance reports, and statewide performance reports on information technology.

Sutton, Ronald E. (1993, January). **Information literacy meets media literacy and visual literacy.** Paper presented at the Annual Conference of the International Visual Literacy Association, Pittsburgh, PA, September 30-October 4, 1992. 11pp. ED 363 307. (Available only as microfiche.) Current definitions of three media literacies are offered from a theoretical and practical standpoint: (1) *information literacy*, which means that a person must be able to recognize when information is needed, and have the ability to locate, evaluate, and use effectively the needed information; (2) *media literacy*, which is the ability to decode, analyze, evaluate, and produce communication in a variety of forms; and (3) *visual literacy*, which may be defined as the ability to recognize and understand ideas conveyed through visible actions or images.

Journal Articles

Creth, Sheila D. (1993). Creating a virtual information organization: Collaborative relationships between libraries and computing centers. **Journal of Library Administration, 19**(3-4), 111-32. EJ 481 814. Discussion of changes in higher education as a result of advances in information technology focuses on the relationship between academic libraries and computing centers.

Davis, Niki. (1993). The development of classroom applications of new technology in pre-service teacher education: A review of the research. **Journal of Technology and Teacher Education,** 1(3), 229-49. EJ 476 256. Reviews the literature dealing with information technology in preservice teacher education in the United Kingdom and the United States.

Goodrum, David A., and others. (1993, November). Defining and building an enriched learning and information environment. **Educational Technology, 33**(11), 10-20. EJ 473 078. (Available UMI). Discussion of the development of an Enriched Learning and Information Environment (ELIE) highlights technology-based and theory-based frameworks for defining ELIEs; a sociotechnical definition; a conceptual prototype; a participatory design process; and design issues for technology systems.

Martinez, Michael E. (1994, July). Access to information technologies among school-age children: Implications for a democratic society. **Journal of the American Society for Information Science, 45**(6), 395-400. EJ 488 234. (Available UMI). Discusses access to information technology among school-age children, based on the National Assessment of Educational Progress (NAEP), and suggests implications of the results for a democratic society.

Schwen, Thomas M., and others. (1993, November). On the design of an enriched learning and information environment (ELIE). **Educational Technology, 33**(11), 5-9. EJ 473 077. (Available UMI). Discusses the concept and design of an enriched learning and information environment that was originally developed at Indiana University in partnership with American Telephone and Telegraph.

Television Documentaries

Media mayhem: More than make believe. Newist/CESA #7, Studio B, University of Wisconsin, Green Bay, WI 54311. 30 min., color; each 1/2" VHS is accompanied by a resource guide. Purchase $195; rental $50. Intended for students in grades 7-12 (especially those "at risk") and teachers of younger students, this entertaining introduction to media literacy argues that the omnipresent violence in today's media is not a reflection of reality. The program includes the perspectives of violent offenders, an ex-television story analyst, and eight young actors portraying themselves in adult positions of authority.

INSTRUCTIONAL DESIGN AND TRAINING

Media-Related Periodicals

Human Computer Interaction. Lawrence Erlbaum Associates, 365 Broadway, Hillsdale, NJ 07642. q.; $39 indiv. U.S. and Canada, $64 elsewhere, $180 inst., $205 elsewhere. A journal of theoretical, empirical, and methodological issues of user science and of system design.

Instructional Science. Kluwer Academic Publishers, 355 Accord Station, Hingham, MA 02018-0358. 6/yr.; $257. Aimed to promote a deeper understanding of the nature, theory, and practice of the instructional process and the learning resulting from this process.

Journal of Educational Multimedia and Hypermedia. Association for the Advancement of Computing in Education, Box 2966, Charlottesville, VA 22902-2966. q.; $65 indiv., $83 inst.; Canada and Mexico add $10, other countries add $15. A multidisciplinary information source presenting research and applications on multimedia and hypermedia tools that allow the integration of images, sounds, text, and data in learning and teaching.

Journal of Educational Technology Systems. Baywood Publishing Co., 26 Austin Ave., Box 337, Amityville, NY 11701. q.; $112 inst. plus $4.50 postage U.S. and Canada, $9.35 postage elsewhere. In-depth articles on completed and ongoing research in all phases of educational technology and its application and future within the teaching profession.

Journal of Interactive Instruction Development. Learning Technology Institute, Society for Applied Learning Technology, 50 Culpeper St., Warrenton, VA 22186. q.; $60 indiv., $75 inst.; add $15 postage outside North America. A showcase of successful programs that will give awareness of innovative, creative, and effective approaches to courseware development for interactive technology.

Journal of Technical Writing and Communication. Baywood Publishing Co., 26 Austin Ave., Box 337, Amityville, NY 11701. q.; $36 indiv., $107 inst. Essays on oral and written communication, for purposes ranging from pure research to needs of business and industry.

Journal of Visual Literacy. International Visual Literacy Association, c/o John C. Belland, 122 Ramseyer Hall, 29 West Woodruff Ave., Ohio State University, Columbus, OH 43210. semi-ann.; $12 indiv., $18 libraries. Interdisciplinary forum on all aspects of visual/verbal languaging.

Performance and Instruction. National Society for Performance and Instruction, 1300 L St., NW, Suite 1250, Washington, DC 20005. 10/yr.; $89 nonmembers. Journal of NSPI, intended to promote the advantage of performance science and technology. Contains articles, research, and case studies relating to improving human performance.

Performance Improvement Quarterly. National Society for Performance and Instruction, 1300 L St., NW, Suite 1250, Washington, DC 20005. q.; $20 nonmembers. Represents the cutting edge in research and theory in performance technology.

Training. Lakewood Publications, Inc., 50 S. Ninth, Minneapolis, MN 55402. mo.; $68 U.S., $78 Canada, $89 elsewhere. Covers all aspects of training, management, and organizational development, motivation, and performance improvement.

Books

Kelly, Leslie, ed. (1995). **The ASTD technical and skills training handbook.** McGraw-Hill, Inc., Princeton Road, Hightstown, NJ 08520. 615pp. $59.50. This handbook is intended to serve as a hands-on reference for technical trainers, many of whom are resident experts in corporations who have been recruited from within the organization rather than individuals with training background. It contains 23 chapters by experts in the field, including information on instructional design, the adult learner, training methods and programs, liability and the technical trainer, growth of technical training professionalism, and colleges, universities, and vocational and technical institutes.

Merrill, M. David, and Twitchell, David G., eds. (1994). **Instructional design theory.** Educational Technology Publications, 700 Palisade Ave., Englewood Cliffs, NJ 07632. 480pp. $39.95. This volume presents the key writings of M. David Merrill over the past two decades as he has developed instructional design theory. Papers are presented in six categories: Instructional Science, Content Structure and Organization, Component Display Theory, Learner Control, Authoring and Authoring Systems, and Automating Instructional Design.

Seels, Barbara B., ed. (1975). **Instructional design fundamentals: A reconsideration.** Educational Technology Publications, 700 Palisade Ave., Englewood Cliffs, NJ 07632. 288pp. $37.95. A revised definition and domain structure for the field of educational technology broadens its scope beyond linear instructional systems design or technology as a systematic process. The articles in this book address four categories of the newly reconceptualized domain of design: ISD (instructional systems design), Message Design, Instructional Strategies, and Learner Characteristics.

ERIC Documents

Li, Ming-Fen. (1993, January). **Empowering learners through metacognitive thinking, instruction, and design.** Paper presented at the Association for Educational Communications and Technology, New Orleans, LA, January 13-17, 1993. 14pp. ED 362 180. A perspective is presented for designing instruction in metacognition, drawing on how human beings acquire metacognitive skills and how these skills are interwoven with other thinking skills.

Litchfield, Brenda C. (1993, April). **Design factors in multimedia environments: Research findings and implications for instructional design.** Paper presented at the American Educational Research Association, Atlanta, GA, April 12-16, 1993. 18pp. ED 363 268. Current literature pertaining to multimedia programs is reviewed and discussed as it relates to the design and development of instructional programs, including instructional strategies and cooperative learning; navigation and learner control; learning styles and motivation; and media, including interactive videodisc, hypermedia, and hypertext.

Mukherjee, Prachee, and Edmonds, Gerald S. (1993). **Screen design: A review of research.** Paper presented at the Annual Conference of the International Visual Literacy Association, Rochester, NY, October 13-17, 1993. 9pp. ED 370 561. Reviews the literature on screen design used for instructional purposes, including the definition, foundations, elements, and functions of screen design; screen design research and problems; and criteria for evaluation.

Richey, Rita C. (1994). **Design 2000: Theory-based design models of the future.** Paper presented at the National Convention of the Association for Educational Communications and Technology, Research and Theory Division, Nashville, TN, February 16-20, 1994. 9pp. ED 373 752. Explores the influence of theory on instructional-design models of the future on the basis of current theoretical developments and anticipated model changes that are expected to result from disparate theoretical thinking in areas such as chaos theory, constructivism, situated learning, cognitive-learning theory, and general systems theory.

Journal Articles

Aarntzen, Diana. (1993, November). Audio in courseware: Design knowledge issues. **Educational and Training Technology International, 30**(4), 354-66. EJ 476 342. (Available UMI). Considers issues that must be addressed when incorporating audio in courseware design, including functions of audio in courseware; the relationship between aural and visual information; learner characteristics in relation to audio; events of instruction; and audio characteristics, including interactivity and speech technology.

Bagdonis, Anthony S., and Salisbury, David F. (1994, April). Development and validation of models in instructional design. **Educational Technology, 34**(4), 26-32. EJ 481 850. (Available UMI). Provides an overview of the use of models in instructional design, including a definition of the term *model*; types of models; procedures for model development; classification of models in the literature; and alternative techniques for model validation.

Blissett, Gillian, and Atkins, Madeleine. (1993, July-September). Are they thinking? Are they learning? A study of the use of interactive video. **Computers and Education, 21**(1-2), 31-39. EJ 473 110. (Available UMI). Relates findings of an empirical study of interactive videodisc use by 12- and 13-year-old students in England to theories of learning and to other research findings.

Cennamo, Katherine S. (1993). Learning from video: Factors influencing learners' preconceptions and invested mental effort. **Educational Technology Research and Development, 41**(3), 33-45. EJ 471 177. (Available UMI). Discusses factors that influence learners' preconceptions of television, the mental effort they invest in processing a video-based lesson, and their achievement.

Damarin, Suzanne K. (1993, Fall). The ascendancy of the visual and issues of gender: Equality versus difference. **Journal of Visual Literacy, 13**(2), 61-71. EJ 486 743. Discusses visual literacy, visual cognition, visual thinking and learning, and visual knowledge, with a focus on women and gender differences.

Milheim, William D. (1994). A comprehensive model for the transfer of training. **Performance Improvement Quarterly, 7**(2), 95-104. EJ 481 874. Presents a model for the effective transfer of skills from training programs to worksite implementation for instructional designers and corporate trainers involved in performance improvement.

Ross, Steven M., and others. (1994, Winter). Preferences for different CBI text screen designs based on the density level and realism of the lesson content viewed. **Computers in Human Behavior, 10**(4), 593-603. EJ 493 289. (Available UMI). Reports on a study of college student preferences for learning from computer-based instruction screen designs representing four levels of screen density, varied by the type of stimulus material and number of frames presented from a single lesson.

Tessmer, Martin. (1994). Formative evaluation alternatives. **Performance Improvement Quarterly, 7**(1), 3-18. EJ 478 010. Discussion of formative evaluation highlights alternative formative evaluation methods and tools and explains their advantages, disadvantages, and applicable contexts.

LIBRARIES AND MEDIA CENTERS

Media-Related Periodicals

Book Report. Linworth Publishing, 480 E. Wilson Bridge Rd., Suite L, Worthington, OH 43085-2372. 5/school yr.; $39 U.S., $47 Canada, $9 single copy. Journal for junior and senior high school librarians provides articles, tips, and ideas for day-to-day school library management, as well as reviews of audiovisuals and software, all written by school librarians.

Collection Building. Neal-Schuman Publishers, 100 Varick St., New York, NY 10013. q.; $58.50 U.S., $63.50 Canada, $65 elsewhere. Focuses on all aspects of collection building, ranging from microcomputers to business collections to popular topics and censorship.

College and Research Libraries. Association of College and Research Libraries, 50 E. Huron St., Chicago, IL 60611. bi-mo.; $50 U.S. nonmembers, $55 Canada and Spain, $60 elsewhere, $12 single copy. Publishes articles of interest to college and research librarians.

Computers in Libraries. Meckler Publishing, 11 Ferry Lane W., Westport, CT 06880-5808. 10/yr.; $80. Covers practical applications of microcomputers to library situations and recent news items.

Electronic Library. Information Today, Inc. (formerly Learned Information, Inc.), 143 Old Marlton Pike, Medford, NJ 08055-8750. 6/yr.; $99. For librarians and information center managers interested in microcomputer and library automation. Features industry news and product announcements.

Emergency Librarian. Emergency Librarian, c/o U.S. Agent-Transborder Mail Unit #103, 34310 9th Ave., Federal Way, WA 98003-6741. bi-mo. (except July-August); $47. Articles, review columns, and critical analyses of management and programming issues for children's and young adult librarians.

Government Information Quarterly. JAI Press, 55 Old Post Rd., No. 2, P.O. Box 1678, Greenwich, CT 06835-1678. q.; $55 indiv. (foreign $65), $135 inst. (foreign $155). International journal of resources, services, policies, and practices.

Information Services and Use. Elsevier Science Publishers, Box 10558, Burke, VA 20009-0558. 4/yr.; $214. Contains data on international developments in information management and its applications. Articles cover online systems, library automation, word processing, micrographics, videotex, and telecommunications.

Journal of Academic Librarianship. JAI Press, 55 Old Post Rd., No. 2, Box 1678, Greenwich, CT 06836. bi-mo.; $29 indiv., $65 inst. (add $8 for foreign). Results of significant research, issues and problems facing academic libraries, book reviews, and innovations in academic libraries.

Journal of Government Information (formerly **Government Publications Review**). Elsevier Science Ltd., Journals Division, 660 White Plains Rd., Tarrytown, NY 10591-5153. 6/yr.; £209 ($320 U.S.). An international journal covering production, distribution, bibliographic control, accessibility, and use of government information in all formats and at all levels.

Journal of Librarianship and Information Science. Bailey Management Services, 127 Sandgate Rd., Folkestone, Kent CT20 2BL, England. q.; $125. Deals with all aspects of library and information work in the United Kingdom and reviews literature from international sources.

Journal of Library Administration. Haworth Press, 10 Alice St., Binghamton, NY 13904-1580. q.; $38 indiv., $95 inst. Provides information on all aspects of effective library management, with emphasis on practical applications.

Library Hi Tech. Pierian Press, Box 1808, Ann Arbor, MI 48106. q.; $55. Concentrates on reporting on the selection, installation, maintenance, and integration of systems and hardware.

Library and Information Science Research. Ablex Publishing Corp., 355 Chestnut St., Norwood, NJ 07648. q.; $45 indiv., $95 inst. Research articles, dissertation reviews, and book reviews on issues concerning information resources management.

Library Journal. Box 59690, Boulder, CO 80322-9690. 21/yr.; $87.50 U.S., $109 Canada, $149 elsewhere. A professional periodical for librarians, with current issues and news, professional reading, lengthy book review section, and classifieds.

Library Quarterly. University of Chicago Press, Journals Division, 5720 S. Woodlawn Ave., Chicago, IL 60637. q.; $29 indiv., $46 inst., $23 students. Scholarly articles of interest to librarians.

Library Resources and Technical Services. Association for Library Collections and Technical Services, 50 E. Huron St., Chicago, IL 60611. q.; $45 nonmembers U.S., Canada, and Mexico; $55 elsewhere. Scholarly papers on bibliographic access and control, preservation, conservation, and reproduction of library materials.

Library Software Review. Sage Periodicals Press, 2455 Teller Rd., Thousand Oaks, CA 91320. q.; $44 indiv., $135 inst. U.S. (foreign add $8). Emphasizes practical aspects of library computing for libraries of all types, including reviews of automated systems ranging from large-scale mainframe-based systems to microcomputer-based systems, and both library-specific and general-purpose software used in libraries.

Library Trends. University of Illinois Press, Journals Dept., 1325 S. Oak St., Champaign, IL 61820. q.; $75 U.S., $82 elsewhere. Each issue is concerned with one aspect of library and information science, analyzing current thought and practice and examining ideas that hold the greatest potential for the field.

LISA: Library and Information Science Abstracts. c/o Butterworth Service Co., Borough Green, Sevenoaks, Kent TN15 8PH, England. mo.; $630. More than 500 abstracts per issue from more than 500 periodicals, reports, books, and conference proceedings.

Microcomputers for Information Management. Ablex Publishing, 355 Chestnut St., Norwood, NJ 07648. q.; $39.50 indiv., $100 inst. Focuses on new developments with microcomputer technology in libraries and in information science in the United States and abroad.

The Public-Access Computer Systems Review. An electronic journal published on an irregular basis by the University Libraries, University of Houston, and sent free of charge to participants of the Public-Access Computer Systems Forum (PACS-L), a computer conference on BITNET. (To join -L, send an e-mail message to LISTSERV@UHUPVM1 (BITNET) or LISTSERV@UHUPVM1.UH.EDU (Internet) that says SUBSCRIBE PACS-L First Name Last Name.) Annual cumulated volume available in print from Order Department, American Library Association, 50 E. Huron St., Chicago, IL 60611. $20; $17 members of the Library and Information Technology Association. Contains articles about all types of computer systems that libraries make available to their patrons and technologies to implement these systems.

Public Libraries. Public Library Association, American Library Association, 50 E. Huron St., Chicago, IL 60611-2795. q.; $50 U.S. nonmembers, $60 elsewhere, $10 single copy. News and articles of interest to public librarians.

Public Library Quarterly. Haworth Press, 10 Alice St., Binghamton, NY 13904. q.; $36 indiv., $75 inst. Addresses the major administrative challenges and opportunities that face the nation's public libraries.

Reference Librarian. Haworth Press, 10 Alice St., Binghamton, NY 13904-9981. 2/yr.; $40 indiv., $95 inst. Each issue focuses on a topic of current concern, interest, or practical value to reference librarians.

RQ. Reference and Adult Services Division, American Library Association, 50 E. Huron St., Chicago, IL 60611-2795. q.; $42 nonmembers U.S., $52 elsewhere, $12 single copy. Covers all aspects of library service to adults, and reference service and collection development at every level and for all types of libraries.

School Library Journal. Box 1978, Marion, OH 43305-1978. mo.; $67 U.S., $91 Canada, $110 elsewhere. For school and youth service librarians. Contains about 2,500 critical book reviews annually.

School Library Media Activities Monthly. LMS Associates, 17 E. Henrietta St., Baltimore, MD 21230. 10/yr.; $44 U.S., $54 elsewhere. A vehicle for distributing ideas for teaching library media skills and for the development and implementation of library media skills programs.

School Library Media Quarterly. American Association of School Librarians, American Library Association, 50 E. Huron St., Chicago, IL 60611-2795. q.; $40 nonmembers U.S., $50 elsewhere, $12 single copy. For library media specialists, district supervisors, and others concerned with the selection and purchase of print and nonprint media and with the development of programs and services for preschool through high school libraries.

Special Libraries. Special Libraries Association, 1700 18th St., NW, Washington, DC 20009-2508. q.; $60 nonmembers (foreign $65), $10 single copy. Discusses administration, organization, and operations. Includes reports on research, technology, and professional standards.

The Unabashed Librarian. Box 2631, New York, NY 10116. q.; $30 U.S., $36 elsewhere. Down-to-earth library items: procedures, forms, programs, cataloging, booklists, software reviews.

Voice of Youth Advocates. Scarecrow Press, 52 Liberty St., Box 4167, Metuchen, NJ 08840. bi-mo.; $32.50 U.S., $37.50 others. Contains articles, bibliographies, and media reviews of materials for or about adolescents.

Wilson Library Bulletin. H. W. Wilson Co., 950 University Ave., Bronx, NY 10452. 10/yr.; $52 U.S., $58 elsewhere. Significant articles on librarianship, news, and reviews of films, books, and professional literature.

Books

Haycock, Ken. (1992). **What works: Research about teaching and learning through the school's library resource center.** Rockland Press, Box C34069, Department 284, Seattle, WA 98124-1069. $20 prepaid. Brings together relevant doctoral research at North American universities related to the instructional effectiveness of the elementary and secondary school librarian and school library.

Kuhlthau, Carol Collier, ed. (1994). **School library media annual, 1994.** Libraries Unlimited, P.O. Box 6633, Englewood, CO 80155-6633. 380pp. $45. The theme of this year's state-of-the-art report focuses on the virtual school library, how it shapes the school library media program, LM_NET and the future, distance education, and the literacy crisis. It also includes summaries of the research of the year; lists of the best books; software; state and national organizations and awards; and reports from various associations.

Journal Articles

AASL position statement on appropriate staffing for school library media centers. (1994, January-February). **Emergency Librarian, 21**(3), 33. EJ 476 348. (Available UMI). Presents the AASL (American Association of School Librarians) position statement on appropriate staffing for school library media centers.

Barron, Daniel D. (1994, February). Site-based management: Background, research, and implications for school library media specialists. **School Library Media Activities Monthly, 10**(6), 48-50. EJ 477 900. Discusses site-based management in schools and suggests implications for school library media specialists.

Boardman, Edna M. (1994, September-October). The Knapp School Libraries Project: The best $1,130,000 ever spent on school libraries. **Book Report, 13**(2), 17-19. EJ 489 785. (Available UMI). Describes the Knapp School Libraries Project, which was developed in the 1960s to create model libraries in elementary and secondary schools by upgrading their materials and adding qualified personnel.

Kovacs, Diane K., and others. (1994, Spring). A model for planning and providing reference services using Internet resources. **Library Trends, 42**(4), 638-47. EJ 489 791. (Available UMI). Discusses the development of practical strategies for library mediation between Internet resources and potential users.

Miller, Marilyn L., and Shontz, Marilyn. (1994, April). Inside high-tech school library media centers: Problems and possibilities. **School Library Journal, 40**(4), 24-29. EJ 481 875. (Available UMI). Examines statistics for school library media centers that have installed both an automated circulation system and an online public access catalog and compares them with other library media centers at other levels of automation.

Minor, Barbara B. (1994). Research from the ERIC files: July 1992 to June 1993. **School Library Media Annual (SLMA), 12,** 143-64. EJ 495 190. Describes research from the ERIC database on school library media programs, including library and information skills instruction; information seeking; educational equity; use of technology; censorship; school library media collections; use studies; role of the library media specialist; collective bargaining and job/certification requirements; and training for media specialists.

MEDIA TECHNOLOGIES

Media-Related Periodicals

Broadcasting and Cable (formerly **Broadcasting**). Box 6399, Torrence, CA 90504. w.; $99 U.S., $300 elsewhere. All-inclusive newsweekly for radio, television, cable, and allied business.

CableVision. Cablevision Magazine, Box 7698, Riverton, NJ 08077-7698. 26/yr.; $55 U.S., $85 Canada, $165 elsewhere. A newsmagazine for the cable television industry. Covers programming, marketing, advertising, business, and other topics.

Communication Abstracts. Sage Publications, Inc., 2455 Teller Rd., Thousand Oaks, CA 91320. bi-mo.; $125 indiv., $380 inst. Abstracts communication-related articles, reports, and books. Cumulated annually.

Communication Booknotes. Center for Advanced Study in Telecommunications (CAST), Ohio State University, 210 E. Baker Systems, 1971 Neil Ave., Columbus, OH 43210-1971. bi-mo.; $45 indiv., $95 inst. (add $5 for foreign). Newsletter that reviews books and periodicals about mass media, telecommunications, and information policy.

Communications News. Nelson Publishing Co., 2504 N. Tamiami Trail, Nokomis, FL 34275. mo.; $50 (free to qualified personnel). Up-to-date information from around the world regarding voice, video, and data communications.

Document and Image Automation (formerly **Optical Information Systems Magazine**). Meckler Publishing, 11 Ferry Lane W., Westport, CT 06880-5808. bi-mo.; $125. Features articles on the applications of videodisc, optical disc, and teletext systems; future implications; system and software compatibilities; and cost comparisons. Also tracks videodisc projects and covers world news.

Document and Image Automation Update (formerly **Optical Information Systems Update**). Meckler Publishing, 11 Ferry Lane W., Westport, CT 06880-5808. 12/yr.; $297. News and facts about technology, software, courseware developments, calendar, conference reports, and job listings.

Educational Media International. Kogan Page, Ltd., Distribution Centre, Blackhorse Road, Letchworth, Herts SG6 1HN, England. q.; £37 ($70 U.S.). The official journal of the International Council for Educational Media.

Federal Communications Commission Reports. Superintendent of Documents, Government Printing Office, Washington, DC 20402. w.; price varies. Decisions, public notices, and other documents pertaining to FCC activities.

Historical Journal of Film, Radio, and Television. Carfax Publishing Co., Box 2025, Dunnellon, FL 34430-2025. 4/yr.; $112 indiv., $298 inst. Articles by international experts in the field, news and notices, and book reviews.

International Journal of Instructional Media. Westwood Press, Inc., 23 E. 22nd St., 4th floor, New York, NY 10010. q.; $105. Articles discuss specific applications and techniques for bringing the advantages of a particular instructional medium to bear on a complete curriculum system or program.

Journal of Broadcasting and Electronic Media. Broadcast Education Association, 1771 N St., NW, Washington, DC 20036. q.; $75 U.S., $90 elsewhere. Includes articles, book reviews, research reports, and analyses. Provides a forum for research relating to telecommunications and related fields.

Journal of Educational Television. Carfax Publishing Co., Box 25, Abingdon, Oxfordshire OX14 3UE, England. 3/yr.; $128 indiv., $352 inst. This journal of the Educational Television Association serves as an international forum for discussions and reports on developments in the field of television and related media in teaching, learning, and training.

Journal of Popular Film and Television. Heldref Publications, 1319 Eighteenth St., NW, Washington, DC 20036-1802. q.; $32 indiv., $62 inst. Articles on film and television, book reviews, and theory.

Media International. Oakfield House, Perrymount Rd., Haywoods Heath, W. Sussex RH16 3ER, England. mo.; $95. Contains features on the major media developments and regional news reports from the international media scene.

Multimedia Monitor (formerly **Multimedia and Videodisc Monitor**). Future Systems, Inc., Box 26, Falls Church, VA 22040. mo.; $395 indiv., $150 educational inst. Describes current events in the videodisc marketplace and in training and development.

Telematics and Informatics. Elsevier Science, Journals Division, 660 White Plains Rd., Tarrytown, NY 10591-5153. q.; £395. Intended for the specialist in telecommunications and information science. Covers the merging of computer and telecommunications technologies worldwide.

Video Systems. Intertec Publishing Corp., 9800 Metcalf, Overland Park, KS 66212-2215. mo.; $45 (free to qualified professionals). For video professionals. Contains state-of-the-art audio and video technology reports.

Videography. PSN Publications, 2 Park Ave., 18th floor, New York, NY 10016. mo.; $30. For the video professional; covers techniques, applications, equipment, technology, and video art.

Books

Barron, Ann E., and Orwig, Gary W. (1994). **Multimedia technologies for training: An introduction.** Libraries Unlimited, P.O. Box 6633, Englewood, CO 80155-6633. 211pp. $29. Designed for trainers, managers, and educators in business, military, and academic environments, this guide presents advances in digitized imagery and audio, virtual reality, expert and authoring systems, networks and optical media. It also addresses the production of CD-ROMs and videodiscs, wireless LANs, HDTV, the Internet, and more.

Boschmann, Erwin, ed. (1994). **The electronic classroom: A handbook for education in the electronic environment.** Information Today, Inc. (formerly Learned Information), 147 Old Marlton Pike, Medford, NJ 08055-8750. 275pp. $42.50. This handbook describes the full range of emerging technologies and their use in secondary and higher education as well an in private, corporate, and government training environments. It provides a detailed description for educators on how to create an electronic site and offers a theoretical framework supporting pedagogical soundness in education.

Dockterman, David. (1994). **Great teaching & the VCR.** Tom Snyder Productions, 80 Coolidge Hill Rd., Watertown, MA 02172-2817. 30pp. Free. This free booklet explores ways teachers can go beyond passive viewing and use the VCR to promote cooperative learning, critical thinking, and other group activities.

Film & video finder 1994/95. (1994). Access Innovations, Inc., P.O. Box 40130, Albuquerque, NM 87196. 4,300pp. $295 plus $10 shipping and handling. This three-volume, hardbound set from NICEM (National Information Center for Educational Media) provides information on 110,000 films and videos, 20,000 of which are new since the 1991 edition. Entries include descriptions of content; color code; format; running time; date of release; recommended audience or grade level; purchase/rental source; and Library of Congress catalog card and number if available.

Gayeski, Dianne M., ed. (1995). **Designing communication and learning environments.** Educational Technology Publications, 700 Palisade Ave., Englewood Cliffs, NJ 07632. 180pp. $34.95. Chapters from professionals actively working with a variety of mediated environments, who present detailed descriptions of their work as case studies and design guidelines. Chapters are presented in four sections: Conceptual Foundations, Design Elements, Selecting Media Support Technologies, and Case Studies.

Heller, Norma. (1994). **Projects for new technologies in education: Grades 6-9.** Libraries Unlimited, P.O. Box 6633, Englewood, CO 80155-6633. 154pp. $23.50. This guide presents step-by-step procedures for planning and implementing technologies in both library and classroom curricula and numerous interdisciplinary projects that use technology to teach research skills. It applies CD-ROMs, online databases, telecommunications, and information networks to the education setting and shows how they can be used to provide new avenues for learning and classroom integration.

Holtz, Matthew. (1995). **The multimedia workshop: Authorware Professional 2.0.** Wadsworth Publishing Co., Distribution Center, 7625 Empire Dr., Florence, KY 41042-2978. 176pp. $20.25. This guide provides state-of-the-art tutorials to introduce students to the latest multimedia software tools for Windows. It explains the how and why of each feature with examples, hands-on activities, and projects at the end of each chapter; notes, troubleshooting advice, previews, and other helpful pointers are included throughout. An instructor's manual is available on disk, and versions of the guide for other software tools are being developed.

Index to AV producers and distributors. (1994). Access Innovations, Inc., P.O. Box 40130, Albuquerque, NM 87196. 545pp. $89.95. This softbound directory from NICEM lists more than 23,300 producers and distributors of audiovisual materials of all kinds. It provides media staff, library personnel, teachers, and other educators with a current as well as an archival directory of companies and institutions involved in the production and dissemination of nonprint media.

Kamil, Bobbi L. (1994). **Delivering the future: Cable and education partnerships for the Information Age.** Cable in the Classroom, 1900 N. Beauregard St., Suite 108, Alexandria, VA 22311. 232pp. $19.95. Explains how the worlds of the educator and the telecommunications provider can intersect effectively to bring the information highway into U.S. schools. Case studies of a number of exemplary programs demonstrate the imaginative partnerships that the cable industry, local school districts, and colleges have created to serve their respective interests. Issues, opportunities, and technology in use in each case are explored.

Multimedia and learning: A school leader's guide. (1994). National School Boards Association, 1680 Duke St., Alexandria, VA 22314-3493. 116pp. $35. This comprehensive reference guide for school leaders seeking to implement multimedia in their school systems covers how to improve teaching and learning experiences through use of multimedia; multimedia technologies and trends; research-based studies and theories of multimedia in learning environments; case studies of multimedia in schools; multimedia applications for education; and facilities planning, staff development, and copyright issues.

Semrau, Penelope, and Boyer, Barbara A. (1994). **Using interactive video in education.** Allyn and Bacon, 160 Gould St., Needham Heights, MA 02194-2310. 324pp. $26. Intended for use in inservice and preservice courses, this book covers uses and benefits of interactive videodiscs in the classroom; using videodisc to teach specific lessons; how to evaluate videodiscs; the use of HyperCard, LinkWay, and Toolbook for creating interactive video programs; and creating a videodisc from scratch.

Stevens, George H., and Stevens, Emily F. (1995). **Designing electronic performance support tools: Improving workplace performance with hypertext, hypermedia, and multimedia.** Educational Technology Publications, 700 Palisade Ave., Englewood Cliffs, NJ 07632. 288pp. $39.95. This practical resource for designers and managers explains how to implement electronic performance and learning support systems using the tools made possible by hypertext, hypermedia, and multimedia technologies. It also details how electronic performance support systems (EPSS) can be used for the full range of business support on the job, as well as more traditional computer-based training applications.

Valmont, William J. (1995). **Creating videos for school use.** Allyn & Bacon, Dept. 894, 160 Gould St., Needham Heights, MA 02194-2315. 225pp. $26. This nontechnical, machine-independent text is designed to help teachers with limited budgets create their own classroom videos and help their students create videos as projects.

ERIC Documents

Couch, John D., and others. (1993, January). **Interdisciplinary study with computer-based multimedia.** (Available only as microfiche.) Paper presented at the Annual Conference of the International Visual Literacy Association, Pittsburgh, PA, September 30-October 4, 1992. 8pp. ED 363 316. Interdisciplinary study with computer-based multimedia in the classroom is reviewed, with emphasis on its potential for science instruction.

Fontana, Lynn A., and others. (1993, January). **Multimedia: A gateway to higher-order thinking skills.** Paper presented at the Association for Educational Communications and Technology, New Orleans, LA, January 13-17, 1993. 15pp. ED 362 165. Describes the design of a multimedia prototype to foster higher-order thinking skills in social studies using the Ken Burns documentary, "The Civil War," at the George Mason University (Virginia) Center for Interactive Educational Technology.

Kotlas, Carolyn, comp. (1993, March). **Computers and copyrights: Bibliography.** 8pp. ED 364 190. University of North Carolina, Chapel Hill. Institute for Academic Technology. This bibliography lists 58 sources of information to help college and university computer center staff to interpret copyright law as it relates to software, optical disks, and other formats used in multimedia development and classroom presentations. Materials listed include books, articles, government documents, ftp (file transfer protocol) files, brochures, and listserv discussion groups.

Leader, Lars F., and Klein, James D. (1994). **The effects of search tool and cognitive style on performance in hypermedia database searches.** Paper presented at the National Convention of the Association for Educational Communications and Technology, Research and Theory Division, Nashville, TN, February 16-20, 1994. 14pp. ED 373 729. This study investigated the effects of interface tools and learner cognitive styles on performance in searches for information within a hypermedia database. Subjects were 75 students in a university English as a Second Language (ESL) program.

Maurer, Hermann, ed. (1993, June). **Educational multimedia and hypermedia annual, 1993. Proceedings of ED-MEDIA 93—World Conference on Educational Media and Hypermedia (Orlando, Florida, June 23-26, 1993).** 673pp. ED 360 949. (Also available from the Association for the Advancement of Computing in Education, P.O. Box 2966, Charlottesville, VA 22902; $45.) Presentations in these proceedings address what is happening in educational multimedia and hypermedia right now and what is to happen in the future, including developments in elementary and secondary education, higher education, and distance education.

Moore, David M., and others. (1993). **Multimedia: Promise, reality and future.** Paper presented at the Annual Conference of the International Visual Literacy Association, Rochester, NY, October 13-17, 1993. 13pp. ED 370 554. This review of the literature on multimedia research focuses on what it says about the role of multimedia in instruction and whether extant research is sufficient and valid.

Schoenmaker, Jan, and Stanchev, Ivan, eds. (1994). **Principles and tools for instructional visualization.** Twente Univ., Enschede (Netherlands). Dept. of Applied Education; Andersen Consulting, Enschede (Netherlands). Educational Computing Consortium. 152pp. ED 367 305. The 11 papers in this report reflect research and development on visualization and the use of multimedia carried out at the Department of Applied Education, Division of Instrumental Science and Technology of the University of Twente (Netherlands) and the Andersen Consulting Educational Computing Consortium, also at the University of Twente.

Journal Articles

Carroll, John M. (1994). Designing scenarios for human action. **Performance Improvement Quarterly, 7**(3), 64-75. EJ 488 349. An approach to the design of computer systems and applications in which scenarios of human-system interaction are a central working design representation. Described and illustrated by examples from the design of a multimedia information system.

Jonassen, David H. (1993). Conceptual frontiers in hypermedia environments for learning. **Journal of Educational Multimedia and Hypermedia, 2**(4), 331-35. (Introduction to selected papers from ED-MEDIA 93—World Conference on Educational Multimedia and Hypermedia.) EJ 481 776. (Available UMI). Provides an overview of the transition from traditional, programmed instruction to computer-assisted instruction, including concepts and history affecting instructional environments.

Kelly, Anthony E., and O'Donnell, Angela. (1994). Hypertext and the study strategies of preservice teachers: Issues in instructional hypertext design. **Journal of Educational Computing Research, 10**(4), 373-87. EJ 489 735. Describes research that investigated the study strategies of preservice teachers through the use of a hypertext program that monitored lecture note review strategies of individuals and dyads.

Kozma, Robert B. (1994). A reply: Media and methods. **Educational Technology Research and Development, 2**(3), 1-14. EJ 493 371. (Available UMI). This response to a previously published article on the replaceability of media and instructional methods focuses on a study that used a chemistry multimedia software package to examine cognitive processes in which learners interact with instructional designs and use media and methods to construct understanding.

Poncelet, Guy M., and Proctor, Len F. (1993, Summer). Design and development factors in the production of hypermedia-based courseware. **Canadian Journal of Educational Communication, 22**(2), 91-111. EJ 471 139. Presents guidelines derived from cognitive and constructivist learning theory and instructional design literature for designing effective hypermedia-based courseware.

Strommen, Erik F. (1993). Is it easier to hop or walk? Development issues in interface design. **Human-Computer Interaction, 8**(4), 337-52. EJ 479 973. Describes a study conducted by the Children's Television Workshop that tested two forms of *Sesame Street* character movement (i.e., discrete movement versus continuous motion) with three-year-old preschool children using a Nintendo controller.

Tiene, Drew. (1994, April-May). Teens react to Channel One: A survey of jr. high school students. **Tech Trends, 39**(3), 17-20. EJ 485 192. (Available UMI). Discusses the results of a survey administered in two midwest suburban junior high schools to explore the students' reactions to Channel One.

Torrence, David R. (1994, March). Training with television. **Performance and Instruction, 33**(3), 26-29. EJ 483 680. (Available UMI). Discussion of the use of video for training; highlights six areas that should be considered for effective video use.

CD-ROMS

Introduction to multimedia. (1995). Wadsworth Publishing Co., Distribution Center, 7625 Empire Dr., Florence, KY 41042-2978. Available in Macintosh and Windows versions. $52.75 each version. The first in a new series of CD-ROM-based learning tools, this fully interactive and user-friendly CD-ROM presents the topics and skills essential to an introductory course, including text, graphics and animation, full-motion video, audio, interface design, principles of interactivity, delivery, theory and criticism, the development process, applications of multimedia, production systems, and future directions. An instructor's guide is included.

Computer Software

HyperStudio. Roger Wagner Publishing, Inc., 1050 Pioneer Way, Suite P, El Cajon, CA 92020. For more information, contact the publisher. The Macintosh version of the multimedia authoring system HyperStudio is designed for the nontechnical user, with a point-and-click interface. Features include full-color graphics, animation, sound recording and playback, and text. In addition, the program has built-in support for CD-ROM, Pioneer laserdisc players, and QuickTime movies. Logo is also built in.

Online Products

A-V ONLINE. Knight-Ridder Information (formerly Dialog), 2440 El Camino Real, Mountain View, CA 94040. (DIALOG File 46; CompuServe KI046. For information on a tape lease agreement, contact Access Innovations, Inc., P.O. Box 40130, Albuquerque, NM 87196.) Updated quarterly, this NICEM database provides information on nonprint media covering all levels of education and instruction. Nonprint formats covered are 16mm films, videos, audiocassettes, CD-ROMs, software, laserdisc, filmstrips, slides, transparencies, motion cartridges, kits, models, and realia. Entries date from 1964 to the present, with approximately 420,000 records as of January 1995.

Videos

Multimedia in education. (1993). Insight Media, 2162 Broadway, New York, NY 10024. 20 min. $179. This program shows how educators are using multimedia technology to explore new ways of teaching and learning. It discusses the use of videotapes, laserdiscs, information networks, virtual reality systems, and computer modeling in education.

The new ABC's: Classrooms of tomorrow. Films for the Humanities & Sciences, P.O. Box 2053, Princeton, NJ 08543-2053. 58 min., color. Purchase $149; rental $75. This program visits several "classrooms of tomorrow" to examine technologies that stimulate smart students to do better, involve very young children with computers before they have learned to read, help reduce truancy rates, give computer-driven mobility to physically disabled students, and provide computer-based analogies of real-world job tasks before students reach the job market.

Touch that dial: Using video technology in the classroom. Films for the Humanities & Sciences, P.O. Box 2053, Princeton, NJ 08543-2053. 40 min., color. Purchase $159; rental $75. Four 10-minute programs explore broadcast television, videocassettes, satellite transmissions, videodisc, and CD-ROMs; describe the basics of using the technology; show how to actively engage students; and give tips on how to design successful, comprehensive lessons using video.

SIMULATION AND VIRTUAL REALITY

Media-Related Periodicals

Aspects of Educational and Training Technology Series. Kogan Page Ltd., 120 Pentonville Rd., London N1 9JN, England. ann. £32. Covers the proceedings of the annual conference of the Association of Educational and Training Technology.

Simulation and Gaming. Sage Publications, Inc., Box 5084, Thousand Oaks, CA 91359. q.; $50 indiv., $157 inst. An international journal of theory, design, and research published by the Association for Business Simulation and Experiential Learning.

Virtual Reality Report. Meckler Publishing, 11 Ferry Lane W., Westport, CT 06880-5808. 12/yr.; $327. Covers developments in the field of virtual reality and cyberspace.

Books

Towne, Douglas M. (1995). **Learning and instruction in simulation environments.** Educational Technology Publications, 700 Palisade Ave., Englewood Cliffs, NJ 07632. 384pp. $39.95. This guide provides information on the capabilities of simulation-oriented training, the kinds of problems that arise, the characteristics of available development systems, and the technical skills required to produce effective training systems. Many examples are included.

ERIC Documents

McLellan, Hilary. (1993). **Avatars, affordances, and interfaces: Virtual reality tools for learning.** Paper presented at the Annual Conference of the International Visual Literacy Association, Rochester, NY, October 13-17, 1993. 11pp. ED 370 586. Explores three interrelated virtual reality design topics—avatars, affordances, and interfaces—that are particularly relevant to visual literacy.

Journal Articles

Franchi, Jorge. (1994, January-February). Virtual reality: An overview. **TechTrends, 39**(1), 23-26. EJ 479 767. (Available UMI). Highlights of this overview of virtual reality include optics; interface devices; virtual worlds; potential applications; problems; current research and development; and future possibilities. Includes a listing of vendors and suppliers of virtual reality products.

Lewis, Joan E. (1994, Spring). Virtual reality: Ready or not! **TECHNOS, 3**(1), 12-17. EJ 483 689. Describes the development and current status of virtual reality (VR) and VR research and discusses its market potentials and educational possibilities.

Lohse, Gerald Lee. (1993). A cognitive model for understanding graphical perception. **Human-Computer Interaction, 8**(4), 353-88. EJ 479 794. Discussion of how we perceive meaning from graphics. Highlights a computer simulation model, UCIE (Understanding Cognitive Information Engineering), and describes an empirical study that compared actual performance to UCIE predictions related to the amount of time required to answer a question in various presentation formats.

Thurman, Richard A. (1993). Instructional simulation from a cognitive psychology viewpoint. **Educational Technology Research and Development, 41**(4), 75-89. EJ 478 002. (Available UMI). Examines implications from cognitive psychology that are important for the design of microcomputer-based instructional simulations. Topics addressed include cognitive structure; cognitive and metacognitive strategies; automaticity of cognitive processes; and affect, or the motivational appeal.

Thurman, Richard A., and Mattoon, Joseph S. (1994, October). Virtual reality: Toward fundamental improvements in simulation-based training. **Educational Technology, 34**(8), 56-64. EJ 491 542. (Available UMI). Considers the role and effectiveness of virtual reality in simulation-based training.

TELECOMMUNICATIONS AND NETWORKING

Media-Related Periodicals

Canadian Journal of Educational Communication. Association for Media and Technology in Education in Canada, 3-1750 The Queensway, Suite 1318, Etobicoke, ON M9C 5H5, Canada. 3/yr.; $42.80 Canada, $40 U.S., $55 elsewhere. Concerned with all aspects of educational systems and technology.

Computer Communications. Turpin Transactions, Ltd., Distribution Centre, Blackhorse Rd., Letchworth, Herts SG6 1HM, England. 10/yr.; £255 in U.K. and Europe, £280 elsewhere. Focuses on networking and distributed computing techniques, communications hardware and software, and standardization.

Data Communications. Box 473, Hightstown, NJ 08520. mo.; $95 U.S., $105 Canada. Provides users with news and analysis of changing technology for the networking of computers.

EDUCOM Review. EDUCOM, 1112 Sixteenth St., NW, Suite 600, Washington, DC 20036-4823. q.; $60 U.S., $75 elsewhere. Features articles on current issues and applications of computing and communications technology in higher education. Reports of EDUCOM consortium activities.

EMMS (Electronic Mail & Micro Systems). Telecommunications Reports, 1333 H Street, NW, 11th floor, Washington, DC 20005. semi-mo.; $535 U.S., $595 elsewhere. Covers technology, user, product, and legislative trends in graphic, record, and microcomputer applications.

Internet Research (previously **Electronic Networking: Research, Applications, and Policy**). Meckler Publishing, 11 Ferry Lane W., Westport, CT 06880. q.; $115. A cross-disciplinary journal presenting research findings related to electronic networks, analyses of policy issues related to networking, and descriptions of current and potential applications of electronic networking for communication, computation, and provision of information services.

Internet World (formerly **Research and Education Networking**). Mecklermedia Corporation. Orders for North and South America, Internet World, P.O. Box 713, Mt. Morris, IL 61054; elsewhere, Mecklermedia Ltd., Artillery House, Artillery Row, London SW1P 1RT, UK. m.; $29 U.S, $41.73 Canada, Central and South America, £29 elsewhere. Analyzes development with National Research and Education Network, Internet, electronic networking, publishing, and scholarly communication, as well as other network issues of interest to a wide range of network users.

Telecommunications. Horizon House Publications, Inc., 685 Canton St., Norwood, MA 02062. mo.; $67 U.S., $120 elsewhere (free to qualified individuals). Feature articles and news for the field of telecommunications.

T.I.E. News (Telecommunications in Education). International Society for Technology in Education, 1787 Agate St., Eugene, OR 97403-1923. q.; $16 members, $25 nonmembers. Contains articles on all aspects of educational telecommunications.

Books

Dern, Daniel P. (1993). **The Internet guide for new users.** McGraw-Hill, Professional Book Group, 11 West 19th St., New York, NY 10011 (1-800-2-MCGRAW). 570pp. $27.95. A practical resource for anyone who wants to join, understand, and use the Internet. This guide not only shows newcomers how to get up and running but also provides key information for experienced users about the Internet's concepts and facilities. It can be used by the owners of any type of computer or terminal that can attach to a modem or network. Interviews with some of the creators of Internet tools provide information not available elsewhere.

Epler, Doris, ed. (1995). **K-12 networking: Breaking down the walls of the learning environment.** Information Today, Inc. (formerly Learned Information, Inc.), 143 Old Marlton Pike, Medford, NJ 08055-8750. 150pp. $39.50. Intended to address the real concerns of educators about implementing types of networks in their schools, this guide focuses on the ability to connect various electronic systems, using a variety of media to share information, materials, and services efficiently and effectively. Benefits of networks for school libraries are featured.

Kochmer, Jonathan. (1993, March). **Internet passport: NorthWestNet's guide to our world online.** Fourth edition (formerly **NorthWestNet User Services Internet Resource Guide [NUSIRG]**). NorthWestNet, Attn: The Internet Passport, 15400 SE 30th Pl., Suite 202, Bellevue, WA 98007. 450pp. $39.95. This guide is designed to help computer network users master the three basic skills needed to use Internet: (1) using electronic mail (e-mail) to communicate with other Internet users; (2) logging in to remote computers with a service called Telnet; and (3) obtaining online documents, software, and other materials via File Transfer Protocol (FTP).

Kurshan, Barbara L., Harrington, Marcia A., and Milbury, Peter G. (1994). **An educator's guide to electronic networking: Creating virtual communities.** Information Resources Publications, 4-194 Center for Science and Technology, Syracuse University, Syracuse, NY 13244-4100. 110pp. IR-96; $10 plus $2 shipping and handling. This guide provides a framework to help think about, choose, create, and design an electronically networked community that can provide easy, inexpensive access to many resources that are not readily available by other means.

Miller, Elizabeth B. (1994). **The Internet directory for K-12 teachers and librarians, 1994-1995.** Libraries Unlimited, P.O. Box 6633, Englewood, CO 80155-6633. 120pp. $25. Designed for use by educators who are beginners on the Internet, this guide specifies what is out there and demonstrates how to find it. Guidelines and tips for getting started are included, as well as examples of teachers and librarians currently using the Internet and resources in various subjects.

Mostafa, Javed, Newell, Thomas, and Trenthem, Richard. (1994). **The easy Internet handbook.** Libraries Unlimited, P.O. Box 6633, Englewood, CO 80155-6633. 140pp. $20. This handbook provides comprehensive coverage of the Internet in a format that is accessible enough to be used as a reference book. The first of two parts explains concepts and provides information on devices and services related to the Internet; the second part provides quick access to instruction information that assists the user in understanding and using Internet tools.

Sachs, David, and Stair, Henry. (1994). **Hands-on Internet—A beginning guide for PC users.** Prentice-Hall (School Div.), 160 Gould St., Needham Heights, MA 02194-2130. 275pp. $29.95. Nine sessions use a step-by-step format to guide the reader through logging in, electronic mail, Usenet, mailing lists, Telnet, and file transfer protocol. The search tools, commands, and steps that are explained apply to any platform. A discussion of ethics and copyright issues, a quick reference section, and communications software are included.

Schrum, Lynne M., and ISTE's Special Interest Group for Telecommunications. (1994). **Directory of educational telecommunications services.** International Society for Technology in Education, 1787 Agate St., Eugene, OR 97403-1923. 40pp. $7. This brief directory provides information on more than 30 educational telecommunications services and 4 information and database services. Each entry includes a description, as well as contact and pricing information. Additional topics include a description of the Internet, U.S. Internet nodes, and suggested Internet and telecommunications tools.

Towney, Charles, and Barclay, Donald A. (1995). **Teaching electronic literacy: A how-to-do-it manual.** Neal-Schuman Publishers, 100 Varick St., New York, NY 10013. 150pp. $39.95. This guide offers clear language, step-by-step instruction, and targeted chapters on learning theory and electronic literacy; teaching basic electronic searching strategies; introducing learners to the Internet; teaching the basic Internet tools; putting together an electronic literacy workshop; using the Internet to teach the Internet; equipment requirements; administration; and recommended readings.

ERIC Documents

Experience the power: Network technology for education. (1994). National Center for Education Statistics (ED), Washington, DC. 20pp. ED 369 418. Provides a basic introduction to the application of electronic telecommunications networks to the challenge of meeting the nation's education goals.

Honey, Margaret, and McMillan, Katherine. (1993, November 24). **Case studies of K-12 educators' use of the Internet: Exploring the relationship between metaphor and practice.** Bank Street College of Education, New York, NY. Center for Children and Technology. 22pp. ED 372 726. Reports on a national telecommunications survey that was conducted to determine the kinds of representations and associations that elementary and secondary educators are building on the Internet and the ways in which these representations vary depending on their use.

Ruberg, Laurie F., and Miller, Mary G. (1993, January). **Moving from U.S. mail to e-mail.** Paper presented at the Annual Conference of the International Visual Literacy Association, Pittsburgh, PA, September 30-October 4, 1992. 9pp. ED 363 312. Both benefits and drawbacks of sending and receiving electronic mail messages—i.e., the capacity to send and receive messages on computer networks—are considered and suggestions are offered for ways to make the technology most effective.

Sivin, Jay P., and Bialo, Ellen R. (1992, May). **Ethical use of information technologies in education: Important issues for America's schools. Issues and practices series.** Institute for Law and Justice, Inc., Alexandria, VA. 42pp. ED 348 989. This paper offers an overview of ethical issues in the use of educational technology for teachers, administrators, and members of the community concerned about school policy.

Journal Articles

Germain, Jack M. (1994, January-February). ERIC goes Internet. **Online Access, 9**(1), 50-60. EJ 477 954. Description of the ERIC database covers suggested uses for teachers, students, parents, and researchers; information available in ERIC; how to access ERIC, including through the Internet; the AskERIC service that is available through the Internet; and steps for searching the database.

Kaman, Geradine M. (1993, Summer). Broadband-ISDN: Personal connections to global resources. **Internet Research, 3**(2), 8-20. EJ 469 217. Discussion of the development and impact of the broadband Integrated Services Digital Network (ISDN) on global telecommunications and society. Covers regulatory policies, ownership and control, content regulation, home access, rural versus urban access, pricing, user groups, barriers, and privacy.

Maule, R. William. (1993, January). The network classroom. **Interpersonal Computing and Technology: An Electronic Journal for the 21st Century, 1**(1). [To retrieve this article, send the following e-mail message to LISTSERV@GUVM.GEORGETOWN.EDU: GET MAULE IPCTV1N1 F=MAIL]. EJ 485 259. Discussion of the role of new computer communications technologies in education. Focuses on modern networking systems, strategies for implementing networked-based communication, and public online information resources for the classroom.

The national information infrastructure: Requirements for education and training. (1994, Spring-Summer). **Educational IRM Quarterly, 3**(3-4), 20-36. EJ 488 367. Includes 19 access, education and training, and technical requirements that must be addressed in the development of the national information infrastructure. The requirements were prepared by national education, training, and trade associations participating in the National Coordinating Committee on Technology in Education and Training (NCC-TET).

Ricart, Glenn. (1993, September-October). Connecting the networking dots. **EDUCOM Review, 28**(5), 36-41. EJ 469 229. (Available UMI). Provides technical recommendations for wiring of college campuses to provide for current and future computer network needs, and discusses the effects of trends in networking costs.

Riel, Margaret. (1990, December). Computer-mediated communication: A tool for reconnecting kids with society. **Interactive Learning Environments, 1**(4), 255-63. EJ 479 859. Discusses the use of computer-mediated communication (CMC) in education and summarizes three studies that demonstrated the positive effect of electronic networking on elementary and secondary students' reading and writing skills and their interest in meaningful educational activities.

Online Resources

Clearinghouse for Subject-Oriented Internet Resource Guides. Jointly sponsored by the University of Michigan's University Library and School of Information and Library Studies. It can be accessed by: anonymous FTP (host: una.hh.lib.umich.edu, path:/inetdirsstacks); Gopher (gopher.lib.umich.edu, under the menus Other Gophers/University of Michigan); and World Wide Web/Mosaic (URL:http://www.lib.umich.edu/chhome.html). WAIS indexing allows full-text searching of the guides. This clearinghouse serves as a central location for a collection of subject-oriented Internet resource guides compiled by individuals throughout the Internet. Volunteers publicize and market the service, process newly submitted guides, obtain updated versions of existing guides, create and label menu items for new guides, answer users' questions, and reindex the collection for full-text searching.

Videos

Interacting with Internet. Produced by BFA Educational Media. Order from Association for Educational Communications and Technology, 1025 Vermont Ave., NW, Suite 820, Washington, DC 20005. VHS, 30 min. $179 AECT members, $200 nonmembers. This video uses advanced graphics, online simulations, and easy-to-understand instructions for accessing and mastering the Internet.

Index

This index lists names of associations and organizations, authors, titles, and subjects (indicated by bold entries). In addition, acronyms for all organizations and associations are cross-referenced to the full name. Please note that a classified list of U.S. organizations and associations appears on pages 183-242.

AACC. *See* American Association of Community Colleges (AACC)

Aarntzen, Diana, 336, 361

AASCU. *See* American Association of State Colleges and Universities (AASCU)

AASL. *See* American Association of School Librarians (AASL)

"AASL position statement on appropriate staffing for school library media centers," 366

Abbott, Andy, 46, 47

Abrams, Arnie H., 332

Academic Lists (electronic file), 68

Academy of Motion Picture Arts and Sciences (AMPAS), 191

Academy One, 55

ACCESS ERIC, 214

ACCESS NETWORK, 243

"Access to information technologies among school-age children: Implications for a democratic society," 358

Accomplished Teachers: Integrating Computers into Classroom Practice, 119

Accountability and education, 9, 12

Accreditation Requirements of the State Board of Education, 145

Accreditation Standards, 148

Accreditation Standards and Procedures for Idaho Elementary Schools, 142

Accreditation Standards and Procedures for Idaho Middle and Junior High Schools, 142

Accreditation Standards and Procedures for Idaho Secondary Schools, 142

"Accrediting prior learning at a distance," 344

ACEI. *See* Association for Childhood Education International (ACEI)

ACHE. *See* Association for Continuing Higher Education (ACHE)

ACRL. *See* Association of College and Research Libraries (ACRL)

"Adapting instruction to individual learner differences: A research paradigm for computer-based instruction," 335

Adaptive Technology Resource Center (World Wide Web site), 73

ADCIS. *See* Association for the Development of Computer-based Instructional Systems (ADCIS)

ADJ/CHP1. *See* ERIC Adjunct Clearinghouse on Chapter 1 (Compensatory Education) (ADJ/CHP1)

ADJ/CL. *See* ERIC Adjunct Clearinghouse on Clinical Schools (ADJ/CL)

ADJ/CN. *See* ERIC Adjunct Clearinghouse for Consumer Education (ADJ/CN)

ADJ/JS. *See* ERIC Adjunct Clearinghouse for United States-Japan Studies (ADJ/JS)

ADJ/LE. *See* ERIC Adjunct Clearinghouse for ESL Literacy Education (ADJ/LE)

ADJ/LR. *See* ERIC Adjunct Clearinghouse for Law-Related Education (ADJ/LR)

ADJ/TC. *See* ERIC Adjunct Clearinghouse for the Test Collection (ADJ/TC)

Advanced Research Projects Agency Network. *See* ARPANET (Advanced Research Projects Agency Network)

AECT. *See* Association for Educational Communications and Technology (AECT)

AECT Gopher, 68

AECT-L (Association for Educational Communications and Technology-List), 68

AEE. *See* Association for Experiential Education (AEE)

AEL. *See* Appalachia Educational Laboratory, Inc. (AEL)

AERA. *See* American Educational Research Association (AERA)

AERA (American Educational Research Association) (LISTSERV), 68

AFB. *See* American Foundation for the Blind (AFB)

AFC. *See* Anthropology Film Center (AFC)

Agency for Instructional Technology (AIT), 191

AIME (amount of invested mental effort), 98, 102-3

AIT. *See* Agency for Instructional Technology (AIT)

AIVF/FIVF. *See* Association of Independent Video and Filmmakers/Foundation for Independent Video and Film (AIVF/FIVF)

Beekman, George, 333
"Behaviorism evolves," 347
Beishuizen, J. J., 353
Bejar, Isaac L., 336
Belland, J. C., 5
Bialo, Ellen R., 378
Big Dummy's Guide to the Internet (electronic
    file). See EFF'S Guide to the Internet
    (electronic file)
"The big wrench versus integrated approaches:
    The great media debate," 338
Biraimah, Karen, 336
Blackman Dornburg, Beverly, 154
Bliss, Joan, 328
Blissett, Gillian, 362
Bloomsburg University, 286
Boardman, Edna M., 366
Boe, Tom, 127
Boeckmann, K., 110, 112, 113
Boise State University, 270
Bonja, R. P., 127
Boohan, Richard, 328
Book Report, 362
Booker, Di, 357
Borenstein, N. S., 93
Bork, Alfred, 76, 78, 79
Boschmann, Erwin, 369
Boston University, 254, 276
Bowers, C. A., 5
Bowers, Gary, 155
Bowers, Richard A., 329
Bowman, Mary Ann, 354
Boyer, Barbara A., 370
Bragg, Charles A., 345
Branson, Robert K., 162-65
Braun, Henry I., 336
Bridgewater State College, 276
Briggs, Leslie J., 3, 163
Brigham Young University, 259, 290
Bright, R. Lewis, 162
British Journal of Educational Technology, 348
"Broadband-ISDN: Personal connections to
    global resources," 378
Broadcasting. See Broadcasting and Cable
Broadcasting and Cable, 367
Brock, Patricia Ann, 349
Brody, Philip J., 349
Broering, Naomi C., 355
Brown, Christine, 336
Brummelhuis, Alfons ten, 334, 336
Brush, Thomas, 344
Bruwelheide, Janis H., 157-60
Buffalo State College, 300
Building Information Literacy Using High
    Technology: A Guide for Schools and
    Libraries, 357
Bulletin of the American Society for Information
    Science, 356
Burrell, G., 5
Burt, Gordon, 5

Butterworth, Christine, 344
Buxton, W. A. S., 100
BYTE, 330

Cable in the Classroom, 206
CableVision, 367
CALICO Journal, 330
California
    doctoral programs in instructional
        technology, 247-48
    graduate programs in educational
        computing, 295
    graduate programs in instructional
        technology, 265-66
    library media standards and guidelines,
        140-41
California State University-Dominguez Hills,
    295
California State University-Los Angeles, 265
California State University-San Bernardino, 265
"Camera placement for recognition of complex
    behaviors," 110
Campion, Lee, 29
Canadian Book Publishers' Council (CBPC), 243
Canadian Broadcasting Corporation (CBC)/
    Société Radio-Canada (SRC), 244
Canadian Education Association/Association
    canadienne d'éducation (CEA), 244
Canadian Film Institute (CFI), 244
Canadian Journal of Educational Communica-
    tion, 348, 375
Canadian Journal of Information and Library
    Science/Revue canadienne des sciences
    de l'information et de bibliothèconomie,
    356
Canadian Library Association, 244
Canadian Museums Association/Association des
    musées canadiens (CMA/AMC), 245
Carlson, Randal D., 336
Carroll, John M., 372
Case studies of K-12 Educators Use of the
    Internet: Exploring the Relationship
    Between Metaphor and Practice, 378
Casey, Bob, 31
Cates, Ward Mitchell, 337
Catholic Library Association (CLA), 206
CBC. See Canadian Broadcasting Corporation
    (CBC)/Société Radio-Canada (SRC)
CBPC. See Canadian Book Publishers' Council
    (CBPC)
CCAIT. See Community College Association for
    Instruction and Technology (CCAIT)
CCC. See Copyright Clearance Center, Inc.
    (CCC)
CCSN. See Community College Satellite Net-
    work (CCSN)
CD-ROM Databases, 329
CD-ROM Finder, 329
CD-ROM Librarian. See CD-ROM World

National Association of Regional Media Centers (NARMC), 203
National Association of Secondary School Principals (NASSP), 225-26
National Association of State Boards of Education (NASBE), 226
National Association of State Textbook Administrators (NASTA), 226
National Audiovisual Center (NAC), 226
National Biological Information Infrastructure, 58
National Cable Television Institute (NCTI), 226
National Center for Education Statistics, 9
The National Center for Improving Science Education, 226-27
National Center for Research in Mathematical Sciences Education (NCRMSE), 227
National Center for Science Teaching and Learning (NCSTL), 227-28
National Center to Improve Practice (NCIP), 228-29
National Challenge Centers, 58
National Clearinghouse for Bilingual Education (NCBE), 228
National Commission on Libraries and Information Science (NCLIS), 229
National Council for Accreditation of Teacher Education (NCATE), 46, 229
National Council for Educational Technology Information Service (UK) (World Wide Web site), 74
National Council of Teachers of English (NCTE), Commission on Media, 229
National Council of the Churches of Christ in the U.S.A., 229
National Defense Education Act (NDEA), 8
National Education Association (NEA)
  Department of Audio Visual Instruction (DAVI), 27-28, 30, 137
  media standards and guidelines, K-12, 136, 137
  Technological Development Project, 27, 29
National Education Telecommunications Organization & Education Satellite Company (NETO/EDSAT), 230
National Endowment for the Humanities (NEH), 230
National Federation of Community Broadcasters (NFCB), 230
National Film Board of Canada (NFBC), 230, 245
National Film Information Service, 230
National Gallery of Art (NGA), 230-31
National Information Center for Educational Media (NICEM), 231
National Information Infrastructure (NII), 8
  education and lifelong learning, 50-53
  equity and access, 60-61
  goals and objectives, 61-63
  important issues, 64-65

roles, 56-59
  federal government, 56-58
  private sector, 56, 57
  state and local agencies, 56, 59
technology, benefits of, 53-54
telecommunications, 55-56, 59-60
"The national information infrastructure. Requirements for education and training," 379
National Institute of Standards and Technology, 57
National ITFS Association (NIA), 203
National Press Photographers Association, Inc. (NPPA), 231
National PTA, 231
National Public Broadcasting Archives (NPBA), 231-32
National Religious Broadcasters (NRB), 232
National Research and Education Network (NREN), 58
National School Supply and Equipment Association (NSSEA), 232
National Science Foundation (NSF), 58, 232
  NFSNET, 58
National Science Teachers Association (NSTA), 232-33
National Society for Performance and Instruction (NSPI), 165, 178-79, 233
National Study of School Evaluation (NSSE), 137, 138
National Task Force on Educational Technology, 127
National Technology Center, 233
National Telemedia Council Inc. (NTC), 233
National University Continuing Education Association (NUCEA), 233-34
NAVH. See National Association for Visually Handicapped (NAVH)
Navigating the Internet: An Interactive Workshop (electronic file), 69
NCATE. See National Council for Accreditation of Teacher Education (NCATE)
NCBE. See National Clearinghouse for Bilingual Education (NCBE)
NCIP. See National Center to Improve Practice (NCIP)
NCLIS. See National Commission on Libraries and Information Science (NCLIS)
NCME. See Network for Continuing Medical Education (NCME)
NCREL. See North Central Regional Educational Laboratory (NCREL)
NCRMSE. See National Center for Research in Mathematical Sciences Education (NCRMSE)
NCSA Mosaic Home Page (World Wide Web site), 74
NCSTL. See National Center for Science Teaching and Learning (NCSTL)